# Ethical and Professional Standards and Quantitative Methods

## CFA® PROGRAM CURRICULUM • VOLUME 1

### LEVEL I
### 2009

PEARSON
Custom
Publishing

Cover photograph courtesy of Corbis.

10  9  8  7  6  5  4  3  2

ISBN 0-536-53703-8

2007160905

AG/NN

Please visit our web site at *www.pearsoncustom.com*

PEARSON CUSTOM PUBLISHING
501 Boylston Street, Suite 900, Boston, MA 02116
A Pearson Education Company

# CONTENTS

iii

indicates an optional segment

indicates an optional segment      www.cfainstitute.org/toolkit—Your online preparation resource

# HOW TO USE THE CFA PROGRAM CURRICULUM

Congratulations on your decision to enter the Chartered Financial Analyst (CFA®) Program. This exciting and rewarding program of study reflects your desire to become a serious investment professional. You are embarking on a program noted for its high ethical standards and the breadth of knowledge, skills, and abilities it develops. Your commitment to the CFA Program should be educationally and professionally rewarding.

The credential you seek is respected around the world as a mark of accomplishment and dedication. Each level of the program represents a distinct achievement in professional development. Successful completion of the program is rewarded with membership in a prestigious global community of investment professionals. CFA charterholders are dedicated to life-long learning and maintaining currency with the ever-changing dynamics of a challenging profession. The CFA Program represents the first step towards a career-long commitment to professional education.

The CFA examination measures your degree of mastery of the assigned CFA Program curriculum. Effective study and preparation based on that curriculum are keys to your success on the examination.

## Curriculum Development

The CFA Program curriculum is grounded in the practice of the investment profession. Utilizing a collaborative website, CFA Institute performs a continuous practice analysis with investment professionals around the world to determine the knowledge, skills, and abilities that are relevant to the profession. Regional panels and targeted surveys are also conducted annually to verify and reinforce the continuous feedback. The practice analysis process ultimately defines the Candidate Body of Knowledge (CBOK™) an inventory of knowledge and responsibilities expected of the investment management professional at the level of a new CFA charterholder. The process also determines how much emphasis each of the major topic areas receives on the CFA examinations.

A committee made up of practicing charterholders, in conjunction with CFA Institute staff, designs the CFA Program curriculum to deliver the CBOK to candidates. The examinations, also written by practicing charterholders, are designed to allow you to demonstrate your mastery of the CBOK as set forth in the CFA Program curriculum. As you structure your personal study program, you should emphasize mastery of the CBOK and the practical application of that knowledge. For more information on the practice analysis, CBOK, and development of the CFA Program curriculum, please visit www.cfainstitute.org/toolkit.

## Organization

The Level I CFA Program curriculum is organized into 10 topic areas. Each topic area begins with a brief statement of the material and the depth of knowledge expected.

Each topic area is then divided into one or more study sessions. These study sessions—18 sessions in the Level I curriculum—should form the basic structure of your reading and preparation.

Each study session includes a statement of its structure and objective, and is further divided into specific reading assignments. The outline on the inside front cover of each volume illustrates the organization of these 18 study sessions.

*The reading assignments are the basis for all examination questions, and are selected or developed specifically to teach the CBOK.* These readings are drawn from CFA Program-commissioned content, textbook chapters, professional journal articles, research analyst reports, and cases. Many readings include problems and solutions as well as appendices to help you learn.

Reading-specific Learning Outcome Statements (LOS) are listed in the pages introducing each study session as well as at the beginning of each reading. These LOS indicate what you should be able to accomplish after studying the reading. We encourage you to review how to properly use LOS, and the descriptions of commonly used LOS "command words," at www.cfainstitute.org/toolkit. The command words signal the depth of learning you are expected to achieve from the reading. You should use the LOS to guide and focus your study, as each examination question is based on an assigned reading and one or more LOS. However, the readings provide context for the LOS and enable you to apply a principle or concept in a variety of scenarios. It is important to study the whole of a required reading.

## Features of the Curriculum

▶ **Required vs. Optional Segments** - You should read all of the pages for an assigned reading. In some cases, however, we have reprinted an entire chapter or article and marked those parts of the reading that are not required as "optional." The CFA examination is based only on the required segments, and the optional segments are included only when they might help you to better understand the required segments (by seeing the required material in its full context). When an optional segment begins, you will see an icon and a solid vertical bar in the outside margin that will continue until the optional segment ends, accompanied by another icon. *Unless the material is specifically marked as optional, you should assume it is required.* Keep in mind that the optional material is provided strictly for your convenience and will not be tested. You should rely on the required segments and the reading-specific LOS in preparing for the examination.

▶ **Problems/Solutions** - *All questions and problems in the readings as well as their solutions (which are provided in an appendix at the end of each volume) are required material.* When appropriate, we have included problems within and after the readings to demonstrate practical application and reinforce your understanding of the concepts presented. The questions and problems are designed to help you learn these concepts. Many of the questions are adapted from past CFA examinations.

Beginning with the 2009 exams, the selected response questions on the CFA exam will have three choices (a correct answer and two distracters). This includes both the multiple choice questions at Level I and the item set questions at Levels II and III. In many cases, the questions provided in the curriculum have been modified to match the new three-choice format.

▶ **Margins** - The wide margins in each volume provide space for your note-taking.

▶ **Two-Color Format** - To enrich the visual appeal and clarity of the exhibits, tables, and text, the curriculum is printed in a two-color format.

► **Six-Volume Structure** - For portability of the curriculum, the material is spread over six volumes.

► **Glossary and Index** - For your convenience, we have printed a comprehensive glossary and index in each volume. Throughout the curriculum, a **bolded blue** word in a reading denotes a term defined in the glossary.

► **Source Material** - The authorship, publisher, and copyright owners are given for each reading for your reference. We recommend that you use this CFA Institute curriculum rather than the original source materials because the curriculum may include only selected pages from outside readings, updated sections within the readings, and may have problems and solutions tailored to the CFA Program.

► **LOS Self-Check** - We have inserted checkboxes next to each LOS that you can use to track your progress in mastering the concepts in each reading.

## Designing Your Personal Study Program

**Create a Schedule** - An orderly, systematic approach to examination preparation is critical. You should dedicate a consistent block of time every week to reading and studying. Complete all reading assignments and the associated problems and solutions in each study session. Review the LOS both before and after you study each reading to ensure that you have mastered the applicable content and can demonstrate the knowledge, skill, or ability described by the LOS and the assigned reading. Use the new LOS self-check to track your progress and highlight areas of weakness for later review.

You will receive periodic e-mail communications that contain important study tips and preparation strategies. Be sure to read these carefully.

CFA Institute estimates that you will need to devote a minimum of 10–15 hours per week for 18 weeks to study the assigned readings. Allow a minimum of one week for each study session, and plan to complete them all at least 30–45 days prior to the examination. This schedule will allow you to spend the final four to six weeks before the examination reviewing the assigned material and taking online sample and mock examinations.

At CFA Institute, we believe that candidates need to commit to a *minimum* of 250 hours reading and reviewing the curriculum, and taking online sample examinations, to master the material. This recommendation, however, may substantially underestimate the hours needed for appropriate examination preparation depending on your individual circumstances, relevant experience, and academic background. You will undoubtedly adjust your study time to conform to your own strengths and weaknesses, and your educational and professional background.

You will probably spend more time on some study sessions than on others. You should allow ample time for both in-depth study of all topic areas and additional concentration on those topic areas for which you feel least prepared.

**Preliminary Readings** - The reading assignments in Economics assume candidates already have a basic mastery of the concepts typically presented in introductory university-level economics courses. Information on suggested readings to improve your knowledge of these topics precedes the relevant study sessions.

**Candidate Preparation Toolkit** - We have created the online toolkit to provide a single comprehensive location with resources and guidance for candidate preparation. In addition to in-depth information on study program planning, the CFA Program curriculum, and the online sample and mock examinations, the toolkit also contains curriculum errata, printable study session outlines, sample examination questions, and more. Errata that we have identified in the curriculum are corrected and listed periodically in the errata listing in the toolkit. We encourage you to use the toolkit as your central preparation resource during your tenure as a candidate. Visit the toolkit at www.cfainstitute.org/toolkit.

**Online Sample Examinations** - As part of your study of the assigned curriculum, use the CFA Institute online sample examinations to assess your exam preparation as you progress toward the end of your study. After each question, you will receive immediate feedback noting the correct response and indicating the relevant assigned reading, so you'll be able to identify areas of weakness for further study. The 120-minute sample examinations reflect the question formats, topics, and level of difficulty of the actual CFA examinations. Aggregate data indicate that the CFA examination pass rate was higher among candidates who took one or more online sample examinations than among candidates who did not take the online sample examinations. For more information on the online sample examinations, please visit www.cfainstitute.org/toolkit.

 **Online Mock Examinations** - In response to candidate requests, CFA Institute has developed mock examinations that mimic the actual CFA examinations not only in question format and level of difficulty, but also in length. The three-hour online mock exams simulate the morning and afternoon sessions of the actual CFA exam, and are intended to be taken after you complete your study of the full curriculum, so you can test your understanding of the CBOK and your readiness for the exam. To further differentiate, feedback is provided at the end of the exam, rather than after each question as with the sample exams. CFA Institute recommends that you take these mock exams at the final stage of your preparation toward the actual CFA examination. For more information on the online mock examinations, please visit www.cfainstitute.org/toolkit.

## Tools to Measure Your Comprehension of the Curriculum

With the addition of the online mock exams, CFA Institute now provides three distinct ways you can practice for the actual CFA exam. The full descriptions are above, but below is a brief summary of each:

**End-of-Reading Questions** - These questions are found at the end of each reading in the printed curriculum, and should be used to test your understanding of the concepts.

**Online Sample Exams** - Typically available two months before the CFA exam, online sample exams are designed to assess your exam preparation, and can help you target areas of weakness for further study.

**Online Mock Exams** - In contrast to the sample exams, mock exams are not available until closer to the actual exam date itself. Mock exams are designed to replicate the exam day experience, and should be taken near the end of your study period to prepare for exam day.

**Preparatory Providers** - After you enroll in the CFA Program, you may receive numerous solicitations for preparatory courses and review materials. Although preparatory courses and notes may be helpful to some candidates, you should view these resources as *supplements* to the assigned CFA Program curriculum. The CFA examinations reference only the CFA Institute assigned curriculum—no preparatory course or review course materials are consulted or referenced. Before you decide on a supplementary prep course, do some research. Determine the experience and expertise of the instructors, the accuracy and currency of their content, the delivery method for their materials, and the provider's claims of success. Most importantly, make sure the provider is in compliance with the CFA Institute Prep Provider Guidelines Program. Three years of prep course products can be a significant investment, so make sure you're getting a sufficient return. Just remember, there are no shortcuts to success on the CFA examinations. Prep products can enhance your learning experience, but the CFA curriculum is the key to success. For more information on the Prep Provider Guidelines Program, visit www.cfainstitute.org/cfaprog/resources/prepcourse.html.

## SUMMARY

Every question on the CFA examination is based on specific pages in the required readings and on one or more LOS. Frequently, an examination question is also tied to a specific example highlighted within a reading or to a specific end-of-reading question/problem and its solution. To make effective use of the curriculum, please remember these key points:

1. All pages printed in the Custom Curriculum are required reading for the examination except for occasional sections marked as optional. You may read optional pages as background, but you will not be tested on them.

2. All questions/problems printed at the end of readings and their solutions in the appendix to each volume are required study material for the examination.

3. Make appropriate use of the CFA Candidate Toolkit, the online sample/mock examinations, and preparatory courses and review materials.

4. Schedule and commit sufficient study time to cover the 18 study sessions, review the materials, and take sample/mock examinations.

5. **Note:** Some of the concepts in the study sessions may be superseded by updated rulings and/or pronouncements issued after a reading was published. Candidates are expected to be familiar with the overall analytical framework contained in the assigned readings. Candidates are not responsible for changes that occur after the material was written.

# Feedback

At CFA Institute, we are committed to delivering a comprehensive and rigorous curriculum for the development of competent, ethically grounded investment professionals. We rely on candidate and member feedback as we work to incorporate content, design, and packaging improvements. You can be assured that we will continue to listen to your suggestions. Please send any comments or feedback to curriculum@cfainstitute.org. Ongoing improvements in the curriculum will help you prepare for success on the upcoming examinations, and for a lifetime of learning as a serious investment professional.

# ETHICAL AND PROFESSIONAL STANDARDS

## TOPIC LEVEL LEARNING OUTCOME

The candidate should be able to demonstrate a thorough knowledge of the CFA Institute Code of Ethics and Standards of Professional Conduct, and familiarity with the Global Investment Performance Standards.

# STUDY SESSION 1
## ETHICAL AND PROFESSIONAL STANDARDS

The readings in this study session present a framework for ethical conduct in the investment profession by focusing on the CFA Institute Code of Ethics and Standards of Professional Conduct as well as the Global Investment Performance Standards (GIPS®).

The principles and guidance presented in the CFA Institute *Standards of Practice Handbook* (SOPH) form the basis for the CFA Institute self-regulatory program to maintain the highest professional standards among investment practitioners. "Guidance" in the SOPH addresses the practical application of the Code of Ethics and Standards of Professional Conduct. The guidance reviews the purpose and scope of each standard, presents recommended procedures for compliance, and provides examples of the standard in practice.

The Global Investment Performance Standards (GIPS) facilitate efficient comparison of investment performance across investment managers and country borders by prescribing methodology and standards that are consistent with a clear and honest presentation of returns. Having a global standard for reporting investment performance minimizes the potential for ambiguous or misleading presentations.

### READING ASSIGNMENTS

**Reading 1**   Code of Ethics and Standards of Professional Conduct
            *Standards of Practice Handbook*, Ninth Edition
**Reading 2**   "Guidance" for Standards I–VII
            *Standards of Practice Handbook*, Ninth Edition
**Reading 3**   Introduction to the Global Investment Performance Standards (GIPS®)
**Reading 4**   Global Investment Performance Standards (GIPS®)

# CODE OF ETHICS AND STANDARDS OF PROFESSIONAL CONDUCT

## LEARNING OUTCOMES

| The candidate should be able to: | Mastery |
|---|---|
| **a.** describe the structure of the CFA Institute Professional Conduct Program and the process for the enforcement of the Code and Standards; | ☐ |
| **b.** state the six components of the Code of Ethics and the seven Standards of Professional Conduct; | ☐ |
| **c.** explain the ethical responsibilities required by the Code and Standards, including the multiple sub-sections of each Standard. | ☐ |

# PREFACE

The purpose of the Code and Standards is to provide up-to-date guidance to the people who grapple with real ethical problems in the investment profession, where theory meets practice and ethics gain meaning. The Code and Standards are intended for a diverse and global audience: CFA Institute members navigating ambiguous ethical situations; supervisors and subordinates determining the nature of their responsibilities to one another, to clients and potential clients, and to the securities markets; and candidates preparing for the Chartered Financial Analyst examinations.

## Ethics in the Investment Profession

Ethical practices by investment professionals benefit all market participants and stakeholders and lead to increased investor confidence in global capital markets. Clients are reassured that the investment professionals they hire have the clients' best interest in mind and investment professionals benefit from the "reputational capital" such integrity generates. Ethical practices instill a public trust in the fairness of markets, allowing them to function efficiently. In short, good ethics is a fundamental requirement of the investment profession.

An important goal of CFA Institute is to ensure that the organization and its members develop, promote, and follow the highest ethical standards in the investment industry. The CFA Institute Code of Ethics and Standards of Professional Conduct (Code and Standards) are the foundation supporting the organization's quest to advance the interests of the global investment community by establishing and maintaining the highest standards of professional excellence and integrity. The Code of Ethics is a set of principles that define the professional conduct CFA Institute expects from its members and candidates in the CFA Program. The Code works in tandem with the Standards of Professional Conduct which outlines conduct that constitutes fair and ethical business practices.

For more than 40 years, CFA Institute members and candidates in the CFA Program have been required to abide by the organization's Code and Standards. Periodically, CFA Institute has revised and updated its Code and Standards to ensure that they remain relevant to the changing nature of the investment profession and representative of the "highest standard" of professional conduct. As the investment profession evolves, the list of ethical issues lengthens, from personal investing and soft commissions to misleading advice and the need to separate objective analysis from company promotion. New challenges are always emerging. As economies become more sophisticated and interconnected, new investment opportunities are constantly being created, along with new financial instruments to make the most of those opportunities for clients. Although the investment world has become a far more complex place since this *Handbook* was first published, distinguishing right from wrong remains the paramount principle of the Code of Ethics and Standards of Professional Conduct.

# Evolution of the CFA Institute
# Code of Ethics and Standards of Professional Conduct

Generally the changes to the Code and Standards, over the years, have been minor. CFA Institute revised the language of the Standards and occasionally tacked on a new standard addressing prominent issues of the day. For instance, in 1992, CFA Institute added the standard addressing performance presentation to the existing list of standards. The last major changes came in 1996 and were mostly structural in nature. CFA Institute organized them to coincide with the constituencies of investment professionals—clients, employers, investors, the public, and the profession.

After a long review process, several revisions, solicitation and careful consideration of public comment from its members, candidates, and investment professionals, CFA Institute has adopted the new and revised version of the Code and Standards included in this book. The changes include a reorganization of the standards, adoption of new standards, and revisions to existing standards. CFA Institute believes that the revisions clarify the requirements of the Code and Standards and effectively convey to its global membership what constitutes "best practice" in a number of areas relating to the investment profession.

These new standards are effective 1 January 2006. CFA Institute has published the 9th edition of the *Standards of Practice Handbook* to offer guidance, interpretation, applications, and recommended procedures for compliance for the new standards.

## Summary of Changes

*Reorganization of Standards.* The organization of past versions of the Standards was based on the CFA Institute member's or candidate's responsibilities to various constituencies: the public, the client, the employer, and the profession. This led to the repetition of concepts in an attempt to fit broad substantive ideas into specific categories even though those ideas have general application. For example, disclosure of conflicts of interest was addressed in two separate standards, one dealing with disclosure of conflicts to employers, the other dealing with disclosure of conflicts to clients. Also, misrepresentation was addressed in several standards relating to investment recommendations, performance and credentials. Multiple references to similar ideas detracted from clarity and comprehension of the ethical concepts contained in the Code and Standards.

The revised Standards are organized by topic to streamline the structure and improve comprehension. Instead of five standards that discuss member and candidate conduct as it relates to various groups, the new Standards are organized into seven general topics:

   I. Professionalism
   II. Integrity of Capital Markets
   III. Duties to Clients
   IV. Duties to Employers
   V. Investment Analysis, Recommendations, and Actions
   VI. Conflicts of Interest
   VII. Responsibilities as a CFA Institute Member or CFA Candidate

*Revising Current Standards.* CFA Institute has expanded the Standards (e.g., misrepresentation, duty to employer, suitability, duty of loyalty to clients, disclosure of conflicts, and material nonpublic information) to better address the state of the investment profession and establish clear "best practices" in these areas.

*Clarifying Requirements.* In some instances, the guidance in prior versions of the Handbook included "requirements" with which all members and candidates had to comply, even though this conduct was not specifically set forth in the Standards themselves. For example, the prior guidance prohibited acceptance of gifts over a specific dollar amount, even though the specific prohibition was not found in the Standards. CFA Institute has eliminated or incorporated these requirements into the new Standards as appropriate so that members and candidates are clearly on notice about what conduct the Code and Standards requires or prohibits. The guidance included in the 9th edition of the Handbook expands on the requirements set forth in the Code and Standards and does not introduce new requirements.

*New Standards.* CFA Institute added standards relating to market manipulation and record retention to better address the state of the investment profession and establish clear "best practices" in these areas.

*Eliminating the Requirement to Inform Employers of the Code and Standards.* Previously the Standards of Professional Conduct included a requirement that members and candidates notify their employer of their responsibility to abide by the Code and Standards. Although it is in the member's or candidate's best interest to notify their employer, and thereby potentially avoid being placed in a compromising position, CFA Institute believes that notification should be a recommendation rather than a requirement in the Standards. Such a recommendation is included in the Preamble to the Code of Ethics.

*Maintaining Relevance to a Global Membership.* In some areas (e.g., use of material nonpublic information and fiduciary duty) the prior versions of the Code and Standards were based on U.S. law and regulation and may not have reflected best practice in the global investment industry. Therefore, CFA Institute has revised the Standards to make them less U.S.-centric to maintain the highest ethical standard on a global basis.

*Text Revisions.* As the investment industry and, as a result, CFA Institute membership has become more global, it is critical for the Code and Standards to use language that, to the extent possible, can be easily understood and translated into different languages. Therefore, in some instances CFA Institute has eliminated, modified, or added language for clarity, even though it is not the intent to change the meaning of a particular provision.

Changes to the Code and Standards have far-reaching implications for CFA Institute membership, the CFA Program, and the investment industry as a whole. Unlike other voluntary ethical standards promulgated by the organization through the CFA Centre for Financial Market Integrity (e.g., the GIPS® standards, Soft Dollar Standards, Trade Management Guidelines, Research Objectivity Standards, Best Practice Guidelines Governing Analyst and Corporate Issuer Relations, Asset Manager Code of Professional Conduct), members and CFA candidates are required to adhere to the Code and Standards. In addition, the Code and Standards are increasingly being adopted, in whole or in part, by firms and regulatory authorities. Their relevance goes well beyond CFA Institute members and CFA candidates.

It is imperative that the Code and Standards be updated if they are to be effective and represent the highest ethical standards in the global investment industry. CFA Institute strongly believes that the revisions and reorganization of the Code and Standards are not undertaken for cosmetic change but add value by addressing legitimate concerns and improving comprehension.

## Standards of Practice Handbook

The periodic revisions to the Code and Standards have come in conjunction with the update of the *Standards of Practice Handbook*. The *Handbook* is the fundamental element of the ethics education effort of CFA Institute and the primary resource for guidance in interpreting and implementing the Code and Standards. The *Handbook* seeks to educate members and candidates on how to apply the Code and Standards to their professional lives and thereby benefit their clients, employers, and the investing public in general. The *Handbook* explains the purpose of the Standards and how they apply in a variety of situations. The guidance discusses and amplifies each standard and suggests procedures to prevent violations.

Examples in the "Application of the Standard" section are meant to illustrate how the standard applies to hypothetical factual situations. The names contained in the examples are fictional and are not meant to refer to any actual person or entity. Unless otherwise stated, individuals in each example are CFA Institute members and/or holders of the Chartered Financial Analyst designation. Because factual circumstances vary so widely and often involve gray areas, the explanatory material and examples are not intended to be all-inclusive. Many examples set forth in the Application of the Standard section involve standards that have legal counterparts; members are strongly urged to discuss with their supervisors and legal and compliance departments the content of the Code and Standards and the members' general obligations under the Code and Standards.

CFA Institute recognizes that the presence of any set of ethical standards can create a false sense of security unless the documents are fully understood, enforced, and made a meaningful part of everyday professional activities. The *Handbook* is intended to provide a useful frame of reference that lends substance to the understanding of professional behavior in the investment decision-making process. This book cannot cover every contingency or circumstance, and it does not attempt to do so. The development and interpretation of the Code and Standards is an evolving process and will be subject to continuing refinement.

## CFA Institute Professional Conduct Program

All CFA Institute members and candidates enrolled in the CFA Program are required to comply with the Code and Standards. The CFA Institute Bylaws and Rules of Procedure for Proceedings Related to Professional Conduct (Rules of Procedure) form the basic structure for enforcing the Code and Standards. The Rules of Procedure are based on two primary principles: (1) fair process to the member and candidate and (2) confidentiality of proceedings. The CFA Institute Board of Governors maintains oversight and responsibility for the Professional Conduct Program (PCP) through the Disciplinary Review Committee (DRC), which is responsible for the enforcement of the Code and Standards.

Professional Conduct staff, under the direction of the CFA Institute Designated Officer, conducts professional conduct inquiries. Several circumstances can prompt an inquiry. Members and candidates must self-disclose on the annual Professional Conduct Statement all matters that question their professional conduct, such as involvement in civil litigation, a criminal investigation, or being the subject of a written complaint. Secondly, written complaints received by Professional Conduct staff can bring about an investigation. Third, CFA Institute staff may become aware of questionable conduct by a member or candidate through the media or other public source. Fourth, CFA examination proctors can submit a violation report for any candidate suspected to have compromised his or her professional conduct during the examination.

When an inquiry is initiated, the Professional Conduct staff conducts an investigation that may include requesting a written explanation from the member or candidate; interviewing the member or candidate, complaining parties, and third parties; and collecting documents and records in support of its investigation. The Designated Officer, upon reviewing the material obtained during the investigation, may conclude the inquiry with no disciplinary sanction, issue a cautionary letter, or continue proceedings to discipline the member or candidate. If the Designated Officer finds that a violation of the Code and Standards occurred, the Designated Officer proposes a disciplinary sanction, which may be rejected or accepted by the member or candidate. If the member or candidate rejects the proposed sanction, the matter is referred to a hearing by a panel of CFA Institute members.

Sanctions imposed by CFA Institute may have significant consequences, including condemnation by the sanctioned members' peers and possible ramifications for employment. Candidates enrolled in the CFA Program who have violated the Code and Standards may be suspended from further participation in the CFA program.

## Adoption of the Code and Standards

The CFA Institute Code and Standards apply to individual members of CFA Institute and candidates for the CFA designation. However, CFA Institute does encourage firms to adopt the Code of Ethics and Standards of Professional Conduct as part of their firm code of ethics. There are no formal procedures for adopting the Code and Standards but those who claim compliance should fully understand the requirements of the Code and Standards.

Although CFA Institute welcomes public acknowledgement, when appropriate, that firms are using the CFA Institute Code and Standards, no attribution is necessary. For firms that would like to distribute the Code and Standards to clients and potential clients, attractive, one-page copies of the Code and Standards, including translations, are available on the CFA Institute website (www.cfainstitute.org).

CFA Institute, through its CFA Centre for Financial Market Integrity, has also published an Asset Manager Code of Professional Conduct (AMC) that is designed, in part, to help U.S. firms comply with the regulations mandating codes of ethics for investment advisers. The AMC provides specific, practical guidelines for asset managers in six areas: loyalty to clients, the investment process, trading, compliance, performance evaluation, and disclosure. Although the Code and Standards are aimed at individual investment professionals who are members of the CFA Institute or candidates for the CFA designation, the Asset Manager Code of Professional Conduct has been drafted for firms. The AMC is included as an appendix and also can be found on the CFA Institute website.

CFA Institute encourages firms adopting either the Code and Standards or the Asset Manager Code of Conduct to notify CFA Institute that they have adopted or are incorporating these standards as part of their firm codes of ethics.

## Acknowledgments

Because CFA Institute is a volunteer organization, its work to promote ethical practice in the investment profession relies to a great degree on the goodwill of its members to devote their time on the organization's behalf. Such goodwill is also in abundance among CFA Institute members acting in an individual capacity to extend ethical integrity.

The CFA Institute Standards of Practice Council (SPC), a group currently consisting of 15 CFA charterholder volunteers from nine different countries, is charged with maintaining and interpreting the Code and Standards and ensuring that they are effective. The SPC draws its membership from a broad spectrum of organizations in the securities field, including brokers, investment advisors, banks, and insurance companies. In most instances, the SPC members also have important supervisory responsibilities within their firms.

The SPC continually evaluates the Code and Standards, as well as the guidance in the Handbook, to ensure that they are:

► Representative of the "highest standard" of professional conduct;
► Relevant to the changing nature of the investment profession;
► Globally applicable;
► Sufficiently comprehensive, practical, and specific;
► Enforceable; and
► Testable for the CFA Program.

Over the last two years, the SPC has spent countless hours reviewing and discussing revisions to the Code and Standards and updates to the Guidance that make up this 9th edition of the *Handbook*. Below is a list of the current members of the SPC who generously donated their time and energy to this effort.

| | |
|---|---|
| Lee Price, CFA, Chair | Mario Eichenberger, CFA |
| Ross E. Hallett, CFA | Toshihiko Saito, CFA |
| Samuel B. Jones, CFA | Richard Wayman, CFA |
| Lynn S. Mander, CFA | Martha Oberndorfer, CFA |
| Todd P. Lowe, CFA | Mark Sinsheimer, CFA |
| Sunil Singhania, CFA | Brian O'Keefe, CFA |
| Miroslaw Panek, CFA | |

Finally, this book is dedicated to the late Jules Huot, CFA, a long-time member of the SPC and volunteer for CFA Institute who tirelessly advocated for ethics in the investment profession and constantly worked to promote ethics and integrity within the industry.

# CFA INSTITUTE CODE OF ETHICS AND STANDARDS OF PROFESSIONAL CONDUCT

## Preamble to the CFA Institute Code of Ethics and Standards of Professional Conduct

The CFA Institute Code of Ethics and Standards of Professional Conduct (Code and Standards) are fundamental to the values of CFA Institute and essential to achieving its mission to lead the investment profession globally by setting high standards of education, integrity, and professional excellence. High ethical standards are critical to maintaining the public's trust in financial markets and in the investment profession. Since their creation in the 1960s, the Code and Standards have promoted the integrity of CFA Institute members and served as a model for measuring the ethics of investment professionals globally, regardless of job function, cultural differences, or local laws and regulations. All CFA Institute members (including holders of the Chartered Financial Analyst® (CFA®) designation) and CFA candidates must abide by the Code and Standards and are encouraged to notify their employer of this responsibility. Violations may result in disciplinary sanctions by CFA Institute. Sanctions can include revocation of membership, candidacy in the CFA Program, and the right to use the CFA designation.

## The Code of Ethics

Members of CFA Institute (including Chartered Financial Analyst® [CFA®] charterholders) and candidates for the CFA designation ("members and candidates") must:

► Act with integrity, competence, diligence, respect, and in an ethical manner with the public, clients, prospective clients, employers, employees, colleagues in the investment profession, and other participants in the global capital markets.

► Place the integrity of the investment profession and the interests of clients above their own personal interests.

► Use reasonable care and exercise independent professional judgment when conducting investment analysis, making investment recommendations, taking investment actions, and engaging in other professional activities.

► Practice and encourage others to practice in a professional and ethical manner that will reflect credit on themselves and the profession.

► Promote the integrity of, and uphold the rules governing, capital markets.

► Maintain and improve their professional competence and strive to maintain and improve the competence of other investment professionals.

## Standards of Professional Conduct

### I. PROFESSIONALISM

**A. Knowledge of the Law.** Members and candidates must understand and comply with all applicable laws, rules, and regulations (including the CFA Institute Code of Ethics and Standards of Professional Conduct) of any government, regulatory organization, licensing agency, or professional association governing their professional activities. In the event of conflict, members and candidates must comply with the more strict law, rule, or regulation. Members and candidates must not knowingly participate or assist in and must dissociate from any violation of such laws, rules, or regulations.

**B. Independence and Objectivity.** Members and candidates must use reasonable care and judgment to achieve and maintain independence and objectivity in their professional activities. Members and candidates must not offer, solicit, or accept any gift, benefit, compensation, or consideration that reasonably could be expected to compromise their own or another's independence and objectivity.

**C. Misrepresentation.** Members and candidates must not knowingly make any misrepresentations relating to investment analysis, recommendations, actions, or other professional activities.

**D. Misconduct.** Members and candidates must not engage in any professional conduct involving dishonesty, fraud, or deceit or commit any act that reflects adversely on their professional reputation, integrity, or competence.

### II. INTEGRITY OF CAPITAL MARKETS

**A. Material Nonpublic Information.** Members and candidates who possess material nonpublic information that could affect the value of an investment must not act or cause others to act on the information.

**B. Market Manipulation.** Members and candidates must not engage in practices that distort prices or artificially inflate trading volume with the intent to mislead market participants.

### III. DUTIES TO CLIENTS

**A. Loyalty, Prudence, and Care.** Members and candidates have a duty of loyalty to their clients and must act with reasonable care and exercise prudent judgment. Members and candidates must act for the benefit of their clients and place their clients' interests before their employer's or their own interests. In relationships with clients, members and candidates must determine applicable fiduciary duty and must comply with such duty to persons and interests to whom it is owed.

**B. Fair Dealing.** Members and candidates must deal fairly and objectively with all clients when providing investment analysis, making investment recommendations, taking investment action, or engaging in other professional activities.

**C. Suitability.**

1. When members and candidates are in an advisory relationship with a client, they must:

   a. Make a reasonable inquiry into a client's or prospective client's investment experience, risk and return objectives, and financial constraints prior to making any investment recommendation or taking investment action and must reassess and update this information regularly.

      b. Determine that an investment is suitable to the client's financial situation and consistent with the client's written objectives, mandates, and constraints before making an investment recommendation or taking investment action.

      c. Judge the suitability of investments in the context of the client's total portfolio.

  2. When members and candidates are responsible for managing a portfolio to a specific mandate, strategy, or style, they must only make investment recommendations or take investment actions that are consistent with the stated objectives and constraints of the portfolio.

**D. Performance Presentation.** When communicating investment performance information, members or candidates must make reasonable efforts to ensure that it is fair, accurate, and complete.

**E. Preservation of Confidentiality.** Members and candidates must keep information about current, former, and prospective clients confidential unless:

  1. The information concerns illegal activities on the part of the client or prospective client,

  2. Disclosure is required by law, or

  3. The client or prospective client permits disclosure of the information.

## IV. DUTIES TO EMPLOYERS

**A. Loyalty.** In matters related to their employment, members and candidates must act for the benefit of their employer and not deprive their employer of the advantage of their skills and abilities, divulge confidential information, or otherwise cause harm to their employer.

**B. Additional Compensation Arrangements.** Members and candidates must not accept gifts, benefits, compensation, or consideration that competes with, or might reasonably be expected to create a conflict of interest with, their employer's interest unless they obtain written consent from all parties involved.

**C. Responsibilities of Supervisors.** Members and candidates must make reasonable efforts to detect and prevent violations of applicable laws, rules, regulations, and the Code and Standards by anyone subject to their supervision or authority.

## V. INVESTMENT ANALYSIS, RECOMMENDATIONS, AND ACTIONS

**A. Diligence and Reasonable Basis.** Members and candidates must:

  1. Exercise diligence, independence, and thoroughness in analyzing investments, making investment recommendations, and taking investment actions.

  2. Have a reasonable and adequate basis, supported by appropriate research and investigation, for any investment analysis, recommendation, or action.

**B. Communication with Clients and Prospective Clients.** Members and candidates must:

  1. Disclose to clients and prospective clients the basic format and general principles of the investment processes used to analyze investments, select securities, and construct portfolios and must promptly disclose any changes that might materially affect those processes.

  2. Use reasonable judgment in identifying which factors are important to their investment analyses, recommendations, or actions and

include those factors in communications with clients and prospective clients.

   3. Distinguish between fact and opinion in the presentation of investment analysis and recommendations.

**C. Record Retention.** Members and candidates must develop and maintain appropriate records to support their investment analysis, recommendations, actions, and other investment-related communications with clients and prospective clients.

## VI. CONFLICTS OF INTEREST

**A. Disclosure of Conflicts.** Members and candidates must make full and fair disclosure of all matters that could reasonably be expected to impair their independence and objectivity or interfere with respective duties to their clients, prospective clients, and employer. Members and candidates must ensure that such disclosures are prominent, are delivered in plain language, and communicate the relevant information effectively.

**B. Priority of Transactions.** Investment transactions for clients and employers must have priority over investment transactions in which a member or candidate is the beneficial owner.

**C. Referral Fees.** Members and candidates must disclose to their employer, clients, and prospective clients, as appropriate, any compensation, consideration, or benefit received from, or paid to, others for the recommendation of products or services.

## VII. RESPONSIBILITIES AS A CFA INSTITUTE MEMBER OR CFA CANDIDATE

**A. Conduct as Members and Candidates in the CFA Program.** Members and candidates must not engage in any conduct that compromises the reputation or integrity of CFA Institute or the CFA designation or the integrity, validity, or security of the CFA examinations.

**B. Reference to CFA Institute, the CFA Designation, and the CFA Program.** When referring to CFA Institute, CFA Institute membership, the CFA designation, or candidacy in the CFA Program, members and candidates must not misrepresent or exaggerate the meaning or implications of membership in CFA Institute, holding the CFA designation, or candidacy in the CFA program.

# "GUIDANCE" FOR STANDARDS I–VII

## LEARNING OUTCOMES

| The candidate should be able to: | Mastery |
| --- | --- |
| **a.** demonstrate a thorough knowledge of the Code of Ethics and Standards of Professional Conduct by applying the Code and Standards to situations involving issues of professional integrity; | ☐ |
| **b.** distinguish between conduct that conforms to the Code and Standards and conduct that violates the Code and Standards; | ☐ |
| **c.** recommend practices and procedures designed to prevent violations of the Code of Ethics and Standards of Professional Conduct. | ☐ |

The "Guidance" statements address the application of the Standards of Professional Conduct. For each standard, the Guidance discusses the purpose and scope of the standard, presents recommended procedures for compliance, and gives examples of application of the standard.

# STANDARD I—PROFESSIONALISM

## A. Knowledge of the Law

**Members and candidates must understand and comply with all applicable laws, rules, and regulations (including the CFA Institute Code of Ethics and Standards of Professional Conduct) of any government, regulatory organization, licensing agency, or professional association governing their professional activities. In the event of conflict, members and candidates must comply with the more strict law, rule, or regulation. Members and candidates must not knowingly participate or assist in and must dissociate from any violation of such laws, rules, or regulations.**

Members and candidates must have an understanding of applicable laws and regulations of all countries in which they trade securities or provide investment advice or other investment services. This standard does not require members and candidates to become experts in compliance. Investment professionals are not required to have detailed knowledge of or be experts on all laws that could potentially govern the member's or candidate's activities. However, members and candidates must comply with the laws and regulations that directly govern their work.

### Relationship between the Code and Standards and Local Law

Some members or candidates may live, work, or provide investment services to clients living in a country that has no law or regulation governing a particular action or that has laws or regulations that differ from the requirements of the Code and Standards. When applicable law and the Code and Standards require different conduct, members and candidates must follow the more strict of the applicable law or the Code and Standards.

"Applicable law" is the law that governs the member's or candidate's conduct. Which law applies will depend on the particular facts and circumstances of each case. The "more strict" law or regulation is the law or regulation that imposes greater restrictions on the action of the member or candidate or calls for the member or candidate to exert a greater degree of action that protects the interests of investors. For example, applicable law or regulation may not require members and candidates to disclose referral fees received from or paid to others for the recommendation of investment products or services. However, because the Code and Standards impose this obligation, members and candidates must disclose the existence of such fees.

Members and candidates must adhere to the following principles:

► Members and candidates must comply with applicable law or regulation related to their professional activities.
► Members and candidates must not engage in conduct that constitutes a violation of the Code and Standards, even though it may otherwise be legal.
► In the absence of any applicable law or regulation or when the Code and Standards impose a higher degree of responsibility than applicable laws and regulations, members and candidates must adhere to the Code and Standards.

Applications of these principles are outlined in Exhibit 1 (on pp. 20–21).

CFA Institute members are obligated to abide by the CFA Institute Articles of Incorporation, Bylaws, Code of Ethics, Standards of Professional Conduct, Rules of Procedure for Proceedings Related to Professional Conduct, Membership Agreement, and other applicable rules promulgated by CFA Institute, all as amended from time to time. CFA candidates who are not members must also abide by these documents (except for the Membership Agreement), as well as rules and regulations related to the administration of the CFA examination, the Candidate Responsibility Statement, and the Candidate Pledge.

### Participation or Association with Violations by Others

Members and candidates are responsible for violations in which they *knowingly* participate or assist. Although members and candidates are presumed to have knowledge of all applicable laws, rules, and regulations, CFA Institute acknowledges that members may not recognize violations if they are not aware of all the facts giving rise to the violations. Standard I applies when members and candidates know or should know that their conduct may contribute to a violation of applicable laws, rules, regulations, or the Code and Standards.

If a member or candidate has reasonable grounds to believe that imminent or ongoing client or employee activities are illegal or unethical, the member or candidate must dissociate, or separate, from the activity. In extreme cases, dissociation may require a member or candidate to leave his or her employer. However, there are intermediate steps that members and candidates may take to dissociate from ethical violations of others. The first step should be to attempt to stop the behavior by bringing it to the attention of the employer through a supervisor or the compliance department. Members and candidates may consider directly confronting the person or persons committing the violation. If these attempts are unsuccessful, then members and candidates have a responsibility to step away and dissociate from the activity by taking such steps as removing their name from written reports or recommendations or asking for a different assignment. Inaction combined with continuing association with those involved in illegal or unethical conduct may be construed as participation or assistance in the illegal or unethical conduct.

Although the Code and Standards do not require that members and candidates report violations to the appropriate governmental or regulatory organizations, such disclosure may be prudent in certain circumstances, and mandated if required by applicable law. Similarly, the Code and Standards do not require that members and candidates report to CFA Institute potential violations of the Code and Standards by fellow members and candidates. However, CFA Institute encourages members, nonmembers, clients, and the investing public to report violations of the Code and Standards by CFA Institute members or CFA candidates by submitting a complaint in writing to the CFA Institute Professional Conduct Program: E-mail pconduct@cfainstitute.org or visit the CFA Institute website at www.cfainstitute.org.

## Recommended Procedures for Compliance

### Members and Candidates

Suggested methods by which members and candidates can acquire and maintain understanding of applicable laws, rules, and regulations include the following:

▶ Stay informed. Members and candidates should establish or encourage their employers to establish a procedure by which employees are regularly informed about changes in applicable laws, rules, regulations, and case law. In many instances, the employer's compliance department or legal counsel can provide such information in the form of memorandums distributed to employees in the organization. Also, participation in an internal or external continuing education program is a practical method of staying current.

▶ Review procedures. Members and candidates should review or encourage their employers to review written compliance procedures on a regular basis in order to ensure that they reflect current law and provide adequate guidance to employees concerning what is permissible conduct under the law and/or the CFA Institute Code and Standards. Recommended compliance procedures for specific items of the CFA Institute Code and Standards are discussed within the guidance associated with each standard.

▶ Maintain current files. Members and candidates should maintain or encourage their employers to maintain readily accessible current reference copies of applicable statutes, rules, regulations, and important cases.

When in doubt, it is recommended that a member or candidate seek the advice of compliance personnel or legal counsel concerning legal requirements. If the potential violation is committed by a fellow employee, it may also be prudent for the member or candidate to seek the advice of the firm's compliance department or legal counsel.

When dissociating from an activity that violates the Code and Standards, members and candidates should document any violations and urge their firms to attempt to persuade the perpetrator(s) to cease such conduct. It may be necessary for a member or candidate to resign his or her employment to dissociate from the conduct.

### Firms

The formality and complexity of compliance procedures for firms depend on the nature and size of the organization and the nature of its investment operations. Members and candidates should encourage their firms to consider the following policies and procedures to support the principles of Standard I:

▶ Develop and/or adopt a code of ethics. The ethical culture of an organization starts at the top. Members and candidates should encourage their supervisors or management to adopt a code of ethics. Adhering to a code of ethics facilitates solutions when faced with ethical dilemmas and can prevent the need of employees to resort to a "whistle-blowing" solution.

▶ Make available and/or distribute to employees pertinent information that highlights applicable laws and regulations. Information sources may include primary information developed by the relevant government, governmental agencies, regulatory organizations, licensing agencies, and professional associations (e.g., from their websites); law firm memorandums or newsletters; and association memorandums or publications (e.g., *CFA Magazine*).

▶ Establish written protocols for reporting suspected violations of laws, regulations, and company policies.

## Application of the Standard

***Example 1:*** Michael Allen works for a brokerage firm and is responsible for an underwriting of securities. A company official gives Allen information indicating that the financial statements Allen filed with the regulator overstate the issuer's earnings. Allen seeks the advice of the brokerage firm's general counsel, who states that it would be difficult for the regulator to prove that Allen has been involved in any wrongdoing.

> *Comment:* Although it is recommended that members and candidates seek the advice of legal counsel, the reliance on such advice does not absolve a member or candidate from the requirement to comply with the law or regulation. Allen should report this situation to his supervisor, seek an independent legal opinion, and determine whether the regulator should be notified of the error.

***Example 2:*** Lawrence Brown's employer, an investment-banking firm, is the principal underwriter for an issue of convertible debentures by the Courtney Company. Brown discovers that Courtney Company has concealed severe third-quarter losses in its foreign operations. The preliminary prospectus has already been distributed.

*Comment:* Knowing that the preliminary prospectus is misleading, Brown should report his findings to the appropriate supervisory persons in his firm. If the matter is not remedied and Brown's employer does not dissociate from the underwriting, Brown should sever all his connections with the underwriting. Brown should also seek legal advice to determine whether additional reporting or other action should be taken.

***Example 3:*** Kamisha Washington's firm advertises its past performance record by showing the 10-year return of a composite of its client accounts. However, Washington discovers that the composite omits the performance of accounts that have left the firm during the 10-year period and that this omission has led to an inflated performance figure. Washington is asked to use promotional material that includes the erroneous performance number when soliciting business for the firm.

*Comment:* Misrepresenting performance is a violation of the Code and Standards. Although she did not calculate the performance herself, Washington would be assisting in violating this standard if she were to use the inflated performance number when soliciting clients. She must dissociate herself from the activity. She can bring the misleading number to the attention of the person responsible for calculating performance, her supervisor, or the compliance department at her firm. If her firm is unwilling to recalculate performance, she must refrain from using the misleading promotional material and should notify the firm of her reasons. If the firm insists that she use the material, she should consider whether her obligation to dissociate from the activity would require her to seek other employment.

***Example 4:*** James Collins is an investment analyst for a major Wall Street brokerage firm. He works in a developing country with a rapidly modernizing economy and a growing capital market. Local securities laws are minimal—in form and content—and include no punitive prohibitions against insider trading.

*Comment:* Collins should be aware of the risks that a small market and the absence of a fairly regulated flow of information to the market represent to his ability to obtain information and make timely judgments. He should include this factor in formulating his advice to clients. In handling material nonpublic information that accidentally comes into his possession, he must follow Standard II(A).

***Example 5:*** Laura Jameson works for a multinational investment advisor based in the United States. Jameson lives and works as a registered investment advisor in the tiny, but wealthy, island nation of Karramba. Karramba's securities laws state that no investment advisor registered and working in that country can participate in initial public offerings (IPOs) for the advisor's personal account. Jameson, believing that as a U.S. citizen working for a U.S.-based company she need comply only with U.S. law, has ignored this Karrambian law. In addition, Jameson believes that, as a charterholder, as long as she adheres to the Code and Standards requirement that she disclose her participation in any IPO to her employer and clients when such ownership creates a conflict of interest, she is operating on ethical high ground.

*Comment:* Jameson is in violation of Standard I(A). As a registered investment advisor in Karramba, Jameson is prevented by Karrambian securities law from participating in IPOs regardless of the law of her home country. In addition, because the law of the country where she is working is stricter than the Code and Standards, she must follow the stricter requirements of the local law rather than the requirements of the Code and Standards.

| EXHIBIT 1 | Global Application of the Code and Standards |
|-----------|----------------------------------------------|

Members and candidates who practice in multiple jurisdictions may be subject to varied securities laws and regulations. If applicable law is stricter than the requirements of the Code and Standards, members and candidates must adhere to applicable law; otherwise, they must adhere to the Code and Standards. The following chart provides illustrations involving a member who may be subject to the securities laws and regulations of three different types of countries. Countries with:

NSL = no securities laws or regulations
LS = *less* strict securities laws and regulations than the Code and Standards
MS = *more* strict securities laws and regulations than the Code and Standards

| Applicable Law | Duties | Explanation |
|----------------|--------|-------------|
| Member resides in NSL country, does business in LS country; LS law applies. | Member must adhere to the Code and Standards. | Because applicable law is less strict than the Code and Standards, the member must adhere to the Code and Standards. |
| Member resides in NSL country, does business in MS country; MS law applies. | Member must adhere to the law of MS country. | Because applicable law is stricter than the Code and Standards, member must adhere to the more strict applicable law. |
| Member resides in LS country, does business in NSL country; LS law applies. | Member must adhere to the Code and Standards. | Because applicable law is less strict than the Code and Standards, the member must adhere to the Code and Standards. |
| Member resides in LS country, does business in MS country; MS law applies. | Member must adhere to the law of MS country. | Because applicable law is stricter than the Code and Standards, the member must adhere to the more strict applicable law. |
| Member resides in LS country, does business in NSL country; LS law applies, but it states that law of locality where business is conducted governs. | Member must adhere to the Code and Standards. | Because applicable law states that the law of the locality where the business is conducted governs and there is no local law, the member must adhere to the Code and Standards. |
| Member resides in LS country, does business in MS country; LS law applies, but it states that law of locality where business is conducted governs. | Member must adhere to the law of MS country. | Because applicable law of the locality where the business is conducted governs and local law is stricter than the Code and Standards, the member must adhere to the more strict applicable law. |

*(Exhibit continued on next page …)*

| EXHIBIT 1 | (continued) | |
|---|---|---|
| **Applicable Law** | **Duties** | **Explanation** |
| Member resides in MS country, does business in LS country; MS law applies. | Member must adhere to the law of MS country. | Because applicable law is stricter than the Code and Standards, member must adhere to the more strict applicable law. |
| Member resides in MS country, does business in LS country; MS law applies, but it states that law of locality where business is conducted governs. | Member must adhere to the Code and Standards. | Because applicable law states that the law of the locality where the business is conducted governs and local law is less strict than the Code and Standards, the member must adhere to the Code and Standards. |
| Member resides in MS country, does business in LS country with a client who is a citizen of LS country; MS law applies, but it states that the law of the client's home country governs. | Member must adhere to the Code and Standards. | Because applicable law states that the law of the client's home country governs (which is less strict than the Code and Standards), the member must adhere to the Code and Standards. |
| Member resides in MS country, does business in LS country with a client who is a citizen of MS country; MS law applies, but it states that the law of the client's home country governs. | Member must adhere to the law of MS country. | Because applicable law states that the law of the client's home country governs and the law of the client's home country is stricter than the Code and Standards, the member must adhere to the more strict applicable law. |

## B. Independence and Objectivity

**Members and candidates must use reasonable care and judgment to achieve and maintain independence and objectivity in their professional activities. Members and candidates must not offer, solicit, or accept any gift, benefit, compensation, or consideration that reasonably could be expected to compromise their own or another's independence and objectivity.**

Standard I(B) states the responsibility of CFA Institute members and candidates in the CFA Program to maintain independence and objectivity so that their clients will have the benefit of their work and opinions unaffected by any potential conflict of interest or other circumstance adversely affecting their judgment. Every member and candidate should endeavor to avoid situations that could cause or be perceived to cause a loss of independence or objectivity in recommending investments or taking investment action.

External sources may try to influence the investment process by offering analysts and portfolio managers a variety of benefits. Corporations may seek expanded research coverage; issuers and underwriters may wish to promote new securities offerings; brokers may want to increase commission business. Benefits may include gifts, invitations to lavish functions, tickets, favors, job referrals, and so on. One type of benefit is the allocation of shares in oversubscribed IPOs to investment managers for their personal accounts. This practice affords managers the opportunity to make quick profits that may not be available to their clients. Such a practice is prohibited under Standard I(B). Modest gifts and entertainment are acceptable, but special care must be taken by members and candidates to resist subtle and not-so-subtle pressures to act in conflict with the interests of their clients. Best practice dictates that members and candidates must reject any offer of gift or entertainment that could be expected to threaten their independence and objectivity.

Receiving a gift, benefit, or consideration from a client can be distinguished from gifts given by entities seeking to influence a member or candidate to the detriment of other clients. In a client relationship, the client has already entered some type of compensation arrangement with the member, candidate, or his or her firm. A gift from a client could be considered supplementary compensation. The potential for obtaining influence to the detriment of other clients, although present, is not as great as in situations where no compensation arrangement exists. Therefore, members and candidates may accept "bonuses" or gifts from clients but must disclose to their employers such benefits from clients. Disclosure allows the employer of a member or candidate to make an independent determination about the extent to which the gift may affect the member's or candidate's independence and objectivity.

Members and candidates may also come under pressure from their own firms to, for example, issue favorable research reports or recommendations for certain companies. The commercial side of a bank may derive substantial revenue from its lending/deposit relationships with a company, and bank managers may be tempted to influence the work of analysts in the investment department. The situation may be aggravated if the head of the company sits on the bank's or investment firm's board and attempts to interfere in investment decision making. Members and candidates acting in a sales or marketing capacity must be especially certain of their objectivity in selecting appropriate investments for their clients.

Left unmanaged, pressures that threaten independence place research analysts in a difficult position and may jeopardize their ability to act independently and objectively. One of the ways that research analysts have coped with these pressures in the past is to use subtle and ambiguous language in their recommendations or to temper the tone of their research reports. Such subtleties are lost on some investors who reasonably expect research reports and recommendations to be straightforward and transparent and to communicate clearly an analyst's views based on unbiased analysis and independent judgment.

Members and candidates are personally responsible for maintaining independence and objectivity when preparing research reports, making investment recommendations, and taking investment action on behalf of clients. Recommendations must convey the member's or candidate's true opinions, free of bias from internal or external pressures, and be stated in clear and unambiguous language.

Members and candidates also should be aware that some of their professional or social activities within CFA Institute or its member societies may subtly threaten their independence or objectivity. When seeking corporate financial support for conventions, seminars, or even weekly society luncheons, the members or candidates responsible for the activities should evaluate both the actual effect of such solicitations on their independence and whether their objectivity might be perceived to be compromised in the eyes of their clients.

## *Investment-Banking Relationships*

Some sell-side firms may exert pressure on their analysts to issue favorable research on current or prospective investment-banking clients. For many of these firms, income from investment banking has become increasingly important to overall firm profitability because brokerage income has declined as a result of price competition. Consequently, firms offering investment-banking services work hard to develop and maintain relationships with investment-banking clients and prospects. These companies are often covered by the firm's research analysts because companies often select their investment bank based on the reputation of its research analysts, the quality of their work, and their standing in the industry.

Research analysts frequently work closely with their investment-banking colleagues to help evaluate prospective investment-banking clients. Although this practice benefits the firm and enhances market efficiency (e.g., by allowing firms to assess risks more accurately and make better pricing assumptions), it requires firms to carefully balance the conflicts of interest inherent in the collaboration of research and investment banking. Having analysts work with investment bankers is appropriate only when the conflicts are adequately and effectively managed and disclosed. Firm management has a responsibility to provide an environment in which analysts are neither coerced nor enticed into issuing research that does not reflect their true opinions. Firms should require public disclosure of actual conflicts of interest to investors.

Given the symbiotic relationship between research and investment banking, the traditional approach to building "firewalls" between these two functions must be managed to minimize resulting conflicts of interest. It is critical that sell-side firms foster and maintain a corporate culture that fully supports independence and objectivity and protects analysts from undue pressure by their investment-banking colleagues. A key element of an enhanced firewall is separate reporting structures for personnel within the research and investment-banking functions. For example, investment-banking personnel should not have any authority to approve, disapprove, or make changes to research reports or recommendations. Another element should be a compensation arrangement that minimizes the pressures and rewards objectivity and accuracy. Compensation arrangements should not link analyst remuneration directly to investment-banking assignments on which the analyst may participate as a team member. Firms should also regularly review their policies and procedures to determine whether analysts are adequately safeguarded and to improve the transparency of disclosures relating to conflicts of interest. The highest level of transparency is achieved when disclosures are prominent and specific, rather than marginalized and generic.

## *Public Companies*

Analysts can also be pressured to issue favorable reports and recommendations by the companies they follow. Company management often believes that the company's stock is undervalued and may find it difficult to accept critical research reports or ratings downgrades. Management compensation may also be dependent on stock performance. Not every stock is a "buy" and not every research report is favorable—for many reasons, including the cyclical nature of many business activities and market fluctuations. For instance, a "good company" does not always translate into a "good stock" rating if the current stock price is fully valued. In making an investment recommendation, the analyst is responsible for anticipating, interpreting, and assessing a company's prospects and stock-price performance in a factual manner.

Due diligence in financial research and analysis involves gathering information from a wide variety of sources, including company management and investor-relations personnel, suppliers, customers, competitors, and other relevant sources in addition to public disclosure documents, such as proxy statements, annual reports, and other regulatory filings. Research analysts may justifiably fear that companies will limit their ability to conduct thorough research by denying "negative" analysts direct access to company management and/or barring them from conference calls and other communication venues. Retaliatory practices include companies bringing legal action against analysts personally and/or their firms to seek monetary damages for the economic effects of negative reports and recommendations. Although few companies engage in such behavior, the perception that a reprisal is possible is a reasonable concern for analysts. This concern may make it difficult for them to conduct the comprehensive research needed to make objective recommendations. For further information and guidance, members and candidates should refer to the CFA Institute *Best Practice Guidelines Covering Analyst/Corporate Issuer Relations* (www.cfainstitute.org).

### Buy-Side Clients

A third source of pressure on sell-side analysts may come from buy-side clients. Institutional clients are traditionally the primary users of sell-side research, either directly or with soft dollar brokerage. Portfolio managers may have significant positions in the security of a company under review. A rating downgrade may adversely affect the portfolio's performance, particularly in the short term, because the sensitivity of stock prices to ratings changes has increased in recent years. A downgrade may also impact the manager's compensation, which is usually tied to portfolio performance. Moreover, portfolio performance is subject to media and public scrutiny, which may affect the manager's professional reputation. Consequently, some portfolio managers may implicitly or explicitly support sell-side ratings inflation.

Portfolio managers have a responsibility to respect and foster the intellectual honesty of sell-side research. Therefore, it is improper for portfolio managers to threaten or engage in retaliatory practices, such as reporting sell-side analysts to the covered company to instigate negative corporate reactions. Although most portfolio managers do not engage in such practices, the perception by the research analyst that a reprisal is possible may cause concern, making it difficult to maintain independence and objectivity.

### Issuer-Paid Research

In light of the recent reduction of sell-side research coverage, many companies, seeking to increase visibility both in the financial markets and with potential investors, hire analysts to produce research reports analyzing their companies. These reports bridge the gap created by the lack of coverage and can be an effective method of communicating with investors.

Issuer-paid research, however, is fraught with potential conflicts. Depending on how the research is written and distributed, investors can be misled into believing that research appears to be from an independent source when, in reality, it has been paid for by the subject company.

It is critical that research analysts adhere to strict standards of conduct that govern how the research is to be conducted and what disclosures must be made in the report. Analysts must engage in thorough, independent, and unbiased analysis and must fully disclose potential conflicts, including the nature of their compensation. Otherwise, analysts risk misleading investors by becoming an extension of an issuer's public relations department while appearing to produce "independent" analysis.

Investors need clear, credible, and thorough information about companies and research based on independent thought. At a minimum, research should include a thorough analysis of the company's financial statements based on publicly disclosed information, benchmarking within a peer group, and industry analysis. Analysts must exercise diligence, independence, and thoroughness in conducting their research in an objective manner. Analysts must distinguish between fact and opinion in their reports. Conclusions must have a reasonable and adequate basis, and must be supported by appropriate research.

Analysts must also strictly limit the type of compensation that they accept for conducting research. Otherwise, the content and conclusions of the reports could reasonably be expected to be determined or affected by compensation from the sponsoring companies. This compensation can be direct, such as payment based on the conclusions of the report or more indirect, such as stock warrants or other equity instruments that could increase in value based on positive coverage in the report. In those instances, analysts would have an incentive to avoid negative information or conclusions that would diminish their potential compensation. Best practice is for analysts to accept only a flat fee for their work prior to writing the report, without regard to their conclusions or the report's recommendations.

## Recommended Procedures for Compliance

Members and candidates should follow certain practices and should encourage their firms to establish certain procedures to avoid violations of Standard I(B):

- ▶ Protect integrity of opinions. Members, candidates, and their firms should establish policies stating that every research report on issues by a corporate client reflects the unbiased opinion of the analyst. Firms should also design compensation systems that protect the integrity of the investment decision process by maintaining the independence and objectivity of analysts.

- ▶ Create a restricted list. If the firm is unwilling to permit dissemination of adverse opinions about a corporate client, members and candidates should encourage the firm to remove the controversial company from the research universe and put it on a restricted list so that the firm disseminates only factual information about the company.

- ▶ Restrict special cost arrangements. When attending meetings at an issuer's headquarters, members or candidates should pay for commercial transportation and hotel charges. No corporate issuer should reimburse members or candidates for air transportation. Members and candidates should encourage issuers to limit the use of corporate aircraft to situations in which commercial transportation is not available or in which efficient movement could not otherwise be arranged. Members and candidates should take particular care that when frequent meetings are held between an individual issuer and an individual member or candidate, the issuer should not always host the member or candidate.

- ▶ Limit gifts. Members and candidates must limit the acceptance of gratuities and/or gifts to token items. Standard I(B) does not preclude customary, ordinary, business-related entertainment so long as its purpose is not to influence or reward members or candidates.

▶ Restrict investments. Members and candidates should restrict (or encourage their investment firms to restrict) employee purchases of equity or equity-related IPOs. Strict limits should be imposed on investment personnel acquiring securities in private placements.

▶ Review procedures. Members and candidates should implement (or encourage their firms to implement) effective supervisory and review procedures to ensure that analysts and portfolio managers comply with policies relating to their personal investment activities.

▶ Firms should establish a formal written policy on the independence and objectivity of research and implement reporting structures and review procedures to ensure that research analysts do not report to and are not supervised or controlled by any department of the firm that could compromise the independence of the analyst. More detailed recommendations related to a firm's policies regarding research objectivity are set forth in the CFA Institute Research Objectivity Standards (www.cfainstitute.org).

## Application of the Standard

**Example 1:** Steven Taylor, a mining analyst with Bronson Brokers, is invited by Precision Metals to join a group of his peers in a tour of mining facilities in several western U.S. states. The company arranges for chartered group flights from site to site and for accommodations in Spartan Motels, the only chain with accommodations near the mines, for three nights. Taylor allows Precision Metals to pick up his tab, as do the other analysts, with one exception—John Adams, an employee of a large trust company who insists on following his company's policy and paying for his hotel room himself.

*Comment:* The policy of Adams's company complies closely with Standard I(B) by avoiding even the appearance of a conflict of interest, but Taylor and the other analysts were not necessarily violating Standard I(B). In general, when allowing companies to pay for travel and/or accommodations under these circumstances, members and candidates must use their judgment—keeping in mind that such arrangements must not impinge on a member's or candidate's independence and objectivity. In this example, the trip was strictly for business and Taylor was not accepting irrelevant or lavish hospitality. The itinerary required chartered flights, for which analysts were not expected to pay. The accommodations were modest. These arrangements are not unusual and did not violate Standard I(B) so long as Taylor's independence and objectivity were not compromised. In the final analysis, members and candidates should consider both whether they can remain objective and whether their integrity might be perceived by their clients to have been compromised.

**Example 2:** Susan Dillon, an analyst in the corporate finance department of an investment services firm, is making a presentation to a potential new business client that includes the promise that her firm will provide full research coverage of the potential client.

*Comment:* Dillon may agree to provide research coverage, but she must not commit her firm's research department to providing a favorable recommendation. The firm's recommendation (favorable, neutral, or unfavorable) must be based on an independent and objective investigation and analysis of the company and its securities.

***Example 3:*** Walter Fritz is an equity analyst with Hilton Brokerage who covers the mining industry. He has concluded that the stock of Metals & Mining is over-priced at its current level, but he is concerned that a negative research report will hurt the good relationship between Metals & Mining and the investment-banking division of his firm. In fact, a senior manager of Hilton Brokerage has just sent him a copy of a proposal his firm has made to Metals & Mining to under-write a debt offering. Fritz needs to produce a report right away and is concerned about issuing a less-than-favorable rating.

> *Comment:* Fritz's analysis of Metals & Mining must be objective and based solely on consideration of company fundamentals. Any pressure from other divisions of his firm is inappropriate. This conflict could have been eliminated if, in anticipation of the offering, Hilton Brokerage had placed Metals & Mining on a restricted list for its sales force.

***Example 4:*** As support for the sales effort of her corporate bond department, Lindsey Warner offers credit guidance to purchasers of fixed-income securities. Her compensation is closely linked to the performance of the corporate bond department. Near the quarter's end, Warner's firm has a large inventory position in the bonds of Milton, Ltd., and has been unable to sell the bonds because of Milton's recent announcement of an operating problem. Salespeople have asked her to contact large clients to push the bonds.

> *Comment:* Unethical sales practices create significant potential violations of the Code and Standards. Warner's opinion of the Milton bonds must not be affected by internal pressure or compensation. In this case, Warner must refuse to push the Milton bonds unless she is able to justify that the market price has already adjusted for the operating problem.

***Example 5:*** Jill Jorund is a securities analyst following airline stocks and a rising star at her firm. Her boss has been carrying a "buy" recommendation on International Airlines and asks Jorund to take over coverage of that airline. He tells Jorund that under no circumstances should the prevailing "buy" recommendation be changed.

> *Comment:* Jorund must be independent and objective in her analysis of International Airlines. If she believes that her boss's instructions have com-promised her, she has two options: Tell her boss that she cannot cover the company under these constraints, or pick up coverage of the company, reach her own independent conclusions, and if they conflict with her boss's opinion, share the conclusions with her boss or other supervisors in the firm so that they can make appropriate recommendations. Jorund must only issue recommendations that reflect only her independent and objective opinion.

***Example 6:*** Edward Grant directs a large amount of his commission business to a New York-based brokerage house. In appreciation for all the business, the bro-kerage house gives Grant two tickets to the World Cup in South Africa, two nights at a nearby resort, several meals, and transportation via limousine to the game. Grant fails to disclose receiving this package to his supervisor.

> *Comment:* Grant has violated Standard I(B) because accepting these substan-tial gifts may impede his independence and objectivity. Every member and candidate should endeavor to avoid situations that might cause or be per-ceived to cause a loss of independence or objectivity in recommending investments or taking investment action. By accepting the trip, Grant has opened himself up to the accusation that he may give the broker favored treatment in return.

*Example 7:* Theresa Green manages the portfolio of Ian Knowlden, a client of Tisbury Investments. Green achieves an annual return for Knowlden that is consistently better than that of the benchmark she and the client previously agreed to. As a reward, Knowlden offers Green two tickets to Wimbledon and the use of Knowlden's flat in London for a week. Green discloses this gift to her supervisor at Tisbury.

> *Comment:* Green is in compliance with Standard I(B) because she disclosed the gift from one of her clients. Members and candidates may accept bonuses or gifts from clients so long as they disclose them to their employers, because gifts in a client relationship are deemed less likely to affect a member's or candidate's objectivity and independence than gifts in other situations. Disclosure is required, however, so that supervisors can monitor such situations to guard against employees favoring a gift-giving client to the detriment of other fee-paying clients (such as by allocating a greater proportion of IPO stock to the gift-giving client's portfolio).

*Example 8:* Tom Wayne is the investment manager of the Franklin City Employees Pension Plan. He recently completed a successful search for a firm to manage the foreign equity allocation of the plan's diversified portfolio. He followed the plan's standard procedure of seeking presentations from a number of qualified firms and recommended that his board select Penguin Advisors because of its experience, well-defined investment strategy, and performance record, which was compiled and verified in accordance with the CFA Institute Global Investment Performance Standards. Following the plan selection of Penguin, a reporter from the Franklin City Record called to ask if there was any connection between this action and the fact that Penguin was one of the sponsors of an "investment fact-finding trip to Asia" that Wayne made earlier in the year. The trip was one of several conducted by the Pension Investment Academy, which had arranged the itinerary of meetings with economic, government, and corporate officials in major cities in several Asian countries. The Pension Investment Academy obtains support for the cost of these trips from a number of investment managers, including Penguin Advisors; the Academy then pays the travel expenses of the various pension plan managers on the trip and provides all meals and accommodations. The president of Penguin Advisors was one of the travelers on the trip.

> *Comment:* Although Wayne can probably put to good use the knowledge he gained from the trip in selecting portfolio managers and in other areas of managing the pension plan, his recommendation of Penguin Advisors may be tainted by the possible conflict incurred when he participated in a trip paid in part by Penguin Advisors and when he was in the daily company of the president of Penguin Advisors. To avoid violating Standard I(B), Wayne's basic expenses for travel and accommodations should have been paid by his employer or the pension plan; contact with the president of Penguin Advisors should have been limited to informational or educational events only; and the trip, the organizer, and the sponsor should have been made a matter of public record. Even if his actions were not in violation of Standard I(B), Wayne should have been sensitive to the public perception of the trip when reported in the newspaper and the extent to which the subjective elements of his decision might have been affected by the familiarity that the daily contact of such a trip would encourage. This advantage would probably not be shared by competing firms.

*Example 9:* Javier Herrero recently left his job as a research analyst for a large investment advisor. While looking for a new position, he is hired by an investor-relations firm to write a research report on one of its clients, a small educational software company. The investor-relations firm hopes to generate investor interest in the technology company. The firm will pay Herrero a flat fee plus a bonus if any new investors buy stock in the company as a result of Herrero's report.

> *Comment:* If Herrero accepts this payment arrangement, he will be in violation of Standard I(B) because the compensation can reasonably be expected to compromise his independence and objectivity. Herrero will receive a bonus for attracting investors, which is an overwhelming incentive to draft a positive report regardless of the facts and to ignore or play down any negative information about the company. Herrero should accept for his work only a flat fee that is not tied to the conclusions or recommendations of the report. Issuer-paid research that is objective and unbiased can be done under the right circumstances so long as the analyst takes steps to maintain his or her objectivity and includes in the report proper disclosures regarding potential conflicts of interest.

## C. Misrepresentation

**Members and candidates must not knowingly make any misrepresentations relating to investment analysis, recommendations, actions, or other professional activities.**

Trust is the foundation of the investment profession. Investors must be able to rely on the statements and information provided to them by those with whom investors trust their financial well being. Investment professionals who make false or misleading statements not only harm investors but also reduce the level of investor confidence in the investment profession and threaten the integrity of capital markets as a whole.

A misrepresentation is any untrue statement or omission of a fact or any statement that is otherwise false or misleading. A member or candidate must not knowingly misrepresent or give a false impression in oral representations, advertising (whether in the press or through brochures), electronic communications, or written materials (whether publicly disseminated or not). In this context, "knowingly" means that a member or candidate either knows or should have known that the misrepresentation was being made.

Written materials for a general audience include, but are not limited to, research reports, market letters, newspaper columns, and books. Electronic communications include, but are not limited to, Internet communications, web pages, chat rooms, and e-mail.

Members and candidates must not misrepresent any aspect of their practice, including (but not limited to) their qualifications or credentials, the qualifications or services provided by their firm, their performance record or the record of their firm, or the characteristics of an investment. Any misrepresentation made by the member or candidate relating to the member or candidate's professional activities is a breach of this standard.

Standard I(C) prohibits members and candidates from guaranteeing clients specific return on investments that are inherently volatile ("I can guarantee that you will earn 8 percent on equities this year," or "I can guarantee that you will not lose money on this investment"). For the most part, the majority of investments contain some element of risk that makes their return inherently unpredictable. In those situations, guaranteeing either a particular rate of return or a guaranteed preservation of investment capital is misleading to investors. Standard I(C) does not prohibit members and candidates from providing clients with information on investment products that have guarantees built into the structure of the product itself or for which an institution has agreed to cover any losses.

Standard I(C) also prohibits plagiarism in the preparation of material for distribution to employers, associates, clients, prospects, or the general public. Plagiarism is defined as copying or using in substantially the same form materials prepared by others without acknowledging the source of the material or identifying the author and publisher of such material. Members and candidates must not copy, or represent as their own, original ideas or material without permission and must acknowledge and identify the source of ideas or material that is not their own.

The investment profession uses a myriad of financial, economic, and statistical data in the investment decision-making process. Through various publications and presentations, the investment professional is constantly exposed to the work of others and to the temptation to use that work without proper acknowledgment.

Misrepresentation through plagiarism in investment management can take various forms. The simplest and most flagrant example is to take a research report or study done by another firm or person, change the names, and release the material as one's own original analysis. This action is a clear violation of Standard I(C). Other practices include (1) using excerpts from articles or reports prepared by others either verbatim or with only slight changes in wording without acknowledgment, (2) citing specific quotations supposedly attributable to "leading analysts" and "investment experts" without specific reference, (3) presenting statistical estimates of forecasts prepared by others with the source identified but without qualifying statements or caveats that may have been used, (4) using charts and graphs without stating their sources, and (5) copying proprietary computerized spreadsheets or algorithms without seeking the cooperation or authorization of their creators.

In the case of distributing third-party, outsourced research, members and candidates can use and distribute these reports so long as they do not represent themselves as the author of the report. The member or candidate may add value to the client by sifting through research and repackaging it for clients. The client should fully understand that he or she is paying for the ability of the member or candidate to find the best research from a wide variety of sources. However, members and candidates must not misrepresent their abilities, the extent of their expertise, or the extent of their work in a way that would mislead their clients or prospective clients. Members and candidates should consider disclosing whether the research being presented to clients comes from an outside source, from either within or outside the member's or candidate's firm. Clients should know who has the expertise behind the report or if the work is being done by the analyst, other members of the firm, or an outside party.

The standard also applies to plagiarism in oral communications, such as through group meetings; visits with associates, clients, and customers; use of audio/video media (which is rapidly increasing); and telecommunications, such as through electronic data transfer and the outright copying of electronic media.

One of the most egregious practices in violation of this standard is the preparation of research reports based on multiple sources of information without acknowledging the sources. Such information would include, for example, ideas, statistical compilations, and forecasts combined to give the appearance of original work. Although there is no monopoly on ideas, members and candidates must give credit when it is clearly due. Analysts should not use undocumented forecasts, earnings projections, asset values, and so on. Sources must be revealed to bring the responsibility directly back to the author of the report or the firm involved.

## Recommended Procedures for Compliance

Members and candidates can prevent unintentional misrepresentations of the qualifications or services they or their firms provide if each member and candidate understands the limit of the firms's or individual's capabilities and the need to be accurate and complete in presentations. Firms can provide guidance for employees who make written or oral presentations to clients or potential clients by providing a written list of the firm's available services and a description of the firm's qualifications. This list should suggest ways of describing the firm's services, qualifications, and compensation that are both accurate and suitable for client or customer presentations. Firms can also help prevent misrepresentation by specifically designating which employees are authorized to speak on behalf of the firm. Whether or not the firm provides guidance, members and candidates should make certain they understand the services the firm can perform and its qualifications.

In addition, in order to ensure accurate presentations to clients, each member and candidate should prepare a summary of his or her own qualifications and experience as well as a list of the services the member or candidate is capable of performing. Firms can assist member and candidate compliance by periodically reviewing employee correspondence and documents that contain representations of individual or firm qualifications.

Members and candidates who publish web pages should regularly monitor materials posted to the site to ensure the site maintains current information. Members and candidates should also ensure that all reasonable precautions have been taken to protect the site's integrity, confidentiality, and security, and that the site does not misrepresent any information and provides full disclosure.

To avoid plagiarism in preparing research reports or conclusions of analysis, members and candidates should take the following steps:

▶ Maintain copies. Keep copies of all research reports, articles containing research ideas, material with new statistical methodology, and other materials that were relied on in preparing the research report.

▶ Attribute quotations. Attribute to their sources any direct quotations, including projections, tables, statistics, model/product ideas, and new methodologies prepared by persons other than recognized financial and statistical reporting services or similar sources.

▶ Attribute summaries. Attribute to their sources paraphrases or summaries of material prepared by others. For example, to support his analysis of Brown's competitive position, the author of a research report on Brown Company may summarize another analyst's report of Brown's chief competitor, but the author of the Brown report must acknowledge in his own report his reliance on the other analyst's report.

## Application of the Standard

*Example 1:* Allison Rogers is a partner in the firm of Rogers and Black, a small firm offering investment advisory services. She assures a prospective client who has just inherited $1 million that "we can perform all the financial and investment services you need." Rogers and Black is well equipped to provide investment advice but, in fact, cannot provide asset allocation assistance or a full array of financial and investment services.

> *Comment:* Rogers has violated Standard I(C) by orally misrepresenting the services her firm can perform for the prospective client. She must limit herself to describing the range of investment advisory services Rogers and Black can provide and offer to help the client obtain elsewhere the financial and investment services that her firm cannot provide.

*Example 2:* Anthony McGuire is an issuer-paid analyst hired by publicly traded companies to electronically promote their stocks. McGuire creates a website that promotes his research efforts as a seemingly independent analyst. McGuire posts a profile and a strong buy recommendation for each company on the website indicating that the stock is expected to increase in value. He does not disclose the contractual relationships with the companies he covers on his website, in the research reports he issues, or in the statements he makes about the companies on Internet chat rooms.

> *Comment:* McGuire has violated Standard I(C) because the Internet site and e-mails are misleading to potential investors. Even if the recommendations are valid and supported with thorough research, his omissions regarding the true relationship between himself and the companies he covers constitute a misrepresentation. McGuire has also violated Standard VI(A) by not disclosing the existence of an arrangement with the companies through which he receives compensation in exchange for his services.

*Example 3:* Hijan Yao is responsible for the creation and distribution of the marketing material for his firm. Yao creates and distributes a performance presentation for the firm's Asian equity composite that complies with GIPS and states that the composite has 350 billion yen in assets. In fact, the composite has only 35 billion yen in assets, and the higher figure on the presentation is a result of a typographical error. Nevertheless, the erroneous material is distributed to a number of clients before Yao catches the mistake.

> *Comment:* Once the error is discovered, Yao must take steps to cease distribution of the incorrect material and correct the error by informing those who have received the erroneous information. However, because Yao did not knowingly make the misrepresentation, he did not violate the Code and Standards.

*Example 4:* Syed Muhammad is the president of an investment management firm. The promotional material for the firm, created by the firm's marketing department, incorrectly claims that Muhammad has an advanced degree in finance from a prestigious business school in addition to the CFA designation. Although Muhammad attended the school for a short period of time, he did not receive a degree. Over the years, Muhammad and others in the firm have distributed this material to numerous prospective clients and consultants.

> *Comment:* Even though Muhammad may not have been directly responsible for the misrepresentation about his credentials contained in the firm's promotional material, he used this material numerous times over an extended period and should have known of the misrepresentation. Thus, Muhammad has violated Standard I(C).

*Example 5:* Cindy Grant, a research analyst for a Canadian brokerage firm, has specialized in the Canadian mining industry for the past 10 years. She recently read an extensive research report on Jefferson Mining, Ltd., by Jeremy Barton, another analyst. Barton provided extensive statistics on the mineral reserves, production capacity, selling rates, and marketing factors affecting Jefferson's operations. He also noted that initial drilling results on a new ore body, which had not been made public, might show the existence of mineral zones that could increase the life of Jefferson's main mines, but Barton cited no specific data as to the initial drilling results. Grant called an officer of Jefferson, who gave her the initial drilling results over the telephone. The data indicated that the expected life of the main mines would be tripled. Grant added these statistics to Barton's report and circulated it as her own report within her firm.

*Comment:* Grant plagiarized Barton's report by reproducing large parts of it in her own report without acknowledgment.

***Example 6:*** When Ricki Marks sells mortgage-backed derivatives called interest-only strips (IOs) to her public pension plan clients, she describes them as "guaranteed by the U.S. government." Purchasers of the IOs, however, are entitled only to the interest stream generated by the mortgages not the notional principal itself. The municipality's investment policies and local law require that securities purchased by the public pension plans be guaranteed by the U.S. government. Although the underlying mortgages are guaranteed, neither the investor's investment nor the interest stream on the IOs is guaranteed. When interest rates decline, causing an increase in prepayment of mortgages, the interest payments to the clients decline, and the clients lose a portion of their investment.

*Comment:* Marks violated Standard I(C) by misrepresenting the terms and character of the investment.

***Example 7:*** Khalouck Abdrabbo manages the investments of several high-net-worth individuals in the United States who are approaching retirement. Abdrabbo advises that a portion of their investments be moved from equity to certificates of deposit and money-market accounts so the principal will be "guaranteed" up to a certain amount. The interest is not guaranteed.

*Comment:* While there is risk that the institution offering the certificates of deposits and money-market accounts could go bankrupt, in the U.S., these accounts are insured by the United States government through the Federal Deposit Insurance Corporation. Therefore, using the term "guaranteed" in this context is not inappropriate as long as the amount is within the government-insured limit. Abdrabbo should explain these facts to the clients.

***Example 8:*** Steve Swanson is a senior analyst in the investment research department of Ballard and Company. Apex Corporation has asked Ballard to assist in acquiring the majority ownership in stock of Campbell Company, a financial consulting firm, and to prepare a report recommending that stockholders of Campbell agree to the acquisition. Another investment firm, Davis and Company, had already prepared a report for Apex analyzing both Apex and Campbell and recommending an exchange ratio. Apex has given the Davis report to Ballard officers, who have passed it on to Swanson, who then reviewed the Davis report along with other available material on Apex and Campbell companies. From his analysis, he concludes that the common stocks of Campbell and Apex represent good value at their current prices; he believes, however, that the Davis report does not consider all the factors a Campbell stockholder would need to know to make a decision. Swanson reports his conclusions to the partner in charge, who tells him to "use the Davis report, change a few words, sign your name, and get it out."

*Comment:* If Swanson does as requested, he will violate Standard I(C). He could refer to those portions of the Davis report that he agrees with if he identifies Davis as the source; he could then add his own analysis and conclusions to the report before signing and distributing it.

***Example 9:*** Claude Browning, a quantitative analyst for Double Alpha, Inc., returns in great excitement from a seminar. In that seminar, Jack Jorrely, a well-publicized quantitative analyst at a national brokerage firm, discussed one of his new models in great detail, and Browning is intrigued by the new concepts. He proceeds to test this model, making some minor mechanical changes but retaining the concept, until he produces some very positive results. Browning quickly announces to his supervisors at Double Alpha that he has discovered a new model and that clients and prospective clients alike should be informed of this positive finding as ongoing proof of Double Alpha's continuing innovation and ability to add value.

> *Comment:* Although Browning tested Jorrely's model on his own and even slightly modified it, he must still acknowledge the original source of the idea. Browning can certainly take credit for the final, practical results; he can also support his conclusions with his own test. The credit for the innovative thinking, however, must be awarded to Jorrely.

**Example 10:** Fernando Zubia would like to include in his firm's marketing materials plain-language descriptions of various concepts, such as the price-to-earnings multiple and why standard deviation is used as a measure of risk, that are taken from other sources without reference to the original author. Is this a violation of Standard I(C)?

> *Comment:* Copying verbatim any material without acknowledgement, including plain-language descriptions of the price-to-earnings multiple and standard deviation, violates Standard I(C). Even though these are general concepts, best practice would be for Zubia to describe them in his own words or cite the source from which the descriptions are quoted. Members and candidates responsible for creating marketing materials and those who knowingly use plagiarized materials could potentially be sanctioned if the matter was brought to the attention of the CFA Institute Professional Conduct Program.

**Example 11:** Through a mainstream media outlet, Erika Schneider learns about a study that she would like to cite in her research. Should she cite both the mainstream intermediary source as well as the author of the study itself when using that information?

> *Comment:* In all instances, it is necessary to cite the actual source of the information. Best practice would be to obtain the information directly from the author and review it before citing it in a report. In that instance, Schneider would not need to report how she found out about the information. For example, suppose Schneider reads in the *Financial Times* about a study issued by CFA Institute; best practice for Schneider would be to obtain a copy of the study from CFA Institute, review it, and then cite it in her report. If she does not use any interpretation from the *Financial Times* and it is not adding value to the report itself, the newspaper is merely a conduit to the original information she wants to use in the report and it need not be cited. If she does not obtain the report and review the information, Schneider runs the risk of relying on second-hand information that may misstate the source. If, for example, the *Financial Times* erroneously reported the information from the original CFA Institute study and Schneider copied that erroneous information without acknowledging CFA Institute, she would open herself to complaint. Best practice would be either to obtain the complete study from its original author and cite only that author or to use the information provided by the intermediary and cite both sources.

**Example 12:** Gary Ostrowski runs a small, two-person investment management firm. Ostrowski's firm subscribes to a service from a large investment research firm that provides research reports that can be repackaged as in-house research from smaller firms. Ostrowski's firm distributes these reports to clients as its own work.

> *Comment:* Ostrowski can rely on third-party research that has a reasonable and adequate basis, but he cannot imply that he is the author of the report. Otherwise, Ostrowski would misrepresent the extent of his work in a way that would mislead the firm's clients or prospective clients.

## D. Misconduct

**Members and candidates must not engage in any professional conduct involving dishonesty, fraud, or deceit or commit any act that reflects adversely on their professional reputation, integrity, or competence.**

Whereas Standard I(A) addresses the obligation of members and candidates to comply with applicable law that governs their professional activities, Standard I(D) addresses conduct that reflects poorly on the professional integrity, good reputation, or competence of members and candidates. Although CFA Institute discourages any sort of unethical behavior by members and candidates, the Code and Standards are aimed at conduct related to a member's or candidate's professional life. Any act that involves lying, cheating, stealing, or other dishonest conduct that reflects adversely on a member's or candidate's professional activities, would violate this standard.

Conduct that damages trustworthiness or competence can include behavior that may not be illegal but could negatively affect a member's or candidate's ability to perform his or her responsibilities. For example, abusing alcohol during business hours could constitute a violation of this standard because it could have a detrimental effect on the member or candidate's ability to fulfill his or her professional responsibilities. Personal bankruptcy may not reflect on the integrity or trustworthiness of the person declaring bankruptcy, but if the circumstances of the bankruptcy involve fraudulent or deceitful business conduct, it may be a violation of this standard.

Individuals may attempt to abuse the CFA Institute Professional Conduct Program by actively seeking CFA Institute enforcement of the Code and Standards, and Standard I(D) in particular, as a method to settle personal, political, or other disputes unrelated to professional ethics. CFA Institute is aware of this issue, and appropriate disciplinary policies, procedures, and enforcement mechanisms are in place to address misuse of the Code and Standards and the Professional Conduct Program in this way.

## Recommended Procedures for Compliance

To prevent general misconduct, members and candidates should encourage their firms to adopt the following policies and procedures to support the principles of Standard I(D):

▶ Develop and/or adopt a code of ethics to which every employee must subscribe and make clear that any personal behavior that reflects poorly on the individual involved, the institution as a whole, or the investment industry will not be tolerated.

▶ Disseminate to all employees a list of potential violations and associated disciplinary sanctions, up to and including dismissal from the firm.

▶ Check references of potential employees to ensure that they are of good character and not ineligible to work in the investment industry because of past infractions of the law.

## Application of the Standard

***Example 1:*** Simon Sasserman is a trust investment officer at a bank in a small affluent town. He enjoys lunching every day with friends at the country club, where his clients have observed him having numerous drinks. Back at work after lunch, he clearly is intoxicated while making investment decisions. His colleagues make a point of handling any business with Sasserman in the morning because they distrust his judgment after lunch.

> *Comment:* Sasserman's excessive drinking at lunch and subsequent intoxication at work constitute a violation of Standard I(D) because this conduct has raised questions about his professionalism and competence. His behavior thus reflects poorly on him, his employer, and the investment industry.

***Example 2:*** Howard Hoffman, a security analyst at ATZ Brothers, Inc., a large brokerage house, submits reimbursement forms over a two-year period to ATZ's self-funded health insurance program for more than two dozen bills, most of which have been altered to increase the amount due. An investigation by the firm's director of employee benefits uncovers the conduct. ATZ subsequently terminates Hoffman's employment and notifies CFA Institute.

> *Comment:* Hoffman violated Standard I(D) because he engaged in intentional conduct involving fraud and deceit in the workplace that adversely reflected on his honesty.

***Example 3:*** Jody Brink, an analyst covering the automotive industry, volunteers much of her spare time to local charities. The board of one of the charitable institutions decides to buy five new vans to deliver hot lunches to low-income elderly people. Brink offers to donate her time to handle purchasing agreements. To pay a long-standing debt to a friend who operates an automobile dealership—and to compensate herself for her trouble—she agrees to a price 20 percent higher than normal and splits the surcharge with her friend. The director of the charity ultimately discovers the scheme and tells Brink that her services, donated or otherwise, are no longer required.

> *Comment:* Brink engaged in conduct involving dishonesty, fraud, and misrepresentation and has violated Standard I(D).

***Example 4:*** Carmen Garcia manages a mutual fund dedicated to socially responsible investing. She is also an environmental activist. As the result of her participation at nonviolent protests, Garcia has been arrested on numerous occasions for trespassing on the property of a large petrochemical plant that is accused of damaging the environment.

> *Comment:* Generally, Standard I(D) is not meant to cover legal transgressions resulting from acts of civil disobedience in support of personal beliefs because such conduct does not reflect poorly on the member's or candidate's professional reputation, integrity, or competence.

# STANDARD II—INTEGRITY OF CAPITAL MARKETS

## A. Material Nonpublic Information

**Members and candidates who possess material nonpublic information that could affect the value of an investment must not act or cause others to act on the information.**

Trading on material nonpublic information erodes confidence in capital markets, institutions, and investment professionals by supporting the idea that those with inside information and special access can take unfair advantage of the general investing public. Although trading on inside information may lead to short-term profits, in the long run, individuals and the profession as a whole will suffer as investors avoid capital markets perceived to be "rigged" in favor of the knowledgeable insider. Standard II(A) promotes and maintains a high level of confidence in market integrity, which is one of the foundations of the investment profession.

Information is "material" if its disclosure would likely have an impact on the price of a security or if reasonable investors would want to know the information before making an investment decision. In other words, information is material if it would significantly alter the total mix of information currently available regarding a security such that the price of the security would be affected.

The specificity of the information, the extent of its difference from public information, its nature, and its reliability are key factors in determining whether a particular piece of information fits the definition of material. For example, material information may include, but is not limited to, information on the following:

▶ earnings;

▶ mergers, acquisitions, tender offers, or joint ventures;

▶ changes in assets;

▶ innovative products, processes, or discoveries;

▶ new licenses, patents, registered trademarks, or regulatory approval/rejection of a product;

▶ developments regarding customers or suppliers (e.g., the acquisition or loss of a contract);

▶ changes in management;

▶ change in auditor notification or the fact that the issuer may no longer rely on an auditor's report or qualified opinion;

▶ events regarding the issuer's securities (e.g., defaults on senior securities, calls of securities for redemption, repurchase plans, stock splits, changes in dividends, changes to the rights of security holders, public or private sales of additional securities, and changes in credit ratings);

▶ bankruptcies;

▶ significant legal disputes;

▶ government reports of economic trends (employment, housing starts, currency information, etc.);

▶ orders for large trades before they are executed.

In addition to the substance and specificity of the information, the source or relative reliability of the information also determines materiality. The less reliable a source, the less likely the information provided would be considered material. For example, factual information from a corporate insider regarding a significant new contract for a company would likely be material, while an assumption based on speculation by a competitor about the same contract might be less reliable and, therefore, not material.

Also, the more ambiguous the effect on price, the less material the information becomes. If it is unclear whether the information will affect the price of a security and to what extent, information may not be considered material. The passage of time may also render information that was once important immaterial.

Information is "nonpublic" until it has been disseminated or is available to the marketplace in general (as opposed to a select group of investors). Dissemination can be defined as "made known to." For example, a company report of profits that is posted on the Internet and distributed widely through a press release or accompanied by a filing has been effectively disseminated to the marketplace. Members and candidates must have a reasonable expectation that people have received the information before it can be considered public. It is not necessary, however, to wait for the slowest method of delivery. Once the information is disseminated to the market, it is public information that is no longer covered by this standard.

Members and candidates must be particularly aware of information that is selectively disclosed by corporations to a small group of investors, analysts, or other market participants. Information that is made available to analysts remains nonpublic until it is made available to investors in general. Corporations that disclose information on a limited basis create the potential for insider-trading violations.

Issues of selective disclosure often arise when a corporate insider provides material information to analysts in a briefing or conference call before that information is released to the public. Analysts must be aware that a disclosure made to a room full of analysts does not necessarily make the disclosed information "public." Analysts should also be alert to the possibility that they are selectively receiving material nonpublic information when a company provides them with guidance or interpretation of such publicly available information as financial statements or regulatory filings.

### Mosaic Theory

A financial analyst gathers and interprets large quantities of information from many sources. The analyst may use significant conclusions derived from the analysis of public and nonmaterial nonpublic information as the basis for investment recommendations and decisions even if those conclusions would have been material inside information had they been communicated directly to the analyst by a company. Under the "mosaic theory," financial analysts are free to act on this collection, or mosaic, of information without risking violation.

The practice of financial analysis depends on the free flow of information. For the fair and efficient operation of the capital markets, analysts and investors must have the greatest amount of information possible to facilitate well-informed investment decisions about how and where to invest capital. Accurate, timely, and intelligible communication are essential if analysts and investors are to obtain the data needed to make informed decisions about how and where to invest capital. These disclosures must go beyond the information mandated by the reporting requirements of the securities laws and should include specific business information about items used to guide a company's future growth, such as new products, capital projects, and the competitive environment. Analysts seek and use such information to compare and contrast investment alternatives.

Much of the information used by analysts comes directly from companies. Analysts often receive such information through contacts with corporate insiders, especially investor relations and finance officers. Information may be disseminated in the form of press releases, through oral presentations by company executives in analysts' meetings or conference calls, or during analysts' visits to company premises. In seeking to develop the most accurate and complete picture of a company, analysts should also reach beyond contacts with companies themselves and collect information from other sources, such as customers, contractors, suppliers, and companies' competitors.

Analysts are in the business of formulating opinions and insights—not obvious to the general investing public—concerning the attractiveness of particular securities. In the course of their work, analysts actively seek out corporate information not generally known to the market for the express purpose of analyzing that information, forming an opinion on its significance, and informing their clients who can be expected to trade on the basis of the recommendation. Analysts' initiatives to discover and analyze information and communicate their findings to their clients significantly enhance market efficiency, thus benefiting all investors (see U.S. Supreme Court case *Dirks v. Securities and Exchange Commission* [463 US 646]).

Accordingly, violations of Standard II(A) will not result when a perceptive analyst reaches a conclusion about a corporate action or event through an analysis of public information and items of nonmaterial nonpublic information. Investment professionals should note, however, that although analysts are free to use mosaic information in their research reports, they should save and document all their research [see Standard V(C)]. Evidence of the analyst's knowledge of public and nonmaterial nonpublic information about a corporation strengthens the assertion that the analyst reached his or her conclusions solely through appropriate methods rather than through the use of material nonpublic information.

When a particularly well-known or respected analyst issues a report or makes changes to his or her recommendation, that information alone could have an effect on the market and, thus, could be considered material. Theoretically, under this standard, such a report would have to be made public before it was distributed to clients. However, the analyst is not a company insider and does not have access to inside information. Presumably, the analyst created the report with information available to the public (mosaic theory) using his or her expertise to interpret the information. The analyst's hard work, paid for by the client, generated the conclusions. Simply because the public in general would find the conclusions material does not require that the analyst make his or her work public. Investors who are not clients of the analyst can either do the work themselves or become a client of the analyst if they want access to the analyst's expertise.

## Recommended Procedures for Compliance

If a member or candidate determines that information is material, the member or candidate should make reasonable efforts to achieve public dissemination of the information. This effort usually entails encouraging the issuer company to make the information public. If public dissemination is not possible, the member or candidate must communicate the information only to the designated supervisory and compliance personnel within the member's or candidate's firm and must not take investment action on the basis of the information. Moreover, members and candidates must not knowingly engage in any conduct that may induce company insiders to privately disclose material nonpublic information.

Members and candidates should encourage their firms to adopt compliance procedures to prevent the misuse of material nonpublic information. Particularly important is improving compliance in such areas as the review of employee and proprietary trading, documentation of firm procedures, and the supervision of interdepartmental communications in multiservice firms. Compliance procedures should suit the particular characteristics of a firm, including its size and the nature of its business.

Members and candidates should encourage their firms to develop and follow disclosure policies designed to ensure that information is disseminated to the marketplace in an equitable manner. For example, analysts from small firms should receive the same information and attention from a company as analysts from large firms receive. Similarly, companies should not provide certain information to buy-side analysts but not to sell-side analysts, or vice versa. Furthermore, a company should not discriminate among analysts in the provision of information or blackball particular analysts who have given negative reports on the company in the past.

Companies should consider issuing press releases prior to analyst meetings and conference calls and scripting those meetings and calls to decrease the chance that further information will be disclosed. If material nonpublic information is disclosed for the first time in an analyst meeting or call, the company should promptly issue a press release or otherwise make the information publicly available.

An information barrier commonly referred to as a "firewall" is the most widely used approach to preventing the communication of material nonpublic information within firms. It restricts the flow of confidential information to those who need to know the information to perform their jobs effectively. The minimum elements of such a system include, but are not limited to, the following:

▶ substantial control of relevant interdepartmental communications, preferably through a clearance area within the firm in either the compliance or legal department;

▶ review of employee trading through the maintenance of "watch," "restricted," and "rumor" lists;

▶ documentation of the procedures designed to limit the flow of information between departments and of the enforcement actions taken pursuant to those procedures;

▶ heightened review or restriction of proprietary trading while a firm is in possession of material nonpublic information.

Although documentation requirements must, for practical reasons, take into account the differences between the activities of small firms and those of large, multiservice firms, firms of all sizes and types benefit by improving the documentation of their internal enforcement of firewall procedures. Therefore, even at small firms, procedures concerning interdepartmental communication, the review of trading activity, and the investigation of possible violations should be compiled and formalized.

As a practical matter, to the extent possible, firms should consider the physical separation of departments and files to prevent the communication of sensitive information. For example, the investment-banking and corporate finance areas of a brokerage firm should be separated from the sales and research departments, and a bank's commercial lending department should be segregated from its trust and research departments.

There should be no overlap of personnel between such departments. A single supervisor or compliance officer should have the specific authority and responsibility to decide whether or not information is material and whether it is sufficiently public to be used as the basis for investment decisions. Ideally, the supervisor or compliance officer responsible for communicating information to a firm's research or brokerage area would not be a member of that area.

For a firewall to be effective in a multiservice firm, an employee can be allowed to be on only one side of the wall at any given time. Inside knowledge may not be limited to information about a specific offering or a current financial condition of the company. Analysts may be exposed to a host of information about the company, including new product developments or future budget projections that clearly constitute inside knowledge and thus preclude the analyst from returning to his or her research function. For example, an analyst who follows a particular company may provide limited assistance to the investment bankers under carefully controlled circumstances when the firm's investment-banking department is involved in a deal with the company. That analyst must then be treated as though he or she were an investment banker; the analyst must remain on the investment-banking side of the wall until any information he or she learns is publicly disclosed. In short, the analyst cannot use any information learned in the course of the project for research purposes and cannot share that information with colleagues in the research department.

A primary objective of an effective firewall procedure is to establish a reporting system in which authorized people review and approve communications between departments. If an employee behind a firewall believes that he or she needs to share confidential information with someone on the other side of the wall, the employee should consult a designated compliance officer to determine whether sharing the information is necessary and how much information should be shared. If the sharing is necessary, the compliance officer should coordinate the process of "looking over the wall" so that the necessary information will be shared and the integrity of the procedure will be maintained.

An information barrier is the minimum procedure a firm should have in place to protect itself from liability. Firms should also consider restrictions or prohibitions on personal trading by employees and should carefully monitor both proprietary trading and personal trading by employees. Firms should require employees to make periodic reports (to the extent that such reporting is not already required by securities laws) of their own transactions and transactions made for the benefit of family members. Securities should be placed on a restricted list when a firm has or may have material nonpublic information. The broad distribution of a restricted list often triggers the sort of trading the list was developed to avoid. Therefore, a watch list shown to only the few people responsible for compliance should be used to monitor transactions in specified securities. The use of a watch list in combination with a restricted list is an increasingly common means of ensuring an effective procedure.

Multiservice firms should maintain written records of the communications between various departments. Firms should place a high priority on training and should consider instituting comprehensive training programs, particularly for employees in sensitive areas.

Procedures concerning the restriction or review of a firm's proprietary trading while it is in the possession of material nonpublic information will necessarily vary depending on the types of proprietary trading in which a firm may engage. A prohibition on all types of proprietary activity when a firm comes into possession of material nonpublic information is *not* appropriate. For example, when a firm acts as a market maker, a proprietary trading prohibition may be counterproductive to the goals of maintaining the confidentiality of information and market liquidity. This concern is particularly keen in the relationships between small, regional broker/dealers and small issuers. In many situations, a firm will take a small issuer public with the understanding that the firm will continue to be a market maker in the stock. In such instances, a withdrawal by the firm from market-making acts would be a clear tip to outsiders. However, firms that continue market-making activity while in the possession of material nonpublic information should instruct their market makers to remain passive to the market—that is, take only the contra side of unsolicited customer trades.

In risk-arbitrage trading, the case for a trading prohibition is more compelling. In contrast to market making, the impetus for arbitrage trading is neither passive nor reactive and the potential for illegal profits is greater. The most prudent course for firms is to suspend arbitrage activity when a security is placed on the watch list. Those firms that do continue arbitrage activity face a high hurdle in proving the adequacy of their internal procedures and must demonstrate stringent review and documentation of firm trades.

Written compliance policies and guidelines should be circulated to all employees of a firm. Policies and guidelines should be used in conjunction with training programs aimed at enabling employees to recognize material nonpublic information. As noted, material nonpublic information is not always clearly identifiable as such. Employees must be given sufficient training to either make an informed decision or consult a supervisor or compliance officer before engaging in questionable transactions.

## Application of the Standard

***Example 1:*** Frank Barnes, the president and controlling shareholder of the SmartTown clothing chain, decides to accept a proposed tender offer and sell the family business at a price almost double the market price of its shares. He describes this decision to his sister (SmartTown's treasurer), who conveys it to her daughter (who owns no stock in the family company at present), who tells her husband, Staple. Staple, however, tells his stockbroker, Alex Halsey, who immediately buys SmartTown stock for himself.

> *Comment:* The information regarding the pending sale is both material and nonpublic. Staple has violated Standard II(A) by communicating the inside information to his broker. Also, Halsey has violated the standard by initiating the transaction to buy the shares based on material nonpublic information.

***Example 2:*** Josephine Walsh is riding an elevator up to her office when she overhears the chief financial officer (CFO) for the Swan Furniture Company tell the president of Swan that he has just calculated the company's earnings for the past quarter and they have unexpectedly and significantly dropped. The CFO adds that this drop will not be released to the public until next week. Walsh immediately calls her broker and tells him to sell her Swan stock.

> *Comment:* Walsh has sufficient information to determine that the information is both material and nonpublic. By trading the inside information, she has violated Standard II(A).

***Example 3:*** Samuel Peter, an analyst with Scotland and Pierce Incorporated, is assisting his firm with a secondary offering for Bright Ideas Lamp Company. Peter participates, via telephone conference call, in a meeting with Scotland and Pierce investment-banking employees and Bright Ideas' CEO. Peter is advised that the company's earnings projections for the next year have significantly dropped. Throughout the telephone conference call, several Scotland and Pierce salespeople and portfolio managers walk in and out of Peter's office, where the telephone call is taking place. As a result, they are aware of the drop in projected earnings for Bright Ideas. Before the conference call is concluded, the salespeople trade the stock of the company on behalf of the firm's clients and other firm personnel trade the stock in a firm proprietary account and in employee personal accounts.

> *Comment:* Peter violated Standard II(A) because he failed to prevent the transfer and misuse of material nonpublic information to others in his firm. Peter's firm should have adopted information barriers to prevent the communication of nonpublic information between departments of the firm. The salespeople and portfolio managers who traded on the information have also violated Standard II(A) by trading on inside information.

***Example 4:*** Madison & Lambeau, a well-respected broker/dealer, submits a weekly column to *Securities Weekly* magazine. Once published, the column usually affects the value of the stocks discussed. Ron George, an employee of Madison & Lambeau, knows that *Securities Weekly* is published by Ziegler Publishing, for which his nephew is the night foreman. George's nephew faxes him an advance copy of the weekly column before it is printed. George regularly trades in the securities mentioned in the Madison & Lambeau column prior to its distribution, and to date, he has realized a personal profit of $42,000 as well as significant profits for his clients.

> *Comment:* George has violated Standard II(A) by trading on material nonpublic information. George's nephew has also violated the standard by communicating the information that causes George to trade.

**Example 5:** Greg Newman and his wife volunteer at a local charitable organization that delivers meals to the elderly. One morning, Newman's wife receives a telephone call from Betsy Sterling, another volunteer, who asks if Newman and his wife can fill in for her and her husband that afternoon. Mrs. Sterling indicates that her husband is busy at work because his company has just fired its chief financial officer for misappropriation of funds. Mrs. Newman agrees to perform the volunteer work for the Sterlings and advises her husband of the situation. Newman knows that Mr. Sterling is the CEO at O'Hara Brothers Incorporated. Newman determines that this information is not public and then sells his entire holding of 3,000 shares of O'Hara Brothers. Three days later, the firing is announced and O'Hara Brothers stock drops in value.

> *Comment:* Because the information is material and nonpublic, Newman has violated Standard II(A) by trading on this information.

**Example 6:** Elizabeth Levenson is based in Taipei and covers the Taiwanese market for her firm, which is based in Singapore. She is invited to meet the finance director of a manufacturing company along with the other 10 largest shareholders of the company. During the meeting, the finance director states that the company expects its workforce to strike next Friday, which will cripple productivity and distribution. Can Levenson use this information as a basis to change her rating on the company from "buy" to "sell"?

> *Comment:* Levenson must first determine whether the material information is public. If the company has not made this information public (a small-group forum does not qualify as a method of public dissemination), she cannot use the information according to Standard II(A).

**Example 7:** Leah Fechtman is trying to decide whether to hold or sell shares of an oil and gas exploration company that she owns in several of the funds she manages. Although the company has underperformed the index for some time already, the trends in the industry sector signal that companies of this type might become takeover targets. In the midst of the decision, her doctor, who casually follows the markets, mentions that she thinks that the company in question will soon be bought out by a large multinational conglomerate and that it would be a good idea to buy the stock right now. After talking to various investment professionals and checking their opinions on the company as well as industry trends, Fechtman decides the next day to accumulate more company stock.

> *Comment:* Although information on an expected takeover bid may be of the type that is generally material and nonpublic, in this case, the source of information is unreliable and could not be considered material. Therefore, Fechtman is not prohibited from trading the stock based on this information.

**Example 8:** Jagdish Teja is a buy-side analyst covering the furniture industry. Looking for an attractive company to recommend as a buy, he analyzed several furniture makers by studying their financial reports and visiting their operations. He also talked to some designers and retailers to find out which furniture styles are trendy and popular. Although none of the companies that he analyzed turned out to be a clear buy, he discovered that one of them, Swan Furniture

Company (SFC), might be in trouble. Swan's extravagant new designs were introduced at substantial costs. Even though these designs initially attracted attention, in the long run, the public is buying more conservative furniture from other makers. Based on that and on P&L analysis, Teja believes that Swan's next-quarter earnings will drop substantially. He then issues a sell recommendation for SFC. Immediately after receiving that recommendation, investment managers start reducing the stock in their portfolios.

> *Comment:* Information on quarterly earnings figures is material and nonpublic. However, Teja arrived at his conclusion about the earnings drop based on public information and on pieces of nonmaterial nonpublic information (such as opinions of designers and retailers). Therefore, trading based on Teja's correct conclusion is not prohibited by Standard II(A).

*Example 9:* Roger Clement is a senior financial analyst who specializes in the European automobile sector at Rivoli Capital. Because he has been repeatedly nominated by many leading industry magazines and newsletters as "best analyst" for the automobile industry, he is widely regarded as an authority on the sector. After speaking with representatives of Turgot Chariots, a European auto manufacturer with sales primarily in Korea, as well as salespeople, labor leaders, his firm's Korean currency analysts, and banking officials, Clement reviewed his analysis of Turgot Chariots and concluded that (1) its newly introduced model will probably not meet sales anticipation, (2) its corporate restructuring strategy might well face serious opposition from the unions, (3) the depreciation of the Korean won should lead to pressure on margins for the industry in general and Turgot's market segment in particular, and (4) banks could take a tougher-than-expected stance in the soon-to-come round of credit renegotiations. For these reasons, he changed his recommendation from market overperform to underperform.

> *Comment:* To reach a conclusion about the value of the company, Clement has pieced together a number of nonmaterial or public bits of information that affect Turgot Chariots. Therefore, under the "mosaic theory," Clement has not violated Standard II(A) in drafting the report.

*Example 10:* The next day, Clement is preparing to be interviewed on a global financial news television program where he will discuss his changed recommendation on Turgot Chariots for the first time in public. While preparing for the program, he mentions to the show's producers and Mary Zito, the journalist who will be interviewing him, the information he will be discussing. Just prior to going on the air, Zito sells her holdings in Turgot Chariots.

> *Comment:* Zito knows that Clement's opinions will have a strong influence on the stock's behavior, so when she receives advanced notice of Clement's change of opinion, she knows it will have a material impact on the stock price, even if she is not totally aware of Clement's underlying reasoning. She is not a client of Clement but obtains early access to the material nonpublic information prior to publication. Her actions are thus trades based on material nonpublic information and violate Standard II(A).

*Example 11:* Timothy Holt is a portfolio manager for the Toro Aggressive Growth Fund, a large mutual fund with an aggressive growth mandate. As a result, the fund is heavily invested in small-cap companies with strong growth potential. Based on an unfavorable analysis of McCardell Industries by his research department, Holt decides to liquidate the fund's holdings in the company. Holt knows that this action will be widely viewed as negative by the market and that the company's stock is likely to plunge. He contacts several family members to tell them to liquidate any of their holdings before Toro's holdings are sold.

*Comment:* Holt knows that Toro's trades have a strong influence on the market. Therefore, when he tells his family to sell stock in advance of Toro's trade, he has violated Standard II(A) by causing others to trade on material nonpublic information.

**Example 12:** Holt executes his sell order of McCardell Industries with Toro's broker, Karim Ahmed. Ahmed immediately recognizes the likely effect this order will have on the stock price of McCardell and sells his own holdings in the company prior to placing the order.

*Comment:* Ahmed has violated Standard II(A) by trading on material nonpublic information.

## B. Market Manipulation

**Members and candidates must not engage in practices that distort prices or artificially inflate trading volume with the intent to mislead market participants.**

Standard II(B) requires that members and candidates uphold market integrity by prohibiting market manipulation. Market manipulation includes practices that distort security prices or trading volume with the intent to deceive people or entities that rely on information in the market. Market manipulation damages the interests of all investors by disrupting the smooth functioning of financial markets and damaging investor confidence. Although it may be less likely to occur in more mature financial markets, cross-border investing increasingly exposes all global investors to the potential for such practices.

Market manipulation can be related to (1) transactions that deceive market participants by distorting the price-setting mechanism of financial instruments or (2) the dissemination of false or misleading information. The development of new products and technologies enhances the incentives, means, and opportunities for market manipulation.

Transaction-based manipulation includes, but is not limited to:

▶ transactions that artificially distort prices or volume to give the impression of activity or price movement in a financial instrument and

▶ securing a controlling, dominant position in a financial instrument to exploit and manipulate the price of a related derivative and/or the underlying asset.

By requiring that violations include the intent to mislead by creating artificial price or volume levels, this standard is not meant to prohibit legitimate trading strategies that exploit a difference in market power, information, or other market inefficiencies. Legitimate orders in a thinly traded security could overwhelm the liquidity for that security, which would be different from efforts to artificially affect the price of the security at the close of trading. In addition, this standard is not meant to prohibit transactions done for tax purposes, such as selling and immediately buying back a particular stock. The intent of the action is critical to determining whether it is a violation of this standard.

Information-based manipulation includes, but is not limited to, spreading false rumors to induce trading by others. For example, members and candidates must refrain from "pumping up" the price of an investment by issuing misleading positive information or overly optimistic projections of a security's worth only to later "dump" ownership in the investment once the price of the stock, fueled by the misleading information's effect on other market participants, reaches an artificially high level.

## Application of the Standard

*Example 1:* The principal owner of Financial Information Services (FIS) entered into an agreement with two microcap companies to promote the companies' stock in exchange for stock and cash compensation. The principal owner caused FIS to disseminate e-mails, design and maintain several Internet websites, and distribute an online investment newsletter—all of which recommended investment in the two companies. The systematic publication of purportedly independent analysis and recommendations containing inaccurate and highly promotional and speculative statements increased public investment in the companies and led to dramatically higher stock prices.

> *Comment:* The principal owner of FIS violated Standard II(B) by using inaccurate reporting and misleading information under the guise of independent analysis to artificially increase the stock price of the companies. Furthermore, the principal owner violated Standard V(A) by not having a reasonable and adequate basis for recommending the two companies and violated Standard VI(A) by not disclosing to investors the compensation agreements (which constituted a conflict of interest).

*Example 2:* An employee of a broker/dealer acquired a significant ownership interest in several publicly traded microcap stocks and held that stock in various brokerage accounts in which the broker/dealer had a controlling interest. The employee orchestrated the manipulation of the stock price by artificially increasing the bid price for the stock through transactions among the various accounts.

> *Comment:* The employee of the broker/dealer violated Standard II(B) by distorting the price of the stock through false trading and manipulative sales practices.

*Example 3:* Matthew Murphy is an analyst at Divisadero Securities & Co., which has a significant number of hedge funds among its most important brokerage clients. Two trading days before the publication of the quarter-end report, Murphy alerts his sales force that he is about to issue a research report on Wirewolf Semiconductor, which will include his opinion that:

▶ quarterly revenues are likely to fall short of management's guidance;

▶ earnings will be as much as 5 cents per share (or more than 10 percent) below consensus; and

▶ Wirewolf's highly respected chief financial officer may be about to join another company.

Knowing that Wirewolf had already entered its declared quarter-end "quiet period" before reporting earnings (and thus would be reluctant to respond to rumors, etc.), Murphy times the release of his research report specifically to sensationalize the negative aspects of the message to create significant downward pressure on Wirewolf's stock to the distinct advantage of Divisadero's hedge fund clients. The report's conclusions are based on speculation, not on fact. The next day, the research report is broadcast to all of Divisadero's clients and to the usual newswire services.

Before Wirewolf's investor-relations department can assess its damage on the final trading day of the quarter and refute Murphy's report, its stock opens trading sharply lower, allowing Divisadero's clients to cover their short positions at substantial gains.

> *Comment:* Murphy violated Standard II(B) by trying to create artificial price volatility designed to have material impact on the price of an issuer's stock.

Moreover, by lacking an adequate basis for the recommendation, Murphy also violated Standard V(A).

**Example 4:** Rajesh Sekar manages two funds—an equity fund and a balanced fund—whose equity components are supposed to be managed following the same model. According to that model, the funds' holdings in stock CD are excessive. Reduction of CD holdings would not be easy because the stock has low liquidity in the stock market. Sekar decides to start trading larger portions of CD stock back and forth between his two funds to slowly increase the price, believing that market participants would see growing volume and increasing price and become interested in the stock. If other investors are willing to buy the CD stock because of such interest, then Sekar would be able to get rid of at least some part of his overweight position without inducing price decreases, so the whole transaction would be for the benefit of fund participants, even if additional brokers' commissions are accounted for.

> *Comment:* Sekar's plan would be beneficial for his funds' participants but is based on artificial distortion of both trading volume and price of CD stock and therefore constitutes a violation of Standard II(B).

**Example 5:** Sergei Gonchar is the chairman of the ACME Futures Exchange, which seeks to launch a new bond futures contract. In order to convince investors, traders, arbitragers, hedgers, and so on to use its contract, the exchange attempts to demonstrate that it has the best liquidity. To do so, it enters into agreements with members so that they commit to a substantial minimum trading volume on the new contract over a specific period in exchange for substantial reductions on their regular commissions.

> *Comment:* Formal liquidity on a market is determined by the obligations set on market makers, but the actual liquidity of a market is better estimated by the actual trading volume and bid-ask spreads. Attempts to mislead participants on the actual liquidity of the market constitute a violation of Standard II(B). In this example, investors have been intentionally misled to believe they chose the most liquid instrument for some specific purpose and could eventually see the actual liquidity of the contract dry up suddenly after the term of the agreement if the "pump-priming" strategy fails. If ACME fully discloses its agreement with members to boost transactions over some initial launch period, it does not violate Standard II(B). ACME's intent is not to harm investors but on the contrary to give them a better service. For that purpose, it may engage in a liquidity-pumping strategy, but it must be disclosed.

**Example 6:** Emily Gordon is a household products analyst employed by a research boutique, Picador & Co. Based on information that she has picked up during a trip through Latin America, she believes that Hygene, Inc., a major marketer of personal care products, has generated better-than-expected sales from its new product initiatives in South America. After modestly boosting her revenue and gross profit margin projections in her worksheet models for Hygene, Gordon estimates that her earnings projection of $2.00 per diluted share for the current year may be as much as 5 percent too low. She contacts the CFO of Hygene to try to gain confirmation of her findings from her trip and to get some feedback regarding her revised models. The CFO declines to comment and reiterates management's most recent guidance of $1.95 to $2.05 for the year.

Gordon decides to try to force a comment from the company by telling Picador & Co. clients who follow a momentum investment style that consensus earnings projections for Hygene are much too low, and that she's considering raising her published estimate by an ambitious $0.15 to $2.15 per share. She believes that, when word of an unrealistically high earnings projection filters back to Hygene's investor relations department, the company will feel compelled to update its earnings guidance. Meanwhile, Gordon hopes that she is at least correct with respect to the earnings direction and that she will help clients that act on her insights to profit from a quick gain trading on her advice.

*Comment:* By exaggerating her earnings projections in order to try to fuel a quick gain in Hygene's stock price, Gordon is in violation of Standard II(B). Furthermore, by virtue of previewing to only a select group of clients her intentions of revising upward her earnings projections, she is in violation of Standard III(B). It would have been acceptable for Gordon to have instead written a report that:

► framed her earnings projection in a range of possible outcomes;
► outlined clearly her assumptions used in her Hygene models that took into consideration the findings from her trip through Latin America; and
► distributed the report to all Picador & Co. clients in an equitable manner.

***Example 7:*** In an effort to pump up the price of his holdings in Moosehead & Belfast Railroad Company, Steve Weinberg logs on to several investor chat rooms on the Internet to start rumors that the company is about to expand its rail network in anticipation of receiving a large contract for shipping lumber.

*Comment:* Weinberg has violated Standard II(B) by disseminating false information about Moosehead & Belfast with the intent to mislead market participants.

# STANDARD III—DUTIES TO CLIENTS

## A. Loyalty, Prudence, and Care

**Members and candidates have a duty of loyalty to their clients and must act with reasonable care and exercise prudent judgment. Members and candidates must act for the benefit of their clients and place their clients' interests before their employer's or their own interests. In relationships with clients, members and candidates must determine applicable fiduciary duty and must comply with such duty to persons and interests to whom it is owed.**

Standard III(A) clarifies that client interests are paramount. A member's or candidate's responsibility to a client includes a duty of loyalty and a duty to exercise reasonable care. Investment actions must be carried out for the sole benefit of the client and in a manner the manager believes to be in the best interest of the client, given the known facts and circumstances. Members and candidates must exercise the same level of prudence, judgment, and care that they would apply in the management and disposition of their own interests under similar circumstances.

Prudence requires caution and discretion. The exercise of prudence by an investment professional requires that they must act with the care, skill, and diligence under the circumstances that a reasonable person acting in a like capacity and familiar with such matters would use. In the context of managing a client's portfolio, prudence requires following the investment parameters set forth by the client and balancing risk and return. Acting with care requires members and candidates to act in a prudent and judicious manner in avoiding harm to clients.

Standard III(A) also requires members and candidates to understand and adhere to any legally imposed fiduciary responsibility they assume with each client. Fiduciary duties are often imposed by law or regulation when an individual or institution is charged with the duty of acting for the benefit of another party, such as managing of investment assets. The duty required in fiduciary relationships exceeds what is acceptable in many other business relationships because the fiduciary is in an enhanced position of trust. Members and candidates must abide by any fiduciary duty legally imposed on them.

The first step for members and candidates in fulfilling their duty of loyalty to clients is to determine the identity of the "client" to whom the duty of loyalty is owed. In the context of an investment manager managing the personal assets of an individual, the client is easily identified. When the manager is responsible for the portfolios of pension plans or trusts, however, the client is not the person or entity who hires the manager but, rather, the beneficiaries of the plan or trust. The duty of loyalty is owed to the ultimate beneficiaries and not just the client.

Members and candidates must also be aware of whether they have "custody" or effective control of client assets. If so, a heightened level of responsibility arises. Members and candidates are considered to have custody if they have any direct or indirect access to client funds. Members and candidates must manage any pool of assets in their control in accordance with the terms of the governing documents (such as trust documents and investment management agreements), which are the primary determinant of the manager's powers and duties. Whenever their actions are contrary to provisions of those instruments or applicable law, members and candidates are exposed to potential violations of the standard.

Situations involving potential conflicts of interest with respect to responsibilities to clients can be extremely complex because they can involve a number of competing interests. The duty of loyalty, prudence, and care applies to a large number of persons in varying capacities, but the exact duties may differ in many respects, depending on the nature of the relationship with the client or the type of account under which the assets are managed. Members and candidates must put their obligation to clients first in all dealings. In addition, members and candidates should endeavor to avoid all real or potential conflicts of interest and forgo using opportunities for their own benefit at the expense of those to whom their duty of loyalty is owed.

The duty of loyalty, prudence, and care owed to the individual client is especially important because the professional investment manager typically possesses greater knowledge than the client. This disparity places the individual client in a vulnerable position of trust. The manager in these situations should ensure that the client's objectives and expectations for the performance of the account are realistic and suitable to the client's circumstances and that the risks involved are appropriate. In most circumstances, recommended investment strategies should relate to the long-term objectives and circumstances of the client. Particular care must be taken to ensure that the goals of the investment manager or the firm in placing business, selling products, or executing security transactions do not conflict with the best interests and objectives of the client.

Members and candidates must follow any guidelines set out by their clients for the management of their assets. Some clients, such as charitable organizations and pension plans, have strict investment policies that limit investment options to certain types or classes of investments or prohibit investments in certain securities. Other organizations have aggressive policies that do not prohibit investments by type but instead set criteria on the basis of the portfolio's total risk and return.

Investment decisions may be judged in the context of the total portfolio rather than by individual investments within the portfolio. The member's or candidate's duty is satisfied with respect to a particular investment if they have thoroughly considered the investment's place in the overall portfolio, the risk of loss and opportunity for gains, tax implications, and the diversification, liquidity, cash flow, and overall return requirements of the assets or the portion of the assets for which the manager is responsible.

The duty of loyalty, prudence, and care can apply in a number of other situations faced by the investment professional other than with issues related directly to investing assets.

Part of a member's or candidate's duty of loyalty includes voting proxies in an informed and responsible manner. Proxies have economic value to a client, and members and candidates must ensure that they properly safeguard and maximize this value. A fiduciary who fails to vote, casts a vote without considering the impact of the question, or votes blindly with management on nonroutine governance issues (e.g., a change in firm capitalization) may violate this standard. Voting of proxies is an integral part of the management of investments. A cost-benefit analysis may show that voting all proxies may not benefit the client, so voting proxies may not be necessary in all instances. Members and candidates should disclose to clients their proxy-voting policies.

An investment manager often has discretion over the selection of brokers executing transactions. Conflicts arise when an investment manager uses client brokerage to purchase research services that benefit the investment manager, a practice commonly called "soft dollars" or "soft commissions." Whenever a manager uses client brokerage to purchase goods or services that do not benefit the client, the manager should disclose to clients the method or policies followed by the manager in addressing the potential conflict. A manager who pays a higher commission than he or she would normally pay to purchase goods or services, without corresponding benefit to the client, violates the duty of loyalty to the client.

From time to time, a manager's client will direct the manager to use the client's brokerage to purchase goods or services for the client, a practice that is commonly called "directed brokerage." Because brokerage is an asset of the client and is used to benefit that client, not the manager, such practice does not violate any duty of loyalty. In such situations, the manager is obligated to seek best price and execution and be assured by the client that the goods or services purchased with brokerage will benefit the account beneficiaries, and the manager should disclose to client that they may not be getting best execution.

## Recommended Procedures for Compliance

Members and candidates with control of client assets should submit to each client, at least quarterly, an itemized statement showing the funds and securities in the custody or possession of the member or candidate, plus all debits, credits, and transactions that occurred during the period; disclose to the client where the assets are to be maintained, as well as where or when they are moved; and separate the client's assets from any other party's assets, including the member's or candidate's own assets.

Members and candidates should review investments periodically to ensure compliance with the terms of the governing documents.

Members and candidates should establish policies and procedures with respect to proxy voting and the use of client brokerage, including soft dollars.

If a member or candidate is uncertain about the appropriate course of action with respect to a client, the member or candidate should ask what he or she would expect or demand if the member or candidate were the client. If in doubt, a member or candidate should disclose the questionable matter in writing and obtain client approval.

Members and candidates should address and encourage their firms to address the following topics when drafting their policies and procedures statements or manuals regarding responsibilities to clients:

- ► Follow all applicable rules and laws. Members and candidates must follow all legal requirements and applicable provisions of the CFA Institute Code of Ethics and Standards of Professional Conduct.

- ► Establish the investment objectives of the client. When taking investment actions, members and candidates must consider the appropriateness and suitability of the portfolio relative to (1) the client's needs and circumstances or (2) the investment's basic characteristics or (3) the basic characteristics of the total portfolio.

- ► Diversify. Members and candidates should diversify investments to reduce the risk of loss, unless diversification is not consistent with plan guidelines or is contrary to the account objectives.

- ► Deal fairly with all clients with respect to investment actions. Members and candidates must not favor some clients over others and should establish policies for allocating trades and disseminating investment recommendations.

- ► Disclose conflicts of interest. Members and candidates must disclose all actual and potential conflicts of interest so that clients can evaluate those conflicts.

- ► Disclose compensation arrangements. Members and candidates should make their clients aware of all forms of manager compensation.

- ► Vote proxies. Members and candidates should determine who is authorized to vote shares and vote proxies in the best interest of the clients and ultimate beneficiaries.

- ► Maintain confidentiality. Members and candidates must preserve the confidentiality of client information.

- ► Seek best execution. Members and candidates must seek best execution for their clients. Best execution refers to the trading process firms apply that seeks to maximize the value of a client's portfolio within the client's stated investment objectives and constraints.

- ► Place client interests first. Members and candidates must serve the best interest of the clients.

## Application of the Standard

*Example 1:* First Country Bank serves as trustee for the Miller Company's pension plan. Miller is the target of a hostile takeover attempt by Newton, Inc. In attempting to ward off Newton, Miller's managers persuade Julian Wiley, an investment manager at First Country Bank, to purchase Miller common stock in the open market for the employee pension plan. Miller's officials indicate that such action would be favorably received and would probably result in other accounts being placed with the bank. Although Wiley believes the stock to be overvalued and would not ordinarily buy it, he purchases the stock to support Miller's managers, to maintain the company's good favor, and to realize additional new business. The heavy stock purchases cause Miller's market price to rise to such a level that Newton retracts its takeover bid.

*Comment:* Standard III(A) requires that a member or candidate, in evaluating a takeover bid, act prudently and solely in the interests of plan participants and beneficiaries. To meet this requirement, a member or candidate must carefully evaluate the long-term prospects of the company against the short-term prospects presented by the takeover offer and by the ability to invest elsewhere. In this instance, Wiley, acting on behalf of his employer, the trustee, clearly violated Standard III(A) by using the profit-sharing plan to perpetuate existing management, perhaps to the detriment of plan participants and the company's shareholders, and to benefit himself. Wiley's responsibilities to the plan participants and beneficiaries should take precedence over any ties to corporate managers and self-interest. A duty exists to examine such a takeover offer on its own merits and to make an independent decision. The guiding principle is the appropriateness of the investment decision to the pension plan, not whether the decision benefits Wiley or the company that hired him.

***Example 2:*** JNI, a successful investment counseling firm, serves as investment manager for the pension plans of several large, regionally based companies. Its trading activities generate a significant amount of commission-related business. JNI uses the brokerage and research services of many firms, but most of its trading activity is handled through a large brokerage company, Thompson, Inc., principally because of close personal relationships between the executives of the two firms. Thompson's commission structure is high in comparison with charges for similar brokerage services from other firms. JNI considers Thompson's research services and execution capabilities average. In exchange for JNI directing its brokerage to Thompson, Thompson absorbs a number of JNI overhead expenses, including those for rent.

*Comment:* JNI executives breached their fiduciary duty by using client brokerage for services that do not benefit JNI clients and by not obtaining best price and execution for their clients. Because JNI executives failed to uphold their duty of loyalty, they violated Standard III(A).

***Example 3:*** Charlotte Everett, a struggling independent investment advisor, serves as investment manager for the pension plans of several companies. One of her brokers, Scott Company, is close to consummating management agreements with prospective new clients whereby Everett would manage the new client accounts and trade the accounts exclusively through Scott. One of Everett's existing clients, Crayton Corporation, has directed Everett to place securities transactions for Crayton's account exclusively through Scott. But to induce Scott to exert efforts to land more new accounts for her, Everett also directs transactions to Scott from other clients without their knowledge.

*Comment:* Everett has an obligation at all times to seek best price and execution on all trades. Everett may direct new client trades exclusively through Scott Company as long as Everett receives best price and execution on the trades or receives a written statement from new clients that she is not to seek best price and execution and that they are aware of the consequence for their accounts. Everett may trade other accounts through Scott as a reward for directing clients to Everett only if the accounts receive best price and execution and the practice is disclosed to the accounts. Because Everett did not disclose the directed trading, Everett has violated Standard III(A).

***Example 4:*** Emilie Rome is a trust officer for Paget Trust Company. Rome's supervisor is responsible for reviewing Rome's trust account transactions and her monthly reports of personal stock transactions. Rome has been using Nathan Gray, a broker, almost exclusively for trust account brokerage transactions.

Where Gray makes a market in stocks, he has been giving Rome a lower price for personal purchases and a higher price for sales than he gives to Rome's trust accounts and other investors.

> *Comment:* Rome is violating her duty of loyalty to the bank's trust accounts by using Gray for brokerage transactions simply because Gray trades Rome's personal account on favorable terms.

**Example 5:** Lauren Parker, an analyst with Provo Advisors, covers South American equities for the firm. She likes to travel to the markets for which she is responsible and decides to go on a briefing trip to Chile, Argentina, and Brazil. The trip is sponsored by SouthAM, Inc., a research firm with a small broker/dealer affiliate that uses the clearing facilities of a larger New York brokerage house. SouthAM specializes in arranging South American trips for analysts during which they can meet with central bank officials, government ministers, local economists, and senior executives of corporations. SouthAM accepts commission dollars at a ratio of 2 to 1 against the hard-dollar cost of the research fee for the trip. Parker is not sure that SouthAM's execution is competitive but, without informing her supervisor, directs the trading desk at Provo to start giving commission business to SouthAM so she can take the trip. SouthAM has conveniently timed the briefing trip to coincide with the beginning of Carnival season, so Parker also decides to spend five days of vacation in Rio de Janeiro at the end of the trip. Parker used commission dollars to pay for the five days of hotel expenses.

> *Comment:* Parker violated Standard III(A) by not exercising her duty of loyalty to her clients to determine whether the commissions charged by SouthAM were reasonable in relation to the benefit of the research provided by the trip and by not determining that best execution and prices can be received from SouthAM. In addition, the five extra days are not part of the research effort because they do not assist in the investment decision-making process and thus should not be paid for with client assets.

**Example 6:** Vida Knauss manages the portfolios of a number of high-net-worth individuals. A major part of her investment management fee is based on trading commissions. Knauss engages in extensive trading for each of her clients to ensure that she attains the minimum commission level set by her firm. While the securities purchased and sold for the clients are appropriate and fall within the acceptable asset classes for the clients, the amount of trading for each account exceeds what is necessary to accomplish the clients' investment objectives.

> *Comment:* Knauss has violated Standard III(A) because she is using the assets of her clients to benefit her firm and herself.

## B. Fair Dealing

**Members and candidates must deal fairly and objectively with all clients when providing investment analysis, making investment recommendations, taking investment action, or engaging in other professional activities.**

Standard III(B) requires members and candidates to treat all clients fairly when disseminating investment recommendations or material changes to prior investment advice or when taking investment action with regard to general purchases, new issues, or secondary offerings. Only through the fair treatment of all parties can the investment management profession maintain the confidence of the investing public.

When an investment advisor has multiple clients, the potential exists for the advisor to favor one client over another. This favoritism may take various forms, from the quality and timing of services provided to the allocation of investment opportunities. The term "fairly" implies that the member or candidate must take care not to discriminate against any clients when disseminating investment recommendations or taking investment action. Standard III(B) does not state "equally" because members and candidates could not possibly reach all clients at exactly the same time—whether by mail, telephone, computer, facsimile, or wire. Each client has unique needs, investment criteria, and investment objectives so that not all investment opportunities are suitable for all clients. In addition, members and candidates may provide more personal, specialized, or in-depth service to clients willing to pay for premium services through higher management fees or higher levels of brokerage. Members and candidates can differentiate their services to clients, but different levels of service must not disadvantage or negatively affect clients. In addition, the different service levels should be disclosed to clients and prospective clients and be available to everyone (i.e., different service levels should not be offered selectively).

Standard III(B) covers the conduct relating to two broadly defined categories of conduct—investment recommendations and investment action.

### Investment Recommendations

The first type of conduct involves members and candidates whose primary function is the preparation of investment recommendations to be disseminated either to the public or within a firm for the use of others in making investment decisions. This group includes members and candidates employed by investment counseling, advisory, or consulting firms as well as banks, brokerage firms, and insurance companies if the member's or candidate's primary responsibility is the preparation of recommendations to be acted on by others, including those in the member's or candidate's organization.

An investment recommendation is any opinion expressed by a member or candidate in regard to purchasing, selling, or holding a given security or other investment. This opinion can be disseminated to customers or clients through an initial detailed research report, through a brief update report, by addition to or deletion from a recommended list, or simply by oral communication. A recommendation that is distributed to anyone outside the organization is considered a communication for general distribution under Standard III(B).

Standard III(B) addresses the manner in which investment recommendations or changes in prior recommendations are disseminated to clients. Each member or candidate is obligated to ensure that information is disseminated in such a manner that all clients have a fair opportunity to act on every recommendation. Communicating with all clients on a uniform basis presents practical problems for members and candidates because of differences in timing and methods of communication with the various types of customers and clients. Members and candidates should encourage their firms to design an equitable system to prevent selective, discriminatory disclosure and should inform clients of what kind of communications they will receive.

The duty to clients imposed by Standard III(B) may be more critical when a member or candidate changes their recommendation than when they make an initial recommendation. Material changes in a member's or candidate's prior investment advice arising from subsequent research should be communicated to all current clients, and particularly those clients who the member or candidate knows may have acted on or been affected by the earlier advice. Clients who don't know that the member or candidate has changed a recommendation and who therefore place orders contrary to a current recommendation should be advised of the changed recommendation before the order is accepted.

### Investment Actions

The second group includes those members and candidates whose primary function is taking investment action (portfolio management) based on research recommendations prepared internally or received from external sources. Investment action, like investment recommendations, can affect market value. Consequently, Standard III(B) requires that members or candidates treat all clients fairly in light of their investment objectives and circumstances. For example, when making investments in new offerings or in secondary financings, members and candidates should distribute the issues to all customers for whom the investments are appropriate in a manner consistent with the block-allocation policies of the firm. If the issue is oversubscribed, then the issue should be prorated to all subscribers. This action should be taken on a round-lot basis to avoid odd-lot distributions. In addition, if the issue is oversubscribed, members and candidates should forgo any sales to themselves or their immediate families to free up additional shares for clients.

Members and candidates must make every effort to treat all individual and institutional clients in a fair and impartial manner. A member or candidate may have multiple relationships with an institution; for example, a bank may hold many positions for a manager, such as corporate trustee, pension fund manager, manager of funds for individuals employed by the customer, loan originator, or creditor. A member or candidate must exercise care to treat clients fairly, including those with whom multiple relationships do not exist.

Members and candidates should disclose to clients and prospects the written allocation procedures they or their firms have in place and how the procedures would affect the client or prospect. The disclosure should be clear and complete so that the client can make an informed investment decision. Even when complete disclosure is made, however, members and candidates must put client interests ahead of their own. A member's or candidate's duty of fairness and loyalty to clients can never be overridden by client consent to patently unfair allocation procedures.

Treating clients fairly also means that members and candidates should not take advantage of their position in the industry to the detriment of clients. For instance, in the context of IPOs, members and candidates must make bona fide public distributions of "hot issue" securities (defined as securities of a public offering that trade at a premium in the secondary market whenever such trading commences because of the great demand for the securities). Members and candidates are prohibited from withholding such securities for their own benefit and must not use such securities as a reward or incentive to gain benefit.

## Recommended Procedures for Compliance

Although Standard III(B) refers to a member's or candidate's responsibility to deal fairly and objectively with clients, members and candidates should also encourage their firms to establish compliance procedures requiring all employees who disseminate investment recommendations or take investment actions to treat customers and clients fairly. At the very least, a member or candidate should recommend appropriate procedures to management if none are in place and make management aware of possible violations of fair-dealing practices within the firm when they come to the attention of the member or candidate.

The extent of the formality and complexity of such compliance procedures depends on the nature and size of the organization and the type of securities involved. An investment advisor who is a sole proprietor and handles only discretionary accounts might not disseminate recommendations to the public, but that advisor should have formal written procedures to ensure that all clients receive fair investment action.

Good business practice dictates that initial recommendations be made available to all customers who indicate an interest. Although a member or candidate need not communicate a recommendation to all customers, the selection process by which customers receive information should be based on suitability and known interest, not on any preferred or favored status. A common practice to assure fair dealing is to communicate recommendations both within the firm and to customers—simultaneously.

Members and candidates should consider the following points when establishing fair-dealing compliance procedures:

### Limit the Number of People Involved

Members and candidates should make reasonable efforts to limit the number of people who are privy to the fact that a recommendation is going to be disseminated.

### Shorten the Time Frame between Decision and Dissemination

Members and candidates should make reasonable efforts to limit the amount of time that elapses between the decision to make an investment recommendation and the time the actual recommendation is disseminated. If a detailed institutional recommendation is in preparation that might take two or three weeks to publish, a short summary report including the conclusion might be published in advance. In an organization where both a research committee and investment policy committee must approve a recommendation, the meetings should be held on the same day if possible. The process of reviewing, printing, and mailing reports or faxing or distributing them by e-mail necessarily involves the passage of time, sometimes long periods of time. In large firms with extensive review processes, the time factor is usually not within the control of the analyst who prepares the report. Thus, many firms and their analysts communicate to customers and firm personnel the new or changed recommendations by an update or "flash" report. The communication technique might be fax, e-mail, wire, or short written report.

### Publish Personnel Guidelines for Predissemination

Members and candidates should establish guidelines that prohibit personnel who have prior knowledge of an investment recommendation from discussing or taking any action on the pending recommendation.

### Simultaneous Dissemination

Members and candidates should establish procedures for dissemination of investment recommendations so that all clients are treated fairly—that is, with the goal of informing them at approximately the same time. For example, if a firm is going to announce a new recommendation, supervisory personnel should time the announcement to avoid placing any client or group of clients at unfair advantage relative to other clients. A communication to all branch offices should be sent at the time of the general announcement. When appropriate, the firm should accompany the announcement of a new recommendation with a statement that trading restrictions for the firm's employees are now in effect. The trading restrictions should stay in effect until the recommendation is widely distributed by communicating the information to all relevant clients. Once this has occurred, the member or candidate may follow up separately with individual clients, but members and candidates should not give favored clients advanced information when such prenotification may disadvantage other clients.

## *Maintain a List of Clients and Their Holdings*

Members and candidates should maintain a list of all clients and the securities or other investments each client holds in order to facilitate notification of customers or clients of a change in an investment recommendation. If a particular security or other investment is to be sold, such a list could be used to ensure that all holders are treated fairly in the liquidation of that particular investment.

## *Develop Written Trade Allocation Procedures*

When formulating procedures for allocating trades, members and candidates should develop a set of guiding principles that ensure:

- ► fairness to advisory clients, both in priority of execution of orders and in the allocation of the price obtained in execution on block orders or trades;
- ► timeliness and efficiency in the execution of orders;
- ► accuracy of the member's or candidate's records as to trade orders and client account positions.

With these principles in mind, members and candidates should develop or encourage their firm to develop written allocation procedures, with particular attention to procedures for block trades and new issues. Members and candidates should consider the following procedures:

- ► requiring orders and modifications or cancellations of orders to be in writing and time stamped;
- ► processing and executing orders on a first-in, first-out basis;
- ► developing a policy to address such issues as calculating execution prices and "partial fills" when trades are grouped, or blocked, for efficiency purposes;
- ► giving all client accounts participating in a block trade the same execution price and charging the same commission;
- ► when the full amount of the block order is not executed, allocating partially executed orders among the participating client accounts pro rata on the basis of order size;
- ► when allocating trades for new issues, obtaining advance indications of interest, allocating securities by client (rather than portfolio manager), and providing for a method for calculating allocations.

## *Disclose Trade Allocation Procedures*

Members and candidates should disclose to clients and prospective clients how they select accounts to participate in an order and how they determine the amount of securities each account will buy or sell. Trade allocation procedures must be fair and equitable, and disclosure of inequitable allocation methods does not relieve this obligation.

### *Establish Systematic Account Review*

Member and candidate supervisors should review each account on a regular basis to ensure that no client or customer is being given preferential treatment and that the investment actions taken for each account are suitable for the account's objectives. Because investments should be based on individual needs and circumstances, an investment manager may have good reasons for placing a given security or other investment in one account while selling it from another account. However, members and candidates should encourage firms to establish review procedures to detect whether trading in one account is being used to benefit a favored client.

### *Disclose Levels of Service*

Members and candidates should disclose to all clients whether or not the organization offers different levels of service to clients for the same fee or different fees. Different levels of service should not be offered to clients selectively.

## Application of the Standard

*Example 1:* Bradley Ames, a well-known and respected analyst, follows the computer industry. In the course of his research, he finds that a small, relatively unknown company whose shares are traded over the counter has just signed significant contracts with some of the companies he follows. After a considerable amount of investigation, Ames decides to write a research report on the company and recommend purchase. While the report is being reviewed by the company for factual accuracy, Ames schedules a luncheon with several of his best clients to discuss the company. At the luncheon, he mentions the purchase recommendation scheduled to be sent early the following week to all the firm's clients.

> *Comment:* Ames violated Standard III(B) by disseminating the purchase recommendation to the clients with whom he had lunch a week before the recommendation was sent to all clients.

*Example 2:* Spencer Rivers, president of XYZ Corporation, moves his company's growth-oriented pension fund to a particular bank primarily because of the excellent investment performance achieved by the bank's commingled fund for the prior five-year period. A few years later, Rivers compares the results of his pension fund with those of the bank's commingled fund. He is startled to learn that, even though the two accounts have the same investment objectives and similar portfolios, his company's pension fund has significantly underperformed the bank's commingled fund. Questioning this result at his next meeting with the pension fund's manager, Rivers is told that, as a matter of policy, when a new security is placed on the recommended list, Morgan Jackson, the pension fund manager, first purchases the security for the commingled account and then purchases it on a pro rata basis for all other pension fund accounts. Similarly, when a sale is recommended, the security is sold first from the commingled account and then sold on a pro rata basis from all other accounts. Rivers also learns that if the bank cannot get enough shares (especially the hot issues) to be meaningful to all the accounts, its policy is to place the new issues only in the commingled account.

Seeing that Rivers is neither satisfied nor pleased by the explanation, Jackson quickly adds that nondiscretionary pension accounts and personal trust accounts have a lower priority on purchase and sale recommendations than discretionary pension fund accounts. Furthermore, Jackson states, the company's pension fund had the opportunity to invest up to 5 percent in the commingled fund.

*Comment:* The bank's policy did not treat all customers fairly, and Jackson violated her duty to her clients by giving priority to the growth-oriented commingled fund over all other funds and to discretionary accounts over nondiscretionary accounts. Jackson must execute orders on a systematic basis that is fair to all clients. In addition, trade allocation procedures should be disclosed to all clients from the beginning. Of course, in this case, disclosure of the bank's policy would not change the fact that the policy is unfair.

*Example 3:* Dominic Morris works for a small regional securities firm. His work consists of corporate finance activities and investing for institutional clients. Arena, Ltd., is planning to go public. The partners have secured rights to buy an arena football league franchise and are planning to use the funds from the issue to complete the purchase. Because arena football is the current rage, Morris believes he has a hot issue on his hands. He has quietly negotiated some options for himself for helping convince Arena to do the financing. When he seeks expressions of interest, the institutional buyers oversubscribe the issue. Morris, assuming that the institutions have the financial clout to drive the stock up, then fills all orders (including his own) and cuts back the institutional blocks.

*Comment:* Morris has violated Standard III(B) by not treating all customers fairly. He should not have taken any shares himself and should have prorated the shares offered among all clients. In addition, he should have disclosed to his firm and to his clients that he had received options as part of the deal [see Standard VI(A)—Disclosure of Conflicts].

*Example 4:* Eleanor Preston, the chief investment officer of Porter Williams Investments (PWI), a medium-sized money management firm, has been trying to retain a difficult client, Colby Company. Management at the disgruntled client, which accounts for almost half of PWI's revenues, recently told Preston that if the performance of its account did not improve, it would find a new money manager. Shortly after this threat, Preston purchases mortgage-backed securities (MBS) for several accounts, including Colby's. Preston is busy with a number of transactions that day, so she fails to allocate the trades immediately or write up the trade tickets. A few days later, when Preston is allocating trades, she notes that some of the MBS have significantly increased in price and some have dropped. Preston decides to allocate the profitable trades to Colby and spread the losing trades among several other PWI accounts.

*Comment:* Preston violated Standard III(B) by failing to deal fairly with her clients in taking these investment actions. Preston should have allocated the trades prior to executing the orders, or she should have had a systematic approach to allocating the trades, such as pro rata, as soon after they were executed as practicable. Among other things, Preston must disclose to the client that the advisor may act as broker for, receive commissions from, and have a potential conflict of interest regarding both parties in agency cross-transactions. After the disclosure, she should obtain from the client consent authorizing such transactions in advance.

*Example 5:* Saunders Industrial Waste Management (SIWM) publicly indicates to analysts that it is comfortable with the somewhat disappointing earnings per share projection of $1.15 for the quarter. Bernard Roberts, an analyst at Coffey Investments, is confident that SIWM management has understated the forecasted earnings so that the real announcement would cause an "upside surprise" and boost the price of SIWM stock. The "whisper number" estimate based on extensive research and discussed among knowledgeable analysts is higher than $1.15. Roberts repeats the $1.15 figure in his research report to all Coffey clients but informally tells his larger clients that he expects the earnings per share to be higher, making SIWM a good buy.

*Comment:* By not sharing his opinion regarding the potential for a significant upside earnings surprise with all clients, Roberts is not treating all clients fairly and has violated Standard III(B).

***Example 6:*** Jenpin Weng uses e-mail to issue a new recommendation to all his clients. He then calls his three biggest institutional clients to discuss the recommendation in detail.

*Comment:* Weng has not violated Standard III(B) because he widely disseminated the recommendation and provided the information to all his clients prior to discussing it with a select few. Weng's larger clients received additional personal service that they presumably pay for through bigger fees or because they have a large amount of assets under Weng's management. Weng would have violated Standard III(B) if he had discussed the report with a select group of clients prior to distributing it to all his clients.

## C. Suitability

1. **When members and candidates are in an advisory relationship with a client, they must:**

   a. **Make a reasonable inquiry into a client's or prospective client's investment experience, risk and return objectives, and financial constraints prior to making any investment recommendation or taking investment action and must reassess and update this information regularly.**

   b. **Determine that an investment is suitable to the client's financial situation and consistent with the client's written objectives, mandates, and constraints prior to making an investment recommendation or taking investment action.**

   c. **Judge the suitability of investments in the context of the client's total portfolio.**

2. **When members and candidates are responsible for managing a portfolio to a specific mandate, strategy, or style, they must only make investment recommendations or take investment actions that are consistent with the stated objectives and constraints of the portfolio.**

Standard III(C) requires that members and candidates who are in an investment advisory relationship with clients consider carefully the needs, circumstances, and objectives of the clients when determining the appropriateness and suitability of a given investment or course of investment action.

The responsibilities conferred upon members and candidates to gather information and make a suitability analysis prior to making a recommendation or taking investment action falls on those members and candidates who provide investment advice in the course of an advisory relationship with a client. Other members and candidates often are simply executing specific instructions for retail clients when buying or selling securities, such as shares in mutual funds. These members and candidates and others, such as sell-side analysts, may not have the opportunity to judge the suitability of the particular investment for the person or entity. In cases of unsolicited trade requests that a member or candidate knows are unsuitable for the client, the member or candidate should refrain from making the trade or seek an affirmative statement from the client that suitability is not a consideration.

When an advisory relationship exists, members and candidates must gather client information at the inception of the relationship. Such information includes the client's financial circumstances, personal data (such as age and occupation) that are relevant to investment decisions, attitudes toward risk, and objectives in investing. This information should be incorporated into a written investment policy statement (IPS) that addresses the client's risk tolerance, return requirements, and all investment constraints (including time horizon, liquidity needs, tax concerns, legal and regulatory factors, and unique circumstances). Without identifying such client factors, members and candidates cannot judge whether a particular investment or strategy is suitable for a particular client. The IPS also should identify and describe the roles and responsibilities of the parties to the advisory relationship and investment process, as well as schedules for review and evaluation. After formulating long-term capital market expectations, members and clients can assist in developing an appropriate strategic asset allocation and investment program for the client, whether these are presented in separate documents or incorporated in the IPS or in appendices to the IPS.

Such an inquiry should be repeated at least annually and prior to material changes to any specific investment recommendations or decisions on behalf of the client. The effort to determine the needs and circumstances of each client is not a one-time occurrence. Investment recommendations or decisions are usually part of an ongoing process that takes into account the diversity and changing nature of portfolio and client characteristics. The passage of time is bound to produce changes that are important with respect to investment objectives.

For an individual client, such changes might include the number of dependents, personal tax status, health, liquidity needs, risk tolerance, the amount of wealth beyond that represented in the portfolio, and the extent to which compensation and other income provide for current income needs. With respect to an institutional client, such changes might relate to the magnitude of unfunded liabilities in a pension fund, the withdrawal privileges in an employee's savings plan, or the distribution requirements of a charitable foundation. Without efforts to update information concerning client factors, one or more factors could change without the investment manager's knowledge.

Suitability review can be done effectively only if the client fully discloses his or her complete financial portfolio, including those portions not managed by the member or candidate. If clients withhold information about their financial portfolio, the suitability analysis conducted by members and candidates cannot be expected to be complete but must be done based on the information provided.

One of the most important factors to be considered in matching appropriateness and suitability of an investment with a client's needs and circumstances is measuring that client's tolerance for risk. The investment professional must consider the possibilities of rapidly changing investment environments and their likely impact on a client's holdings, both individual securities and the collective portfolio. The risk of many investment strategies can and should be analyzed and quantified in advance.

The use of synthetic investment vehicles and derivative investment products has introduced particular issues of risk. Members and candidates should pay careful attention to the leverage often inherent in such vehicles or products when considering them for use in a client's investment program. Such leverage and limited liquidity, depending on the degree to which they are hedged, bear directly on the issue of suitability for the client.

The investment profession has long recognized that the combination of several different investments is likely to provide a more acceptable level of risk exposure than having all assets in a single investment. The unique characteristics (or risks) of an individual investment may become partially or entirely neutralized when combined with other individual investments within a portfolio. Some reasonable amount of diversification is the norm for many portfolios, especially those managed by individuals or institutions that have some degree of fiduciary responsibility. An investment with high relative risk on its own may be a suitable investment in the context of the entire portfolio or when the client's stated objectives contemplate speculative or risky investments. It may be the case that the manager is responsible for only a portion of the client's total portfolio or that the client has not provided the full financial picture of the client to the manager. Members and candidates can be responsible only for assessing suitability of an investment given the information and criteria provided by the clients.

Some members and candidates do not manage money for individuals but are responsible for managing a fund to an index or an expected mandate. In those cases, the member's or candidate's responsibility is to invest consistent with the stated mandate. For example, a member or candidate who serves as the fund manager for a large-cap income fund would not be following the fund mandate by investing heavily in small-cap or start-up companies whose stock is speculative in nature. Members and candidates who manage pooled assets to a specific mandate are not responsible for determining the suitability of the fund as an investment for investors who may be purchasing shares in the fund. The responsibility for determining the suitability of an investment for clients can only be conferred on members and candidates who have an advisory relationship with clients.

## Recommended Procedures for Compliance

To fulfill the basic provisions of Standard III(C), a member or candidate should put the needs and circumstances of each client and the client's investment objectives into a written investment policy statement (IPS) for each client. In formulating an investment policy for the client, the member or candidate should take the following into consideration:

▶ Client identification—(1) type and nature of clients, (2) the existence of separate beneficiaries, and (3) approximate portion of total client assets.

▶ Investor objectives—(1) return objectives (income, growth in principal, maintenance of purchasing power) and (2) risk tolerance (suitability, stability of values).

▶ Investor constraints—(1) liquidity needs, (2) expected cash flows (patterns of additions and/or withdrawals), (3) investable funds (assets and liabilities or other commitments), (4) time horizon, (5) tax considerations, (6) regulatory and legal circumstances, (7) investor preferences, prohibitions, circumstances, and unique needs, and (8) proxy-voting responsibilities and guidance.

▶ Performance measurement benchmarks.

The investor's objectives and constraints should be maintained and reviewed periodically to reflect any changes in the client's circumstances. Members and candidates should regularly compare client constraints with capital market expectations to arrive at an appropriate asset allocation. Changes in either factor may result in a fundamental change in asset allocation. Annual review is reasonable unless business or other reasons, such as a major change in market conditions, dictate more frequent review. Members and candidates should document attempts at such a review if circumstances prevent it.

## Application of the Standard

*Example 1:* Caleb Smith, an investment advisor, has two clients: Larry Robertson, 60 years old, and Gabriel Lanai, 40 years old. Both clients earn roughly the same salary, but Robertson has a much higher risk tolerance because he has a large asset base. Robertson is willing to invest part of his assets very aggressively; Lanai wants only to achieve a steady rate of return with low volatility to pay for his children's education. Smith recommends investing 20 percent of both portfolios in zero-yield, small-cap, high-technology issues.

> *Comment:* In Robertson's case, the investment may be appropriate given his financial circumstances and aggressive investment position, but this investment would not be suitable for Lanai. Smith would violate Standard III(C) by applying Robertson's investment strategy to Lanai because Lanai's financial circumstances and objectives are different.

*Example 2:* Jessica Walters, an investment advisor, suggests to Brian Crosby, a risk-averse client, that covered call options be used in his equity portfolio. The purpose would be to enhance Crosby's income and partially offset any untimely depreciation in value should the stock market or other circumstances affect his holdings unfavorably. Walters educates Crosby about all possible outcomes, including the risk of incurring an added tax liability if a stock rises in price and is called away and, conversely, the risk of his holdings losing protection on the downside if prices drop sharply.

> *Comment:* When determining suitability of an investment, the primary focus should be on the characteristics of the client's entire portfolio, not on an issue-by-issue analysis. The basic characteristics of the entire portfolio will largely determine whether the investment recommendations are taking client factors into account. Therefore, the most important aspects of a particular investment will be those that will affect the characteristics of the total portfolio. In this case, Walters properly considered the investment in the context of the entire portfolio and thoroughly explained the investment to the client.

*Example 3:* In a regular meeting with Seth Jones, the portfolio managers at Blue Chip Investment Advisors are careful to allow some time to review his current needs and circumstances. In doing so, they learn that some significant changes have recently taken place. A wealthy uncle left Jones an inheritance that increased his net worth fourfold, to $1,000,000.

> *Comment:* The inheritance significantly increased Jones's ability and possibly his willingness to assume risk and diminished the average yield required to meet his current income needs. Jones's financial circumstances have definitely changed, so Blue Chip managers must update Jones's investment policy statement to understand how his investment objectives have changed. Accordingly, the Blue Chip portfolio managers should consider a somewhat higher equity ratio for his portfolio than was called for by the previous circumstances, and the managers' specific common stock recommendations might be heavily tilted toward low-yield, growth-oriented issues.

*Example 4:* Louis Perkowski manages a high-income mutual fund. He purchases zero-dividend stock in a financial services company because he believes the stock is undervalued and is in a potential growth industry, making it an attractive investment.

> *Comment:* A zero-dividend stock does not seem to fit the mandate of the fund that Perkowski is managing. Unless Perkowski's investment fits within

the mandate or is within the realm of investments allowable under the disclosures of the fund, Perkowski has violated Standard III(C).

*Example 5:* Max Gubler, CIO of a property/casualty insurance subsidiary of a large financial conglomerate, wants to better diversify the company's investment portfolio and increase its returns. The company's investment policy statement (IPS) provides for highly liquid investments, such as large-caps, governments, and supra-nationals, as well as corporate bonds with a minimum credit rating of AA– and maturity of no more than five years. In a recent presentation, a venture capital group offered very attractive prospective returns on some of their private equity funds providing seed capital. An exit strategy is already contemplated but investors will first have to observe a minimum three-year lock-up period, with a subsequent laddered exit option for a maximum of one-third of shares per year. Gubler does not want to miss this opportunity, and after an extensive analysis and optimization of this asset class with the company's current portfolio, he invests 4 percent in this seed fund, leaving the portfolio's total equity exposure still well below its upper limit.

> *Comment:* Gubler violates Standards III(A) and III(C). His new investment locks up part of the company's assets for at least three and for up to as many as five years and possibly beyond. Since the IPS requires investments in highly liquid investments and describes accepted asset classes, private equity investments with a lock-up period certainly do not qualify. Even without such a lock-up period, an asset class with only an occasional, and thus implicitly illiquid, market may not be suitable. Although an IPS typically describes objectives and constraints in great detail, the manager must make every effort to understand the client's business and circumstances. Doing so should also enable the manager to recognize, understand, and discuss with the client other factors that may be or may become material in the investment management process.

## D. Performance Presentation

**When communicating investment performance information, members and candidates must make reasonable efforts to make sure that it is fair, accurate, and complete.**

Standard III(D) requires members and candidates to provide credible performance information to clients and prospective clients and to avoid misstating performance or misleading clients and prospective clients about the investment performance of members or candidates or their firms. This standard encourages full disclosure of investment performance data to clients and prospective clients.

Standard III(D) covers any practice that would lead to misrepresentation of a member's or candidate's performance record, whether the practice involves performance presentation or performance measurement. This standard prohibits misrepresentations of past performance or reasonably expected performance. A member or candidate must give a fair and complete presentation of performance information whenever communicating data with respect to the performance history of individual accounts, composites of groups of accounts, or composites of an analyst's or firm's performance results. Further, members and candidates should not state or imply that clients will obtain or benefit from a rate of return that was generated in the past.

The requirements of this standard are not limited to members and candidates managing separate accounts. Anytime a member or candidate provides performance information for which the manager is claiming responsibility, such as for pooled funds, the history must be accurate. Research analysts promoting the success or accuracy of their recommendations must ensure that their claims are fair, accurate, and complete.

If the presentation is brief, the member or candidate must make available to clients and prospects, upon request, the detailed information supporting that communication.

## Recommended Procedures for Compliance

For members and candidates seeking to show the performance history of the assets they manage, compliance with the Global Investment Performance Standards (GIPS) is the best method to meet their obligations under Standard III(D). Members and candidates should encourage their firms to adhere to the GIPS standards.

Members and candidates can also meet their obligations under Standard III(D) by:

▶ considering the knowledge and sophistication of the audience to whom a performance presentation is addressed;

▶ presenting the performance of the weighted composite of similar portfolios rather than using a single representative account;

▶ including terminated accounts as part of performance history;

▶ including disclosures that would fully explain the performance results being reported (for example, stating, when appropriate, that results are simulated when model results are used, clearly indicating when the performance record is that of a prior entity, or disclosing whether the performance is gross of fees, net of fees, or after tax); and

▶ maintaining the data and records used to calculate the performance being presented.

## Application of the Standard

*Example 1:* Kyle Taylor of Taylor Trust Company, noting the performance of Taylor's common trust fund for the past two years, states in a brochure sent to his potential clients that "You can expect steady 25 percent annual compound growth of the value of your investments over the year." Taylor Trust's common trust fund did increase at the rate of 25 percent per annum for the past year, which mirrored the increase of the entire market. The fund, however, never averaged that growth for more than one year, and the average rate of growth of all of its trust accounts for five years was 5 percent per annum.

> *Comment:* Taylor's brochure is in violation of Standard III(D). Taylor should have disclosed that the 25 percent growth occurred only in one year. Additionally, Taylor did not include client accounts other than those in the firm's common trust fund. A general claim of firm performance should take into account the performance of all categories of accounts. Finally, by stating that clients can expect a steady 25 percent annual compound growth rate, Taylor also violated Standard I(C), which prohibits statements of assurances or guarantees regarding an investment.

*Example 2:* Anna Judd, a senior partner of Alexander Capital Management, circulates a performance sheet listing performance figures for capital appreciation accounts for the years 1988 through 2004 and claiming compliance with the Global Investment Performance Standards (GIPS). Returns are not calculated in accordance with the Global Investment Performance Standards (GIPS) because the composites are not asset weighted, which is a violation of GIPS.

> *Comment:* Judd is in violation of Standard III(D). When claiming compliance with GIPS, firms must meet all the requirements and mandatory disclosures and any other additional requirements or disclosures necessary to that firm's specific situation. Judd's violation is not from any misuse of the data but from a false claim of GIPS compliance.

**Example 3:** Aaron McCoy is vice president and managing partner of the equity investment group of Mastermind Financial Advisors, a new business. Mastermind recruited McCoy because he had a proven six-year track record with G&P Financial. In developing Mastermind's advertising and marketing campaign, McCoy prepared an advertisement that included the equity investment performance he achieved at G&P Financial. The advertisement for Mastermind did not identify the equity performance as being earned while at G&P. The advertisement was distributed to existing clients and prospective clients of Mastermind.

> *Comment:* McCoy violated Standard III(D) by distributing an advertisement that contained material misrepresentations regarding the historical performance of Mastermind. Standard III(D) requires that members and candidates make every reasonable effort to ensure that performance information is a fair, accurate, and complete representation of an individual's or firm's performance. As a general matter, this standard does not prohibit showing past performance of funds managed at a prior firm as part of a performance track record so long as it is accompanied by appropriate disclosures detailing where the performance comes from and the person's specific role in achieving that performance. If McCoy chooses to use his past performance from G&P in Mastermind's advertising, he should make full disclosure as to the source of the historical performance.

**Example 4:** Jed Davis developed a mutual fund selection product based on historical information from the 1990–95 period. Davis tested his methodology by applying it retroactively to data from the 1996–2003 period, thus producing simulated performance results for those years. In January 2004, Davis's employer decided to offer the product, and Davis began promoting it through trade journal advertisements and direct dissemination to clients. The advertisements included the performance results for the 1996–2003 period but did not indicate that the results were simulated.

> *Comment:* Davis violated Standard III(D) by failing to clearly identify simulated performance results. Standard III(D) prohibits members and candidates from making any statements that misrepresent the performance achieved by them or their firms and requires members and candidates to make every reasonable effort to ensure that performance information presented to clients is fair, accurate, and complete. Use of the simulated results should be accompanied by full disclosure as to the source of the performance data, including the fact that the results from 1995 through 2003 were the result of applying the model retroactively to that time period.

**Example 5:** In a presentation prepared for prospective clients, William Kilmer shows the rates of return realized over a five-year period by a "composite" of his firm's discretionary accounts with a balanced objective. This "composite," however, consisted of only a few of the accounts that met the balanced criteria set by the firm, excluded accounts under a certain asset level without disclosing the fact of their exclusion, and included nonbalanced accounts that would boost investment results. In addition, to achieve better results, Kilmer manipulated the narrow range of accounts included in the composite by changing the accounts that made up the composite over time.

> *Comment:* Kilmer violated Standard III(D) by misrepresenting the facts in the promotional material sent to prospective clients, distorting his firm's performance record, and failing to include disclosure that would have clarified the presentation.

## E. Preservation of Confidentiality

**Members and candidates must keep information about current, former, and prospective clients confidential unless:**

1. **The information concerns illegal activities on the part of the client;**
2. **Disclosure is required by law; or**
3. **The client or prospective client permits disclosure of the information.**

Standard III(E) requires that members and candidates preserve the confidentiality of information communicated to them by their clients, prospective clients, and former clients. This standard is applicable when (1) the member or candidate receives information on the basis of his or her special ability to conduct a portion of the client's business or personal affairs and (2) the member or candidate receives information that arises from or is relevant to that portion of the client's business that is the subject of the special or confidential relationship. If disclosure of the information is required by law or the information concerns illegal activities by the client, however, the member or candidate may have an obligation to report the activities to the appropriate authorities.

As a general matter, members and candidates must comply with applicable law. If applicable law requires disclosure of client information in certain circumstances, members and candidates must comply with the law. Similarly, if applicable law requires members and candidates to maintain confidentiality, even if the information concerns illegal activities on the part of the client, members and candidates should not disclose such information. When in doubt, members and candidates should consult with their employer's compliance personnel or outside counsel before disclosing confidential information about clients.

This standard protects the confidentiality of client information even if the person or entity is no longer a client of the member or candidate. Therefore, members and candidates must continue to maintain the confidentiality of client records even after the client relationship has ended. However, if a client or former client expressly authorizes the member or candidate to disclose information, the member or candidate may follow the terms of the authorization and provide the information.

### *Professional Conduct Investigations by CFA Institute*

The requirements of Standard III(E) are not intended to prevent members and candidates from cooperating with an investigation by the CFA Institute Professional Conduct Program (PCP). When permissible under applicable law members and candidates shall consider the PCP an extension of themselves when requested to provide information about a client in support of a PCP investigation into their own conduct. Members and candidates are encouraged to cooperate with investigations into the conduct of others. Any information turned over to the PCP is kept in the strictest confidence.

## Recommended Procedures for Compliance

The simplest, most conservative, and most effective way to comply with Standard III(E) is to avoid disclosing any information received from a client except to authorized fellow employees who are also working for the client. In some instances, however, a member or candidate may want to disclose information received from clients that is outside the scope of the confidential relationship and does not involve illegal activities. Before making such a disclosure, a member or candidate should ask the following:

▶ In what context was the information disclosed? If disclosed in a discussion of work being performed for the client, is the information relevant to the work?

▶ Is the information background material that, if disclosed, will enable the member or candidate to improve service to the client?

## Application of the Standard

*Example 1:* Sarah Connor, a financial analyst employed by Johnson Investment Counselors, Inc., provides investment advice to the trustees of City Medical Center. The trustees have given her a number of internal reports concerning City Medical's needs for physical plant renovation and expansion. They have asked Connor to recommend investments that would generate capital appreciation in endowment funds to meet projected capital expenditures. Connor is approached by a local businessman, Thomas Kasey, who is considering a substantial contribution either to City Medical Center or to another local hospital. Kasey wants to find out the building plans of both institutions before making a decision, but he does not want to speak to the trustees.

> *Comment:* The trustees gave Connor the internal reports so she could advise them on how to manage their endowment funds. Because the information in the reports is clearly both confidential and within the scope of the confidential relationship, Standard III(E) requires that Connor refuse to divulge information to Kasey.

*Example 2:* Lynn Moody is an investment officer at the Lester Trust Company. She has an advisory customer who has talked to her about giving approximately $50,000 to charity to reduce her income taxes. Moody is also treasurer of the Home for Indigent Widows (HIW), which is planning its annual giving campaign. HIW hopes to expand its list of prospects, particularly those capable of substantial gifts. Moody recommends that HIW's vice president for corporate gifts call on her customer and ask for a donation in the $50,000 range.

> *Comment:* Even though the attempt to help the Home for Indigent Widows was well intended, Moody violated Standard III(E) by revealing confidential information about her client.

*Example 3:* Government officials approach Casey Samuel, the portfolio manager for Garcia Company's pension plan, to examine pension fund records. They tell her that Garcia's corporate tax returns are being audited and the pension fund reviewed. Two days earlier Samuel learned in a regular investment review meeting with Garcia officers that potentially excessive and improper charges are being made to the pension plan by Garcia. Samuel consults her employer's general counsel and is advised that Garcia has probably violated tax and fiduciary regulations and laws.

*Comment:* Samuel should inform her supervisor of these activities, and her employer should take steps, with Garcia, to remedy the violations. If that approach is not successful, Samuel and her employer should seek advice of legal counsel to determine the appropriate steps to be taken. Samuel may well have a duty to disclose the evidence she has of the continuing legal violations and to resign as asset manager for Garcia.

**Example 4:** David Bradford manages money for a family-owned real estate development corporation. He also manages the individual portfolios of several of the family members and officers of the corporation, including the chief financial officer (CFO). Based on the financial records from the corporation, as well as some questionable practices of the CFO that he has observed, Bradford believes that the CFO is embezzling money from the corporation and putting it into his personal investment account.

*Comment:* Bradford should check with his firm's compliance department as well as outside counsel to determine whether applicable securities regulations require reporting the CFO's financial records.

# STANDARD IV—DUTIES TO EMPLOYERS

## A. Loyalty

**In matters related to their employment, members and candidates must act for the benefit of their employer and not deprive their employer of the advantage of their skills and abilities, divulge confidential information, or otherwise cause harm to their employer.**

Standard IV(A) requires members and candidates to protect the interests of their firm by refraining from any conduct that would injure the firm, deprive it of profit, or deprive it of the advantage of the member's or candidate's skills and ability. Members and candidates must always place the interests of clients above the interests of their employer. Otherwise, in matters related to their employment, members and candidates must not engage in conduct that harms the interests of the employer. Implicit in this standard is the obligation of members and candidates to comply with the policies and procedures established by their employers that govern the employer-employee relationship—to the extent that such policies and procedures do not conflict with applicable laws, rules, regulations, or the Code and Standards.

This standard is not meant to be a blanket requirement to place employer interests ahead of personal interests in all matters. This standard does not require members and candidates to subordinate important personal and family obligations to their work. Members and candidates should enter into a dialogue with their employer about balancing personal and employment obligations when personal matters may interfere with their work on a regular or significant basis.

In addition, the employer-employee relationship imposes duties and responsibilities on both parties. Employers must adhere to the duties and responsibilities that they owe to their employees if they expect to have contented and productive employees.

### Independent Practice

Included in Standard IV(A) is the requirement that members and candidates abstain from independent competitive activity that could conflict with the interests of their employer. Although Standard IV(A) does not preclude members or candidates from entering into an independent business while still employed, members and candidates who plan to engage in independent practice for compensation must provide notification to their employer describing the types of service the members or candidates will render to prospective independent clients, the expected duration of the services, and the compensation for the services. Members and candidates should not render services until receiving consent from their employer to all of the terms of the arrangement. "Practice" means any service that the employer currently makes available for remuneration. "Undertaking independent practice" means engaging in competitive business, as opposed to making preparations to begin such practice.

### Leaving an Employer

When investment professionals plan to leave their current employer, they must continue to act in the employer's best interest and must not engage in any activities that would conflict with this duty until their resignation becomes effective. It is difficult to define specific guidelines for those members and candidates who plan to compete with their employer as part of a new venture. The circumstances of each situation must be reviewed to distinguish permissible preparations from violations of duty. Activities that might constitute a violation, especially in combination, include the following:

▶ misappropriation of trade secrets,

▶ misuse of confidential information,

▶ solicitation of employer's clients prior to cessation of employment,

▶ self-dealing (appropriating for one's own property a business opportunity, or information belonging to one's employer),

▶ misappropriation of clients or client lists.

A departing employee is generally free to make arrangements or preparations to go into a competitive business before terminating the relationship with his or her employer provided that such preparations do not breach the employee's duty of loyalty. However, members and candidates contemplating seeking other employment must not contact existing clients or potential clients prior to leaving their employer for purposes of soliciting their business for the new employer. In addition, they must not take records or files to a new employer without the written permission of the previous employer.

Once an employee has left the firm, the skills and experience that an employee obtains while employed are not "confidential" or "privileged" information. Similarly, simple knowledge of the names and existence of former clients is generally not confidential information unless deemed such by an agreement or by law. Standard IV(A) does not impose a prohibition on the use of experience or knowledge gained at one employer from being used at another employer. However, firm records or work performed on behalf of the firm stored on a home computer for the member's or candidate's convenience while employed should be erased or returned to the employer unless the firm gives permission to keep those records after employment ends.

Nor does the standard prohibit former employees from contacting clients of their previous firm so long as the contact information does not come from the records of the former employer or violate an applicable non-compete agreement. Members and candidates are free to use public information about their former firm after departing to contact former clients without violating Standard IV(A), absent a specific agreement not to do so.

Employers often require employees to sign "non-compete" agreements that preclude a departing employee from engaging in certain conduct. Members and candidates should take care to review the terms of any such agreements when leaving their employer to determine what, if any, conduct those agreements may prohibit.

### Whistleblowing

A member's or candidate's personal interests, as well as the interests of his or her employer, are secondary to protecting the integrity of capital markets and the interests of the clients. Therefore, there may be circumstances in which members and candidates act contrary to their employer interests in an effort to comply with their duties to the market and clients (e.g., when an employer is engaged in illegal or unethical activity). In such instances, activities that would normally violate a member's or candidate's duty to his or her employer (such as contradicting employer instructions, violating certain policies and procedures, or preserving a record by copying employer records) may be justified. Such action would be permitted only if the intent is clearly aimed at protecting clients or the integrity of the market and not for personal gain.

### Nature of Employment

A wide variety of business relationships exist within the investment industry. For instance, a member or candidate can be retained as an employee or independent contractor. Members and candidates must determine whether they are employees or independent contractors in order to determine the applicability of Standard IV(A). This issue will be decided largely by the degree of control exercised by the employing entity over the member or candidate. Factors determining control include whether the member's or candidate's hours, work location, and other parameters of the job are set; whether facilities are provided to the member or candidate; whether the member's or candidate's expenses are reimbursed; whether the member or candidate holds himself or herself out to other employers for additional work; and the number of clients or employers the member or candidate works for.

A member's or candidate's duties within an independent contractor relationship are governed by the oral or written agreement between the member and the client. Members and candidates should take care to define clearly the scope of their responsibilities and the expectations of each client within the context of each relationship. Once the member or candidate establishes a relationship with a client, they have a duty to abide by the terms of the agreement.

## Application of the Standard

*Example 1:* Samuel Magee manages pension accounts for Trust Assets, Inc., but has become frustrated with the working environment and has been offered a position with Fiduciary Management. Before resigning from Trust Assets, Magee asks four big accounts to leave that firm and open accounts with Fiduciary. Magee also persuades several prospective clients to sign agreements with Fiduciary Management. Magee had previously made presentations to these prospects on behalf of Trust Assets, Inc.

*Comment:* Magee violated the employee-employer principle requiring him to act solely for his employer's benefit. Magee's duty is to Trust Assets as long as he is employed there. The solicitation of Trust Assets' current clients and prospective clients is unethical and violates Standard IV(A).

***Example 2:*** James Hightower has been employed by Jason Investment Management Corporation for 15 years. He began as an analyst but assumed increasing responsibilities and is now a senior portfolio manager and a member of the firm's investment policy committee. Hightower has decided to leave Jason Investment and start his own investment management business. He has been careful not to tell any of Jason's clients that he is leaving, because he does not want to be accused of breaching his duty to Jason by soliciting Jason's clients before his departure. Hightower is planning to copy and take with him the following documents and information he developed or worked on while at Jason: (1) the client list, with addresses, telephone numbers, and other pertinent client information; (2) client account statements; (3) sample marketing presentations to prospective clients containing Jason's performance record; (4) Jason's recommended list of securities; (5) computer models to determine asset allocations for accounts with different objectives; (6) computer models for stock selection; and (7) personal computer spreadsheets for Hightower's major corporate recommendations which he developed when he was an analyst.

> *Comment:* Except with the consent of their employer, departing employees may not take employer property, which includes books, records, reports, and other materials, and may not interfere with their employer's business opportunities. Taking any employer records, even those the member or candidate prepared, violates Standard IV(A).

***Example 3:*** Rueben Winston manages all-equity portfolios at Target Asset Management (TAM), a large, established investment counselor. Ten years ago, Philpott & Company, which manages a family of global bond mutual funds, acquired TAM in a diversification move. After the merger, the combined operations prospered in the fixed-income business while the equity management business at TAM languished. Lately, a few of the equity pension accounts that had been with TAM before the merger have terminated their relationships with TAM. One day, Winston finds on his voice mail a message from a concerned client, "Hey! I just heard that Philpott is close to announcing the sale of your firm's equity management business to Rugged Life. What is going on?" Not being aware of any such deal, Winston and his associates are stunned. Their internal inquiries are met with denials from Philpott management, but the rumors persist. Feeling left in the dark, Winston contemplates leading an employee buyout of TAM's equity management business.

> *Comment:* An employee-led buyout of TAM's equity asset management business would be consistent with Standard IV(A) because it would rest on the permission of the employer and, ultimately, the clients. In this case, however, in which employees suspect the senior managers or principals are not truthful or forthcoming, members should consult legal counsel to determine appropriate action.

***Example 4:*** Laura Clay, who is unemployed, wants part-time consulting work while seeking a full-time analyst position. During an interview at Phere Associates, a large institutional asset manager, Clay is told that the firm has no immediate research openings but would be willing to pay her a flat fee to complete a study of the wireless communications industry within a given period of time. Clay would be allowed unlimited access to Phere's research files and would be welcome to come to the offices and use whatever support facilities are available during normal working hours. Phere's research director does not seek any exclusivity for Clay's output, and the two agree to the arrangement on a handshake. As Clay nears completion of the study, she is offered an analyst job in the research department of Dowt & Company, a brokerage firm, and she is pondering submitting the draft of her wireless study for publication by Dowt.

> *Comment:* Although she is under no written contractual obligation to Phere, Clay has an obligation to let Phere act on the output of her study before Dowt & Company or Clay uses the information to its own advantage. That is, unless Phere gives permission to Clay waiving rights to her wireless report, Clay would be in violation of Standard IV(A) if she were to immediately recommend to Dowt the same transactions recommended in the report to Phere. Furthermore, Clay must not take from Phere any research file material or other property that she may have used.

**Example 5:** Emma Madeline, a recent college graduate and a candidate in the CFA Program, spends her summer as an unpaid intern at Murdoch and Lowell. Murdoch and Lowell is attempting to bring the firm into compliance with the GIPS standards, and Madeline is assigned to assist in its efforts. Two months into her internship, Madeline applies for a job at McMillan & Company, which has plans to become GIPS compliant. Madeline accepts the job with McMillan. Before leaving Murdoch, she copies the firm's software that she helped develop, as she believes this software will assist her in her new position.

> *Comment:* Even though Madeline does not receive monetary compensation for her services at Murdoch, she has used firm resources in creating the software and she is considered an employee because she receives compensation and benefits in the form of work experience and knowledge. By copying the software, Madeline violated Standard IV(A) because she misappropriated Murdoch's property without permission.

**Example 6:** Dennis Elliot has hired Sam Chisolm who previously worked for a competing firm. Chisolm left his former firm after 18 years of employment. When Chisolm begins working for Elliot, he wants to contact his former clients because he knows them well and is certain that many will follow him to his new employer. Is Chisolm in violation of the Standard IV(A) if he contacts his former clients?

> *Comment:* Because client records are the property of the firm, contacting former clients for any reason through the use of client lists or other information taken from a former employer without permission would be a violation of Standard IV(A). In addition, the nature and extent of the contact with former clients may be governed by the terms of any non-compete agreement signed by the employee and the former employer that covers contact with former clients after employment.
>
> But, simple knowledge of the names and existence of former clients is not confidential information, just as skills or experience that an employee obtains while employed is not "confidential" or "privileged" information. The Code and Standards do not impose a prohibition on the use of experience or knowledge gained at one employer from being used at another employer. The Code and Standards also do not prohibit former employees from contacting clients of their previous firm, absent a non-compete agreement. Members and candidates are free to use public information about their former firm after departing to contact former clients without violating Standard IV(A).

In the absence of a non-compete agreement, as long as Chisolm maintains his duty of loyalty to his employer before joining Elliot's firm, does not take steps to solicit clients until he has left his former firm, and does not make use of material from his former employer without its permission after he has left, he would not be in violation of the Code and Standards.

***Example 7:*** Gardner Allen currently works at a registered investment company as an equity analyst. Without notice to her employer, she registers with government authorities to start an investment company that will compete with her employer. However, she has not actively sought clients. Does registration of this competing company with the appropriate regulatory authorities constitute a violation of Standard IV(A)?

*Comment:* Allen's preparations for the new business by registering with the regulatory authorities do not conflict with the work for her employer if the preparations have been done on Allen's own time outside of the office and if Allen will not be getting clients for the business or otherwise operating the new company until she has left her current employer.

***Example 8:*** Several employees are planning to depart their current employer within a few weeks and have been careful to not engage in any activities that would conflict with their duty to their current employer. They have just learned that one of their employer's clients has undertaken a request for proposal (RFP) to review and possibly hire a new investment consultant. The RFP has been sent to the employer and all of its competitors. The group believes that the new entity to be formed would be qualified to respond to the RFP and eligible for the business. The RFP submission period is likely to conclude before the employees' resignations are effective. Is it permissible for the group of departing employees to respond to the RFP under their anticipated new firm?

*Comment:* A group of employees responding to an RFP that their employer is also responding to would lead to direct competition between the employees and the employer. Such conduct would violate Standard IV(A) unless the group of employees received permission from their employer as well as the entity sending out the RFP.

***Example 9:*** Alfonso Mota is a research analyst with Tyson Investments. He works part time as a mayor for his hometown, a position for which he receives compensation. Must Mota seek permission from Tyson to serve as mayor?

*Comment:* If Mota's mayoral duties are so extensive and time consuming that they might detract from his ability to fulfill his responsibilities at Tyson, he should discuss his outside activities with his employer and come to a mutual agreement regarding how to manage his personal commitments with his responsibilities to his employer.

***Example 10:*** After leaving her employer, Shawna McQuillen establishes her own money management business. While with her former employer, she did not sign a non-compete agreement that would have prevented her from soliciting former clients. Upon her departure, she does not take any of her client lists or contact information and clears her personal computer of any employer records, including client contact information. She obtains the phone numbers of her former clients through public records and contacts them to solicit their business.

*Comment:* McQuillen is not in violation of Standard IV(A) because she has not used information or records from her former employer and is not prevented by an agreement with her former employer from soliciting her former clients.

## B. Additional Compensation Arrangements

**Members and candidates must not accept gifts, benefits, compensation, or consideration that competes with, or might reasonably be expected to create a conflict of interest with, their employers' interest unless they obtain written consent from all parties involved.**

Standard IV(B) requires members and candidates to obtain permission from their employer before accepting compensation or other benefits from third parties for the services rendered to the employer or for any services that might create a conflict of interest with their employers' interest. Compensation and benefits include direct compensation by the client and any indirect compensation or other benefits received from third parties. "Written consent" includes any form of communication that can be documented (for example, communication via computer e-mail that can be retrieved and documented).

Members and candidates must obtain permission for additional compensation/benefits because such arrangements may affect loyalties and objectivity and create potential conflicts of interest. Disclosure allows an employer to consider the outside arrangements when evaluating the actions and motivations of members and candidates. Moreover, the employer is entitled to have full knowledge of compensation/benefit arrangements to assess the true cost of the services members or candidates are providing.

## Recommended Procedures for Compliance

Members and candidates should make an immediate written report to their employers specifying any compensation they propose to receive for services in addition to the compensation or benefits received from their employers. This written report should state the terms of any agreement under which a member or candidate will receive additional compensation; terms include the nature of the compensation, the approximate amount of compensation, and the duration of the agreement.

## Application of the Standard

***Example 1:*** Geoff Whitman, a portfolio analyst for Adams Trust Company, manages the account of Carol Cochran, a client. Whitman is paid a salary by his employer, and Cochran pays the trust company a standard fee based on the market value of assets in her portfolio. Cochran proposes to Whitman that "any year that my portfolio achieves at least a 15 percent return before taxes, you and your wife can fly to Monaco at my expense and use my condominium during the third week of January." Whitman does not inform his employer of the arrangement and vacations in Monaco the following January as Cochran's guest.

> *Comment:* Whitman violated Standard IV(B) by failing to inform his employer in writing of this supplemental, contingent compensation arrangement. The nature of the arrangement could have resulted in partiality to Cochran's account, which could have detracted from Whitman's performance with respect to other accounts he handles for Adams Trust. Whitman must obtain the consent of his employer to accept such a supplemental benefit.

***Example 2:*** Terry Jones sits on the board of directors of Exercise Unlimited, Inc. In return for his services on the board, Jones receives unlimited membership privileges for his family at all Exercise Unlimited facilities. Jones purchases Exercise Unlimited stock for the client accounts for which it is appropriate.

Jones does not disclose this arrangement to his employer, as he does not receive monetary compensation for his services to the board.

> *Comment:* Jones violated Standard IV(B) by failing to disclose to his employer benefits received in exchange for his services on the board of directors.

## C. Responsibilities of Supervisors

**Members and candidates must make reasonable efforts to detect and prevent violations of applicable laws, rules, regulations, and the Code and Standards by anyone subject to their supervision or authority.**

Standard IV(C) states that members and candidates must take steps to prevent persons acting under their supervision from violating the law, rules, regulations, or the Code and Standards.

Any investment professionals who have employees subject to their control or influence—whether or not the employees are CFA Institute members, CFA charterholders, or candidates in the CFA Program—exercise supervisory responsibility. Members and candidates acting as supervisors must have in-depth knowledge of the Code and Standards and must apply this knowledge in discharging their supervisory responsibilities.

The conduct that constitutes reasonable supervision in a particular case depends on the number of employees supervised and the work performed by those employees. Members and candidates who supervise large numbers of employees cannot personally evaluate the conduct of their employees on a continuing basis. Although these members and candidates may delegate supervisory duties, such delegation does not relieve them of their supervisory responsibility. Their responsibilities under Standard IV(C) include instructing those subordinates to whom supervision is delegated regarding methods to prevent and detect violations.

Members and candidates with supervisory responsibility must make reasonable efforts to detect violations of laws, rules, regulations, and the Code and Standards. They exercise reasonable supervision by establishing and implementing written compliance procedures and ensuring that those procedures are followed through periodic review. If a member or candidate has adopted reasonable procedures and taken steps to institute an effective compliance program, then the member or candidate may not be in violation of Standard IV(C) if they do not detect violations that occur despite these efforts. The fact that violations do occur may indicate, however, that the compliance procedures are inadequate. In addition, in some cases, merely enacting such procedures may not be sufficient to fulfill the duty required by Standard IV(C). A member or candidate may be in violation of Standard IV(C) if he or she knows or should know that the procedures designed to detect and prevent violations are not being followed.

### Compliance Procedures

Members and candidates with supervisory responsibility also must understand what constitutes an adequate compliance system for their firms and make reasonable efforts to see that appropriate compliance procedures are established, documented, communicated to covered personnel, and followed. "Adequate" procedures are those designed to meet industry standards, regulatory requirements, the requirements of the Code and Standards, and the circumstances of the firm. Once compliance procedures are established, the supervisor must also make reasonable efforts to ensure that the procedures are monitored and enforced.

To be effective, compliance procedures must be in place prior to the occurrence of a violation of the law or the Code and Standards. Although compliance procedures cannot be designed to anticipate every potential violation, they should be designed to anticipate the activities most likely to result in misconduct. Each compliance program must be appropriate for the size and nature of the organization. Model compliance procedures or other industry programs should be reviewed to ensure that procedures meet the minimum industry standards.

A member or candidate with supervisory responsibility should bring an inadequate compliance system to the attention of the firm's senior managers and recommend corrective action. If the member or candidate clearly cannot discharge supervisory responsibilities because of the absence of a compliance system or because of an inadequate compliance system, the member or candidate should decline in writing to accept supervisory responsibility until the firm adopts reasonable procedures to allow them to adequately exercise such responsibility.

Once a supervisor learns that an employee has violated or may have violated the law or the Code and Standards, the supervisor must promptly initiate an investigation to ascertain the extent of the wrongdoing. Relying on an employee's statements about the extent of the violation or assurances that the wrongdoing will not reoccur is not enough. Reporting the misconduct up the chain of command and warning the employee to cease the activity are also not enough. Pending the outcome of the investigation, a supervisor should take steps to ensure the violations will not be repeated, such as placing limits on the employee's activities or increasing the monitoring of the employee's activities.

## Recommended Procedures for Compliance

Members and candidates are encouraged to recommend that their employers adopt a code of ethics. Adoption of a code of ethics is critical to establishing a strong ethical foundation for investment adviser firms and their employees. Codes of ethics formally emphasize and reinforce the fiduciary responsibilities of investment firm personnel, protect investing clients by deterring misconduct, and protect the firm's reputation for integrity.

There is a distinction between codes of ethics and the necessary specific policies and procedures needed to ensure compliance with the code of conduct and securities laws and regulations. While both are important, codes of ethics should consist of fundamental, principle-based ethical and fiduciary concepts that are applicable to all of the firm's employees. In this way, firms can best convey to employees and clients the ethical ideals that investment advisers strive to achieve. These concepts can then be implemented by detailed, firmwide compliance policies and procedures. Compliance procedures will assist the firm's personnel in fulfilling the responsibilities enumerated in the code of ethics and ensure that the ideals expressed in the code of ethics are adhered to in the day-to-day operation of the firm.

Commingling compliance procedures in the firm's code of ethics will diminish the goal of reinforcing with the firm's employees their ethical obligations. Stand-alone codes of ethics should be written in plain language and address general fiduciary concepts, unencumbered by numerous detailed procedures directed to the day-to-day operation of the firm. In this way codes will be most effective in stressing to employees that they are in positions of trust and must act with integrity at all times.

Separating the codes of ethics from compliance procedures will also reduce, if not eliminate, the legal terminology and boilerplate language that can make the underlying ethical principles incomprehensible to the average person. Above all, the principles in the codes of ethics must be accessible and understandable to everyone in the firm to ensure that a culture of ethics and integrity is created rather than merely a focus on attention to the rules.

In addition, members and candidates should encourage their employers to provide their codes of ethics to clients. But only simple, straightforward codes of ethics will be understandable to clients and thus be effective in conveying the message that the firm is committed to conducting business in an ethical manner and in the best interests of the clients.

A supervisor complies with Standard IV(C) by identifying situations in which legal violations or violations of the Code and Standards are likely to occur and by establishing and enforcing compliance procedures to prevent such violations. Adequate compliance procedures should:

- ▶ be contained in a clearly written and accessible manual that is tailored to the member's or candidate's operations;
- ▶ be drafted so that the procedures are easy to understand;
- ▶ designate a compliance officer whose authority and responsibility are clearly defined and who has the necessary resources and authority to implement the firm's compliance procedures;
- ▶ describe the hierarchy of supervision and assign duties among supervisors;
- ▶ implement a system of checks and balances;
- ▶ outline the scope of the procedures;
- ▶ outline procedures to document the monitoring and testing of compliance procedures;
- ▶ outline permissible conduct; and
- ▶ delineate procedures for reporting violations and sanctions.

Once a compliance program is in place, a supervisor should:

- ▶ disseminate the contents of the program to appropriate personnel;
- ▶ periodically update procedures to ensure that the measures are adequate under the law;
- ▶ continually educate personnel regarding the compliance procedures;
- ▶ issue periodic reminders of the procedures to appropriate personnel;
- ▶ incorporate a professional conduct evaluation as part of an employee's performance review;
- ▶ review the actions of employees to ensure compliance and identify violators; and
- ▶ take the necessary steps to enforce the procedures once a violation has occurred.

Once a violation is discovered, a supervisor should:

- ▶ respond promptly;
- ▶ conduct a thorough investigation of the activities to determine the scope of the wrongdoing; and
- ▶ increase supervision or place appropriate limitations on the wrongdoer pending the outcome of the investigation.

# Application of the Standard

*Example 1:* Jane Mattock, senior vice president and head of the research department of H&V, Inc., a regional brokerage firm, has decided to change her recommendation for Timber Products from buy to sell. In line with H&V's procedures, she orally advises certain other H&V executives of her proposed actions before the report is prepared for publication. As a result of his conversation with Mattock, Dieter Frampton, one of the executives of H&V accountable to Mattock, immediately sells Timber's stock from his own account and from certain discretionary client accounts. In addition, other personnel inform certain institutional customers of the changed recommendation before it is printed and disseminated to all H&V customers who have received previous Timber reports.

> *Comment:* Mattock failed to supervise reasonably and adequately the actions of those accountable to her. She did not prevent or establish reasonable procedures designed to prevent dissemination of or trading on the information by those who knew of her changed recommendation. She must ensure that her firm has procedures for reviewing or recording trading in the stock of any corporation that has been the subject of an unpublished change in recommendation. Adequate procedures would have informed the subordinates of their duties and detected sales by Frampton and selected customers.

*Example 2:* Deion Miller is the research director for Jamestown Investment Programs. The portfolio managers have become critical of Miller and his staff because the Jamestown portfolios do not include any stock that has been the subject of a merger or tender offer. Georgia Ginn, a member of Miller's staff, tells Miller that she has been studying a local company, Excelsior, Inc., and recommends its purchase. Ginn adds that the company has been widely rumored to be the subject of a merger study by a well-known conglomerate and discussions between them are under way. At Miller's request, Ginn prepares a memo recommending the stock. Miller passes along Ginn's memo to the portfolio managers prior to leaving for vacation, noting that he has not reviewed the memo. As a result of the memo, the portfolio managers buy Excelsior stock immediately. The day Miller returns to the office, Miller learns that Ginn's only sources for the report were her brother, who is an acquisitions analyst with Acme Industries and the "well-known conglomerate" and that the merger discussions were planned but not held.

> *Comment:* Miller violated Standard IV(C) by not exercising reasonable supervision when he disseminated the memo without checking to ensure that Ginn had a reasonable and adequate basis for her recommendations and that Ginn was not relying on material nonpublic information.

*Example 3:* David Edwards, a trainee trader at Wheeler & Company, a major national brokerage firm, assists a customer in paying for the securities of Highland, Inc., by using anticipated profits from the immediate sale of the same securities. Despite the fact that Highland is not on Wheeler's recommended list, a large volume of its stock is traded through Wheeler in this manner. Roberta Ann Mason is a Wheeler vice president responsible for supervising compliance with the securities laws in the trading department. Part of her compensation from Wheeler is based on commission revenues from the trading department. Although she notices the increased trading activity, she does nothing to investigate or halt it.

> *Comment:* Mason's failure to adequately review and investigate purchase orders in Highland stock executed by Edwards and her failure to supervise the trainee's activities violated Standard IV(C). Supervisors should be especially sensitive to actual or potential conflicts between their own self-interests and their supervisory responsibilities.

*Example 4:* Samantha Tabbing is senior vice president and portfolio manager for Crozet, Inc., a registered investment advisory and registered broker/dealer firm. She reports to Charles Henry, the president of Crozet. Crozet serves as the investment advisor and principal underwriter for ABC and XYZ public mutual funds. The two funds' prospectuses allow Crozet to trade financial futures for the funds for the limited purpose of hedging against market risks. Henry, extremely impressed with Tabbing's performance in the past two years, directs Tabbing to act as portfolio manager for the funds. For the benefit of its employees, Crozet has also organized the Crozet Employee Profit-Sharing Plan (CEPSP), a defined-contribution retirement plan. Henry assigns Tabbing to manage 20 percent of the assets of CEPSP. Tabbing's investment objective for her portion of CEPSP's assets is aggressive growth. Unbeknownst to Henry, Tabbing frequently places S&P 500 Index purchase and sale orders for the funds and the CEPSP without providing the futures commission merchants (FCMs) who take the orders with any prior or simultaneous designation of the account for which the trade has been placed. Frequently, neither Tabbing nor anyone else at Crozet completes an internal trade ticket to record the time an order was placed or the specific account for which the order was intended. FCMs often designate a specific account only after the trade, when Tabbing provides such designation. Crozet has no written operating procedures or compliance manual concerning its futures trading, and its compliance department does not review such trading. After observing the market's movement, Tabbing assigns to CEPSP the S&P 500 positions with more-favorable execution prices and assigns positions with less-favorable execution prices to the funds.

*Comment:* Henry violated Standard IV(C) by failing to adequately supervise Tabbing with respect to her S&P 500 trading. Henry further violated Standard IV(C) by failing to establish record-keeping and reporting procedures to prevent or detect Tabbing's violations.

# STANDARD V—INVESTMENT ANALYSIS, RECOMMENDATIONS, AND ACTIONS

## A. Diligence and Reasonable Basis

**Members and candidates must:**
1. **Exercise diligence, independence, and thoroughness in analyzing investments, making investment recommendations, and taking investment actions.**
2. **Have a reasonable and adequate basis, supported by appropriate research and investigation, for any investment analysis, recommendation, or action.**

The application of Standard V(A) is dependent on the investment philosophy followed, the role of the member or candidate in the investment decision-making process, and the support and resources provided by the member's or candidate's employer. These factors will dictate the nature of the diligence, thoroughness of the research, and level of investigation required by Standard V(A).

The requirements for issuing conclusions on research will vary based on the member's or candidate's role in the investment decision-making process, but the member or candidate must make reasonable efforts to cover all pertinent issues when arriving at the recommendation. Members and candidates enhance transparency by providing or offering to provide supporting information to clients when recommending a purchase or sale or when changing a recommendation.

### Using Secondary or Third-Party Research

If members and candidates rely on secondary or third-party research, they must make reasonable and diligent efforts to determine whether such research is sound. Secondary research is defined as research conducted by someone else in the member's or candidate's firm. Third-party research is research conducted by entities outside the member's or candidate's firm, such as a brokerage firm, bank, or research firm. If a member or candidate has reason to suspect that either secondary or third-party research or information comes from a source that lacks a sound basis, the member or candidate must refrain from relying on that information. This requirement also applies in situations involving quantitatively oriented research, such as computer-generated screening or ranking of universes of equity securities based on various sets of prescribed criteria. Examples of criteria that a member or candidate can use in forming his or her opinion that research is sound include:

▶ review of the assumptions used,

▶ rigor of analysis performed,

▶ date/timeliness of the research,

▶ evaluation of the objectivity and independence of recommendations.

When a member or candidate relies on others within his or her firm to determine whether secondary or third-party research is sound, the information can be used in good faith unless the member or candidate has reason to question its validity or the processes and procedures used by those responsible for the investigation. An example of this situation would be a portfolio manager who does not have a choice over a data source because the firm's senior management conducted due diligence to determine which vendor would provide services.

### Group Research and Decision Making

Commonly, members and candidates may be part of a group or team that is collectively responsible for producing investment analysis or research. The conclusions or recommendations of the report represent the consensus of the group and are not necessarily the views of the member or candidate, even though the name of the member or candidate is included on the report. There may be many instances when the member or candidate does not agree with the independent and objective view of the group. If the member or candidate believes that consensus opinion has a reasonable and adequate basis, then the member or candidate does not necessarily have to decline to be identified with the report. There should be a presumption that the group members are independent and objective and have a reasonable basis for the opinions. If the member or candidate is confident in the process, the member or candidate does not have to dissociate from the report if it does not reflect his or her opinion. The member or candidate should, however, document his or her difference of opinion with the team.

## Recommended Procedures for Compliance

Members and candidates should encourage their firms to consider the following policies and procedures to support the principles of Standard V(A):

▶ Establish a policy requiring that research reports and recommendations have a basis that can be substantiated as reasonable and adequate. An individual employee (supervisory analyst) or a group of employees (review committee) should be appointed to review and approve all research reports and recommendations to determine whether they meet the criteria as established in the policy.

▶ Develop detailed, written guidance for research analysts, supervisory analysts, and review committees that establishes due-diligence procedures for judging whether a particular recommendation has a reasonable and adequate basis.

▶ Develop measurable criteria for assessing the quality of research, including the reasonableness and adequacy of the basis for any recommendation and the accuracy of recommendations over time, and implement compensation arrangements that depend on these measurable criteria and that are applied consistently to all research analysts.

## Application of the Standard

*Example 1:* Helen Hawke manages the corporate finance department of Sarkozi Securities, Ltd. The firm is anticipating that the government will soon close a tax loophole that currently allows oil and gas exploration companies to pass on drilling expenses to holders of a certain class of shares. Because market demand for this tax-advantaged class of stock is currently high, Sarkozi convinces several companies to undertake new equity financings at once before the loophole closes. Time is of the essence, but Sarkozi lacks sufficient resources to conduct adequate research on all the prospective issuing companies. Hawke decides to estimate the IPO prices based on the relative size of each company and to justify the pricing later when her staff has time.

> *Comment:* Sarkozi should have taken on only the work that it could adequately handle. By categorizing the issuers as to general size, Hawke has bypassed researching all the other relevant aspects that should be considered when pricing new issues and thus has not performed sufficient due diligence. Such an omission can result in investors purchasing shares at prices that have no actual basis. Hawke has violated Standard V(A).

*Example 2:* Babu Dhaliwal works for Heinrich Brokerage in the corporate finance group. He has just persuaded Feggans Resources, Ltd., to allow his firm to do a secondary equity financing at Feggans Resources' current stock price. Because the stock has been trading at higher multiples than similar companies with equivalent production, Dhaliwal presses the Feggans Resources managers to project what would be the maximum production they could achieve in an optimal scenario. Based on these numbers, he is able to justify the price his firm will be asking for the secondary issue. During a sales pitch to the brokers, Dhaliwal then uses these numbers as the base-case production levels that Feggans Resources will achieve.

> *Comment:* When presenting information to the brokers, Dhaliwal should have given a range of production scenarios and the probability of Feggans Resources achieving each level. By giving the maximum production level as the likely level of production, he has misrepresented the chances of achieving that production level and seriously misled the brokers.

*Example 3:* Brendan Witt creates an Internet site with a chat-room area to publish his stock recommendations. He views the site as a chance to attract new clients. In the chat room, he almost always writes positively about technology stocks and recommends purchasing based on what the conventional wisdom of the markets has deemed the "hot" securities of the day.

*Comment:* Witt's exuberance about technology and the conventional wisdom of the markets, without more information, do not constitute a reasonable and adequate basis, supported by appropriate research and investigation, on which to base a recommendation. Therefore, Witt has violated Standard V(A).

***Example 4:*** Carsten Dunlop is an investment consultant in the London office of EFG, a major global investment consultant firm. One of her U.K. pension funds has decided to appoint a specialist U.S. equity manager. EFG's global manager research relies on local consultants to cover managers within their region and, after conducting thorough due diligence, post their views and ratings on EFG's manager database. Dunlop accesses EFG's global manager research database and conducts a screen of all U.S. equity managers based on the client's desired match for philosophy/style, performance, and tracking-error targets and those that are rated "buy." She selects the five managers meeting these criteria and puts them in a briefing report that is delivered to the client 10 days later. In between the time of Dunlop's database search and delivery of the report to the client, EFG updated the database with the information that one of the firms that Dunlop has recommended for consideration lost its chief investment officer, head of U.S. equity research, and the majority of portfolio managers on the U.S. equity product—all of whom have left to establish their own firm, and she does not provide the client with this updated information. Although EFG has updated its database, Dunlop's report to the client does not reflect this new information.

*Comment:* Dunlop has failed to satisfy the requirement of Standard V(A) by not checking the database in a timely manner and updating her report to the client. Although EFG updated the manager ratings to reflect the personnel turnover at the firm, Dunlop did not update her report to reflect the new information.

***Example 5:*** Evelyn Mastakis is a junior analyst asked by her firm to write a research report predicting the expected interest rate for residential mortgages over the next six months. Mastakis submits her report to the fixed-income investment committee of her firm for review, as required by firm procedures. Although some committee members support Mastakis's conclusion, the majority of the committee disagrees with her conclusion, and the report is significantly changed to indicate that interest rates are likely to increase more than originally predicted by Mastakis.

*Comment:* The results of research are not always clear, and different people may have different opinions based on the same factual evidence. In this case, the majority of the committee may have valid reasons for issuing a report that differs from the analyst's original research. The firm can issue a report different from the original report of the analyst as long as there is a reasonable or adequate basis for its conclusions. Generally, analysts must write research reports that reflect their own opinion and can ask the firm not to put their name on reports that ultimately differ from that opinion. When the work is a group effort, however, not all members of the team may agree with all aspects of the report. Ultimately, members and candidates can ask to have their names removed from the report, but if they are satisfied that the process has produced results or conclusions that have a reasonable or adequate basis, members or candidates do not have to dissociate from the report even when they do not agree with its contents. The member or candidate should document the difference of opinion and any request to remove his or her name from the report.

***Example 6:*** Gary McDermott runs a small, two-person investment management firm. McDermott's firm subscribes to a service from a large investment research firm that provides research reports. McDermott's firm makes investment recommendations based on these reports.

> *Comment:* Members and candidates can rely on third-party research but must make reasonable and diligent efforts to determine that such research is sound. If McDermott undertakes due diligence efforts on a regular basis to ensure that the research produced by the large firm is objective and reasonably based, McDermott can rely on that research when making investment recommendations to clients.

## B. Communication with Clients and Prospective Clients

**Members and candidates must:**

1. **Disclose to clients and prospective clients the basic format and general principles of the investment processes used to analyze investments, select securities, and construct portfolios and must promptly disclose any changes that might materially affect those processes.**

2. **Use reasonable judgment in identifying which factors are important to their investment analyses, recommendations, or actions and include those factors in communications with clients and prospective clients.**

3. **Distinguish between fact and opinion in the presentation of investment analysis and recommendations.**

Standard V(B) addresses members' and candidates' conduct with respect to communicating with clients. Developing and maintaining clear, frequent, and thorough communication practices is critical to providing high-quality financial services to clients. When clients can understand the information communicated to them, they also can understand exactly how members and candidates are acting on their behalf, which gives clients the opportunity to make well-informed decisions regarding their investments. Such understanding can be accomplished only through clear communication.

Standard V(B) states the responsibility of members and candidates to include in their communications those key factors that are instrumental to the investment recommendation presented. A critical part of this requirement is to distinguish clearly between opinions and facts. In preparing a research report, the member or candidate must present the basic characteristics of the security being analyzed, which will allow the reader to evaluate the report and incorporate information the reader deems relevant to his or her investment decision-making process.

Members and candidates must adequately illustrate to clients and prospective clients the manner in which the member or candidate conducts the investment decision-making process. The member or candidate must keep existing clients and other interested parties informed with respect to changes to the chosen investment process on an ongoing basis. Only by thoroughly understanding the nature of the investment product or service can a client determine whether changes to that product or service could materially affect the client's investment objectives.

Understanding the basic characteristics of the investment is of great importance in judging the suitability of each investment on a stand-alone basis, but it is especially important in determining the impact each investment will have on the characteristics of the portfolio. For instance, although the risk and return characteristics of shares of a common stock might seem to be essentially the same for any investor when the stock is viewed in isolation, the implications of such an investment vary greatly depending on the other investments held. If the particular stock represents 90 percent of an individual's investments, the stock's importance in the portfolio is vastly different from what it would be to an investor who holds the same amount of the stock in a highly diversified portfolio in which the stock represents only 2 percent of the holdings.

For purposes of Standard V(B), communication is not confined to a written report of the type traditionally generated by an analyst researching a particular security, company, or industry. A presentation of information can be made via any means of communication, including in-person recommendation, telephone conversation, media broadcast, or transmission by computer (e.g., on the Internet). Furthermore, the nature of these communications is highly diverse—from one word ("buy" or "sell") to in-depth reports of more than 100 pages. Brief communications must be supported by background reports or data that can be made available to interested parties on request.

A communication may contain a general recommendation about the market, asset allocation, or classes of investments (e.g., stocks, bonds, real estate) or relate to a specific security. If recommendations are contained in capsule form (such as a recommended stock list), members and candidates should notify clients that additional information and analyses are available from the producer of the report. Investment advice based on quantitative research and analysis must be supported by readily available reference material and should be applied in a manner consistent with previously applied methodology or with changes in methodology highlighted. Members and candidates should outline known limitations of the analysis and conclusions contained in their investment analysis. In evaluating the basic characteristics of the investment being recommended, members and candidates should consider in the report the principal risks inherent in the expected cash returns, which may include credit risk, financial risk (specifically the use of leverage or financial derivatives), and overall market risk.

Once the process has been completed, the member or candidate who prepares the report must include those elements important to the analysis and conclusions of the report so that the user can follow and challenge the report's reasoning. A report writer who has done adequate investigation may emphasize certain areas, touch briefly on others, and omit certain aspects deemed unimportant. For instance, a report may dwell on a quarterly earnings release or new-product introduction at the sacrifice of examining other fundamental matters in depth so long as the analyst clearly stipulates the limits to the scope of the report.

Standard V(B) requires that opinion be separated from fact. Violations are most likely to occur when reports fail to separate the past from the future by not indicating that earnings estimates, changes in the outlook for dividends, and/or future market price information are opinions subject to future circumstances. In the case of complex quantitative analysis, analysts must clearly separate fact from statistical conjecture and should identify the known limitations of the analysis.

## Recommended Procedures for Compliance

Because the selection of relevant factors is an analytical skill, determination of whether a member or candidate has used reasonable judgment in excluding and including information in research reports depends heavily on case-by-case review rather than a specific checklist. To assist in the after-the-fact review of a report, the member or candidate must maintain records indicating the nature of the research and should, if asked, be able to supply additional information to the client (or any user of the report) covering factors not included.

## Application of the Standard

*Example 1:* Sarah Williamson, director of marketing for Country Technicians, Inc., is convinced that she has found the perfect formula for increasing Country Technicians' income and diversifying its product base. Williamson plans to build on Country Technicians' reputation as a leading money manager by marketing an exclusive and expensive investment advice letter to high-net-worth individuals. One hitch in the plan is the complexity of Country Technicians' investment system—a combination of technical trading rules (based on historical price and volume fluctuations) and portfolio-construction rules designed to minimize risk. To simplify the newsletter, she decides to include only each week's top-five buy and sell recommendations and to leave out details of the valuation models and the portfolio-structuring scheme.

> *Comment:* Williamson's plans for the newsletter violate Standard V(B). Williamson need not describe the investment system in detail in order to implement the advice effectively, clients must be informed of Country Technicians' basic process and logic. Without understanding the basis for a recommendation, clients cannot possibly understand its limitations or its inherent risks.

*Example 2:* Richard Dox is a mining analyst for East Bank Securities. He has just finished his report on Boisy Bay Minerals. Included in his report is his own assessment of the geological extent of mineral reserves likely to be found on the company's land. Dox completed this calculation based on the core samples from the company's latest drilling. According to Dox's calculations, the company has in excess of 500,000 ounces of gold on the property. Dox concludes his research report as follows: "Based on the fact that the company has 500,000 ounces of gold to be mined, I recommend a strong BUY."

> *Comment:* If Dox issues the report as written, he will violate Standard V(B). His calculation of the total gold reserves for the property is an opinion not a fact. Opinion must be distinguished from fact in research reports.

*Example 3:* Olivia Thomas, an analyst at Government Brokers, Inc., which is a brokerage firm specializing in government bond trading, has produced a report that describes an investment strategy designed to benefit from an expected decline in U.S. interest rates. The firm's derivative products group has designed a structured product that will allow the firm's clients to benefit from this strategy. Thomas's report describing the strategy indicates that high returns are possible if various scenarios for declining interest rates are assumed. Citing the proprietary nature of the structured product underlying the strategy, the report does not describe in detail how the firm is able to offer such returns in the scenarios, nor does the report address the likely returns of the strategy if, contrary to expectations, interest rates rise.

> *Comment:* Thomas has violated Standard V(B) because her report fails to describe properly the basic characteristics of the investment strategy, including how the structure was created and the degree to which leverage was embedded in the structure. The report should include a balanced discussion of how the strategy would perform in the case of rising as well as falling interest rates.

*Example 4:* May & Associates is an aggressive growth manager that has represented itself since its inception as a specialist at investing in small-capitalization domestic stocks. One of May's selection criteria is a maximum capitalization of $250 million for any given company. After a string of successful years of superior relative performance, May expanded its client base significantly, to the point at which assets under management now exceed $3 billion. For liquidity purposes, May's chief investment officer (CIO) decides to lift the maximum permissible market-cap ceiling to $500 million and change the firm's sales and marketing literature accordingly to inform prospective clients and third-party consultants.

> *Comment:* Although May's CIO is correct about informing potentially interested parties as to the change in investment process, he must also notify May's existing clients. Among the latter group might be a number of clients who not only retained May as a small-cap manager but also retained mid-cap and large-cap specialists in a multiple-manager approach. Such clients could regard May's change of criteria as a style change that could distort their overall asset allocations.

**Example 5:** Rather than lifting the ceiling for its universe from $250 million to $500 million, May & Associates extends its small-cap universe to include a number of non-U.S. companies.

> *Comment:* Standard V(B) requires that May's CIO advise May's clients of this change because the firm may have been retained by some clients specifically for its prowess at investing in domestic small-cap stocks. Other variations requiring client notification include introducing derivatives to emulate a certain market sector or relaxing various other constraints, such as portfolio beta. In all such cases, members and candidates must disclose changes to all interested parties.

**Example 6:** RJZ Capital Management is a value-style active equity manager that selects stocks using a combination of four multifactor models. Because of favorable results gained from back-testing the most recent 10 years of available market data, the president of RJZ decides to replace its simple model of price to trailing 12-months earnings with a new dividend discount model designed by the firm that is a function of projected inflation rates, earnings growth rates, and interest rates.

> *Comment:* Because the introduction of a new and different valuation model represents a material change in the investment process, RJZ's president must communicate the change to the firm's clients. RJZ is moving away from a model based on hard data toward a new model that is at least partly dependent on the firm's forecasting skills. Clients would likely view such a model as a significant change rather than a mere refinement of RJZ's process.

**Example 7:** RJZ Capital Management loses the chief architect of its multifactor valuation system. Without informing its clients, the president of RJZ decides to redirect the firm's talents and resources toward developing a product for passive equity management—a product that will emulate the performance of a major market index.

> *Comment:* The president of RJZ failed to disclose to clients a substantial change to its investment process, which is a violation of Standard V(B).

**Example 8:** At Fundamental Asset Management, Inc., the responsibility for selecting stocks for addition to the firm's "approved" list has just shifted from individual security analysts to a committee consisting of the research director and three senior portfolio managers. Eleanor Morales, a portfolio manager with Fundamental Asset Management, fails to notify her clients of the change.

> *Comment:* Morales must disclose the process change to all her clients. Some of Fundamental's clients might be concerned about the morale and motivation among the firm's best research analysts following the change. Moreover, clients might challenge the stock-picking track record of the portfolio managers and might even want to monitor the situation closely.

## C. Record Retention

**Members and candidates must develop and maintain appropriate records to support their investment analysis, recommendations, actions, and other investment-related communications with clients and prospective clients.**

Members and candidates must retain records that substantiate the scope of their research and reasons for their actions or conclusions. The records required to support recommendations and/or investment actions depend on the role of the member or candidate in the investment decision-making process. Records can be maintained either in hard copy or electronic form.

As a general matter, records created as part of a member's or candidate's professional activity on behalf of his or her employer are the property of the member's or candidate's firm. When a member or candidate leaves a firm to seek other employment, the member or candidate cannot take the property of the firm, including originals or copies of supporting records of the member's or candidate's work, to the new employer without the express consent of the previous employer. Without re-creating the records at the new firm, the member or candidate cannot use historical recommendations or research reports created at the previous firm because the supporting documentation is unavailable.

Local regulators often impose requirements on members, candidates, and their firms related to record retention that must be followed. Fulfilling such regulatory requirements also may satisfy the requirements of Standard V(C), but members and candidates must explicitly determine whether it does. In the absence of regulatory guidance, CFA Institute recommends maintaining records for at least seven years.

## Recommended Procedures for Compliance

The responsibility to maintain records that support investment action generally falls with the firm rather than individuals. However, members and candidates must retain research notes and other documents supporting current investment-related communications to assist their firms in complying with internal or external record preservation requirements.

## Application of the Standard

***Example 1:*** One of Nikolas Lindstrom's clients is upset by the negative investment returns in his equity portfolio. The investment policy statement for the client requires that the portfolio manager follow a benchmark-oriented approach. The benchmark for the client included a 35 percent investment allocation in the technology sector, which the client acknowledged was appropriate. Over the past three years, the portion put into the segment of technology stocks suffered severe losses. The client complains to the investment manager that so much money was allocated to this sector.

> *Comment:* For Lindstrom, it is important to have appropriate records to show that over the past three years the percentage of technology stocks in the benchmark index was 35 percent. Therefore, the amount of money invested in the technology sector was appropriate according to the investment policy statement. Lindstrom should also have the investment policy statement for the client stating that the benchmark was appropriate for the client's investment objectives. He should also have records indicating that the investment had been explained appropriately to the client and that the investment policy statement was updated on a regular basis.

*Example 2:* Malcolm Young is a research analyst who writes numerous reports rating companies in the luxury retail industry. His reports are based on a variety of sources, including interviews with company management, manufacturers, and economists; onsite company visits; customer surveys; and secondary research from analysts covering related industries.

> *Comment:* Young must carefully document and keep copies of all the information that goes into his report, including the secondary or third-party research of other analysts.

*Example 3:* Martin Blank develops an analytical model while employed by Grosse Point Investment Management, LLP (GPIM). While at the firm, he systematically documents the assumptions that make up the model as well as his reasoning for the assumptions. As the result of the success of his model, Blank is hired to be the head of the research department of one of GPIM's competitors. Blank takes copies of the records supporting his model to his new firm.

> *Comment:* The records created by Blank supporting the research model he developed at GPIM are the records of GPIM. He cannot take the documents with him to his new employer without GPIM's permission. Blank must re-create the records supporting his model at the new firm.

# STANDARD VI—CONFLICTS OF INTEREST

## A. Disclosure of Conflicts

**Members and candidates must make full and fair disclosure of all matters that could reasonably be expected to impair their independence and objectivity or interfere with respective duties to their clients, prospective clients, and their employer. Members and candidates must ensure that such disclosures are prominent, are delivered in plain language, and communicate the relevant information effectively.**

Conflicts of interest often arise in the investment management profession. Conflicts can occur between the interests of clients, the interests of employers, and the member's or candidate's own personal interest. Managing these conflicts is a critical part of working in the investment industry and can take many forms. Best practice is to avoid conflicts of interest when possible. When conflicts cannot be reasonably avoided, disclosure of their existence is necessary.

Standard VI(A) protects investors and employers by requiring members and candidates to fully disclose to clients, potential clients, and employers all actual and potential conflicts of interest. Once a member or candidate has made full disclosure, the member's or candidate's employer, clients, and prospects will have the information needed to evaluate the objectivity of the investment advice or action taken on their behalf.

To be effective, disclosures must be prominent and must be made in plain language and in a manner designed to effectively communicate the information to clients and prospective clients. It is up to members and candidates to determine how often, in what manner, or under what particular circumstances disclosure of conflicts must be made. Members and candidates have the responsibility to assess when and how they meet their obligations under this standard in each particular case. Members and candidates should err on the side of caution or repetition to ensure that conflicts of interest are effectively communicated.

### Disclosure to Clients

Members and candidates must maintain their objectivity when rendering investment advice or taking investment action. Investment advice or actions may be perceived to be tainted in numerous situations. Can a member or candidate remain objective if, on behalf of the firm, the member or candidate obtains or assists in obtaining fees for services? Can a member or candidate give objective advice if he or she owns stock in the company that is the subject of an investment recommendation or if the member or candidate has a close personal relationship with the company managers? Requiring members and candidates to disclose all matters that reasonably could be expected to impair the member's or candidate's objectivity allows clients and prospects to judge motives and possible biases for themselves.

In the investment industry, a conflict, or the perception of a conflict, often cannot be avoided. The most obvious conflicts of interest, which should always be disclosed, are relationships between the member, candidate, or their firm and an issuer (such as a directorship or consultancy), investment banking, underwriting and financial relationships, broker/dealer market-making activities, and material beneficial ownership of stock. A member or candidate must take reasonable steps to determine if a conflict of interest exists and disclose to clients any conflicts of the member's or candidate's firm when known. Disclosure of broker/dealer market-making activities alerts clients that a purchase or sale might be made from or to the firm's principal account and that the firm has a special interest in the price of the stock.

Service as a director poses three basic conflicts of interest. First, a conflict may exist between the duties owed to clients and the duties owed to shareholders of the company. Second, investment personnel who serve as directors may receive the securities or the option to purchase securities of the company as compensation for serving on the board, which could raise questions about trading actions that could increase the value of those securities. Third, board service creates the opportunity to receive material nonpublic information involving the company. Even though the information is confidential, the perception could be that information not available to the public might be communicated to a director's firm—whether a broker, investment advisor, or other type of organization. When members or candidates providing investment services also serve as directors, they should be isolated from those making investment decisions by the use of firewalls or similar restrictions.

Many other circumstances give rise to actual or potential conflicts of interest. For instance, a sell-side analyst working for a broker/dealer may be encouraged, not only by members of her or his own firm but by corporate issuers themselves, to write research reports about particular companies. The buy-side analyst is likely to be faced with similar conflicts as banks exercise their underwriting and securities-dealing powers. The marketing division may ask an analyst to recommend the stock of a certain company in order to obtain business from that company.

The potential for conflicts of interest also exists with broker-sponsored limited partnerships formed to invest venture capital. Increasingly, members and candidates are expected not only to follow issues from these partnerships once they are offered to the public but also to promote the issues in the secondary market after public offerings. Members, candidates, and their firms should attempt to resolve situations presenting potential conflicts of interest or disclose them in accordance with the principles set forth in Standard VI(A).

The most prevalent conflict requiring disclosure under Standard VI(A) is a member's or candidate's ownership of stock in companies that they recommend to clients and/or that clients hold. Clearly, the easiest method for preventing a conflict is to prohibit members and candidates from owning any such securities, but this approach is over burdensome and discriminates against members and candidates. Therefore, sell-side members and candidates should disclose any materially beneficial ownership interest in a security or other investment that the member or candidate is recommending. Buy-side members and candidates should disclose their procedures for reporting requirements for personal transactions. For the purposes of Standard VI(A), members and candidates beneficially own securities or other investments if they have a direct or indirect pecuniary interest in the securities; have the power to vote or direct the voting of the shares of the securities or investments; or have the power to dispose or direct the disposition of the security or investment. Conflicts arising from personal investing are discussed more fully in the guidance for Standard VI(B)—Priority of Transactions.

### *Disclosure of Conflicts to Employers*

Disclosure of conflicts to employers may also be appropriate in many instances. When reporting conflicts of interest to employers, members and candidates should give their employer enough information to assess the impact of the conflict. By complying with employer guidelines, members and candidates allow their employers to avoid potentially embarrassing and costly ethical or regulatory violations.

Reportable situations include conflicts that would interfere with rendering unbiased investment advice and conflicts that would cause a member or candidate not to act in the employer's best interest. The same circumstances that generate conflicts to be reported to clients and prospects also would dictate reporting to employers. Ownership of stocks analyzed or recommended, participation in outside boards, and financial and other pressures that may influence a decision are to be promptly reported to the employer so that their impact can be assessed and a decision made on how to resolve the conflict.

The mere appearance of conflict of interest may create problems for members, candidates, and their employers. Therefore, many of the conflicts previously mentioned could be explicitly prohibited by the employer. For example, many employers restrict personal trading, outside board membership, and related activities to prevent situations that might not normally be considered problematic from a conflict-of-interest point of view but that could give the appearance of a conflict of interest. Members and candidates must comply with these restrictions. Members and candidates must take reasonable steps to avoid conflicts and, if they occur inadvertently, must report them promptly so that the employer and the member or candidate can resolve them as quickly and effectively as possible.

Standard VI(A) also deals with a member's and candidate's conflicts of interest that might be detrimental to the employer's business. Any potential conflict situation that could prevent clear judgment in or full commitment to the execution of the member's or candidate's duties to the employer should be reported to the member's or candidate's employer and promptly resolved.

## Recommended Procedures for Compliance

Members or candidates should disclose special compensation arrangements with the employer that might conflict with client interests, such as bonuses based on short-term performance criteria, commissions, incentive fees, performance fees, and referral fees. If the member's or candidate's firm does not permit such disclosure, the member or candidate should document the request and may consider dissociating from the activity.

Members' or candidates' firms are encouraged to include information on compensation packages in firms' promotional literature. If a member or candidate manages a portfolio for which the fee is based on a share of capital gains or capital appreciation (a performance fee), this information should be disclosed to clients. If a member, candidate, or a member's or candidate's firm has outstanding agent options to buy stock as part of the compensation package for corporate financing activities, the amount and expiration date of these options should be disclosed as a footnote to any research report published by the member's or candidate's firm.

## Application of the Standard

**Example 1:** Hunter Weiss is a research analyst with Farmington Company, a broker and investment-banking firm. Farmington's merger and acquisition department has represented Vimco, a conglomerate, in all of its acquisitions for 20 years. From time to time, Farmington officers sit on the boards of directors of various Vimco subsidiaries. Weiss is writing a research report on Vimco.

> *Comment:* Weiss must disclose in his research report Farmington's special relationship with Vimco. Broker/dealer management of and participation in public offerings must be disclosed in research reports. Because the position of underwriter to a company presents a special past and potential future relationship with a company that is the subject of investment advice, it threatens the independence and objectivity of the report and must be disclosed.

**Example 2:** The investment management firm of Dover & Roe sells a 25 percent interest in its partnership to a multinational bank holding company, First of New York. Immediately thereafter, Margaret Hobbs, president of Dover & Roe, changes her recommendation of First of New York's common stock from "sell" to "buy" and adds First of New York's commercial paper to Dover & Roe's approved list for purchase.

> *Comment:* Hobbs must disclose the new relationship with First of New York to all Dover & Roe clients. This relationship must also be disclosed to clients by the firm's portfolio managers when they make specific investment recommendations or take investment actions with respect to First of New York's securities.

**Example 3:** Carl Fargmon, a research analyst who follows firms producing office equipment, has been recommending purchase of Kincaid Printing because of its innovative new line of copiers. After his initial report on the company, Fargmon's wife inherits from a distant relative $3 million of Kincaid stock. He has been asked to write a follow-up report on Kincaid.

> *Comment:* Fargmon must disclose his wife's ownership of the Kincaid stock to his employer and in his follow-up report. Best practice would be to avoid the conflict by asking his employer to assign another analyst to draft the follow-up report.

**Example 4:** Betty Roberts is speculating in penny stocks for her own account and purchases 100,000 shares of Drew Mining, Inc., for 30 cents a share. She intends to sell these shares at the sign of any substantial upward price movement of the stock. A week later, her employer asks her to write a report on penny stocks in the mining industry to be published in two weeks. Even without owning the Drew stock, Roberts would recommend it in her report as a "buy." A surge of the price of the stock to the $2 range is likely to result once the report is issued.

> *Comment:* Although this holding may not be material, Roberts must disclose it in the report and to her employer before writing the report because the gain for her will be substantial if the market responds strongly to her recommendation. The fact that she has only recently purchased the stock adds to the appearance that she is not entirely objective.

***Example 5:*** Samantha Dyson, a portfolio manager for Thomas Investment Counsel, Inc., specializes in managing defined-benefit pension plan accounts, all of which are in the accumulative phase and have long-term investment objectives. A year ago, Dyson's employer, in an attempt to motivate and retain key investment professionals, introduced a bonus compensation system that rewards portfolio managers on the basis of quarterly performance relative to their peers and certain benchmark indexes. Dyson changes her investment strategy and purchases several high-beta stocks for client portfolios in an attempt to improve short-term performance. These purchases are seemingly contrary to the client investment policy statement. Now, an officer of Griffin Corporation, one of Dyson's pension fund clients, asks why Griffin Corporation's portfolio seems to be dominated by high-beta stocks of companies that often appear among the most actively traded issues. No change in objective or strategy has been recommended by Dyson during the year.

> *Comment:* Dyson violated Standard VI(A) by failing to inform her clients of the changes in her compensation arrangement with her employer that created a conflict of interest. Firms may pay employees on the basis of performance, but pressure by Thomas Investment Counsel to achieve short-term performance goals is in basic conflict with the objectives of Dyson's accounts.

***Example 6:*** Wayland Securities works with small companies doing IPOs and/or secondary offerings. Typically, these deals are in the $10 million to $50 million range and, as a result, the corporate finance fees are quite small. In order to compensate for the small fees, Wayland Securities usually takes "agents options"—that is, rights (exercisable within a two-year time frame) to acquire up to an additional 10 percent of the current offering. Following an IPO performed by Wayland for Falk Resources, Ltd., Darcy Hunter, the head of corporate finance at Wayland, is concerned about receiving value for her Falk Resources options. The options are one month from expiring, and the stock is not doing well. She contacts John Fitzpatrick in the research department of Wayland Securities, reminds him that he is eligible for 30 percent of these options and indicates that now would be a good time to give some additional coverage to Falk Resources. Fitzpatrick agrees and immediately issues a favorable report.

> *Comment:* In order for Fitzpatrick not to be in violation of Standard VI(A), he must indicate in the report the volume and expiration date of agent options outstanding. Furthermore, because he is personally eligible for some of the options, Fitzpatrick must disclose the extent of this compensation. He also must be careful that he does not violate his duty of independence and objectivity under Standard I(B).

***Example 7:*** Gary Carter is a representative with Bengal International, a registered broker/dealer. Carter is approached by a stock promoter for Badger Company, who offers to pay Carter additional compensation for sales to his clients of Badger Company's stock. Carter accepts the stock promoter's offer but does not disclose the arrangements to his clients or to his employer. Carter sells shares of the stock to his clients.

> *Comment:* Carter has violated Standard VI(A) by failing to disclose to clients that he was receiving additional compensation for recommending and selling Badger stock. Because he did not disclose the arrangement with Badger to his clients, the clients were unable to evaluate whether Carter's recommendations to buy Badger were affected by this arrangement. Carter's conduct also violated Standard VI(A) by failing to disclose to his employer monetary compensation received in addition to the compensation and benefits conferred by his employer. Carter was required by Standard VI(A) to disclose the

arrangement with Badger to his employer so that his employer could evaluate whether the arrangement affected his objectivity and loyalty.

*Example 8:* Carol Corky, a senior portfolio manager for Universal Management, recently became involved as a trustee with the Chelsea Foundation, a very large not-for-profit foundation in her hometown. Universal is a small money manager (with assets under management of approximately $100 million) that caters to individual investors. Chelsea has assets in excess of $2 billion. Corky does not believe informing Universal of her involvement with Chelsea is necessary.

*Comment:* By failing to inform Universal of her involvement with Chelsea, Corky violated Standard VI(A). Given the large size of the endowment at Chelsea, Corky's new role as a trustee can reasonably be expected to be time-consuming, to the possible detriment of Corky's portfolio responsibilities with Universal. As a trustee, Corky also may become involved with the investment decisions at Chelsea. Therefore, Standard VI(A) obligates Corky to discuss becoming a trustee at Chelsea with her compliance officer or supervisor at Universal before accepting the position, and she should have disclosed the degree to which she would be involved in investment decisions at Chelsea.

*Example 9:* Bruce Smith covers East European equities for Marlborough investments, an investment management firm with a strong presence in emerging markets. While on a business trip to Russia, Smith learns that investing in Russian equity directly is difficult but that equity-linked notes that replicate the performance of the underlying Russian equity can be purchased from a New York-based investment bank. Believing that his firm would not be interested in such a security, Smith purchases a note linked to a Russian telecommunications company for his own account without informing Marlborough. A month later, Smith decides that the firm should consider investing in Russian equities using equity-linked notes, and he prepares a write-up on the market that concludes with a recommendation to purchase several of the notes. One note recommended is linked to the same Russian telecom company that Smith holds in his personal account.

*Comment:* Smith violated Standard VI(A) by failing to disclose his ownership of the note linked to the Russian telecom company. Smith is required by the standard to disclose the investment opportunity to his employer and look to his company's policies on personal trading to determine whether it was proper for him to purchase the note for his own account. By purchasing the note, Smith may or may not have impaired his ability to make an unbiased and objective assessment of the appropriateness of the derivative instrument for his firm, but Smith's failure to disclose the purchase to his employer impaired his employer's ability to render an opinion regarding whether the ownership of the security constituted a conflict of interest that might have affected future recommendations. Once he recommended the notes to his firm, Smith compounded his problems by not disclosing that he owned the notes in his personal account—a clear conflict of interest.

## B. Priority of Transactions

**Investment transactions for clients and employers must have priority over investment transactions in which a member or candidate is the beneficial owner.**

Standard VI(B) reinforces the responsibility of members and candidates to give the interests of their clients and employers priority over their personal financial interests. This standard is designed to prevent any potential conflict of interest or the appearance of a conflict of interest with respect to personal transactions. Client interests have priority. Client transactions must take precedence over transactions made on behalf of the member's or candidate's firm or personal transactions.

Standard VI(B) states that transactions for clients and employers must have priority over transactions in securities or other investments of which a member or candidate is the beneficial owner so that such personal transactions do not adversely affect the interests of their clients or employers. For purposes of the Code and Standards, a member or candidate is a "beneficial owner" if the member or candidate has a direct or indirect personal interest in the securities. A member or candidate having the same investment positions or being coinvested with their clients does not always create a conflict. Some clients in certain investment situations require members or candidates to have aligned interests. However, personal investment positions or transactions of a member or candidate or their firm should never adversely affect client investments.

Conflicts between the client's interest and an investment professional's personal interest may occur. Although conflicts of interest exist, there is nothing inherently unethical about individual managers, advisors, or mutual fund employees making money from personal investments as long as (1) the client is not disadvantaged by the trade, (2) the investment professional does not benefit personally from trades undertaken for clients, and (3) the investment professional complies with applicable regulatory requirements.

Standard VI(B) covers the activities of all members and candidates who have knowledge of pending transactions that may be made on behalf of their clients or employers. Standard VI(B) also applies to members and candidates who have access to information during the normal preparation of research recommendations or who take investment actions. Members and candidates are prohibited from conveying such information to any person whose relationship to the member or candidate makes the member or candidate a beneficial owner of the person's securities. Members and candidates must not convey this information to any other person if the information can be deemed material nonpublic information.

Members or candidates may undertake transactions in accounts for which they are a beneficial owner only after their clients and employers have had an adequate opportunity to act on the recommendation. Personal transactions include those made for the member's or candidate's own account, for family (including spouse, children, and other immediate family members) accounts, and for accounts in which the member or candidate has a direct or indirect pecuniary interest, such as a trust or retirement account. Family accounts that are client accounts should be treated like any other firm account and should neither be given special treatment nor be disadvantaged because of an existing family relationship with the member or candidate. If a member or candidate has a beneficial ownership in the account, however, the member or candidate may still be subject to preclearance or reporting requirements of their employer or applicable law.

## Recommended Procedures for Compliance

Policies and procedures designed to prevent potential conflicts of interest, or even the appearance of a conflict of interest, with respect to personal transactions are critical to establishing investor confidence in the securities industry. Because investment firms vary greatly in assets under management, types of clients, number of employees, and so on, each firm should establish policies regarding personal investing that are best suited to the firm. Members and candidates should then prominently disclose those policies to clients and prospective clients.

The specific provisions of each firm's standards will vary, but all firms should adopt certain basic procedures to address the conflict areas created by personal investing. These include:

### Limited Participation in Equity IPOs

Some eagerly awaited IPOs may significantly rise in value shortly after the issue is brought to market. Because the new issue may be highly attractive and sought after, the opportunity to participate in the IPO may be limited. Therefore, purchases of IPOs by investment personnel create conflicts of interest in two principal ways. First, participation in an IPO may have the appearance of appropriating an attractive investment opportunity from clients for personal gain—a clear breach of the duty of loyalty to clients. Second, because opportunities to participate in IPOs are limited, there may be an appearance that the investment opportunity is being bestowed as an incentive to make future investment decisions for the benefit of the party providing the opportunity. Members and candidates can avoid these conflicts or the appearance of a conflict of interest by not participating in IPOs.

Reliable and systematic review procedures should be established to ensure that conflicts relating to IPOs are identified and appropriately dealt with by supervisors. Members and candidates should preclear their participation in IPOs, even in situations were there are no conflicts of interest between a member's or candidate's participation in an IPO and the client's interests. Members and candidates should not benefit from the position that their clients occupy in the marketplace—through preferred trading, the allocation of limited offerings, and/or oversubscription.

### Restrictions on Private Placements

Strict limits should be placed on investment personnel acquiring securities in private placements, and appropriate supervisory and review procedures should be established to prevent noncompliance.

Firms do not routinely use private placements for clients (e.g., venture capital deals) because of the high risk associated with them. Conflicts relating to private placements are more significant to members and candidates who manage large pools of assets or act as plan sponsors because these managers may be offered special opportunities, such as private placements, as a reward or an enticement for continuing to do business with a particular broker.

Participation in private placements raises conflict-of-interest issues that are similar to issues surrounding IPOs. Investment personnel should not be involved in transactions, including (but not limited to) private placements that could be perceived as favors or gifts that seem designed to influence future judgment or to reward past business deals.

Whether the venture eventually proves to be good or bad, managers have an immediate conflict concerning private placement opportunities. Participants in private placements have an incentive to recommend these investments to clients if and when they go public, regardless of the suitability of the investments for their clients, in order to increase the value of the participants' personal portfolios.

### Establish Blackout/Restricted Periods

Investment personnel involved in the investment decision-making process should establish blackout periods prior to trades for clients so that managers cannot take advantage of their knowledge of client activity by "front-running" client trades.

Individual firms must decide who within the firm should be required to comply with the trading restrictions. At a minimum, all individuals who are involved in the investment decision-making process should be subject to the same restricted period. Each firm must determine specific requirements relating to blackout and restricted periods that are most relevant to the firm while ensuring that the procedures are governed by the guiding principles set forth in the Code and Standards. Size of firm and type of securities purchased are relevant factors. For example, in a large firm, a blackout requirement is, in effect, a total trading ban because the firm is continually trading in most securities. In a small firm, the blackout period is more likely to prevent the investment manager from front-running.

## Reporting Requirements

Supervisors should establish reporting procedures for investment personnel, including duplicate confirmations, disclosure of personal holdings/beneficial ownerships, and preclearance procedures. Once trading restrictions are in place, they must be enforced. The best method for monitoring and enforcing procedures established to eliminate conflicts of interest relating to personal trading is through reporting requirements, including the following:

- ► Disclosure of holdings in which the employee has a beneficial interest. Disclosure by investment personnel to the firm should be made upon commencement of the employment relationship and at least annually thereafter. To address privacy considerations, disclosure of personal holdings should be handled in a confidential manner by the firm.

- ► Providing duplicate confirmations of transactions. Investment personnel should be required to direct their brokers to supply duplicate copies or confirmations to their firms of all their personal securities transactions and copies of periodic statements for all securities accounts. Firms should establish additional reporting requirements, including the frequency of such reporting, that emphasize the firm's intention to promote full and complete disclosure and that explain the role and responsibilities of supervisors. The duplicate confirmation requirement has two purposes: (1) The requirement sends a message that "people are looking" and makes it difficult for an individual to act unethically, and (2) it enables verification of the accounting of the flow of personal investments that cannot be determined from merely looking at transactions or holdings.

- ► Preclearance procedures. Investment personnel should clear all personal investments to identify possible conflicts prior to the execution of personal trades. Preclearance procedures are designed to identify possible conflicts before a problem arises. Preclearance procedures are consistent with the CFA Institute Code and Standards and demonstrate that members, candidates, and their firms place the interests of their clients ahead of their own personal investing interests.

## Disclosure of Policies

Upon request, members and candidates should fully disclose to investors their firms' personal investing policies. The infusion of information on employees' personal investment activities and policies into the marketplace will foster an atmosphere of full and complete disclosure and calm the public's legitimate concerns about the conflicts of interest posed by investment personnel's personal trading. The disclosure must be helpful to investors, however, not simply boiler-plate language containing some vague admonition that investment personnel are "subject to policies and procedures regarding their personal trading."

## Application of the Standard

***Example 1:*** A research analyst, Marlon Long, does not recommend purchase of a common stock for his employer's account because he wants to purchase the stock personally and does not want to wait until the recommendation is approved and the stock purchased by his employer.

> *Comment:* Long violated Standard VI(B) by taking advantage of his knowl-edge of the stock's value before allowing his employer to benefit from that information.

***Example 2:*** Carol Baker, the portfolio manager of an aggressive-growth mutual fund, maintains an account in her husband's name at several brokerage firms with which the fund and a number of Baker's other individual clients do a substantial amount of business. Whenever a new hot issue becomes available, she instructs the brokers to buy it for her husband's account. Because such issues normally are scarce, Baker often acquires shares while her clients are not able to participate.

> *Comment:* Baker must acquire shares for her mutual fund first and, only after doing so, acquire them for her husband's account, even though she might miss out on participating in new issues via her husband's account. She also must disclose the trading for her husband's account to her employer because this activity creates a conflict between her personal interests and her employer's interests [Standard VI(A)—Disclosure of Conflicts].

***Example 3:*** Erin Toffler, a portfolio manager at Esposito Investments, manages the retirement account established with the firm by her parents. Whenever IPOs become available, she first allocates shares to all her other clients for whom the investment is appropriate; only then does she place any remaining portion in her parents' account, if the issue is appropriate for them. She has adopted this procedure so that no one can accuse her of favoring her parents.

> *Comment:* Toffler has breached her duty to her parents by treating them dif-ferently from her other accounts simply because of the family relationship. As fee-paying clients of Esposito Investments, Toffler's parents are entitled to the same treatment as any other client of the firm. If Toffler has beneficial ownership in the account, however, and Esposito Investments has preclear-ance and reporting requirements for personal transactions, she may have to preclear the trades and report the transactions to Esposito.

***Example 4:*** Gary Michaels is an entry-level employee who holds a relatively low-paying job serving both the research and investment management departments of an active investment management company. He purchases a sports car and begins to wear expensive clothes after only a year of employment with the firm. The director of the investment management department, who has responsibility for monitoring the personal stock transactions of all employees, investigates and discovers that Michaels has made substantial investment gains by purchasing stocks just before they were put on the firm's recommended purchase list. Michaels was regularly given the firm's quarterly personal transaction form but declined to complete it.

> *Comment:* Michaels violated Standard VI(B) by placing personal transac-tions ahead of client transactions. In addition, his supervisor violated the

Standards by permitting Michaels to continue to perform his assigned tasks without first having signed the quarterly personal transaction form [Standard IV(C)—Responsibilities of Supervisors]. Note also that if Michaels had communicated information about the firm's recommendations to a person who traded the security, that action would be a misappropriation of the information and a violation of Standard II(A)—Material Nonpublic Information.

***Example 5:*** A brokerage's insurance analyst, Denise Wilson, makes a closed-circuit report to her firm's branches around the country. During the broadcast, she includes negative comments about a major company within the industry. The following day, Wilson's report is printed and distributed to the sales force and public customers. The report recommends that both short-term traders and intermediate investors take profits by selling that company's stocks. Seven minutes after the broadcast, Ellen Riley, head of the firm's trading department, closes out a long call position in the stock. Shortly thereafter, Riley establishes a sizable "put" position in the stock. Riley claims she took this action to facilitate anticipated sales by institutional clients.

> *Comment:* Riley expected that both the stock and option markets would respond to the "sell" recommendation, but she did not give customers an opportunity to buy or sell in the options market before the firm itself did. By taking action before the report was disseminated, Riley's firm could have depressed the price of the "calls" and increased the price of the "puts." The firm could have avoided a conflict of interest if it had waited to trade for its own account until its clients had an opportunity to receive and assimilate Wilson's recommendations. As it is, Riley's actions violated Standard VI(B).

## C. Referral Fees

**Members and candidates must disclose to their employer, clients, and prospective clients, as appropriate, any compensation, consideration, or benefit received from, or paid to, others for the recommendation of products or services.**

Standard VI(C) states the responsibility of members and candidates to inform employer, clients, and prospective clients of any benefit received for referrals of customers and clients. Such disclosure will allow the client or employer to evaluate (1) any partiality shown in any recommendation of services and (2) the full cost of the services.

Appropriate disclosure means that members and candidates must advise the client or prospective client, before entry into any formal agreement for services, of any benefit given or received for the recommendation of any services provided by the member or candidate. In addition, the member or candidate must disclose the nature of the consideration or benefit—for example, flat fee or percentage basis, one-time or continuing benefit, based on performance, benefit in the form of provision of research or other noncash benefit—together with the estimated dollar value. Consideration includes all fees, whether paid in cash, in soft dollars, or in kind.

## Application of the Standard

***Example 1:*** Brady Securities, Inc., a broker/dealer, has established a referral arrangement with Lewis Brothers, Ltd., an investment counseling firm. Under this arrangement, Brady Securities refers all prospective tax-exempt accounts, including pension, profit-sharing, and endowment accounts, to Lewis Brothers. In return, Lewis Brothers makes available to Brady Securities on a regular basis the security recommendations and reports of its research staff, which registered representatives of Brady Securities use in serving customers. In addition, Lewis Brothers conducts monthly economic and market reviews for Brady Securities personnel and directs all stock commission business generated by referral accounts to Brady Securities. Willard White, a partner in Lewis Brothers, calculates that the incremental costs involved in functioning as the research department of Brady Securities amount to $20,000 annually. Referrals from Brady Securities last year resulted in fee income of $200,000, and directing all stock trades through Brady Securities resulted in additional costs to Lewis Brothers' clients of $10,000.

Diane Branch, the chief financial officer of Maxwell, Inc., contacts White and says that she is seeking an investment manager for Maxwell's profit-sharing plan. She adds, "My friend Harold Hill at Brady Securities recommended your firm without qualification, and that's good enough for me. Do we have a deal?" White accepts the new account but does not disclose his firm's referral arrangement with Brady Securities.

> *Comment:* White violated Standard VI(C) by failing to inform the prospective customer of the referral fee payable in services and commissions for an indefinite period to Brady Securities. Such disclosure could have caused Branch to reassess Hill's recommendation and make a more critical evaluation of Lewis Brothers' services.

*Example 2:* James Handley works for the Trust Department of Central Trust Bank. He receives compensation for each referral he makes to Central Trust's brokerage and personal financial management department that results in a sale. He refers several of his clients to the personal financial management department but does not disclose the arrangement within Central Trust to his clients.

> *Comment:* Handley has violated Standard VI(C) by not disclosing the referral arrangement at Central Trust Bank to his clients. The Standard does not distinguish between referral fees paid by a third party for referring clients to the third party and internal compensation arrangements paid within the firm to attract new business to a subsidiary. Members and candidates must disclose all such referral fees. Therefore, Handley would be required to disclose, at the time of referral, any referral fee agreement in place between Central Trust Bank's departments. The disclosure should include the nature and the value of the benefit and should be made in writing.

*Example 3:* Katherine Roberts is a portfolio manager at Katama Investments, an advisory firm specializing in managing assets for high-net-worth individuals. Katama's trading desk uses a variety of brokerage houses to execute trades on behalf of its clients. Roberts asks the trading desk to direct a large portion of its commissions to Naushon, Inc., a small broker/dealer run by one of Roberts's business school classmates. Katama's traders have found that Naushon is not very competitive on pricing, and although Naushon generates some research for its trading clients, Katama's other analysts have found most of Naushon's research not especially useful. Nevertheless, the traders do as Roberts asks, and in return for receiving a large portion of Katama's business, Naushon recommends the investment services of Roberts and Katama to its wealthiest clients. This arrangement is not disclosed to either Katama or the clients referred by Naushon.

> *Comment:* Roberts violated Standard VI(C) by failing to inform her employer of the referral arrangement.

*Example 4:* Yeshao Wen is a portfolio manager for a bank. He receives additional monetary compensation from his employer when he is successful in assisting in the sales process and generation of assets under management. The assets in question will be invested in proprietary product offerings such as affiliate company mutual funds.

> *Comment:* Standard VI(C) is meant to address instances where the investment advice provided by a member or candidate appears to be objective and independent but in fact is influenced by an unseen referral arrangement. It is not meant to cover compensation by employers to employees for generating new business when it would be obvious to potential clients that the employees are "referring" potential clients to the services of their employers.
>
> If Wen is selling the bank's investment management services in general, he does not need to disclose to potential clients that he will receive a bonus for finding new clients and acquiring new assets under management for the bank. Potential clients are likely aware that it would be financially beneficial both to the portfolio manager and the manager's firm for the portfolio manager to sell the services of the firm and attract new clients. Therefore, sales efforts attempting to attract new investment management clients need not disclose this fact.
>
> However, in this example, the assets will be managed in "proprietary product offerings" of the manager's company (for example, an in-house mutual fund) and Wen will receive additional compensation for selling firm products. Some sophisticated investors may realize that it would be financially beneficial to the portfolio manager and the manager's firm if the investor buys the product offerings of the firm.
>
> Best practice, however, dictates that the portfolio manager must disclose to clients that they are compensated for referring clients to firm products. Such disclosure will meet the purpose of Standard VI(C), which is to allow investors to determine whether there is any partiality on the part of the portfolio manager when making investment advice.

# STANDARD VII—RESPONSIBILITIES AS A CFA INSTITUTE MEMBER OR CFA CANDIDATE

## A. Conduct as Members and Candidates in the CFA Program

**Members and candidates must not engage in any conduct that compromises the reputation or integrity of CFA Institute or the CFA designation or the integrity, validity, or security of the CFA examinations.**

Standard VII(A) covers the conduct of CFA Institute members and candidates involved with the CFA Program and prohibits any conduct that undermines the public's confidence that the CFA charter represents a level of achievement based on merit and ethical conduct. The standard's function is to hold members and candidates to a high ethical standard while they are participating in or involved with the CFA Program. Conduct covered includes, but is not limited to:

- ▶ cheating on the CFA examination or any other examination;
- ▶ disregarding the rules and policies of the CFA Program related to examination administration;

▶ providing confidential program information to candidates or the public;

▶ disregarding or attempting to circumvent security measures established by CFA Institute for the CFA examination;

▶ improperly using the CFA designation or other association with CFA Institute to further personal or professional goals; and

▶ misrepresenting information on the Professional Conduct Statement or the CFA Institute Professional Development Program.

This standard does not cover expressing opinions regarding the CFA Program or CFA Institute. Members and candidates are free to disagree and express their disagreement with CFA Institute on its policies, procedures, or any advocacy positions taken by the organization.

## Application of the Standard

*Example 1:* Travis Nero serves as a proctor for the administration of the CFA examination in his city. In the course of his service, he reviews a copy of the Level II examination on the evening prior to the examination's administration and provides information concerning the examination questions to two candidates who use it to prepare for the exam.

*Comment:* Nero and the two candidates violated Standard VII(A). By giving information concerning the examination questions to two candidates, Nero provided an unfair advantage to the two candidates and undermined the integrity and validity of the Level II examination as an accurate measure of the knowledge, skills, and abilities necessary to earn the right to use the CFA designation. By accepting the information, the candidates also compromised the integrity and validity of the Level II examination and undermined the ethical framework that is a key part of the designation.

*Example 2:* Loren Sullivan is enrolled to take the Level II CFA examination. He has been having difficulty remembering a particular formula, so prior to entering the examination room, he writes the formula on the palm of his hand. During the afternoon section of the examination, a proctor notices Sullivan looking at the palm of his hand. She asks to see his hand and finds the formula to be a bit smudged but readable.

*Comment:* Because Sullivan wrote down information from the Candidate Body of Knowledge and took that written information into the examination, his conduct compromised the validity of his examination and violated Standard VII(A). Sullivan's conduct was also in direct contradiction of the rules and regulations of the CFA Program, the Candidate Pledge, and the CFA Institute Code and Standards.

*Example 3:* Prior to participating in the CFA Examination Grading Program, Wesley Whitcomb is required to sign a CFA Institute Grader Agreement. As part of the Grader Agreement, Whitcomb agrees not to reveal or discuss the examination materials with anyone except CFA Institute staff or other graders. Several weeks after the conclusion of the CFA examination grading, Whitcomb tells several colleagues who are candidates in the CFA Program which question he graded. He also discusses the guideline answer and adds that few candidates scored well on the question.

*Comment:* Whitcomb violated Standard VII(A) by breaking the Grader Agreement and disclosing information related to a specific question on the examination, which compromised the integrity of the examination process.

***Example 4:*** At the conclusion of the morning section of the Level I CFA examination, the proctors announce that all candidates are to stop writing immediately. John Davis has not completed the examination, so he continues to randomly fill in ovals on his answer sheet. A proctor approaches Davis's desk and reminds him that he should stop writing immediately; Davis, however, continues to complete the answer sheet. After the proctor asks him to stop writing two additional times, Davis finally puts down his pencil.

> *Comment:* By continuing to complete his examination after time was called, Davis violated Standard VII(A). By continuing to write, Davis had an unfair advantage over other candidates, and his conduct compromised the validity of his examination. Additionally, by not heeding the proctor's repeated instructions, Davis violated the rules and regulations of the CFA Program.

***Example 5:*** Ashlie Hocking is writing Level II of the CFA examination in London. After completing the exam, she immediately attempts to contact her friend in Sydney, Australia, to tip him off to specific questions on the exam.

> *Comment:* Hocking has violated Standard VII(A) by attempting to give her friend an unfair advantage, thereby compromising the integrity of the CFA examination process.

***Example 6:*** Jose Ramirez is an investment-relations consultant for several small companies that are seeking greater exposure to investors. He is also the program chair for the CFA Institute society in the city where he works. To the exclusion of other companies, Ramirez only schedules companies that are his clients to make presentations to the society.

> *Comment:* Ramirez, by using his volunteer position at CFA Institute to benefit himself and his clients, compromises the reputation and integrity of CFA Institute and, thus, violates Standard VII(A).

***Example 7:*** Marguerite Warrenski is a member of the CFA Institute Investment Performance Council (IPC), which oversees the creation, implementation, and revision of the CFA Institute performance presentation standards: the AIMR-PPS and GIPS. As a member of the IPC, she has advance knowledge of confidential information regarding both standards, including any new or revised standards the committee is considering. She tells her clients that her IPC membership will allow her to assist her clients in keeping up with changes to the standards and facilitating their compliance with the changes.

> *Comment:* Warrenski, by using her volunteer position at CFA Institute to benefit herself and her clients, compromises the reputation and integrity of CFA Institute and, thus, violates Standard VII(A).

## B. Reference to CFA Institute, the CFA Designation, and the CFA Program

**When referring to CFA Institute, CFA Institute membership, the CFA designation, or candidacy in the CFA Program, members and candidates must not misrepresent or exaggerate the meaning or implications of membership in CFA Institute, holding the CFA designation, or candidacy in the CFA Program.**

Individuals may reference their CFA designation, CFA Institute membership, or candidacy in the CFA Program but must not exaggerate the meaning or implications of membership in CFA Institute, holding the CFA designation, or candidacy in the CFA Program.

This standard is intended to prevent promotional efforts that make promises or guarantees that are tied to the designation. Statements referencing CFA Institute, the CFA designation, or the CFA Program must not:

▶ over-promise the competency of an individual, or

▶ over-promise future investment results (e.g., higher performance, lower risk).

Statements that highlight or emphasize the commitment of CFA Institute members, CFA charterholders, and CFA candidates to ethical and professional conduct as well as the thoroughness and rigor of the CFA Program are appropriate. Members and candidates may make claims about the relative merits of CFA Institute, the CFA Program, or the Code of Ethics as long as those statements are the opinion of the speaker, whether implicitly or explicitly stated as opinion. Otherwise, statements that do not express opinion have to be supported by facts.

Standard VII(B) applies to any form of communication, including but not limited to that made in electronic or written form (such as on firm letterhead, business cards, professional biographies, directory listings, printed advertising, firm brochures, or personal resumes) and oral statements made to the public, clients, or prospects.

### CFA Institute Membership

The term "CFA Institute members" refers to Regular and Affiliate members of CFA Institute who have met the membership requirements as defined in the CFA Institute Bylaws. Once accepted as a CFA Institute member, the member must satisfy the following requirements to maintain his or her status:

▶ remit annually to CFA Institute a completed Professional Conduct Statement, which renews the commitment to abide by the requirements of the CFA Institute Code of Ethics and Standards of Professional Conduct and the CFA Institute Professional Conduct Program, and

▶ pay applicable CFA Institute membership dues on an annual basis.

If a CFA Institute member fails to meet any one of the requirements listed above, then the individual is no longer considered an active member. Until their membership is reactivated, individuals must not hold themselves out as active members. They may state, for example, that they were CFA Institute members in the past or reference the years when their membership was active.

### Using the Chartered Financial Analyst Designation

Those who have earned the right to use the Chartered Financial Analyst designation may use the marks "Chartered Financial Analyst" or "CFA" and are encouraged to do so but only in a manner that does not misrepresent or exaggerate the meaning or implications of the designation. The use of the designation may be accompanied by an accurate explanation of the requirements that have been met to earn the right to use the designation.

"CFA charterholders" are those individuals who have earned the right to use the Chartered Financial Analyst designation granted by CFA Institute. These are people who have satisfied certain requirements, including completion of the CFA Program and required years of acceptable work experience. Once granted the right to use the designation, individuals must also satisfy the CFA Institute membership requirements (see above) to maintain their right to use the designation.

If a CFA charterholder fails to meet any one of the membership requirements, he or she forfeits the right to use the CFA designation. Until reactivated, individuals must not hold themselves out as CFA charterholders. They may state, for example, that they were charterholders in the past.

## *Referencing Candidacy in the CFA Program*

Candidates in the CFA Program may reference their participation in the CFA Program, but the reference must clearly state that an individual is a candidate in the CFA Program and must not imply that the candidate has achieved any type of partial designation. A person is a candidate in the CFA Program if:

► the person's application for registration in the CFA Program has been accepted by CFA Institute, as evidenced by issuance of a notice of acceptance, and the person is enrolled to sit for a specified examination; or

► the registered person has sat for a specified examination but exam results have not yet been received.

If an individual is registered for the CFA Program but declines to sit for an exam or otherwise does not meet the definition of a candidate as described in the CFA Institute Bylaws, then that individual is no longer considered an active candidate. Once the person is enrolled to sit for a future examination, his or her CFA candidacy resumes.

CFA candidates must never state or imply a partial designation for passing one or more levels or cite an expected completion date of any level of the CFA Program. Final award of the charter is subject to meeting the CFA Program requirements and approval by the CFA Institute Board.

If a candidate passes each level of the exam on the first try and wants to state that he or she did so, that is not a violation of Standard VII(B) because it is a statement of fact. If the candidate then goes on to claim or imply superior ability by obtaining the designation in only three years, he or she is in violation of the standard.

The following statements and Exhibit 2 (on pp. 106–107) illustrate proper and improper references to the CFA designation:

### Improper References

► "CFA charterholders achieve better performance results."

► "John Smith is among the elite, having passed all three CFA examinations in three consecutive attempts."

► "As a CFA charterholder, I am the most qualified to manage client investments."

► "CFA, Level II."

► "CFA, Expected 2005."

### Proper References

► "Completion of the CFA Program has enhanced my portfolio management skills."

► "John Smith passed all three CFA examinations in three consecutive years."

► "The CFA designation is globally recognized and attests to a charterholder's success in a rigorous and comprehensive study program in the field of investment management and research analysis."

| EXHIBIT 2 | Correct and Incorrect Use of the Chartered Financial Analyst and CFA Marks | |
|---|---|---|

| Incorrect | Principle | Correct |
|---|---|---|
| He is one of two CFAs in the company. He is a Chartered Financial Analyst. | The CFA and Chartered Financial Analyst designations must always be used as adjectives, never as nouns or common names. | He is one of two CFA charterholders in the company. He earned the right to use the Chartered Financial Analyst designation. |
| Jane Smith, C.F.A. John Doe, cfa | No periods. Always capitalize the letters "CFA". | Jane Smith, CFA |
| John, a CFA-type portfolio manager. The focus is on Chartered Financial Analysis. CFA-equivalent program Swiss-CFA | Do not alter the designation to create new words or phrases. | John Jones, CFA |
| Jones Chartered Financial Analysts, Inc. | The designation must not be used as part of the name of a firm. | John Jones, Chartered Financial Analyst |
| Jane Smith, **CFA** John Doe, **Chartered Financial Analyst** | The CFA designation should not be given more prominence (e.g., larger, bold) than the charterholder's name. | Jane Smith, CFA John Doe, Chartered Financial Analyst |
| Chartered Financial Analyst (CFA), September 2007 | Candidates in the CFA Program must not cite the expected date of exam completion and award of charter. | Level I candidate in the CFA Program. |
| CFA Level I. CFA degree expected in 2006. | No designation exists for someone who has passed Level I, Level II, or Level III of the exam. The CFA designation should not be referred to as a degree. | Passed Level I of the CFA examination in 2002. |
| CFA (Passed Finalist) | A candidate who has passed Level III but has not yet received his or her charter cannot use the CFA or Chartered Financial Analyst designation. | I have passed all three levels of the CFA Program and may be eligible for the CFA charter upon completion of the required work experience. |

*(Exhibit continued on next page …)*

| EXHIBIT 2 | (continued) | |
|---|---|---|
| CFA, 2001, UK Society of Investment Professionals | In citing the designation in a resume, a charterholder should use the date that he or she received the designation and should cite CFA Institute as the conferring body. | CFA, 2001, CFA Institute (optional: Charlottesville, Virginia, USA) |

▶ "The credibility that the CFA designation affords and the skills the CFA Program cultivates are key assets for my future career development."

▶ "As a CFA charterholder, I am committed to the highest ethical standards."

▶ "I enrolled in the CFA Program to obtain the highest set of credentials in the global investment management industry."

▶ "I passed Level I of the CFA examination."

▶ "I am a 2003 Level III CFA candidate."

▶ "I passed all three levels of the CFA Program and will be eligible for the CFA charter upon completion of the required work experience."

### *Proper Usage of the CFA Marks*

Upon obtaining the CFA charter from CFA Institute, charterholders are given the right to use the CFA trademarks, including Chartered Financial Analyst®, CFA®, and the CFA Logo (a certification mark). These trademarks are registered by CFA Institute in countries around the world.

▶ The Chartered Financial Analyst and CFA marks must always be used either after a charterholder's name or as adjectives (never as nouns) in written documents or oral conversations. For example, to refer to oneself as "a CFA" or "a Chartered Financial Analyst" is improper.

▶ The CFA Logo certification mark is used by charterholders as a distinctive visual symbol of the CFA designation that can be easily recognized by employers, colleagues, and clients. As a certification mark, it must only be used to directly reference an individual charterholder or group of charterholders.

CFA charterholders should refer to guidelines published by CFA Institute that provide additional information and examples illustrating proper and improper use of the CFA Logo, Chartered Financial Analyst, and CFA marks. These guidelines and the CFA Logo are available on the CFA Institute website at www.cfainstitute.org/memservices/cfaguide.html.

## Recommended Procedures for Compliance

It is common for references to a member's CFA designation or CFA candidacy to be misused or improperly referenced by others within a member's or candidate's firm who do not possess knowledge of the requirements of Standard VII(B). As an appropriate step to reduce this risk, members and candidates should disseminate written information on Standard VII(B) and the accompanying guidance to their firm's legal, compliance, public relations, and marketing departments. Information on proper use of the designation can be found on the CFA Institute website at: www.cfainstitute.org/memservices/pdf/trademark_usage.pdf. For materials that reference employees' affiliation with CFA Institute, members and candidates should encourage their firms to create templates that are approved by a central authority (such as the compliance department) as being consistent with Standard VII(B). This practice would promote consistency and accuracy of references to CFA Institute membership, the CFA designation, and CFA candidacy within the firm.

## Application of the Standard

*Example 1:* An advertisement for AZ Investment Advisors states that all the firm's principals are CFA charterholders and all passed the three examinations on their first attempt. The advertisement prominently links this fact to the notion that AZ's mutual funds have achieved superior performance.

> *Comment:* AZ may state that all principals passed the three examinations on the first try as long as this statement is true and is not linked to performance or does not imply superior ability. Implying that (1) CFA charterholders achieve better investment results and (2) those who pass the exams on the first try may be more successful than those who do not violates Standard VII(B).

*Example 2:* Five years after receiving his CFA charter, Louis Vasseur resigns his position as an investment analyst and spends the next two years traveling abroad. Because he is not actively engaged in the investment profession, he does not file a completed Professional Conduct Statement with CFA Institute and does not pay his CFA Institute membership dues. At the conclusion of his travels, Vasseur becomes a self-employed analyst, accepting assignments as an independent contractor. Without reinstating his CFA Institute membership by filing his Professional Conduct Statement and paying his dues, he prints business cards that display "CFA" after his name.

> *Comment:* Vasseur has violated Standard VII(B) because Vasseur's right to use the CFA designation was suspended when he failed to file his Professional Conduct Statement and stopped paying dues. Therefore, he no longer is able to state or imply that he is an active CFA charterholder. When Vasseur files his Professional Conduct Statement and resumes paying CFA Institute dues to activate his membership, he will be eligible to use the CFA designation upon satisfactory completion of CFA Institute reinstatement procedures.

*Example 3:* After a 25-year career, James Simpson retires from his firm. Because he is not actively engaged in the investment profession, he does not file a completed Professional Conduct Statement with CFA Institute and does not pay his CFA Institute membership dues. Simpson designs a plain business card (without a corporate logo) to hand out to friends with his new contact details, and he continues to put "CFA" after his name.

> *Comment:* Simpson has violated Standard VII(B). If he wants to obtain "retired" status in terms of his CFA Institute membership and CFA charter status, he needs to file the appropriate paperwork with CFA Institute to be recognized as such. By failing to file his Professional Conduct Statement and ceasing to pay dues, his membership is suspended and he gives up his right to use the CFA designation. When Simpson receives his notification from

CFA Institute that his membership has been reclassified as "retired" and he resumes paying reduced dues, his membership will be reactivated and his right to use the CFA designation will be reinstated.

***Example 4:*** Asia Futures Ltd. is a small quantitative investment advisory firm. The firm takes great pride in the fact that all its employees are CFA charterholders. To underscore this fact, the firm's senior partner is proposing to change the firm's letterhead to include the following:

# Asia Futures Ltd.

*Comment:* The CFA Logo is a certification mark intended to identify individual charterholders and must not be incorporated into a company name, confused with a company logo, or placed in such close proximity to a company name or logo as to give the reader the idea that the certification mark certifies the company. It would only be appropriate to use the CFA Logo on the business card or letterhead of each individual CFA charterholder.

***Example 5:*** Rhonda Reese has been a CFA charterholder since 2000. In a conversation with a friend who is considering enrolling in the CFA Program, she states that she has learned a great deal from the CFA Program and that many firms require their employees to be CFA charterholders. She would recommend the CFA Program to anyone pursuing a career in investment management.

*Comment:* Reese's comments comply with Standard VII(B). Her statements refer to enhanced knowledge and the fact that many firms require the CFA designation for their investment professionals.

***Example 6:*** Tatiana Prittima has earned both her CFA designation and a Ph.D. in finance. She would like to cite both her accomplishments on her business card but is unsure of the proper method for doing so.

*Comment:* The order of designations cited on such items as resumes and business cards is a matter of personal preference. Prittima is free to cite the CFA designation either before or after listing her Ph.D.

## PRACTICE PROBLEMS FOR READING 2

Unless otherwise stated in the question, all individuals in the following questions are CFA Institute members or candidates in the CFA program and, therefore, are subject to the CFA Institute Code of Ethics and Standards of Professional Conduct.

1. Smith, a research analyst with a brokerage firm, decides to change his recommendation on the common stock of Green Company, Inc., from a buy to a sell. He mails this change in investment advice to all the firm's clients on Wednesday. The day after the mailing, a client calls with a buy order for 500 shares of Green Company. In this circumstance, Smith should:
   A. accept the order.
   B. advise the customer of the change in recommendation before accepting the order.
   C. not accept the order until five days have elapsed after the communication of the change in recommendation.
   D. not accept the order because it is contrary to the firm's recommendation.

2. All of the following statements about a manager's use of clients' brokerage commissions are true *except*:
   A. a client may direct a manager to use that client's brokerage commissions to purchase goods and services for that client.
   B. client brokerage commissions may be used by the manager to pay for securities research used in managing the client's portfolio.
   C. client brokerage commissions should be used to benefit the client and should be commensurate with the value of the brokerage and research services received.
   D. client brokerage commissions may be directed to pay for the investment manager's operating expenses.

3. Jamison is a junior research analyst with Howard & Howard, a brokerage and investment-banking firm. Howard & Howard's mergers and acquisitions department has represented the Britland Company in all of its acquisitions for the past 20 years. Two of Howard & Howard's senior officers are directors of various Britland subsidiaries. Jamison has been asked to write a research report on Britland. What is the best course of action for her to follow?
   A. Jamison may write the report but must refrain from expressing any opinions because of the special relationships between the two companies.
   B. Jamison may write the report so long as the officers agree not to alter it.
   C. Jamison may write the report if she discloses the special relationships with the company in the report.
   D. Jamison should not write the report because the two Howard & Howard officers are constructive insiders.

**4.** Which of the following statements clearly *conflicts* with the recommended procedures for compliance presented in the CFA Institute *Standards of Practice Handbook*?

   **A.** Firms should disclose to clients the personal investing policies and procedures established for their employees.

   **B.** Prior approval must be obtained for the personal investment transactions of all employees.

   **C.** For confidentiality reasons, personal transactions and holdings should not be reported to employers unless mandated by regulatory organizations.

   **D.** Personal transactions should be defined as including transactions in securities owned by the employee and members of his or her immediate family and transactions involving securities in which the employee has a beneficial interest.

**5.** Bronson provides investment advice to the board of trustees of a private university endowment fund. The trustees have provided Bronson with the fund's financial information, including planned expenditures. Bronson receives a phone call on Friday afternoon from Murdock, a prominent alumnus, requesting that Bronson fax him comprehensive financial information about the fund. According to Murdock, he has a potential contributor but needs the information that day to close the deal and cannot contact any of the trustees. Based on CFA Institute Standards, Bronson should:

   **A.** send Murdock the information because disclosure would benefit the client.

   **B.** not send Murdock the information to preserve confidentiality.

   **C.** send Murdock the information, provided Bronson promptly notifies the trustees.

   **D.** send Murdock the information because it is not material nonpublic information.

**6.** Miller heads the research department of a large brokerage firm. The firm has many analysts, some of whom are subject to the Code and Standards. If Miller delegates some supervisory duties, which statement best describes her responsibilities under the Code and Standards?

   **A.** Miller's supervisory responsibilities do not apply to those subordinates who are not subject to the Code and Standards.

   **B.** Miller no longer has supervisory responsibility for those duties delegated to her subordinates.

   **C.** Miller retains supervisory responsibility for all subordinates despite her delegation of some duties.

   **D.** CFA Institute Standards prevent Miller from delegating supervisory duties to subordinates.

7. Willier is the research analyst responsible for following Company X. All the information he has accumulated and documented suggests that the outlook for the company's new products is poor, so the stock should be rated a weak hold. During lunch, however, Willier overhears a financial analyst from another firm whom he respects offer opinions that conflict with Willier's forecasts and expectations. Upon returning to his office, Willier releases a strong buy recommendation to the public. Willier:

   A. was in full compliance with the Standards.

   B. violated the Standards by failing to distinguish between facts and opinions in his recommendation.

   C. violated the Standards because he did not seek approval of the change from his firm's compliance department.

   D. violated the Standards because he did not have a reasonable and adequate basis for his recommendation.

8. An investment management firm has been hired by ETV Corporation to work on an initial public offering for the company. The firm's brokerage unit now has a sell recommendation on ETV, but the head of the investment-banking department has asked the head of the brokerage unit to change the recommendation from sell to buy. According to the Standards, the head of the brokerage unit would be permitted to:

   A. increase the recommendation by no more than one increment (in this case, to a hold recommendation).

   B. place the company on a restricted list and give only factual information about the company.

   C. assign a new analyst to decide if the stock deserves a higher rating.

   D. reassign responsibility for rating the stock to the head of the investment-banking unit.

9. Albert and Tye, who recently started their own investment advisory business, have registered to take the Level III CFA examination. Albert's business card reads, "Judy Albert, CFA Level II." Tye has not put anything about the CFA designation on his business card, but promotional material that he designed for the business describes the CFA requirements and indicates that Tye participates in the CFA Program and has completed Levels I and II. According to the Standards:

   A. Albert has violated the Standards but Tye has not.

   B. Tye has violated the Standards but Albert has not.

   C. both Albert and Tye have violated the Standards.

   D. neither Albert nor Tye has violated the Standards.

**10.** Scott works for a regional brokerage firm. He estimates that Walkton Industries will increase its dividend by $1.50 a share during the next year. He realizes that this increase is contingent on pending legislation that would, if enacted, give Walkton a substantial tax break. The U.S. representative for Walkton's home district has told Scott that, although she is lobbying hard for the bill and prospects for passage look good, Congress's concern over the federal deficit could cause the tax bill to be voted down. Walkton has not made any statements regarding a change in dividend policy. Scott writes in his research report, "We expect Walkton's stock price to rise by at least $8.00 a share by the end of the year. Because the dividend will increase by $1.50 a share, the stock price gain will be fueled, in large part, by the increase in the dividend. Investors buying the stock at the current time should expect to realize a total return of at least 15 percent on the stock." According to the Standards:

**A.** Scott violated the Standards because he used material inside information.

**B.** Scott violated the Standards because he failed to separate opinion from fact.

**C.** Scott violated the Standards by basing his research on uncertain predictions of future government action.

**D.** Scott did not violate the Standards.

**11.** Which *one* of the following actions will *not* help to ensure the fair treatment of brokerage firm clients when a new investment recommendation is made?

**A.** Limit the number of people in the firm who are aware in advance that a recommendation is to be disseminated.

**B.** Distribute recommendations to institutional clients prior to individual accounts.

**C.** Minimize elapsed time between the decision and the dissemination of a recommendation.

**D.** Monitor the trading activities of firm personnel.

**12.** The mosaic theory holds that an analyst:

**A.** violates the Code and Standards if the analyst fails to have knowledge of and comply with applicable laws.

**B.** can use material public information or nonmaterial nonpublic information in the analyst's analysis.

**C.** should use all available and relevant information in support of an investment recommendation.

**D.** should distinguish between facts and opinions in research reports.

**13.** Jurgens is a portfolio manager. One of her firm's clients has told Jurgens that he will compensate her beyond that provided by her firm on the basis of the capital appreciation of his portfolio each year. Jurgens should:

**A.** turn down the additional compensation because it will result in conflicts with the interests of other clients' accounts.

**B.** receive permission from CFA Institute for the compensation arrangement.

**C.** obtain permission from her employer prior to accepting the compensation arrangement.

**D.** turn down the additional compensation because it will create undue pressure on her to achieve strong short-term performance.

**14.** One of the discretionary accounts managed by Farnsworth is the Jones Corporation employee profit-sharing plan. Jones, the company president, recently asked Farnsworth to vote the shares in the profit-sharing plan in favor of the company-nominated slate of directors and against the directors sponsored by a dissident stockholder group. Farnsworth does not want to lose this account because he directs all the account's trades to a brokerage firm that provides Farnsworth with useful information about tax-free investments. Although this information is not of value in managing the Jones Corporation account, it does help in managing several other accounts. The brokerage firm providing this information also offers the lowest commissions for trades and best execution. Farnsworth investigates the director issue, concludes that management's slate is better for the long-run performance of the firm than the dissident group's slate, and votes accordingly. Farnsworth:

   **A.** violated the Standards in voting the shares in the manner requested by Jones but not in directing trades to the brokerage firm.

   **B.** did not violate the Standards in voting the shares in the manner requested by Jones or in directing trades to the brokerage firm.

   **C.** violated the Standards in directing trades to the brokerage firm but not in voting the shares as requested by Jones.

   **D.** violated the Standards in voting the shares in the manner requested by Jones and in directing trades to the brokerage firm.

**15.** Brown works for an investment counseling firm. Green, a new client of the firm, is meeting with Brown for the first time. Green used another counseling firm for financial advice for years, but she has switched her account to Brown's firm. After spending a few minutes getting acquainted, Brown explains to Green that she has discovered a highly undervalued stock that offers large potential gains. She recommends that Green purchase the stock. Brown has committed a violation of the Standards. What should she have done differently?

   **A.** Brown should have determined Green's needs, objectives, and tolerance for risk before making a recommendation for any type of security.

   **B.** Brown should have asked Green her reasons for changing counseling firms. If the discovery process indicated that Green had been treated unfairly at the other firm, Brown should have notified CFA Institute of any violation.

   **C.** Brown should have thoroughly explained the characteristics of the company to Green, including the characteristics of the industry in which the company operates.

   **D.** Brown should have explained her qualifications, including her education, training, experience, and the meaning of the CFA designation.

**16.** Grey recommends the purchase of a mutual fund that invests solely in long-term U.S. Treasury bonds. Grey makes the following statements to his clients:

Statement 1   "The payment of the bonds is guaranteed by the U.S. government; therefore, the default risk of the bonds is virtually zero."

Statement 2   "If you invest in the mutual fund, you will earn a 10 percent rate of return each year for the next several years based on historical performance of the stock market."

Do Grey's Statement 1 and Statement 2, respectively, violate the CFA Institute Code and Standards?

|  | Statement 1 | Statement 2 |
|---|---|---|
| **A.** | No | No |
| **B.** | No | Yes |
| **C.** | Yes | No |
| **D.** | Yes | Yes |

**17.** Anderb, a portfolio manager for XYZ Investment Management Company—a registered investment organization that advises investment companies and private accounts—was promoted to that position three years ago. Bates, her supervisor, is responsible for reviewing Anderb's portfolio account transactions and her required monthly reports of personal stock transactions. Anderb has been using Jonelli, a broker, almost exclusively for portfolio account brokerage transactions. For securities in which Jonelli's firm makes a market, Jonelli has been giving Anderb lower prices for personal purchases and higher prices for personal sales than Jonelli gives to Anderb's portfolio accounts and other investors. Anderb has been filing monthly reports with Bates only for those months in which she has no personal transactions, which is about every fourth month. Which of the following is *least likely* to be a violation of the Code and Standards?

**A.** Anderb failed to disclose to her employer her personal transactions.

**B.** Anderb breached her fiduciary responsibility to her clients.

**C.** Bates failed to enforce reasonable procedures for supervising and monitoring Anderb's trading for her own account.

**D.** Bates allowed Anderb to use Jonelli as her broker for personal trades.

**18.** Which of the following is a correct statement of a member's or candidate's duty under the Code and Standards?

   **A.** In the absence of specific applicable law or other regulatory requirements, the Code and Standards govern the member's or candidate's actions.

   **B.** A member or candidate is required to comply only with applicable local laws, rules, regulations, or customs even though the CFA Institute Code and Standards may impose a higher degree of responsibility or a higher duty on the member or candidate.

   **C.** A member or candidate who trades securities in a securities market where no applicable local laws or stock exchange rules regulate the use of material nonpublic information may take investment action based on material nonpublic information.

   **D.** A member or candidate must comply with the CFA Institute Code of Ethics and Standards of Professional Conduct when they conflict with local law.

**19.** Ward is scheduled to visit the corporate headquarters of Evans Industries. Ward expects to use the information obtained to complete his research report on Evans stock. Ward learns that Evans plans to pay all of Ward's expenses for the trip, including costs of meals, hotel room, and air transportation. Which of the following actions would be the *best* course for Ward to take under the Code and Standards?

   **A.** Accept the expense-paid trip and write an objective report.

   **B.** Pay for all travel expenses, including costs of meals and incidental items.

   **C.** Accept the expense-paid trip but disclose the value of the services accepted in the report.

   **D.** Write the report without taking the trip.

**20.** Which of the following statements is *incorrect* under the Code and Standards?

   **A.** CFA Institute members and candidates are prohibited from undertaking independent practice in competition with their employer.

   **B.** Written consent from the employer is necessary to permit independent practice that could result in compensation or other benefit in competition with a member's or candidate's employer.

   **C.** Prior to leaving an employer to work for another firm or start an independent practice, members and candidates may not contact their clients to solicit their business for the new venture.

   **D.** Members and candidates are allowed to make arrangements or preparations to go into a competitive business before terminating their relationship with their employer.

**21.** Smithers is a financial analyst with XYZ Brokerage Company. She is preparing a purchase recommendation on JNI Corporation. Which of the following situations is *least likely* to represent a conflict of interest for Smithers that would have to be disclosed?

   **A.** Smithers is on retainer as a consultant to JNI.

   **B.** XYZ holds for its own account a substantial common stock position in JNI.

   **C.** Smithers has material beneficial ownership of JNI through a family trust.

   **D.** Smithers's brother-in-law is a supplier to JNI.

**22.** Michelieu tells a prospective client, "I may not have a long-term track record yet, but I'm sure that you'll be very pleased with my recommendations and service. In the three years that I've been in the business, my equity-oriented clients have averaged a total return of more than 26 percent a year." The statement is true, but Michelieu only has a few clients, and one of his clients took a large position in a penny stock (against Michelieu's advice) and realized a huge gain. This large return caused the average of all of Michelieu's clients to exceed 26 percent a year. Without this one investment, the average gain would have been 8 percent a year. Has Michelieu violated the Standards?

   **A.** Yes, because the statement about return ignores the risk preferences of his clients.

   **B.** No, because Michelieu is not promising that he can earn a 26 percent return in the future.

   **C.** No, because the statement is a true and accurate description of Michelieu's track record.

   **D.** Yes, because the statement misrepresents Michelieu's track record.

**23.** An investment-banking department of a brokerage firm often receives material nonpublic information that could have considerable value if used in advising the firm's brokerage clients. In order to conform to the Code and Standards, which one of the following is the best policy for the brokerage firm?

   **A.** Permanently prohibit both purchase and sell recommendations of the stocks of clients of the investment-banking department.

   **B.** Establish physical and informational barriers within the firm to prevent the exchange of information between the investment-banking and brokerage operations.

   **C.** Prohibit purchase recommendations when the investment banking department has access to material nonpublic information but, in view of the fiduciary obligation to clients, allow sale of current holdings.

   **D.** Monitor the exchange of information between the investment-banking department and the brokerage operation.

**24.** Stewart has been hired by Goodner Industries, Inc., to manage its pension fund. Stewart's fiduciary duty is owed to:

   **A.** the management of Goodner.

   **B.** the shareholders of Goodner.

   **C.** the participants and beneficiaries of Goodner's pension plan.

   **D.** each of the above equally.

**25.** Which of the following statements is *inconsistent* with Standard VI(C)—Disclosure of Referral Fees?

   **A.** Disclosure will help the client evaluate the full cost of the services.

   **B.** Disclosure will help the client evaluate any possible partiality shown in the recommendation of services.

   **C.** Disclosure means advising a prospective client about the referral arrangement once a formal client relationship has been established.

   **D.** Disclosure includes a description of the nature of the consideration or benefit received by or paid to the investment professional.

26. Martin Bogwell, CFA, conducted a thorough analysis and issued a research report on a manufacturing company. In the report, Bogwell included his opinion that he was uncertain about the ability of the company to perform on a contract. The Chief Executive Officer of the company disagreed and submitted a complaint to Bogwell's supervisor. The complaint alleged that employees of the manufacturing company explained the contract to Bogwell, but that he did not accept their explanation. According to the *Standards of Practice Handbook*, Bogwell violated the CFA Institute Standard of Professional Conduct relating to:

   A.  research reports.

   B.  reasonable basis.

   C.  Bogwell did not violate the CFA Institute Standards of Professional Conduct.

27. According to the *Standards of Practice Handbook*, which of the following activities is *least likely* to breach a member's duty to a client?

   A.  Failing to disclose all forms of manager compensation.

   B.  Using soft dollar arrangements to pay firm management expenses.

   C.  Disclosing confidential client information to the CFA Institute Professional Conduct Program.

28. Darla Stone, CFA, disclosed confidential information concerning illegal activities on the part of her client to local regulatory authorities, after consulting with her employer's compliance department. According to the *Standards of Practice Handbook*, did Stone violate any CFA Institute Standards of Professional Conduct?

   A.  Stone did not violate any standards.

   B.  Stone did violate standards in regard to her duties to her clients.

   C.  Stone did violate standards in regard to her knowledge of the law.

29. Anastasia Fleur, CFA, discovers that Dan Notori, CFA, a fellow employee, has been altering trade order records to conceal his method of allocating trades. Notori's actions discriminate against certain clients and violate the firm's policies. Fleur informs her firm's compliance officer about Notori's activities. Several weeks later, Fleur becomes aware that the trade order records continue to be altered by Notori. According to the *Standards of Practice Handbook*, Fleur must:

   A.  directly confront Notori.

   B.  dissociate herself from an unethical activity.

   C.  report the violation to the appropriate regulatory authorities.

**30.** Theodore Flasky, CFA, is one of several analysts covering the technology sector for a large independent provider of research services. Flasky completes an initial report recommending the purchase of Avantoch because of the company's innovative solutions to data management. Following the distribution of his initial report on the company, Flasky's wife is informed that she has received a substantial inheritance from a distant relative the Flasky's have not contacted in recent years. Flasky has just learned that over $1 million worth of Avantoch stock is included in the inheritance. Before Flasky has an opportunity to inform his employer about the inheritance, he is asked to write a follow-up report on Avantoch. According to the *Standards of Practice Handbook*, Flasky's *best* course of action would be to:

    **A.** immediately sell his wife's Avantoch stock.

    **B.** encourage his employer to place Avantoch on a restricted list.

    **C.** ask his employer to assign another analyst to draft the follow-up report.

**31.** After submitting his resignation, but prior to his departure from Creek Investment Advisors, Otto Cavanagh, CFA, spends his time after normal business hours making plans to start his own investment advisory firm. Following his departure from Creek, Cavanagh contacts several personal friends who are also Creek clients and solicits their business. According to the *Standards of Practice Handbook*, did Cavanagh violate the CFA Institute Standard of Professional Conduct relating to duties to employers?

    **A.** No.

    **B.** Yes, by soliciting clients of Creek Investment Advisors.

    **C.** Yes, by using privileged information that belongs to his employer.

**32.** With respect to the Standard relating to responsibilities of supervisors, which of the following statements is *least* appropriate? According to the *Standards of Practice Handbook*, members with supervisory responsibilities should encourage their employers to adopt codes of ethics that:

    **A.** are provided to the firm's clients.

    **B.** are applicable to all the firm's employees.

    **C.** incorporate the firm's compliance procedures.

**33.** Jarrod Brenner, CFA, is a portfolio manager at Northstone Capital who has a beneficial interest in the account that he manages for his parents. Brenner discloses to his employer his beneficial interest in his parents' account and follows the firm's pre-clearance and reporting requirements for all transactions related to that account. He is careful to undertake transactions in the account only after his clients and employer have had an adequate opportunity to act. With respect to managing his parents' account, according to the *Standards of Practice Handbook*, has Brenner violated any CFA Institute Standards of Professional Conduct?

    **A.** No.

    **B.** Yes, with respect to duties to clients.

    **C.** Yes, with respect to duties to employer.

**34.** If a current or former client has not authorized the disclosure of confidential information and disclosure of that confidential information does not conflict with applicable law, which of the following statements is *most* accurate? According to the *Standards of Practice Handbook*, a member will breach his duties by disclosing confidential client information that relates to:

   **A.** an individual who has ended the client relationship with that member.

   **B.** illegal activities on the part of an entity that is currently that member's client.

   **C.** illegal activities on the part of an individual who is currently that member's client.

**35.** Muriel LeMay, CFA, is a research analyst for a large investment management firm. She is invited to attend a luncheon with the top executives of a large pharmaceutical company and three other buy-side analysts representing firms that also hold substantial positions in the company's stock. During the luncheon, material information is disclosed that has not yet been made available to the marketplace. According to the *Standards of Practice Handbook*, LeMay's *most* appropriate initial course of action would be to:

   **A.** refrain from discussing the information with anyone.

   **B.** encourage the company to make the information public.

   **C.** disclose the information to her firm's compliance personnel.

# INTRODUCTION TO THE GLOBAL INVESTMENT PERFORMANCE STANDARDS (GIPS®)

LEARNING OUTCOMES

| The candidate should be able to: | Mastery |
|---|---|
| **a.** explain why the GIPS standards were created, what parties the GIPS standards apply to and who is served by the standards; | ☐ |
| **b.** explain the construction and purpose of composites in performance reporting; | ☐ |
| **c.** explain the requirements for verification of compliance with GIPS standards. | ☐ |

The objective of this reading is to orient the Level I candidate approaching the assigned sections of the GIPS® standards. It explains why the GIPS standards were created, who can claim compliance, and who benefits from compliance. It also introduces the key notion of "composites," states the purpose of verification, and previews the structure of the Standards.

## I. Why Were the GIPS Standards Created?

Institutions and individuals are constantly scrutinizing past investment performance returns in search of the best manager to achieve their investment objectives.

In the past, the investment community had great difficulty making meaningful comparisons on the basis of accurate investment performance data. Several performance measurement practices hindered the comparability of performance returns from one firm to another, while others called into question the accuracy and credibility of performance reporting overall. Misleading practices included:

► <u>Representative Accounts</u>: Selecting a top performing portfolio to represent the firm's overall investment results for a specific mandate.

► <u>Survivorship Bias</u>: Presenting an "average" performance history that *excludes* accounts whose poor performance was weak enough to result in termination of the firm.

▶ <u>Varying Time Periods</u>: Presenting performance for a selected time period during which the mandate produced excellent returns or out-performed its benchmark—making comparison with other firms' results impossible.

Making a valid comparison of investment performance among even the most ethical investment management firms was problematic. For example, a pension fund seeking to hire an investment management firm might receive proposals from several firms, all using different methodologies for calculating their results.

The GIPS standards are a practitioner-driven set of ethical principles that establish a standardized, industry-wide approach for investment firms to follow in calculating and reporting their historical investment results to prospective clients. The GIPS standards ensure fair representation and full disclosure of performance information. In other words, the GIPS standards lead investment management firms to avoid misrepresentations of performance and to communicate all relevant information that prospective clients should know in order to evaluate past results.

## II. Who Can Claim Compliance?

First, any investment management firm may choose to comply with the GIPS standards. Complying with the GIPS standards is voluntary. Compliance with the GIPS standards is not required by any legal or regulatory authorities.

Second, only investment management firms that *actually manage* assets can claim compliance with the Standards. Plan sponsors and consultants cannot make a claim of compliance unless they actually manage assets for which they are making a claim of compliance. They can claim to endorse the Standards and/or require that their investment managers comply with the Standards. Similarly, software (and the vendors who supply software) cannot be "compliant." Software can assist firms in achieving GIPS compliance (e.g., by calculating performance in a manner consistent with the calculation requirements of the Standards) but only an investment management firm can claim compliance once the firm has satisfied all requirements of the Standards.

Third, compliance is a firm-wide process that cannot be achieved on a single product or composite. A firm has only two options with regard to compliance with the GIPS standards: fully comply with *all* requirements of the GIPS standards and claim compliance through the use of the GIPS Compliance Statement; or not comply with all requirements of the GIPS standards and not claim compliance with, or make any reference to, the GIPS standards.

## III. Who Benefits from Compliance?

The GIPS standards benefit two main groups: investment management firms and prospective clients.

▶ By choosing to comply with the GIPS standards, investment management firms assure prospective clients that the historical "track record" they report is both complete and fairly presented. Compliance enables the GIPS-compliant firm to participate in competitive bids against other compliant firms throughout the world. Achieving and maintaining compliance may also strengthen the firm's internal controls over performance-related processes and procedures.

▶ Investors have a greater level of confidence in the integrity of performance presentations of a GIPS-compliant firm and can more easily compare performance presentations from different investment management firms. While the GIPS standards certainly do not eliminate the need for in-depth due diligence on the part of the investor, compliance with the Standards enhances the credibility of investment management firms that have chosen to undertake this responsibility.

## IV. Composites

One of the key concepts of the Standards is the required use of "composites." A composite is an aggregation of discretionary portfolios into a single group that represents a particular investment objective or strategy. A composite must include all actual, fee-paying, discretionary portfolios managed in accordance with the same investment objective or strategy. For example, if a GIPS-compliant firm presents its track record for a Global Equity Composite, the Composite must include all portfolios that are managed, or have historically been managed, in the firm's Global Equity strategy. The firm may not subjectively select which Global Equity portfolios will be included in or excluded from the calculation and presentation of the Global Equity Composite. The determination of which port-folios to include in the Composite should be done according to pre-established criteria (i.e., on an ex-ante basis), not after the fact. This prevents a firm from including only their best performing portfolios in the Composite.

## V. Verification

Firms that claim compliance with the GIPS standards are responsible for their claim of compliance and for maintaining that compliance. That is, firms self-regulate their claim of compliance. Once a firm claims compliance with the Standards, they may voluntarily hire an independent third party to verify their claim of compliance to increase confidence in the validity of the firm's claim of compliance.

The primary purpose of verification is to provide assurance that a firm claiming compliance with the GIPS standards has adhered to the Standards on a firm-wide basis. Verification is performed with respect to an entire firm, not on specific composites. Verification tests:

▶ Whether the investment firm has complied with all the composite construction requirements of GIPS on a firm-wide basis; and

▶ Whether the firm's processes and procedures are designed to calculate and present performance results in compliance with the GIPS standards.

Verification must be performed by an independent third party. A firm cannot perform its own verification.

Third-party verification brings credibility to a firm's claim of compliance. A verified firm may provide a prospective client with greater assurance about its claim of compliance with the GIPS standards. Additionally, by voluntarily under-going verification, a firm may improve its internal policies and procedures with regard to all aspects of complying with the GIPS standards.

## VI. The Structure of the GIPS Standards

The GIPS standards (as revised by the Investment Performance Council and adopted by the CFA Institute Board of Governors in February 2005) are divided into eight sections that reflect the basic elements involved in calculating and presenting performance information: Fundamentals of Compliance, Input Data, Calculation Methodology, Composite Construction, Disclosures, Presentation and Reporting, Real Estate, and Private Equity. There are both requirements and recommendations within the provisions of each section.

# GLOBAL INVESTMENT PERFORMANCE STANDARDS (GIPS®)

## LEARNING OUTCOMES

| The candidate should be able to: | Mastery |
|---|:---:|
| **a.** describe the key characteristics of the GIPS standards and the fundamentals of compliance; | ☐ |
| **b.** describe the scope of the GIPS standards with respect to an investment firm's definition and historical performance record; | ☐ |
| **c.** explain how the GIPS standards are implemented in countries with existing standards for performance reporting and describe the appropriate response when the GIPS standards and local regulations conflict; | ☐ |
| **d.** characterize the eight major sections of the GIPS standards. | ☐ |

## PREFACE: BACKGROUND OF THE GIPS STANDARDS

OPTIONAL SEGMENT BEGINS

Investment practices, regulation, performance measurement, and reporting of performance results have historically varied considerably from country to country. Some countries have established performance calculation and presentation guidelines that are domestically accepted, and others have few standards for presenting investment performance. These practices have limited the comparability of performance results between firms in different countries and have hindered the ability of firms to penetrate markets on a global basis.

CFA Institute (formerly known as the Association for Investment Management and Research or AIMR[1]) recognized the need for a global set of performance presentation standards, and in 1995, it sponsored and funded the Global Investment Performance Standards (GIPS®) Committee to develop a single standard for presenting investment performance. In February 1999, the GIPS committee finalized the GIPS standards and presented them to the AIMR Board of Governors, who formally endorsed them.

---

[1] In May 2004, AIMR changed its name to CFA Institute.

**125**

Although CFA Institute is funding and supporting the activities of the GIPS standards, the success of the Standards is the result of an alliance among experts from a variety of fields within the global investment industry. The following key industry groups have been involved in and contributed significantly to promoting and developing the GIPS standards:

**Australia**—Performance Analyst Group of Australia (P Group)

**Austria**—Österreichischen Verreinigung für Finanzanalyse und Asset Management und der Vereinigung Österreichischer Investmentgesellschaften

**Belgium**—Belgian Association for Pension Institutions

**Denmark**—Danish Society of Financial Analysts and Danish Society of Investment Professionals

**France**—Société Francaise des Analystes Financiers (SFAF) and Association Francaise de la Gestion Financiere (AFG)

**Hungary**—Hungarian Society of Investment Professionals

**Ireland**—Irish Association of Investment Managers

**Italy**—Italian Investment Performance Committee (IIPC)

**Japan**—The Security Analysts Association of Japan (SAAJ)

**Luxembourg**—Association Luxembourgeoise des Fonds d'Investissement (ALFI) and Association Luxembourgeoise des gestionnaires de portefeuilles et analystes financiers (ALGAFI)

**Netherlands**—Vereniging van Beleggings Analisten (VBA)

**New Zealand**—CFA Society of New Zealand

**Norway**—The Norwegian Society of Financial Analysts

**Poland**—Polski Komitet Wyników Inwestycyjnych

**Portugal**—Associação Portuguesa de Analistas Financeiros (APAF)

**Spain**—CFA Spain

**South Africa**—Investment Management Association of South Africa (IMASA)

**Sweden**—Swedish Society of Financial Analysts (SFF)

**Switzerland**—Swiss Bankers Association (SBA)

**United Kingdom**—National Association of Pension Funds Ltd (NAPF)

**United States and Canada**—CFA Institute

With the release of the GIPS standards in 1999, the GIPS committee was replaced by the Investment Performance Council (IPC), which serves as the global committee responsible for the Standards. It consists of 36 members from 15 countries. The IPC's members have diverse and in-depth investment experience. They come from firms of all sizes and specialize in mutual funds, private wealth management, insurance, pension funds, private equity and venture capital, real estate, investment consulting services, and performance measurement and verification.

The principal goal of the IPC is to have all countries adopt the GIPS standards as *the* standard for investment firms seeking to present historical investment performance. The IPC envisions GIPS compliance acting as a "passport" that allows firms to enter the arena of investment management competition on a global basis and to compete on an equal footing. The GIPS passport will level the playing field and promote global competition among investment firms, which will, in turn, provide prospective clients with a greater level of confidence in the integrity of performance presentations as well as the general practices of a compliant firm.

In order to achieve this goal, over the past 5 years, the IPC has used a dual approach convergence strategy to (1) transition the existing local standards to the GIPS standards and (2) evolve the GIPS standards to incorporate local best practices from all regional standards so as to form one improved standard for investment performance calculation and reporting.

In addition to improving the original GIPS standards, this version includes new sections to address real estate and private equity investments as well as new provisions to address fees. It also includes guidelines for claiming compliance with the GIPS standards in advertisements and formalizes positions resulting from the development of guidance statements (such as firm definition, composite definition, and portability) and incorporates local best practices for performance measurement and reporting from around the world. Several examples have been included to assist with the application of the GIPS standards. The GIPS standards are no longer a *minimum* worldwide standard. Instead, this version promotes the highest performance measurement and presentation practices and eliminates the need for separate local standards.

The IPC strongly encourages countries without an investment performance standard in place to accept the GIPS standards as the local standard and translate them into the native language when necessary, thus promoting a "translation of GIPS" (TG). However, to effectively transition existing regional standards, the IPC acknowledges that some countries need to adopt certain long-standing requirements in addition to the GIPS standards.

Since 1999, the IPC has promoted the "Country Version of GIPS" (CVG) approach, whereby countries that had existing performance standards could adopt the GIPS standards as the core. This core was only to be supplemented to satisfy local regulatory or legal requirements and well-established practices. Any other differences were to be transitioned out of the CVG so that the CVG would converge with the GIPS standards.

Today, 25 countries throughout North America, Europe, Africa, and the Asia Pacific region have adopted the GIPS standards, encouraging investment management firms to follow the Standards when calculating and reporting their performance results. Out of these 25 countries, 9 have an IPC-endorsed CVG (Australia, Canada, Ireland, Italy, Japan, South Africa, Switzerland, United Kingdom, and United States). The remaining IPC-endorsed standards are either translations of GIPS or GIPS (in English).

We are now entering the second phase of the convergence strategy to the GIPS standards—namely to evolve the GIPS standards to incorporate local best practices from all regional standards. To effectively move toward one globally accepted standard for investment performance calculation and presentation, the IPC strongly encourages countries without an investment performance standard in place to accept the GIPS standards in English or translate them into the local language, adopting a TG approach.

By revising the GIPS standards, it is the IPC's hope that CVGs will no longer be necessary. Instead, all CVG-compliant firms will be granted reciprocity for periods prior to 1 January 2006. Their CVG-compliant history will satisfy the GIPS requirement to show at least a 5-year track record. In this way, firms from all countries will comply with one standard, the GIPS standards, from 1 January 2006 and the industry will achieve convergence of all standards.

# GLOBAL INVESTMENT PERFORMANCE STANDARDS

## I. INTRODUCTION

### A. PREAMBLE—WHY IS A GLOBAL STANDARD NEEDED?

1. The financial markets and the investment management industry are becoming increasingly global in nature. Given the variety of financial entities and countries involved, this globalization of the investment process and the exponential growth of assets under management demonstrate the need to standardize the calculation and presentation of investment performance.

2. Prospective clients and investment management firms will benefit from an established standard for investment performance measurement and presentation that is recognized worldwide. Investment practices, regulation, performance measurement, and reporting of performance results vary considerably from country to country. Some countries have guidelines that are widely accepted within their borders, and others have few recognized standards for presenting investment performance.

3. Requiring investment management firms to adhere to performance presentation standards will help assure investors that the performance information is both complete and fairly presented. Investment management firms in countries with minimal presentation standards will be able to compete for business on an equal footing with investment management firms from countries with more developed standards. Investment management firms from countries with established practices will have more confidence that they are being fairly compared with "local" investment management firms when competing for business in countries that have not previously adopted performance standards.

4. Both prospective and existing clients of investment management firms will benefit from a global investment performance standard by having a greater degree of confidence in the performance numbers presented by the investment management firms. Performance standards that are accepted in all countries enable all investment management firms to measure and present their investment performance so that clients can readily compare investment performance among investment management firms.

### B. VISION STATEMENT

5. A global investment performance standard leads to readily accepted presentations of investment performance that (1) present performance results that are readily comparable among investment management firms without regard to geographical location and (2) facilitate a dialogue between investment managers and their prospective clients about the critical issues of how the investment management firm achieved performance results and determines future investment strategies.

### C. OBJECTIVES

6. To obtain worldwide acceptance of a standard for the calculation and presentation of investment performance in a fair, comparable format that provides full disclosure.

7. To ensure accurate and consistent investment performance data for reporting, record keeping, marketing, and presentations.

8. To promote fair, global competition among investment management firms for all markets without creating barriers to entry for new investment management firms.

9. To foster the notion of industry "self-regulation" on a global basis.

## D. OVERVIEW

10. The Global Investment Performance Standards ("GIPS standards" or "Standards") have several key characteristics:

   a. For the purpose of claiming compliance with the GIPS standards, investment management firms must define an entity that claims compliance ("FIRM"). The FIRM MUST be defined as an investment firm, subsidiary, or division held out to clients or potential clients as a DISTINCT BUSINESS ENTITY.

   b. The GIPS standards are ethical standards for investment performance presentation to ensure fair representation and full disclosure of a FIRM's performance.

   c. The GIPS standards REQUIRE FIRMS to include all actual fee-paying, discretionary PORTFOLIOS in COMPOSITES defined according to similar strategy and/or investment objective and REQUIRE FIRMS to initially show GIPS-compliant history for a minimum of five (5) years or since inception of the FIRM or COMPOSITE if in existence less than 5 years. After presenting at least 5 years of compliant history, the FIRM MUST add annual performance each year going forward up to ten (10) years, at a minimum.

   d. The GIPS standards REQUIRE FIRMS to use certain calculation and presentation methods and to make certain disclosures along with the performance record.

   e. The GIPS standards rely on the integrity of input data. The accuracy of input data is critical to the accuracy of the performance presentation. For example, BENCHMARKS and COMPOSITES SHOULD be created/selected on an EX-ANTE basis, not after the fact.

   f. The GIPS standards consist of provisions that FIRMS are REQUIRED to follow in order to claim compliance. FIRMS are encouraged to adopt the RECOMMENDED provisions to achieve best practice in performance presentation.

   g. The GIPS standards MUST be applied with the goal of full disclosure and fair representation of investment performance. Meeting the objectives of full disclosure and fair representation will likely require more than compliance with the minimum REQUIREMENTS of the GIPS standards. If an investment FIRM applies the GIPS standards in a performance situation that is not addressed specifically by the Standards or is open to interpretation, disclosures other than those REQUIRED by the GIPS standards may be necessary. To fully explain the performance included in a presentation, FIRMS are encouraged to present all relevant ADDITIONAL INFORMATION and SUPPLEMENTAL INFORMATION.

   h. All requirements, clarifications, updated information, and guidance MUST be adhered to when determining a FIRM's claim of compliance and will be made available via the GIPS *Handbook* and the CFA Institute website (www.cfainstitute.org).

i. In cases where applicable local or country-specific law or regulation conflicts with the GIPS standards, the Standards REQUIRE FIRMS to comply with the local law or regulation and make full disclosure of the conflict.

j. The GIPS standards do not address every aspect of performance measurement, valuation, attribution, or coverage of all asset classes. The GIPS standards will evolve over time to address additional aspects of investment performance. Certain RECOMMENDED elements in the GIPS standards may become REQUIREMENTS in the future.

k. Within the GIPS standards are supplemental PRIVATE EQUITY and REAL ESTATE provisions that must be applied to these asset classes. (See sections II.6 and II.7.)

### E.  SCOPE

11. <u>Application of the GIPS Standards</u>: FIRMS from any country may come into compliance with the GIPS standards. Compliance with the GIPS standards will facilitate a FIRM'S participation in the investment management industry on a global level.

12. <u>Historical Performance Record</u>:

a. FIRMS are REQUIRED to present, at a minimum, 5 years of annual investment performance that is compliant with the GIPS standards. If the FIRM or COMPOSITE has been in existence less than 5 years, the FIRM MUST present performance since the inception of the FIRM or COMPOSITE; and

b. After a FIRM presents 5 years of compliant history, the FIRM MUST present additional annual performance up to 10 years, at a minimum. For example, after a FIRM presents 5 years of compliant history, the FIRM MUST add an additional year of performance each year so that after 5 years of claiming compliance, the FIRM presents a 10-year performance record.

c. FIRMS may link a non-GIPS-compliant performance record to their compliant history so long as no noncompliant performance is presented after 1 January 2000 and the FIRM discloses the periods of noncompliance and explains how the presentation is not in compliance with the GIPS standards.

d. FIRMS previously claiming compliance with an Investment Performance Council-endorsed Country Version of GIPS (CVG) are granted reciprocity to claim compliance with the GIPS standards for historical periods prior to 1 January 2006. (See "Background of GIPS Standards" for more details on CVGs.) If the FIRM previously claimed compliance with a CVG, at a minimum, the FIRM MUST continue to show the historical CVG-compliant track record up to 10 years (or since inception).

Nothing in this section shall prevent FIRMS from initially presenting more than 5 years of performance results.

### F.  COMPLIANCE

13. <u>Effective Date</u>: The GIPS standards were amended by the IPC on 7 December 2004 and adopted by the CFA Institute Board of Governors on 4 February 2005. The effective date of the revised Standards is 1 January 2006. All presentations that include performance results for periods after 31 December 2005 MUST meet all the

REQUIREMENTS of the revised GIPS standards. Performance presentations that include results through 31 December 2005 may be prepared in compliance with the 1999 version of the GIPS standards. Early adoption of these revised GIPS standards is encouraged.

14. REQUIREMENTS: FIRMS MUST meet all the REQUIREMENTS set forth in the GIPS standards to claim compliance with the GIPS standards. Although the REQUIREMENTS MUST be met immediately by a FIRM claiming compliance, the following REQUIREMENTS do not go into effect until a future date:

    a. For periods beginning 1 January 2008, REAL ESTATE investments must be valued at least quarterly.

    b. For periods beginning 1 January 2010, FIRMS MUST VALUE PORTFOLIOS on the date of all LARGE EXTERNAL CASH FLOWS.

    c. For periods beginning 1 January 2010, FIRMS MUST value PORTFOLIOS as of the calendar month-end or the last business day of the month.

    d. For periods beginning 1 January 2010, COMPOSITE returns MUST be calculated by asset weighting the individual PORTFOLIO returns at least monthly.

    e. For periods beginning 1 January 2010, CARVE-OUT returns are not permitted to be included in single asset class COMPOSITE returns unless the CARVE-OUTS are actually managed separately with their own cash balances.

    Until these future REQUIREMENTS become effective, these provisions SHOULD be considered RECOMMENDATIONS. FIRMS are encouraged to implement these future REQUIREMENTS prior to their effective dates. To ease compliance with the GIPS standards when the future REQUIREMENTS take effect, the industry should immediately begin to design performance software to incorporate these future REQUIREMENTS.

15. Compliance Check: FIRMS MUST take all steps necessary to ensure that they have satisfied all the REQUIREMENTS of the GIPS standards before claiming compliance with the GIPS standards. FIRMS are strongly encouraged to perform periodic internal compliance checks and implement adequate business controls on all stages of the investment performance process—from data input to presentation material—to ensure the validity of compliance claims.

16. Third-Party Performance Measurement and COMPOSITE Construction: The GIPS standards recognize the role of independent third-party performance measurers and the value they can add to the FIRM'S performance measurement activities. Where third-party performance measurement is an established practice or is available, FIRMS are encouraged to use this service as it applies to the FIRM. Similarly, where the practice is to allow third parties to construct COMPOSITES for FIRMS, FIRMS can use such COMPOSITES in a GIPS-compliant presentation only if the COMPOSITES meet the REQUIREMENTS of the GIPS standards.

17. Sample Presentations: Sample presentations, shown in Appendix 4A, provide examples of what a compliant presentation might look like.

## G. IMPLEMENTING A GLOBAL STANDARD

18. In 1999, the Investment Performance Council (IPC) was created and given the responsibility to meet the ongoing needs for maintaining

and developing a high-quality global investment performance standard. The IPC provides a practical and effective implementation structure for the GIPS standards and encourages wider public participation in an industry-wide standard.

19. One of the principal objectives of the IPC is for all countries to adopt the GIPS standards as the common method for calculating and presenting investment performance. As of December 2004, more than 25 countries around the world had adopted or were in the process of adopting the GIPS standards. The IPC believes the establishment and acceptance of the GIPS standards are vital steps in facilitating the availability of comparable investment performance history on a global basis. GIPS compliance provides FIRMS with a "passport" and creates a level playing field where all FIRMS can compete on equal footing.

20. The presence of a local sponsoring organization for investment performance standards is essential for their effective implementation and on-going operation within a country. Such country sponsors also provide an important link between the IPC, the governing body for the GIPS standards, and the local markets where investment managers operate.

   The country sponsor, by actively supporting the GIPS standards and the work of the IPC, will ensure that the country's interests can and will be taken into account as the GIPS standards are developed going forward. Compliance with the GIPS standards is voluntary, but support from the local country sponsor will help drive the success of the GIPS standards.

21. The IPC strongly encourages countries without an investment performance standard in place to accept the GIPS standards as the local standard and translate them into the local language when necessary, thus promoting a "translation of GIPS" (TG).

22. Compliance with the GIPS standards will provide FIRMS with a "right of access" to be considered alongside all investment managers, thereby allowing all FIRMS to be evaluated on equal terms.

23. Although the GIPS standards may be translated into many languages, if a discrepancy arises between the different versions of the Standards (e.g., TGs), the English version of GIPS standards is controlling.

24. The IPC will continue to develop the GIPS standards so that they maintain their relevance within the changing investment management industry and has committed to evaluating the Standards every 5 years.

25. The self-regulatory nature of the GIPS standards necessitates a strong commitment to ethical integrity. Self-regulation also assists regulators in exercising their responsibility for ensuring the fair disclosure of information to and within the financial markets in general. Regulators are encouraged to:

   ▶ recognize the benefit of voluntary compliance with standards that represent global best practices,

   ▶ give consideration to adopting a function favored by some regulators, namely to enforce sanctions upon false claims of compliance with the GIPS standards as fraudulent advertising, and

   ▶ recognize and encourage independent verification services.

26. Where existing laws or regulations already impose performance presentation standards, FIRMS are strongly encouraged to comply with the GIPS standards in addition to those local requirements. Compliance with applicable law or regulation does not necessarily lead to compliance with the GIPS standards. When complying with the GIPS standards and local law or regulation, FIRMS must disclose any local laws and regulations that conflict with the GIPS standards.

## II. PROVISIONS OF THE GLOBAL INVESTMENT PERFORMANCE STANDARDS

The GIPS standards are divided into eight sections that reflect the basic elements involved in presenting performance information: fundamentals of compliance, input data, calculation methodology, COMPOSITE construction, disclosures, presentation and reporting, REAL ESTATE, and PRIVATE EQUITY.

The provisions for each section are divided between REQUIREMENTS, listed first in each section, and RECOMMENDATIONS. FIRMS MUST meet all the REQUIREMENTS to claim compliance with the GIPS standards. FIRMS are strongly encouraged to adopt and implement the recommendations to ensure that the FIRM fully adheres to the spirit and intent of the GIPS standards. Examples of GIPS-compliant presentations are included as Appendix 4A.

0.  **Fundamentals of Compliance:** Critical issues that a FIRM MUST consider when claiming compliance with the GIPS standards are defining the FIRM, documenting FIRM policies and procedures, maintaining compliance with updates to the GIPS standards, and properly using the claim of compliance and references to verification. The definition of the FIRM is the foundation for FIRM-wide compliance and creates defined boundaries whereby TOTAL FIRM ASSETS can be determined. Once a FIRM meets all of the REQUIREMENTS of the GIPS standards, it MUST appropriately use the claim of compliance to state compliance with the GIPS standards.

1.  **Input Data:** Consistency of input data is critical to effective compliance with the GIPS standards and establishes the foundation for full, fair, and comparable investment performance presentations.

2.  **Calculation Methodology:** Achieving comparability among FIRMS' performance presentations REQUIRES uniformity in methods used to calculate returns. The Standards mandate the use of certain calculation methodologies for both PORTFOLIOS and COMPOSITES.

3.  **Composite Construction:** A COMPOSITE is an aggregation of one or more PORTFOLIOS into a single group that represents a particular investment objective or strategy. The COMPOSITE return is the asset-weighted average of the performance results of all the PORTFOLIOS in the COMPOSITE. Creating meaningful, asset-weighted COMPOSITES is critical to the fair presentation, consistency, and comparability of results over time and among FIRMS.

4.  **Disclosures:** Disclosures allow FIRMS to elaborate on the raw numbers provided in the presentation and give the end user of the presentation the proper context in which to understand the performance results. To comply with the GIPS standards, FIRMS MUST disclose certain information about their performance presentation and policies adopted by the FIRM. Disclosures are to be considered static information that does not normally change from period to period. Although some disclosures are REQUIRED of all FIRMS, others are specific to certain circumstances and thus may not be REQUIRED. No "negative assurance" language is needed for nonapplicable disclosures.

5. **Presentation and Reporting:** After gathering the input data, calculating returns, constructing the COMPOSITES, and determining the necessary disclosures, the FIRM MUST incorporate this information in presentations based on the REQUIREMENTS set out in the GIPS standards for presenting the investment performance returns. No finite set of provisions can cover all potential situations or anticipate future developments in investment industry structure, technology, products, or practices. When appropriate, FIRMS have the responsibility to include other information not necessarily covered by the Standards in a GIPS-compliant presentation.

6. **REAL ESTATE:** These provisions apply to all investments where returns are primarily from the holding, trading, development, or management of REAL ESTATE assets. REAL ESTATE includes land, buildings under development, completed buildings, and other structures or improvements held for investment purposes. The provisions apply regardless of the level of control the FIRM has over management of the investment. The provisions apply irrespective of whether a REAL ESTATE asset or investment is producing revenue. They also apply to REAL ESTATE investments with leverage or gearing.

7. **PRIVATE EQUITY:** These provisions apply to all PRIVATE EQUITY investments other than OPEN-END or EVERGREEN FUNDS (which MUST follow the main GIPS provisions). PRIVATE EQUITY investments MUST be valued according to the GIPS PRIVATE EQUITY Valuation Principles found in Appendix 4D. PRIVATE EQUITY refers to investments in nonpublic companies that are in various stages of development and encompasses venture investing, buyout investing, and mezzanine investing. Fund-of-funds investing as well as secondary investing are also included in PRIVATE EQUITY. Investors typically invest in PRIVATE EQUITY assets either directly or through a fund of funds or LIMITED PARTNERSHIP.

## 0. FUNDAMENTALS OF COMPLIANCE

### 0.A Definition of the Firm—Requirements

0.A.1   The GIPS standards MUST be applied on a FIRM-wide basis.

0.A.2   FIRMS must be defined as an investment firm, subsidiary, or division held out to clients or potential clients as a DISTINCT BUSINESS ENTITY.

0.A.3   TOTAL FIRM ASSETS MUST be the aggregate of the MARKET VALUE of all discretionary and nondiscretionary assets under management within the defined FIRM. This includes both fee-paying and non-fee-paying assets.

0.A.4   FIRMS MUST include the performance of assets assigned to a subadvisor in a COMPOSITE provided the FIRM has discretion over the selection of the subadvisor.

0.A.5   Changes in a FIRM'S organization are not permitted to lead to alteration of historical COMPOSITE results.

### 0.B Definition of the Firm—Recommendations

0.B.1   FIRMS are encouraged to adopt the broadest, most meaningful definition of the FIRM. The scope of this definition should include all geographical (country, regional, etc.) offices operating under the same brand name regardless of the actual name of the individual investment management company.

**0.A  Document Policies and Procedures—Requirements**

0.A.6   FIRMS MUST document, in writing, their policies and procedures used in establishing and maintaining compliance with all the applicable REQUIREMENTS of the GIPS standards.

**0.A  Claim of Compliance—Requirements**

0.A.7   Once a FIRM has met all the REQUIRED elements of the GIPS standards, the FIRM MUST use the following compliance statement to indicate that the FIRM is in compliance with the GIPS standards:

> "[Insert name of FIRM] has prepared and presented this report in compliance with the Global Investment Performance Standards (GIPS®)."

0.A.8   If the FIRM does not meet all the REQUIREMENTS of the GIPS standards, the FIRM cannot represent that it is "in compliance with the Global Investment Performance Standards except for . . .".

0.A.9   Statements referring to the calculation methodology used in a COMPOSITE presentation as being "in accordance [or compliance] with the Global Investment Performance Standards" are prohibited.

0.A.10  Statements referring to the performance of a single, existing client as being "calculated in accordance with the Global Investment Performance Standards" are prohibited except when a GIPS-compliant FIRM reports the performance of an individual account to the existing client.

**0.A  Firm Fundamental Responsibilities—Requirements**

0.A.11  FIRMS MUST make every reasonable effort to provide a compliant presentation to all prospective clients. That is, FIRMS cannot choose to whom they want to present compliant performance. (As long as a prospective client has received a compliant presentation within the previous 12 months, the FIRM has met this REQUIREMENT.)

0.A.12  FIRMS MUST provide a COMPOSITE list and COMPOSITE DESCRIPTION to any prospective client that makes such a request (a sample list and COMPOSITE DESCRIPTION are included in Appendix 4B). FIRMS MUST list "discontinued" COMPOSITES on the FIRM'S list of COMPOSITES for at least 5 years after discontinuation.

0.A.13  FIRMS MUST provide a compliant presentation for any COMPOSITE listed on the FIRM'S list and a COMPOSITE DESCRIPTION to any prospective client that makes such a request.

0.A.14  When the FIRM jointly markets with other FIRMS, the FIRM claiming compliance with the GIPS standards MUST be sure that it is clearly defined and separate relative to any other FIRMS being marketed and that it is clear which FIRM is claiming compliance.

0.A.15  FIRMS are encouraged to comply with the RECOMMENDATIONS and MUST comply with all applicable REQUIREMENTS of the GIPS standards, including any updates, reports, guidance statements, interpretations, or clarifications published by CFA Institute and the Investment Performance Council, which will be made available via the CFA Institute website (www.cfainstitute.org) as well as the *GIPS Handbook*.

### 0.B Verification—Recommendations

0.B.2 FIRMS are encouraged to undertake the verification process, defined as the review of a FIRM's performance measurement processes and procedures by an independent third-party verifier. A single verification report is issued in respect to the whole FIRM; verification cannot be carried out for a single COMPOSITE. The primary purpose of verification is to establish that a FIRM claiming compliance with the GIPS standards has adhered to the Standards.

0.B.3 FIRMS that have been verified are encouraged to add a disclosure to COMPOSITE presentations or advertisements stating that the FIRM has been verified. FIRMS MUST disclose the periods of verification if the COMPOSITE presentation includes results for periods that have not been subject to FIRM-wide verification. The verification disclosure language SHOULD read:

> "[Insert name of FIRM] has been verified for the periods [insert dates] by [name of verifier]. A copy of the verification report is available upon request."

### 1. INPUT DATA

*OPTIONAL SEGMENT BEGINS*

#### 1.A Input Data—Requirements

1.A.1 All data and information necessary to support a FIRM's performance presentation and to perform the REQUIRED calculations MUST be captured and maintained.

1.A.2 PORTFOLIO valuations MUST be based on MARKET VALUES (not cost basis or book values).

1.A.3 For periods prior to 1 January 2001, PORTFOLIOS MUST be valued at least quarterly. For periods between 1 January 2001 and 1 January 2010, PORTFOLIOS MUST be valued at least monthly. For periods beginning 1 January 2010, FIRMS MUST value PORTFOLIOS on the date of all LARGE EXTERNAL CASH FLOWS.

1.A.4 For periods beginning 1 January 2010, FIRMS MUST value PORTFOLIOS as of the calendar month-end or the last business day of the month.

1.A.5 For periods beginning 1 January 2005, FIRMS MUST use TRADE DATE ACCOUNTING.

1.A.6 ACCRUAL ACCOUNTING MUST be used for fixed-income securities and all other assets that accrue interest income. MARKET VALUES of fixed-income securities MUST include accrued income.

1.A.7 For periods beginning 1 January 2006, COMPOSITES MUST have consistent beginning and ending annual valuation dates. Unless the COMPOSITE is reported on a noncalendar fiscal year, the beginning and ending valuation dates MUST be at calendar year-end (or on the last business day of the year).

#### 1.B Input Data—Recommendations

1.B.1 ACCRUAL ACCOUNTING SHOULD be used for dividends (as of the ex-dividend date).

1.B.2 When presenting NET-OF-FEES RETURNS, FIRMS SHOULD accrue INVESTMENT MANAGEMENT FEES.

1.B.3 Calendar month-end valuations or valuations on the last business day of the month are RECOMMENDED.

## 2. CALCULATION METHODOLOGY

### 2.A Calculation Methodology—Requirements

2.A.1 TOTAL RETURN, including realized and unrealized gains and losses plus income, MUST be used.

2.A.2 TIME-WEIGHTED RATES OF RETURN that adjust for EXTERNAL CASH FLOWS MUST be used. Periodic returns MUST be geometrically linked. EXTERNAL CASH FLOWS MUST be treated in a consistent manner with the FIRM'S documented, COMPOSITE-specific policy. At a minimum:

    a. For periods beginning 1 January 2005, FIRMS MUST use approximated rates of return that adjust for daily-weighted EXTERNAL CASH FLOWS.

    b. For periods beginning 1 January 2010, FIRMS MUST value PORTFOLIOS on the date of all LARGE EXTERNAL CASH FLOWS.

2.A.3 COMPOSITE returns MUST be calculated by asset weighting the individual PORTFOLIO returns using beginning-of-period values or a method that reflects both beginning-of-period values and EXTERNAL CASH FLOWS.

2.A.4 Returns from cash and cash equivalents held in PORTFOLIOS MUST be included in TOTAL RETURN calculations.

2.A.5 All returns MUST be calculated after the deduction of the actual TRADING EXPENSES incurred during the period. Estimated TRADING EXPENSES are not permitted.

2.A.6 For periods beginning 1 January 2006, FIRMS MUST calculate COMPOSITE returns by asset weighting the individual PORTFOLIO returns at least quarterly. For periods beginning 1 January 2010, COMPOSITE returns MUST be calculated by asset weighting the individual PORTFOLIO returns at least monthly.

2.A.7 If the actual direct TRADING EXPENSES cannot be identified and segregated from a BUNDLED FEE:

    a. when calculating GROSS-OF-FEES RETURNS, returns MUST be reduced by the entire BUNDLED FEE or the portion of the BUNDLED FEE that includes the direct TRADING EXPENSES. The use of estimated TRADING EXPENSES is not permitted.

    b. when calculating NET-OF-FEES RETURNS, returns MUST be reduced by the entire BUNDLED FEE or the portion of the BUNDLED FEE that includes the direct TRADING EXPENSES and the INVESTMENT MANAGEMENT FEE. The use of estimated TRADING EXPENSES is not permitted.

### 2.B Calculation Methodology—Recommendations

2.B.1 Returns SHOULD be calculated net of nonreclaimable withholding taxes on dividends, interest, and capital gains. Reclaimable withholding taxes SHOULD be accrued.

2.B.2 FIRMS SHOULD calculate COMPOSITE returns by asset weighting the member PORTFOLIOS at least monthly.

2.B.3 FIRMS SHOULD value PORTFOLIOS on the date of all LARGE EXTERNAL CASH FLOWS.

## 3. COMPOSITE CONSTRUCTION

### 3.A Composite Construction—Requirements

3.A.1   All actual, fee-paying, discretionary PORTFOLIOS MUST be included in at least one COMPOSITE. Although non-fee-paying discretionary PORTFOLIOS may be included in a COMPOSITE (with appropriate disclosures), nondiscretionary PORTFOLIOS are not permitted to be included in a FIRM'S COMPOSITES.

3.A.2   COMPOSITES MUST be defined according to similar investment objectives and/or strategies. The full COMPOSITE DEFINITION MUST be made available on request.

3.A.3   COMPOSITES MUST include new PORTFOLIOS on a timely and consistent basis after the PORTFOLIO comes under management unless specifically mandated by the client.

3.A.4   Terminated PORTFOLIOS MUST be included in the historical returns of the appropriate COMPOSITES up to the last full measurement period that the PORTFOLIO was under management.

3.A.5   PORTFOLIOS are not permitted to be switched from one COMPOSITE to another unless documented changes in client guidelines or the redefinition of the COMPOSITE make it appropriate. The historical record of the PORTFOLIO MUST remain with the appropriate COMPOSITE.

3.A.6   Convertible and other hybrid securities MUST be treated consistently across time and within COMPOSITES.

3.A.7   CARVE-OUT segments excluding cash are not permitted to be used to represent a discretionary PORTFOLIO and, as such, are not permitted to be included in COMPOSITE returns. When a single asset class is carved out of a multiple asset class PORTFOLIO and the returns are presented as part of a single asset COMPOSITE, cash must be allocated to the CARVE-OUT returns in a timely and consistent manner. Beginning 1 January 2010, CARVE-OUT returns are not permitted to be included in single asset class COMPOSITE returns unless the CARVE-OUT is actually managed separately with its own cash balance.

3.A.8   COMPOSITES must include only assets under management within the defined FIRM. FIRMS are not permitted to link simulated or model PORTFOLIOS with actual performance.

3.A.9   If a FIRM sets a minimum asset level for PORTFOLIOS to be included in a COMPOSITE, no PORTFOLIOS below that asset level can be included in that COMPOSITE. Any changes to a COMPOSITE-specific minimum asset level are not permitted to be applied retroactively.

### 3.B Composite Construction—Recommendations

3.B.1   CARVE-OUT returns SHOULD not be included in single asset class COMPOSITE returns unless the CARVE-OUTS are actually managed separately with their own cash balance.

3.B.2   To remove the effect of a significant EXTERNAL CASH FLOW, the use of a TEMPORARY NEW ACCOUNT is RECOMMENDED (as opposed to adjusting the COMPOSITE composition to remove PORTFOLIOS with significant EXTERNAL CASH FLOWS).

3.B.3   FIRMS SHOULD not market a COMPOSITE to a prospective client who has assets less than the COMPOSITE'S minimum asset level.

## 4. DISCLOSURES

### 4.A Disclosures—Requirements

4.A.1 FIRMS MUST disclose the definition of "FIRM" used to determine the TOTAL FIRM ASSETS and FIRM-WIDE compliance.

4.A.2 FIRMS MUST disclose the availability of a complete list and description of all of the FIRM'S COMPOSITES.

4.A.3 FIRMS MUST disclose the minimum asset level, if any, below which PORTFOLIOS are not included in a COMPOSITE. FIRMS MUST also disclose any changes to the minimum asset level.

4.A.4 FIRMS MUST disclose the currency used to express performance.

4.A.5 FIRMS MUST disclose the presence, use, and extent of leverage or derivatives (if material), including a sufficient description of the use, frequency, and characteristics of the instruments to identify risks.

4.A.6 FIRMS MUST clearly label returns as GROSS-OF-FEES or NET-OF-FEES.

4.A.7 FIRMS MUST disclose relevant details of the treatment of withholding tax on dividends, interest income, and capital gains. If using indexes that are net-of-taxes, the FIRM MUST disclose the tax basis of the BENCHMARK (e.g., Luxembourg based or U.S. based) versus that of the COMPOSITE.

4.A.8 FIRMS MUST disclose and describe any known inconsistencies in the exchange rates used among the PORTFOLIOS within a COMPOSITE and between the COMPOSITE and the BENCHMARK.

4.A.9 If the presentation conforms with local laws and regulations that differ from the GIPS REQUIREMENTS, FIRMS MUST disclose this fact and disclose the manner in which the local laws and regulations conflict with the GIPS standards.

4.A.10 For any performance presented for periods prior to 1 January 2000 that does not comply with the GIPS standards, FIRMS MUST disclose the period of noncompliance and how the presentation is not in compliance with the GIPS standards.

4.A.11 For periods prior to 1 January 2010, when a single asset class is carved out of a multiple asset PORTFOLIO and the returns are presented as part of a single asset COMPOSITE, FIRMS MUST disclose the policy used to allocate cash to the CARVE-OUT returns.

4.A.12 FIRMS MUST disclose the FEE SCHEDULE appropriate to the presentation.

4.A.13 If a COMPOSITE contains PORTFOLIOS with BUNDLED FEES, FIRMS MUST disclose for each annual period shown the percentage of COMPOSITE assets that is BUNDLED FEE PORTFOLIOS.

4.A.14 If a COMPOSITE contains PORTFOLIOS with BUNDLED FEES, FIRMS MUST disclose the various types of fees that are included in the BUNDLED FEE.

4.A.15 When presenting GROSS-OF-FEES RETURNS, FIRMS MUST disclose if any other fees are deducted in addition to the direct TRADING EXPENSES.

4.A.16 When presenting NET-OF-FEES RETURNS, FIRMS MUST disclose if any other fees are deducted in addition to the INVESTMENT MANAGEMENT FEE and direct TRADING EXPENSES.

4.A.17 FIRMS MUST disclose that ADDITIONAL INFORMATION regarding policies for calculating and reporting returns is available upon request.

4.A.18 Beginning 1 January 2006, FIRMS MUST disclose the use of a subadvisor(s) and the periods a subadvisor(s) was used.

4.A.19 FIRMS MUST disclose all significant events that would help a prospective client interpret the performance record.

4.A.20 FIRMS MUST disclose the COMPOSITE DESCRIPTION.

4.A.21 If a FIRM is redefined, the FIRM MUST disclose the date and reason for the redefinition.

4.A.22 If a FIRM has redefined a COMPOSITE, the FIRM MUST disclose the date and nature of the change. Changes to COMPOSITES are not permitted to be applied retroactively.

4.A.23 FIRMS MUST disclose any changes to the name of a COMPOSITE.

4.A.24 FIRMS MUST disclose the COMPOSITE CREATION DATE.

4.A.25 FIRMS MUST disclose if, prior to 1 January 2010, calendar month-end PORTFOLIO valuations or valuations on the last business day of the month are not used.

4.A.26 FIRMS MUST disclose which DISPERSION measure is presented.

**4.B Disclosures—Recommendations**

4.B.1 If a parent company contains multiple defined FIRMS, each FIRM within the parent company is encouraged to disclose a list of the other FIRMS contained within the parent company.

4.B.2 FIRMS SHOULD disclose when a change in a calculation methodology or valuation source results in a material impact on the performance of a COMPOSITE RETURN.

4.B.3 FIRMS that have been verified SHOULD add a disclosure to their COMPOSITE presentation stating that the FIRM has been verified and clearly indicating the periods the verification covers if the COMPOSITE presentation includes results for periods that have not been subject to FIRM-wide verification.

## 5. PRESENTATION AND REPORTING

**5.A Presentation and Reporting—Requirements**

5.A.1 The following items MUST be reported for each COMPOSITE presented:

a. At least 5 years of performance (or a record for the period since FIRM or COMPOSITE inception if the FIRM or COMPOSITE has been in existence less than 5 years) that meets the REQUIREMENTS of the GIPS standards; after presenting 5 years of performance, the FIRM MUST present additional annual performance up to 10 years. (For example, after a FIRM presents 5 years of compliant history, the FIRM MUST add an additional year of performance each year so that after 5 years of claiming compliance, the FIRM presents a 10-year performance record.)

b. Annual returns for all years.

c. The number of PORTFOLIOS and amount of assets in the COMPOSITE, and either the percentage of the TOTAL FIRM ASSETS represented by the COMPOSITE or the amount of TOTAL FIRM

ASSETS at the end of each annual period. If the COMPOSITE contains 5 PORTFOLIOS or less, the number of PORTFOLIOS is not REQUIRED.

d. A measure of DISPERSION of individual PORTFOLIO returns for each annual period. If the COMPOSITE contains 5 PORTFOLIOS or less for the full year, a measure of DISPERSION is not REQUIRED.

5.A.2 FIRMS may link non-GIPS-compliant returns to their compliant history so long as the FIRMS meet the disclosure REQUIREMENTS for noncompliant performance and only compliant returns are presented for periods after 1 January 2000. (For example, a FIRM that has been in existence since 1995 and that wants to present its entire performance history and claim compliance beginning 1 January 2005 MUST present returns that meet the REQUIREMENTS of the GIPS standards at least from 1 January 2000 and MUST meet the disclosure REQUIREMENTS for any noncompliant history prior to 1 January 2000.)

5.A.3 Returns of PORTFOLIOS and COMPOSITES for periods of less than 1 year are not permitted to be annualized.

5.A.4  a. Performance track records of a past FIRM or affiliation MUST be linked to or used to represent the historical record of a new FIRM or new affiliation if:

  i. Substantially all the investment decision makers are employed by the new FIRM (e.g., research department, PORTFOLIO managers, and other relevant staff),

  ii. The staff and decision-making process remain intact and independent within the new FIRM, and

  iii. The new FIRM has records that document and support the reported performance.

b. The new FIRM MUST disclose that the performance results from the past FIRM are linked to the performance record of the new FIRM.

c. In addition to 5.A.4.a and 5.A.4.b, when one FIRM joins an existing FIRM, performance of COMPOSITES from both FIRMS MUST be linked to the ongoing returns if substantially all the assets from the past FIRM'S COMPOSITE transfer to the new FIRM.

d. If a compliant FIRM acquires or is acquired by a noncompliant FIRM, the FIRMS have 1 year to bring the noncompliant assets into compliance.

5.A.5 Beginning 1 January 2006, if a COMPOSITE includes or is formed using single asset class CARVE-OUTS from multiple asset class PORTFOLIOS, the presentation MUST include the percentage of the COMPOSITE that is composed of CARVE-OUTS prospectively for each period.

5.A.6 The TOTAL RETURN for the BENCHMARK (or BENCHMARKS) that reflects the investment strategy or mandate represented by the COMPOSITE MUST be presented for each annual period. If no BENCHMARK is presented, the presentation MUST explain why no BENCHMARK is disclosed. If the FIRM changes the BENCHMARK that is used for a given COMPOSITE in the performance presentation, the FIRM MUST disclose both the date and the reasons for the

change. If a custom BENCHMARK or combination of multiple BENCHMARKS is used, the FIRM MUST describe the BENCHMARK creation and re-balancing process.

5.A.7 If a COMPOSITE contains any non-fee-paying PORTFOLIOS, the FIRM MUST present, as of the end of each annual period, the percentage of the COMPOSITE assets represented by the non-fee-paying PORTFOLIOS.

**5.B Presentation and Reporting—Recommendations**

5.B.1 It is RECOMMENDED that FIRMS present the following items:

a. COMPOSITE returns gross of INVESTMENT MANAGEMENT FEES and ADMINISTRATIVE FEES and before taxes (except for nonreclaimable withholding taxes),

b. Cumulative returns for COMPOSITE and BENCHMARKS for all periods,

c. Equal-weighted mean and median returns for each COMPOSITE,

d. Graphs and charts presenting specific information REQUIRED or RECOMMENDED under the GIPS standards,

e. Returns for quarterly and/or shorter time periods,

f. Annualized COMPOSITE and BENCHMARK returns for periods greater than 12 months,

g. COMPOSITE-level country and sector weightings.

5.B.2 It is RECOMMENDED that FIRMS present relevant COMPOSITE-level risk measures, such as beta, tracking error, modified duration, information ratio, Sharpe ratio, Treynor ratio, credit ratings, value at risk (VaR), and volatility, over time of the COMPOSITE and BENCHMARK.

5.B.3 After presenting the REQUIRED 5 years of compliant historical performance, the FIRM is encouraged to bring any remaining portion of its *historical* track record into compliance with the GIPS standards. (This does not preclude the REQUIREMENT that the FIRM MUST add annual performance to its track record on an *on-going* basis to build a 10-year track record.)

## 6. REAL ESTATE

Following are provisions that apply to the calculation and presentation of REAL ESTATE assets. The REAL ESTATE provisions supplement all the REQUIRED and RECOMMENDED elements of the GIPS standards (outlined in Section II.0. through Section II.5.), except the REAL ESTATE provisions that override the existing GIPS provisions for valuation: II.6.A.1, II.6.A.2, II.6.B.1, and II.6.B.2. Investment types not considered as REAL ESTATE and, therefore, are addressed elsewhere in the general provisions of the GIPS standards include:

▶ Publicly traded REAL ESTATE securities, including any listed securities issued by public companies,

▶ Commercial mortgage-backed securities (CMBS),

▶ Private debt investments, including commercial and residential loans where the expected return is solely related to contractual interest rates without any participation in the economic performance of the underlying REAL ESTATE.

If a PORTFOLIO includes a mix of REAL ESTATE and other investments that are not REAL ESTATE, then these REQUIREMENTS and RECOMMENDATIONS only apply to the REAL ESTATE portion of the PORTFOLIO, and when the FIRM CARVES-OUT the REAL ESTATE portion of the PORTFOLIO, the GIPS CARVE-OUT provisions (see II.3.A.7) MUST also be applied.

### 6.A  Real Estate Input Data—Requirements

6.A.1  REAL ESTATE investments MUST be valued at MARKET VALUE at least once every 12 months. For periods beginning 1 January 2008, REAL ESTATE investments MUST be valued at least quarterly.

6.A.2  REAL ESTATE investments MUST be valued by an external PROFESSIONALLY DESIGNATED, CERTIFIED, or LICENSED COMMERCIAL PROPERTY VALUER/APPRAISER at least once every 36 months. In markets where neither professionally designated nor appropriately sanctioned valuers or appraisers are available and valuers or appraisers from other countries bearing such credentials do not commonly operate, then the party responsible for engaging such services locally shall take necessary steps to ensure that only well-qualified property valuers are used.

### 6.B  Real Estate Input Data—Recommendations

6.B.1  REAL ESTATE investments SHOULD be valued at least quarterly.

6.B.2  REAL ESTATE investments SHOULD be valued by an external valuer or appraiser at least once every 12 months.

6.B.3  If calculating the INTERNAL RATE OF RETURN, FIRMS SHOULD use quarterly cash flows at a minimum.

### 6.A  Real Estate Disclosures—Requirements

6.A.3  In addition to the other disclosure REQUIREMENTS of the GIPS standards, performance presentations for REAL ESTATE investments MUST disclose:

a. The calculation methodology for component returns—that is, component returns are (1) calculated separately using chain-linked TIME-WEIGHTED RATES OF RETURN or (2) adjusted such that the sum of the INCOME RETURN and the CAPITAL RETURN is equal to the TOTAL RETURN,

b. The FIRM'S description of discretion,

c. The valuation methods and procedures (e.g., discounted cash flow valuation model, capitalized income approach, sales comparison approach, the valuation of debt payable in determining the value of leveraged REAL ESTATE),

d. The range of performance returns for the individual accounts in the COMPOSITE,

e. The source of the valuation (whether valued by an external valuer or INTERNAL VALUATION or whether values are obtained from a third-party manager) for each period,

f. The percent of total MARKET VALUE of COMPOSITE assets (asset weighted not equally weighted) to total REAL ESTATE assets valued by an EXTERNAL VALUATION for each period, and

g. The frequency REAL ESTATE investments are valued by external valuers.

### 6.B  Real Estate Disclosures—Recommendations

6.B.4  If since-inception INTERNAL RATE OF RETURN performance results are shown, the FIRM SHOULD disclose the time period that is covered as well as the frequency of the cash flows used in the calculation.

### 6.A  Presentation and Reporting—Requirements

6.A.4  The income and capital appreciation component returns MUST be presented in addition to TOTAL RETURN.

### 6.B  Presentation and Reporting—Recommendations

6.B.5  When available, the capital and income segments of the appropriate REAL ESTATE BENCHMARK SHOULD be presented.

6.B.6  It is RECOMMENDED that FIRMS present the since-inception INTERNAL RATE OF RETURN for the COMPOSITE.

6.B.7  It is RECOMMENDED that the following items be presented, especially in those circumstances when the investment manager has the ability to control the timing of investor capital call tranches during the fund's or PORTFOLIO's initial acquisition period:

a.  GROSS- and NET-OF-FEES (including incentive allocations) annualized since inception TIME-WEIGHTED RATE OF RETURN and INTERNAL RATE OF RETURN (terminal value based on ENDING MARKET VALUE net assets of the COMPOSITE) to the last year reported for the COMPOSITE.

b.  GROSS- and NET-OF-FEES (including incentive allocations) annualized since inception TIME-WEIGHTED RATE OF RETURN and INTERNAL RATE OF RETURN (based on realized cash flows only, excluding unrealized gains) to the last year reported for the COMPOSITE.

c.  In addition, other performance measures may provide additional useful information for both prospective and existing investors. The GIPS PRIVATE EQUITY Provisions (see GIPS standards II.7) provide guidance with regard to such additional measures as investment and REALIZATION MULTIPLES and ratios relating to PAID-IN-CAPITAL.

## 7.  PRIVATE EQUITY

Following are provisions that apply to the calculation and presentation of PRIVATE EQUITY investments other than OPEN-END or EVERGREEN FUNDS (which MUST follow the main GIPS provisions). The PRIVATE EQUITY provisions supplement all the REQUIRED and RECOMMENDED elements of the GIPS standards (outlined in Section II.1 through Section II.5), except these PRIVATE EQUITY provisions that override the existing GIPS provisions for valuation (II.7.A.1 and II.7.B.1), calculation methodology (II.7.A.2 and II.7.A.3), fees (II.7.A.4 and II.7.A.5), and presentation and reporting of returns (II.7.A.20).

### 7.A  Private Equity Input Data—Requirements

7.A.1  PRIVATE EQUITY investments MUST be valued (preferably quarterly but at least annually) according to the GIPS PRIVATE EQUITY Valuation Principles provided in Appendix 4D.

### 7.B  Private Equity Input Data—Recommendations

7.B.1  PRIVATE EQUITY investments SHOULD be valued quarterly.

### 7.A  Private Equity Calculation Methodology—Requirements

7.A.2  FIRMS MUST calculate the annualized since-inception INTERNAL RATE OF RETURN (SI-IRR).

7.A.3  The annualized SI-IRR MUST be calculated using either daily or monthly cash flows and the period-end valuation of the unliquidated remaining holdings. Stock DISTRIBUTIONS MUST be valued at the time of DISTRIBUTION.

7.A.4  NET-OF-FEES RETURNS MUST be net of INVESTMENT MANAGEMENT FEES, CARRIED INTEREST, and TRANSACTION EXPENSES.

7.A.5  For INVESTMENT ADVISORS, all returns MUST be net of all underlying partnership and/or fund fees and CARRIED INTEREST. NET-OF-FEES RETURNS MUST, in addition, be net of all the INVESTMENT ADVISOR's fees, expenses, and CARRIED INTEREST.

## 7.A  Private Equity Composite Construction—Requirements

7.A.6  All CLOSED-END PRIVATE EQUITY investments, including, but not limited to, fund of funds, partnerships, or DIRECT INVESTMENTS, MUST be included in a COMPOSITE defined by strategy and VINTAGE YEAR.

7.A.7  Partnership/fund investments, DIRECT INVESTMENTS, and OPEN-END PRIVATE EQUITY investments (e.g., EVERGREEN FUNDS) MUST be in separate COMPOSITES.

## 7.A  Private Equity Disclosures—Requirements

7.A.8  FIRMS MUST disclose the VINTAGE YEAR of the COMPOSITE.

7.A.9  For all closed (discontinued) COMPOSITES, FIRMS MUST disclose the final realization (liquidation) date of the COMPOSITE.

7.A.10  FIRMS MUST disclose the unrealized appreciation/depreciation of the COMPOSITE for the most recent period.

7.A.11  FIRMS MUST disclose the total COMMITTED CAPITAL of the COMPOSITE for the most recent period.

7.A.12  For the most recent period, FIRMS MUST disclose the valuation methodologies used to value their PRIVATE EQUITY investments. If any change occurs in either valuation basis or methodology from the prior period, the change MUST be disclosed.

7.A.13  If the presentation complies with any local or regional valuation guidelines in addition to the GIPS PRIVATE EQUITY Valuation Principles, FIRMS MUST disclose which local or regional guidelines have been used.

7.A.14  FIRMS MUST document the FIRM's valuation review procedures and disclose that the procedures are available upon request.

7.A.15  FIRMS MUST disclose the definition of the COMPOSITE investment strategy (e.g., early stage, development, buy-outs, generalist, turnaround, mezzanine, geography, middle market, and large transaction).

7.A.16  If a BENCHMARK is used, FIRMS MUST disclose the calculation methodology used for the BENCHMARK.

7.A.17  If a valuation basis other than FAIR VALUE is used to value investments within the COMPOSITE, FIRMS MUST disclose for the most recent period presented their justification for why FAIR VALUE is not applicable. Additionally, FIRMS MUST disclose the following:

a.  The carrying value of non-FAIR-VALUE-basis investments relative to total fund.

b.  The number of holdings valued on a non-FAIR-VALUE basis.

c.  The absolute value of the non-FAIR-VALUE-basis investments.

7.A.18 FIRMS MUST disclose whether they are using daily or monthly cash flows in the SI-IRR calculation.

7.A.19 If a FIRM does not use a calendar year period-end, a disclosure MUST be made indicating the period-end used.

**7.A  Private Equity Presentation and Reporting—Requirements**

7.A.20 FIRMS MUST present both the NET-OF-FEES and GROSS-OF-FEES annualized SI-IRR of the COMPOSITE for each year since inception.

7.A.21 For each period presented, FIRMS MUST report:

a. PAID-IN CAPITAL to date (cumulative DRAWDOWN),

b. Total current INVESTED CAPITAL, and

c. Cumulative DISTRIBUTIONS to date.

7.A.22 For each period presented, FIRMS MUST report the following multiples:

a. TOTAL VALUE to PAID-IN CAPITAL (INVESTMENT MULTIPLE or TVPI),

b. Cumulative DISTRIBUTIONS to PAID-IN CAPITAL (REALIZATION MULTIPLE or DPI),

c. PAID-IN CAPITAL to COMMITTED CAPITAL (PIC MULTIPLE), and

d. RESIDUAL VALUE TO PAID-IN CAPITAL (RVPI).

7.A.23 If a BENCHMARK is shown, the cumulative annualized SI-IRR for the BENCHMARK that reflects the same strategy and VINTAGE YEAR of the COMPOSITE MUST be presented for the same periods for which the COMPOSITE is presented. If no BENCHMARK is shown, the presentation MUST explain why no BENCHMARK is disclosed.

**7.B  Private Equity Presentation and Reporting—Recommendations**

7.B.2 FIRMS SHOULD present the average holding period of the investments (PORTFOLIO companies) over the life of the COMPOSITE.

## III.  VERIFICATION

The primary purpose of verification is to establish that a FIRM claiming compliance with the GIPS standards has adhered to the Standards. Verification will also increase the understanding and professionalism of performance measurement teams and consistency of presentation of performance results.

The verification procedures attempt to strike a balance between ensuring the quality, accuracy, and relevance of performance presentations and minimizing the cost to FIRMS of independent review of performance results. FIRMS SHOULD assess the benefits of improved internal processes and procedures, which are as significant as the marketing advantages of verification.

The goal of the IPC in drafting the verification procedures is to encourage broad acceptance of verification.

Verification is strongly encouraged and is expected to become mandatory at a future date. The IPC will re-evaluate all aspects of mandatory verification by 2010 and provide the industry sufficient time to implement any changes.

### A.  SCOPE AND PURPOSE OF VERIFICATION

1. Verification is the review of an investment management FIRM'S performance measurement processes and procedures by an independent third-party "verifier." Verification tests:

a. Whether the FIRM has complied with all the COMPOSITE construction REQUIREMENTS of the GIPS standards on a FIRM-wide basis, and

b. Whether the FIRM's processes and procedures are designed to calculate and present performance results in compliance with the GIPS standards.

A single verification report is issued in respect of the whole FIRM; verification cannot be carried out for a single COMPOSITE.

2. Third-party verification brings credibility to the claim of compliance and supports the overall guiding principles of full disclosure and fair representation of investment performance.

3. The initial minimum period for which verification can be performed is 1 year of a FIRM's presented performance. The RECOMMENDED period over which verification is performed is that part of the FIRM's track record for which GIPS compliance is claimed.

4. A verification report must confirm that:

  a. The FIRM has complied with all the COMPOSITE construction REQUIREMENTS of the GIPS standards on a FIRM-wide basis, and

  b. The FIRM's processes and procedures are designed to calculate and present performance results in compliance with the GIPS standards.

Without such a report from the verifier, the FIRM cannot state that its claim of compliance with the GIPS standards has been verified.

5. After performing the verification, the verifier may conclude that the FIRM is not in compliance with the GIPS standards or that the records of the FIRM cannot support a complete verification. In such situations, the verifier must issue a statement to the FIRM clarifying why a verification report was not possible.

6. A principal verifier may accept the work of a local or previous verifier as part of the basis for the principal verifier's opinion.

7. The minimum GIPS verification procedures are described in section III.B Required Verification Procedures.

## B. REQUIRED VERIFICATION PROCEDURES

The following are the minimum procedures that verifiers must follow when verifying an investment FIRM's compliance with the GIPS standards. Verifiers must follow these procedures prior to issuing a verification report to the FIRM:

1. Preverification Procedures

  a. <u>Knowledge of the FIRM</u>: Verifiers must obtain selected samples of the FIRM's investment performance reports and other available information regarding the FIRM to ensure appropriate knowledge of the FIRM.

  b. <u>Knowledge of GIPS Standards</u>: Verifiers must understand all the REQUIREMENTS and RECOMMENDATIONS of the GIPS standards, including any updates, reports, guidance statements, interpretations, and clarifications published by CFA Institute and the Investment Performance Council, which will be made available via the CFA Institute website (www.cfainstitute.org) as well as the *GIPS Handbook*. All clarification and update information must be considered when determining a FIRM's claim of compliance.

  c. <u>Knowledge of the Performance Standards</u>: Verifiers must be knowledgeable of country-specific laws and regulations applicable to the FIRM and must determine any differences between the GIPS standards and the country-specific laws and regulations.

d. <u>Knowledge of FIRM Policies</u>: Verifiers must determine the FIRM's assumptions and policies for establishing and maintaining compliance with all applicable REQUIREMENTS of the GIPS standards. At a minimum, verifiers must determine the following policies and procedures of the FIRM:

   i. Policy with regard to investment discretion. The verifier must receive from the FIRM, in writing, the FIRM's definition of investment discretion and the FIRM's guidelines for determining whether accounts are fully discretionary;

   ii. Policy with regard to the definition of COMPOSITES according to investment strategy. The verifier must obtain the FIRM's list of COMPOSITE DEFINITIONS with written criteria for including accounts in each COMPOSITE;

   iii. Policy with regard to the timing of inclusion of new accounts in the COMPOSITES;

   iv. Policy with regard to timing of exclusion of closed accounts in the COMPOSITES;

   v. Policy with regard to the accrual of interest and dividend income;

   vi. Policy with regard to the market valuation of investment securities;

   vii. Method for computing the TIME-WEIGHTED-RATE OF RETURN for the portfolio;

   viii. Assumptions on the timing of capital inflows/outflows;

   ix. Method for computing COMPOSITE returns;

   x. Policy with regard to the presentation of COMPOSITE returns;

   xi. Policies regarding timing of implied taxes due on income and realized capital gains for reporting performance on an after-tax basis;

   xii. Policies regarding use of securities/countries not included in a COMPOSITE'S BENCHMARK;

   xiii. Use of leverage and other derivatives; and

   xiv. Any other policies and procedures relevant to performance presentation.

e. <u>Knowledge of Valuation Basis for Performance Calculations</u>: Verifiers must ensure that they understand the methods and policies used to record valuation information for performance calculation purposes. In particular, verifiers must determine that:

   i. The FIRM's policy on classifying fund flows (e.g., injections, disbursements, dividends, interest, fees, and taxes) is consistent with the desired results and will give rise to accurate returns;

   ii. The FIRM's accounting treatment of income, interest, and dividend receipts is consistent with cash account and cash accruals definitions;

   iii. The FIRM's treatment of taxes, tax reclaims, and tax accruals is correct and the manner used is consistent with the desired method (i.e., gross- or net-of-tax return);

   iv. The FIRM's policies on recognizing purchases, sales, and the opening and closing of other positions are internally consistent and will produce accurate results; and

   v. The FIRM's accounting for investments and derivatives is consistent with the GIPS standards.

2. Verification Procedures

 a. <u>Definition of the FIRM</u>: Verifiers must determine that the FIRM is, and has been, appropriately defined.

 b. <u>COMPOSITE Construction</u>. Verifiers must be satisfied that:

   i. The FIRM has defined and maintained COMPOSITES according to reasonable guidelines in compliance with the GIPS standards;

   ii. All the FIRM's actual discretionary fee-paying PORTFOLIOS are included in a COMPOSITE;

   iii. The FIRM's definition of discretion has been consistently applied over time;

   iv. At all times, all accounts are included in their respective COMPOSITES and no accounts that belong in a particular COMPOSITE have been excluded;

   v. COMPOSITE BENCHMARKS are consistent with COMPOSITE DEFINITIONS and have been consistently applied over time;

   vi. The FIRM's guidelines for creating and maintaining COMPOSITES have been consistently applied; and

   vii. The FIRM's list of COMPOSITES is complete.

 c. <u>Nondiscretionary Accounts</u>: Verifiers must obtain a listing of all FIRM PORTFOLIOS and determine on a sampling basis whether the manager's classification of the account as discretionary or nondiscretionary is appropriate by referring to the account's agreement and the FIRM's written guidelines for determining investment discretion.

 d. <u>Sample Account Selection</u>: Verifiers must obtain a listing of open and closed accounts for all COMPOSITES for the years under examination. Verifiers may check compliance with the GIPS standards using a selected sample of a FIRM's accounts. Verifiers SHOULD consider the following criteria when selecting the sample accounts for examination:

   i. Number of COMPOSITES at the FIRM;

   ii. Number of PORTFOLIOS in each COMPOSITE;

   iii. Nature of the COMPOSITE;

   iv. Total assets under management;

   v. Internal control structure at the FIRM (system of checks and balances in place);

   vi. Number of years under examination; and

   vii. Computer applications, software used in the construction and maintenance of COMPOSITES, the use of external performance measurers, and the calculation of performance results.

This list is not all-inclusive and contains only the minimum criteria that SHOULD be used in the selection and evaluation of a sample for testing. For example, one potentially useful approach would be to choose a PORTFOLIO for the study sample that has the largest impact on COMPOSITE performance because of its size or because of extremely good or bad performance. The lack of explicit record keeping or the presence of errors may warrant selecting a larger sample or applying additional verification procedures.

e. <u>Account Review</u>: For selected accounts, verifiers must determine:

   i. Whether the timing of the initial inclusion in the COMPOSITE is in accordance with policies of the FIRM;

   ii. Whether the timing of exclusion from the COMPOSITE is in accordance with policies of the FIRM for closed accounts;

   iii. Whether the objectives set forth in the account agreement are consistent with the manager's COMPOSITE DEFINITION as indicated by the account agreement, PORTFOLIO summary, and COMPOSITE DEFINITION;

   iv. The existence of the accounts by tracing selected accounts from account agreements to the COMPOSITES;

   v. That all PORTFOLIOS sharing the same guidelines are included in the same COMPOSITE; and

   vi. That shifts from one COMPOSITE to another are consistent with the guidelines set forth by the specific account agreement or with documented guidelines of the FIRM'S clients.

f. <u>Performance Measurement Calculation</u>: Verifiers must determine whether the FIRM has computed performance in accordance with the policies and assumptions adopted by the FIRM and disclosed in its presentations. In doing so, verifiers SHOULD:

   i. Recalculate rates of return for a sample of accounts in the FIRM using an acceptable return formula as prescribed by the GIPS standards (e.g., TIME-WEIGHTED RATE OF RETURN); and

   ii. Take a reasonable sample of COMPOSITE calculations to assure themselves of the accuracy of the asset weighting of returns, the geometric linking of returns to produce annual rates of returns, and the calculation of the DISPERSION of individual returns around the aggregate COMPOSITE return.

g. <u>Disclosures</u>: Verifiers must review a sample of COMPOSITE presentations to ensure that the presentations include the information and disclosures REQUIRED by the GIPS standards.

h. <u>Maintenance of Records</u>: The verifier must maintain sufficient information to support the verification report. The verifier must obtain a representation letter from the client FIRM confirming major policies and any other specific representations made to the verifier during the examination.

## C. DETAILED EXAMINATIONS OF INVESTMENT PERFORMANCE PRESENTATIONS

Separate from a GIPS verification, a firm may choose to have a further, more extensive, specifically focused examination (or performance audit) of a specific COMPOSITE presentation.

FIRMS cannot make any claim that a particular COMPOSITE has been independently examined with respect to the GIPS standards unless the verifier has also followed the GIPS verification procedures set forth in section III.B. FIRMS cannot state that a particular COMPOSITE presentation has been "GIPS verified" or make any claim to that effect. GIPS verification relates only to FIRM-WIDE verification. FIRMS can make a claim of verification only after a verifier has issued a GIPS verification report.

To assert a verification report has been received, a detailed examination of a COMPOSITE presentation is not REQUIRED. Examinations of this type are unlikely to become a REQUIREMENT of the GIPS standards or become mandatory.

OPTIONAL SEGMENT ENDS

# APPENDIX 4A—SAMPLE GIPS-COMPLIANT PRESENTATIONS

## EXAMPLE 1

### Sample 1 Investment Firm Balanced Composite

#### 1 January 1995 through 31 December 2004

| Year | Gross-of-Fees Return (Percent) | Net-of-Fees Return (Percent) | Benchmark Return (Percent) | Number of Portfolios | Internal Dispersion (Percent) | Total Composite Assets (CAD Million) | Total Firm Assets (CAD Million) |
|------|------|------|------|------|------|------|------|
| 1995 | 16.0 | 15.0 | 14.1 | 26 | 4.5 | 165 | 236 |
| 1996 | 2.2 | 1.3 | 1.8 | 32 | 2.0 | 235 | 346 |
| 1997 | 22.4 | 21.5 | 24.1 | 38 | 5.7 | 344 | 529 |
| 1998 | 7.1 | 6.2 | 6.0 | 45 | 2.8 | 445 | 695 |
| 1999 | 8.5 | 7.5 | 8.0 | 48 | 3.1 | 520 | 839 |
| 2000 | −8.0 | −8.9 | −8.4 | 49 | 2.8 | 505 | 1014 |
| 2001 | −5.9 | −6.8 | −6.2 | 52 | 2.9 | 499 | 995 |
| 2002 | 2.4 | 1.6 | 2.2 | 58 | 3.1 | 525 | 1125 |
| 2003 | 6.7 | 5.9 | 6.8 | 55 | 3.5 | 549 | 1225 |
| 2004 | 9.4 | 8.6 | 9.1 | 59 | 2.5 | 575 | 1290 |

**Sample 1 Investment Firm has prepared and presented this report in compliance with the Global Investment Performance Standards (GIPS®).**

*Notes:*

1. Sample 1 Investment Firm is a balanced portfolio investment manager that invests solely in Canadian securities. Sample 1 Investment Firm is defined as an independent investment management firm that is not affiliated with any parent organization. For the periods from 2000 through 2004, Sample 1 Investment Firm has been verified by Verification Services Inc. A copy of the verification report is available upon request. Additional information regarding the firm's policies and procedures for calculating and reporting performance results is available upon request.

2. The composite includes all nontaxable balanced portfolios with an asset allocation of 30% S&P TSX and 70% Scotia Canadian Bond Index Fund, which allow up to a 10% deviation in asset allocation.

3. The benchmark: 30% S&P TSX; 70% Scotia Canadian Bond Index Fund rebalanced monthly.

4. Valuations are computed and performance reported in Canadian dollars.

5. Gross-of-fees performance returns are presented before management and custodial fees but after all trading expenses. Returns are presented net of nonreclaimable withholding taxes. Net-of-fees performance returns are calculated by deducting the highest fee of 0.25% from the quarterly gross composite return. The management fee schedule is as follows: 1.00% on first CAD25M; 0.60% thereafter.

6. This composite was created in February 1995. A complete list and description of firm composites is available upon request.

7. For the periods 1995 and 1996, Sample 1 Investment Firm was not in compliance with the GIPS standards because portfolios were valued annually.

8. Internal dispersion is calculated using the equal-weighted standard deviation of all portfolios that were included in the composite for the entire year.

**EXAMPLE 2**

**Sample 2 Asset Management Company**

### Equities World BM MSCI Active Mandates Direct

| | Reporting Currency CHF | | Creation Date 1 July 1999 | | | |
|---|---|---|---|---|---|---|
| Period | Total Return (%) | MSCI World (ri) in CHF Benchmark Return (%) | Number of Portfolios | Composite Dispersion (Range) | Total Composite Assets (Millions) | Percentage of Firm Assets (%) |
| 2004 | 18.0 | 19.6 | 6 | 0.2 | 84.3 | <0.1 |
| 2003 | −35.3 | −33.0 | 8 | 0.7 | 126.6 | 0.1 |
| 2002 | −16.0 | −14.5 | 8 | 1.5 | 233.0 | 0.2 |
| 2001 | −13.5 | −11.8 | 7 | 1.3 | 202.1 | 0.2 |
| 2000 | 60.2 | 46.1 | <5 | N/A | 143.7 | 0.2 |
| 1999 | 21.3 | 17.5 | <5 | N/A | 62.8 | <0.1 |
| 1998 | 22.5 | 26.3 | <5 | N/A | 16.1 | <0.1 |

**Compliance Statement**

Sample 2 Asset Management Company has prepared and presented this report in compliance with the Global Investment Performance Standards (GIPS®).

**Definition of the Firm**

Sample 2 Asset Management Company is an independent investment management firm established in 1997. Sample 2 Asset Management Company manages a variety of equity, fixed income, and balanced assets for primarily Swiss and European clients. Additional information regarding the firm's policies and procedures for calculating and reporting performance returns is available upon request.

**Benchmark**

Sources of foreign exchange rates may be different between the composite and the benchmark.

**Fees**

Performance figures are presented gross of management fees, custodial fees, and withholding taxes but net of all trading expenses.

**List of Composites**

A complete listing and description of all composites is available on request.

**Verification**

Sample 2 Asset Management Company has been verified by an independent verifier on an annual basis from 1998 through 2003.

**Fee Schedule**

The standard fixed management fee for accounts with assets under management of up to CHF50 million is 0.35% per annum.

**Minimum Account Size**

The minimum portfolio size for inclusion in Equities World BM MSCI composite is CHF1 million.

## EXAMPLE 3

### Schedule of Performance Results
### Sample 3 Realty Management Firm

## Core Real Estate Composite

### 1 January 1995 through 31 December 2004

| Year | Gross-of-Fees Returns | | | Range of Returns | Composite Dispersion | NCREIF Property Index Benchmark | Number of Portfolios | Year-End Composite | | | Firm Total Net Assets (USD Million) | Percent of Firm Assets |
|------|------------------|-------------------|-------|-------|-------|-------|-------|-------|-------|-------|-------|-------|
| | Income Return | Capital Return | TOTAL | | | | | Net Assets (USD Million) | Percent Leveraged | External Valuation | | |
| 1995 | 5.1% | –4.0% | 0.8% | 0.7–1.0 | NA | –5.6% | <5 | $ 79 | 43% | 100% | $ 950 | 8% |
| 1996 | 5.5% | –0.9% | 4.5% | 4.0–5.0 | NA | –4.3% | <5 | $ 143 | 49% | 100% | $ 989 | 14% |
| 1997 | 6.9% | –1.5% | 5.3% | 5.0–5.4 | NA | 1.4% | <5 | $ 217 | 56% | 100% | $ 1,219 | 18% |
| 1998 | 8.1% | 0.9% | 9.1% | 8.9–9.7 | NA | 6.4% | <5 | $ 296 | 54% | 100% | $ 1,375 | 22% |
| 1999 | 8.9% | 1.7% | 10.8% | 9.9–11.0 | NA | 7.5% | <5 | $ 319 | 50% | 100% | $ 1,425 | 22% |
| 2000 | 9.0% | 0.5% | 9.6% | 9.1–10.9 | 0.7 | 10.3% | 5 | $ 367 | 45% | 100% | $ 1,532 | 24% |
| 2001 | 9.1% | 1.2% | 10.5% | 10.0–10.7 | 0.3 | 13.9% | 5 | $ 349 | 39% | 100% | $ 1,712 | 20% |
| 2002 | 7.9% | 1.8% | 9.9% | 9.8–10.5 | 0.3 | 16.3% | 6 | $ 398 | 31% | 100% | $ 1,796 | 22% |
| 2003 | 8.5% | 2.9% | 11.5% | 10.9–12.0 | 0.5 | 11.1% | 6 | $ 425 | 28% | 100% | $ 1,924 | 22% |
| 2004 | 8.2% | 2.5% | 10.8% | 9.9–11.8 | 0.8 | 12.0% | 7 | $ 432 | 22% | 100% | $ 1,954 | 22% |

Annualized Since Inception Time-Weighted Returns:

| | | | | | | |
|------|------|------|---|---|------|---|
| | 7.7% | 0.5% | 8.0% | | 6.7% | |

Annualized Since Inception Internal Rate of Return:

7.8%

## DISCLOSURES

### Compliance Statement
Sample 3 Realty Management Firm has prepared and presented this report in compliance with the Global Investment Performance Standards (GIPS®).

### The Firm
Sample 3 Realty Management Firm (the "Firm"), a subsidiary of ABC Capital, Inc., is a registered investment adviser under the Investment Advisors Act of 1940. The Firm exercises complete discretion over the selection, capitalization, asset management, and disposition of investments in wholly-owned properties and joint ventures. A complete list and description of the Firm's composites is available upon request.

### The Composite
The Core Real Estate Composite (the "Composite") comprises all actual fee-paying discretionary portfolios managed by the Firm with a core investment and risk strategy with an income focus having a minimum initial portfolio size of $10 million. Portfolios that initially qualify are excluded later from the composite if their asset size decreases below the minimum requirement due to capital distributions. The Composite was created in 1998. Composite dispersion is measured using an asset-weighted standard deviation of returns of the portfolios.

### Valuation
Assets are valued quarterly by the Firm and appraised annually by an independent Member of the Appraisal Institute. Both the internal and external property valuations rely primarily on the application of market discount rates to future projections of free cash flows (unleveraged cash flows) and capitalized terminal values over the expected holding period for each property. Property mortgages, notes, and loans are marked to market using prevailing interest rates for comparable property loans if the terms of existing loans preclude the immediate repayment of such loans. Loan repayment fees, if any, are considered in the projected year of sale.

## Calculation of Performance Returns

Returns presented are denominated in United States dollars. Returns are presented net of leverage. Composite returns are calculated on an asset-weighted average basis using beginning-of-period values. Returns include cash and cash equivalents and related interest income. Income return is based on accrual recognition of earned income. Capital expenditures, tenant improvements, and lease commissions are capitalized and included in the cost of the property, are not amortized, and are reconciled through the valuation process and reflected in the capital return component. Income and capital returns may not equal total returns due to chain-linking of quarterly returns. Annual returns are time-weighted rates of return calculated by linking quarterly returns. For the annualized since-inception time-weighted return, terminal value is based on ending market value of net assets of the Composite. For the since-inception internal rate of return, contributions from and distributions to investors since January 1, 1995, and a terminal value equal to the composite's ending market value of net assets as of December 31, 2004, are used. The IRR is calculated using monthly cash flows. Additional information regarding policies for calculating and reporting returns in compliance with the GIPS standards is available upon request.

## Investment Management Fees

Some of the portfolios pay incentive fees ranging between 10% and 20% of IRR in excess of established benchmarks. Current annual investment advisory fees are as follows:

| | |
|---|---|
| Up to $30 million: | 1.6% |
| $30 – $50 million: | 1.3% |
| over $50 million: | 1.0% |

## NCREIF Property Index Benchmark

The National Council of Real Estate Investment Fiduciaries (NCREIF) Property Index benchmark has been taken from published sources. The NCREIF Property Index is unleveraged, includes various real estate property types, excludes cash and other nonproperty related assets and liabilities, income, and expenses. The calculation methodology for the index is not consistent with calculation methodology employed for the Composite because the benchmark computes the total return by adding the income and capital appreciation return on a quarterly basis.

## EXAMPLE 4

### Sample 4 Private Equity Partners Buy-Out Composite

#### 1 January 1995 through 31 December 2002

| Year | Annualized SI-IRR Gross-of-Fees (%) | Annualized SI-IRR Net-of-Fees (%) | Benchmark Return (%) | Composite Assets (USD$ Mil) | Total Firm Assets (USD$ Mil) |
|---|---|---|---|---|---|
| 1995 | (7.5) | (11.07) | (9.42) | 4.31 | 357.36 |
| 1996 | 6.2 | 4.53 | 2.83 | 10.04 | 402.78 |
| 1997 | 13.8 | 10.10 | 14.94 | 14.25 | 530.51 |
| 1998 | 13.1 | 9.28 | 14.22 | 25.21 | 613.73 |
| 1999 | 53.2 | 44.53 | 37.43 | 54.00 | 871.75 |

*(Table continued on next page . . .)*

*(continued)*

## Sample 4 Private Equity Partners Buy-Out Composite

### 1 January 1995 through 31 December 2002

| Year | Annualized SI-IRR Gross-of-Fees (%) | Annualized SI-IRR Net-of-Fees (%) | Benchmark Return (%) | Composite Assets (USD$ Mil) | Total Firm Assets (USD$ Mil) |
|---|---|---|---|---|---|
| 2000 | 40.6 | 26.47 | 32.97 | 24.25 | 1,153.62 |
| 2001 | 29.9 | 21.86 | 27.42 | 8.25 | 1,175.69 |
| 2002 | 25.3 | 17.55 | 25.24 | 10.25 | 1,150.78 |

| Year | Paid-In Capital (USD$ Mil) | Invested Capital (USD$ Mil) | Cumulative Distributions (USD$ Mil) | Investment Multiple (TVPI) | Realization Multiple (DPI) | PIC | RVPI |
|---|---|---|---|---|---|---|---|
| 1995 | 4.68 | 4.68 | 0 | 0.92 | 0.00 | 0.19 | 0.92 |
| 1996 | 9.56 | 9.56 | 0 | 1.05 | 0.00 | 0.38 | 1.05 |
| 1997 | 14.54 | 12.91 | 2.55 | 1.16 | 0.18 | 0.58 | 0.98 |
| 1998 | 23.79 | 22.15 | 2.55 | 1.17 | 0.11 | 0.95 | 1.06 |
| 1999 | 25.00 | 19.08 | 15.78 | 2.79 | 0.63 | 1.00 | 2.16 |
| 2000 | 25.00 | 17.46 | 27.44 | 2.07 | 1.10 | 1.00 | 0.97 |
| 2001 | 25.00 | 14.89 | 39.10 | 1.89 | 1.56 | 1.00 | 0.33 |
| 2002 | 25.00 | 13.73 | 41.25 | 2.06 | 1.65 | 1.00 | 0.41 |

TVPI = Total Value to Paid-In Capital

DPI = Distributed Capital to Paid-In Capital

PIC = Paid-In Capital to Committed Capital

RVPI = Residual Value to Paid-In Capital

**Sample 4 Private Equity Partners has prepared and presented this report in compliance with the Global Investment Performance Standards (GIPS®).**

Sample 4 Private Equity Partners is an independent private equity investment firm, having offices in London, New York, and San Francisco. The Sample 4 Buy-Out Composite invests in private equity buyouts and was created in January 1995.

The Sample 4 Buy-Out Composite complies with the XYZ Venture Capital Association's valuation guidelines. Valuations are prepared by Sample 4's valuations committee and reviewed by an independent advisory board. Sample 4 follows the fair value basis of valuation as recommended in the GIPS Private Equity Valuation Principles. All investments within the Sample 4 Buy-Out Composite are valued either using a most recent transaction or an earnings multiple. Sample 4's valuation review procedures are available upon request.

The GP-BO index is used as the benchmark and is constructed as the QRS index return plus 500 basis points. The benchmark return is calculated using monthly cash flows. There is only one fund in the composite for all time periods, and the dispersion of portfolio returns within the composite, therefore, is zero for all years.

The vintage year of the Sample 4 Buy-Out Fund is 1995, and total committed capital is USD$25 million. The total composite assets (unrealized gains) are USD$10.25 million as of 31 December 2002.

The fund's SI-IRR calculation incorporates monthly cash flows.

A complete list of firm composites and composite performance results is available upon request. Additional information regarding the firm's policies and procedures for calculating and reporting performance results is available upon request.

The standard fee schedule currently in effect is as follows: 1.00% of assets under management. In addition, there is a 20% incentive fee for all assets. The incentive fee is applied to the value added in excess of fees, expenses, and the return of the GP-BO index.

# APPENDIX 4B—SAMPLE LIST AND DESCRIPTION OF COMPOSITES

## Sample Asset Management Firm

### List and Description of Composites

The **Small Cap Growth Composite** includes all institutional portfolios invested in U.S. equities with strong earnings and growth characteristics and small capitalizations. The benchmark is the Russell 2000® Growth Index.

The **Large Cap Growth Composite** includes all institutional portfolios invested in U.S. equities with strong earnings and growth characteristics and large capitalizations. The benchmark is the Russell 1000® Growth Index.

The **Core Fixed Income Composite** includes all institutional portfolios invested in fixed securities. Portfolios within the composite will have a duration that is plus or minus 20 percent of the benchmark. The benchmark is the Lehman Brothers Aggregate Bond Index.

The **Intermediate Fixed Income Composite** includes all institutional portfolios invested in fixed securities. Portfolios within the composite will have a duration that is plus or minus 20 percent of the benchmark. The benchmark is the Lehman Brothers Intermediate Aggregate Bond Index.

The **High Yield Fixed Income Composite** includes all institutional portfolios invested in high yield debt securities. The benchmark is the Lehman Brothers U.S. Corporate High Yield Bond Index.

The **Balanced Growth Composite** includes all institutional balanced portfolios that have a 50–70% allocation to growth equities, with a typical allocation between 55–65%. The benchmark is 60% S&P 500® and 40% Lehman Brothers Aggregate Bond Index. Only portfolios greater than $5 million are included in the composite.

### Terminated Composites

The **GARP Equity Composite** includes all institutional portfolios invested in growth stocks that are reasonably priced and valued "cheap" compared with their peers. The benchmark is the S&P 500® Index. The composite terminated in November 2003.

The **Small-Mid Cap Growth Composite** includes all institutional portfolios invested in U.S. equities with strong earnings and growth characteristics. The benchmark is the Russell 2500® Growth Index. The composite terminated in February 2004.

# APPENDIX 4C—GIPS ADVERTISING GUIDELINES

### A.  PURPOSE OF THE GIPS ADVERTISING GUIDELINES

The Global Investment Performance Standards provide the investment community with a set of ethical standards for FIRMS to follow when presenting their performance results to potential clients. The Standards serve to provide greater uniformity and comparability among investment managers without regard to geographical location and to facilitate a dialogue between FIRMS and their prospective clients about the critical issues of how the FIRM achieved historical performance results and determines future investment strategies.

The GIPS Advertising Guidelines attempt to serve as industry global best practice for the advertisement of performance results. The GIPS Advertising Guidelines do not replace the GIPS standards nor do they absolve FIRMS from presenting performance presentations that adhere to the REQUIREMENTS of the full GIPS standards. The guidelines only apply to firms that already satisfy all the REQUIREMENTS of the Standards on a FIRM-wide basis and claim compliance with the Standards. FIRMS that claim compliance can choose to advertise that claim using the GIPS Advertising Guidelines.

The guidelines are mandatory for FIRMS that include a claim of compliance with the GIPS Advertising Guidelines in their advertisements. The guidelines are voluntary for FIRMS that do not include a claim of compliance in their advertisements. All FIRMS are encouraged to abide by these ethical guidelines.

### Definition of Advertisement

For the purposes of these guidelines, an advertisement includes any materials that are distributed to or designed for use in newspapers, magazines, FIRM brochures, letters, media, or any other written or electronic material addressed to more than one prospective client. Any written material (other than one-on-one presentations and individual client reporting) distributed to maintain existing clients or solicit new clients for an advisor is considered an advertisement.

### Relationship of GIPS Advertising Guidelines to Regulatory Requirements

The GIPS Advertising Guidelines are guidelines that promote an ethical framework for advertisements. They do not change the scope of the activities of local regulatory bodies regarding the regulation of advertisements. FIRMS advertising performance results MUST also adhere to all applicable regulatory rules and requirements governing advertisements. FIRMS are encouraged to seek legal or regulatory counsel because it is likely that additional disclosures are REQUIRED. In cases where applicable law or regulation conflicts with the GIPS Advertising Guidelines, the guidelines REQUIRE FIRMS to comply with the law or regulation. FIRMS MUST disclose any conflicts between laws/regulations and the GIPS Advertising Guidelines.

The calculation and advertisement of pooled unitized products, such as mutual funds and open-ended investment companies, are regulated in most markets. These advertising guidelines are not intended to replace the regulations when a FIRM is advertising performance solely for a pooled unitized product. However, should a GIPS-compliant FIRM choose to advertise performance results, the FIRM MUST apply all applicable laws and regulations as well as the GIPS Advertising Guidelines in order to include a claim of compliance with the GIPS standards.

## B. REQUIREMENTS OF THE GIPS ADVERTISING GUIDELINES

**All advertisements that include a claim of compliance with the GIPS Advertising Guidelines must include the following:**

1. A description of the FIRM.

2. How an interested party can obtain a presentation that complies with the REQUIREMENTS of GIPS standards and/or a list and description of all FIRM COMPOSITES.

3. The GIPS Advertising Guidelines compliance statement:

   [Insert name of firm] claims compliance with the Global Investment Performance Standards (GIPS®).

**All advertisements that include a claim of compliance with the GIPS Advertising Guidelines and that present performance results MUST also include the following information (the relevant information MUST be taken/derived from a presentation that adheres to the REQUIREMENTS of the GIPS standards):**

4. A description of the strategy of the COMPOSITE being advertised.

5. Period-to-date COMPOSITE performance results in addition to either:

   a. 1-, 3-, and 5-year cumulative annualized COMPOSITE returns with the end-of-period date clearly identified (or annualized period since COMPOSITE inception if inception is greater than 1 and less than 5 years). Periods of less than 1 year are not permitted to be annualized. The annualized returns MUST be calculated through the same period of time as presented in the corresponding compliant presentation; or

   b. 5 years of annual COMPOSITE returns with the end-of-period date clearly identified (or since COMPOSITE inception if inception is less than 5 years). The annual returns MUST be calculated through the same period of time as presented in the corresponding compliant presentation.

6. Whether performance is shown gross and/or net of INVESTMENT MANAGEMENT FEES.

7. The BENCHMARK TOTAL RETURN for the same periods for which the COMPOSITE return is presented and a description of that BENCHMARK. (The appropriate COMPOSITE BENCHMARK return is the same BENCHMARK TOTAL RETURN as presented in the corresponding GIPS-compliant presentation.) If no BENCHMARK is presented, the advertisement MUST disclose why no BENCHMARK is presented.

8. The currency used to express returns.

9. The description of the use and extent of leverage and derivatives if leverage or derivatives are used as an active part of the investment strategy (i.e., not merely for efficient PORTFOLIO management) of the COMPOSITE. Where leverage/derivatives do not have a material effect on returns, no disclosure is REQUIRED.

10. When presenting noncompliant performance information for periods prior to 1 January 2000 in an advertisement, FIRMS MUST disclose the period(s) and which specific information is not compliant as well as provide the reason(s) the information is not in compliance with the GIPS standards.

## Additional and Supplemental Information

FIRMS are encouraged to present SUPPLEMENTAL INFORMATION or ADDITIONAL INFORMATION (in addition to the information REQUIRED under the GIPS Advertising Guidelines) provided the SUPPLEMENTAL INFORMATION is clearly labeled as such and shown with equal or lesser prominence than the information REQUIRED under the guidelines. Where such SUPPLEMENTAL INFORMATION is included for noncompliant periods, these periods MUST be disclosed together with an explanation of what information is not compliant and why it is not in compliance with the GIPS standards.

SUPPLEMENTAL and ADDITIONAL INFORMATION is the subject of the "Guidance Statement on the Use of Supplemental Information" and users should refer to that guidance for further clarification on how to disclose such data.

# SAMPLE ADVERTISEMENTS

## Sample Advertisement without Performance Returns

**Sample 4 Investments**

Sample 4 Investments is the institutional asset management division of Sample 4 Plc and is a registered investment advisory firm specializing in qualitative, growth-oriented investment management.

> Sample 4 Investments claims compliance with the Global Investment Performance Standards (GIPS®).

To receive a complete list and description of Sample 4 Investments' composites and/or a presentation that adheres to the GIPS standards, contact John Doe at (800) 555-1234, or write to Sample 4 Investments, 123 Main Street, Resultland 12345, or e-mail jdoe@sample4investments.com

## Sample Advertisement Including Performance Returns (1-, 3-, and 5-Year Annualized)

**Sample 4 Investments: Global Equity Growth Composite Performance**

| Results Shown in US $ before Fees | Ending 31 Mar 04 | | Ending 31 Dec 03 | |
| --- | --- | --- | --- | --- |
| | Period to Date (3 Mths) | 1 Year | 3 Years per Annum | 5 Years per Annum |
| Global Equity Growth | –3.84% | –19.05% | –14.98% | 0.42% |
| MSCI World Index | –4.94% | –19.54% | –16.37% | –1.76% |

Sample 4 Investments is the institutional asset management subsidiary of Sample 4 plc and is a registered investment advisor specializing in qualitative, growth-oriented investment management. The Global Equity Growth Composite strategy focuses on earnings, growth of earnings, and key valuation metrics.

Sample 4 Investments claims compliance with the Global Investment Performance Standards (GIPS®).

To receive a complete list and description of Sample 4 Investments' composites and/or a presentation that adheres to the GIPS standards, contact Jean Paul at +12 (034) 5678910, or write Sample 4 Investments, One Plain Street, Resultland 12KJ4, or jpaul@sample4inv.com.re.

**OR the firm may present:**

## Sample Advertisement Including Performance Returns (5 Years of Annual Returns)

| Sample 4 Investments: Global Equity Growth Composite Performance | | | | | | |
|---|---|---|---|---|---|---|
| Results Shown in US $ before Fees | Period to Date (3 Mths to 31 Mar 04) | 31 Dec 2003 | 31 Dec 2002 | 31 Dec 2001 | 31 Dec 2000 | 31 Dec 1999 |
| Global Equity Growth Composite | −3.84% | −19.05% | −17.05% | −8.47% | 31.97% | 25.87% |
| MSCI World Index | −4.94% | −19.54% | −16.52% | −12.92% | 25.34% | 24.80% |

Sample 4 Investments is the institutional asset management subsidiary of Sample 4 plc and is a registered investment advisor specializing in qualitative, growth-oriented investment management. The Global Equity Growth Composite strategy focuses on earnings, growth of earnings, and key valuation metrics.

Sample 4 Investments claims compliance with the Global Investment Performance Standards (GIPS®).

To receive a complete list and description of Sample 4 Investments' composites and/or a presentation that adheres to the GIPS standards, contact Jean Paul at +12 (034) 5678910, or write Sample 4 Investments, One Plain Street, Resultland 12KJ4, or jpaul@sample4inv.com.re.

# APPENDIX 4D—PRIVATE EQUITY VALUATION PRINCIPLES

## INTRODUCTION

Opinions among INVESTMENT ADVISORS, practitioners, and investors differ regarding the valuation of PRIVATE EQUITY assets. The margin of error for a particular valuation methodology may often be greater than the difference between alternative methodologies. The volatility of asset values is also often high, increasing the perception that a historical valuation was "wrong." Although cash-to-cash returns are the principal metric, PRIVATE EQUITY funds raise capital in part based on unrealized interim returns. The valuation of unrealized assets underpinning these interim returns is critical to this analysis.

Although many points are contested, some common ground exists:

▶ The PRIVATE EQUITY industry must strive to promote integrity and professionalism in order to improve investor confidence and self-regulation.

▶ Consistency and comparability are important in reporting to investors, and many aspects of valuation SHOULD be transparent. More information, however, does not always equal greater transparency, and there are legal and practical constraints on the dissemination of information.

▶ Each PRIVATE EQUITY investment is based on a set of assumptions. It is reasonable for investors to expect interim valuations to reflect factors that, at a minimum, adversely impact these assumptions.

▶ When a PRIVATE EQUITY asset becomes publicly traded, arguments against interim valuations fall away, although practical considerations may remain where there are restrictions on trading or trading volumes are low.

Beyond these issues are the debates on valuation basis and methodology. The move toward a FAIR VALUE basis has been gathering momentum in most areas of financial reporting. Particularly for early stage venture investments that may not achieve profitability for a number of years, practical problems remain and the utility of the FAIR VALUE basis must garner greater support before a consensus on detailed guidelines is likely to be possible.

## GUIDELINES FOR VALUATION

The following MUST be applied to all forms of investment vehicles making PRIVATE EQUITY investments. These principles do not apply to OPEN-END or EVERGREEN FUNDS.

1. Valuations MUST be prepared with integrity and professionalism by individuals with appropriate experience and ability under the direction of senior management.

2. FIRMS MUST document their valuation review procedures.

3. FIRMS MUST create as much transparency as deemed possible in relation to the valuation basis used to value fund investments. For the latest period presented, the valuation methodologies used to value PRIVATE EQUITY investments MUST be clearly disclosed, including all key assumptions.

4. The basis of valuation MUST be logically cohesive and applied rigorously. Although a FAIR VALUE basis is RECOMMENDED, all valuations MUST, at a minimum, recognize when assets have suffered a diminution in value. (Please see the Additional Considerations section for further guidance on diminution circumstances.)

5. Valuations MUST be prepared on a consistent and comparable basis from one reporting period to the next. If any change is deemed appropriate in either valuation basis or method, the change MUST be explained. When such a change gives rise to a material alteration in the valuation of the investments, the effect of the change SHOULD also be disclosed.

6. Valuations MUST be prepared at least annually. (Quarterly valuations are RECOMMENDED.)

## FAIR VALUE RECOMMENDATION

It is RECOMMENDED that the FAIR VALUE basis, which is consistent with international financial reporting principles, be used to value PRIVATE EQUITY investments. This valuation SHOULD represent the amount at which an asset could be acquired or sold in a current transaction between willing parties in which the parties each acted knowledgeably, prudently, and without compulsion.

The accuracy with which the value of an individual PRIVATE EQUITY asset can be determined will generally have substantial uncertainty. Consequently, it is RECOMMENDED that a valuation method that involves the least number of estimates is preferred over another method that introduces additional subjective assumptions. However, if the latter method results in more accurate and meaningful valuation, then it SHOULD be used instead of the former method.

### Valuation Hierarchy

The following hierarchy of FAIR VALUE methodologies SHOULD be followed when valuing PRIVATE EQUITY investments:

1. <u>Market Transaction</u>
   Where a recent independent third-party transaction has occurred involving a material investment as part of a new round of financing or sale of equity, it would provide the most appropriate indication of FAIR VALUE.

2. <u>Market-Based Multiples</u>
   In the absence of any such third-party transactions continuing to have relevance, the FAIR VALUE of an investment may be calculated using earnings or other market-based multiples. The particular multiple used SHOULD be appropriate for the business being valued. Market-based multiples include, but are not limited to, the following: price to earnings, enterprise value to EBIT, enterprise value to EBITDA, and so on.

3. <u>Discounted Expected Future Cash Flows</u>
   This method SHOULD represent the present value of risk-adjusted expected cash flows, discounted at the risk-free rate.

### Additional Considerations

1. Where a third-party transaction has taken place other than at arm's length, or where the new investor's objectives in making the investment are largely strategic in nature (i.e. the new investor was not acting solely as a financial

investor), the manager SHOULD consider ignoring the valuation or applying an appropriate discount to it.

2. A material diminution in the value of an investment may result from, among other things, a breach of covenant, failure to service debt, a filing for creditor protection or bankruptcy, major lawsuit (particularly concerning intellectual property rights), or a loss or change of management. Other events may include fraud within the company, a material devaluation in an investment currency that is different from the fund currency, substantial changes in quoted market conditions, or any event resulting in profitability falling significantly below the levels at the time of investment or the company performing substantially and consistently behind plan. Estimating the extent of the diminution in most cases will generally involve both quantitative and qualitative analysis and SHOULD be performed with as much diligence as possible.

3. The FIRM SHOULD have policies in place for informing clients/prospects when a material diminution has taken place within the PORTFOLIO. Waiting until a quarterly update may often not provide the prospective investor with this critical information soon enough to make an informed decision.

4. Within the valuation hierarchy there will be certain industries where very specific valuation methodologies become applicable. Within the correct industry, either of these methods could be considered the primary valuation methodology in the absence of an applicable third-party transaction. Whenever one of these methods is used, the FIRM MUST justify the measure as representing the most appropriate and accurate method for calculating a FAIR VALUE.

    a. <u>Net Assets:</u> For FIRMS that derive a majority of their value from their underlying assets rather than the company's earnings, this method may be preferred.

    b. <u>Industry BENCHMARKS:</u> In particular industries, there are metrics, such as "price per subscriber," that can be used to derive the value of a FIRM. These measures are very specialized to the industries they represent and must not be carried over to more diversified FIRMS.

5. It is RECOMMENDED that valuations be reviewed by a qualified person or entity that is independent from the valuer. Such parties would include third-party experts, an independent advisory board, or a committee independent of the executives responsible for the valuations.

6. As stated in the Valuation Hierarchy section of this document, FAIR VALUE allows for the use of a recent transaction as the primary methodology for valuation. Accordingly, when an investment is first made, this "cost" represents the most recent transaction and, therefore, the FAIR VALUE. In this case, the cost is permitted to be used not because it represents the cost of the investment but, rather, because it represents the value of the most recent transaction.

    Cost as a *basis* of valuation is only permitted when an estimate of FAIR VALUE cannot be reliably determined. Although a FAIR VALUE basis should always be attempted, the PRIVATE EQUITY Provisions do recognize that there may be situations when a non-FAIR-VALUE basis is necessary. Ultimately, FIRMS must keep in mind that investors make decisions based on FAIR VALUES, not out-of-date historical cost-based measures.

    In any case, when a non-FAIR-VALUE basis is used, the FIRM MUST disclose its justification for why a FAIR VALUE basis cannot be applied. In addition, for each COMPOSITE, the FIRM MUST disclose the number of holdings to which a non-FAIR-

VALUE basis is applied, the TOTAL VALUE of those holdings, and the value of those holdings as a percentage of the total COMPOSITE/fund assets.

7. Where companies have activities that span more than one sector, making it impractical to find comparable companies or sectors, each earnings stream may be valued independently. Sector average multiples, based on companies of comparable size, can be used where it is not practical or possible to identify a sufficient number of directly comparable companies.

8. The entry multiple(s) for an investment SHOULD only be used as a last resort when comparable quoted companies are not available.

9. All quasi-equity investments SHOULD be valued as equity unless their realizable value can be demonstrated to be other than the equity value.

10. When a PRIVATE EQUITY FIRM has invested in loan stock and preference shares alongside an equity investment, these instruments SHOULD not generally be valued on the basis of their yield. They SHOULD be valued at cost plus any premium or rolled up interest only to the extent it has fully accrued, less any provision/discount where appropriate.

OPTIONAL SEGMENT ENDS

## PRACTICE PROBLEM FOR READING 4

**1.** With respect to the Global Investment Performance Standards, which of the following is one of the eight major sections that reflect the elements involved in presenting performance information?

   **A.** Real Estate.

   **B.** Derivatives.

   **C.** Legal and Ethical Considerations.

# QUANTITATIVE METHODS

## STUDY SESSIONS

**Study Session 2**    Basic Concepts
**Study Session 3**    Application

### TOPIC LEVEL LEARNING OUTCOME

The candidate should be able to demonstrate a thorough knowledge of elementary statistics, data collection and analysis, probability theory and distributions, the time value of money, and performance measurement.

# STUDY SESSION 2
## QUANTITATIVE METHODS:
### Basic Concepts

This introductory study session presents the fundamentals of those quantitative techniques that are essential in almost any type of financial analysis, and which will be used throughout the remainder of the CFA Program curriculum. This session introduces two main building blocks of the quantitative analytical tool kit: (1) the time value of money and (2) statistics and probability theory.

The time value of money concept is one of the main principles of financial valuation. The calculations based on this principle (e.g., present value, future value, and internal rate of return) are the basic tools used to support corporate finance decisions and estimate the fair value of fixed income, equity, or any other type of security or investment.

Similarly, the basic concepts of statistics and probability theory constitute the essential tools used in describing the main statistical properties of a population and understanding and applying various probability concepts in practice.

## READING ASSIGNMENTS

**Reading 5**    The Time Value of Money
*Quantitative Methods for Investment Analysis*, Second Edition, by Richard A. DeFusco, CFA, Dennis W. McLeavey, CFA, Jerald E. Pinto, CFA, and David E. Runkle, CFA

**Reading 6**    Discounted Cash Flow Applications
*Quantitative Methods for Investment Analysis*, Second Edition, by Richard A. DeFusco, CFA, Dennis W. McLeavey, CFA, Jerald E. Pinto, CFA, and David E. Runkle, CFA

**Reading 7**    Statistical Concepts and Market Returns
*Quantitative Methods for Investment Analysis*, Second Edition, by Richard A. DeFusco, CFA, Dennis W. McLeavey, CFA, Jerald E. Pinto, CFA, and David E. Runkle, CFA

**Reading 8**    Probability Concepts
*Quantitative Methods for Investment Analysis*, Second Edition, by Richard A. DeFusco, CFA, Dennis W. McLeavey, CFA, Jerald E. Pinto, CFA, and David E. Runkle, CFA

# THE TIME VALUE OF MONEY

by Richard A. DeFusco, CFA, Dennis W. McLeavey, CFA, Jerald E. Pinto, CFA, and David E. Runkle, CFA

## LEARNING OUTCOMES

| The candidate should be able to: | Mastery |
|---|:---:|
| **a.** interpret interest rates as required rate of return, discount rate or opportunity cost; | ☐ |
| **b.** explain an interest rate as the sum of a real risk-free rate, expected inflation, and premiums that compensate investors for distinct types of risk; | ☐ |
| **c.** calculate and interpret the effective annual rate, given the stated annual interest rate and the frequency of compounding, and solve time value of money problems when compounding periods are other than annual; | ☐ |
| **d.** calculate and interpret the future value (FV) and present value (PV) of a single sum of money, an ordinary annuity, an annuity due, a perpetuity (PV only), and a series of unequal cash flows; | ☐ |
| **e.** draw a time line, and solve time value of money applications (for example, mortgages and savings for college tuition or retirement). | ☐ |

## INTRODUCTION          1

As individuals, we often face decisions that involve saving money for a future use, or borrowing money for current consumption. We then need to determine the amount we need to invest, if we are saving, or the cost of borrowing, if we are shopping for a loan. As investment analysts, much of our work also involves evaluating transactions with present and future cash flows. When we place a value on any security, for example, we are attempting to determine the worth of a stream of future cash flows. To carry out all the above tasks accurately, we must understand the mathematics of time value of money problems. Money has time value in that individuals value a given amount of money more highly the earlier it is received. Therefore, a smaller amount of money

*Quantitative Methods for Investment Analysis*, Second Edition, by Richard A. DeFusco, CFA, Dennis W. McLeavey, CFA, Jerald E. Pinto, CFA, and David E. Runkle, CFA. Copyright © 2004 by CFA Institute. Reprinted with permission.

now may be equivalent in value to a larger amount received at a future date. The **time value of money** as a topic in investment mathematics deals with equivalence relationships between cash flows with different dates. Mastery of time value of money concepts and techniques is essential for investment analysts.

The reading is organized as follows: Section 2 introduces some terminology used throughout the reading and supplies some economic intuition for the variables we will discuss. Section 3 tackles the problem of determining the worth at a future point in time of an amount invested today. Section 4 addresses the future worth of a series of cash flows. These two sections provide the tools for calculating the equivalent value at a future date of a single cash flow or series of cash flows. Sections 5 and 6 discuss the equivalent value today of a single future cash flow and a series of future cash flows, respectively. In Section 7, we explore how to determine other quantities of interest in time value of money problems.

## 2    INTEREST RATES: INTERPRETATION

In this reading, we will continually refer to interest rates. In some cases, we assume a particular value for the interest rate; in other cases, the interest rate will be the unknown quantity we seek to determine. Before turning to the mechanics of time value of money problems, we must illustrate the underlying economic concepts. In this section, we briefly explain the meaning and interpretation of interest rates.

Time value of money concerns equivalence relationships between cash flows occurring on different dates. The idea of equivalence relationships is relatively simple. Consider the following exchange: You pay $10,000 today and in return receive $9,500 today. Would you accept this arrangement? Not likely. But what if you received the $9,500 today and paid the $10,000 one year from now? Can these amounts be considered equivalent? Possibly, because a payment of $10,000 a year from now would probably be worth less to you than a payment of $10,000 today. It would be fair, therefore, to **discount** the $10,000 received in one year; that is, to cut its value based on how much time passes before the money is paid. An **interest rate**, denoted $r$, is a rate of return that reflects the relationship between differently dated cash flows. If $9,500 today and $10,000 in one year are equivalent in value, then $10,000 − $9,500 = $500 is the required compensation for receiving $10,000 in one year rather than now. The interest rate—the required compensation stated as a rate of return—is $500/$9,500 = 0.0526 or 5.26 percent.

Interest rates can be thought of in three ways. First, they can be considered required rates of return—that is, the minimum rate of return an investor must receive in order to accept the investment. Second, interest rates can be considered discount rates. In the example above, 5.26 percent is that rate at which we discounted the $10,000 future amount to find its value today. Thus, we use the terms "interest rate" and "discount rate" almost interchangeably. Third, interest rates can be considered opportunity costs. An **opportunity cost** is the value that investors forgo by choosing a particular course of action. In the example, if the party who supplied $9,500 had instead decided to spend it today, he would have forgone earning 5.26 percent on the money. So we can view 5.26 percent as the opportunity cost of current consumption.

Economics tells us that interest rates are set in the marketplace by the forces of supply and demand, where investors are suppliers of funds and borrowers are demanders of funds. Taking the perspective of investors in analyzing market-determined interest rates, we can view an interest rate *r* as being composed of a real risk-free interest rate plus a set of four premiums that are required returns or compensation for bearing distinct types of risk:

$$r = \text{Real risk-free interest rate} + \text{Inflation premium}$$
$$+ \text{Default risk premium} + \text{Liquidity premium} + \text{Maturity premium}$$

▶ The **real risk-free interest rate** is the single-period interest rate for a completely risk-free security if no inflation were expected. In economic theory, the real risk-free rate reflects the time preferences of individuals for current versus future real consumption.

▶ The **inflation premium** compensates investors for expected inflation and reflects the average inflation rate expected over the maturity of the debt. Inflation reduces the purchasing power of a unit of currency—the amount of goods and services one can buy with it. The sum of the real risk-free interest rate and the inflation premium is the **nominal risk-free interest rate**.[1] Many countries have governmental short-term debt whose interest rate can be considered to represent the nominal risk-free interest rate in that country. The interest rate on a 90-day U.S. Treasury bill (T-bill), for example, represents the nominal risk-free interest rate over that time horizon.[2] U.S. T-bills can be bought and sold in large quantities with minimal **transaction costs** and are backed by the full faith and credit of the U.S. government.

▶ The **default risk premium** compensates investors for the possibility that the borrower will fail to make a promised payment at the contracted time and in the contracted amount.

▶ The **liquidity premium** compensates investors for the risk of loss relative to an investment's fair value if the investment needs to be converted to cash quickly. U.S. T-bills, for example, do not bear a liquidity premium because large amounts can be bought and sold without affecting their market price. Many bonds of small issuers, by contrast, trade infrequently after they are issued; the interest rate on such bonds includes a liquidity premium reflecting the relatively high costs (including the impact on price) of selling a position.

▶ The **maturity premium** compensates investors for the increased sensitivity of the market value of debt to a change in market interest rates as maturity is extended, in general (holding all else equal). The difference between the interest rate on longer-maturity, liquid Treasury debt and that on short-term Treasury debt reflects a positive maturity premium for the longer-term debt (and possibly different inflation premiums as well).

---

[1] Technically, 1 plus the nominal rate equals the product of 1 plus the real rate and 1 plus the inflation rate. As a quick approximation, however, the nominal rate is equal to the real rate plus an inflation premium. In this discussion we focus on approximate additive relationships to highlight the underlying concepts.

[2] Other developed countries issue securities similar to U.S. Treasury bills. The French government issues BTFs or negotiable fixed-rate discount Treasury bills (*Bons du Trésor à taux fixe et à intérêts précomptés*) with maturities of 3, 6, and 12 months. The Japanese government issues a short-term Treasury bill with maturities of 6 and 12 months. The German government issues at discount both Treasury financing paper (*Finanzierungsschätze des Bundes* or, for short, *Schätze*) and Treasury discount paper (*Bubills*) with maturities up to 24 months. In the United Kingdom, the British government issues gilt-edged Treasury bills with maturities ranging from 1 to 364 days. The Canadian government bond market is closely related to the U.S. market; Canadian Treasury bills have maturities of 3, 6, and 12 months.

Using this insight into the economic meaning of interest rates, we now turn to a discussion of solving time value of money problems, starting with the future value of a single cash flow.

# THE FUTURE VALUE OF A SINGLE CASH FLOW

In this section, we introduce time value associated with a single cash flow or lump-sum investment. We describe the relationship between an initial investment or **present value** (PV), which earns a rate of return (the interest rate per period) denoted as $r$, and its **future value** (FV), which will be received $N$ years or periods from today.

The following example illustrates this concept. Suppose you invest $100 (PV = $100) in an interest-bearing bank account paying 5 percent annually. At the end of the first year, you will have the $100 plus the interest earned, $0.05 \times \$100 = \$5$, for a total of $105. To formalize this one-period example, we define the following terms:

PV = present value of the investment
$FV_N$ = future value of the investment $N$ periods from today
$r$ = rate of interest per period

For $N = 1$, the expression for the future value of amount PV is

$$FV_1 = PV(1 + r)$$                                    **(5-1)**

For this example, we calculate the future value one year from today as FV1 = $100(1.05) = $105.

Now suppose you decide to invest the initial $100 for two years with interest earned and credited to your account annually (annual compounding). At the end of the first year (the beginning of the second year), your account will have $105, which you will leave in the bank for another year. Thus, with a beginning amount of $105 (PV = $105), the amount at the end of the second year will be $105(1.05) = $110.25. Note that the $5.25 interest earned during the second year is 5 percent of the amount invested at the beginning of Year 2.

Another way to understand this example is to note that the amount invested at the beginning of Year 2 is composed of the original $100 that you invested plus the $5 interest earned during the first year. During the second year, the original principal again earns interest, as does the interest that was earned during Year 1. You can see how the original investment grows:

| | |
|---|---:|
| Original investment | $100.00 |
| Interest for the first year ($100 × 0.05) | 5.00 |
| Interest for the second year based on original investment ($100 × 0.05) | 5.00 |
| Interest for the second year based on interest earned in the first year | |
| (0.05 × $5.00 interest on interest) | 0.25 |
| Total | $110.25 |

The $5 interest that you earned each period on the $100 original investment is known as **simple interest** (the interest rate times the principal). **Principal** is the amount of funds originally invested. During the two-year period, you earn $10 of simple interest. The extra $0.25 that you have at the end of Year 2 is the interest you earned on the Year 1 interest of $5 that you reinvested.

The interest earned on interest provides the first glimpse of the phenomenon known as **compounding**. Although the interest earned on the initial investment is important, for a given interest rate it is fixed in size from period to period. The compounded interest earned on reinvested interest is a far more powerful force because, for a given interest rate, it grows in size each period. The importance of compounding increases with the magnitude of the interest rate. For example, $100 invested today would be worth about $13,150 after 100 years if compounded annually at 5 percent, but worth more than $20 million if compounded annually over the same time period at a rate of 13 percent.

To verify the $20 million figure, we need a general formula to handle compounding for any number of periods. The following general formula relates the present value of an initial investment to its future value after $N$ periods:

$$FV_N = PV(1 + r)^N \qquad \text{(5-2)}$$

where $r$ is the stated interest rate per period and $N$ is the number of compounding periods. In the bank example, $FV_2 = \$100(1 + 0.05)^2 = \$110.25$. In the 13 percent investment example, $FV_{100} = \$100(1.13)^{100} = \$20,316,287.42$.

The most important point to remember about using the future value equation is that the stated interest rate, $r$, and the number of compounding periods, $N$, must be compatible. Both variables must be defined in the same time units. For example, if $N$ is stated in months, then $r$ should be the one-month interest rate, unannualized.

A time line helps us to keep track of the compatibility of time units and the interest rate per time period. In the time line, we use the time index $t$ to represent a point in time a stated number of periods from today. Thus the present value is the amount available for investment today, indexed as $t = 0$. We can now refer to a time $N$ periods from today as $t = N$. The time line in Figure 1 shows this relationship.

**FIGURE 1   The Relationship between an Initial Investment, PV, and Its Future Value, FV**

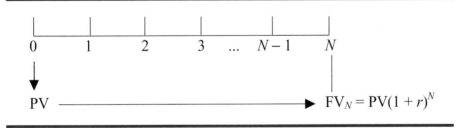

In Figure 1, we have positioned the initial investment, PV, at $t = 0$. Using Equation 5-2, we move the present value, PV, forward to $t = N$ by the factor $(1 + r)^N$. This factor is called a future value factor. We denote the future value on the time line as FV and position it at $t = N$. Suppose the future value is to be received exactly 10 periods from today's date ($N = 10$). The present value, PV, and the future value, FV, are separated in time through the factor $(1 + r)^{10}$.

The fact that the present value and the future value are separated in time has important consequences:

▶ We can add amounts of money only if they are indexed at the same point in time.

> ► For a given interest rate, the future value increases with the number of periods.

> ► For a given number of periods, the future value increases with the interest rate.

To better understand these concepts, consider three examples that illustrate how to apply the future value formula.

## EXAMPLE 1

### The Future Value of a Lump Sum with Interim Cash Reinvested at the Same Rate

You are the lucky winner of your state's lottery of $5 million after taxes. You invest your winnings in a five-year certificate of deposit (CD) at a local financial institution. The CD promises to pay 7 percent per year compounded annually. This institution also lets you reinvest the interest at that rate for the duration of the CD. How much will you have at the end of five years if your money remains invested at 7 percent for five years with no withdrawals?

**Solution:** To solve this problem, compute the future value of the $5 million investment using the following values in Equation 5-2:

$$PV = \$5,000,000$$
$$r = 7\% = 0.07$$
$$N = 5$$

$$
\begin{aligned}
FV_N &= PV(1 + r)^N \\
&= \$5,000,000(1.07)^5 \\
&= \$5,000,000(1.402552) \\
&= \$7,012,758.65
\end{aligned}
$$

At the end of five years, you will have $7,012,758.65 if your money remains invested at 7 percent with no withdrawals.

*In this and most examples in this reading, note that the factors are reported at six decimal places but the calculations may actually reflect greater precision. For example, the* reported 1.402552 has been rounded up from 1.40255173 (the calculation is actually carried out with more than eight decimal places of precision by the calculator or spreadsheet). Our final result reflects the higher number of decimal places carried by the calculator or spreadsheet.[3]

---

[3] We could also solve time value of money problems using tables of interest rate factors. Solutions using tabled values of interest rate factors are generally less accurate than solutions obtained using calculators or spreadsheets, so practitioners prefer calculators or spreadsheets.

## EXAMPLE 2

### The Future Value of a Lump Sum with No Interim Cash

An institution offers you the following terms for a contract: For an investment of ¥2,500,000, the institution promises to pay you a lump sum six years from now at an 8 percent annual interest rate. What future amount can you expect?

**Solution:** Use the following data in Equation 5-2 to find the future value:

$$PV = ¥2,500,000$$
$$r = 8\% = 0.08$$
$$N = 6$$

$$\begin{aligned} FV_N &= PV(1 + r)^N \\ &= ¥2,500,000(1.08)^6 \\ &= ¥2,500,000(1.586874) \\ &= ¥3,967,186 \end{aligned}$$

You can expect to receive ¥3,967,186 six years from now.

Our third example is a more complicated future value problem that illustrates the importance of keeping track of actual calendar time.

## EXAMPLE 3

### The Future Value of a Lump Sum

A pension fund manager estimates that his corporate sponsor will make a $10 million contribution five years from now. The rate of return on plan assets has been estimated at 9 percent per year. The pension fund manager wants to calculate the future value of this contribution 15 years from now, which is the date at which the funds will be distributed to retirees. What is that future value?

**Solution:** By positioning the initial investment, PV, at $t = 5$, we can calculate the future value of the contribution using the following data in Equation 5-2:

$$PV = \$10 \text{ million}$$
$$r = 9\% = 0.09$$
$$N = 10$$

$$\begin{aligned} FV_N &= PV(1 + r)^N \\ &= \$10,000,000(1.09)^{10} \\ &= \$10,000,000(2.367364) \\ &= \$23,673,636.75 \end{aligned}$$

This problem looks much like the previous two, but it differs in one important respect: its timing. From the standpoint of today ($t = 0$), the future amount of \$23,673,636.75 is 15 years into the future. Although the future value is 10 years from its present value, the present value of \$10 million will not be received for another five years.

### FIGURE 2   The Future Value of a Lump Sum, Initial Investment Not at $t = 0$

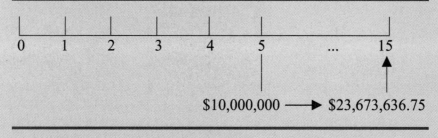

$10,000,000 ⟶ $23,673,636.75

As Figure 2 shows, we have followed the convention of indexing today as $t = 0$ and indexing subsequent times by adding 1 for each period. The additional contribution of \$10 million is to be received in five years, so it is indexed as $t = 5$ and appears as such in the figure. The future value of the investment in 10 years is then indexed at $t = 15$; that is, 10 years following the receipt of the \$10 million contribution at $t = 5$. Time lines like this one can be extremely useful when dealing with more-complicated problems, especially those involving more than one cash flow.

In a later section of this reading, we will discuss how to calculate the value today of the \$10 million to be received five years from now. For the moment, we can use Equation 5-2. Suppose the pension fund manager in Example 3 above were to receive \$6,499,313.86 today from the corporate sponsor. How much will that sum be worth at the end of five years? How much will it be worth at the end of 15 years?

$$PV = \$6{,}499{,}313.86$$
$$r = 9\% = 0.09$$
$$N = 5$$
$$\begin{aligned}FV_N &= PV(1 + r)^N\\ &= \$6{,}499{,}313.86(1.09)^5\\ &= \$6{,}499{,}313.86(1.538624)\\ &= \$10{,}000{,}000 \text{ at the five-year mark}\end{aligned}$$

and

$$PV = \$6{,}499{,}313.86$$
$$r = 9\% = 0.09$$
$$N = 15$$

$$FV_N = PV(1 + r)^N$$
$$= \$6,499,313.86(1.09)^{15}$$
$$= \$6,499,313.86(3.642482)$$
$$= \$23,673,636.74 \text{ at the 15-year mark}$$

These results show that today's present value of about $6.5 million becomes $10 million after five years and $23.67 million after 15 years.

## 3.1 The Frequency of Compounding

In this section, we examine investments paying interest more than once a year. For instance, many banks offer a monthly interest rate that compounds 12 times a year. In such an arrangement, they pay interest on interest every month. Rather than quote the periodic monthly interest rate, financial institutions often quote an annual interest rate that we refer to as the **stated annual interest rate** or **quoted interest rate**. We denote the stated annual interest rate by $r_s$. For instance, your bank might state that a particular CD pays 8 percent compounded monthly. The stated annual interest rate equals the monthly interest rate multiplied by 12. In this example, the monthly interest rate is $0.08/12 = 0.0067$ or 0.67 percent.[4] This rate is strictly a quoting convention because $(1 + 0.0067)^{12} = 1.083$, not 1.08; the term $(1 + r_s)$ is not meant to be a future value factor when compounding is more frequent than annual.

With more than one compounding period per year, the future value formula can be expressed as

$$FV_N = PV\left(1 + \frac{r_s}{m}\right)^{mN} \qquad\qquad \textbf{(5-3)}$$

where $r_s$ is the stated annual interest rate, $m$ is the number of compounding periods per year, and $N$ now stands for the number of years. Note the compatibility here between the interest rate used, $r_s/m$, and the number of compounding periods, $mN$. The periodic rate, $r_s/m$, is the stated annual interest rate divided by the number of compounding periods per year. The number of compounding periods, $mN$, is the number of compounding periods in one year multiplied by the number of years. The periodic rate, $r_s/m$, and the number of compounding periods, $mN$, must be compatible.

### EXAMPLE 4

**The Future Value of a Lump Sum with Quarterly Compounding**

Continuing with the CD example, suppose your bank offers you a CD with a two-year maturity, a stated annual interest rate of 8 percent compounded quarterly, and a feature allowing reinvestment of the interest at the same interest rate. You decide to invest $10,000. What will the CD be worth at maturity?

---

[4] To avoid rounding errors when using a financial calculator, divide 8 by 12 and then press the $\%i$ key, rather than simply entering 0.67 for $\%i$, so we have $(1 + 0.08/12)^{12} = 1.083000$.

**Solution:** Compute the future value with Equation 5-3 as follows:

$$
\begin{aligned}
PV &= \$10,000 \\
r_s &= 8\% = 0.08 \\
m &= 4 \\
r_s/m &= 0.08/4 = 0.02 \\
N &= 2 \\
mN &= 4(2) = 8 \text{ interest periods}
\end{aligned}
$$

$$
\begin{aligned}
FV_N &= PV\left(1 + \frac{r_s}{m}\right)^{mN} \\
&= \$10,000(1.02)^8 \\
&= \$10,000(1.171659) \\
&= \$11,716.59
\end{aligned}
$$

At maturity, the CD will be worth \$11,716.59.

The future value formula in Equation 5-3 does not differ from the one in Equation 5-2. Simply keep in mind that the interest rate to use is the rate per period and the exponent is the number of interest, or compounding, periods.

## EXAMPLE 5

### The Future Value of a Lump Sum with Monthly Compounding

An Australian bank offers to pay you 6 percent compounded monthly. You decide to invest A\$1 million for one year. What is the future value of your investment if interest payments are reinvested at 6 percent?

**Solution:** Use Equation 5-3 to find the future value of the one-year investment as follows:

$$
\begin{aligned}
PV &= A\$1,000,000 \\
r_s &= 6\% = 0.06 \\
m &= 12 \\
r_s/m &= 0.06/12 = 0.0050 \\
N &= 1 \\
mN &= 12(1) = 12 \text{ interest periods}
\end{aligned}
$$

$$
\begin{aligned}
FV_N &= PV\left(1 + \frac{r_s}{m}\right)^{mN} \\
&= A\$1,000,000(1.005)^{12} \\
&= A\$1,000,000(1.061678) \\
&= A\$1,061,677.81
\end{aligned}
$$

If you had been paid 6 percent with annual compounding, the future amount would be only A\$1,000,000(1.06) = A\$1,060,000 instead of A\$1,061,677.81 with monthly compounding.

## 3.2 Continuous Compounding

The preceding discussion on compounding periods illustrates discrete compounding, which credits interest after a discrete amount of time has elapsed. If the number of compounding periods per year becomes infinite, then interest is said to compound continuously. If we want to use the future value formula with continuous compounding, we need to find the limiting value of the future value factor for $m \to \infty$ (infinitely many compounding periods per year) in Equation 5-3. The expression for the future value of a sum in $N$ years with continuous compounding is

$$FV_N = PVe^{r_s N} \tag{5-4}$$

The term $e^{r_s N}$ is the transcendental number $e \approx 2.7182818$ raised to the power $r_s N$. Most financial calculators have the function $e^x$.

---

### EXAMPLE 6

**The Future Value of a Lump Sum with Continuous Compounding**

Suppose a $10,000 investment will earn 8 percent compounded continuously for two years. We can compute the future value with Equation 5-4 as follows:

$$PV = \$10,000$$

$$r_s = 8\% = 0.08$$

$$N = 2$$

$$\begin{aligned}
FV_N &= PVe^{r_s N} \\
&= \$10,000e^{0.08(2)} \\
&= \$10,000(1.173511) \\
&= \$11,735.11
\end{aligned}$$

With the same interest rate but using continuous compounding, the $10,000 investment will grow to $11,735.11 in two years, compared with $11,716.59 using quarterly compounding as shown in Example 4.

---

Table 1 shows how a stated annual interest rate of 8 percent generates different ending dollar amounts with annual, semiannual, quarterly, monthly, daily, and continuous compounding for an initial investment of $1 (carried out to six decimal places).

As Table 1 shows, all six cases have the same stated annual interest rate of 8 percent; they have different ending dollar amounts, however, because of differences in the frequency of compounding. With annual compounding, the ending amount is $1.08. More frequent compounding results in larger ending amounts. The ending dollar amount with continuous compounding is the maximum amount that can be earned with a stated annual rate of 8 percent.

### TABLE 1 The Effect of Compounding Frequency on Future Value

| Frequency | $r_s/m$ | $mN$ | Future Value of $1 |
|---|---|---|---|
| Annual | $8\%/1 = 8\%$ | $1 \times 1 = 1$ | $\$1.00(1.08) = \$1.08$ |
| Semiannual | $8\%/2 = 4\%$ | $2 \times 1 = 2$ | $\$1.00(1.04)^2 = \$1.081600$ |
| Quarterly | $8\%/4 = 2\%$ | $4 \times 1 = 4$ | $\$1.00(1.02)^4 = \$1.082432$ |
| Monthly | $8\%/12 = 0.6667\%$ | $12 \times 1 = 12$ | $\$1.00(1.006667)^{12} = \$1.083000$ |
| Daily | $8\%/365 = 0.0219\%$ | $365 \times 1 = 365$ | $\$1.00(1.000219)^{365} = \$1.083278$ |
| Continuous | | | $\$1.00e^{0.08(1)} = \$1.083287$ |

Table 1 also shows that a $1 investment earning 8.16 percent compounded annually grows to the same future value at the end of one year as a $1 investment earning 8 percent compounded semiannually. This result leads us to a distinction between the stated annual interest rate and the **effective annual rate** (EAR).[5] For an 8 percent stated annual interest rate with semiannual compounding, the EAR is 8.16 percent.

## 3.3 Stated and Effective Rates

The stated annual interest rate does not give a future value directly, so we need a formula for the EAR. With an annual interest rate of 8 percent compounded semiannually, we receive a periodic rate of 4 percent. During the course of a year, an investment of $1 would grow to $1(1.04)^2 = $1.0816, as illustrated in Table 1. The interest earned on the $1 investment is $0.0816 and represents an effective annual rate of interest of 8.16 percent. The effective annual rate is calculated as follows

$$\text{EAR} = (1 + \text{Periodic interest rate})^m - 1 \qquad \textbf{(5-5)}$$

The periodic interest rate is the stated annual interest rate divided by $m$, where $m$ is the number of compounding periods in one year. Using our previous example, we can solve for EAR as follows: $(1.04)^2 - 1 = 8.16$ percent.

The concept of EAR extends to continuous compounding. Suppose we have a rate of 8 percent compounded continuously. We can find the EAR in the same way as above by finding the appropriate future value factor. In this case, a $1 investment would grow to $1e^{0.08(1.0)} = $1.0833. The interest earned for one year represents an effective annual rate of 8.33 percent and is larger than the 8.16 percent EAR with semiannual compounding because interest is compounded

---

[5] Among the terms used for the effective annual return on interest-bearing bank deposits are annual percentage yield (APY) in the United States and equivalent annual rate (EAR) in the United Kingdom. By contrast, the **annual percentage rate** (APR) measures the cost of borrowing expressed as a yearly rate. In the United States, the APR is calculated as a periodic rate times the number of payment periods per year and, as a result, some writers use APR as a general synonym for the stated annual interest rate. Nevertheless, APR is a term with legal connotations; its calculation follows regulatory standards that vary internationally. Therefore, "stated annual interest rate" is the preferred general term for an annual interest rate that does not account for compounding within the year.

more frequently. With continuous compounding, we can solve for the effective annual rate as follows:

$$\text{EAR} = e^{r_s} - 1$$

**(5-6)**

We can reverse the formulas for EAR with discrete and continuous compounding to find a periodic rate that corresponds to a particular effective annual rate. Suppose we want to find the appropriate periodic rate for a given effective annual rate of 8.16 percent with semiannual compounding. We can use Equation 5-5 to find the periodic rate:

$$0.0816 = (1 + \text{Periodic rate})^2 - 1$$
$$1.0816 = (1 + \text{Periodic rate})^2$$
$$(1.0816)^{1/2} - 1 = \text{Periodic rate}$$
$$(1.04) - 1 = \text{Periodic rate}$$
$$4\% = \text{Periodic rate}$$

To calculate the continuously compounded rate (the stated annual interest rate with continuous compounding) corresponding to an effective annual rate of 8.33 percent, we find the interest rate that satisfies Equation 5-6:

$$0.0833 = e^{r_s} - 1$$

$$1.0833 = e^{r_s}$$

To solve this equation, we take the natural logarithm of both sides. (Recall that the natural log of $e^{r_s}$ is $\ln e^{r_s} = r_s$.) Therefore, $\ln 1.0833 = r_s$, resulting in $r_s = 8$ percent. We see that a stated annual rate of 8 percent with continuous compounding is equivalent to an EAR of 8.33 percent.

# THE FUTURE VALUE OF A SERIES OF CASH FLOWS

**4**

In this section, we consider series of cash flows, both even and uneven. We begin with a list of terms commonly used when valuing cash flows that are distributed over many time periods.

▶ An **annuity** is a finite set of level sequential cash flows.

▶ An **ordinary annuity** has a first cash flow that occurs one period from now (indexed at $t = 1$).

▶ An **annuity due** has a first cash flow that occurs immediately (indexed at $t = 0$).

▶ A **perpetuity** is a perpetual annuity, or a set of level never-ending sequential cash flows, with the first cash flow occurring one period from now.

## 4.1 Equal Cash Flows—Ordinary Annuity

Consider an ordinary annuity paying 5 percent annually. Suppose we have five separate deposits of $1,000 occurring at equally spaced intervals of one year, with the first payment occurring at $t = 1$. Our goal is to find the future value of this ordinary annuity after the last deposit at $t = 5$. The increment in the time counter is one year, so the last payment occurs five years from now. As the time

**FIGURE 3    The Future Value of a Five-Year Ordinary Annuity**

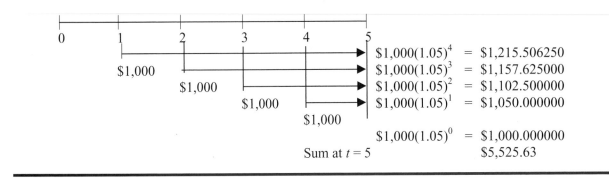

line in Figure 3 shows, we find the future value of each $1,000 deposit as of $t = 5$ with Equation 5-2, $FV_N = PV(1 + r)^N$. The arrows in Figure 3 extend from the payment date to $t = 5$. For instance, the first $1,000 deposit made at $t = 1$ will compound over four periods. Using Equation 5-2, we find that the future value of the first deposit at $t = 5$ is $1,000(1.05)^4 = $1,215.51$. We calculate the future value of all other payments in a similar fashion. (Note that we are finding the future value at $t = 5$, so the last payment does not earn any interest.) With all values now at $t = 5$, we can add the future values to arrive at the future value of the annuity. This amount is $5,525.63.

We can arrive at a general annuity formula if we define the annuity amount as $A$, the number of time periods as $N$, and the interest rate per period as $r$. We can then define the future value as

$$FV_N = A[(1 + r)^{N-1} + (1 + r)^{N-2} + (1 + r)^{N-3} + \ldots + (1 + r)^1 + (1 + r)^0]$$

which simplifies to

$$FV_N = A\left[\frac{(1 + r)^N - 1}{r}\right] \qquad \textbf{(5-7)}$$

The term in brackets is the future value annuity factor. This factor gives the future value of an ordinary annuity of $1 per period. Multiplying the future value annuity factor by the annuity amount gives the future value of an ordinary annuity. For the ordinary annuity in Figure 3, we find the future value annuity factor from Equation 5-7 as

$$\left[\frac{(1.05)^5 - 1}{0.05}\right] = 5.525631$$

With an annuity amount $A = $1,000$, the future value of the annuity is $1,000(5.525631) = $5,525.63$, an amount that agrees with our earlier work.

The next example illustrates how to find the future value of an ordinary annuity using the formula in Equation 5-7.

**EXAMPLE 7**

### The Future Value of an Annuity

Suppose your company's defined contribution retirement plan allows you to invest up to €20,000 per year. You plan to invest €20,000 per year in a stock index fund for the next 30 years. Historically, this fund has earned 9 percent per year on average. Assuming that you actually earn 9 percent a year, how much money will you have available for retirement after making the last payment?

**Solution:** Use Equation 5-7 to find the future amount:

$$A = €20,000$$
$$r = 9\% = 0.09$$
$$N = 30$$

$$\text{FV annuity factor} = \frac{(1 + r)^N - 1}{r} = \frac{(1.09)^{30} - 1}{0.09} = 136.307539$$

$$\text{FV}_N = €20,000(136.307539)$$
$$= €2,726,150.77$$

Assuming the fund continues to earn an average of 9 percent per year, you will have €2,726,150.77 available at retirement.

## 4.2 Unequal Cash Flows

In many cases, cash flow streams are unequal, precluding the simple use of the future value annuity factor. For instance, an individual investor might have a savings plan that involves unequal cash payments depending on the month of the year or lower savings during a planned vacation. One can always find the future value of a series of unequal cash flows by compounding the cash flows one at a time. Suppose you have the five cash flows described in Table 2, indexed relative to the present ($t = 0$).

**TABLE 2  A Series of Unequal Cash Flows and Their Future Values at 5 Percent**

| Time | Cash Flow | Future Value at Year 5 | |
|------|-----------|------------------------|---|
| $t = 1$ | $1,000 | $1,000(1.05)^4 =$ | $1,215.51 |
| $t = 2$ | $2,000 | $2,000(1.05)^3 =$ | $2,315.25 |
| $t = 3$ | $4,000 | $4,000(1.05)^2 =$ | $4,410.00 |
| $t = 4$ | $5,000 | $5,000(1.05)^1 =$ | $5,250.00 |
| $t = 5$ | $6,000 | $6,000(1.05)^0 =$ | $6,000.00 |
| | | Sum | $= $19,190.76 |

All of the payments shown in Table 2 are different. Therefore, the most direct approach to finding the future value at $t = 5$ is to compute the future value of each payment as of $t = 5$ and then sum the individual future values. The total future value at Year 5 equals \$19,190.76, as shown in the third column. Later in this reading, you will learn shortcuts to take when the cash flows are close to even; these shortcuts will allow you to combine annuity and single-period calculations.

## 5   THE PRESENT VALUE OF A SINGLE CASH FLOW

### 5.1 Finding the Present Value of a Single Cash Flow

Just as the future value factor links today's present value with tomorrow's future value, the present value factor allows us to discount future value to present value. For example, with a 5 percent interest rate generating a future payoff of \$105 in one year, what current amount invested at 5 percent for one year will grow to \$105? The answer is \$100; therefore, \$100 is the present value of \$105 to be received in one year at a discount rate of 5 percent.

Given a future cash flow that is to be received in $N$ periods and an interest rate per period of $r$, we can use the formula for future value to solve directly for the present value as follows:

$$FV_N = PV(1 + r)^N$$

$$PV = FV_N \left[ \frac{1}{(1 + r)^N} \right]$$

$$PV = FV_N(1 + r)^{-N} \tag{5-8}$$

We see from Equation 5-8 that the present value factor, $(1 + r)^{-N}$, is the reciprocal of the future value factor, $(1 + r)^N$.

### EXAMPLE 8

#### The Present Value of a Lump Sum

An insurance company has issued a Guaranteed Investment Contract (GIC) that promises to pay \$100,000 in six years with an 8 percent return rate. What amount of money must the insurer invest today at 8 percent for six years to make the promised payment?

**Solution:** We can use Equation 5-8 to find the present value using the following data:

$$FV_N = \$100,000$$

$$r = 8\% = 0.08$$

$$N = 6$$

$$PV = FV_N(1 + r)^{-N}$$

$$= \$100,000\left[\frac{1}{(1.08)^6}\right]$$

$$= \$100,000(0.6301696)$$

$$= \$63,016.96$$

We can say that \$63,016.96 today, with an interest rate of 8 percent, is equivalent to \$100,000 to be received in six years. Discounting the \$100,000 makes a future \$100,000 equivalent to \$63,016.96 when allowance is made for the time value of money. As the time line in Figure 4 shows, the \$100,000 has been discounted six full periods.

**FIGURE 4    The Present Value of a Lump Sum to Be Received at Time _t_ = 6**

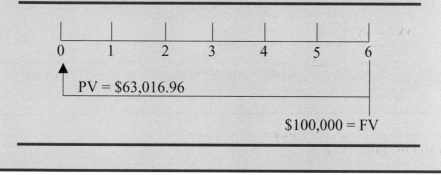

## EXAMPLE 9

### The Projected Present Value of a More Distant Future Lump Sum

Suppose you own a liquid financial asset that will pay you \$100,000 in 10 years from today. Your daughter plans to attend college four years from today, and you want to know what the asset's present value will be at that time. Given an 8 percent discount rate, what will the asset be worth four years from today?

**Solution:** The value of the asset is the present value of the asset's promised payment. At $t = 4$, the cash payment will be received six years later. With this information, you can solve for the value four years from today using Equation 5-8:

$$FV_N = \$100,000$$

$$r = 8\% = 0.08$$

$$N = 6$$

$$PV = FV_N(1 + r)^{-N}$$

$$= \$100,000 \frac{1}{(1.08)^6}$$

$$= \$100,000(0.6301696)$$

$$= \$63,016.96$$

**FIGURE 5     The Relationship between Present Value and Future Value**

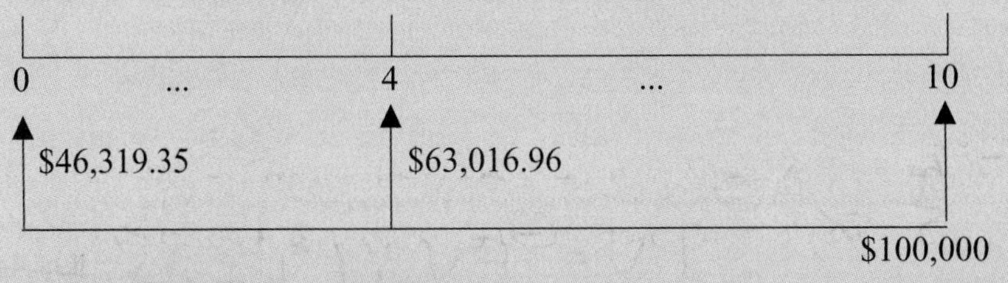

| 0 | ... | 4 | ... | 10 |

$46,319.35                    $63,016.96

$100,000

The time line in Figure 5 shows the future payment of $100,000 that is to be received at $t = 10$. The time line also shows the values at $t = 4$ and at $t = 0$. Relative to the payment at $t = 10$, the amount at $t = 4$ is a projected present value, while the amount at $t = 0$ is the present value (as of today).

Present value problems require an evaluation of the present value factor, $(1 + r)^{-N}$. Present values relate to the discount rate and the number of periods in the following ways:

► For a given discount rate, the farther in the future the amount to be received, the smaller that amount's present value.

► Holding time constant, the larger the discount rate, the smaller the present value of a future amount.

## 5.2   The Frequency of Compounding

Recall that interest may be paid semiannually, quarterly, monthly, or even daily. To handle interest payments made more than once a year, we can modify the present value formula (Equation 5-8) as follows. Recall that $r_s$ is the quoted interest rate and equals the periodic interest rate multiplied by the number of compounding periods in each year. In general, with more than one compounding period in a year, we can express the formula for present value as

$$PV = FV_N \left(1 + \frac{r_s}{m}\right)^{-mN}$$

**(5-9)**

where

    $m$ = number of compounding periods per year

    $r_s$ = quoted annual interest rate

    $N$ = number of years

The formula in Equation 5-9 is quite similar to that in Equation 5-8. As we have already noted, present value and future value factors are reciprocals. Changing the frequency of compounding does not alter this result. The only difference is the use of the periodic interest rate and the corresponding number of compounding periods.

    The following example illustrates Equation 5-9.

## EXAMPLE 10

### The Present Value of a Lump Sum with Monthly Compounding

The manager of a Canadian pension fund knows that the fund must make a lump-sum payment of C\$5 million 10 years from now. She wants to invest an amount today in a GIC so that it will grow to the required amount. The current interest rate on GICs is 6 percent a year, compounded monthly. How much should she invest today in the GIC?

**Solution:** Use Equation 5-9 to find the required present value:

$$FV_N = \text{C\$}5,000,000$$
$$r_s = 6\% = 0.06$$
$$m = 12$$
$$r_s/m = 0.06/12 = 0.005$$
$$N = 10$$
$$mN = 12(10) = 120$$
$$PV = FV_N \left(1 + \frac{r_s}{m}\right)^{-mN}$$
$$= \text{C\$}5,000,000(1.005)^{-120}$$
$$= \text{C\$}5,000,000(0.549633)$$
$$= \text{C\$}2,748,163.67$$

In applying Equation 5-9, we use the periodic rate (in this case, the monthly rate) and the appropriate number of periods with monthly compounding (in this case, 10 years of monthly compounding, or 120 periods).

## 6    THE PRESENT VALUE
## OF A SERIES OF CASH FLOWS

Many applications in investment management involve assets that offer a series of cash flows over time. The cash flows may be highly uneven, relatively even, or equal. They may occur over relatively short periods of time, longer periods of time, or even stretch on indefinitely. In this section, we discuss how to find the present value of a series of cash flows.

### 6.1 The Present Value of a Series of Equal Cash Flows

We begin with an ordinary annuity. Recall that an ordinary annuity has equal annuity payments, with the first payment starting one period into the future. In total, the annuity makes $N$ payments, with the first payment at $t = 1$ and the last at $t = N$. We can express the present value of an ordinary annuity as the sum of the present values of each individual annuity payment, as follows:

$$\text{PV} = \frac{A}{(1 + r)} + \frac{A}{(1 + r)^2} + \frac{A}{(1 + r)^3} + \ldots + \frac{A}{(1 + r)^{N-1}} + \frac{A}{(1 + r)^N} \quad \textbf{(5-10)}$$

where

> $A$ = the annuity amount
>
> $r$ = the interest rate per period corresponding to the frequency of annuity payments (for example, annual, quarterly, or monthly)
>
> $N$ = the number of annuity payments

Because the annuity payment ($A$) is a constant in this equation, it can be factored out as a common term. Thus the sum of the interest factors has a shortcut expression:

$$\text{PV} = A \left[ \frac{1 - \dfrac{1}{(1 + r)^N}}{r} \right] \quad \textbf{(5-11)}$$

In much the same way that we computed the future value of an ordinary annuity, we find the present value by multiplying the annuity amount by a present value annuity factor (the term in brackets in Equation 5-11).

---

### EXAMPLE 11

**The Present Value of an Ordinary Annuity**

Suppose you are considering purchasing a financial asset that promises to pay €1,000 per year for five years, with the first payment one year from now. The required rate of return is 12 percent per year. How much should you pay for this asset?

---

**Solution:** To find the value of the financial asset, use the formula for the present value of an ordinary annuity given in Equation 5-11 with the following data:

$$A = €1,000$$

$$r = 12\% = 0.12$$

$$N = 5$$

$$PV = A\left[\frac{1 - \dfrac{1}{(1 + r)^N}}{r}\right]$$

$$= €1,000\left[\frac{1 - \dfrac{1}{(1.12)^5}}{0.12}\right]$$

$$= €1,000(3.604776)$$

$$= €3,604.78$$

The series of cash flows of €1,000 per year for five years is currently worth €3,604.78 when discounted at 12 percent.

Keeping track of the actual calendar time brings us to a specific type of annuity with level payments: the annuity due. An annuity due has its first payment occurring today ($t = 0$). In total, the annuity due will make $N$ payments. Figure 6 presents the time line for an annuity due that makes four payments of $100.

**FIGURE 6    An Annuity Due of $100 per Period**

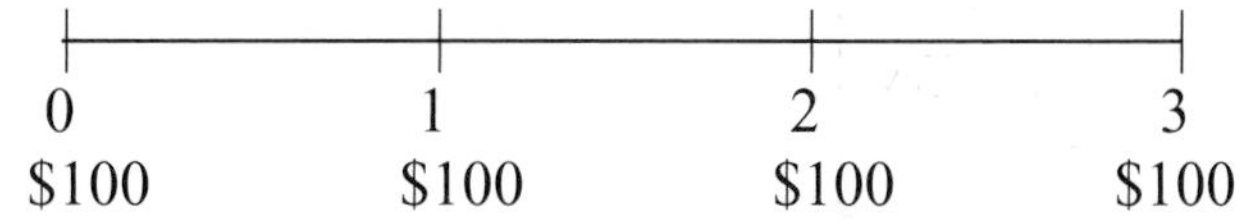

| 0 | 1 | 2 | 3 |
|---|---|---|---|
| $100 | $100 | $100 | $100 |

As Figure 6 shows, we can view the four-period annuity due as the sum of two parts: a $100 lump sum today and an ordinary annuity of $100 per period for three periods. At a 12 percent discount rate, the four $100 cash flows in this annuity due example will be worth $340.18.[6]

Expressing the value of the future series of cash flows in today's dollars gives us a convenient way of comparing annuities. The next example illustrates this approach.

---

[6] There is an alternative way to calculate the present value of an annuity due. Compared to an ordinary annuity, the payments in an annuity due are each discounted one less period. Therefore, we can modify Equation 5-11 to handle annuities due by multiplying the right-hand side of the equation by $(1 + r)$:

$$PV(\text{Annuity due}) = A\{[1 - (1 + r)^{-N}]/r\}(1 + r).$$

## EXAMPLE 12

### The Present Value of an Immediate Cash Flow Plus an Ordinary Annuity

You are retiring today and must choose to take your retirement benefits either as a lump sum or as an annuity. Your company's benefits officer presents you with two alternatives: an immediate lump sum of $2 million or an annuity with 20 payments of $200,000 a year with the first payment starting today. The interest rate at your bank is 7 percent per year compounded annually. Which option has the greater present value? (Ignore any tax differences between the two options.)

**Solution:** To compare the two options, find the present value of each at time $t = 0$ and choose the one with the larger value. The first option's present value is $2 million, already expressed in today's dollars. The second option is an annuity due. Because the first payment occurs at $t = 0$, you can separate the annuity benefits into two pieces: an immediate $200,000 to be paid today ($t = 0$) and an ordinary annuity of $200,000 per year for 19 years. To value this option, you need to find the present value of the ordinary annuity using Equation 5-11 and then add $200,000 to it.

$$
\begin{aligned}
A &= \$200,000 \\
N &= 19 \\
r &= 7\% = 0.07 \\
PV &= A\left[\frac{1 - \dfrac{1}{(1 + r)^N}}{r}\right] \\
&= \$200,000\left[\frac{1 - \dfrac{1}{(1.07)^{19}}}{0.07}\right] \\
&= \$200,000(10.335595) \\
&= \$2,067,119.05
\end{aligned}
$$

The 19 payments of $200,000 have a present value of $2,067,119.05. Adding the initial payment of $200,000 to $2,067,119.05, we find that the total value of the annuity option is $2,267,119.05. The present value of the annuity is greater than the lump sum alternative of $2 million.

We now look at another example reiterating the equivalence of present and future values.

**EXAMPLE 13**

### The Projected Present Value of an Ordinary Annuity

A German pension fund manager anticipates that benefits of €1 million per year must be paid to retirees. Retirements will not occur until 10 years from now at time $t = 10$. Once benefits begin to be paid, they will extend until $t = 39$ for a total of 30 payments. What is the present value of the pension liability if the appropriate annual discount rate for plan liabilities is 5 percent compounded annually?

**Solution:** This problem involves an annuity with the first payment at $t = 10$. From the perspective of $t = 9$, we have an ordinary annuity with 30 payments. We can compute the present value of this annuity with Equation 5-11 and then look at it on a time line.

$$A = €1,000,000$$

$$r = 5\% = 0.05$$

$$N = 30$$

$$PV = A\left[\frac{1 - \dfrac{1}{(1 + r)^N}}{r}\right]$$

$$= €1,000,000\left[\frac{1 - \dfrac{1}{(1.05)^{30}}}{0.05}\right]$$

$$= €1,000,000(15.372451)$$

$$= €15,372,451.03$$

**FIGURE 7    The Present Value of an Ordinary Annuity
with First Payment at Time $t = 10$ (in Millions)**

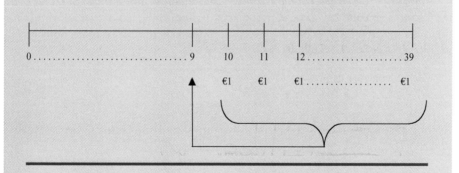

On the time line, we have shown the pension payments of €1 million extending from $t = 10$ to $t = 39$. The bracket and arrow indicate the process of finding the present value of the annuity, discounted back to $t = 9$. The present value of the pension benefits as of $t = 9$ is €15,372,451.03. The problem is to find the present value today (at $t = 0$).

Now we can rely on the equivalence of present value and future value. As Figure 7 shows, we can view the amount at $t = 9$ as a future value from the vantage point of $t = 0$. We compute the present value of the amount at $t = 9$ as follows:

$$FV_N = €15{,}372{,}451.03 \text{ (the present value at } t = 9)$$

$$N = 9$$

$$r = 5\% = 0.05$$

$$
\begin{aligned}
PV &= FV_N(1 + r)^{-N} \\
&= €15{,}372{,}451.03 \, (1.05)^{-9} \\
&= €15{,}372{,}451.03 \, (0.644609) \\
&= €9{,}909{,}219.00
\end{aligned}
$$

The present value of the pension liability is €9,909,219.00.

Example 13 illustrates three procedures emphasized in this reading:

► finding the present or future value of any cash flow series;

► recognizing the equivalence of present value and appropriately discounted future value; and

► keeping track of the actual calendar time in a problem involving the time value of money.

## 6.2 The Present Value of an Infinite Series of Equal Cash Flows—Perpetuity

Consider the case of an ordinary annuity that extends indefinitely. Such an ordinary annuity is called a perpetuity (a perpetual annuity). To derive a formula for the present value of a perpetuity, we can modify Equation 5-10 to account for an infinite series of cash flows:

$$PV = A \sum_{t=1}^{\infty} \left[ \frac{1}{(1 + r)^t} \right] \tag{5-12}$$

As long as interest rates are positive, the sum of present value factors converges and

$$PV = \frac{A}{r} \tag{5-13}$$

To see this, look back at Equation 5-11, the expression for the present value of an ordinary annuity. As $N$ (the number of periods in the annuity) goes to infinity, the term $1/(1 + r)^N$ approaches 0 and Equation 5-11 simplifies to Equation 5-13. This equation will reappear when we value dividends from stocks because stocks have no predefined life span. (A stock paying constant dividends is similar to a perpetuity.) With the first payment a year from now, a perpetuity of $10 per year with a 20 percent required rate of return has a present value of $10/0.2 = $50.

Equation 5-13 is valid only for a perpetuity with level payments. In our development above, the first payment occurred at $t = 1$; therefore, we compute the present value as of $t = 0$.

Other assets also come close to satisfying the assumptions of a perpetuity. Certain government bonds and preferred stocks are typical examples of financial assets that make level payments for an indefinite period of time.

## EXAMPLE 14

### The Present Value of a Perpetuity

The British government once issued a type of security called a consol bond, which promised to pay a level cash flow indefinitely. If a consol bond paid £100 per year in perpetuity, what would it be worth today if the required rate of return were 5 percent?

**Solution:** To answer this question, we can use Equation 5-13 with the following data:

$$A = £100$$
$$r = 5\% = 0.05$$
$$PV = A/r$$
$$= £100/0.05$$
$$= £2,000$$

The bond would be worth £2,000.

## 6.3 Present Values Indexed at Times Other than $t = 0$

In practice with investments, analysts frequently need to find present values indexed at times other than $t = 0$. Subscripting the present value and evaluating a perpetuity beginning with $100 payments in Year 2, we find $PV_1 = \$100/0.05 = \$2,000$ at a 5 percent discount rate. Further, we can calculate today's PV as $PV_0 = \$2,000/1.05 = \$1,904.76$.

Consider a similar situation in which cash flows of $6 per year begin at the end of the 4th year and continue at the end of each year thereafter, with the last cash flow at the end of the 10th year. From the perspective of the end of the third year, we are facing a typical seven-year ordinary annuity. We can find the present value of the annuity from the perspective of the end of the third year and then discount that present value back to the present. At an interest rate of 5 percent, the cash flows of $6 per year starting at the end of the fourth year will be worth $34.72 at the end of the third year ($t = 3$) and $29.99 today ($t = 0$).

The next example illustrates the important concept that an annuity or perpetuity beginning sometime in the future can be expressed in present value terms one period prior to the first payment. That present value can then be discounted back to today's present value.

**EXAMPLE 15**

### The Present Value of a Projected Perpetuity

Consider a level perpetuity of £100 per year with its first payment beginning at $t = 5$. What is its present value today (at $t = 0$), given a 5 percent discount rate?

**Solution:** First, we find the present value of the perpetuity at $t = 4$ and then discount that amount back to $t = 0$. (Recall that a perpetuity or an ordinary annuity has its first payment one period away, explaining the $t = 4$ index for our present value calculation.)

i.  Find the present value of the perpetuity at $t = 4$:

$$A = £100$$

$$r = 5\% = 0.05$$

$$\begin{aligned} PV &= A/r \\ &= £100/0.05 \\ &= £2,000 \end{aligned}$$

ii.  Find the present value of the future amount at $t = 4$. From the perspective of $t = 0$, the present value of £2,000 can be considered a future value. Now we need to find the present value of a lump sum:

$$FV_N = £2,000 \text{ (the present value at } t = 4)$$

$$r = 5\% = 0.05$$

$$N = 4$$

$$\begin{aligned} PV &= FV_N (1 + r)^{-N} \\ &= £2,000(1.05)^{-4} \\ &= £2,000(0.822702) \\ &= £1,645.40 \end{aligned}$$

Today's present value of the perpetuity is £1,645.40.

As discussed earlier, an annuity is a series of payments of a fixed amount for a specified number of periods. Suppose we own a perpetuity. At the same time, we issue a perpetuity obligating us to make payments; these payments are the same size as those of the perpetuity we own. However, the first payment of the perpetuity we issue is at $t = 5$; payments then continue on forever. The payments on this second perpetuity exactly offset the payments received from the perpetuity we own at $t = 5$ and all subsequent dates. We are left with level nonzero net cash flows at $t = 1, 2, 3$, and 4. This outcome exactly fits the definition of an annuity with four payments. Thus we can construct an annuity as the difference between two perpetuities with equal, level payments but differing starting dates. The next example illustrates this result.

**EXAMPLE 16**

**The Present Value of an Ordinary Annuity
as the Present Value of a Current Minus Projected Perpetuity**

Given a 5 percent discount rate, find the present value of a four-year ordinary annuity of £100 per year starting in Year 1 as the difference between the following two level perpetuities:

Perpetuity 1    £100 per year starting in Year 1 (first payment at $t = 1$)

Perpetuity 2    £100 per year starting in Year 5 (first payment at $t = 5$)

**Solution:** If we subtract Perpetuity 2 from Perpetuity 1, we are left with an ordinary annuity of £100 per period for four years (payments at $t = 1, 2, 3, 4$). Subtracting the present value of Perpetuity 2 from that of Perpetuity 1, we arrive at the present value of the four-year ordinary annuity:

i. $PV_0(\text{Perpetuity 1}) = £100/0.05 = £2,000$

ii. $PV_4(\text{Perpetuity 2}) = £100/0.05 = £2,000$

iii. $PV_0(\text{Perpetuity 2}) = £2,000/(1.05)^4 = £1,645.40$

iv. $PV_0(\text{Annuity}) \quad = PV_0(\text{Perpetuity 1}) - PV_0(\text{Perpetuity 2})$

$\qquad\qquad\qquad\quad = £2,000 - £1,645.40$

$\qquad\qquad\qquad\quad = £354.60$

The four-year ordinary annuity's present value is equal to £2,000 − £1,645.40 = £354.60.

## 6.4 The Present Value of a Series of Unequal Cash Flows

When we have unequal cash flows, we must first find the present value of each individual cash flow and then sum the respective present values. For a series with many cash flows, we usually use a spreadsheet. Table 3 lists a series of cash flows with the time periods in the first column, cash flows in the second column, and each cash flow's present value in the third column. The last row of Table 3 shows the sum of the five present values.

**TABLE 3  A Series of Unequal Cash Flows and Their Present Values at 5 Percent**

| Time Period | Cash Flow | Present Value at Year 0 | |
|:---:|:---:|:---|:---:|
| 1 | $1,000 | $1,000(1.05)^{-1} = | $952.38 |
| 2 | $2,000 | $2,000(1.05)^{-2} = | $1,814.06 |
| 3 | $4,000 | $4,000(1.05)^{-3} = | $3,455.35 |
| 4 | $5,000 | $5,000(1.05)^{-4} = | $4,113.51 |
| 5 | $6,000 | $6,000(1.05)^{-5} = | $4,701.16 |
| | | Sum = | $15,036.46 |

We could calculate the future value of these cash flows by computing them one at a time using the single-payment future value formula. We already know the present value of this series, however, so we can easily apply time-value equivalence. The future value of the series of cash flows from Table 2, $19,190.76, is equal to the single $15,036.46 amount compounded forward to $t = 5$:

$$PV = \$15,036.46$$

$$N = 5$$

$$r = 5\% = 0.05$$

$$\begin{aligned} FV_N &= PV(1 + r)^N \\ &= \$15,036.46(1.05)^5 \\ &= \$15,036.46(1.276282) \\ &= \$19,190.76 \end{aligned}$$

## 7    SOLVING FOR RATES, NUMBER OF PERIODS, OR SIZE OF ANNUITY PAYMENTS

In the previous examples, certain pieces of information have been made available. For instance, all problems have given the rate of interest, $r$, the number of time periods, $N$, the annuity amount, $A$, and either the present value, PV, or future value, FV. In real-world applications, however, although the present and future values may be given, you may have to solve for either the interest rate, the number of periods, or the annuity amount. In the subsections that follow, we show these types of problems.

## 7.1 Solving for Interest Rates and Growth Rates

Suppose a bank deposit of €100 is known to generate a payoff of €111 in one year. With this information, we can infer the interest rate that separates the present value of €100 from the future value of €111 by using Equation 5-2, $FV_N = PV(1 + r)^N$, with $N = 1$. With PV, FV, and $N$ known, we can solve for $r$ directly:

$$1 + r = FV/PV$$

$$1 + r = €111/€100 = 1.11$$

$$r = 0.11, \text{ or } 11\%$$

The interest rate that equates €100 at $t = 0$ to €111 at $t = 1$ is 11 percent. Thus we can state that €100 grows to €111 with a growth rate of 11 percent.

As this example shows, an interest rate can also be considered a growth rate. The particular application will usually dictate whether we use the term "interest rate" or "growth rate." Solving Equation 5-2 for $r$ and replacing the interest rate $r$ with the growth rate $g$ produces the following expression for determining growth rates:

$$g = (FV_N/PV)^{1/N} - 1 \qquad \textbf{(5-14)}$$

Below are two examples that use the concept of a growth rate.

---

### EXAMPLE 17

**Calculating a Growth Rate (1)**

For 1998, Limited Brands, Inc., recorded net sales of $8,436 million. For 2002, Limited Brands recorded net sales of $8,445 million, only slightly higher than in 1998. Over the four-year period from the end of 1998 to the end of 2002, what was the rate of growth of Limited Brands' net sales?

**Solution:** To solve this problem, we can use Equation 5-14, $g = (FV_N/PV)^{1/N} - 1$. We denote net sales in 1998 as PV and net sales in 2002 as $FV_4$. We can then solve for the growth rate as follows:

$$g = \sqrt[4]{\$8,445/\$8,436} - 1$$
$$= \sqrt[4]{1.001067} - 1$$
$$= 1.000267 - 1$$
$$= 0.000267$$

The calculated growth rate of approximately 0.03 percent a year, barely more than zero, confirms the initial impression that Limited Brands' net sales were essentially flat during the 1998–2002 period.

---

**EXAMPLE 18**

### Calculating a Growth Rate (2)

In Example 17, we found that Limited Brands' compound growth rate of net sales was close to zero for 1998 to 2002. As a retailer, Limited Brands' sales depend both on the number of stores (or selling square feet or meters) and sales per store (or sales per average selling square foot or meter). In fact, Limited Brands decreased its number of stores during the 1998–2002 period. In 1998, Limited Brands operated 5,382 stores, whereas in 2002 it operated 4,036 stores. In this case, we can speak of a positive compound rate of decrease or a negative compound growth rate. What was the growth rate in number of stores operated?

**Solution:** Using Equation 5-14, we find

$$
\begin{aligned}
g &= \sqrt[4]{4{,}036/5{,}382} - 1 \\
  &= \sqrt[4]{0.749907} - 1 \\
  &= 0.930576 - 1 \\
  &= -0.069424
\end{aligned}
$$

The rate of growth in stores operated was approximately −6.9 percent during the 1998–2002 period. Note that we can also refer to −6.9 percent as the compound annual growth rate because it is the single number that compounds the number of stores in 1998 forward to the number of stores in 2002. Table 4 lists the number of stores operated by Limited Brands from 1998 to 2002.

| Table 4 | Number of Limited Brands Stores, 1998–2002 | | |
|---|---|---|---|
| Year | Number of Stores | $(1 + g)_t$ | $t$ |
| 1998 | 5,382 | | 0 |
| 1999 | 5,023 | 5,023/5,382 = 0.933296 | 1 |
| 2000 | 5,129 | 5,129/5,023 = 1.021103 | 2 |
| 2001 | 4,614 | 4,614/5,129 = 0.899591 | 3 |
| 2002 | 4,036 | 4,036/4,614 = 0.874729 | 4 |

*Source*: www.limited.com.

Table 4 also shows 1 plus the one-year growth rate in number of stores. We can compute the 1 plus four-year cumulative growth in number of stores from 1998 to 2002 as the product of quantities (1 + one-year growth rate). We arrive at the same result as when we divide the ending number of stores, 4,036, by the beginning number of stores, 5,382:

$$\frac{4,036}{5,382} = \left(\frac{5,023}{5,382}\right)\left(\frac{5,129}{5,023}\right)\left(\frac{4,614}{5,129}\right)\left(\frac{4,036}{4,614}\right)$$
$$= (1 + g_1)(1 + g_2)(1 + g_3)(1 + g_4)$$
$$0.749907 = (0.933296)(1.021103)(0.899591)(0.874729)$$

The right-hand side of the equation is the product of 1 plus the one-year growth rate in number of stores operated for each year. Recall that, using Equation 5-14, we took the fourth root of $4,036/5,382 = 0.749907$. In effect, we were solving for the single value of $g$ which, when compounded over four periods, gives the correct product of 1 plus the one-year growth rates.[7]

In conclusion, we do not need to compute intermediate growth rates as in Table 4 to solve for a compound growth rate $g$. Sometimes, however, the intermediate growth rates are interesting or informative. For example, during one year (2000), Limited Brands increased its number of stores. We can also analyze the variability in growth rates when we conduct an analysis as in Table 4. How did Limited Brands maintain approximately the same revenues during the period although it operated increasingly fewer stores? Elsewhere in Limited Brands' disclosures, the company noted that its sales per average selling square foot increased during the period.

The compound growth rate is an excellent summary measure of growth over multiple time periods. In our Limited Brands example, the compound growth rate of $-6.9$ percent is the single growth rate that, when added to 1, compounded over four years, and multiplied by the 1998 number of stores operated, yields the 2002 number of stores operated.

## 7.2 Solving for the Number of Periods

In this section, we demonstrate how to solve for the number of periods given present value, future value, and interest or growth rates.

**EXAMPLE 19**

**The Number of Annual Compounding Periods Needed for an Investment to Reach a Specific Value**

You are interested in determining how long it will take an investment of €10,000,000 to double in value. The current interest rate is 7 percent

---

[7] The compound growth rate that we calculate here is an example of a geometric mean, specifically the geometric mean of the growth rates. We define the geometric mean in the reading on statistical concepts.

compounded annually. How many years will it take €10,000,000 to double to €20,000,000?

**Solution:** Use Equation 5-2, $FV_N = PV(1 + r)^N$, to solve for the number of periods, $N$, as follows:

$$(1 + r)^N = FV_N/PV = 2$$

$$N \ln(1 + r) = \ln(2)$$

$$N = \ln(2)/\ln(1 + r)$$
$$= \ln(2)/\ln(1.07) = 10.24$$

With an interest rate of 7 percent, it will take approximately 10 years for the initial €10,000,000 investment to grow to €20,000,000. Solving for $N$ in the expression $(1.07)^N = 2.0$ requires taking the natural logarithm of both sides and using the rule that $\ln(x^N) = N\ln(x)$. Generally, we find that $N = [\ln(FV/PV)]/\ln(1 + r)$. Here, $N = \ln(€20,000,000/€10,000,000/\ln(1.07) = \ln(2)/\ln(1.07) = 10.24$.[8]

## 7.3 Solving for the Size of Annuity Payments

In this section, we discuss how to solve for annuity payments. Mortgages, auto loans, and retirement savings plans are classic examples of applications of annuity formulas.

### EXAMPLE 20

**The Annuity Payments Needed to Reach a Future Value with Monthly Compounding**

You are planning to purchase a $120,000 house by making a down payment of $20,000 and borrowing the remainder with a 30-year fixed-rate mortgage with monthly payments. The first payment is due at $t = 1$. Current mortgage interest rates are quoted at 8 percent with monthly compounding. What will your monthly mortgage payments be?

**Solution:** The bank will determine the mortgage payments such that at the stated periodic interest rate, the present value of the payments will be

---

[8] To quickly approximate the number of periods, practitioners sometimes use an ad hoc rule called the **Rule of 72**: Divide 72 by the stated interest rate to get the approximate number of years it would take to double an investment at the interest rate. Here, the approximation gives $72/7 = 10.3$ years. The Rule of 72 is loosely based on the observation that it takes 12 years to double an amount at a 6 percent interest rate, giving $6 \times 12 = 72$. At a 3 percent rate, one would guess it would take twice as many years, $3 \times 24 = 72$.

equal to the amount borrowed (in this case, $100,000). With this fact in mind, we can use Equation 5-11,

$$PV = A \left[ \frac{1 - \frac{1}{(1 + r)^N}}{r} \right], \text{ to solve for the annuity amount, } A, \text{ as the present}$$

value divided by the present value annuity factor:

$$PV = \$100,000$$
$$r_s = 8\% = 0.08$$
$$m = 12$$
$$r_s/m = 0.08/12 = 0.006667$$
$$N = 30$$
$$mN = 12 \times 30 = 360$$

$$\text{Present value annuity factor} = \frac{1 - \frac{1}{[1 + (r_s/m)]^{mN}}}{r_s/m} = \frac{1 - \frac{1}{(1.006667)^{360}}}{0.006667}$$
$$= 136.283494$$

$$A = PV/\text{Present value annuity factor}$$
$$= \$100,000/136.283494$$
$$= \$733.76$$

The amount borrowed, $100,000, is equivalent to 360 monthly payments of $733.76 with a stated interest rate of 8 percent. The mortgage problem is a relatively straightforward application of finding a level annuity payment.

Next, we turn to a retirement-planning problem. This problem illustrates the complexity of the situation in which an individual wants to retire with a specified retirement income. Over the course of a life cycle, the individual may be able to save only a small amount during the early years but then may have the financial resources to save more during later years. Savings plans often involve uneven cash flows, a topic we will examine in the last part of this reading. When dealing with uneven cash flows, we take maximum advantage of the principle that dollar amounts indexed at the same point in time are additive—the **cash flow additivity principle**.

## EXAMPLE 21

### The Projected Annuity Amount Needed to Fund a Future-Annuity Inflow

Jill Grant is 22 years old (at $t = 0$) and is planning for her retirement at age 63 (at $t = 41$). She plans to save $2,000 per year for the next 15 years ($t = 1$ to $t = 15$). She wants to have retirement income of $100,000 per year for 20 years, with the first retirement payment starting at $t = 41$. How much must Grant save each year from $t = 16$ to $t = 40$ in order to achieve her retirement goal? Assume she plans to invest in a diversified stock-and-bond mutual fund that will earn 8 percent per year on average.

**Solution:** To help solve this problem, we set up the information on a time line. As Figure 8 shows, Grant will save $2,000 (an outflow) each year for Years 1 to 15. Starting in Year 41, Grant will start to draw retirement income of $100,000 per year for 20 years. In the time line, the annual savings is recorded in parentheses ($2) to show that it is an outflow. The problem is to find the savings, recorded as X, from Year 16 to Year 40.

### FIGURE 8    Solving for Missing Annuity Payments (in Thousands)

| 0 | 1 | 2 | 15 | 16 | 17 | 40 | 41 | 42 | 60 |
|---|---|---|----|----|----|----|----|----|----|
|   | ($2) | ($2) ... ($2) | | (X) | (X) ... (X) | | $100 | $100 ... $100 | |

Solving this problem involves satisfying the following relationship: the present value of savings (outflows) equals the present value of retirement income (inflows). We could bring all the dollar amounts to $t = 40$ or to $t = 15$ and solve for X.

Let us evaluate all dollar amounts at $t = 15$ (we encourage the reader to repeat the problem by bringing all cash flows to $t = 40$). As of $t = 15$, the first payment of X will be one period away (at $t = 16$). Thus we can value the stream of Xs using the formula for the present value of an ordinary annuity.

This problem involves three series of level cash flows. The basic idea is that the present value of the retirement income must equal the present value of Grant's savings. Our strategy requires the following steps:

1. Find the future value of the savings of $2,000 per year and index it at $t = 15$. This value tells us how much Grant will have saved.

2. Find the present value of the retirement income at $t = 15$. This value tells us how much Grant needs to meet her retirement goals (as of $t = 15$). Two substeps are necessary. First, calculate the present value of the annuity of $100,000 per year at $t = 40$. Use the formula for the present value of an annuity. (Note that the present value is indexed at $t = 40$ because the first payment is at $t = 41$.) Next, discount the present value back to $t = 15$ (a total of 25 periods).

3. Now compute the difference between the amount Grant has saved (Step 1) and the amount she needs to meet her retirement goals (Step 2). Her savings from $t = 16$ to $t = 40$ must have a present value equal to the difference between the future value of her savings and the present value of her retirement income.

Our goal is to determine the amount Grant should save in each of the 25 years from $t = 16$ to $t = 40$. We start by bringing the $2,000 savings to $t = 15$, as follows:

$$A = \$2,000$$

$$r = 8\% = 0.08$$

$$N = 15$$

$$\text{FV} = A\left[\frac{(1 + r)^N - 1}{r}\right]$$

$$= \$2,000\left[\frac{(1.08)^{15} - 1}{0.08}\right]$$

$$= \$2,000(27.152114)$$

$$= \$54,304.23$$

At $t = 15$, Grant's initial savings will have grown to \$54,304.23.

Now we need to know the value of Grant's retirement income at $t = 15$. As stated earlier, computing the retirement present value requires two substeps. First, find the present value at $t = 40$ with the formula in Equation 5-11; second, discount this present value back to $t = 15$. Now we can find the retirement income present value at $t = 40$:

$$A = \$100,000$$

$$r = 8\% = 0.08$$

$$N = 20$$

$$\text{PV} = A\left[\frac{1 - \dfrac{1}{(1 + r)^N}}{r}\right]$$

$$= \$100,000\left[\frac{1 - \dfrac{1}{(1.08)^{20}}}{0.08}\right]$$

$$= \$100,000(9.818147)$$

$$= \$981,814.74$$

The present value amount is as of $t = 40$, so we must now discount it back as a lump sum to $t = 15$:

$$\text{FV}_N = \$981,814.74$$

$$N = 25$$

$$r = 8\% = 0.08$$

$$\text{PV} = \text{FV}_N(1 + r)^{-N}$$

$$= \$981,814.74(1.08)^{-25}$$

$$= \$981,814.74(0.146018)$$

$$= \$143,362.53$$

Now recall that Grant will have saved \$54,304.23 by $t = 15$. Therefore, in present value terms, the annuity from $t = 16$ to $t = 40$ must equal the difference between the amount already saved (\$54,304.23) and the amount required for retirement (\$143,362.53). This amount is equal to \$143,362.53 − \$54,304.23 = \$89,058.30. Therefore, we must now find the annuity payment, $A$, from $t = 16$ to $t = 40$ that has a present value of $89,058.30. We find the annuity payment as follows:

$$PV = \$89{,}058.30$$

$$r = 8\% = 0.08$$

$$N = 25$$

$$\text{Present value annuity factor} = \left[ \frac{1 - \dfrac{1}{(1 + r)^N}}{r} \right]$$

$$= \left[ \frac{1 - \dfrac{1}{(1.08)^{25}}}{0.08} \right]$$

$$= 10.674776$$

$$A = PV/\text{Present value annuity factor}$$

$$= \$89{,}058.30/10.674776$$

$$= \$8{,}342.87$$

Grant will need to increase her savings to $8,342.87 per year from $t = 16$ to $t = 40$ to meet her retirement goal of having a fund equal to $981,814.74 after making her last payment at $t = 40$.

## 7.4 Review of Present and Future Value Equivalence

As we have demonstrated, finding present and future values involves moving amounts of money to different points on a time line. These operations are possible because present value and future value are equivalent measures separated in time. Table 5 illustrates this equivalence; it lists the timing of five cash flows, their present values at $t = 0$, and their future values at $t = 5$.

To interpret Table 5, start with the third column, which shows the present values. Note that each $1,000 cash payment is discounted back the appropriate number of periods to find the present value at $t = 0$. The present value of

**TABLE 5 The Equivalence of Present and Future Values**

| Time | Cash Flow | Present Value at $t = 0$ | Future Value at $t = 5$ |
|---|---|---|---|
| 1 | $1,000 | $1,000(1.05)^{-1} = \$952.38$ | $1,000(1.05)^{4} = \$1{,}215.51$ |
| 2 | $1,000 | $1,000(1.05)^{-2} = \$907.03$ | $1,000(1.05)^{3} = \$1{,}157.63$ |
| 3 | $1,000 | $1,000(1.05)^{-3} = \$863.84$ | $1,000(1.05)^{2} = \$1{,}102.50$ |
| 4 | $1,000 | $1,000(1.05)^{-4} = \$822.70$ | $1,000(1.05)^{1} = \$1{,}050.00$ |
| 5 | $1,000 | $1,000(1.05)^{-5} = \$783.53$ | $1,000(1.05)^{0} = \$1{,}000.00$ |
| | | Sum: $4,329.48 | Sum: $5,525.64 |

$4,329.48 is exactly equivalent to the series of cash flows. This information illustrates an important point: A lump sum can actually generate an annuity. If we place a lump sum in an account that earns the stated interest rate for all periods, we can generate an annuity that is equivalent to the lump sum. Amortized loans, such as mortgages and car loans, are examples of this principle.

To see how a lump sum can fund an annuity, assume that we place $4,329.48 in the bank today at 5 percent interest. We can calculate the size of the annuity payments by using Equation 5-11. Solving for $A$, we find

$$A = \frac{PV}{\frac{1 - [1/(1 + r)^N]}{r}}$$

$$= \frac{\$4,329.48}{\frac{1 - [1/(1.05)^5]}{0.05}}$$

$$= \$1,000$$

Table 6 shows how the initial investment of $4,329.48 can actually generate five $1,000 withdrawals over the next five years.

To interpret Table 6, start with an initial present value of $4,329.48 at $t = 0$. From $t = 0$ to $t = 1$, the initial investment earns 5 percent interest, generating a future value of $4,329.48(1.05) = $4,545.95. We then withdraw $1,000 from our account, leaving $4,545.95 − $1,000 = $3,545.95 (the figure reported in the last column for time period 1). In the next period, we earn one year's worth of interest and then make a $1,000 withdrawal. After the fourth withdrawal, we have $952.38, which earns 5 percent. This amount then grows to $1,000 during the year, just enough for us to make the last withdrawal. Thus the initial present value, when invested at 5 percent for five years, generates the $1,000 five-year ordinary annuity. The present value of the initial investment is exactly equivalent to the annuity.

Now we can look at how future value relates to annuities. In Table 5, we reported that the future value of the annuity was $5,525.64. We arrived at this figure by compounding the first $1,000 payment forward four periods, the second $1,000 forward three periods, and so on. We then added the five future amounts at $t = 5$. The annuity is equivalent to $5,525.64 at $t = 5$ and $4,329.48 at $t = 0$. These two dollar measures are thus equivalent. We can verify the equivalence by finding the present value of $5,525.64, which is $5,525.64 \times (1.05)^{-5} = $4,329.48$. We found this result above when we showed that a lump sum can generate an annuity.

## TABLE 6 How an Initial Present Value Funds an Annuity

| Time Period | Amount Available at the Beginning of the Time Period | Ending Amount before Withdrawal | Withdrawal | Amount Available after Withdrawal |
|---|---|---|---|---|
| 1 | $4,329.48 | $4,329.48(1.05) = $4,545.95 | $1,000 | $3,545.95 |
| 2 | $3,545.95 | $3,545.95(1.05) = $3,723.25 | $1,000 | $2,723.25 |
| 3 | $2,723.25 | $2,723.25(1.05) = $2,859.41 | $1,000 | $1,859.41 |
| 4 | $1,859.41 | $1,859.41(1.05) = $1,952.38 | $1,000 | $952.38 |
| 5 | $952.38 | $952.38(1.05)    = $1,000 | $1,000 | $0 |

To summarize what we have learned so far: A lump sum can be seen as equivalent to an annuity, and an annuity can be seen as equivalent to its future value. Thus present values, future values, and a series of cash flows can all be considered equivalent as long as they are indexed at the same point in time.

## 7.5 The Cash Flow Additivity Principle

The cash flow additivity principle—the idea that amounts of money indexed at the same point in time are additive—is one of the most important concepts in time value of money mathematics. We have already mentioned and used this principle; this section provides a reference example for it.

Consider the two series of cash flows shown on the time line in Figure 9. The series are denoted A and B. If we assume that the annual interest rate is 2 percent, we can find the future value of each series of cash flows as follows. Series A's future value is $100(1.02) + $100 = $202. Series B's future value is $200(1.02) + $200 = $404. The future value of (A + B) is $202 + $404 = $606 by the method we have used up to this point. The alternative way to find the future value is to add the cash flows of each series, A and B (call it A + B), and then find the future value of the combined cash flow, as shown in Figure 9.

The third time line in Figure 9 shows the combined series of cash flows. Series A has a cash flow of $100 at $t = 1$, and Series B has a cash flow of $200 at $t = 1$. The combined series thus has a cash flow of $300 at $t = 1$. We can similarly calculate the cash flow of the combined series at $t = 2$. The future value of the combined series (A + B) is $300(1.02) + $300 = $606—the same result we found when we added the future values of each series.

The additivity and equivalence principles also appear in another common situation. Suppose cash flows are $4 at the end of the first year and $24 (actually separate payments of $4 and $20) at the end of the second year. Rather than finding present values of the first year's $4 and the second year's $24, we can treat this situation as a $4 annuity for two years and a second-year $20 lump sum. If the discount rate were 6 percent, the $4 annuity would have a present value of $7.33 and the $20 lump sum a present value of $17.80, for a total of $25.13.

## FIGURE 9    The Additivity of Two Series of Cash Flows

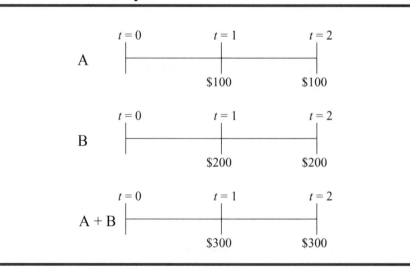

# SUMMARY

In this reading, we have explored a foundation topic in investment mathematics, the time value of money. We have developed and reviewed the following concepts for use in financial applications:

▶ The interest rate, $r$, is the required rate of return; $r$ is also called the discount rate or opportunity cost.

▶ An interest rate can be viewed as the sum of the real risk-free interest rate and a set of premiums that compensate lenders for risk: an inflation premium, a default risk premium, a liquidity premium, and a maturity premium.

▶ The future value, FV, is the present value, PV, times the future value factor, $(1 + r)^N$.

▶ The interest rate, $r$, makes current and future currency amounts equivalent based on their time value.

▶ The stated annual interest rate is a quoted interest rate that does not account for compounding within the year.

▶ The periodic rate is the quoted interest rate per period; it equals the stated annual interest rate divided by the number of compounding periods per year.

▶ The effective annual rate is the amount by which a unit of currency will grow in a year with interest on interest included.

▶ An annuity is a finite set of level sequential cash flows.

▶ There are two types of annuities, the annuity due and the ordinary annuity. The annuity due has a first cash flow that occurs immediately; the ordinary annuity has a first cash flow that occurs one period from the present (indexed at $t = 1$).

▶ On a time line, we can index the present as 0 and then display equally spaced hash marks to represent a number of periods into the future. This representation allows us to index how many periods away each cash flow will be paid.

▶ Annuities may be handled in a similar fashion as single payments if we use annuity factors instead of single-payment factors.

▶ The present value, PV, is the future value, FV, times the present value factor, $(1 + r)^{-N}$.

▶ The present value of a perpetuity is $A/r$, where $A$ is the periodic payment to be received forever.

▶ It is possible to calculate an unknown variable, given the other relevant variables in time value of money problems.

▶ The cash flow additivity principle can be used to solve problems with uneven cash flows by combining single payments and annuities.

## PRACTICE PROBLEMS FOR READING 5

**1.** The table below gives current information on the interest rates for two two-year and two eight-year maturity investments. The table also gives the maturity, liquidity, and default risk characteristics of a new investment possibility (Investment 3). All investments promise only a single payment (a payment at maturity). Assume that premiums relating to inflation, liquidity, and default risk are constant across all time horizons.

| Investment | Maturity (in Years) | Liquidity | Default Risk | Interest Rate (%) |
|---|---|---|---|---|
| 1 | 2 | High | Low | 2.0 |
| 2 | 2 | Low | Low | 2.5 |
| 3 | 7 | Low | Low | $r_3$ |
| 4 | 8 | High | Low | 4.0 |
| 5 | 8 | Low | High | 6.5 |

Based on the information in the above table, address the following:

**A.** Explain the difference between the interest rates on Investment 1 and Investment 2.

**B.** Estimate the default risk premium.

**C.** Calculate upper and lower limits for the interest rate on Investment 3, $r_3$.

**2.** A client has a $5 million portfolio and invests 5 percent of it in a money market fund projected to earn 3 percent annually. Estimate the value of this portion of his portfolio after seven years.

**3.** A client invests $500,000 in a bond fund projected to earn 7 percent annually. Estimate the value of her investment after 10 years.

**4.** For liquidity purposes, a client keeps $100,000 in a bank account. The bank quotes a stated annual interest rate of 7 percent. The bank's service representative explains that the stated rate is the rate one would earn if one were to cash out rather than invest the interest payments. How much will your client have in his account at the end of one year, assuming no additions or withdrawals, using the following types of compounding?

**A.** Quarterly.

**B.** Monthly.

**C.** Continuous.

**5.** A bank quotes a rate of 5.89 percent with an effective annual rate of 6.05 percent. Does the bank use annual, quarterly, or monthly compounding?

**6.** A bank pays a stated annual interest rate of 8 percent. What is the effective annual rate using the following types of compounding?

**A.** Quarterly.

**B.** Monthly.

**C.** Continuous.

**7.** A couple plans to set aside $20,000 per year in a conservative portfolio projected to earn 7 percent a year. If they make their first savings contribution one year from now, how much will they have at the end of 20 years?

**8.** Two years from now, a client will receive the first of three annual payments of $20,000 from a small business project. If she can earn 9 percent annually on her investments and plans to retire in six years, how much will the three business project payments be worth at the time of her retirement?

**9.** To cover the first year's total college tuition payments for his two children, a father will make a $75,000 payment five years from now. How much will he need to invest today to meet his first tuition goal if the investment earns 6 percent annually?

**10.** A client has agreed to invest €100,000 one year from now in a business planning to expand, and she has decided to set aside the funds today in a bank account that pays 7 percent compounded quarterly. How much does she need to set aside?

**11.** A client can choose between receiving 10 annual $100,000 retirement payments, starting one year from today, or receiving a lump sum today. Knowing that he can invest at a rate of 5 percent annually, he has decided to take the lump sum. What lump sum today will be equivalent to the future annual payments?

**12.** A perpetual preferred stock position pays quarterly dividends of $1,000 indefinitely (forever). If an investor has a required rate of return of 12 percent per year compounded quarterly on this type of investment, how much should he be willing to pay for this dividend stream?

**13.** At retirement, a client has two payment options: a 20-year annuity at €50,000 per year starting after one year or a lump sum of €500,000 today. If the client's required rate of return on retirement fund investments is 6 percent per year, which plan has the higher present value and by how much?

**14.** You are considering investing in two different instruments. The first instrument will pay nothing for three years, but then it will pay $20,000 per year for four years. The second instrument will pay $20,000 for three years and $30,000 in the fourth year. All payments are made at year-end. If your required rate of return on these investments is 8 percent annually, what should you be willing to pay for:

   **A.** The first instrument.

   **B.** The second instrument (use the formula for a four-year annuity).

**15.** Suppose you plan to send your daughter to college in three years. You expect her to earn two-thirds of her tuition payment in scholarship money, so you estimate that your payments will be $10,000 a year for four years. To estimate whether you have set aside enough money, you ignore possible inflation in tuition payments and assume that you can earn 8 percent annually on your investments. How much should you set aside now to cover these payments?

**16.** A client is confused about two terms on some certificate-of-deposit rates quoted at his bank in the United States. You explain that the stated annual interest rate is an annual rate that does not take into account compounding within a year. The rate his bank calls APY (annual percentage yield) is the effective annual rate taking into account compounding. The bank's customer service representative mentioned monthly compounding, with $1,000 becoming $1,061.68 at the end of a year. To prepare to explain the terms to your client, calculate the stated annual interest rate that the bank must be quoting.

**17.** A client seeking liquidity sets aside €35,000 in a bank account today. The account pays 5 percent compounded monthly. Because the client is concerned about the fact that deposit insurance covers the account for only up to €100,000, calculate how many months it will take to reach that amount.

**18.** A client plans to send a child to college for four years starting 18 years from now. Having set aside money for tuition, she decides to plan for room and board also. She estimates these costs at $20,000 per year, payable at the beginning of each year, by the time her child goes to college. If she starts next year and makes 17 payments into a savings account paying 5 percent annually, what annual payments must she make?

**19.** A couple plans to pay their child's college tuition for 4 years starting 18 years from now. The current annual cost of college is C$7,000, and they expect this cost to rise at an annual rate of 5 percent. In their planning, they assume that they can earn 6 percent annually. How much must they put aside each year, starting next year, if they plan to make 17 equal payments?

**20.** You are analyzing the last five years of earnings per share data for a company. The figures are $4.00, $4.50, $5.00, $6.00, and $7.00. At what compound annual rate did EPS grow during these years?

**21.** An analyst expects that a company's net sales will double and the company's net income will triple over the next five-year period starting now. Based on the analyst's expectations, which of the following *best* describes the expected compound annual growth?

  **A.** Net sales will grow 15% annually and net income will grow 25% annually.

  **B.** Net sales will grow 20% annually and net income will grow 40% annually.

  **C.** Net sales will grow 25% annually and net income will grow 50% annually.

# DISCOUNTED CASH FLOW APPLICATIONS

by Richard A. DeFusco, CFA, Dennis W. McLeavey, CFA,
Jerald E. Pinto, CFA, and David E. Runkle, CFA

## LEARNING OUTCOMES

| The candidate should be able to: | Mastery |
|---|---|
| **a.** calculate and interpret the net present value (NPV) and the internal rate of return (IRR) of an investment, contrast the NPV rule to the IRR rule, and identify problems associated with the IRR rule; | ☐ |
| **b.** define, calculate, and interpret a holding period return (total return); | ☐ |
| **c.** calculate, interpret, and distinguish between the money-weighted and time-weighted rates of return of a portfolio and appraise the performance of portfolios based on these measures; | ☐ |
| **d.** calculate and interpret the bank discount yield, holding period yield, effective annual yield, and money market yield for a U.S. Treasury bill; and convert among holding period yields, money market yields, effective annual yields, and bond equivalent yields. | ☐ |

## INTRODUCTION 1

As investment analysts, much of our work includes evaluating transactions involving present and future cash flows. In the reading on the time value of money (TVM), we presented the mathematics needed to solve those problems and illustrated the techniques for the major problem types. In this reading we turn to applications. Analysts must master the numerous applications of TVM or discounted cash flow analysis in equity, fixed income, and derivatives analysis as they study each of those topics individually. In this reading, we present a selection of important TVM applications: net present value and internal rate of return as tools for evaluating cash flow streams, portfolio return measurement, and the calculation of money market yields. Important in themselves, these applications also introduce concepts that reappear in many other investment contexts.

The reading is organized as follows. Section 2 introduces two key TVM concepts, net present value and internal rate of return. Building on these concepts, Section 3 discusses a key topic in investment management, portfolio return measurement. Investment managers often face the task of investing funds for the short term; to understand the choices available, they need to understand the calculation of money market yields. The reading thus concludes with a discussion of that topic in Section 4.

## 2 NET PRESENT VALUE AND INTERNAL RATE OF RETURN

In applying discounted cash flow analysis in all fields of finance, we repeatedly encounter two concepts, net present value and internal rate of return. In the following sections we present these keystone concepts.

We could explore the concepts of net present value and internal rate of return in many contexts, because their scope of application covers all areas of finance. Capital budgeting, however, can serve as a representative starting point. Capital budgeting is important not only in corporate finance but also in security analysis, because both equity and fixed income analysts must be able to assess how well managers are investing the assets of their companies. There are three chief areas of financial decision-making in most businesses. **Capital budgeting** is the allocation of funds to relatively long-range projects or investments. From the perspective of capital budgeting, a company is a portfolio of projects and investments. **Capital structure** is the choice of long-term financing for the investments the company wants to make. **Working capital management** is the management of the company's short-term assets (such as inventory) and short-term liabilities (such as money owed to suppliers).

### 2.1 Net Present Value and the Net Present Value Rule

Net present value (NPV) describes a way to characterize the value of an investment, and the net present value rule is a method for choosing among alternative investments. The **net present value** of an investment is the present value of its cash inflows minus the present value of its cash outflows. The word "net" in net present value refers to subtracting the present value of the investment's outflows (costs) from the present value of its inflows (benefits) to arrive at the net benefit.

The steps in computing NPV and applying the NPV rule are as follows:

1. Identify all cash flows associated with the investment—all inflows and outflows.[1]

2. Determine the appropriate discount rate or opportunity cost, $r$, for the investment project.[2]

---

[1] In developing cash flow estimates, we observe two principles. First, we include only the **incremental cash flows** resulting from undertaking the project; we do not include sunk costs (costs that have been committed prior to the project). Second, we account for tax effects by using after-tax cash flows. For a full discussion of these and other issues in capital budgeting, see Brealey and Myers (2003).

[2] The **weighted-average cost of capital** (WACC) is often used to discount cash flows. This value is a weighted average of the after-tax required rates of return on the company's common stock, preferred stock, and long-term debt, where the weights are the fraction of each source of financing in the company's target capital structure. For a full discussion of the issues surrounding the cost of capital, see Brealey and Myers (2003).

3. Using that discount rate, find the present value of each cash flow. (Inflows have a positive sign and increase NPV; outflows have a negative sign and decrease NPV.)

4. Sum all present values. The sum of the present values of all cash flows (inflows and outflows) is the investment's net present value.

5. Apply the **NPV rule**: If the investment's NPV is positive, an investor should undertake it; if the NPV is negative, the investor should not undertake it. If an investor has two candidates for investment but can only invest in one (i.e., **mutually exclusive projects**), the investor should choose the candidate with the higher positive NPV.

What is the meaning of the NPV rule? In calculating the NPV of an investment proposal, we use an estimate of the opportunity cost of capital as the discount rate. The opportunity cost of capital is the alternative return that investors forgo in undertaking the investment. When NPV is positive, the investment adds value because it more than covers the opportunity cost of the capital needed to undertake it. So a company undertaking a positive NPV investment increases shareholders' wealth. An individual investor making a positive NPV investment increases personal wealth, but a negative NPV investment decreases wealth.

When working problems using the NPV rule, it will be helpful to refer to the following formula:

$$NPV = \sum_{t=0}^{N} \frac{CF_t}{(1 + r)^t}$$

(6-1)

where

$CF_t$ = the expected net cash flow at time $t$
$N$ = the investment's projected life
$r$ = the discount rate or opportunity cost of capital

As always, we state the inputs on a compatible time basis: If cash flows are annual, $N$ is the project's life in years and $r$ is an annual rate. For instance, suppose you are reviewing a proposal that requires an initial outlay of \$2 million ($CF_0$ = −\$2 million). You expect that the proposed investment will generate net positive cash flows of $CF_1$ = \$0.50 million at the end of Year 1, $CF_2$ = \$0.75 million at the end of Year 2, and $CF_3$ = \$1.35 million at the end of Year 3. Using 10 percent as a discount rate, you calculate the NPV as follows:

$$NPV = -\$2 + \$0.50/(1.10) + \$0.75/(1.10)^2 + \$1.35/(1.10)^3$$
$$= -\$2 + \$0.454545 + \$0.619835 + \$1.014275$$
$$= \$0.088655 \text{ million}$$

Because the NPV of \$88,655 is positive, you accept the proposal under the NPV rule.

Consider an example in which a research and development program is evaluated using the NPV rule.

## EXAMPLE 1

### Evaluating a Research and Development Program Using the NPV Rule

As an analyst covering the RAD Corporation, you are evaluating its research and development (R&D) program for the current year.

Management has announced that it intends to invest \$1 million in R&D. Incremental net cash flows are forecasted to be \$150,000 per year in perpetuity. RAD Corporation's opportunity cost of capital is 10 percent.

1. State whether RAD's R&D program will benefit shareholders, as judged by the NPV rule.

2. Evaluate whether your answer to Part 1 changes if RAD Corporation's opportunity cost of capital is 15 percent rather than 10 percent.

**Solution to 1:** The constant net cash flows of \$150,000, which we can denote as $\overline{CF}$, form a perpetuity. The present value of the perpetuity is $\overline{CF}/r$, so we calculate the project's NPV as

$$\text{NPV} = CF_0 + \overline{CF}/r = -\$1,000,000 + \$150,000/0.10 = \$500,000$$

With an opportunity cost of 10 percent, the present value of the program's cash inflows is \$1.5 million. The program's cost is an immediate outflow of \$1 million; therefore, its net present value is \$500,000. As NPV is positive, you conclude that RAD Corporation's R&D program will benefit shareholders.

**Solution to 2:** With an opportunity cost of capital of 15 percent, you compute the NPV as you did above, but this time you use a 15 percent discount rate:

$$\text{NPV} = -\$1,000,000 + \$150,000/0.15 = \$0$$

With a higher opportunity cost of capital, the present value of the inflows is smaller and the program's NPV is smaller: At 15 percent, the NPV exactly equals \$0. At NPV = 0, the program generates just enough cash flow to compensate shareholders for the opportunity cost of making the investment. When a company undertakes a zero-NPV project, the company becomes larger but shareholders' wealth does not increase.

## 2.2 The Internal Rate of Return and the Internal Rate of Return Rule

Financial managers often want a single number that represents the rate of return generated by an investment. The rate of return computation most often used in investment applications (including capital budgeting) is the internal rate of return (IRR). The internal rate of return rule is a second method for choosing among investment proposals. The **internal rate of return** is the discount rate that makes net present value equal to zero. It equates the present value of the investment's costs (outflows) to the present value of the investment's benefits (inflows). The rate is "internal" because it depends only on the cash flows of the investment; no external data are needed. As a result, we can apply the IRR concept to any investment that can be represented as a series of cash flows. In the study of bonds, we encounter IRR under the name of yield to maturity. Later in this reading, we will explore IRR as the money-weighted rate of return for portfolios.

Before we continue, however, we must add a note of caution about interpreting IRR: Even if our cash flow projections are correct, we will realize a compound rate of return that is equal to IRR over the life of the investment *only if* we can reinvest all interim cash flows at exactly the IRR. Suppose the IRR for a project is 15 percent but we consistently reinvest the cash generated by the project at a lower rate. In this case, we will realize a return that is less than 15 percent. (This principle can work in our favor if we can reinvest at rates above 15 percent.)

To return to the definition of IRR, in mathematical terms we said the following:

$$NPV = CF_0 + \frac{CF_1}{(1 + IRR)^1} + \frac{CF_2}{(1 + IRR)^2} + \ldots + \frac{CF_N}{(1 + IRR)^N} = 0 \qquad \textbf{(6-2)}$$

Again, the IRR in Equation 6-2 must be compatible with the timing of the cash flows. If the cash flows are quarterly, we have a quarterly IRR in Equation 6-2. We can then state the IRR on an annual basis. For some simple projects, the cash flow at $t = 0$, $CF_0$, captures the single capital outlay or initial investment; cash flows after $t = 0$ are the positive returns to the investment. In such cases, we can say $CF_0 = -$Investment (the negative sign indicates an outflow). Thus we can rearrange Equation 6-2 in a form that is helpful in those cases:

$$Investment = \frac{CF_1}{(1 + IRR)^1} + \frac{CF_2}{(1 + IRR)^2} + \ldots + \frac{CF_N}{(1 + IRR)^N}$$

For most real-life problems, financial analysts use software, spreadsheets, or financial calculators to solve this equation for IRR, so you should familiarize yourself with such tools.[3]

The investment decision rule using IRR, the **IRR rule**, states the following: "Accept projects or investments for which the IRR is greater than the opportunity cost of capital." The IRR rule uses the opportunity cost of capital as a **hurdle rate**, or rate that a project's IRR must exceed for the project to be accepted. Note that if the opportunity cost of capital is equal to the IRR, then the NPV is equal to 0. If the project's opportunity cost is less than the IRR, the NPV is greater than 0 (using a discount rate less than the IRR will make the NPV positive). With these comments in mind, we work through two examples that involve the internal rate of return.

---

### EXAMPLE 2

**Evaluating a Research and Development Program Using the IRR Rule**

In the previous RAD Corporation example, the initial outlay is $1 million and the program's cash flows are $150,000 in perpetuity. Now you are interested in determining the program's internal rate of return. Address the following:

**1.** Write the equation for determining the internal rate of return of this R&D program.

**2.** Calculate the IRR.

---

[3] In some real-world capital budgeting problems, the initial investment (which has a minus sign) may be followed by subsequent cash inflows (which have plus signs) and outflows (which have minus signs). In these instances, the project can have more than one IRR. The possibility of multiple solutions is a theoretical limitation of IRR.

**Solution to 1:** Finding the IRR is equivalent to finding the discount rate that makes the NPV equal to 0. Because the program's cash flows are a perpetuity, you can set up the NPV equation as

$$NPV = -\text{Investment} + \overline{CF}/IRR = 0$$
$$NPV = -\$1,000,000 + \$150,000/IRR = 0$$

or as

$$\text{Investment} = \overline{CF}/IRR$$
$$\$1,000,000 = \$150,000/IRR$$

**Solution to 2:** We can solve for IRR as IRR = $150,000/$1,000,000 = 0.15 or 15 percent. The solution of 15 percent accords with the definition of IRR. In Example 1, you found that a discount rate of 15 percent made the program's NPV equal to 0. By definition, therefore, the program's IRR must be 15 percent. If the opportunity cost of capital is also 15 percent, the R&D program just covers its opportunity costs and neither increases nor decreases shareholder wealth. If it is less than 15 percent, the IRR rule indicates that management should invest in the program because it more than covers its opportunity cost. If the opportunity cost is greater than 15 percent, the IRR rule tells management to reject the R&D program. For a given opportunity cost, the IRR rule and the NPV rule lead to the same decision in this example.

## EXAMPLE 3

### The IRR and NPV Rules Side by Side

The Japanese company Kageyama Ltd. is considering whether or not to open a new factory to manufacture capacitors used in cell phones. The factory will require an investment of ¥1,000 million. The factory is expected to generate level cash flows of ¥294.8 million per year in each of the next five years. According to information in its financial reports, Kageyama's opportunity cost of capital for this type of project is 11 percent.

1. Determine whether the project will benefit Kageyama's shareholders using the NPV rule.

2. Determine whether the project will benefit Kageyama's shareholders using the IRR rule.

**Solution to 1:** The cash flows can be grouped into an initial outflow of ¥1,000 million and an ordinary annuity of five inflows of ¥294.8 million. The expression for the present value of an annuity is $A[1 - (1 + r)^{-N}]/r$, where $A$ is the level annuity payment. Therefore, with amounts shown in millions of Japanese yen,

$$NPV = -1,000 + 294.8[1 - (1.11)^{-5}]/0.11$$
$$NPV = -1,000 + 1,089.55 = 89.55$$

Because the project's NPV is positive ¥89.55 million, it should benefit Kageyama's shareholders.

**Solution to 2:** The IRR of the project is the solution to

$$\text{NPV} = -1,000 + 294.8[1 - (1 + \text{IRR})^{-5}]/\text{IRR} = 0$$

This project's positive NPV tells us that the internal rate of return must be greater than 11 percent. Using a calculator, we find that IRR is 0.145012 or 14.50 percent. Table 1 gives the keystrokes on most financial calculators.

**TABLE 1  Computing IRR**

| Notation Used on Most Calculators | Numerical Value for This Problem |
|---|---|
| $N$ | 5 |
| $\%i$ compute | $X$ |
| PV | −1,000 |
| PMT | 294.8 |
| FV | n/a (=0) |

Because the IRR of 14.50 percent is greater than the opportunity cost of the project, the project should benefit Kageyama's shareholders. Whether it uses the IRR rule or the NPV rule, Kageyama makes the same decision: Build the factory.

In the previous example, value creation is evident: For a single ¥1,000 million payment, Kageyama creates a project worth ¥1,089.55 million, a value increase of ¥89.55 million. Another perspective on value creation comes from converting the initial investment into a capital charge against the annual operating cash flows that the project generates. Recall that the project generates an annual operating cash flow of ¥294,800,000. If we subtract a capital charge of ¥270,570,310 (the amount of a five-year annuity having a present value of ¥1,000 million at 11 percent), we find ¥294,800,000 − ¥270,570,310 = ¥24,229,690. The amount of ¥24,229,690 represents the profit in each of the next five years after taking into account opportunity costs. The present value of a five-year annuity of ¥24,229,690 at an 11 percent cost of capital is exactly what we calculated as the project's NPV: ¥89.55 million. Therefore, we can also calculate NPV by converting the initial investment to an annual capital charge against cash flow.

## 2.3 Problems with the IRR Rule

The IRR and NPV rules give the same accept or reject decision when projects are independent—that is, when the decision to invest in one project does not affect the decision to undertake another. When a company cannot finance all the projects it would like to undertake—that is, when projects are mutually exclusive—it must rank the projects from most profitable to least. However, rankings according to IRR and NPV may not be the same. The IRR and NPV rules rank projects differently when

▶ the size or scale of the projects differs (measuring size by the investment needed to undertake the project), or

▶ the timing of the projects' cash flows differs.

When the IRR and NPV rules conflict in ranking projects, we should take directions from the NPV rule. Why that preference? The NPV of an investment represents the expected addition to shareholder wealth from an investment, and we take the maximization of shareholder wealth to be a basic financial objective of a company. To illustrate the preference for the NPV rule, consider first the case of projects that differ in size. Suppose that a company has only €30,000 available to invest.[4] The company has available two one-period investment projects described as A and B in Table 2.

| Project | Investment at $t = 0$ | Cash Flow at $t = 1$ | IRR | NPV at 8% |
|---------|---------|---------|---------|---------|
| TABLE 2 IRR and NPV for Mutually Exclusive Projects of Different Size | | | | |
| A | −€10,000 | €15,000 | 50% | €3,888.89 |
| B | −€30,000 | €42,000 | 40% | €8,888.89 |

Project A requires an immediate investment of €10,000. This project will make a single cash payment of $15,000 at $t = 1$. Because the IRR is the discount rate that equates the present value of the future cash flow with the cost of the investment, the IRR equals 50 percent. If we assume that the opportunity cost of capital is 8 percent, then the NPV of Project A is €3,888.89. We compute the IRR and NPV of Project B as 40 percent and €8,888.89, respectively. The IRR and NPV rules indicate that we should undertake both projects, but to do so we would need €40,000—more money than is available. So we need to rank the projects. How do the projects rank according to IRR and NPV?

The IRR rule ranks Project A, with the higher IRR, first. The NPV rule, however, ranks Project B, with the higher NPV, first—a conflict with the IRR rule's ranking. Choosing Project A because it has the higher IRR would not lead to the largest increase in shareholders' wealth. Investing in Project A effectively leaves €20,000 (€30,000 minus A's cost) uninvested. Project A increases wealth by almost €4,000, but Project B increases wealth by almost €9,000. The difference between the two projects' scale creates the inconsistency in the ranking between the two rules.

IRR and NPV can also rank projects of the same scale differently when the timing of cash flows differs. We can illustrate this principle with Projects A and D, presented in Table 3.

| Project | CF0 | CF1 | CF2 | CF3 | IRR | NPV at 8% |
|---------|-----|-----|-----|-----|-----|-----------|
| TABLE 3 IRR and NPV for Mutually Exclusive Projects with Different Timing of Cash Flows | | | | | | |
| A | −€10,000 | €15,000 | 0 | 0 | 50.0% | €3,888.89 |
| D | −€10,000 | 0 | 0 | €21,220 | 28.5% | €6,845.12 |

---

[4] Or suppose the two projects require the same physical or other resources, so that only one can be undertaken.

The terms $CF_0$, $CF_1$, $CF_2$, and $CF_3$ represent the cash flows at time periods 0, 1, 2, and 3. The IRR for Project A is the same as it was in the previous example. The IRR for Project D is found as follows:

$$-10{,}000 + \frac{21{,}220}{(1 + IRR)^3} = 0$$

The IRR for Project D is 28.5 percent, compared with 50 percent for Project A. IRRs and IRR rankings are not affected by any external interest rate or discount rate because a project's cash flows alone determine the internal rate of return. The IRR calculation furthermore assumes reinvestment at the IRR, so we generally cannot interpret them as achievable rates of return. For Project D, for example, to achieve a 28.5 percent return we would need to earn 28.5 percent on €10,000 for the first year, earn 28.5 percent on €10,000(1.285) = €12,850 the second year, and earn 28.5 percent on €10,000(1.285)$^2$ = €16,512.25 the third year.[5] A reinvestment rate such as 50 percent or 28.5 percent may be quite unrealistic. By contrast, the calculation of NPV uses an external market-determined discount rate, and reinvestment is assumed to take place at that discount rate. NPV rankings can depend on the external discount rate chosen. Here, Project D has a larger but more distant cash inflow (€21,220 versus €15,000). As a result, Project D has a higher NPV than Project A at lower discount rates.[6] The NPV rule's assumption about reinvestment rates is more realistic and more economically relevant because it incorporates the market-determined opportunity cost of capital as a discount rate. As a consequence, the NPV is the expected addition to shareholder wealth from an investment.

In summary, when dealing with mutually exclusive projects, choose among them using the NPV rule when the IRR rule and NPV rule conflict.[7]

# PORTFOLIO RETURN MEASUREMENT

**3**

Suppose you are an investor and you want to assess the success of your investments. You face two related but distinct tasks. The first is **performance measurement**, which involves calculating returns in a logical and consistent manner. Accurate performance measurement provides the basis for your second task, **performance appraisal**.[8] Performance measurement is thus of great importance for all investors and investment managers because it is the foundation for all further analysis.

In our discussion of portfolio return measurement, we will use the fundamental concept of **holding period return (HPR)**, the return that an investor earns over a specified holding period. For an investment that makes one cash payment at the end of the holding period, HPR = $(P_1 - P_0 + D_1)/P_0$, where $P_0$ is the initial investment, $P_1$ is the price received at the end of the holding period, and $D_1$ is the cash paid by the investment at the end of the holding period.

---

[5] The ending amount €10,000(1.285)$^3$ = €21,218 differs from the €21,220 amount listed in Table 3 because we rounded IRR.

[6] There is a crossover discount rate above which Project A has a higher NPV than Project D. This crossover rate is 18.94 percent.

[7] Technically, different reinvestment rate assumptions account for this conflict between the IRR and NPV rules. The IRR rule assumes that the company can earn the IRR on all reinvested cash flows, but the NPV rule assumes that cash flows are reinvested at the company's opportunity cost of capital. The NPV assumption is far more realistic. For further details on this and other topics in capital budgeting, see Brealey and Myers (2003).

[8] The term "performance evaluation" has been used as a synonym for performance appraisal.

Particularly when we measure performance over many periods, or when the portfolio is subject to additions and withdrawals, portfolio performance measurement is a challenging task. Two of the measurement tools available are the money-weighted rate of return measure and the time-weighted rate of return measure. The first measure we discuss, the money-weighted rate of return, implements a concept we have already covered in the context of capital budgeting: internal rate of return.

## 3.1 Money-Weighted Rate of Return

The first performance measurement concept that we will discuss is an internal rate of return calculation. In investment management applications, the internal rate of return is called the money-weighted rate of return because it accounts for the timing and amount of all dollar flows into and out of the portfolio.[9]

To illustrate the money-weighted return, consider an investment that covers a two-year horizon. At time $t = 0$, an investor buys one share at $200. At time $t = 1$, he purchases an additional share at $225. At the end of Year 2, $t = 2$, he sells both shares for $235 each. During both years, the stock pays a per-share dividend of $5. The $t = 1$ dividend is not reinvested. Table 4 shows the total cash inflows and outflows.

### TABLE 4 Cash Flows

| Time | Outlay |
|------|--------|
| 0 | $200 to purchase the first share |
| 1 | $225 to purchase the second share |

| Time | Proceeds |
|------|----------|
| 1 | $5 dividend received from first share (and not reinvested) |
| 2 | $10 dividend ($5 per share × 2 shares) received |
| 2 | $470 received from selling two shares at $235 per share |

The money-weighted return on this portfolio is its internal rate of return for the two-year period. The portfolio's internal rate of return is the rate, $r$, for which the present value of the cash inflows minus the present value of the cash outflows equals 0, or

$$PV \text{ (outflows)} = PV \text{ (inflows)}$$

$$\$200 + \frac{\$225}{(1 + r)} = \frac{\$5}{(1 + r)} + \frac{\$480}{(1 + r)^2}$$

The left-hand side of this equation details the outflows: $200 at time $t = 0$ and $225 at time $t = 1$. The $225 outflow is discounted back one period because it occurs at $t = 1$. The right-hand side of the equation shows the present value of the inflows: $5 at time $t = 1$ (discounted back one period) and $480 (the $10 dividend plus the $470 sale proceeds) at time $t = 2$ (discounted back two periods).

---

[9] In the United States, the money-weighted return is frequently called the dollar-weighted return. We follow a standard presentation of the money-weighted return as an IRR concept.

To solve for the money-weighted return, we use either a financial calculator that allows us to enter cash flows or a spreadsheet with an IRR function.[10] The first step is to group net cash flows by time. For this example, we have −$200 for the $t = 0$ net cash flow, −$220 = −$225 + $5 for the $t = 1$ net cash flow, and $480 for the $t = 2$ net cash flow. After entering these cash flows, we use the spreadsheet's or calculator's IRR function to find that the money-weighted rate of return is 9.39 percent.[11]

Now we take a closer look at what has happened to the portfolio during each of the two years. In the first year, the portfolio generated a one-period holding period return of ($5 + $225 − $200)/$200 = 15 percent. At the beginning of the second year, the amount invested is $450, calculated as $225 (per share price of stock) $\times$ 2 shares, because the $5 dividend was spent rather than reinvested. At the end of the second year, the proceeds from the liquidation of the portfolio are $470 (as detailed in Table 4) plus $10 in dividends (as also detailed in Table 4). So in the second year the portfolio produced a holding period return of ($10 + $470 − $450)/$450 = 6.67 percent. The mean holding period return was (15% + 6.67%)/2 = 10.84 percent. The money-weighted rate of return, which we calculated as 9.39 percent, puts a greater weight on the second year's relatively poor performance (6.67 percent) than the first year's relatively good performance (15 percent), as more money was invested in the second year than in the first. That is the sense in which returns in this method of calculating performance are "money weighted."

As a tool for evaluating investment managers, the money-weighted rate of return has a serious drawback. Generally, the investment manager's clients determine when money is given to the investment manager and how much money is given. As we have seen, those decisions may significantly influence the investment manager's money-weighted rate of return. A general principle of evaluation, however, is that a person or entity should be judged only on the basis of their own actions, or actions under their control. An evaluation tool should isolate the effects of the investment manager's actions. The next section presents a tool that is effective in that respect.

## 3.2 Time-Weighted Rate of Return

An investment measure that is not sensitive to the additions and withdrawals of funds is the time-weighted rate of return. In the investment management industry, the time-weighted rate of return is the preferred performance measure. The **time-weighted rate of return** measures the compound rate of growth of $1 initially invested in the portfolio over a stated measurement period. In contrast to the money-weighted rate of return, the time-weighted rate of return is not affected by cash withdrawals or additions to the portfolio. The term "time-weighted" refers to the fact that returns are averaged over time. To compute an exact time-weighted rate of return on a portfolio, take the following three steps:

**1.** Price the portfolio immediately prior to any significant addition or withdrawal of funds. Break the overall evaluation period into subperiods based on the dates of cash inflows and outflows.

**2.** Calculate the holding period return on the portfolio for each subperiod.

---

[10] In this particular case we could solve for $r$ by solving the quadratic equation $480x^2 − 220x − 200 = 0$ with $x = 1/(1 + r)$, using standard results from algebra. In general, however, we rely on a calculator or spreadsheet software to compute a money-weighted rate of return.

[11] Note that the calculator or spreadsheet will give the IRR as a periodic rate. If the periods are not annual, we annualize the periodic rate.

**3.** Link or compound holding period returns to obtain an annual rate of return for the year (the time-weighted rate of return for the year). If the investment is for more than one year, take the geometric mean of the annual returns to obtain the time-weighted rate of return over that measurement period.

Let us return to our money-weighted example and calculate the time-weighted rate of return for that investor's portfolio. In that example, we computed the holding period returns on the portfolio, Step 2 in the procedure for finding time-weighted rate of return. Given that the portfolio earned returns of 15 percent during the first year and 6.67 percent during the second year, what is the portfolio's time-weighted rate of return over an evaluation period of two years?

We find this time-weighted return by taking the geometric mean of the two holding period returns, Step 3 in the procedure above. The calculation of the geometric mean exactly mirrors the calculation of a compound growth rate. Here, we take the product of 1 plus the holding period return for each period to find the terminal value at $t = 2$ of \$1 invested at $t = 0$. We then take the square root of this product and subtract 1 to get the geometric mean. We interpret the result as the annual compound growth rate of \$1 invested in the portfolio at $t = 0$. Thus we have

$$(1 + \text{Time-weighted return})^2 = (1.15)(1.0667)$$

$$\text{Time-weighted return} \ = \ \sqrt{(1.15)(1.0667)} \ - 1 = 10.76\%$$

The time-weighted return on the portfolio was 10.76 percent, compared with the money-weighted return of 9.39 percent, which gave larger weight to the second year's return. We can see why investment managers find time-weighted returns more meaningful. If a client gives an investment manager more funds to invest at an unfavorable time, the manager's money-weighted rate of return will tend to be depressed. If a client adds funds at a favorable time, the money-weighted return will tend to be elevated. The time-weighted rate of return removes these effects.

In defining the steps to calculate an exact time-weighted rate of return, we said that the portfolio should be valued immediately prior to any significant addition or withdrawal of funds. With the amount of cash flow activity in many portfolios, this task can be costly. We can often obtain a reasonable approximation of the time-weighted rate of return by valuing the portfolio at frequent, regular intervals, particularly if additions and withdrawals are unrelated to market movements. The more frequent the valuation, the more accurate the approximation. Daily valuation is commonplace. Suppose that a portfolio is valued daily over the course of a year. To compute the time-weighted return for the year, we first compute each day's holding period return:

$$r_t = \frac{\text{MVE}_t - \text{MVB}_t}{\text{MVB}_t}$$

where $\text{MVB}_t$ equals the market value at the beginning of day $t$ and $\text{MVE}_t$ equals the market value at the end of day $t$. We compute 365 such daily returns, denoted $r_1, r_2, \ldots, r_{365}$. We obtain the annual return for the year by linking the daily holding period returns in the following way: $(1 + r_1) \times (1 + r_2) \times \ldots \times (1 + r_{365}) - 1$. If withdrawals and additions to the portfolio happen only at day's end, this annual return is a precise time-weighted rate of return for the year. Otherwise, it is an approximate time-weighted return for the year.

If we have a number of years of data, we can calculate a time-weighted return for each year individually, as above. If $r_i$ is the time-weighted return for year $i$, we calculate an annualized time-weighted return as the geometric mean of $N$ annual returns, as follows:

$$r_{TW} = [(1 + r_1) \times (1 + r_2) \times \ldots \times (1 + r_N)]^{1/N} - 1$$

Example 4 illustrates the calculation of the time-weighted rate of return.

## EXAMPLE 4

### Time-Weighted Rate of Return

Strubeck Corporation sponsors a pension plan for its employees. It manages part of the equity portfolio in-house and delegates management of the balance to Super Trust Company. As chief investment officer of Strubeck, you want to review the performance of the in-house and Super Trust portfolios over the last four quarters. You have arranged for outflows and inflows to the portfolios to be made at the very beginning of the quarter. Table 5 summarizes the inflows and outflows as well as the two portfolios' valuations. In the table, the ending value is the portfolio's value just prior to the cash inflow or outflow at the beginning of the quarter. The amount invested is the amount each portfolio manager is responsible for investing.

**TABLE 5  Cash Flows for the In-House Strubeck Account and the Super Trust Account**

|  | Quarter | | | |
|---|---|---|---|---|
|  | **1** | **2** | **3** | **4** |
| *In-House Account* | | | | |
| Beginning value | $4,000,000 | $6,000,000 | $5,775,000 | $6,720,000 |
| Beginning of period inflow (outflow) | $1,000,000 | ($500,000) | $225,000 | ($600,000) |
| Amount invested | $5,000,000 | $5,500,000 | $6,000,000 | $6,120,000 |
| Ending value | $6,000,000 | $5,775,000 | $6,720,000 | $5,508,000 |
| *Super Trust Account* | | | | |
| Beginning value | $10,000,000 | $13,200,000 | $12,240,000 | $5,659,200 |
| Beginning of period inflow (outflow) | $2,000,000 | ($1,200,000) | ($7,000,000) | ($400,000) |
| Amount invested | $12,000,000 | $12,000,000 | $5,240,000 | $5,259,200 |
| Ending value | $13,200,000 | $12,240,000 | $5,659,200 | $5,469,568 |

Based on the information given, address the following.

1. Calculate the time-weighted rate of return for the in-house account.

2. Calculate the time-weighted rate of return for the Super Trust account.

**Solution to 1:** To calculate the time-weighted rate of return for the in-house account, we compute the quarterly holding period returns for the account and link them into an annual return. The in-house account's time-weighted rate of return is 27 percent, calculated as follows:

1Q HPR: $r_1 = (\$6{,}000{,}000 - \$5{,}000{,}000)/\$5{,}000{,}000 = 0.20$

2Q HPR: $r_2 = (\$5{,}775{,}000 - \$5{,}500{,}000)/\$5{,}500{,}000 = 0.05$

3Q HPR: $r_3 = (\$6{,}720{,}000 - \$6{,}000{,}000)/\$6{,}000{,}000 = 0.12$

4Q HPR: $r_4 = (\$5{,}508{,}000 - \$6{,}120{,}000)/\$6{,}120{,}000 = -0.10$

$$(1 + r_1)(1 + r_2)(1 + r_3)(1 + r_4) - 1 = (1.20)(1.05)(1.12)(0.90) - 1 = 0.27 \text{ or } 27\%$$

**Solution to 2:** The account managed by Super Trust has a time-weighted rate of return of 26 percent, calculated as follows:

1Q HPR: $r_1 = (\$13{,}200{,}000 - \$12{,}000{,}000)/\$12{,}000{,}000 = 0.10$

2Q HPR: $r_2 = (\$12{,}240{,}000 - \$12{,}000{,}000)/\$12{,}000{,}000 = 0.02$

3Q HPR: $r_3 = (\$5{,}659{,}200 - \$5{,}240{,}000)/\$5{,}240{,}000 = 0.08$

4Q HPR: $r_4 = (\$5{,}469{,}568 - \$5{,}259{,}200)/\$5{,}259{,}200 = 0.04$

$$(1 + r_1)(1 + r_2)(1 + r_3)(1 + r_4) - 1 = (1.10)(1.02)(1.08)(1.04) - 1 = 0.26 \text{ or } 26\%$$

The in-house portfolio's time-weighted rate of return is higher than the Super Trust portfolio's by 100 basis points.

Having worked through this exercise, we are ready to look at a more detailed case.

## EXAMPLE 5

**Time-Weighted and Money-Weighted Rates of Return Side by Side**

Your task is to compute the investment performance of the Walbright Fund during 2003. The facts are as follows:

▶ On 1 January 2003, the Walbright Fund had a market value of $100 million.

▶ During the period 1 January 2003 to 30 April 2003, the stocks in the fund showed a capital gain of $10 million.

▶ On 1 May 2003, the stocks in the fund paid a total dividend of $2 million. All dividends were reinvested in additional shares.

▶ Because the fund's performance had been exceptional, institutions invested an additional $20 million in Walbright on 1 May 2003, raising assets under management to $132 million ($100 + $10 + $2 + $20).

▶ On 31 December 2003, Walbright received total dividends of $2.64 million. The fund's market value on 31 December 2003, not including the $2.64 million in dividends, was $140 million.

▶ The fund made no other interim cash payments during 2003.

Based on the information given, address the following.

**1.** Compute the Walbright Fund's time-weighted rate of return.

**2.** Compute the Walbright Fund's money-weighted rate of return.

**3.** Interpret the differences between the time-weighted and money-weighted rates of return.

**Solution to 1:**  Because interim cash flows were made on 1 May 2003, we must compute two interim total returns and then link them to obtain an annual return. Table 6 lists the relevant market values on 1 January, 1 May, and 31 December as well as the associated interim four-month (1 January to 1 May) and eight-month (1 May to 31 December) holding period returns.

### TABLE 6  Cash Flows for the Walbright Fund

| | |
|---|---|
| 1 January 2003 | Beginning portfolio value = $100 million |
| 1 May 2003 | Dividends received before additional investment = $2 million |
| | Ending portfolio value = $110 million |
| | Holding period return $= \dfrac{\$2 + \$10}{\$100} = 12\%$ |
| | New investment = $20 million |
| | Beginning market value for last 2/3 of year = $132 million |
| 31 December 2003 | Dividends received = $2.64 million |
| | Ending portfolio value = $140 million |
| | Holding period return $= \dfrac{\$2.64 + \$140 - \$132}{\$132}$ |
| | $= 8.06\%$ |

Now we must geometrically link the four- and eight-month returns to compute an annual return. We compute the time-weighted return as follows:

$$\text{Time-weighted return} = 1.12 \times 1.0806 - 1 = 0.2103$$

In this instance, we compute a time-weighted rate of return of 21.03 percent for one year. The four-month and eight-month intervals combine to equal one year. (Taking the square root of the product $1.12 \times 1.0806$ would be appropriate only if 1.12 and 1.0806 each applied to one full year.)

**Solution to 2:** To calculate the money-weighted return, we find the discount rate that sets the present value of the outflows (purchases) equal to the present value of the inflows (dividends and future payoff). The initial market value of the fund and all additions to it are treated as cash outflows. (Think of them as expenditures.) Withdrawals, receipts, and the ending market value of the fund are counted as inflows. (The ending market value is the amount investors receive on liquidating the fund.) Because interim cash flows have occurred at four-month intervals, we must solve for the four-month internal rate of return. Table 6 details the cash flows and their timing.

The present value equation (in millions) is as follows:

$$PV\ (outflows) = PV\ (inflows)$$

$$\$100 + \frac{\$2}{(1+r)^1} + \frac{\$20}{(1+r)^1} = \frac{\$2}{(1+r)^1} + \frac{\$2.64}{(1+r)^3} + \frac{\$140}{(1+r)^3}$$

The left-hand side of the equation shows the investments in the fund or outflows: a $100 million initial investment followed by the $2 million dividend reinvested and an additional $20 million of new investment (both occurring at the end of the first four-month interval, which makes the exponent in the denominator 1). The right-hand side of the equation shows the payoffs or inflows: the $2 million dividend at the first four-month interval followed by the $2.64 million dividend and the terminal market value of $140 million (both occurring at the end of the third four-month interval, which makes the exponent in the denominator 3). The second four-month **interval** has no cash flow. We can bring all the terms to the right of the equal sign, arranging them in order of time. After simplification,

$$0 = -\$100 - \frac{\$20}{(1+r)^1} + \frac{\$142.64}{(1+r)^3}$$

Using a spreadsheet or IRR-enabled calculator, we use $-100, -20, 0,$ and $\$142.64$ for the $t = 0$, $t = 1$, $t = 2$, and $t = 3$ net cash flows, respectively.[12] Using either tool, we get a four-month IRR of 6.28 percent. The quick way to annualize this is to multiply by 3. A more accurate way is $(1.0628)^3 - 1 = 0.20$ or 20 percent.

**Solution to 3:** In this example, the time-weighted return (21.03 percent) is greater than the money-weighted return (20 percent). The Walbright Fund's performance was relatively poorer during the eight-month period, when the fund owned more shares, than it was overall. This fact is reflected in a lower money-weighted rate of return compared with time-weighted rate of return, as the money-weighted return is sensitive to the timing and amount of withdrawals and additions to the portfolio.

---

[12] By convention, we denote outflow with a negative sign, and we need 0 as a placeholder for the $t = 2$.

The accurate measurement of portfolio returns is important to the process of evaluating portfolio managers. In addition to considering returns, however, analysts must also weigh risk. When we worked through Example 4, we stopped short of suggesting that in-house management was superior to Super Trust because it earned a higher time-weighted rate of return. With risk in focus, we can talk of risk-adjusted performance and make comparisons—but only cautiously. In other readings, we will discuss the Sharpe ratio, an important risk-adjusted performance measure that we might apply to an investment manager's time-weighted rate of return. For now, we have illustrated the major tools for measuring the return on a portfolio.

# MONEY MARKET YIELDS    4

In our discussion of internal rate of return and net present value, we referred to the opportunity cost of capital as a market-determined rate. In this section, we begin a discussion of discounted cash flow analysis in actual markets by considering short-term debt markets.

To understand the various ways returns are presented in debt markets, we must discuss some of the conventions for quoting yields on money-market instruments. The **money market** is the market for short-term debt instruments (one-year maturity or less). Some instruments require the issuer to repay the lender the amount borrowed plus interest. Others are **pure discount instruments** that pay interest as the difference between the amount borrowed and the amount paid back.

In the U.S. money market, the classic example of a pure discount instrument is the U.S. Treasury bill (T-bill) issued by the federal government. The **face value** of a T-bill is the amount the U.S. government promises to pay back to a T-bill investor. In buying a T-bill, investors pay the face amount less the discount, and receive the face amount at maturity. The **discount** is the reduction from the face amount that gives the price for the T-bill. This discount becomes the interest that accumulates, because the investor receives the face amount at maturity. Thus, investors earn a dollar return equal to the discount if they hold the instrument to maturity. T-bills are by far the most important class of money-market instruments in the United States. Other types of money-market instruments include commercial paper and bankers' acceptances, which are discount instruments, and negotiable certificates of deposit, which are interest-bearing instruments. The market for each of these instruments has its own convention for quoting prices or yields. The remainder of this section examines the quoting conventions for T-bills and other money-market instruments. In most instances, the quoted yields must be adjusted for use in other present value problems.

Pure discount instruments such as T-bills are quoted differently from U.S. government bonds. T-bills are quoted on a **bank discount basis**, rather than on a price basis. The bank discount basis is a quoting convention that annualizes, based on a 360-day year, the discount as a percentage of face value. Yield on a bank discount basis is computed as follows:

$$r_{BD} = \frac{D}{F}\frac{360}{t} \qquad (6\text{-}3)$$

where

$$
\begin{aligned}
r_{BD} &= \text{the annualized yield on a bank discount basis} \\
D &= \text{the dollar discount, which is equal to the difference between the} \\
&\quad\ \text{face value of the bill, } F, \text{ and its purchase price, } P_0 \\
F &= \text{the face value of the T-bill} \\
t &= \text{the actual number of days remaining to maturity} \\
360 &= \text{bank convention of the number of days in a year}
\end{aligned}
$$

The bank discount yield (often called simply the discount yield) takes the dollar discount from par, $D$, and expresses it as a fraction of the face value (not the price) of the T-bill. This fraction is then multiplied by the number of periods of length $t$ in one year (that is, $360/t$), where the year is assumed to have 360 days. Annualizing in this fashion assumes simple interest (no compounding). Consider the following example.

## EXAMPLE 6

### The Bank Discount Yield

Suppose a T-bill with a face value (or par value) of $100,000 and 150 days until maturity is selling for $98,000. What is its bank discount yield?

**Solution:** For this example, the dollar discount, $D$, is $2,000. The yield on a bank discount basis is 4.8 percent, as computed with Equation 6-3:

$$r_{BD} = \frac{\$2,000}{\$100,000} \frac{360}{150} = 4.8\%$$

The bank discount formula takes the T-bill's dollar discount from face or par as a fraction of face value, 2 percent, and then annualizes by the factor $360/150 = 2.4$. The price of discount instruments such as T-bills is quoted using discount yields, so we typically translate discount yield into price.

Suppose we know the bank discount yield of 4.8 percent but do not know the price. We solve for the dollar discount, $D$, as follows:

$$D = r_{BD} F \frac{t}{360}$$

With $r_{BD} = 4.8$ percent, the dollar discount is $D = 0.048 \times \$100,000 \times 150/360 = \$2,000$. Once we have computed the dollar discount, the purchase price for the T-bill is its face value minus the dollar discount, $F - D = \$100,000 - \$2,000 = \$98,000$.

Yield on a bank discount basis is not a meaningful measure of investors' return, for three reasons. First, the yield is based on the face value of the bond, not on its purchase price. Returns from investments should be evaluated relative to the amount that is invested. Second, the yield is annualized based on a 360-day year rather than a 365-day year. Third, the bank discount yield annualizes with simple interest, which ignores the opportunity to earn interest on interest (compound interest).

We can extend Example 6 to discuss three often-used alternative yield measures. The first is the holding period return over the remaining life of the instrument (150 days in the case of the T-bill in Example 6). It determines the return that an investor will earn by holding the instrument to maturity; as used here, this measure refers to an unannualized rate of return (or periodic rate of return). In fixed income markets, this holding period return is also called a **holding period yield (HPY)**.[13] For an instrument that makes one cash payment during its life, HPY is

---

[13] Bond-market participants often use the term "yield" when referring to total returns (returns incorporating both price change and income), as in yield to maturity. In other cases, yield refers to returns from income alone (as in current yield, which is annual interest divided by price). As used in this volume and by many writers, holding period yield is a bond market synonym for holding period return, total return, and horizon return.

$$HPY = \frac{P_1 - P_0 + D_1}{P_0}$$

**(6-4)**

where

$P_0$ = the initial purchase price of the instrument
$P_1$ = the price received for the instrument at its maturity
$D_1$ = the cash distribution paid by the instrument at its maturity
(i.e., interest)

When we use this expression to calculate the holding period yield for an interest-bearing instrument (for example, coupon-bearing bonds), we need to observe an important detail: The purchase and sale prices must include any **accrued interest** added to the trade price because the bond was traded between interest payment dates. Accrued interest is the coupon interest that the seller earns from the last coupon date but does not receive as a coupon, because the next coupon date occurs after the date of sale.[14]

For pure discount securities, all of the return is derived by redeeming the bill for more than its purchase price. Because the T-bill is a pure discount instrument, it makes no interest payment and thus $D_1 = 0$. Therefore, the holding period yield is the dollar discount divided by the purchase price, $HPY = D/P_0$, where $D = P_1 - P_0$. The holding period yield is the amount that is annualized in the other measures. For the T-bill in Example 6, the investment of \$98,000 will pay \$100,000 in 150 days. The holding period yield on this investment using Equation 6-4 is (\$100,000 − \$98,000)/\$98,000 = \$2,000/\$98,000 = 2.0408 percent. For this example, the periodic return of 2.0408 percent is associated with a 150-day period. If we were to use the T-bill rate of return as the opportunity cost of investing, we would use a discount rate of 2.0408 percent for the 150-day T-bill to find the present value of any other cash flow to be received in 150 days. As long as the other cash flow has risk characteristics similar to those of the T-bill, this approach is appropriate. If the other cash flow were riskier than the T-bill, then we could use the T-bill's yield as a base rate, to which we would add a risk premium. The formula for the holding period yield is the same regardless of the currency of denomination.

The second measure of yield is the **effective annual yield (EAY)**. The EAY takes the quantity 1 plus the holding period yield and compounds it forward to one year, then subtracts 1 to recover an annualized return that accounts for the effect of interest-on-interest.[15]

$$EAY = (1 + HPY)^{365/t} - 1$$

**(6-5)**

In our example, we can solve for EAY as follows:

$$EAY = (1.020408)^{365/150} - 1 = 1.050388 - 1 = 5.0388\%$$

This example illustrates a general rule: The bank discount yield is less than the effective annual yield.

The third alternative measure of yield is the **money market yield** (also known as the **CD equivalent yield**). This convention makes the quoted yield on a T-bill comparable to yield quotations on interest-bearing money market instruments that pay interest on a 360-day basis. In general, the money market yield is equal

---

[14] The price with accrued interest is called the **full price**. Trade prices are quoted "clean" (without accrued interest), but accrued interest, if any, is added to the purchase price. For more on accrued interest, see Fabozzi (2004).

[15] Effective annual yield was called the effective annual rate (Equation 5-5) in the reading on the time value of money.

to the annualized holding period yield; assuming a 360-day year, $r_{MM} = (HPY)(360/t)$. Compared to the bank discount yield, the money market yield is computed on the purchase price, so $r_{MM} = (r_{BD})(F/P_0)$. This equation shows that the money market yield is larger than the bank discount yield. In practice, the following expression is more useful because it does not require knowing the T-bill price:

$$r_{MM} = \frac{360 r_{BD}}{360 - (t)(r_{BD})} \qquad \text{(6-6)}$$

For the T-bill example, the money market yield is $r_{MM} = (360)(0.048)/[360 - (150)(0.048)] = 4.898$ percent.[16]

Table 7 summarizes the three yield measures we have discussed.

### TABLE 7  Three Commonly Used Yield Measures

| Holding Period Yield (HPY) | Effective Annual Yield (EAY) | Money Market Yield (CD Equivalent Yield) |
|---|---|---|
| $HPY = \dfrac{P_1 - P_0 + D_1}{P_0}$ | $EAY = (1 + HPY)^{365/t} - 1$ | $r_{MM} = \dfrac{360 r_{BD}}{360 - (t)(r_{BD})}$ |

The next example will help you consolidate your knowledge of these yield measures.

### EXAMPLE 7

**Using the Appropriate Discount Rate**

You need to find the present value of a cash flow of $1,000 that is to be received in 150 days. You decide to look at a T-bill maturing in 150 days to determine the relevant interest rate for calculating the present value. You have found a variety of yields for the 150-day bill. Table 8 presents this information.

### TABLE 8  Short-Term Money Market Yields

| | |
|---|---|
| Holding period yield | 2.0408% |
| Bank discount yield | 4.8% |
| Money market yield | 4.898% |
| Effective annual yield | 5.0388% |

Which yield or yields are appropriate for finding the present value of the $1,000 to be received in 150 days?

---

[16] Some national markets use the money market yield formula, rather than the bank discount yield formula, to quote the yields on discount instruments such as T-bills. In Canada, the convention is to quote Treasury bill yields using the money market formula assuming a 365-day year. Yields for German Treasury discount paper with a maturity less than one year and French BTFs (T-bills) are computed with the money market formula assuming a 360-day year.

**Solution:** The holding period yield is appropriate, and we can also use the money market yield and effective annual yield after converting them to a holding period yield.

▶ *Holding period yield* (2.0408 percent). This yield is exactly what we want. Because it applies to a 150-day period, we can use it in a straightforward fashion to find the present value of the $1,000 to be received in 150 days. (Recall the principle that discount rates must be compatible with the time period.) The present value is

$$PV = \frac{\$1,000}{1.020408} = \$980.00$$

Now we can see why the other yield measures are inappropriate or not as easily applied.

▶ *Bank discount yield* (4.8 percent). We should not use this yield measure to determine the present value of the cash flow. As mentioned earlier, the bank discount yield is based on the face value of the bill and not on its price.

▶ *Money market yield* (4.898 percent). To use the money market yield, we need to convert it to the 150-day holding period yield by dividing it by (360/150). After obtaining the holding period yield 0.04898/(360/150) = 0.020408, we use it to discount the $1,000 as above.

▶ *Effective annual yield* (5.0388 percent). This yield has also been annualized, so it must be adjusted to be compatible with the timing of the cash flow. We can obtain the holding period yield from the EAY as follows:

$$(1.050388)^{150/365} - 1 = 0.020408$$

Recall that when we found the effective annual yield, the exponent was 365/150, or the number of 150-day periods in a 365-day year. To shrink the effective annual yield to a 150-day yield, we use the reciprocal of the exponent that we used to annualize.

In Example 7, we converted two short-term measures of annual yield to a holding period yield for a 150-day period. That is one type of conversion. We frequently also need to convert periodic rates to annual rates. The issue can arise both in money markets and in longer-term debt markets. As an example, many bonds (long-term debt instruments) pay interest semiannually. Bond investors compute IRRs for bonds, known as yields to maturity (YTM). If the semiannual yield to maturity is 4 percent, how do we annualize it? An exact approach, taking account of compounding, would be to compute $(1.04)^2 - 1 = 0.0816$ or 8.16 percent. This is what we have been calling an effective annual yield. An approach used in U.S. bond markets, however, is to double the semiannual YTM: $4\% \times 2 = 8\%$. The yield to maturity calculated this way, ignoring compounding, has been called a **bond-equivalent yield**. Annualizing a semiannual yield by doubling is putting the yield on a bond-equivalent basis. In practice the result, 8 percent, would be referred to simply as the bond's yield to maturity. In money markets, if we annualized a six-month period yield by doubling it, in order to make the result comparable to bonds' YTMs we would also say that the result was a bond-equivalent yield.

# SUMMARY

In this reading, we applied the concepts of present value, net present value, and internal rate of return to the fundamental problem of valuing investments. We applied these concepts first to corporate investment, the well-known capital budgeting problem. We then examined the fundamental problem of calculating the return on a portfolio subject to cash inflows and outflows. Finally we discussed money market yields and basic bond market terminology. The following summarizes the reading's key concepts:

► The net present value (NPV) of a project is the present value of its cash inflows minus the present value of its cash outflows. The internal rate of return (IRR) is the discount rate that makes NPV equal to 0. We can interpret IRR as an expected compound return only when all interim cash flows can be reinvested at the internal rate of return and the investment is maintained to maturity.

► The NPV rule for decision making is to accept all projects with positive NPV or, if projects are mutually exclusive, to accept the project with the higher positive NPV. With mutually exclusive projects, we rely on the NPV rule. The IRR rule is to accept all projects with an internal rate of return exceeding the required rate of return. The IRR rule can be affected by problems of scale and timing of cash flows.

► Money-weighted rate of return and time-weighted rate of return are two alternative methods for calculating portfolio returns in a multiperiod setting when the portfolio is subject to additions and withdrawals. Time-weighted rate of return is the standard in the investment management industry. Money-weighted rate of return can be appropriate if the investor exercises control over additions and withdrawals to the portfolio.

► The money-weighted rate of return is the internal rate of return on a portfolio, taking account of all cash flows.

► The time-weighted rate of return removes the effects of timing and amount of withdrawals and additions to the portfolio and reflects the compound rate of growth of one unit of currency invested over a stated measurement period.

► The bank discount yield for U.S. Treasury bills (and other money-market instruments sold on a discount basis) is given by $r_{BD} = (F - P_0)/F \times 360/t = D/F \times 360/t$, where $F$ is the face amount to be received at maturity, $P_0$ is the price of the Treasury bill, $t$ is the number of days to maturity, and $D$ is the dollar discount.

► For a stated holding period or horizon, holding period yield (HPY) = (Ending price − Beginning price + Cash distributions)/(Beginning price). For a U.S. Treasury bill, HPY = $D/P_0$.

► The effective annual yield (EAY) is $(1 + HPY)^{365/t} - 1$.

► The money market yield is given by $r_{MM} = HPY \times 360/t$, where $t$ is the number of days to maturity.

► For a Treasury bill, money market yield can be obtained from the bank discount yield using $r_{MM} = (360 \times r_{BD})/(360 - t \times r_{BD})$.

► We can convert back and forth between holding period yields, money market yields, and equivalent annual yields by using the holding period yield, which is common to all the calculations.

► The bond-equivalent yield of a yield stated on a semiannual basis is that yield multiplied by 2.

# PRACTICE PROBLEMS FOR READING 6

1. Waldrup Industries is considering a proposal for a joint venture that will require an investment of C$13 million. At the end of the fifth year, Waldrup's joint venture partner will buy out Waldrup's interest for C$10 million. Waldrup's chief financial officer has estimated that the appropriate discount rate for this proposal is 12 percent. The expected cash flows are given below.

| Year | Cash Flow |
|------|-----------|
| 0 | −C$13,000,000 |
| 1 | C$3,000,000 |
| 2 | C$3,000,000 |
| 3 | C$3,000,000 |
| 4 | C$3,000,000 |
| 5 | C$10,000,000 |

   **A.** Calculate this proposal's NPV.

   **B.** Make a recommendation to the CFO (chief financial officer) concerning whether Waldrup should enter into this joint venture.

2. Waldrup Industries has committed to investing C$5,500,000 in a project with expected cash flows of C$1,000,000 at the end of Year 1, C$1,500,000 at the end of Year 4, and C$7,000,000 at the end of Year 5.

   **A.** Demonstrate that the internal rate of return of the investment is 13.51 percent.

   **B.** State how the internal rate of return of the investment would change if Waldrup's opportunity cost of capital were to increase by 5 percentage points.

3. Bestfoods, Inc. is planning to spend $10 million on advertising. The company expects this expenditure to result in annual incremental cash flows of $1.6 million in perpetuity. The corporate opportunity cost of capital for this type of project is 12.5 percent.

   **A.** Calculate the NPV for the planned advertising.

   **B.** Calculate the internal rate of return.

   **C.** Should the company go forward with the planned advertising? Explain.

4. Trilever is planning to establish a new factory overseas. The project requires an initial investment of $15 million. Management intends to run this factory for six years and then sell it to a local entity. Trilever's finance department has estimated the following yearly cash flows:

| Year | Cash Flow |
|------|-----------|
| 0 | −$15,000,000 |
| 1 | $4,000,000 |
| 2 | $4,000,000 |
| 3 | $4,000,000 |
| 4 | $4,000,000 |
| 5 | $4,000,000 |
| 6 | $7,000,000 |

Trilever's CFO decides that the company's cost of capital of 19 percent is an appropriate hurdle rate for this project.

   A. Calculate the internal rate of return of this project.

   B. Make a recommendation to the CFO concerning whether to undertake this project.

5. Westcott–Smith is a privately held investment management company. Two other investment counseling companies, which want to be acquired, have contacted Westcott–Smith about purchasing their business. Company A's price is £2 million. Company B's price is £3 million. After analysis, Westcott–Smith estimates that Company A's profitability is consistent with a perpetuity of £300,000 a year. Company B's prospects are consistent with a perpetuity of £435,000 a year. Westcott–Smith has a budget that limits acquisitions to a maximum purchase cost of £4 million. Its opportunity cost of capital relative to undertaking either project is 12 percent.

   A. Determine which company or companies (if any) Westcott–Smith should purchase according to the NPV rule.

   B. Determine which company or companies (if any) Westcott–Smith should purchase according to the IRR rule.

   C. State which company or companies (if any) Westcott–Smith should purchase. Justify your answer.

6. John Wilson buys 150 shares of ABM on 1 January 2002 at a price of $156.30 per share. A dividend of $10 per share is paid on 1 January 2003. Assume that this dividend is not reinvested. Also on 1 January 2003, Wilson sells 100 shares at a price of $165 per share. On 1 January 2004, he collects a dividend of $15 per share (on 50 shares) and sells his remaining 50 shares at $170 per share.

   A. Write the formula to calculate the money-weighted rate of return on Wilson's portfolio.

   B. Using any method, compute the money-weighted rate of return.

   C. Calculate the time-weighted rate of return on Wilson's portfolio.

   D. Describe a set of circumstances for which the money-weighted rate of return is an appropriate return measure for Wilson's portfolio.

   E. Describe a set of circumstances for which the time-weighted rate of return is an appropriate return measure for Wilson's portfolio.

**7.** Mario Luongo and Bob Weaver both purchase the same stock for €100. One year later, the stock price is €110 and it pays a dividend of €5 per share. Weaver decides to buy another share at €110 (he does not reinvest the €5 dividend, however). Luongo also spends the €5 per share dividend but does not transact in the stock. At the end of the second year, the stock pays a dividend of €5 per share but its price has fallen back to €100. Luongo and Weaver then decide to sell their entire holdings of this stock. The performance for Luongo and Weaver's investments are as follows:

> Luongo:  Time-weighted return = 4.77 percent
> Money-weighted return = 5.00 percent
>
> Weaver:  Money-weighted return = 1.63 percent

Briefly explain any similarities and differences between the performance of Luongo's and Weaver's investments.

**8.** A Treasury bill with a face value of $100,000 and 120 days until maturity is selling for $98,500.

  **A.** What is the T-bill's bank discount yield?

  **B.** What is the T-bill's money market yield?

  **C.** What is the T-bill's effective annual yield?

**9.** Jane Cavell has just purchased a 90-day U.S. Treasury bill. She is familiar with yield quotes on German Treasury discount paper but confused about the bank discount quoting convention for the U.S. T-bill she just purchased.

  **A.** Discuss three reasons why bank discount yield is not a meaningful measure of return.

  **B.** Discuss the advantage of money market yield compared with bank discount yield as a measure of return.

  **C.** Explain how the bank discount yield can be converted to an estimate of the holding period return Cavell can expect if she holds the T-bill to maturity.

# STATISTICAL CONCEPTS AND MARKET RETURNS

by Richard A. DeFusco, CFA, Dennis W. McLeavey, CFA, Jerald E. Pinto, CFA, and David E. Runkle, CFA

READING

7

## LEARNING OUTCOMES

| The candidate should be able to: | Mastery |
|---|---|
| **a.** differentiate between descriptive statistics and inferential statistics, between a population and a sample, and among the types of measurement scales; | ☐ |
| **b.** explain a parameter, a sample statistic, and a frequency distribution; | ☐ |
| **c.** calculate and interpret relative frequencies and cumulative relative frequencies, given a frequency distribution, and describe the properties of a dataset presented as a histogram or a frequency polygon; | ☐ |
| **d.** define, calculate, and interpret measures of central tendency, including the population mean, sample mean, arithmetic mean, weighted average or mean (including a portfolio return viewed as a weighted mean), geometric mean, harmonic mean, median, and mode; | ☐ |
| **e.** describe, calculate and interpret quartiles, quintiles, deciles, and percentiles; | ☐ |
| **f.** define, calculate, and interpret 1) a range and a mean absolute deviation, and 2 ) the variance and standard deviation of a population and of a sample; | ☐ |
| **g.** calculate and interpret the proportion of observations falling within a specified number of standard deviations of the mean, using Chebyshev's inequality; | ☐ |
| **h.** define, calculate, and interpret the coefficient of variation and the Sharpe ratio; | ☐ |
| **i.** define and interpret skewness, explain the meaning of a positively or negatively skewed return distribution, and describe the relative locations of the mean, median, and mode for a nonsymmetrical distribution; | ☐ |
| **j.** define and interpret measures of sample skewness and kurtosis. | ☐ |

1

# INTRODUCTION

Statistical methods provide a powerful set of tools for analyzing data and drawing conclusions from them. Whether we are analyzing asset returns, earnings growth rates, commodity prices, or any other financial data, statistical tools help us quantify and communicate the data's important features. This reading presents the basics of describing and analyzing data, the branch of statistics known as descriptive statistics. The reading supplies a set of useful concepts and tools, illustrated in a variety of investment contexts. One theme of our presentation, reflected in the reading's title, is the demonstration of the statistical methods that allow us to summarize return distributions.[1] We explore four properties of return distributions:

▶ where the returns are centered (central tendency),

▶ how far returns are dispersed from their center (dispersion),

▶ whether the distribution of returns is symmetrically shaped or lopsided (skewness), and

▶ whether extreme outcomes are likely (kurtosis).

These same concepts are generally applicable to the distributions of other types of data, too.

The reading is organized as follows. After defining some basic concepts in Section 2, in Sections 3 and 4 we discuss the presentation of data: Section 3 describes the organization of data in a table format, and Section 4 describes the graphic presentation of data. We then turn to the quantitative description of how data are distributed: Section 5 focuses on measures that quantify where data are centered, or measures of central tendency. Section 6 presents other measures that describe the location of data. Section 7 presents measures that quantify the degree to which data are dispersed. Sections 8 and 9 describe additional measures that provide a more accurate picture of data. Section 10 provides investment applications of concepts introduced in Section 5.

2

# SOME FUNDAMENTAL CONCEPTS

Before starting the study of statistics with this reading, it may be helpful to examine a picture of the overall field. In the following, we briefly describe the scope of statistics and its branches of study. We explain the concepts of population and sample. Data come in a variety of types, affecting the ways they can be measured and the appropriate statistical methods for analyzing them. We conclude by discussing the basic types of data measurement.

---

[1] Ibbotson Associates (www.ibbotson.com) generously provided much of the data used in this reading. We also draw on Dimson, Marsh, and Staunton's (2002) history and study of world markets as well as other sources.

## 2.1 The Nature of Statistics

The term **statistics** can have two broad meanings, one referring to data and the other to method. A company's average earnings per share (EPS) for the last 20 quarters, or its average returns for the past 10 years, are statistics. We may also analyze historical EPS to forecast future EPS, or use the company's past returns to infer its risk. The totality of methods we employ to collect and analyze data is also called statistics.

Statistical methods include descriptive statistics and statistical inference (inferential statistics). **Descriptive statistics** is the study of how data can be summarized effectively to describe the important aspects of large data sets. By consolidating a mass of numerical details, descriptive statistics turns data into information. **Statistical inference** involves making forecasts, estimates, or judgments about a larger group from the smaller group actually observed. The foundation for statistical inference is probability theory, and both statistical inference and probability theory will be discussed in later readings. Our focus in this reading is solely on descriptive statistics.

## 2.2 Populations and Samples

Throughout the study of statistics we make a critical distinction between a population and a sample. In this section, we explain these two terms as well as the related terms "**parameter**" and "sample statistic."[2]

▶ **Definition of Population.** A **population** is defined as all members of a specified group.

Any descriptive measure of a population characteristic is called a **parameter**. Although a population can have many parameters, investment analysts are usually concerned with only a few, such as the mean value, the range of investment returns, and the variance.

Even if it is possible to observe all the members of a population, it is often too expensive in terms of time or money to attempt to do so. For example, if the population is all telecommunications customers worldwide and an analyst is interested in their purchasing plans, she will find it too costly to observe the entire population. The analyst can address this situation by taking a sample of the population.

▶ **Definition of Sample.** A **sample** is a subset of a population.

In taking a sample, the analyst hopes it is characteristic of the population. The field of statistics known as sampling deals with taking samples in appropriate ways to achieve the objective of representing the population well. A later reading addresses the details of sampling.

Earlier, we mentioned statistics in the sense of referring to data. Just as a parameter is a descriptive measure of a population characteristic, a sample statistic (statistic, for short) is a descriptive measure of a sample characteristic.

▶ **Definition of Sample Statistic.** A **sample statistic** (or **statistic**) is a quantity computed from or used to describe a sample.

We devote much of this reading to explaining and illustrating the use of statistics in this sense. The concept is critical also in statistical inference, which

---

[2] This reading introduces many statistical concepts and formulas. To make it easy to locate them, we have set off some of the more important ones with bullet points.

addresses such problems as estimating an unknown population parameter using a sample statistic.

## 2.3 Measurement Scales

To choose the appropriate statistical methods for summarizing and analyzing data, we need to distinguish among different **measurement scales** or levels of measurement. All data measurements are taken on one of four major scales: nominal, ordinal, interval, or ratio.

**Nominal scales** represent the weakest level of measurement: They categorize data but do not rank them. If we assigned integers to mutual funds that follow different investment strategies, the number 1 might refer to a small-cap value fund, the number 2 to a large-cap value fund, and so on for each possible style. This nominal scale categorizes the funds according to their style but does not rank them.

**Ordinal scales** reflect a stronger level of measurement. Ordinal scales sort data into categories that are ordered with respect to some characteristic. For example, the Morningstar and Standard & Poor's star ratings for mutual funds represent an ordinal scale in which one star represents a group of funds judged to have had relatively the worst performance, with two, three, four, and five stars representing groups with increasingly better performance, as evaluated by those services.

An ordinal scale may also involve numbers to identify categories. For example, in ranking balanced mutual funds based on their five-year cumulative return, we might assign the number 1 to the top 10 percent of funds, and so on, so that the number 10 represents the bottom 10 percent of funds. The ordinal scale is stronger than the nominal scale because it reveals that a fund ranked 1 performed better than a fund ranked 2. The scale tells us nothing, however, about the difference in performance between funds ranked 1 and 2 compared with the difference in performance between funds ranked 3 and 4, or 9 and 10.

**Interval scales** provide not only ranking but also assurance that the differences between scale values are equal. As a result, scale values can be added and subtracted meaningfully. The Celsius and Fahrenheit scales are interval measurement scales. The difference in temperature between 10°C and 11°C is the same amount as the difference between 40°C and 41°C. We can state accurately that 12°C = 9°C + 3°C, for example. Nevertheless, the zero point of an interval scale does not reflect complete absence of what is being measured; it is not a true zero point or natural zero. Zero degrees Celsius corresponds to the freezing point of water, not the absence of temperature. As a consequence of the absence of a true zero point, we cannot meaningfully form ratios on interval scales.

As an example, 50°C, although five times as large a number as 10°C, does not represent five times as much temperature. Also, questionnaire scales are often treated as interval scales. If an investor is asked to rank his risk aversion on a scale from 1 (extremely risk-averse) to 7 (extremely risk-loving), the difference between a response of 1 and a response of 2 is sometimes assumed to represent the same difference in risk aversion as the difference between a response of 6 and a response of 7. When that assumption can be justified, the data are measured on interval scale.

**Ratio scales** represent the strongest level of measurement. They have all the characteristics of interval measurement scales as well as a true zero point as the origin. With ratio scales, we can meaningfully compute ratios as well as meaningfully add and subtract amounts within the scale. As a result, we can apply the widest range of statistical tools to data measured on a ratio scale. Rates of return are measured on a ratio scale, as is money. If we have twice as much money, then we have twice the purchasing power. Note that the scale has a natural zero—zero means no money.

Now that we have addressed the important preliminaries, we can discuss summarizing and describing data.

## EXAMPLE 1

### Identifying Scales of Measurement

State the scale of measurement for each of the following:

1. Credit ratings for bond issues.[3]
2. Cash dividends per share.
3. Hedge fund classification types.[4]
4. Bond maturity in years.

**Solution to 1:** Credit ratings are measured on an ordinal scale. A rating places a bond issue in a category, and the categories are ordered with respect to the expected probability of default. But the difference in the expected probability of default between AA− and A+, for example, is not necessarily equal to that between BB− and B+. In other words, letter credit ratings are not measured on an interval scale.

**Solution to 2:** Cash dividends per share are measured on a ratio scale. For this variable, 0 represents the complete absence of dividends; it is a true zero point.

**Solution to 3:** Hedge fund classification types are measured on a nominal scale. Each type groups together hedge funds with similar investment strategies. In contrast to credit ratings for bonds, however, hedge fund classification schemes do not involve a ranking. Thus such classification schemes are not measured on an ordinal scale.

**Solution to 4:** Bond maturity is measured on a ratio scale.

# SUMMARIZING DATA USING FREQUENCY DISTRIBUTIONS

3

In this section, we discuss one of the simplest ways to summarize data—the frequency distribution.

► **Definition of Frequency Distribution.** A **frequency distribution** is a tabular display of data summarized into a relatively small number of intervals.

Frequency distributions help in the analysis of large amounts of statistical data, and they work with all types of measurement scales.

---

[3] Credit ratings for a bond issue gauge the bond issuer's ability to meet the promised principal and interest payments on the bond. For example, one rating agency, Standard & Poor's, assigns bond issues to one of the following ratings, given in descending order of credit quality (increasing probability of default): AAA, AA+, AA, AA−, A+, A, A−, BBB+, BBB, BBB−, BB+, BB, BB−, B, CCC+, CCC−, CC, C, CI, D. For more information on credit risk and credit ratings, see Fabozzi (2004a).

[4] "Hedge fund" refers to investment vehicles with legal structures that result in less regulatory oversight than other pooled investment vehicles such as mutual funds. Hedge fund classification types group hedge funds by the kind of investment strategy they pursue.

Rates of return are the fundamental units that analysts and portfolio managers use for making investment decisions and we can use frequency distributions to summarize rates of return. When we analyze rates of return, our starting point is the holding period return (also called the total return).

▶ **Holding Period Return Formula.** The holding period return for time period $t$, $R_t$, is

$$R_t = \frac{P_t - P_{t-1} + D_t}{P_{t-1}} \qquad \textbf{(7-1)}$$

where

$P_t$ = price per share at the end of time period $t$

$P_{t-1}$ = price per share at the end of time period $t-1$, the time period immediately preceding time period $t$

$D_t$ = cash distributions received during time period $t$

Thus the holding period return for time period $t$ is the capital gain (or loss) plus distributions divided by the beginning-period price. (For common stocks, the distribution is a dividend; for bonds, the distribution is a coupon payment.) Equation 7-1 can be used to define the holding period return on any asset for a day, week, month, or year simply by changing the interpretation of the time interval between successive values of the time index, $t$.

The holding period return, as defined in Equation 7-1, has two important characteristics. First, it has an element of time attached to it. For example, if a monthly time interval is used between successive observations for price, then the rate of return is a monthly figure. Second, rate of return has no currency unit attached to it. For instance, suppose that prices are denominated in euros. The numerator and denominator of Equation 7-1 would be expressed in euros, and the resulting ratio would not have any units because the units in the numerator and denominator would cancel one another. This result holds regardless of the currency in which prices are denominated.[5]

With these concerns noted, we now turn to the frequency distribution of the holding period returns on the S&P 500 Index.[6] First, we examine annual rates of return; then we look at monthly rates of return. The annual rates of return on the S&P 500 calculated with Equation 7-1 span the period January 1926 to December 2002, for a total of 77 annual observations. Monthly return data cover the period January 1926 to December 2002, for a total of 924 monthly observations.

We can state a basic procedure for constructing a frequency distribution as follows.

▶ **Construction of a Frequency Distribution.**

**1.** Sort the data in ascending order.

**2.** Calculate the range of the data, defined as Range = Maximum value − Minimum value.

**3.** Decide on the number of intervals in the frequency distribution, $k$.

---

[5] Note, however, that if price and cash distributions in the expression for holding period return were not in one's home currency, one would generally convert those variables to one's home currency before calculating the holding period return. Because of exchange rate fluctuations during the holding period, holding period returns on an asset computed in different currencies would generally differ.

[6] We use the total return series on the S&P 500 from January 1926 to December 2002 provided by Ibbotson Associates.

**4.** Determine interval width as Range/$k$.

**5.** Determine the intervals by successively adding the interval width to the minimum value, to determine the ending points of intervals, stopping after reaching an interval that includes the maximum value.

**6.** Count the number of observations falling in each interval.

**7.** Construct a table of the intervals listed from smallest to largest that shows the number of observations falling in each interval.

In Step 4, when rounding the interval width, round up rather than down, to ensure that the final interval includes the maximum value of the data.

As the above procedure makes clear, a frequency distribution groups data into a set of intervals.[7] An **interval** is a set of values within which an observation falls. Each observation falls into only one interval, and the total number of intervals covers all the values represented in the data. The actual number of observations in a given interval is called the **absolute frequency**, or simply the frequency. The frequency distribution is the list of intervals together with the corresponding measures of frequency.

To illustrate the basic procedure, suppose we have 12 observations sorted in ascending order: $-4.57$, $-4.04$, $-1.64$, $0.28$, $1.34$, $2.35$, $2.38$, $4.28$, $4.42$, $4.68$, $7.16$, and $11.43$. The minimum observation is $-4.57$ and the maximum observation is $+11.43$, so the range is $+11.43 - (-4.57) = 16$. If we set $k = 4$, the interval width is $16/4 = 4$. Table 1 shows the repeated addition of the interval width of 4 to determine the endpoints for the intervals (Step 5).

### TABLE 1    Endpoints of Intervals

$$-4.57 + 4.00 = -0.57$$
$$-0.57 + 4.00 = \phantom{-}3.43$$
$$\phantom{-}3.43 + 4.00 = \phantom{-}7.43$$
$$\phantom{-}7.43 + 4.00 = 11.43$$

Thus the intervals are $[-4.57 \text{ to } -0.57)$, $[-0.57 \text{ to } 3.43)$, $[3.43 \text{ to } 7.43)$, and $[7.43 \text{ to } 11.43]$.[8] Table 2 summarizes Steps 5 through 7.

### TABLE 2    Frequency Distribution

| Interval | | Absolute Frequency |
|---|---|---|
| A | $-4.57 \leq$ observation $< -0.57$ | 3 |
| B | $-0.57 \leq$ observation $< \phantom{-}3.43$ | 4 |
| C | $\phantom{-}3.43 \leq$ observation $< \phantom{-}7.43$ | 4 |
| D | $\phantom{-}7.43 \leq$ observation $\leq 11.43$ | 1 |

Note that the intervals do not overlap, so each observation can be placed uniquely into one interval.

---

[7] Intervals are also sometimes called classes, ranges, or bins.

[8] The notation $[-4.57 \text{ to } -0.57)$ means $-4.57 \leq$ observation $< -0.57$. In this context, a square bracket indicates that the endpoint is included in the interval.

In practice, we may want to refine the above basic procedure. For example, we may want the intervals to begin and end with whole numbers for ease of interpretation. We also need to explain the choice of the number of intervals, $k$. We turn to these issues in discussing the construction of frequency distributions for the S&P 500.

We first consider the case of constructing a frequency distribution for the annual returns on the S&P 500 over the period 1926 to 2002. During that period, the return on the S&P 500 had a minimum value of $-43.34$ percent (in 1931) and a maximum value of $+53.99$ percent (in 1933). Thus the range of the data was $+54\% - (-43\%) = 97\%$, approximately. The question now is the number $k$ of intervals into which we should group observations. Although some guidelines for setting $k$ have been suggested in statistical literature, the setting of a useful value for $k$ often involves inspecting the data and exercising judgment. How much detail should we include? If we use too few intervals, we will summarize too much and lose pertinent characteristics. If we use too many intervals, we may not summarize enough.

We can establish an appropriate value for $k$ by evaluating the usefulness of the resulting interval width. A large number of empty intervals may indicate that we are trying to organize the data to present too much detail. Starting with a relatively small interval width, we can see whether or not the intervals are mostly empty and whether or not the value of $k$ associated with that interval width is too large. If intervals are mostly empty or $k$ is very large, we can consider increasingly larger intervals (smaller values of $k$) until we have a frequency distribution that effectively summarizes the distribution. For the annual S&P 500 series, return intervals of 1 percent width would result in 97 intervals and many of them would be empty because we have only 77 annual observations. We need to keep in mind that the purpose of a frequency distribution is to *summarize* the data. Suppose that for ease of interpretation we want to use an interval width stated in whole rather than fractional percents. A 2 percent interval width would have many fewer empty intervals than a 1 percent interval width and effectively summarize the data. A 2 percent interval width would be associated with $97/2 = 48.5$ intervals, which we can round up to 49 intervals. That number of intervals will cover $2\% \times 49 = 98\%$. We can confirm that if we start the smallest 2 percent interval at the whole number $-44.0$ percent, the final interval ends at $-44.0\% + 98\% = 54\%$ and includes the maximum return in the sample, 53.99 percent. In so constructing the frequency distribution, we will also have intervals that end and begin at a value of 0 percent, allowing us to count the negative and positive returns in the data. Without too much work, we have found an effective way to summarize the data. We will use return intervals of 2 percent, beginning with $-44\% \le R_t < -42\%$ (given as "$-44\%$ to $-42\%$" in the table) and ending with $52\% \le R_t \le 54\%$. Table 3 shows the frequency distribution for the annual total returns on the S&P 500.

Table 3 includes three other useful ways to present data, which we can compute once we have established the frequency distribution: the relative frequency, the cumulative frequency (also called the cumulative absolute frequency), and the cumulative relative frequency.

> ▶ **Definition of Relative Frequency.** The **relative frequency** is the absolute frequency of each interval divided by the total number of observations.

The **cumulative relative frequency** cumulates (adds up) the relative frequencies as we move from the first to the last interval. It tells us the fraction of observations that are less than the upper limit of each interval. Examining the frequency distribution given in Table 3, we see that the first return interval, $-44$ percent to $-42$ percent, has one observation; its relative frequency is $1/77$ or 1.30 percent. The cumulative frequency for this interval is 1 because only one observation is less than $-42$ percent. The cumulative relative frequency is thus $1/77$ or 1.30 percent. The next return interval has zero observations; therefore,

**TABLE 3   Frequency Distribution for the Annual Total Return on the S&P 500, 1926–2002**

| Return Interval | Frequency | Relative Frequency | Cumulative Frequency | Cumulative Relative Frequency |
|---|---|---|---|---|
| −44.0% to −42.0% | 1 | 1.30% | 1 | 1.30% |
| −42.0% to −40.0% | 0 | 0.00% | 1 | 1.30% |
| −40.0% to −38.0% | 0 | 0.00% | 1 | 1.30% |
| −38.0% to −36.0% | 0 | 0.00% | 1 | 1.30% |
| −36.0% to −34.0% | 1 | 1.30% | 2 | 2.60% |
| −34.0% to −32.0% | 0 | 0.00% | 2 | 2.60% |
| −32.0% to −30.0% | 0 | 0.00% | 2 | 2.60% |
| −30.0% to −28.0% | 0 | 0.00% | 2 | 2.60% |
| −28.0% to −26.0% | 1 | 1.30% | 3 | 3.90% |
| −26.0% to −24.0% | 1 | 1.30% | 4 | 5.19% |
| −24.0% to −22.0% | 1 | 1.30% | 5 | 6.49% |
| −22.0% to −20.0% | 0 | 0.00% | 5 | 6.49% |
| −20.0% to −18.0% | 0 | 0.00% | 5 | 6.49% |
| −18.0% to −16.0% | 0 | 0.00% | 5 | 6.49% |
| −16.0% to −14.0% | 1 | 1.30% | 6 | 7.79% |
| −14.0% to −12.0% | 0 | 0.00% | 6 | 7.79% |
| −12.0% to −10.0% | 4 | 5.19% | 10 | 12.99% |
| −10.0% to −8.0% | 7 | 9.09% | 17 | 22.08% |
| −8.0% to −6.0% | 1 | 1.30% | 18 | 23.38% |
| −6.0% to −4.0% | 1 | 1.30% | 19 | 24.68% |
| −4.0% to −2.0% | 1 | 1.30% | 20 | 25.97% |
| −2.0% to 0.0% | 3 | 3.90% | 23 | 29.87% |
| 0.0% to 2.0% | 2 | 2.60% | 25 | 32.47% |
| 2.0% to 4.0% | 0 | 0.00% | 25 | 32.47% |
| 4.0% to 6.0% | 4 | 5.19% | 29 | 37.66% |
| 6.0% to 8.0% | 4 | 5.19% | 33 | 42.86% |
| 8.0% to 10.0% | 1 | 1.30% | 34 | 44.16% |
| 10.0% to 12.0% | 3 | 3.90% | 37 | 48.05% |
| 12.0% to 14.0% | 1 | 1.30% | 38 | 49.35% |
| 14.0% to 16.0% | 1 | 1.30% | 39 | 50.65% |
| 16.0% to 18.0% | 2 | 2.60% | 41 | 53.25% |
| 18.0% to 20.0% | 6 | 7.79% | 47 | 61.04% |
| 20.0% to 22.0% | 3 | 3.90% | 50 | 64.94% |
| 22.0% to 24.0% | 5 | 6.49% | 55 | 71.43% |
| 24.0% to 26.0% | 2 | 2.60% | 57 | 74.03% |
| 26.0% to 28.0% | 1 | 1.30% | 58 | 75.32% |
| 28.0% to 30.0% | 1 | 1.30% | 59 | 76.62% |
| 30.0% to 32.0% | 5 | 6.49% | 64 | 83.12% |
| 32.0% to 34.0% | 4 | 5.19% | 68 | 88.31% |
| 34.0% to 36.0% | 0 | 0.00% | 68 | 88.31% |
| 36.0% to 38.0% | 4 | 5.19% | 72 | 93.51% |
| 38.0% to 40.0% | 0 | 0.00% | 72 | 93.51% |
| 40.0% to 42.0% | 0 | 0.00% | 72 | 93.51% |
| 42.0% to 44.0% | 2 | 2.60% | 74 | 96.10% |
| 44.0% to 46.0% | 0 | 0.00% | 74 | 96.10% |
| 46.0% to 48.0% | 1 | 1.30% | 75 | 97.40% |
| 48.0% to 50.0% | 0 | 0.00% | 75 | 97.40% |
| 50.0% to 52.0% | 0 | 0.00% | 75 | 97.40% |
| 52.0% to 54.0% | 2 | 2.60% | 77 | 100.00% |

*Note:* The lower class limit is the weak inequality ($\leq$) and the upper class limit is the strong inequality ($<$).
*Source:* Frequency distribution generated with Ibbotson Associates EnCorr Analyzer.

its cumulative frequency is 0 plus 1 and its cumulative relative frequency is 1.30 percent (the cumulative relative frequency from the previous interval). We can find the other cumulative frequencies by adding the (absolute) frequency to the previous cumulative frequency. The cumulative frequency, then, tells us the number of observations that are less than the upper limit of each return interval.

As Table 3 shows, return intervals have frequencies from 0 to 7 in this sample. The interval encompassing returns between −10 percent and −8 percent $(-10\% \le R_t < -8\%)$ has the most observations, seven. Next most frequent are returns between 18 percent and 20 percent $(18\% \le R_t < 20\%)$, with six observations. From the cumulative frequency column, we see that the number of negative returns is 23. The number of positive returns must then be equal to 77 − 23, or 54. We can express the number of positive and negative outcomes as a percentage of the total to get a sense of the risk inherent in investing in the stock market. During the 77-year period, the S&P 500 had negative annual returns 29.9 percent of the time (that is, 23/77). This result appears in the fifth column of Table 3, which reports the cumulative relative frequency.

The frequency distribution gives us a sense of not only where most of the observations lie but also whether the distribution is evenly distributed, lopsided, or peaked. In the case of the S&P 500, we can see that more than half of the outcomes are positive and most of those annual returns are larger than 10 percent. (Only 11 of the 54 positive annual returns—about 20 percent—were between 0 and 10 percent.)

Table 3 permits us to make an important further point about the choice of the number of intervals related to equity returns in particular. From the frequency distribution in Table 3, we can see that only five outcomes fall between −44 percent to −16 percent and between 38 percent to 54 percent. Stock return data are frequently characterized by a few very large or small outcomes. We could have collapsed the return intervals in the tails of the frequency distribution by choosing a smaller value of $k$, but then we would have lost the information about how extremely poorly or well the stock market had performed. A risk manager may need to know the worst possible outcomes and thus may want to have detailed information on the tails (the extreme values). A frequency distribution with a relatively large value of $k$ is useful for that. A portfolio manager or analyst may be equally interested in detailed information on the tails; however, if the manager or analyst wants a picture only of where most of the observations lie, he might prefer to use an interval width of 4 percent (25 intervals beginning at −44 percent), for example.

The frequency distribution for monthly returns on the S&P 500 looks quite different from that for annual returns. The monthly return series from January 1926 to December 2002 has 924 observations. Returns range from a minimum of approximately −30 percent to a maximum of approximately +43 percent. With such a large quantity of monthly data we must summarize to get a sense of the distribution, and so we group the data into 37 equally spaced return intervals of 2 percent. The gains from summarizing in this way are substantial. Table 4 presents the resulting frequency distribution. The absolute frequencies appear in the second column, followed by the relative frequencies. The relative frequencies are rounded to two decimal places. The cumulative absolute and cumulative relative frequencies appear in the fourth and fifth columns, respectively.

The advantage of a frequency distribution is evident in Table 4, which tells us that the vast majority of observations (599/924 = 65 percent) lie in the four intervals spanning −2 percent to +6 percent. Altogether, we have 355 negative returns and 569 positive returns. Almost 62 percent of the monthly outcomes are positive. Looking at the cumulative relative frequency in the last column, we see that the interval −2 percent to 0 percent shows a cumulative frequency of 38.42 percent, for an upper return limit of 0 percent. This means that 38.42 percent of the observations lie below the level of 0 percent. We can also see that not many observations are greater than +12 percent or less than −12 percent. Note that the frequency distributions of

**TABLE 4  Frequency Distribution for the Monthly Total Return on the S&P 500, January 1926 to December 2002**

| Return Interval | Absolute Frequency | Relative Frequency | Cumulative Absolute Frequency | Cumulative Relative Frequency |
|---|---|---|---|---|
| −30.0% to −28.0% | 1 | 0.11% | 1 | 0.11% |
| −28.0% to −26.0% | 0 | 0.00% | 1 | 0.11% |
| −26.0% to −24.0% | 1 | 0.11% | 2 | 0.22% |
| −24.0% to −22.0% | 1 | 0.11% | 3 | 0.32% |
| −22.0% to −20.0% | 2 | 0.22% | 5 | 0.54% |
| −20.0% to −18.0% | 2 | 0.22% | 7 | 0.76% |
| −18.0% to −16.0% | 2 | 0.22% | 9 | 0.97% |
| −16.0% to −14.0% | 3 | 0.32% | 12 | 1.30% |
| −14.0% to −12.0% | 5 | 0.54% | 17 | 1.84% |
| −12.0% to −10.0% | 6 | 0.65% | 23 | 2.49% |
| −10.0% to −8.0% | 20 | 2.16% | 43 | 4.65% |
| −8.0% to −6.0% | 30 | 3.25% | 73 | 7.90% |
| −6.0% to −4.0% | 54 | 5.84% | 127 | 13.74% |
| −4.0% to −2.0% | 90 | 9.74% | 217 | 23.48% |
| −2.0% to 0.0% | 138 | 14.94% | 355 | 38.42% |
| 0.0% to 2.0% | 182 | 19.70% | 537 | 58.12% |
| 2.0% to 4.0% | 153 | 16.56% | 690 | 74.68% |
| 4.0% to 6.0% | 126 | 13.64% | 816 | 88.31% |
| 6.0% to 8.0% | 58 | 6.28% | 874 | 94.59% |
| 8.0% to 10.0% | 21 | 2.27% | 895 | 96.86% |
| 10.0% to 12.0% | 14 | 1.52% | 909 | 98.38% |
| 12.0% to 14.0% | 6 | 0.65% | 915 | 99.03% |
| 14.0% to 16.0% | 2 | 0.22% | 917 | 99.24% |
| 16.0% to 18.0% | 3 | 0.32% | 920 | 99.57% |
| 18.0% to 20.0% | 0 | 0.00% | 920 | 99.57% |
| 20.0% to 22.0% | 0 | 0.00% | 920 | 99.57% |
| 22.0% to 24.0% | 0 | 0.00% | 920 | 99.57% |
| 24.0% to 26.0% | 1 | 0.11% | 921 | 99.68% |
| 26.0% to 28.0% | 0 | 0.00% | 921 | 99.68% |
| 28.0% to 30.0% | 0 | 0.00% | 921 | 99.68% |
| 30.0% to 32.0% | 0 | 0.00% | 921 | 99.68% |
| 32.0% to 34.0% | 0 | 0.00% | 921 | 99.68% |
| 34.0% to 36.0% | 0 | 0.00% | 921 | 99.68% |
| 36.0% to 38.0% | 0 | 0.00% | 921 | 99.68% |
| 38.0% to 40.0% | 2 | 0.22% | 923 | 99.89% |
| 40.0% to 42.0% | 0 | 0.00% | 923 | 99.89% |
| 42.0% to 44.0% | 1 | 0.11% | 924 | 100.00% |

*Note*: The lower class limit is the weak inequality ($\leq$) and the upper class limit is the strong inequality ($<$). The relative frequency is the absolute frequency or cumulative frequency divided by the total number of observations.
*Source*: Frequency distribution generated with Ibbotson Associates EnCorr Analyzer.

annual and monthly returns are not directly comparable. On average, we should expect the returns measured at shorter intervals (for example, months) to be smaller than returns measured over longer periods (for example, years).

Next, we construct a frequency distribution of average inflation-adjusted returns over 1900–2000 for 16 major equity markets.

## EXAMPLE 2

### Constructing a Frequency Distribution

How have equities rewarded investors in different countries in the long run? To answer this question, we could examine the average annual returns directly.[9] The worth of a nominal level of return depends on changes in the purchasing power of money, however, and internationally there have been a variety of experiences with price inflation. It is preferable, therefore, to compare the average real or inflation-adjusted returns earned by investors in different countries. Dimson, Marsh, and Staunton (2002) presented authoritative evidence on asset returns in 16 countries for the 101 years 1900–2000. Table 5 excerpts their findings for average inflation-adjusted returns.

**TABLE 5    Real (Inflation-Adjusted) Equity Returns: Sixteen Major Equity Markets, 1900–2000**

| Country | Arithmetic Mean |
|---|---|
| Australia | 9.0% |
| Belgium | 4.8% |
| Canada | 7.7% |
| Denmark | 6.2% |
| France | 6.3% |
| Germany | 8.8% |
| Ireland | 7.0% |
| Italy | 6.8% |
| Japan | 9.3% |
| Netherlands | 7.7% |
| South Africa | 9.1% |
| Spain | 5.8% |
| Sweden | 9.9% |
| Switzerland | 6.9% |
| United Kingdom | 7.6% |
| United States | 8.7% |

*Source*: Dimson, Marsh, and Staunton (2002), Table 9-3. Swiss equities date from 1911.

Table 6 summarizes the data in Table 5 into six intervals spanning 4 percent to 10 percent.

---

[9] The average or arithmetic mean of a set of values equals the sum of the values divided by the number of values summed. To find the arithmetic mean of 101 annual returns, for example, we sum the 101 annual returns and then divide the total by 101. Among the most familiar of statistical concepts, the arithmetic mean is explained in more detail later in the reading.

| TABLE 6 | Frequency Distribution of Average Real Equity Returns | | | |
| --- | --- | --- | --- | --- |
| Return Interval | Absolute Frequency | Relative Frequency | Cumulative Absolute Frequency | Cumulative Relative Frequency |
| 4.0% to 5.0% | 1 | 6.25% | 1 | 6.25% |
| 5.0% to 6.0% | 1 | 6.25% | 2 | 12.50% |
| 6.0% to 7.0% | 4 | 25.00% | 6 | 37.50% |
| 7.0% to 8.0% | 4 | 25.00% | 10 | 62.50% |
| 8.0% to 9.0% | 2 | 12.50% | 12 | 75.00% |
| 9.0% to 10% | 4 | 25.00% | 16 | 100.00% |

*Note*: Relative frequencies are rounded to sum to 100%.

As Table 6 shows, there is substantial variation internationally of average real equity returns. Three-fourths of the observations fall in one of three intervals: 6.0 to 7.0 percent, 7.0 to 8.0 percent, or 9.0 to 10.0 percent. Most average real equity returns are between 6.0 percent and 10 percent; the cumulative relative frequency of returns less than 6.0 percent was only 12.50 percent.

# THE GRAPHIC PRESENTATION OF DATA                    4

A graphical display of data allows us to visualize important characteristics quickly. For example, we may see that the distribution is symmetrically shaped, and this finding may influence which probability distribution we use to describe the data. In this section, we discuss the histogram, the frequency polygon, and the cumulative frequency distribution as methods for displaying data graphically. We construct all of these graphic presentations with the information contained in the frequency distribution of the S&P 500 shown in either Table 3 or Table 4.

## 4.1 The Histogram

A histogram is the graphical equivalent of a frequency distribution.

▶ **Definition of Histogram.** A **histogram** is a bar chart of data that have been grouped into a frequency distribution.

The advantage of the visual display is that we can see quickly where most of the observations lie. To see how a histogram is constructed, look at the return interval $18\% \leq R_t < 20\%$ in Table 3. This interval has an absolute frequency of 6. Therefore, we erect a bar or rectangle with a height of 6 over that return interval on the horizontal axis. Continuing with this process for all other return intervals yields a histogram. Figure 1 presents the histogram of the annual total return series on the S&P 500 from 1926 to 2002.

In the histogram in Figure 1, the height of each bar represents the absolute frequency for each return interval. The return interval $-10\% \leq R_t < -8\%$ has a frequency of 7 and is represented by the tallest bar in the histogram. Because there are no gaps between the interval limits, there are no gaps between the bars

**FIGURE 1   Histogram of S&P 500 Annual Total Returns: 1926 to 2002**

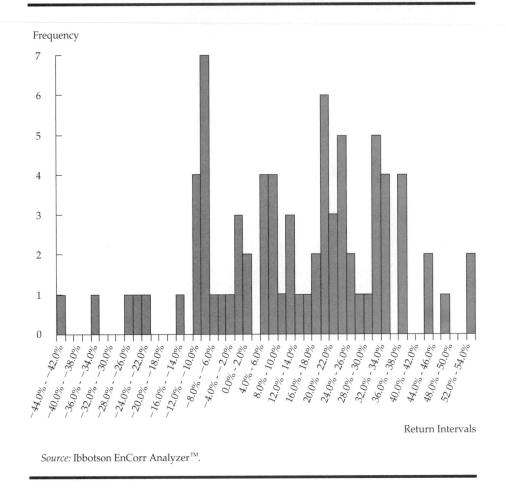

*Source:* Ibbotson EnCorr Analyzer™.

of the histogram. Many of the return intervals have zero frequency; therefore, they have no height in the histogram.

Figure 2 presents the histogram for the distribution of monthly returns on the S&P 500. Somewhat more symmetrically shaped than the histogram of annual returns shown in Figure 1, this histogram also appears more bell-shaped than the distribution of annual returns.

## 4.2 The Frequency Polygon and the Cumulative Frequency Distribution

Two other graphical tools for displaying data are the frequency polygon and the cumulative frequency distribution. To construct a **frequency polygon**, we plot the midpoint of each interval on the *x*-axis and the absolute frequency for that interval on the *y*-axis; we then connect neighboring points with a straight line. Figure 3 shows the frequency polygon for the 924 monthly returns for the S&P 500 from January 1926 to December 2002.

In Figure 3, we have replaced the bars in the histogram with points connected with straight lines. For example, the return interval 0 percent to 2 percent has an absolute frequency of 182. In the frequency polygon, we plot the return-interval midpoint of 1 percent and a frequency of 182. We plot all other

**FIGURE 2    Histogram of S&P 500 Monthly Total Returns:
January 1926 to December 2002**

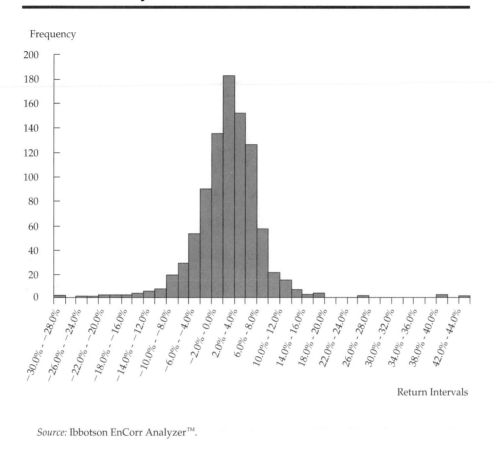

*Source:* Ibbotson EnCorr Analyzer™.

points in a similar way.[10] This form of visual display adds a degree of continuity to the representation of the distribution.

Another form of line graph is the cumulative frequency distribution. Such a graph can plot either the cumulative absolute or cumulative relative frequency against the upper interval limit. The cumulative frequency distribution allows us to see how many or what percent of the observations lie below a certain value. To construct the cumulative frequency distribution, we graph the returns in the fourth or fifth column of Table 4 against the upper limit of each return interval. Figure 4 presents a graph of the cumulative absolute distribution for the monthly returns on the S&P 500. Notice that the cumulative distribution tends to flatten out when returns are extremely negative or extremely positive. The steep slope in the middle of Figure 4 reflects the fact that most of the observations lie in the neighborhood of −2 percent to 6 percent.

We can further examine the relationship between the relative frequency and the cumulative relative frequency by looking at the two return intervals reproduced in Table 7. The first return interval (0 percent to 2 percent) has a cumulative relative frequency of 58.12 percent. The next return interval (2 percent to 4 percent) has a cumulative relative frequency of 74.68 percent. The change in the cumulative relative frequency as we move from one interval to the next is the next interval's relative

---

[10] Even though the upper limit on the interval is not a return falling in the interval, we still average it with the lower limit to determine the midpoint.

**FIGURE 3    Frequency Polygon of S&P 500 Monthly Total Returns: January 1926 to December 2002**

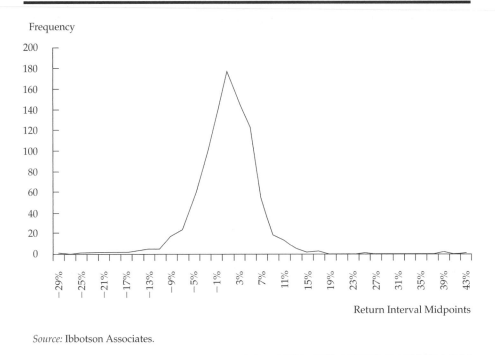

Frequency

*Source:* Ibbotson Associates.

**FIGURE 4    Cumulative Absolute Frequency Distribution of S&P 500 Monthly Total Returns: January 1926 to December 2002**

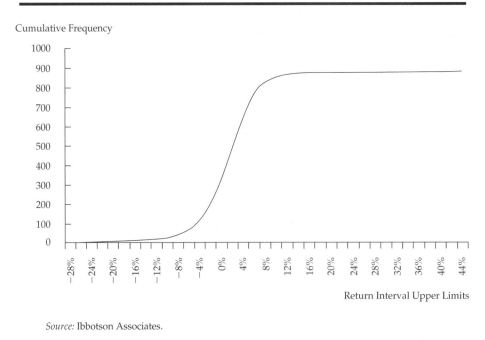

Cumulative Frequency

*Source:* Ibbotson Associates.

frequency. For instance, as we go from the first return interval (0 percent to 2 percent) to the next return interval (2 percent to 4 percent), the change in the cumulative relative frequency is $74.68\% - 58.12\% = 16.56\%$. (Values in the table have been rounded to two decimal places.) The fact that the slope is steep indicates that these frequencies are large. As you can see in the graph of the cumulative distribution, the slope of the curve changes as we move from the first return interval to the last. A fairly small slope for the cumulative distribution for the first few return intervals tells us that these return intervals do not contain many observations. You can go back to the frequency distribution in Table 4 and verify that the cumulative absolute frequency is only 23 observations (the cumulative relative frequency is 2.49 percent) up to the 10th return interval ($-12$ percent to $-10$ percent). In essence, the slope of the cumulative absolute distribution at any particular interval is proportional to the number of observations in that interval.

| **TABLE 7** Selected Class Frequencies for the S&P 500 Monthly Returns | | | | |
|---|---|---|---|---|
| **Return Interval** | **Absolute Frequency** | **Relative Frequency** | **Cumulative Absolute Frequency** | **Cumulative Relative Frequency** |
| 0.0% to 2.0% | 182 | 19.70% | 537 | 58.12% |
| 2.0% to 4.0% | 153 | 16.56% | 690 | 74.68% |

# MEASURES OF CENTRAL TENDENCY     5

So far, we have discussed methods we can use to organize and present data so that they are more understandable. The frequency distribution of an asset class's return series, for example, reveals the nature of the risks that investors may encounter in a particular asset class. As an illustration, the histogram for the annual returns on the S&P 500 clearly shows that large positive and negative annual returns are common. Although frequency distributions and histograms provide a convenient way to summarize a series of observations, these methods are just a first step toward describing the data. In this section we discuss the use of quantitative measures that explain characteristics of data. Our focus is on measures of central tendency and other measures of location or location parameters. A **measure of central tendency** specifies where the data are centered. Measures of central tendency are probably more widely used than any other statistical measure because they can be computed and applied easily. **Measures of location** include not only measures of central tendency but other measures that illustrate the location or distribution of data.

In the following subsections we explain the common measures of central tendency—the arithmetic mean, the median, the mode, the weighted mean, and the geometric mean. We also explain other useful measures of location, including quartiles, quintiles, deciles, and percentiles.

## 5.1 The Arithmetic Mean

Analysts and portfolio managers often want one number that describes a representative possible outcome of an investment decision. The arithmetic mean is by far the most frequently used measure of the middle or center of data.

▶ **Definition of Arithmetic Mean.** The **arithmetic mean** is the sum of the observations divided by the number of observations.

We can compute the arithmetic mean for both populations and samples, known as the population mean and the sample mean, respectively.

### 5.1.1    The Population Mean

The population mean is the arithmetic mean computed for a population. If we can define a population adequately, then we can calculate the population mean as the arithmetic mean of all the observations or values in the population. For example, analysts examining the fiscal 2002 year-over-year growth in same-store sales of major U.S. wholesale clubs might define the population of interest to include only three companies: BJ's Wholesale Club (NYSE: BJ), Costco Wholesale Corporation (Nasdaq: COST), and Sam's Club, part of Wal-Mart Stores (NYSE: WMT).[11] As another example, if a portfolio manager's investment universe (the set of securities she must choose from) is the Nikkei–Dow Jones Average, the relevant population is the 225 shares on the First Section of the Tokyo Stock Exchange that compose the Nikkei.

▶ **Population Mean Formula.** The **population mean**, $\mu$, is the arithmetic mean value of a population. For a finite population, the population mean is

$$\mu = \frac{\sum_{i=1}^{N} X_i}{N} \tag{7-2}$$

where $N$ is the number of observations in the entire population and $X_i$ is the $i$th observation.

The population mean is an example of a parameter. The population mean is unique; that is, a given population has only one mean. To illustrate the calculation, we can take the case of the population mean of current price-to-earnings ratio (P/E) of stocks of U.S. companies running major wholesale clubs as of the beginning of September 2003. As of that date, the current P/Es for BJ, COST, and WMT were 16.73, 22.02, and 29.30, respectively, according to First Call/Thomson Financial. Thus the population mean current P/E on that date was $\mu = (16.73 + 22.02 + 29.30)/3 = 68.05/3 = 22.68$.

### 5.1.2    The Sample Mean

The sample mean is the arithmetic mean computed for a sample. Many times we cannot observe every member of a set; instead, we observe a subset or sample of the population. The concept of the mean can be applied to the observations in a sample with a slight change in notation.

▶ **Sample Mean Formula.** The **sample mean** or average, $\overline{X}$ (read "X-bar"), is the arithmetic mean value of a sample:

$$\overline{X} = \frac{\sum_{i=1}^{n} X_i}{n} \tag{7-3}$$

where $n$ is the number of observations in the sample.

---

[11] A wholesale club implements a store format dedicated mostly to bulk sales in warehouse-sized stores to customers who pay membership dues. As of the early 2000s, those three wholesale clubs dominated the segment in the United States.

Equation 7-3 tells us to sum the values of the observations ($X_i$) and divide the sum by the number of observations. For example, if the sample of P/E multiples contains the values 35, 30, 22, 18, 15, and 12, the sample mean P/E is 132/6 = 22. The sample mean is also called the arithmetic average.[12] As we discussed earlier, the sample mean is a statistic (that is, a descriptive measure of a sample).

Means can be computed for individual units or over time. For instance, the sample might be the 2003 return on equity (ROE) for the 300 companies in the Financial Times Stock Exchange (FTSE) Eurotop 300, an index of Europe's 300 largest companies. In this case, we calculate mean ROE in 2003 as an average across 300 individual units. When we examine the characteristics of some units at a specific point in time (such as ROE for the FTSE Eurotop 300), we are examining **cross-sectional data**. The mean of these observations is called a cross-sectional mean. On the other hand, if our sample consists of the historical monthly returns on the FTSE Eurotop 300 for the past five years, then we have **time-series data**. The mean of these observations is called a time-series mean. We will examine specialized statistical methods related to the behavior of time series in the reading on times-series analysis.

Next, we show an example of finding the sample mean return for equities in 16 European countries for 2002. In this case, the mean is cross-sectional because we are averaging individual country returns.

## EXAMPLE 3

### Calculating a Cross-Sectional Mean

The MSCI EAFE (Europe, Australasia, and Far East) Index is a free float-adjusted market capitalization index designed to measure developed-market equity performance excluding the United States and Canada.[13] As of the end of 2002, the EAFE consisted of 21 developed market country indexes, including indexes for 16 European markets, 2 Australasian markets (Australia and New Zealand), and 3 Far Eastern markets (Hong Kong, Japan, and Singapore).

Suppose we are interested in the local currency performance of the 16 European markets in the EAFE in 2002, a severe bear market year. We want to find the sample mean total return for 2002 across these 16 markets. The return series reported in Table 8 are in local currency (that is, returns are for investors living in the country). Because this return is not stated in any single investor's home currency, it is not a return any single investor would earn. Rather, it is an average of returns in 16 local currencies.

| TABLE 8 | Total Returns for European Equity Markets, 2002 |
| --- | --- |
| **Market** | **Total Return in Local Currency** |
| Austria | −2.97% |
| Belgium | −29.71% |
| *(Table continued on next page . . .)* | |

[12] Statisticians prefer the term "mean" to "average." Some writers refer to all measures of central tendency (including the median and mode) as averages. The term "mean" avoids any possibility of confusion.

[13] The term "free float adjusted" means that the weights of companies in the index reflect the value of the shares actually available for investment.

| TABLE 8 (continued) | |
| --- | --- |
| **Market** | **Total Return in Local Currency** |
| Denmark | −29.67% |
| Finland | −41.65% |
| France | −33.99% |
| Germany | −44.05% |
| Greece | −39.06% |
| Ireland | −38.97% |
| Italy | −23.64% |
| Netherlands | −34.27% |
| Norway | −29.73% |
| Portugal | −28.29% |
| Spain | −29.47% |
| Sweden | −43.07% |
| Switzerland | −25.84% |
| United Kingdom | −25.66% |

*Source*: www.mscidata.com.

Using the data in Table 8, calculate the sample mean return for the 16 equity markets in 2002.

**Solution:** The calculation applies Equation 7-3 to the returns in Table 8: $(-2.97 - 29.71 - 29.67 - 41.65 - 33.99 - 44.05 - 39.06 - 38.97 - 23.64 - 34.27 - 29.73 - 28.29 - 29.47 - 43.07 - 25.84 - 25.66)/16 = -500.04/16 = -31.25$ percent.

In Example 3, we can verify that seven markets had returns less than the mean and nine had returns that were greater. We should not expect any of the actual observations to equal the mean, because sample means provide only a summary of the data being analyzed. As an analyst, you will often need to find a few numbers that describe the characteristics of the distribution. The mean is generally the statistic that you will use as a measure of the typical outcome for a distribution. You can then use the mean to compare the performance of two different markets. For example, you might be interested in comparing the stock market performance of investments in Pacific Rim countries with investments in European countries. You can use the mean returns in these markets to compare investment results.

### 5.1.3 Properties of the Arithmetic Mean

The arithmetic mean can be likened to the center of gravity of an object. Figure 5 expresses this analogy graphically by plotting nine hypothetical observations on a bar. The nine observations are 2, 4, 4, 6, 10, 10, 12, 12, and 12; the arith-

**FIGURE 5    Center of Gravity Analogy for the Arithmetic Mean**

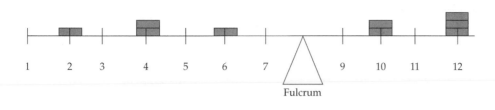

When the fulcrum is placed at 8, the bar is perfectly balanced.

metic mean is $72/9 = 8$. The observations are plotted on the bar with various heights based on their frequency (that is, 2 is one unit high, 4 is two units high, and so on). When the bar is placed on a fulcrum, it balances only when the fulcrum is located at the point on the scale that corresponds to the arithmetic mean.

As analysts, we often use the mean return as a measure of the typical outcome for an asset. As in the example above, however, some outcomes are above the mean and some are below it. We can calculate the distance between the mean and each outcome and call it a deviation. Mathematically, it is always true that the sum of the deviations around the mean equals to 0. We can see this by using the definition of the arithmetic mean shown in Equation 7-3, multiplying both sides of the equation by $n$: $n\overline{X} = \sum_{i=1}^{n} X_i$. The sum of the deviations from the mean can thus be calculated as follows:

$$\sum_{i=1}^{n} (X_i - \overline{X}) = \sum_{i=1}^{n} X_i - \sum_{i=1}^{n} \overline{X} = \sum_{i=1}^{n} X_i - n\overline{X} = 0$$

Deviations from the arithmetic mean are important information because they indicate risk. The concept of deviations around the mean forms the foundation for the more complex concepts of variance, skewness, and kurtosis, which we will discuss later in this reading.

An advantage of the arithmetic mean over two other measures of central tendency, the median and mode, is that the mean uses all the information about the size and magnitude of the observations. The mean is also easy to work with mathematically.

A property and potential drawback of the arithmetic mean is its sensitivity to extreme values. Because all observations are used to compute the mean, the arithmetic mean can be pulled sharply upward or downward by extremely large or small observations, respectively. For example, suppose we compute the arithmetic mean of the following seven numbers: 1, 2, 3, 4, 5, 6, and 1,000. The mean is $1,021/7 = 145.86$ or approximately 146. Because the magnitude of the mean, 146, is so much larger than that of the bulk of the observations (the first six), we might question how well it represents the location of the data. In practice, although an extreme value or outlier in a financial dataset may only represent a rare value in the population, it may also reflect an error in recording the value of an observation, or an observation generated from a different population from that producing the other observations in the sample. In the latter two cases in particular, the arithmetic mean could be misleading. Perhaps the most common approach in such cases is to report the median in place of or in addition to the mean.[14] We discuss the median next.

## 5.2 The Median

A second important measure of central tendency is the median.

> ▶ **Definition of Median.** The **median** is the value of the middle item of a set of items that has been sorted into ascending or descending order. In an odd-numbered sample of $n$ items, the median occupies the $(n + 1)/2$ position. In an even-numbered sample, we define the median as the mean of the values of items occupying the $n/2$ and $(n + 2)/2$ positions (the two middle items).[15]

Earlier we gave the current P/Es of three wholesale clubs as 16.73, 22.02, and 29.30. With an odd number of observations ($n = 3$), the median occupies the $(n + 1)/2 = 4/2 = 2$nd position. The median P/E was 22.02. The P/E value of 22.02 is the "middlemost" observation: One lies above it, and one lies below it. Whether we use the calculation for an even- or odd-numbered sample, an equal number of observations lie above and below the median. A distribution has only one median.

A potential advantage of the median is that, unlike the mean, extreme values do not affect it. The median, however, does not use all the information about the size and magnitude of the observations; it focuses only on the relative position of the ranked observations. Calculating the median is also more complex; to do so, we need to order the observations from smallest to largest, determine whether the sample size is even or odd and, on that basis, apply one of two calculations. Mathematicians express this disadvantage by saying that the median is less mathematically tractable than the mean.

To demonstrate finding the median, we use the data from Example 3, reproduced in Table 9 in ascending order of the 2002 total return for European equities. Because this sample has 16 observations, the median is the mean of the values in the sorted array that occupy the $16/2 = 8$th and $18/2 = 9$th positions. Norway's return occupies the eighth position with a return of $-29.73$ percent, and Belgium's return occupies the ninth position with a return of $-29.71$ percent. The median, as the mean of these two returns, is $(-29.73 - 29.71)/2 = -29.72$ percent. Note that the median is not influenced by extremely large or small outcomes. Had Germany's total return been a much lower value or Austria's total return a much larger value, the median would not have changed. Using a context that arises often in practice, Example 4 shows how to use the mean and median in a sample with extreme values.

---

[14] Other approaches to handling extreme values involve variations of the arithmetic mean. The **trimmed mean** is computed by excluding a stated small percentage of the lowest and highest values and then computing an arithmetic mean of the remaining values. For example, a 5 percent trimmed mean discards the lowest 2.5 percent and the largest 2.5 percent of values and computes the mean of the remaining 95 percent of values. A trimmed mean is used in sports competitions when judges' lowest and highest scores are discarded in computing a contestant's score. A **Winsorized mean** assigns a stated percent of the lowest values equal to one specified low value, and a stated percent of the highest values equal to one specified high value, then computes a mean from the restated data. For example, a 95 percent Winsorized mean sets the bottom 2.5 percent of values equal to the 2.5th percentile value and the upper 2.5 percent of values equal to the 97.5th percentile value. (Percentile values are defined later.)

[15] The notation $M_d$ is occasionally used for the median. Just as for the mean, we may distinguish between a population median and a sample median. With the understanding that a population median divides a population in half while a sample median divides a sample in half, we follow general usage in using the term "median" without qualification, for the sake of brevity.

### TABLE 9    Total Returns for European Equity Markets, 2002 (in Ascending Order)

| No. | Market | Total Return in Local Currency |
|---|---|---|
| 1 | Germany | −44.05% |
| 2 | Sweden | −43.07% |
| 3 | Finland | −41.65% |
| 4 | Greece | −39.06% |
| 5 | Ireland | −38.97% |
| 6 | Netherlands | −34.27% |
| 7 | France | −33.99% |
| 8 | Norway | −29.73% |
| 9 | Belgium | −29.71% |
| 10 | Denmark | −29.67% |
| 11 | Spain | −29.47% |
| 12 | Portugal | −28.29% |
| 13 | Switzerland | −25.84% |
| 14 | United Kingdom | −25.66% |
| 15 | Italy | −23.64% |
| 16 | Austria | −2.97% |

*Source*: www.mscidata.com.

### EXAMPLE 4

**Median and Arithmetic Mean: The Case of the Price–Earnings Ratio**

Suppose a client asks you for a valuation analysis on the seven-stock U.S. common stock portfolio given in Table 10. The stocks are equally weighted in the portfolio. One valuation measure that you use is P/E, the ratio of share price to earnings per share (EPS). Many variations exist for the denominator in the P/E, but you are examining P/E defined as current price divided by the current mean of all analysts' EPS estimates for the company for the current fiscal year ("Consensus Current EPS" in the table).[16] The values in Table 10 are as of 11 September 2003. For comparison purposes, the consensus current P/E on the S&P 500 was 23.63 at that time.

### TABLE 10    P/Es for a Client Portfolio

| Stock | Consensus Current EPS | Consensus Current P/E |
|---|---|---|
| Exponent Inc. (Nasdaq: EXPO) | 1.23 | 13.68 |
| Express Scripts (Nasdaq: ESRX) | 3.19 | 19.07 |
| General Dynamics (NYSE: GD) | 4.95 | 17.56 |

*(Table continued on next page . . .)*

---

[16] For more information on price multiples, see Stowe, Robinson, Pinto, and McLeavey (2002).

| TABLE 10    (continued) | | |
| --- | --- | --- |
| **Stock** | **Consensus Current EPS** | **Consensus Current P/E** |
| Limited Brands (NYSE: LTD) | 1.06 | 15.60 |
| Merant plc (Nasdaq: MRNT) | 0.03 | 443.33 |
| Microsoft Corporation (Nasdaq: MSFT) | 1.11 | 25.61 |
| O'Reilly Automotive, Inc. (Nasdaq: ORLY) | 1.84 | 21.01 |

*Source*: First Call/Thomson Financial.

Using the data in Table 10, address the following:

1. Calculate the arithmetic mean P/E.
2. Calculate the median P/E.
3. Evaluate the mean and median P/Es as measures of central tendency for the above portfolio.

**Solution to 1:** The mean P/E is (13.68 + 19.07 + 17.56 + 15.60 + 443.33 + 25.61 + 21.01)/7 = 555.86/7 = 79.41.

**Solution to 2:** The P/Es listed in ascending order are:

13.68    15.60    17.56    19.07    21.01    25.61    443.33

The sample has an odd number of observations with $n = 7$, so the median occupies the $(n + 1)/2 = 8/2 = $ 4th position in the sorted list. Therefore, the median P/E is 19.07.

**Solution to 3:** Merant's P/E of approximately 443 tremendously influences the value of the portfolio's arithmetic mean P/E. The mean P/E of 79 is much larger than the P/E of six of the seven stocks in the portfolio. The mean P/E also misleadingly suggests an orientation to stocks with high P/Es. The mean P/E of the stocks excluding Merant, or excluding the largest- and smallest-P/E stocks (Merant and Exponent), is below the S&P 500's P/E of 23.63. The median P/E of 19.07 appears to better represent the central tendency of the P/Es.

It frequently happens that when a company's EPS is close to zero—at a low point in the business cycle, for example—its P/E is extremely high. The high P/E in those circumstances reflects an anticipated future recovery of earnings. Extreme P/E values need to be investigated and handled with care. For reasons related to this example, analysts often use the median of price multiples to characterize the valuation of industry groups.

## 5.3 The Mode

The third important measure of central tendency is the mode.

▶ **Definition of Mode.** The **mode** is the most frequently occurring value in a distribution.[17]

---

[17] The notation $M_o$ is occasionally used for the mode. Just as for the mean and the median, we may distinguish between a population mode and a sample mode. With the understanding that a population mode is the value with the greatest probability of occurrence, while a sample mode is the most frequently occurring value in the sample, we follow general usage in using the term "mode" without qualification, for the sake of brevity.

A distribution can have more than one mode, or even no mode. When a distribution has one most frequently occurring value, the distribution is said to be unimodal. If a distribution has two most frequently occurring values, then it has two modes and we say it is bimodal. If the distribution has three most frequently occurring values, then it is trimodal. When all the values in a data set are different, the distribution has no mode because no value occurs more frequently than any other value.

Stock return data and other data from continuous distributions may not have a modal outcome. When such data are grouped into intervals, however, we often find an interval (possibly more than one) with the highest frequency: the **modal interval** (or intervals). For example, the frequency distribution for the monthly returns on the S&P 500 has a modal interval of 0 percent to 2 percent, as shown in Figure 2; this return interval has 182 observations out of a total of 924. The modal interval always has the highest bar in the histogram.

The mode is the only measure of central tendency that can be used with nominal data. When we categorize mutual funds into different styles and assign a number to each style, the mode of these categorized data is the most frequent mutual fund style.

## 5.4 Other Concepts of Mean

Earlier we explained the arithmetic mean, which is a fundamental concept for describing the central tendency of data. Other concepts of mean are very important in investments, however. In the following, we discuss such concepts.

---

### EXAMPLE 5

#### Calculating a Mode

Table 11 gives the credit ratings on senior unsecured debt as of September 2002 of nine U.S. department stores rated by Moody's Investors Service. In descending order of credit quality (increasing expected probability of default), Moody's ratings are Aaa, Aa1, Aa2, Aa3, A1, A2, A3, Baa1, Baa2, Baa3, Ba1, Ba2, Ba3, B1, B2, B3, Caa, Ca, and C.[18]

TABLE 11    Senior Unsecured Debt Ratings:
            U.S. Department Stores, September 2002

| Company | Credit Rating |
| --- | --- |
| Dillards, Inc. | Ba3 |
| Federated Department Stores, Inc. | Baa1 |
| Kohl's Corporation | A3 |
| May's Department Stores Company | A2 |
| Neiman Marcus Group, Inc. | Baa2 |
| Nordstrom, Inc. | Baa1 |
| Penney, JC, Company, Inc. | Ba2 |

*(Table continued on next page . . .)*

---

[18] For more information on credit risk and credit ratings, see Fabozzi (2004a).

| TABLE 11 (continued) | |
| --- | --- |
| **Company** | **Credit Rating** |
| Saks Incorporated | B1 |
| Sears, Roebuck and Co. | Baa1 |

*Source*: Moody's Investors Service.

Using the data in Table 11, address the following concerning the senior unsecured debt of U.S. department stores.

**1.** State the modal credit rating.

**2.** State the median credit rating.

**Solution to 1:** The group of companies represents seven distinct credit ratings, ranging from A2 to B1. To make our task easy, we first organize the ratings into a frequency distribution.

| TABLE 12 | Senior Unsecured Debt Ratings: U.S. Department Stores, Distribution of Credit Ratings |
| --- | --- |
| **Credit Rating** | **Frequency** |
| A2 | 1 |
| A3 | 1 |
| Baa1 | 3 |
| Baa2 | 1 |
| Ba2 | 1 |
| Ba3 | 1 |
| B1 | 1 |

All credit ratings have a frequency of 1 except for Baa1, which has a frequency of 3. Therefore, the modal credit rating of U.S. department stores as of the date of the Moody's report was Baa1. Moody's considers bonds rated Baa1 to be medium-grade obligations—they are neither highly protected nor poorly secured.

**Solution to 2:** For the group $n = 9$, an odd number. The group's median occupies the $(n + 1)/2 = 10/2 = $ 5th position. We see from Table 12 that Baa1 occupies the fifth position. Therefore the median credit rating at September 2002 was Baa1.

### 5.4.1 The Weighted Mean

The concept of weighted mean arises repeatedly in portfolio analysis. In the arithmetic mean, all observations are equally weighted by the factor $1/n$ (or $1/N$). In working with portfolios, we need the more general concept of weighted mean to allow different weights on different observations.

To illustrate the weighted mean concept, an investment manager with $100 million to invest might allocate $70 million to equities and $30 million to bonds. The portfolio has a weight of 0.70 on stocks and 0.30 on bonds. How do we calculate the return on this portfolio? The portfolio's return clearly involves an averaging of the returns on the stock and bond investments. The mean that we compute, however, must reflect the fact that stocks have a 70 percent weight in the portfolio and bonds have a 30 percent weight. The way to reflect this weighting is to multiply the return on the stock investment by 0.70 and the return on the bond investment by 0.30, then sum the two results. This sum is an example of a weighted mean. It would be incorrect to take an arithmetic mean of the return on the stock and bond investments, equally weighting the returns on the two asset classes.

Consider a portfolio invested in Canadian stocks and bonds in which the stock component is indexed on the S&P/TSX Composite Index and the bond component is indexed on the RBC Capital Markets Canadian Bond Market Index. These indexes represent the broad Canadian equity and bond markets, respectively. The portfolio manager allocates 60 percent of the portfolio to Canadian stocks and 40 percent to Canadian bonds. Table 13 presents total returns for these indexes for 1998 to 2002.

### TABLE 13   Total Returns for Canadian Equities and Bonds, 1998–2002

| Year | Equities | Bonds |
|------|----------|-------|
| 1998 | −1.6% | 9.1% |
| 1999 | 31.7% | −1.1% |
| 2000 | 7.4% | 10.3% |
| 2001 | −12.6% | 8.0% |
| 2002 | −12.4% | 8.7% |

*Source*: www.fidelity.ca and www.money.msn.ca.

▶ **Weighted Mean Formula.** The **weighted mean** $\overline{X}_w$ (read "$X$-bar sub-$w$"), for a set of observations $X_1, X_2, \ldots, X_n$ with corresponding weights of $w_1, w_2, \ldots, w_n$ is computed as

$$\overline{X}_w = \sum_{i=1}^{n} w_i X_i$$

(7-4)

where the sum of the weights equals 1; that is, $\sum_i w_i = 1$.

In the context of portfolios, a positive weight represents an asset held long and a negative weight represents an asset held short.[19]

The return on the portfolio under consideration is the weighted average of the return on Canadian stocks and Canadian bonds (the weight on stocks is 0.60;

---

[19] The formula for the weighted mean can be compared to the formula for the arithmetic mean. For a set of observations $X_1, X_2, \ldots, X_n$, let the weights $w_1, w_2, \ldots, w_n$ all equal $1/n$. Under this assumption, the formula for the weighted mean is $(1/n)\sum_{i=1}^{n} X_i$. This is the formula for the arithmetic mean. Therefore, the arithmetic mean is a special case of the weighted mean in which all the weights are equal.

that on bonds is 0.40). Apart from expenses, if the portfolio tracks the indexes perfectly, we find, using Equation 7-4, that

$$
\begin{aligned}
\text{Portfolio return for 1998} &= w_{\text{stock}}R_{\text{stock}} + w_{\text{bonds}}R_{\text{bonds}} \\
&= 0.60(-1.6\%) + 0.40(9.1\%) \\
&= 2.7\%
\end{aligned}
$$

It should be clear that the correct mean to compute in this example is the weighted mean and not the arithmetic mean. If we had computed the arithmetic mean for 1998, we would have calculated a return equal to ½(−1.6%) + ½(9.1%) = (−1.6% + 9.1%)/2 = 3.8%. Given that the portfolio manager invested 60 percent in stocks and 40 percent in bonds, the arithmetic mean would underweight the investment in stocks and overweight the investment in bonds, resulting in a number for portfolio return that is too high by 1.1 percentage points (3.8% − 2.7%).

Now suppose that the portfolio manager maintains constant weights of 60 percent in stocks and 40 percent in bonds for all five years. This method is called a constant-proportions strategy. Because value is price multiplied by quantity, price fluctuation causes portfolio weights to change. As a result, the constant-proportions strategy requires rebalancing to restore the weights in stocks and bonds to their target levels. Assuming that the portfolio manager is able to accomplish the necessary rebalancing, we can compute the portfolio returns in 1999, 2000, 2001, and 2002 with Equation 7-4 as follows:

Portfolio return for 1999 = 0.60(31.7) + 0.40(−1.1) = 18.6%

Portfolio return for 2000 = 0.60(7.4) + 0.40(10.3) = 8.6%

Portfolio return for 2001 = 0.60(−12.6) + 0.40(8.0) = −4.4%

Portfolio return for 2002 = 0.60(−12.4) + 0.40(8.7) = −4.0%

We can now find the time-series mean of the returns for 1998 through 2002 using Equation 7-3 for the arithmetic mean. The time-series mean total return for the portfolio is (2.7 + 18.6 + 8.6 − 4.4 − 4.0)/5 = 21.5/5 = 4.3 percent.

Instead of calculating the portfolio time-series mean return from portfolio annual returns, we can calculate the arithmetic mean bond and stock returns for the five years and then apply the portfolio weights of 0.60 and 0.40, respectively, to those values. The mean stock return is (−1.6 + 31.7 + 7.4 − 12.6 − 12.4)/5 = 12.5/5 = 2.5 percent. The mean bond return is (9.1 − 1.1 + 10.3 + 8.0 + 8.7)/5 = 35.0/5 = 7.0 percent. Therefore, the mean total return for the portfolio is 0.60(2.5) + 0.40(7.0) = 4.3 percent, which agrees with our previous calculation.

### EXAMPLE 6

#### Portfolio Return as a Weighted Mean

Table 14 gives information on the estimated average asset allocation of Canadian pension funds as well as four-year asset class returns.[20]

---

[20] In Table 14, equities are represented by the S&P/TSX Composite Index, U.S. equities by the S&P 500, international (non-North American) equities by the MSCI EAFE Index, bonds by the Scotia Capital Markets Universe Bond Index, mortgages by the Scotia Capital Markets Mortgage Index, real estate by the Standard Life Investments pooled real estate fund, and cash and equivalents by 91-day T-bills.

**TABLE 14  Asset Allocation for Average Canadian Pension Fund, as of 31 March 2003**

| Asset Class | Asset Allocation (Weight) | Asset Class Return (%) |
|---|---|---|
| Equities | 34.6 | 0.6 |
| U.S. equities | 10.8 | −9.3 |
| International equities | 6.4 | −10.5 |
| Bonds | 34.0 | 6.0 |
| Mortgages | 1.3 | 9.0 |
| Real estate | 4.5 | 10.2 |
| Cash and equivalents | 8.4 | 4.2 |

*Source*: Standard Life Investments, Inc.

Using the information in Table 14, calculate the mean return earned by the average Canadian pension fund over the four years ending 31 March 2003.

**Solution:** Converting the percent asset allocation to decimal form, we find the mean return as a weighted average of the asset class returns. We have

$$
\begin{aligned}
\text{Mean portfolio return} &= 0.346(0.6\%) + 0.108(-9.3\%) + \\
&\quad 0.064(-10.5\%) + 0.340(6.0\%) + \\
&\quad 0.013(9.0\%) + 0.045(10.2\%) + 0.084(4.2\%) \\
&= 0.208\% - 1.004\% - 0.672\% + 2.040\% + \\
&\quad 0.117\% + 0.459\% + 0.353\% \\
&= 1.5 \text{ percent}
\end{aligned}
$$

The previous examples illustrate the general principle that a portfolio return is a weighted sum. Specifically, a portfolio's return is the weighted average of the returns on the assets in the portfolio; the weight applied to each asset's return is the fraction of the portfolio invested in that asset.

Market indexes are computed as weighted averages. For market-capitalization indexes such as the CAC-40 in France or the S&P 500 in the United States, each included stock receives a weight corresponding to its outstanding market value divided by the total market value of all stocks in the index.

Our illustrations of weighted mean use past data, but they might just as well use forward-looking data. When we take a weighted average of forward-looking data, the weighted mean is called **expected value**. Suppose we make one forecast for the year-end level of the S&P 500 assuming economic expansion and another forecast for the year-end level of the S&P 500 assuming economic contraction. If we multiply the first forecast by the probability of expansion and the second forecast by the probability of contraction and then add these weighted forecasts, we are calculating the expected value of the S&P 500 at year-end. If we take a weighted average of possible future returns on the S&P 500, we are computing the S&P 500's expected return. The probabilities must sum to 1, satisfying the condition on the weights in the expression for weighted mean, Equation 7-4.

### 5.4.2  The Geometric Mean

The geometric mean is most frequently used to average rates of change over time or to compute the growth rate of a variable. In investments, we frequently use the geometric mean to average a time series of rates of return on an asset or a portfolio, or to compute the growth rate of a financial variable such as earnings or sales. In the reading on the time value of money, for instance, we computed a sales growth rate (Example 17). That growth rate was a geometric mean. Because of the subject's importance, in a later section we will return to the use of the geometric mean and offer practical perspectives on its use. The geometric mean is defined by the following formula.

▶ **Geometric Mean Formula.** The **geometric mean**, $G$, of a set of observations $X_1, X_2, \ldots, X_n$ is

$$G = \sqrt[n]{X_1 X_2 X_3 \ldots X_n}$$

(7-5)

with $X_i \geq 0$ for $i = 1, 2, \ldots, n$.

Equation 7-5 has a solution, and the geometric mean exists, only if the product under the radical sign is non-negative. We impose the restriction that all the observations $X_i$ in Equation 7-5 are greater than or equal to zero. We can solve for the geometric mean using Equation 7-5 directly with any calculator that has an exponentiation key (on most calculators, $y^x$). We can also solve for the geometric mean using natural logarithms. Equation 7-5 can also be stated as

$$\ln G = \frac{1}{n} \ln(X_1 X_2 X_3 \ldots X_n)$$

or as

$$\ln G = \frac{\sum_{i=1}^{n} \ln X_i}{n}$$

When we have computed $\ln G$, then $G = e^{\ln G}$ (on most calculators, the key for this step is $e^x$).

Risky assets can have negative returns up to $-100$ percent (if their price falls to zero), so we must take some care in defining the relevant variables to average in computing a geometric mean. We cannot just use the product of the returns for the sample and then take the $n$th root because the returns for any period could be negative. We must redefine the returns to make them positive. We do this by adding 1.0 to the returns expressed as decimals. The term $(1 + R_t)$ represents the year-ending value relative to an initial unit of investment at the beginning of the year. As long as we use $(1 + R_t)$, the observations will never be negative because the biggest negative return is $-100$ percent. The result is the geometric mean of $1 + R_t$; by then subtracting 1.0 from this result, we obtain the geometric mean of the individual returns $R_t$. For example, the returns on Canadian stocks as represented by the S&P/TSX Composite Index during the 1998–2002 period were given in Table 13 as $-0.016, 0.317, 0.074, -0.126$, and $-0.124$, putting the returns into decimal form. Adding 1.0 to those returns produces 0.9840, 1.317, 1.074, 0.874, and 0.876. Using Equation 7-5 we have $\sqrt[5]{(0.9840)(1.317)(1.074)(0.874)(0.876)} = \sqrt[5]{1.065616} = 1.012792$. This number is 1 plus the geometric mean rate of return. Subtracting 1.0 from this result, we have $1.012792 - 1.0 = 0.012792$ or approximately 1.3 percent. The geometric mean return for Canadian stocks during the 1998–2002 period was 1.3 percent.

An equation that summarizes the calculation of the geometric mean return, $R_G$, is a slightly modified version of Equation 7-5 in which the $X_i$ represent "1 + return in decimal form." Because geometric mean returns use time series, we use a subscript $t$ indexing time as well.

$$1 + R_G = \sqrt[T]{(1 + R_1)(1 + R_2) \ldots (1 + R_T)}$$

$$1 + R_G = \left[ \prod_{t=1}^{T} (1 + R_t) \right]^{\frac{1}{T}}$$

which leads to the following formula.

▶ **Geometric Mean Return Formula.** Given a time series of holding period returns $R_t$, $t = 1, 2, \ldots, T$, the geometric mean return over the time period spanned by the returns $R_1$ through $R_T$ is

$$R_G = \left[ \prod_{t=1}^{T} (1 + R_t) \right]^{\frac{1}{T}} - 1 \qquad\qquad \textbf{(7-6)}$$

We can use Equation 7-6 to solve for the geometric mean return for any return data series. Geometric mean returns are also referred to as compound returns. If the returns being averaged in Equation 7-6 have a monthly frequency, for example, we may call the geometric mean monthly return the compound monthly return. The next example illustrates the computation of the geometric mean while contrasting the geometric and arithmetic means.

## EXAMPLE 7

### Geometric and Arithmetic Mean Returns (1)

As a mutual fund analyst, you are examining, as of early 2003, the most recent five years of total returns for two U.S. large-cap value equity mutual funds.

**TABLE 15   Total Returns for Two Mutual Funds, 1998–2002**

| Year | Selected American Shares (SLASX) | T. Rowe Price Equity Income (PRFDX) |
|------|-----------------------------------|--------------------------------------|
| 1998 | 16.2% | 9.2% |
| 1999 | 20.3% | 3.8% |
| 2000 | 9.3% | 13.1% |
| 2001 | −11.1% | 1.6% |
| 2002 | −17.0% | −13.0% |

*Source*: American Association of Individual Investors (AAII).

Based on the data in Table 15, address the following:

**1.** Calculate the geometric mean return of SLASX.

**2.** Calculate the arithmetic mean return of SLASX and contrast it to the fund's geometric mean return.

**3.** Calculate the geometric mean return of PRFDX.

**4.** Calculate the arithmetic mean return of PRFDX and contrast it to the fund's geometric mean return.

**Solution to 1:** Converting the returns on SLASX to decimal form and adding 1.0 to each return produces 1.162, 1.203, 1.093, 0.889, and 0.830. We use Equation 7-6 to find SLASX's geometric mean return:

$$R_G = \sqrt[5]{(1.162)(1.203)(1.093)(0.889)(0.830)} - 1$$
$$= \sqrt[5]{1.127384} - 1 = 1.024270 - 1 = 0.024270$$
$$= 2.43\%$$

**Solution to 2:** For SLASX, $\bar{R} = (16.2 + 20.3 + 9.3 - 11.1 - 17.0)/5 = 17.7/5 = 3.54\%$. The arithmetic mean return for SLASX exceeds the geometric mean return by $3.54 - 2.43 = 1.11\%$ or 111 basis points.

**Solution to 3:** Converting the returns on PRFDX to decimal form and adding 1.0 to each return produces 1.092, 1.038, 1.131, 1.016, and 0.870. We use Equation 7-6 to find PRFDX's geometric mean return:

$$R_G = \sqrt[5]{(1.092)(1.038)(1.131)(1.016)(0.870)} - 1$$
$$= \sqrt[5]{1.133171} - 1 = 1.025319 - 1 = 0.025319$$
$$= 2.53\%$$

**Solution to 4:** PRFDX, $\bar{R} = (9.2 + 3.8 + 13.1 + 1.6 - 13.0)/5 = 14.7/5 = 2.94\%$. The arithmetic mean for PRFDX exceeds the geometric mean return by $2.94 - 2.53 = 0.41\%$ or 41 basis points. The table below summarizes the findings.

**TABLE 16     Mutual Fund Arithmetic and Geometric Mean Returns: Summary of Findings**

| Fund | Arithmetic Mean | Geometric Mean |
|------|-----------------|----------------|
| SLASX | 3.54% | 2.43% |
| PRFDX | 2.94% | 2.53% |

In Example 7, for both mutual funds, the geometric mean return was less than the arithmetic mean return. In fact, the geometric mean is always less than or equal to the arithmetic mean.[21] The only time that the two means will be equal is when there is no variability in the observations—that is, when all the observations in the series are the same.[22] In Example 7, there was variability in the funds' returns; thus for both funds, the geometric mean was strictly less than the arithmetic mean. In

---

[21] This statement can be proved using Jensen's inequality that the average value of a function is less than or equal to the function evaluated at the mean if the function is concave from below—the case for $\ln(X)$.

[22] For instance, suppose the return for each of the three years is 10 percent. The arithmetic mean is 10 percent. To find the geometric mean, we first express the returns as $(1 + R_t)$ and then find the geometric mean: $[(1.10)(1.10)(1.10)]^{1/3} - 1.0 = 10$ percent. The two means are the same.

general, the difference between the arithmetic and geometric means increases with the variability in the period-by-period observations.[23] This relationship is also illustrated by Example 7. Even casual inspection reveals that the returns of SLASX are more variable than those of PRFDX, and consequently, the spread between the arithmetic and geometric mean returns is larger for SLASX (111 basis points) than for PRFDX (41 basis points).[24] The arithmetic and geometric mean also rank the two funds differently. Although SLASX has the higher arithmetic mean return, PRFDX has the higher geometric mean return. How should the analyst interpret this result?

The geometric mean return represents the growth rate or compound rate of return on an investment. One dollar invested in SLASX at the beginning of 1998 would have grown to $(1.162)(1.203)(1.093)(0.889)(0.830) = \$1.127$, which is equal to 1 plus the geometric mean return compounded over five periods: $(1.0243)^5 = \$1.127$, confirming that the geometric mean is the compound rate of return. For PRFDX, one dollar would have grown to a larger amount, $(1.092)(1.038)(1.131)(1.016)(0.870) = \$1.133$, equal to $(1.0253)^5$. With its focus on the profitability of an investment over a multiperiod horizon, the geometric mean is of key interest to investors. The arithmetic mean return, focusing on average single-period performance, is also of interest. Both arithmetic and geometric means have a role to play in investment management, and both are often reported for return series. Example 8 highlights these points in a simple context.

## EXAMPLE 8

### Geometric and Arithmetic Mean Returns (2)

A hypothetical investment in a single stock initially costs €100. One year later, the stock is trading at €200. At the end of the second year, the stock price falls back to the original purchase price of €100. No dividends are paid during the two-year period. Calculate the arithmetic and geometric mean annual returns.

**Solution:**  First, we need to find the Year 1 and Year 2 annual returns with Equation 7-1.

Return in Year 1 = 200/100 −1 = 100%

Return in Year 2 = 100/200 −1 = −50%

The arithmetic mean of the annual returns is $(100\% - 50\%)/2 = 25\%$.
Before we find the geometric mean, we must convert the percentage rates of return to $(1 + R_t)$. After this adjustment, the geometric mean from Equation 7-6 is $\sqrt{2.0 \times 0.50} - 1 = 0$ percent.
The geometric mean return of 0 percent accurately reflects that the ending value of the investment in Year 2 equals the starting value in Year 1. The compound rate of return on the investment is 0 percent. The arithmetic mean return reflects the average of the one-year returns.

---

[23] We will soon introduce standard deviation as a measure of variability. Holding the arithmetic mean return constant, the geometric mean return decreases for an increase in standard deviation.

[24] We will introduce formal measures of variability later. But note, for example, the 20.4 percentage point swing in returns between 2000 and 2001 for SLASX versus the 11.5 percentage point for PRFDX.

### 5.4.3 The Harmonic Mean

The arithmetic mean, the weighted mean, and the geometric mean are the most frequently used concepts of mean in investments. A fourth concept, the **harmonic mean**, $\overline{X}_H$, is appropriate in a limited number of applications.[25]

▶ **Harmonic Mean Formula.** The **harmonic mean** of a set of observations $X_1, X_2, \ldots, X_n$ is

$$\overline{X}_H = n / \sum_{i=1}^{n} (1/X_i) \tag{7-7}$$

with $X_i > 0$ for $i = 1, 2, \ldots, n$.

The harmonic mean is the value obtained by summing the reciprocals of the observations—terms of the form $1/X_i$—then averaging that sum by dividing it by the number of observations $n$, and, finally, taking the reciprocal of the average.

The harmonic mean may be viewed as a special type of weighted mean in which an observation's weight is inversely proportional to its magnitude. The harmonic mean is a relatively specialized concept of the mean that is appropriate when averaging ratios ("amount per unit") when the ratios are repeatedly applied to a fixed quantity to yield a variable number of units. The concept is best explained through an illustration. A well-known application arises in the investment strategy known as **cost averaging**, which involves the periodic investment of a fixed amount of money. In this application, the ratios we are averaging are prices per share at purchases dates, and we are applying those prices to a constant amount of money to yield a variable number of shares.

Suppose an investor purchases €1,000 of a security each month for $n = 2$ months. The share prices are €10 and €15 at the two purchase dates. What is the average price paid for the security?

In this example, in the first month we purchase €1,000/€10 = 100 shares and in the second month we purchase €1,000/€15 = 66.67, or 166.67 shares in total. Dividing the total euro amount invested, €2,000, by the total number of shares purchased, 166.67, gives an average price paid of €2,000/166.67 = €12. The average price paid is in fact the harmonic mean of the asset's prices at the purchase dates. Using Equation 7-7, the harmonic mean price is $2/[(1/10) + (1/15)] = €12$. The value €12 is less than the arithmetic mean purchase price $(€10 + €15)/2 = €12.5$. However, we could find the correct value of €12 using the weighted mean formula, where the weights on the purchase prices equal the shares purchased at a given price as a proportion of the total shares purchased. In our example, the calculation would be $(100/166.67)€10.00 + (66.67/166.67)€15.00 = €12$. If we had invested varying amounts of money at each date, we could not use the harmonic mean formula. We could, however, still use the weighted mean formula in a manner similar to that just described.

A mathematical fact concerning the harmonic, geometric, and arithmetic means is that unless all the observations in a dataset have the same value, the harmonic mean is less than the geometric mean, which in turn is less than the arithmetic mean. In the illustration given, the harmonic mean price was indeed less than the arithmetic mean price.

---

[25] The terminology "harmonic" arises from its use relative to a type of series involving reciprocals known as a harmonic series.

# OTHER MEASURES OF LOCATION: QUANTILES

Having discussed measures of central tendency, we now examine an approach to describing the location of data that involves identifying values at or below which specified proportions of the data lie. For example, establishing that 25, 50, and 75 percent of the annual returns on a portfolio are at or below the values −0.05, 0.16, and 0.25, respectively, provides concise information about the distribution of portfolio returns. Statisticians use the word **quantile** (or **fractile**) as the most general term for a value at or below which a stated fraction of the data lies. In the following, we describe the most commonly used quantiles—quartiles, quintiles, deciles, and percentiles—and their application in investments.

## 6.1 Quartiles, Quintiles, Deciles, and Percentiles

We know that the median divides a distribution in half. We can define other dividing lines that split the distribution into smaller sizes. **Quartiles** divide the distribution into quarters, **quintiles** into fifths, deciles into tenths, and **percentiles** into hundredths. Given a set of observations, the $y$th percentile is the value at or below which $y$ percent of observations lie. Percentiles are used frequently, and the other measures can be defined with respect to them. For example, the first quartile ($Q_1$) divides a distribution such that 25 percent of the observations lie at or below it; therefore, the first quartile is also the 25th percentile. The second quartile ($Q_2$) represents the 50th percentile, and the third quartile ($Q_3$) represents the 75th percentile because 75 percent of the observations lie at or below it.

When dealing with actual data, we often find that we need to approximate the value of a percentile. For example, if we are interested in the value of the 75th percentile, we may find that no observation divides the sample such that exactly 75 percent of the observations lie at or below that value. The following procedure, however, can help us determine or estimate a percentile. The procedure involves first locating the position of the percentile within the set of observations and then determining (or estimating) the value associated with that position.

Let $P_y$ be the value at or below which $y$ percent of the distribution lies, or the $y$th percentile. (For example, $P_{18}$ is the point at or below which 18 percent of the observations lie; $100 - 18 = 82$ percent are greater than $P_{18}$.) The formula for the position of a percentile in an array with $n$ entries sorted in ascending order is

$$L_y = (n + 1)\frac{y}{100}$$ **(7-8)**

where $y$ is the percentage point at which we are dividing the distribution and $L_y$ is the location ($L$) of the percentile ($P_y$) in the array sorted in ascending order. The value of $L_y$ may or may not be a whole number. In general, as the sample size increases, the percentile location calculation becomes more accurate; in small samples it may be quite approximate.

As an example of the case in which $L_y$ is not a whole number, suppose that we want to determine the third quartile of returns for 2002 ($Q_3$ or $P_{75}$) for the 16 European equity markets given in Table 8. According to Equation 7-8, the position of the third quartile is $L_{75} = (16 + 1)75/100 = 12.75$, or between the 12th and 13th items in Table 9, which ordered the returns into ascending order. The 12th item in Table 9 is the return to equities in Portugal in 2002, −28.29 percent. The 13th item is the return to equities in Switzerland in 2002, −25.84 percent. Reflecting the "0.75" in "12.75," we would conclude that $P_{75}$ lies 75 percent of the distance between −28.29 percent and −25.84 percent.

To summarize:

▶ When the location, $L_y$, is a whole number, the location corresponds to an actual observation. For example, if Italy had not been included in the sample, then $n+1$ would have been 16 and, with $L_{75} = 12$, the third quartile would be $P_{75} = X_{12}$, where $X_i$ is defined as the value of the observation in the $i$th ($i = L_{75}$) position of the data sorted in ascending order (i.e., $P_{75} = -28.29$).

▶ When $L_y$ is not a whole number or integer, $L_y$ lies between the two closest integer numbers (one above and one below), and we use **linear interpolation** between those two places to determine $P_y$. Interpolation means estimating an unknown value on the basis of two known values that surround it (lie above and below it); the term "linear" refers to a straight-line estimate. Returning to the calculation of $P_{75}$ for the equity returns, we found that $L_y = 12.75$; the next lower whole number is 12 and the next higher whole number is 13. Using linear interpolation, $P_{75} \approx X_{12} + (12.75 - 12)(X_{13} - X_{12})$. As above, in the 12th position is the return to equities in Portugal, so $X_{12} = -28.29$ percent; $X_{13} = -25.84$ percent, the return to equities in Switzerland. Thus our estimate is $P_{75} \approx X_{12} + (12.75 - 12)(X_{13} - X_{12}) = -28.29 + 0.75[-25.84 - (-28.29)] = -28.29 + 0.75(2.45) = -28.29 + 1.84 = -26.45$ percent. In words, $-28.29$ and $-25.84$ bracket $P_{75}$ from below and above, respectively. Because $12.75 - 12 = 0.75$, using linear interpolation we move 75 percent of the distance from $-28.29$ to $-25.84$ as our estimate of $P_{75}$. We follow this pattern whenever $L_y$ is non-integer: The nearest whole numbers below and above $L_y$ establish the positions of observations that bracket $P_y$ and then interpolate between the values of those two observations.

Example 9 illustrates the calculation of various quantiles for the dividend yield on the components of a major European equity index.

**EXAMPLE 9**

**Calculating Percentiles, Quartiles, and Quintiles**

The DJ EuroSTOXX 50 is an index of Europe's 50 largest publicly traded companies as measured by market capitalization. Table 17 shows the dividend yields on the 50 component stocks in the index as of mid-2003, ranked in ascending order.

**TABLE 17    Dividend Yields on the Components of the DJ EuroSTOXX 50**

| No. | Company | Dividend Yield | No. | Company | Dividend Yield |
|---|---|---|---|---|---|
| 1 | AstraZeneca | 0.00% | 8 | Roche Holding | 1.33% |
| 2 | BP | 0.00% | 9 | Munich Re Group | 1.36% |
| 3 | Deutsche Telekom | 0.00% | 10 | General Assicurazioni | 1.39% |
| 4 | HSBC Holdings | 0.00% | | | |
| 5 | Credit Suisse Group | 0.26% | 11 | Vodafone Group | 1.41% |
| 6 | L'Oréal | 1.09% | 12 | Carrefour | 1.51% |
| 7 | SwissRe | 1.27% | 13 | Nokia | 1.75% |

*(Table continued on next page . . .)*

| TABLE 17 (continued) | | | | |
|---|---|---|---|---|
| No. | Company | Dividend Yield | No. | Company | Dividend Yield |
| 14 | Novartis | 1.81% | 33 | Santander Central Hispano | 3.66% |
| 15 | Allianz | 1.92% | | | |
| 16 | Koninklije Philips Electronics | 2.01% | 34 | Banco Bilbao Vizcaya Argentaria | 3.67% |
| 17 | Siemens | 2.16% | 35 | Diageo | 3.68% |
| 18 | Deutsche Bank | 2.27% | 36 | HBOS | 3.78% |
| 19 | Telecom Italia | 2.27% | 37 | E.ON | 3.87% |
| 20 | AXA | 2.39% | 38 | Shell Transport and Co. | 3.88% |
| 21 | Telefonica | 2.49% | | | |
| 22 | Nestlé | 2.55% | 39 | Barclays | 4.06% |
| 23 | Royal Bank of Scotland Group | 2.60% | 40 | Royal Dutch Petroleum Co. | 4.27% |
| 24 | ABN-AMRO Holding | 2.65% | 41 | Fortis | 4.28% |
| | | | 42 | Bayer | 4.45% |
| 25 | BNP Paribas | 2.65% | 43 | DaimlerChrysler | 4.68% |
| 26 | UBS | 2.65% | 44 | Suez | 5.13% |
| 27 | Tesco | 2.95% | 45 | Aviva | 5.15% |
| 28 | Total | 3.11% | 46 | Eni | 5.66% |
| 29 | GlaxoSmithKline | 3.31% | 47 | ING Group | 6.16% |
| 30 | BT Group | 3.34% | 48 | Prudential | 6.43% |
| 31 | Unilever | 3.53% | 49 | Lloyds TSB | 7.68% |
| 32 | BASF | 3.59% | 50 | AEGON | 8.14% |

*Source*: france.finance.yahoo.com accessed 8 July 2003.

Using the data in Table 17, address the following:

**1.** Calculate the 10th and 90th percentiles.

**2.** Calculate the first, second, and third quartiles.

**3.** State the value of the median.

**4.** How many quintiles are there, and to what percentiles do the quintiles correspond?

**5.** Calculate the value of the first quintile.

**Solution to 1:** In this example, $n = 50$. Using Equation 7-8, $L_y = (n + 1)y/100$ for position of the $y$th percentile, so for the 10th percentile we have

$$L_{10} = (50 + 1)(10/100) = 5.1$$

$L_{10}$ is between the fifth and sixth observations with values $X_5 = 0.26$ and $X_6 = 1.09$. The estimate of the 10th percentile (first decile) for dividend yield is

$$P_{10} \approx X_5 + (5.1 - 5)(X_6 - X_5) = 0.26 + 0.1(1.09 - 0.26)$$
$$= 0.26 + 0.1(0.83) = 0.34\%$$

For the 90th percentile,

$$L_{90} = (50 + 1)(90/100) = 45.9$$

$L_{90}$ is between the 45th and 46th observations with values $X_{45} = 5.15$ and $X_{46} = 5.66$, respectively. The estimate of the 90th percentile (ninth decile) is

$$P_{90} \approx X_{45} + (45.9 - 45)(X_{46} - X_{45}) = 5.15 + 0.9(5.66 - 5.15)$$
$$= 5.15 + 0.9(0.51) = 5.61\%$$

**Solution to 2:** The first, second, and third quartiles correspond to $P_{25}$, $P_{50,}$ and $P_{75}$, respectively.

$$L_{25} = (51)(25/100) = 12.75 \qquad$$ $L_{25}$ is between the 12th and 13th entries with values $X_{12} = 1.51$ and $X_{13} = 1.75$.

$$P_{25} = Q_1 \approx X_{12} + (12.75 - 12)(X_{13} - X_{12})$$
$$= 1.51 + 0.75(1.75 - 1.51)$$
$$= 1.51 + 0.75(0.24) = 1.69\%$$

$$L_{50} = (51)(50/100) = 25.5 \qquad$$ $L_{25}$ is between the 25th and 26th entries. But these entries share the same value, $X_{25} = X_{26} = 2.65$, so no interpolation is needed.

$$P_{50} = Q_2 = 2.65\%$$

$$L_{75} = (51)(75/100) = 38.25 \qquad$$ $L_{75}$ is between the 38th and 39th entries with values $X_{38} = 3.88$ and $X_{39} = 4.06$.

$$P_{75} = Q_3 \approx X_{38} + (38.25 - 38)(X_{39} - X_{38})$$
$$= 3.88 + 0.25(4.06 - 3.88)$$
$$= 3.88 + 0.25(0.18) = 3.93\%$$

**Solution to 3:** The median is the 50th percentile, 2.65 percent. This is the same value that we would obtain by taking the mean of the $n/2 = 50/2 = 25$th item and $(n + 2)/2 = 52/2 = 26$th items, consistent with the procedure given earlier for the median of an even-numbered sample.

**Solution to 4:** There are four quintiles, and they correspond to $P_{20}$, $P_{40}$, $P_{60}$, and $P_{80}$.

**Solution to 5:** The first quintile is $P_{20}$.

$$L_{20} = (50 + 1)(20/100) = 10.2 \qquad$$ $L_{20}$ is between the 10th and 11th observations with values $X_{10} = 1.39$ and $X_{11} = 1.41$.

The estimate of the first quintile is

$$P_{20} \approx X_{10} + (10.2 - 10)(X_{11} - X_{10})$$
$$= 1.39 + 0.2(1.41 - 1.39)$$
$$= 1.39 + 0.2(0.02) = 1.394\% \text{ or } 1.39\%.$$

## 6.2 Quantiles in Investment Practice

In this section, we discuss the use of quantiles in investments. Quantiles are used in portfolio performance evaluation as well as in investment strategy development and research.

Investment analysts use quantiles every day to rank performance—for example, the performance of portfolios. The performance of investment managers is often characterized in terms of the quartile in which they fall relative to the performance of their peer group of managers. The Morningstar mutual fund star rankings, for example, associates the number of stars with percentiles of performance relative to similar-style mutual funds.

Another key use of quantiles is in investment research. Analysts refer to a group defined by a particular quantile as that quantile. For example, analysts often refer to the set of companies with returns falling below the 10th percentile cutoff point as the bottom return decile. Dividing data into quantiles based on some characteristic allows analysts to evaluate the impact of that characteristic on a quantity of interest. For instance, empirical finance studies commonly rank companies based on the market value of their equity and then sort them into deciles. The 1st decile contains the portfolio of those companies with the smallest market values, and the 10th decile contains those companies with the largest market value. Ranking companies by decile allows analysts to compare the performance of small companies with large ones.

### TABLE 18 Mean Annual Returns of Value and Growth Stocks Based on Selected Characteristics, 1986–1996

| Selection Criteria | Total Observations | $Q_1$ (Value) | $Q_2$ | $Q_3$ | $Q_4$ (Growth) | Spread in Return, $Q_1$ to $Q_4$ |
|---|---|---|---|---|---|---|
| *Classification by P/E* | 28,463 | | | | | |
| Median P/E | | 8.7 | 15.2 | 24.2 | 72.5 | |
| Return | | 15.0% | 13.6% | 13.5% | 10.6% | +4.4% |
| Standard deviation | | 46.5 | 38.3 | 42.5 | 50.4 | |
| *Classification by P/CF* | 30,240 | | | | | |
| Median P/CF | | 4.4 | 8.2 | 13.3 | 34.2 | |
| Return | | 15.5% | 13.7% | 12.9% | 11.2% | +4.3% |
| Standard deviation | | 48.7 | 41.2 | 41.9 | 51.4 | |
| *Classification by P/B* | 32,265 | | | | | |
| Median P/B | | 0.8 | 1.4 | 2.2 | 4.3 | |
| Return | | 18.1% | 14.4% | 12.6% | 12.4% | +5.7% |
| Standard deviation | | 69.6 | 45.9 | 45.1 | 57.0 | |
| *Classification by D/P* | 25,394 | | | | | |
| Median D/P | | 5.6% | 3.2% | 1.9% | 0.6% | |
| Return | | 14.1% | 14.1% | 12.5% | 9.3% | +4.8% |
| Standard deviation | | 40.5 | 38.7 | 38.9 | 42.0 | |

*Source*: Bauman et al.

We can illustrate the use of quantiles, in particular quartiles, in investment research using the example of Bauman, Conover, and Miller (1998). That study compared the performance of international growth stocks to value stocks. Typically, value stocks are defined as those for which the market price is relatively low in relation to earnings per share, book value per share, or dividends per share. Growth stocks, on the other hand, have comparatively high prices in relation to those same measures. The Bauman et al. classification criteria were the following valuation measures: price-to-earnings (P/E), price-to-cash flow (P/CF), price-to-book value (P/B), and dividend yield (D/P). They assigned one-fourth of the total sample with the lowest P/E on 30 June of each year from 1986 to 1996 (the value group) to Quartile 1, and the one-fourth with the highest P/E of each year (the growth group) to Quartile 4. The stocks with the second-highest P/E formed Quartile 3, and the stocks with the second-lowest P/E, Quartile 2. The authors repeated this process for each of the four fundamental factors. Treating each quartile group as a portfolio composed of equally weighted stocks, they were able to compare the performance of the various value/growth quartiles. Table 1 from their study is reproduced as Table 18 on the previous page.

Table 18 reports each valuation factor's median, mean return, and standard deviation for each quartile grouping. Moving from Quartile 1 to Quartile 4, P/E, P/CF, and P/B increase, but D/P decreases. Regardless of the selection criteria, international value stocks outperformed international growth stocks during the sample period.

Bauman, Conover, and Miller also divided companies into one of four quartiles based on market value of equity. Then they examined the returns to the stocks in the quartiles. Table 7 from their article is reproduced here as Table 19. As the table shows, the small-company portfolio had a median market value of $46.6 million and the large company portfolio had a median value of $2,472.3 million. Large companies were more than 50 times larger than small companies, yet their mean stock returns were less than half those of the small companies (small, 22.0 percent; large, 10.8 percent). Overall, Bauman et al. found two effects. First, international value stocks (as the authors defined them) outperformed international growth stocks. Second, international small stocks outperformed international large stocks.

The authors' next step was to examine how value and growth stocks performed while controlling for size. This step involved constructing 16 different value/growth and size portfolios ($4 \times 4 = 16$) and investigating the interaction between these two fundamental factors. They found that international value stocks outperformed international growth stocks except when market capitalization was very small. For portfolio managers, these findings suggest that value stocks offered investors relatively more favorable returns than did growth stocks in international markets during the specific time period studied.

**TABLE 19   Mean Annual Returns of International Stocks Grouped by Market Capitalization, 1986–1996**

| Selection Criteria | Total Observations | $Q_1$ (Small) | $Q_2$ | $Q_3$ | $Q_4$ (Large) | Spread in Return, $Q_1$ to $Q_4$ |
|---|---|---|---|---|---|---|
| *Classification by size* | 32,555 | | | | | |
| Median size (millions) | | $46.6 | $209.9 | $583.7 | $2,472.3 | |
| Return | | 22.0% | 13.6% | 11.1% | 10.8% | +11.2% |
| Standard deviation | | 87.8 | 45.2 | 39.5 | 34.0 | |

*Source*: Bauman et al.

# MEASURES OF DISPERSION

As the well-known researcher Fischer Black has written, "[t]he key issue in investments is estimating expected return."[26] Few would disagree with the importance of expected return or mean return in investments: The mean return tells us where returns, and investment results, are centered. To completely understand an investment, however, we also need to know how returns are dispersed around the mean. **Dispersion** is the variability around the central tendency. If mean return addresses reward, dispersion addresses risk.

In this section, we examine the most common measures of dispersion: range, mean absolute deviation, variance, and standard deviation. These are all measures of **absolute dispersion**. Absolute dispersion is the amount of variability present without comparison to any reference point or benchmark.

These measures are used throughout investment practice. The variance or standard deviation of return is often used as a measure of risk pioneered by Nobel laureate Harry Markowitz. William Sharpe, another winner of the Nobel Prize in economics, developed the Sharpe ratio, a measure of risk-adjusted performance. That measure makes use of standard deviation of return. Other measures of dispersion, mean absolute deviation and range, are also useful in analyzing data.

## 7.1 The Range

We encountered range earlier when we discussed the construction of frequency distribution. The simplest of all the measures of dispersion, range can be computed with interval or ratio data.

▶ **Definition of Range.** The **range** is the difference between the maximum and minimum values in a data set:

$$\text{Range} = \text{Maximum value} - \text{Minimum value} \qquad \textbf{(7-9)}$$

As an illustration of range, the largest monthly return for the S&P 500 in the period from January 1926 to December 2002 is 42.56 percent (in April 1933) and the smallest is −29.73 percent (in September 1931). The range of returns is thus 72.29 percent [42.56 percent − (−29.73 percent)]. An alternative definition of range reports the maximum and minimum values. This alternative definition provides more information than does the range as defined in Equation 7-9.

One advantage of the range is ease of computation. A disadvantage is that the range uses only two pieces of information from the distribution. It cannot tell us how the data are distributed (that is, the shape of the distribution). Because the range is the difference between the maximum and minimum returns, it can reflect extremely large or small outcomes that may not be representative of the distribution.[27]

## 7.2 The Mean Absolute Deviation

Measures of dispersion can be computed using all the observations in the distribution rather than just the highest and lowest. The question is, how should we measure dispersion? Our previous discussion on properties of the arithmetic

---

[26] Black (1993).

[27] Another distance measure of dispersion that we may encounter, the interquartile range, focuses on the middle rather than the extremes. The **interquartile range** (IQR) is the difference between the third and first quartiles of a dataset: $\text{IQR} = Q_3 - Q_1$. The IQR represents the length of the interval containing the middle 50 percent of the data, with a larger interquartile range indicating greater dispersion, all else equal.

mean introduced the notion of distance or deviation from the mean $(X_i - \overline{X})$ as a fundamental piece of information used in statistics. We could compute measures of dispersion as the arithmetic average of the deviations around the mean, but we would encounter a problem: The deviations around the mean always sum to 0. If we computed the mean of the deviations, the result would also equal 0. Therefore, we need to find a way to address the problem of negative deviations canceling out positive deviation.

One solution is to examine the absolute deviations around the mean as in the mean absolute deviation.

▶ **Mean Absolute Deviation Formula.** The **mean absolute deviation** (MAD) for a sample is:

$$\text{MAD} = \frac{\sum_{i=1}^{n} \left| X_i - \overline{X} \right|}{n}$$

(7-10)

where $\overline{X}$ is the sample mean and $n$ is the number of observations in the sample.

In calculating MAD, we ignore the signs of the deviations around the mean. For example, if $X_i = -11.0$ and $\overline{X} = 4.5$, the absolute value of the difference is $|-11.0 - 4.5| = |-15.5| = 15.5$. The mean absolute deviation uses all of the observations in the sample and is thus superior to the range as a measure of dispersion. One technical drawback of MAD is that it is difficult to manipulate mathematically compared with the next measure we will introduce, variance.[28] Example 10 illustrates the use of the range and the mean absolute deviation in evaluating risk.

---

### EXAMPLE 10

**The Range and the Mean Absolute Deviation**

Having calculated mean returns for the two mutual funds in Example 7, the analyst is now concerned with evaluating risk.

**TABLE 15   (Repeated) Total Returns for Two Mutual Funds, 1998–2002**

| Year | Selected American Shares (SLASX) | T. Rowe Price Equity Income (PRFDX) |
|------|------|------|
| 1998 | 16.2% | 9.2% |
| 1999 | 20.3% | 3.8% |
| 2000 | 9.3% | 13.1% |
| 2001 | −11.1% | 1.6% |
| 2002 | −17.0% | −13.0% |

*Source*: AAII.

---

[28] In some analytic work such as optimization, the calculus operation of differentiation is important. Variance as a function can be differentiated, but absolute value cannot.

Based on the data in Table 15 repeated on the previous page, answer the following:

1. Calculate the range of annual returns for (A) SLASX and (B) PRFDX, and state which mutual fund appears to be riskier based on these ranges.

2. Calculate the mean absolute deviation of returns on (A) SLASX and (B) PRFDX, and state which mutual fund appears to be riskier based on MAD.

## Solution to 1:

A. For SLASX, the largest return was 20.3 percent and the smallest was −17.0 percent. The range is thus $20.3 - (-17.0) = 37.3\%$.

B. For PFRDX, the range is $13.1 - (-13.0) = 26.1\%$. With a larger range of returns than PRFDX, SLASX appeared to be the riskier fund during the 1998–2002 period.

## Solution to 2:

A. The arithmetic mean return for SLASX as calculated in Example 7 is 3.54 percent. The MAD of SLASX returns is

$$MAD =$$
$$\frac{|16.2 - 3.54| + |20.3 - 3.54| + |9.3 - 3.54| + |-11.1 - 3.54| + |-17.0 - 3.54|}{5}$$

$$= \frac{12.66 + 16.76 + 5.76 + 14.64 + 20.54}{5}$$

$$= \frac{70.36}{5} = 14.1\%$$

B. The arithmetic mean return for PRFDX as calculated in Example 7 is 2.94 percent. The MAD of PRFDX returns is

$$MAD =$$
$$\frac{|9.2 - 2.94| + |3.8 - 2.94| + |13.1 - 2.94| + |1.6 - 2.94| + |-13.0 - 2.94|}{5}$$

$$= \frac{6.26 + 0.86 + 10.16 + 1.34 + 15.94}{5}$$

$$= \frac{34.56}{5} = 6.9\%$$

SLASX, with a MAD of 14.1 percent, appears to be much riskier than PRFDX, with a MAD of 6.9 percent.

## 7.3 Population Variance and Population Standard Deviation

The mean absolute deviation addressed the issue that the sum of deviations from the mean equals zero by taking the absolute value of the deviations. A second approach to the treatment of deviations is to square them. The variance and standard deviation, which are based on squared deviations, are the two most widely used measures of dispersion. **Variance** is defined as the average of the squared deviations around the mean. **Standard deviation** is the positive square root of the variance. The following discussion addresses the calculation and use of variance and standard deviation.

### 7.3.1   Population Variance

If we know every member of a population, we can compute the **population variance**. Denoted by the symbol $\sigma^2$, the population variance is the arithmetic average of the squared deviations around the mean.

▶ **Population Variance Formula.** The **population variance** is

$$\sigma^2 = \frac{\sum_{i=1}^{N} (X_i - \mu)^2}{N} \tag{7-11}$$

where $\mu$ is the population mean and $N$ is the size of the population.

Given knowledge of the population mean, $\mu$, we can use Equation 7-11 to calculate the sum of the squared differences from the mean, taking account of all $N$ items in the population, and then to find the mean squared difference by dividing the sum by $N$. Whether a difference from the mean is positive or negative, squaring that difference results in a positive number. Thus variance takes care of the problem of negative deviations from the mean canceling out positive deviations by the operation of squaring those deviations. The P/Es for BJ, COST, and WMT were given earlier as 16.73, 22.02, and 29.30, respectively. We calculated the mean P/E as 22.68. Therefore, the population variance of the P/Es is $(1/3)[(16.73 - 22.68)^2 + (22.02 - 22.68)^2 + (29.30 - 22.68)^2] = (1/3)(-5.95^2 + -0.66^2 + 6.62^2) = (1/3)(35.4025 + 0.4356 + 43.8244) = (1/3)(79.6625) = 26.5542$.

### 7.3.2   Population Standard Deviation

Because the variance is measured in squared units, we need a way to return to the original units. We can solve this problem by using standard deviation, the square root of the variance. Standard deviation is more easily interpreted than the variance because standard deviation is expressed in the same unit of measurement as the observations.

▶ **Population Standard Deviation Formula.** The **population standard deviation**, defined as the positive square root of the population variance, is

$$\sigma = \sqrt{\frac{\sum_{i=1}^{N} (X_i - \mu)^2}{N}} \tag{7-12}$$

where $\mu$ is the population mean and $N$ is the size of the population.

Using the example of the P/Es for BJ, COST, and WMT, according to Equation 7-12 we would calculate the variance, 26.5542, then take the square root: $\sqrt{26.5542} = 5.1531$ or approximately 5.2.

Both the population variance and standard deviation are examples of parameters of a distribution. In later readings, we will introduce the notion of variance and standard deviation as risk measures.

In investments, we often do not know the mean of a population of interest, usually because we cannot practically identify or take measurements from each member of the population. We then estimate the population mean with the mean from a sample drawn from the population, and we calculate a sample variance or standard deviation using formulas different from Equations 7-11 and 7-12. We shall discuss these calculations in subsequent sections. However, in investments we sometimes have a defined group that we can consider to be a population. With well-defined populations, we use Equations 7-11 and 7-12, as in the following example.

## EXAMPLE 11

### Calculating the Population Standard Deviation

Table 20 gives the yearly portfolio turnover for the 10 U.S. equity funds that composed the 2002 Forbes Magazine Honor Roll.[29] Portfolio turnover, a measure of trading activity, is the lesser of the value of sales or purchases over a year divided by average net assets during the year. The number and identity of the funds on the Forbes Honor Roll changes from year to year.

**TABLE 20    Portfolio Turnover: 2002 Forbes Honor Roll Mutual Funds**

| Fund | Yearly Portfolio Turnover |
| --- | --- |
| FPA Capital Fund (FPPTX) | 23% |
| Mairs & Power Growth Fund (MPGFX) | 8% |
| Muhlenkamp Fund (MUHLX) | 11% |
| Longleaf Partners Fund (LLPFX) | 18% |
| Heartland Value Fund (HRTVX) | 56% |
| Scudder–Dreman High Return Equity-A (KDHAX) | 29% |
| Clipper Fund (CFIMX) | 23% |
| Weitz Value Fund (WVALX) | 13% |
| Third Avenue Value Fund (TAVFX) | 16% |
| Dodge & Cox Stock Fund (DODGX) | 10% |

*Source: Forbes (2003).*

Based on the data in Table 20, address the following:

**1.** Calculate the population mean portfolio turnover for the period used by *Forbes* for the ten 2002 Honor Roll funds.

---

[29] *Forbes* magazine annually selects U.S. equity mutual funds meeting certain criteria for its Honor Roll. The criteria relate to capital preservation (performance in bear markets), continuity of management (the fund must have a manager with at least six years' tenure), diversification, accessibility (disqualifying funds that are closed to new investors), and after-tax long-term performance.

**2.** Calculate the population variance and population standard deviation of portfolio turnover.

**3.** Explain the use of the population formulas in this example.

**Solution to 1:** $\mu = (23 + 8 + 11 + 18 + 56 + 29 + 23 + 13 + 16 + 10)/10 = 207/10 = 20.7$ percent.

**Solution to 2:** Having established that $\mu = 20.7$, we can calculate $\sigma^2 = \dfrac{\sum_{i=1}^{N} (X_i - \mu)^2}{N}$ by first calculating the numerator in the expression and then dividing by $N = 10$. The numerator (the sum of the squared differences from the mean) is

$(23 - 20.7)^2 + (8 - 20.7)^2 + (11 - 20.7)^2 + (18 - 20.7)^2 +$
$(56 - 20.7)^2 + (29 - 20.7)^2 + (23 - 20.7)^2 + (13 - 20.7)^2 +$
$(16 - 20.7)^2 + (10 - 20.7)^2 = 1,784.1$
Thus $\sigma^2 = 1,784.1/10 = 178.41$.
To calculate standard deviation, $\sigma = \sqrt{178.41} = 13.357$ percent. (The unit of variance is percent squared so the unit of standard deviation is percent.)

**Solution to 3:** If the population is clearly defined to be the Forbes Honor Roll funds in one specific year (2002), and if portfolio turnover is understood to refer to the specific one-year period reported upon by *Forbes*, the application of the population formulas to variance and standard deviation is appropriate. The results of 178.41 and 13.357 are, respectively, the cross-sectional variance and standard deviation in yearly portfolio turnover for the 2002 Forbes Honor Roll Funds.[30]

## 7.4   Sample Variance and Sample Standard Deviation

### 7.4.1   Sample Variance

In many instances in investment management, a subset or sample of the population is all that we can observe. When we deal with samples, the summary measures are called statistics. The statistic that measures the dispersion in a sample is called the sample variance.

▶ **Sample Variance Formula.** The **sample variance** is

$$s^2 = \frac{\sum_{i=1}^{n} (X_i - \overline{X})^2}{n - 1} \tag{7-13}$$

where $\overline{X}$ is the sample mean and $n$ is the number of observations in the sample.

---

[30] In fact, we could not properly use the Honor Roll funds to estimate the population variance of portfolio turnover (for example) of any other differently defined population, because the Honor Roll funds are not a random sample from any larger population of U.S. equity mutual funds.

Equation 7-13 tells us to take the following steps to compute the sample variance:

**i.** Calculate the sample mean, $\overline{X}$.

**ii.** Calculate each observation's squared deviation from the sample mean, $(X_i - \overline{X})^2$.

**iii.** Sum the squared deviations from the mean: $\sum_{i=1}^{n} (X_i - \overline{X})^2$.

**iv.** Divide the sum of squared deviations from the mean by $n - 1$: $\sum_{i=1}^{n} (X_i - \overline{X})^2 / (n - 1)$.

We will illustrate the calculation of the sample variance and the sample standard deviation in Example 12.

We use the notation $s^2$ for the sample variance to distinguish it from population variance, $\sigma^2$. The formula for sample variance is nearly the same as that for population variance except for the use of the sample mean, $\overline{X}$, in place of the population mean, $\mu$, and a different divisor. In the case of the population variance, we divide by the size of the population, $N$. For the sample variance, however, we divide by the sample size minus 1, or $n - 1$. By using $n - 1$ (rather than $n$) as the divisor, we improve the statistical properties of the sample variance. In statistical terms, the sample variance defined in Equation 7-13 is an unbiased estimator of the population variance.[31] The quantity $n - 1$ is also known as the number of degrees of freedom in estimating the population variance. To estimate the population variance with $s^2$, we must first calculate the mean. Once we have computed the sample mean, there are only $n - 1$ independent deviations from it.

### 7.4.2  Sample Standard Deviation

Just as we computed a population standard deviation, we can compute a sample standard deviation by taking the positive square root of the sample variance.

▶ **Sample Standard Deviation Formula.** The **sample standard deviation**, $s$, is

$$s = \sqrt{\frac{\sum_{i=1}^{n} (X_i - \overline{X})^2}{n - 1}} \qquad \textbf{(7-14)}$$

where $\overline{X}$ is the sample mean and $n$ is the number of observations in the sample.

To calculate the sample standard deviation, we first compute the sample variance using the steps given. We then take the square root of the sample variance. Example 12 illustrates the calculation of the sample variance and standard deviation for the two mutual funds introduced earlier.

### EXAMPLE 12

**Calculating Sample Variance and Sample Standard Deviation**
After calculating the geometric and arithmetic mean returns of two mutual funds in Example 7, we calculated two measures of dispersions for those funds, the range and mean absolute deviation of returns, in

---

[31] We discuss this concept further in the reading on sampling.

Example 10. We now calculate the sample variance and sample standard deviation of returns for those same two funds.

| | **TABLE 15 (Repeated) Total Returns for Two Mutual Funds, 1998–2002** | |
|---|---|---|
| **Year** | **Selected American Shares (SLASX)** | **T. Rowe Price Equity Income (PRFDX)** |
| 1998 | 16.2% | 9.2% |
| 1999 | 20.3% | 3.8% |
| 2000 | 9.3% | 13.1% |
| 2001 | −11.1% | 1.6% |
| 2002 | −17.0% | −13.0% |

*Source*: AAII.

Based on the data in Table 15 repeated above, answer the following:

1. Calculate the sample variance of return for (A) SLASX and (B) PRFDX.

2. Calculate sample standard deviation of return for (A) SLASX and (B) PRFDX.

3. Contrast the dispersion of returns as measured by standard deviation of return and mean absolute deviation of return for each of the two funds.

**Solution to 1:** To calculate the sample variance, we use Equation 7-13. (Deviation answers are all given in percent squared.)

**A.** SLASX
   i. The sample mean is $\overline{R} = (16.2 + 20.3 + 9.3 - 11.1 - 17.0)/5 = 17.7/5 = 3.54\%$.

   ii. The squared deviations from the mean are
   $(16.2 - 3.54)^2 = (12.66)^2 = 160.2756$
   $(20.3 - 3.54)^2 = (16.76)^2 = 280.8976$
   $(9.3 - 3.54)^2 = (5.76)^2 = 33.1776$
   $(-11.1 - 3.54)^2 = (-14.64)^2 = 214.3296$
   $(-17.0 - 3.54)^2 = (-20.54)^2 = 421.8916$

   iii. The sum of the squared deviations from the mean is $160.2756 + 280.8976 + 33.1776 + 214.3296 + 421.8916 = 1,110.5720$.

   iv. Divide the sum of the squared deviations from the mean by $n - 1$: $1,110.5720/(5 - 1) = 1,110.5720/4 = 277.6430$

**B.** PRFDX
   i. The sample mean is $\overline{R} = (9.2 + 3.8 + 13.1 + 1.6 - 13.0)/5 = 14.7/5 = 2.94\%$.

   ii. The squared deviations from the mean are
   $(9.2 - 2.94)^2 = (6.26)^2 = 39.1876$
   $(3.8 - 2.94)^2 = (0.86)^2 = 0.7396$
   $(13.1 - 2.94)^2 = (10.16)^2 = 103.2256$
   $(1.6 - 2.94)^2 = (-1.34)^2 = 1.7956$
   $(-13.0 - 2.94)^2 = (-15.94)^2 = 254.0836$

iii. The sum of the squared deviations from the mean is 39.1876 + 0.7396 + 103.2256 + 1.7956 + 254.0836 = 399.032.

iv. Divide the sum of the squared deviations from the mean by $n - 1$: 399.032/4 = 99.758

**Solution to 2:** To find the standard deviation, we take the positive square root of variance.

**A.** For SLASX, $\sigma = \sqrt{277.6430} = 16.66\%$ or 16.7 percent.

**B.** For PRFDX, $\sigma = \sqrt{99.758} = 9.99\%$ or 10.0 percent.

**Solution to 3:** Table 21 summarizes the results from Part 2 for standard deviation and incorporates the results for MAD from Example 10.

| TABLE 21 | Two Mutual Funds: Comparison of Standard Deviation and Mean Absolute Deviation | |
|---|---|---|
| **Fund** | **Standard Deviation** | **Mean Absolute Deviation** |
| SLASX | 16.7% | 14.1% |
| PRFDX | 10.0% | 6.9% |

Note that the mean absolute deviation is less than the standard deviation. The mean absolute deviation will always be less than or equal to the standard deviation because the standard deviation gives more weight to large deviations than to small ones (remember, the deviations are squared).

Because the standard deviation is a measure of dispersion about the arithmetic mean, we usually present the arithmetic mean and standard deviation together when summarizing data. When we are dealing with data that represent a time series of percent changes, presenting the geometric mean—representing the compound rate of growth—is also very helpful. Table 22 presents the historical geometric and arithmetic mean returns, along with the historical standard deviation of returns, for various equity return series. We present these statistics for nominal (rather than inflation-adjusted) returns so we can observe the original magnitudes of the returns.

| TABLE 22 | Equity Market Returns: Means and Standard Deviations | | |
|---|---|---|---|
| **Return Series** | **Geometric Mean** | **Arithmetic Mean** | **Standard Deviation** |
| *I. Ibbotson Associates Series: 1926–2002* | | | |
| S&P 500 (Annual) | 10.20% | 12.20% | 20.49 |
| S&P 500 (Monthly) | 0.81% | 0.97% | 5.65 |

*(Table continued on next page . . .)*

| | **TABLE 22   (continued)** | | |
|---|---|---|---|
| **Return Series** | **Geometric Mean** | **Arithmetic Mean** | **Standard Deviation** |
| *II. Dimson et al. (2002) Series (Annual): 1900–2000* | | | |
| Australia | 11.9% | 13.3% | 18.2% |
| Belgium | 8.2% | 10.5% | 24.1% |
| Canada | 9.7% | 11.0% | 16.6% |
| Denmark | 8.9% | 10.7% | 21.7% |
| France | 12.1% | 14.5% | 24.6% |
| Germany | 9.7% | 15.2% | 36.4% |
| Ireland | 9.5% | 11.5% | 22.8% |
| Italy | 12.0% | 16.1% | 34.2% |
| Japan | 12.5% | 15.9% | 29.5% |
| Netherlands | 9.0% | 11.0% | 22.7% |
| South Africa | 12.0% | 14.2% | 23.7% |
| Spain | 10.0% | 12.1% | 22.8% |
| Sweden | 11.6% | 13.9% | 23.5% |
| Switzerland | 7.6% | 9.3% | 19.7% |
| United Kingdom | 10.1% | 11.9% | 21.8% |
| United States | 10.1% | 12.0% | 19.9% |

*Source*: Ibbotson EnCorr Analyzer™; Dimson et al.

## 7.5 Semivariance, Semideviation, and Related Concepts

An asset's variance or standard deviation of returns is often interpreted as a measure of the asset's risk. Variance and standard deviation of returns take account of returns above and below the mean, but investors are concerned only with downside risk, for example returns below the mean. As a result, analysts have developed semivariance, semideviation, and related dispersion measures that focus on downside risk. **Semivariance** is defined as the average squared deviation below the mean. **Semideviation** (sometimes called semistandard deviation) is the positive square root of semivariance. To compute the sample semivariance, for example, we take the following steps:

  i. Calculate the sample mean.

 ii. Identify the observations that are smaller than or equal to the mean (discarding observations greater than the mean).

iii. Compute the sum of the squared negative deviations from the mean (using the observations that are smaller than or equal to the mean).

iv. Divide the sum of the squared negative deviations from Step iii by $n - 1$. A formula for semivariance approximating the unbiased estimator is

$$\sum_{\text{for all } X_i \leq \bar{X}} (X_i - \bar{X})^2 / (n - 1)$$

To take the case of Selected American Shares with returns (in percent) of 16.2, 20.3, 9.3, −11.1, and −17.0, we earlier calculated a mean return of 3.54 percent. Two returns, −11.1 and −17.0, are smaller than 3.54. We compute the sum of the squared negative deviations from the mean as $(-11.1 - 3.54)^2 + (-17.0 - 3.54)^2 = -14.64^2 + -20.54^2 = 214.3296 + 421.8916 = 636.2212$. With $n - 1 = 4$, we conclude that semivariance is $636.2212/4 = 159.0553$ and that semideviation is $\sqrt{159.0553} = 12.6$ percent, approximately. The semideviation of 12.6 percent is less than the standard deviation of 16.7 percent. From this downside risk perspective, therefore, standard deviation overstates risk.

In practice, we may be concerned with values of return (or another variable) below some level other than the mean. For example, if our return objective is 10 percent annually, we may be concerned particularly with returns below 10 percent a year. We can call 10 percent the target. The name **target semivariance** has been given to average squared deviation below a stated target, and **target semideviation** is its positive square root. To calculate a sample target semivariance, we specify the target as a first step. After identifying observations below the target, we find the sum of the squared negative deviations from the target and divide that sum by the number of observations below the target minus 1. A formula for target semivariance is

$$\sum_{\text{for all } X_i \leq B} (X_i - B)^2/(n - 1)$$

where $B$ is the target and $n$ is the number of observations. With a target return of 10 percent, we find in the case of Selected American Shares that three returns (9.3, −11.1, and −17.0) were below the target. The target semivariance is $[(9.3 - 10.0)^2 + (-11.1 - 10.0)^2 + (-17.0 - 10.0)^2]/(5 - 1) = 293.675$, and the target semideviation is $\sqrt{293.675} = 17.14$ percent, approximately.

When return distributions are symmetric, semivariance and variance are effectively equivalent. For asymmetric distributions, variance and semivariance rank prospects' risk differently.[32] Semivariance (or semideviation) and target semivariance (or target semideviation) have intuitive appeal, but they are harder to work with mathematically than variance.[33] Variance or standard deviation enters into the definition of many of the most commonly used finance risk concepts, such as the Sharpe ratio and beta. Perhaps because of these reasons, variance (or standard deviation) is much more frequently used in investment practice.

## 7.6 Chebyshev's Inequality

The Russian mathematician Pafnuty Chebyshev developed an inequality using standard deviation as a measure of dispersion. The inequality gives the proportion of values within $k$ standard deviations of the mean.

▶ **Definition of Chebyshev's Inequality.** According to Chebyshev's inequality, the proportion of the observations within $k$ standard deviations of the arithmetic mean is at least $1 - 1/k^2$ for all $k > 1$.

---

[32] See Estrada (2003). We discuss skewness later in this reading.

[33] As discussed in the reading on probability concepts and the various readings on portfolio concepts, we can find a portfolio's variance as a straightforward function of the variances and correlations of the component securities. There is no similar procedure for semivariance and target semivariance. We also cannot take the derivative of semivariance or target semivariance.

Table 23 illustrates the proportion of the observations that must lie within a certain number of standard deviations around the sample mean.

**TABLE 23   Proportions from Chebyshev's Inequality**

| k | Interval around the Sample Mean | Proportion |
|---|---|---|
| 1.25 | $\overline{X} \pm 1.25s$ | 36% |
| 1.50 | $\overline{X} \pm 1.50s$ | 56% |
| 2.00 | $\overline{X} \pm 2s$ | 75% |
| 2.50 | $\overline{X} \pm 2.50s$ | 84% |
| 3.00 | $\overline{X} \pm 3s$ | 89% |
| 4.00 | $\overline{X} \pm 4s$ | 94% |

*Note:* Standard deviation is denoted as *s*.

When $k = 1.25$, for example, the inequality states that the minimum proportion of the observations that lie within $\pm 1.25s$ is $1 - 1/(1.25)^2 = 1 - 0.64 = 0.36$ or 36 percent.

The most frequently cited facts that result from Chebyshev's inequality are that a two-standard-deviation interval around the mean must contain at least 75 percent of the observations, and a three-standard-deviation interval around the mean must contain at least 89 percent of the observations, no matter how the data are distributed.

The importance of Chebyshev's inequality stems from its generality. The inequality holds for samples and populations and for discrete and continuous data regardless of the shape of the distribution. As we shall see in the reading on sampling, we can make much more precise interval statements if we can assume that the sample is drawn from a population that follows a specific distribution called the normal distribution. Frequently, however, we cannot confidently assume that distribution.

The next example illustrates the use of Chebyshev's inequality.

**EXAMPLE 13**

**Applying Chebyshev's Inequality**

According to Table 22, the arithmetic mean monthly return and standard deviation of monthly returns on the S&P 500 were 0.97 percent and 5.65 percent, respectively, during the 1926–2002 period, totaling 924 monthly observations. Using this information, address the following:

1. Calculate the endpoints of the interval that must contain at least 75 percent of monthly returns according to Chebyshev's inequality.

2. What are the minimum and maximum number of observations that must lie in the interval computed in Part 1, according to Chebyshev's inequality?

**Solution to 1:** According to Chebyshev's inequality, at least 75 percent of the observations must lie within two standard deviations of the mean,

$\overline{X} \pm 2s$. For the monthly S&P 500 return series, we have $0.97\% \pm 2(5.65\%)$ = $0.97\% \pm 11.30\%$. Thus the lower endpoint of the interval that must contain at least 75 percent of the observations is $0.97\% - 11.30\%$ = $-10.33\%$, and the upper endpoint is $0.97\% + 11.30\% = 12.27\%$.

**Solution to 2:** For a sample size of 924, at least $0.75(924) = 693$ observations must lie in the interval from $-10.33\%$ to $12.27\%$ that we computed in Part 1. Chebyshev's inequality gives the minimum percentage of observations that must fall within a given interval around the mean, but it does not give the maximum percentage. Table 4, which gave the frequency distribution of monthly returns on the S&P 500, is excerpted below. The data in the excerpted table are consistent with the prediction of Chebyshev's inequality. The set of intervals running from $-10.0\%$ to $12.0\%$ is just slightly narrower than the two-standard-deviation interval $-10.33\%$ to $12.27\%$. A total of 886 observations (approximately 96 percent of observations) fall in the range from $-10.0\%$ to $12.0\%$.

| TABLE 4 | Frequency Distribution for the Monthly Total Return on the S&P 500, January 1926 to December 2002 (Excerpt) |
|---|---|
| **Return Interval** | **Absolute Frequency** |
| $-10.0\%$ to $-8.0\%$ | 20 |
| $-8.0\%$ to $-6.0\%$ | 30 |
| $-6.0\%$ to $-4.0\%$ | 54 |
| $-4.0\%$ to $-2.0\%$ | 90 |
| $-2.0\%$ to $0.0\%$ | 138 |
| $0.0\%$ to $2.0\%$ | 182 |
| $2.0\%$ to $4.0\%$ | 153 |
| $4.0\%$ to $6.0\%$ | 126 |
| $6.0\%$ to $8.0\%$ | 58 |
| $8.0\%$ to $10.0\%$ | 21 |
| $10.0\%$ to $12.0\%$ | $\underline{14}$ |
| | 886 |

## 7.7 Coefficient of Variation

We noted earlier that standard deviation is more easily interpreted than variance because standard deviation uses the same units of measurement as the observations. We may sometimes find it difficult to interpret what standard deviation means in terms of the relative degree of variability of different sets of data, however, either because the data sets have markedly different means or because the data sets have different units of measurement. In this section we explain a measure of relative dispersion, the coefficient of variation that can be useful in such situations. **Relative dispersion** is the amount of dispersion relative to a reference value or benchmark.

We can illustrate the problem of interpreting the standard deviation of data sets with markedly different means using two hypothetical samples of companies. The first sample, composed of small companies, includes companies with 2003 sales of €50 million, €75 million, €65 million, and €90 million. The second sample, composed of large companies, includes companies with 2003 sales of €800 million, €825 million, €815 million, and €840 million. We can verify using Equation 7-14 that the standard deviation of sales in both samples is €16.8 million.[34] In the first sample, the largest observation, €90 million, is 80 percent larger than the smallest observation, €50 million. In the second sample, the largest observation is only 5 percent larger than the smallest observation. Informally, a standard deviation of €16.8 million represents a high degree of variability relative to the first sample, which reflects mean 2003 sales of €70 million, but a small degree of variability relative to the second sample, which reflects mean 2003 sales of €820 million.

The coefficient of variation is helpful in situations such as that just described.

▶ **Coefficient of Variation Formula.** The **coefficient of variation**, CV, is the ratio of the standard deviation of a set of observations to their mean value:[35]

$$CV = s/\overline{X} \tag{7-15}$$

where $s$ is the sample standard deviation and $\overline{X}$ is the sample mean.

When the observations are returns, for example, the coefficient of variation measures the amount of risk (standard deviation) per unit of mean return. Expressing the magnitude of variation among observations relative to their average size, the coefficient of variation permits direct comparisons of dispersion across different data sets. Reflecting the correction for scale, the coefficient of variation is a scale-free measure (that is, it has no units of measurement).

We can illustrate the application of the coefficient of variation using our earlier example of two samples of companies. The coefficient of variation for the first sample is (€16.8 million)/(€70 million) = 0.24; the coefficient of variation for the second sample is (€16.8 million)/(€820 million) = 0.02. This confirms our intuition that the first sample had much greater variability in sales than the second sample. Note that 0.24 and 0.02 are pure numbers in the sense that they are free of units of measurement (because we divided the standard deviation by the mean, which is measured in the same units as the standard deviation). If we need to compare the dispersion among data sets stated in different units of measurement, the coefficient of variation can be useful because it is free from units of measurement. Example 14 illustrates the calculation of the coefficient of variation.

**EXAMPLE 14**

**Calculating the Coefficient of Variation**

Table 24 summarizes annual mean returns and standard deviations for several major U.S. asset classes, using an option in Ibbotson Encorr Analyzer to convert monthly return statistics to annual ones.

---

[34] The second sample was created by adding €750 million to each observation in the first sample. Standard deviation (and variance) has the property of remaining unchanged if we add a constant amount to each observation.

[35] The reader will also encounter CV defined as $100(s/\overline{X})$, which states CV as a percentage.

**TABLE 24  Arithmetic Mean Annual Return and Standard Deviation of Returns, U.S. Asset Classes, 1926–2002**

| Asset Class | Arithmetic Mean Return | Standard Deviation of Return |
|---|---|---|
| S&P 500 | 12.3% | 21.9% |
| U.S. small stock | 16.9% | 35.1% |
| U.S. long-term corporate | 6.1% | 7.2% |
| U.S. long-term government | 5.8% | 8.2% |
| U.S. 30-day T-bill | 3.8% | 0.9% |

*Source*: Ibbotson EnCorr Analyzer™.

Using the information in Table 24, address the following:

1. Calculate the coefficient of variation for each asset class given.

2. Rank the asset classes from most risky to least risky using CV as a measure of relative dispersion.

3. Determine whether there is more difference between the absolute or the relative riskiness of the S&P 500 and U.S. small stocks. Use the standard deviation as a measure of absolute risk and CV as a measure of relative risk.

**Solution to 1:**
S&P 500: CV = 21.9%/12.3% = 1.780
U.S. small stock: CV = 35.1%/16.9% = 2.077
U.S. long-term corporate: CV = 7.2%/6.1% = 1.180
U.S. long-term government: CV = 8.2%/5.8% = 1.414
U.S. 30-day T-bill: CV = 0.9%/3.8% = 0.237

**Solution to 2:**  Based on CV, the ranking is U.S. small stocks (most risky), S&P 500, U.S. long-term governments, U.S. long-term corporates, and U.S. 30-day T-bills (least risky).

**Solution to 3:**  As measured both by standard deviation and CV, U.S. small stocks were riskier than the S&P 500. However, the CVs reveal less difference between small-stock and S&P 500 return variability than that suggested by the standard deviations alone. The standard deviation of small stock returns was $(35.1 - 21.9)/21.9 = 0.603$ or about 60 percent larger than S&P 500 returns, compared with a difference in the CV of $(2.077 - 1.780)/1.780 = 0.167$ or 17 percent.

## 7.8  The Sharpe Ratio

Although CV was designed as a measure of relative dispersion, its inverse reveals something about return per unit of risk because the standard deviation of returns is commonly used as a measure of investment risk. For example, a portfolio with a mean monthly return of 1.19 percent and a standard deviation of 4.42 percent has an inverse CV of 1.19%/4.42% = 0.27. This result indicates that each unit of standard deviation represents a 0.27 percent return.

A more precise return–risk measure recognizes the existence of a risk-free return, a return for virtually zero standard deviation. With a risk-free asset, an investor can choose a risky portfolio, $p$, and then combine that portfolio with the risk-free asset to achieve any desired level of absolute risk as measured by standard deviation of return, $s_p$. Consider a graph with mean return on the vertical axis and standard deviation of return on the horizontal axis. Any combination of portfolio $p$ and the risk-free asset lies on a ray (line) with slope equal to the quantity (Mean return − Risk-free return) divided by $s_p$. The ray giving investors choices offering the most reward (return in excess of the risk-free rate) per unit of risk is the one with the highest slope. The ratio of excess return to standard deviation of return for a portfolio $p$—the slope of the ray passing through $p$—is a single-number measure of a portfolio's performance known as the Sharpe ratio, after its developer, William F. Sharpe.

▶ **Sharpe Ratio Formula.** The **Sharpe ratio** for a portfolio $p$, based on historical returns, is defined as

$$S_h = \frac{\overline{R}_p - \overline{R}_F}{s_p}$$

(7-16)

where $\overline{R}_p$ is the mean return to the portfolio, $\overline{R}_F$ is the mean return to a risk-free asset, and $s_p$ is the standard deviation of return on the portfolio.[36]

The numerator of the Sharpe measure is the portfolio's mean return minus the mean return on the risk-free asset over the sample period. The $\overline{R}_p - \overline{R}_F$ term measures the extra reward that investors receive for the added risk taken. We call this difference the **mean excess return** on portfolio $p$. Thus the Sharpe ratio measures the reward, in terms of mean excess return, per unit of risk, as measured by standard deviation of return. Those risk-averse investors who make decisions only in terms of mean return and standard deviation of return prefer portfolios with larger Sharpe ratios to those with smaller Sharpe ratios.

To illustrate the calculation of the Sharpe ratio, consider the performance of the S&P 500 and U.S. small stocks during the 1926–2002 period, as given previously in Table 24. Using the mean U.S. T-bill return to represent the risk-free rate, we find

$$\text{S\&P 500: } S_h = \frac{12.3 - 3.8}{21.9} = 0.39$$

$$\text{U.S. small stocks: } S_h = \frac{16.9 - 3.8}{35.1} = 0.37$$

Although U.S. small stocks earned higher mean returns, they performed slightly less well than the S&P 500, as measured by the Sharpe ratio.

---

[36] The equation presents the *ex post* or historical Sharpe ratio. We can also think of the Sharpe ratio for a portfolio going forward based on our expectations for mean return, the risk-free return, and the standard deviation of return; this would be the *ex ante* Sharpe ratio. One may also encounter an alternative calculation for the Sharpe ratio in which the denominator is the standard deviation of the series (Portfolio return − Risk-free return) rather than the standard deviation of portfolio return; in practice, the two standard deviation calculations generally yield very similar results. For more information on the Sharpe ratio (which has also been called the Sharpe measure, the reward-to-variability ratio, and the excess return to variability measure), see Elton, Gruber, Brown, and Goetzmann (2003) and Sharpe (1994).

The Sharpe ratio is a mainstay of performance evaluation. We must issue two cautions concerning its use, one related to interpreting negative Sharpe ratios and the other to conceptual limitations.

Finance theory tells us that in the long run, investors should be compensated with additional mean return above the risk-free rate for bearing additional risk, at least if the risky portfolio is well diversified. If investors are so compensated, the numerator of the Sharpe ratio will be positive. Nevertheless, we often find that portfolios exhibit negative Sharpe ratios when the ratio is calculated over periods in which bear markets for equities dominate. This raises a caution when dealing with negative Sharpe ratios. With positive Sharpe ratios, a portfolio's Sharpe ratio decreases if we increase risk, all else equal. That result is intuitive for a risk-adjusted performance measure. With negative Sharpe ratios, however, increasing risk results in a numerically larger Sharpe ratio (for example, doubling risk may increase the Sharpe ratio from $-1$ to $-0.5$). Therefore, in a comparison of portfolios with negative Sharpe ratios, we cannot generally interpret the larger Sharpe ratio (the one closer to zero) to mean better risk-adjusted performance.[37] Practically, to make an interpretable comparison in such cases using the Sharpe ratio, we may need to increase the evaluation period such that one or more of the Sharpe ratios becomes positive; we might also consider using a different performance evaluation metric.

The conceptual limitation of the Sharpe ratio is that it considers only one aspect of risk, standard deviation of return. Standard deviation is most appropriate as a risk measure for portfolio strategies with approximately symmetric return distributions. Strategies with option elements have asymmetric returns. Relatedly, an investment strategy may produce frequent small gains but have the potential for infrequent but extremely large losses.[38] Such a strategy is sometimes described as picking up coins in front of a bulldozer; for example, some hedge fund strategies tend to produce that return pattern. Calculated over a period in which the strategy is working (a large loss has not occurred), this type of strategy would have a high Sharpe ratio. In this case, the Sharpe ratio would give an overly optimistic picture of risk-adjusted performance because standard deviation would incompletely measure the risk assumed.[39] Therefore, before applying the Sharpe ratio to evaluate a manager, we should judge whether standard deviation adequately describes the risk of the manager's investment strategy.

Example 15 illustrates the calculation of the Sharpe ratio in a portfolio performance evaluation context.

## EXAMPLE 15

### Calculating the Sharpe Ratio

In earlier examples, we computed the various statistics for two mutual funds, Selected American Shares (SLASX) and T. Rowe Price Equity Income (PRFDX), for a five-year period ending in December 2002. Table 25 summarizes selected statistics for these two mutual funds for a longer period, the 10-year period ending in 2002.

---

[37] If the standard deviations are equal, however, the portfolio with the negative Sharpe ratio closer to zero is superior.

[38] This statement describes a return distribution with negative skewness. We discuss skewness later in this reading.

[39] For more information, see Amin and Kat (2003).

| TABLE 25 | Mutual Fund Mean Return and Standard Deviation of Return, 1993–2002 | |
| --- | --- | --- |
| **Fund** | **Arithmetic Mean** | **Standard Deviation of Return** |
| SLASX | 12.58% | 19.44% |
| PRFDX | 11.64% | 13.65% |

*Source*: AAII.

The U.S. 30-day T-bill rate is frequently used as a proxy for the risk-free rate. Table 26 gives the annual return on T-bills for the 1993–2002 period.

| TABLE 26 | Annualized U.S. 30-Day T-Bill Rates of Return, 1993–2002 |
| --- | --- |
| **Year** | **Return** |
| 1993 | 2.90% |
| 1994 | 3.90% |
| 1995 | 5.60% |
| 1996 | 5.21% |
| 1997 | 5.26% |
| 1998 | 4.86% |
| 1999 | 4.68% |
| 2000 | 5.89% |
| 2001 | 3.83% |
| 2002 | 1.65% |

*Source*: Ibbotson Associates.

Using the information in Tables 25 and 26, address the following.

1. Calculate the Sharpe ratios for SLASX and PRFDX during the 1993–2002 period.

2. State which fund had superior risk-adjusted performance during this period, as measured by the Sharpe ratio.

**Solution to 1:** We already have in hand the means of the portfolio return and standard deviations of returns. The mean annual risk-free rate of return from 1993 to 2002, using U.S. T-bills as a proxy, is (2.90 + 3.90 + 5.60 + 5.21 + 5.26 + 4.86 + 4.68 + 5.89 + 3.83 + 1.65)/10 = 43.78/10 = 4.38 percent.

$$\text{SLASX: } S_{h,\text{SLASX}} = \frac{12.58 - 4.38}{19.44} = 0.42$$

$$\text{PRFDX: } S_{h,\text{PRFDX}} = \frac{11.64 - 4.38}{13.65} = 0.53$$

**Solution to 2:** PRFDX had a higher positive Sharpe ratio than SLASX during the period. As measured by the Sharpe ratio, PRFDX's performance was superior.

# SYMMETRY AND SKEWNESS IN RETURN DISTRIBUTIONS

Mean and variance may not adequately describe an investment's distribution of returns. In calculations of variance, for example, the deviations around the mean are squared, so we do not know whether large deviations are likely to be positive or negative. We need to go beyond measures of central tendency and dispersion to reveal other important characteristics of the distribution. One important characteristic of interest to analysts is the degree of symmetry in return distributions.

If a return distribution is symmetrical about its mean, then each side of the distribution is a mirror image of the other. Thus equal loss and gain intervals exhibit the same frequencies. Losses from −5 percent to −3 percent, for example, occur with about the same frequency as gains from 3 percent to 5 percent.

One of the most important distributions is the normal distribution, depicted in Figure 6. This symmetrical, bell-shaped distribution plays a central role in the mean–variance model of portfolio selection; it is also used extensively in financial risk management. The normal distribution has the following characteristics:

▶ Its mean and median are equal.

▶ It is completely described by two parameters—its mean and variance.

▶ Roughly 68 percent of its observations lie between plus and minus one standard deviation from the mean; 95 percent lie between plus and minus two standard deviations; and 99 percent lie between plus and minus three standard deviations.

A distribution that is not symmetrical is called **skewed**. A return distribution with positive skew has frequent small losses and a few extreme gains. A return distribution with negative skew has frequent small gains and a few extreme losses. Figure 7 shows positively and negatively skewed distributions. The positively skewed distribution shown has a long tail on its right side; the negatively skewed distribution has a long tail on its left side. For the positively skewed unimodal distribution, the mode is less than the median, which is less than the mean. For the negatively skewed unimodal distribution, the mean is less than the median, which is less than the mode.[40] Investors should be attracted by a positive skew because the mean return falls above the median. Relative to the mean return, positive skew amounts to a limited, though frequent, downside compared with a somewhat unlimited, but less frequent, upside.

Skewness is the name given to a statistical measure of skew. (The word "skewness" is also sometimes used interchangeably for "skew.") Like variance, skewness is computed using each observation's deviation from its mean. **Skewness** (sometimes referred to as relative skewness) is computed as the average cubed deviation from the mean standardized by dividing by the standard deviation cubed to

---

[40] As a mnemonic, in this case the mean, median, and mode occur in the same order as they would be listed in a dictionary.

## FIGURE 6    Properties of a Normal Distribution (EV 5 Expected Value)

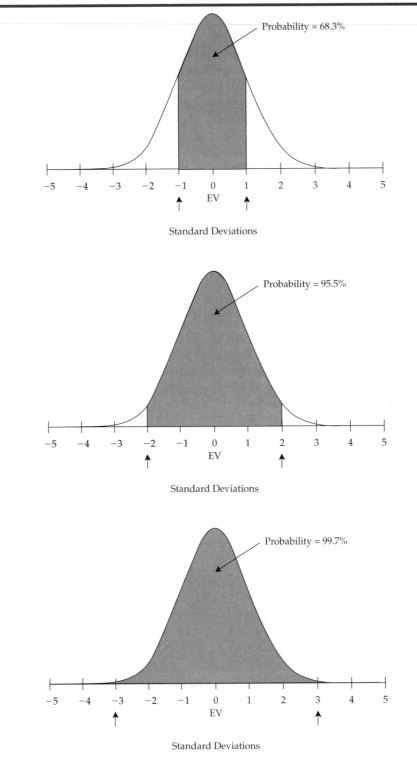

*Source*: Reprinted with permission from *Fixed Income Readings for the Chartered Financial Analyst® Program*. Copyright 2000, Frank J. Fabozzi Associates, New Hope, PA.

**FIGURE 7   Properties of a Skewed Distribution**

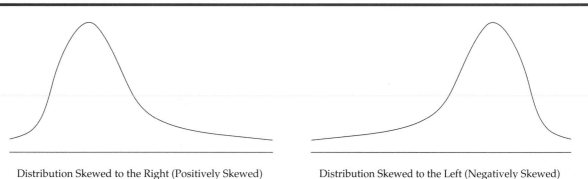

Distribution Skewed to the Right (Positively Skewed)          Distribution Skewed to the Left (Negatively Skewed)

*Source*: Reprinted with permission from *Fixed Income Readings for the Chartered Financial Analyst*® *Program.* Copyright 2000, Frank J. Fabozzi Associates, New Hope, PA.

make the measure free of scale.[41] A symmetric distribution has skewness of 0, a positively skewed distribution has positive skewness, and a negatively skewed distribution has negative skewness, as given by this measure.

We can illustrate the principle behind the measure by focusing on the numerator. Cubing, unlike squaring, preserves the sign of the deviations from the mean. If a distribution is positively skewed with a mean greater than its median, then more than half of the deviations from the mean are negative and less than half are positive. In order for the sum to be positive, the losses must be small and likely, and the gains less likely but more extreme. Therefore, if skewness is positive, the average magnitude of positive deviations is larger than the average magnitude of negative deviations.

A simple example illustrates that a symmetrical distribution has a skewness measure equal to 0. Suppose we have the following data: 1, 2, 3, 4, 5, 6, 7, 8, and 9. The mean outcome is 5, and the deviations are $-4, -3, -2, -1, 0, 1, 2, 3,$ and 4. Cubing the deviations yields $-64, -27, -8, -1, 0, 1, 8, 27,$ and 64, with a sum of 0. The numerator of skewness (and so skewness itself) is thus equal to 0, supporting our claim. Below we give the formula for computing skewness from a sample.

▶ **Sample Skewness Formula.** Sample skewness (also called sample relative skewness), $S_K$, is

$$S_K = \left[ \frac{n}{(n-1)(n-2)} \right] \frac{\sum_{i=1}^{n} (X_i - \overline{X})^3}{s^3} \qquad \textbf{(7-17)}$$

where $n$ is the number of observations in the sample and $s$ is the sample standard deviation.[42]

The algebraic sign of Equation 7-17 indicates the direction of skew, with a negative $S_K$ indicating a negatively skewed distribution and a positive $S_K$ indicating a

---

[41] We are discussing a moment coefficient of skewness. Some textbooks present the Pearson coefficient of skewness, equal to 3(Mean − Median)/Standard deviation, which has the drawback of involving the calculation of the median.

[42] The term $n/[(n-1)(n-2)]$ in Equation 7-17 corrects for a downward bias in small samples.

positively skewed distribution. Note that as $n$ becomes large, the expression reduces to the mean cubed deviation,

$$S_K \approx \left(\frac{1}{n}\right) \frac{\sum_{i=1}^{n} (X_i - \overline{X})^3}{s^3}.$$ As a frame of reference, for a sample size of

100 or larger taken from a normal distribution, a skewness coefficient of $\pm 0.5$ would be considered unusually large.

**TABLE 27   S&P 500 Annual and Monthly Total Returns, 1926–2002: Summary Statistics**

| Return Series | Number of Periods | Arithmetic Mean | Standard Deviation | Skewness | Excess Kurtosis |
|---|---|---|---|---|---|
| S&P 500 (Annual) | 77 | 12.20% | 20.49% | −0.2943 | −0.2207 |
| S&P 500 (Monthly) | 924 | 0.97% | 5.65% | 0.3964 | 9.4645 |

*Source*: Ibbotson EnCorr Analyzer™.

Table 27 shows several summary statistics for the annual and monthly returns on the S&P 500. Earlier we discussed the arithmetic mean return and standard deviation of return, and we shall shortly discuss kurtosis.

Table 27 reveals that S&P 500 annual returns during this period were negatively skewed while monthly returns were positively skewed, and the magnitude of skewness was greater for the monthly series. We would find for other market series that the shape of the distribution of returns often depends on the holding period examined.

Some researchers believe that investors should prefer positive skewness, all else equal—that is, they should prefer portfolios with distributions offering a relatively large frequency of unusually large payoffs.[43] Different investment strategies may tend to introduce different types and amounts of skewness into returns. Example 16 illustrates the calculation of skewness for a managed portfolio.

---

**EXAMPLE 16**

**Calculating Skewness for a Mutual Fund**

Table 28 presents 10 years of annual returns on the T. Rowe Price Equity Income Fund (PRFDX).

**TABLE 28   Annual Rates of Return: T. Rowe Price Equity Income, 1993–2002**

| Year | Return |
|---|---|
| 1993 | 14.8% |
| 1994 | 4.5% |

*(Table continued on next page . . .)*

---

[43] For more on the role of skewness in portfolio selection, see Reilly and Brown (2003) and Elton et al. (2003) and the references therein.

## TABLE 28   (continued)

| Year | Return |
|------|--------|
| 1995 | 33.3% |
| 1996 | 20.3% |
| 1997 | 28.8% |
| 1998 | 9.2% |
| 1999 | 3.8% |
| 2000 | 13.1% |
| 2001 | 1.6% |
| 2002 | −13.0% |

*Source*: AAII.

Using the information in Table 28, address the following.

**1.** Calculate the skewness of PRFDX showing two decimal places.

**2.** Characterize the shape of the distribution of PRFDX returns based on your answer to Part 1.

**Solution to 1:** To calculate skewness, we find the sum of the cubed deviations from the mean, divide by the standard deviation cubed, and then multiply that result by $n/[(n-1)(n-2)]$. Table 29 gives the calculations.

## TABLE 29   Calculating Skewness for PRFDX

| Year | $R_t$ | $R_t - \bar{R}$ | $(R_t - \bar{R})^3$ |
|------|-------|-----------------|---------------------|
| 1993 | 14.8% | 3.16 | 31.554 |
| 1994 | 4.5% | −7.14 | −363.994 |
| 1995 | 33.3% | 21.66 | 10,161.910 |
| 1996 | 20.3% | 8.66 | 649.462 |
| 1997 | 28.8% | 17.16 | 5,053.030 |
| 1998 | 9.2% | −2.44 | −14.527 |
| 1999 | 3.8% | −7.84 | −481.890 |
| 2000 | 13.1% | 1.46 | 3.112 |
| 2001 | 1.6% | −10.04 | −1,012.048 |
| 2002 | −13.0% | −24.64 | −14,959.673 |

| | | | |
|------|-------|-----------------|---------------------|
| $n =$ | 10 | | |
| $\bar{R} =$ | 11.64% | | |
| | | Sum $=$ | −933.064 |
| $s =$ | 13.65% | $s^3 =$ | 2,543.302 |
| | | Sum$/s^3 =$ | −0.3669 |
| | | $n/[(n-1)(n-2)] =$ | 0.1389 |
| | | **Skewness $=$** | **−0.05** |

*Source*: AAII.

Using Equation 7-17, the calculation is:

$$S_K = \left[\frac{10}{(9)(8)}\right]\frac{-933.064}{13.65^3} = -0.05$$

> In this example, five deviations are negative and five are positive. Two large positive deviations, in 1995 and 1997, are more than offset by a very large negative deviation in 2002 and a moderately large negative deviation in 2001, both bear market years. The result is that skewness is a very small negative number.
>
> **Solution to 2:** Based on this small sample, the distribution of annual returns for the fund appears to be approximately symmetric (or very slightly negatively skewed). The negative and positive deviations from the mean are equally frequent, and large positive deviations approximately offset large negative deviations.

## 9    KURTOSIS IN RETURN DISTRIBUTIONS

In the previous section, we discussed how to determine whether a return distribution deviates from a normal distribution because of skewness. One other way in which a return distribution might differ from a normal distribution is by having more returns clustered closely around the mean (being more peaked) and more returns with large deviations from the mean (having fatter tails). Relative to a normal distribution, such a distribution has a greater percentage of small deviations from the mean return (more small surprises) and a greater percentage of extremely large deviations from the mean return (more big surprises). Most investors would perceive a greater chance of extremely large deviations from the mean as increasing risk.

**Kurtosis** is the statistical measure that tells us when a distribution is more or less peaked than a normal distribution. A distribution that is more peaked than normal is called **leptokurtic** (*lepto* from the Greek word for slender); a distribution that is less peaked than normal is called **platykurtic** (*platy* from the Greek word for broad); and a distribution identical to the normal distribution in this respect is called **mesokurtic** (*meso* from the Greek word for middle). The situation of more-frequent extremely large surprises that we described is one of leptokurtosis.[44]

Figure 8 illustrates a leptokurtic distribution. It is more peaked and has fatter tails than the normal distribution.

The calculation for kurtosis involves finding the average of deviations from the mean raised to the fourth power and then standardizing that average by dividing by the standard deviation raised to the fourth power.[45] For all normal distributions, kurtosis is equal to 3. Many statistical packages report estimates of **excess kurtosis**, which is kurtosis minus 3.[46] Excess kurtosis thus characterizes kurtosis relative to the normal distribution. A normal or other mesokurtic distribution has excess kurtosis equal to 0. A leptokurtic distribution has excess kurtosis greater than 0, and a platykurtic distribution has excess kurtosis less than 0. A return distribution with positive excess kurtosis—a leptokurtic return distribution—has more frequent extremely large deviations from the mean than a normal distribution. Below is the expression for computing kurtosis from a sample.

---

[44] Kurtosis has been described as an illness characterized by episodes of extremely rude behavior.

[45] This measure is free of scale. It is always positive because the deviations are raised to the fourth power.

[46] Ibbotson and some software packages, such as Microsoft Excel, label "excess kurtosis" as simply "kurtosis." This highlights the fact that one should familiarize oneself with the description of statistical quantities in any software packages that one uses.

**FIGURE 8    Leptokurtic: Fat Tailed**

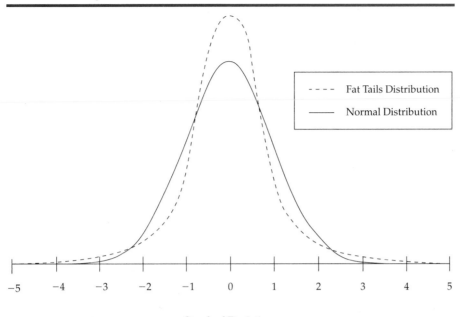

Standard Deviations

*Source*: Reprinted with permission from *Fixed Income Readings for the Chartered Financial Analyst® Program*. Copyright 2000, Frank J. Fabozzi Associates, New Hope, PA.

▶ **Sample Excess Kurtosis Formula.** The **sample excess kurtosis** is

$$K_E = \left( \frac{n(n+1)}{(n-1)(n-2)(n-3)} \frac{\sum_{i=1}^{n} (X_i - \overline{X})^4}{s^4} \right) - \frac{3(n-1)^2}{(n-2)(n-3)} \quad \textbf{(7-18)}$$

where $n$ is the sample size and $s$ is the sample standard deviation.

In Equation 7-18, **sample kurtosis** is the first term. Note that as $n$ becomes large,

Equation 7-18 approximately equals $\dfrac{n^2}{n^3} \dfrac{\sum (X - \overline{X})^4}{s^4} - \dfrac{3n^2}{n^2} = \dfrac{1}{n} \dfrac{\sum (X - \overline{X})^4}{s^4} - 3.$

For a sample of 100 or larger taken from a normal distribution, a sample excess kurtosis of 1.0 or larger would be considered unusually large.

Most equity return series have been found to be leptokurtic. If a return distribution has positive excess kurtosis (leptokurtosis) and we use statistical models that do not account for the fatter tails, we will underestimate the likelihood of very bad or very good outcomes. For example, the return on the S&P 500 for 19 October 1987 was 20 standard deviations away from the mean daily return. Such an outcome is possible with a normal distribution, but its likelihood is almost equal to 0. If daily returns are drawn from a normal distribution, a return four standard deviations or more away from the mean is expected once every 50 years; a return greater than five standard deviations away is expected once every 7,000 years. The return for October 1987 is more likely to have come from a distribution that had fatter tails than from a normal distribution. Looking at Table 27 given earlier, the monthly return series for the S&P 500 has very large excess kurtosis, approximately 9.5. It is extremely fat-tailed relative to the normal distribution. By contrast, the annual return series has very slightly negative excess kurtosis (roughly −0.2). The results for excess kurtosis in the table are consistent with research findings that the normal distribution is a better approximation for U.S. equity returns for annual holding periods than for shorter ones (such as monthly).[47]

The following example illustrates the calculations for sample excess kurtosis for one of the two mutual funds we have been examining.

**EXAMPLE 17**

**Calculating Sample Excess Kurtosis**

Having concluded in Example 16 that the annual returns on T. Rowe Price Equity Income Fund were approximately symmetrically distributed during the 1993–2002 period, what can we say about the kurtosis of the fund's return distribution? Table 28 (repeated below) recaps the annual returns for the fund.

**TABLE 28    Annual Rates of Return: T. Rowe Price Equity Income, 1993–2002 (Repeated)**

| Year | Return |
|------|--------|
| 1993 | 14.8% |
| 1994 | 4.5% |
| 1995 | 33.3% |
| 1996 | 20.3% |
| 1997 | 28.8% |
| 1998 | 9.2% |
| 1999 | 3.8% |
| 2000 | 13.1% |
| 2001 | 1.6% |
| 2002 | −13.0% |

*Source*: AAII.

Using the information from Table 28 repeated above, address the following.

1. Calculate the sample excess kurtosis of PRFDX showing two decimal places.
2. Characterize the shape of the distribution of PRFDX returns based on your answer to Part 1 as leptokurtic, mesokurtic, or platykurtic.

**Solution to 1:** To calculate excess kurtosis, we find the sum of the deviations from the mean raised to the fourth power, divide by the

---

[47] See Campbell, Lo, and MacKinlay (1997) for more details.

standard deviation raised to the fourth power, and then multiply that result by $n(n+1)/[(n-1)(n-2)(n-3)]$. This calculation determines kurtosis. Excess kurtosis is kurtosis minus $3(n-1)^2/[(n-2)(n-3)]$. Table 30 gives the calculations.

**TABLE 30    Calculating Kurtosis for PRFDX**

| Year | $R_t$ | $R_t - \bar{R}$ | $(R_t - \bar{R})^4$ |
|------|-------|-----------------|---------------------|
| 1993 | 14.8% | 3.16 | 99.712 |
| 1994 | 4.5% | −7.14 | 2,598.920 |
| 1995 | 33.3% | 21.66 | 220,106.977 |
| 1996 | 20.3% | 8.66 | 5,624.340 |
| 1997 | 28.8% | 17.16 | 86,709.990 |
| 1998 | 9.2% | −2.44 | 35.445 |
| 1999 | 3.8% | −7.84 | 3,778.020 |
| 2000 | 13.1% | 1.46 | 4.544 |
| 2001 | 1.6% | −10.04 | 10,160.963 |
| 2002 | −13.0% | −24.64 | 368,606.351 |

| | | | |
|---|---|---|---|
| $n =$ | 10 | | |
| $\bar{R} =$ | 11.64% | | |
| | | Sum = | 697,725.261 |
| $s =$ | 13.65% | $s^4 =$ | 34,716.074 |
| | | Sum/$s^4 =$ | 20.098 |
| | $n(n+1)/[(n-1)(n-2)(n-3)] =$ | | 0.2183 |
| | | **Kurtosis =** | **4.39** |
| | $3(n-1)^2/[(n-2)(n-3)] =$ | | 4.34 |
| | | **Excess Kurtosis =** | **0.05** |

*Source*: AAII.

Using Equation 7-18, the calculation is:

$$K_E = \left[ \frac{110}{(9)(8)(7)} \frac{697,725.261}{13.65^4} \right] - \frac{3(9)^2}{(8)(7)}$$

$$= 4.39 - 4.34$$

$$= 0.05$$

**Solution to 2:** The distribution of PRFDX's annual returns appears to be mesokurtic, based on a sample excess kurtosis close to zero. With skewness and excess kurtosis both close to zero, PRFDX's annual returns appear to have been approximately normally distributed during the period.[48]

---

[48] It is useful to know that we can conduct a Jarque–Bera (JB) statistical test of normality based on sample size $n$, sample skewness, and sample excess kurtosis. We can conclude that a distribution is not normal with no more than a 5 percent chance of being wrong if the quantity JB = $n[(S_K^2/6) + (K_E^2/24)]$ is 6 or greater for a sample with at least 30 observations. In this mutual fund example, we have only 10 observations and the test described is only correct based on large samples (as a guideline, for $n \geq 30$). Gujarati (2003) provides more details on this test.

**10** **USING GEOMETRIC AND ARITHMETIC MEANS**

With the concepts of descriptive statistics in hand, we will see why the geometric mean is appropriate for making investment statements about past performance. We will also explore why the arithmetic mean is appropriate for making investment statements in a forward-looking context.

For reporting historical returns, the geometric mean has considerable appeal because it is the rate of growth or return we would have had to earn each year to match the actual, cumulative investment performance. In our simplified Example 8, for instance, we purchased a stock for €100 and two years later it was worth €100, with an intervening year at €200. The geometric mean of 0 percent is clearly the compound rate of growth during the two years. Specifically, the ending amount is the beginning amount times $(1 + R_G)^2$. The geometric mean is an excellent measure of past performance.

Example 8 illustrated how the arithmetic mean can distort our assessment of historical performance. In that example, the total performance for the two-year period was unambiguously 0 percent. With a 100 percent return for the first year and −50 percent for the second, however, the arithmetic mean was 25 percent. As we noted previously, the arithmetic mean is always greater than or equal to the geometric mean. If we want to estimate the average return over a one-period horizon, we should use the arithmetic mean because the arithmetic mean is the average of one-period returns. If we want to estimate the average returns over more than one period, however, we should use the geometric mean of returns because the geometric mean captures how the total returns are linked over time.

As a corollary to using the geometric mean for performance reporting, the use of **semilogarithmic** rather than arithmetic scales is more appropriate when graphing past performance.[49] In the context of reporting performance, a semilogarithmic graph has an arithmetic scale on the horizontal axis for time and a logarithmic scale on the vertical axis for the value of the investment. The vertical axis values are spaced according to the differences between their logarithms. Suppose we want to represent £1, £10, £100, and £1,000 as values of an investment on the vertical axis. Note that each successive value represents a 10-fold increase over the previous value, and each will be equally spaced on the vertical axis because the difference in their logarithms is roughly 2.30; that is, ln 10 − ln 1 = ln 100 − ln 10 = ln 1,000 − ln 100 = 2.30. On a semilogarithmic scale, equal movements on the vertical axis reflect equal percentage changes, and growth at a constant compound rate plots as a straight line. A plot curving upward reflects increasing growth rates over time. The slopes of a plot at different points may be compared in order to judge relative growth rates.

In addition to reporting historical performance, financial analysts need to calculate expected equity risk premiums in a forward-looking context. For this purpose, the arithmetic mean is appropriate.

We can illustrate the use of the arithmetic mean in a forward-looking context with an example based on an investment's future cash flows. In contrasting the geometric and arithmetic means for discounting future cash flows, the essential issue concerns uncertainty. Suppose an investor with $100,000 faces an equal chance of a 100 percent return or a −50 percent return, represented on the tree diagram as a 50/50 chance of a 100 percent return or a −50 percent return per period. With 100 percent return in one period and −50 percent return in the other, the geometric mean return is $\sqrt{2(0.5)} - 1 = 0$.

---

[49] See Campbell (1974) for more information.

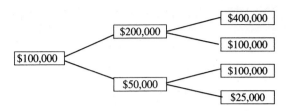

The geometric mean return of 0 percent gives the mode or median of ending wealth after two periods and thus accurately predicts the modal or median ending wealth of $100,000 in this example. Nevertheless, the arithmetic mean return better predicts the arithmetic mean ending wealth. With equal chances of 100 percent or −50 percent returns, consider the four equally likely outcomes of $400,000, $100,000, $100,000, and $25,000 as if they actually occurred. The arithmetic mean ending wealth would be $156,250 = ($400,000 + $100,000 + $100,000 + $25,000)/4. The actual returns would be 300 percent, 0 percent, 0 percent, and −75 percent for a two-period arithmetic mean return of (300 + 0 + 0 −75)/4 = 56.25 percent. This arithmetic mean return predicts the arithmetic mean ending wealth of $100,000 × 1.5625 = $156,250. Noting that 56.25 percent for two periods is 25 percent per period, we then must discount the expected terminal wealth of $156,250 at the 25 percent arithmetic mean rate to reflect the uncertainty in the cash flows.

Uncertainty in cash flows or returns causes the arithmetic mean to be larger than the geometric mean. The more uncertain the returns, the more divergence exists between the arithmetic and geometric means. The geometric mean return approximately equals the arithmetic return minus half the variance of return.[50] Zero variance or zero uncertainty in returns would leave the geometric and arithmetic return approximately equal, but real-world uncertainty presents an arithmetic mean return larger than the geometric. For example, Dimson et al. (2002) reported that from 1900 to 2000, U.S. equities had nominal annual returns with an arithmetic mean of 12 percent and standard deviation of 19.9 percent. They reported the geometric mean as 10.1 percent. We can see the geometric mean is approximately the arithmetic mean minus half of the variance of returns: $R_G \approx 0.12 - (1/2)(0.199^2) = 0.10$.

---

[50] See Bodie, Kane, and Marcus (2001).

# SUMMARY

In this reading, we have presented descriptive statistics, the set of methods that permit us to convert raw data into useful information for investment analysis.

► A population is defined as all members of a specified group. A sample is a subset of a population.

► A parameter is any descriptive measure of a population. A sample statistic (statistic, for short) is a quantity computed from or used to describe a sample.

► Data measurements are taken using one of four major scales: nominal, ordinal, interval, or ratio. Nominal scales categorize data but do not rank them. Ordinal scales sort data into categories that are ordered with respect to some characteristic. Interval scales provide not only ranking but also assurance that the differences between scale values are equal. Ratio scales have all the characteristics of interval scales as well as a true zero point as the origin. The scale on which data are measured determines the type of analysis that can be performed on the data.

► A frequency distribution is a tabular display of data summarized into a relatively small number of intervals. Frequency distributions permit us to evaluate how data are distributed.

► The relative frequency of observations in an interval is the number of observations in the interval divided by the total number of observations. The cumulative relative frequency cumulates (adds up) the relative frequencies as we move from the first interval to the last, thus giving the fraction of the observations that are less than the upper limit of each interval.

► A histogram is a bar chart of data that have been grouped into a frequency distribution. A frequency polygon is a graph of frequency distributions obtained by drawing straight lines joining successive points representing the class frequencies.

► Sample statistics such as measures of central tendency, measures of dispersion, skewness, and kurtosis help with investment analysis, particularly in making probabilistic statements about returns.

► Measures of central tendency specify where data are centered and include the (arithmetic) mean, median, and mode (most frequently occurring value). The mean is the sum of the observations divided by the number of observations. The median is the value of the middle item (or the mean of the values of the two middle items) when the items in a set are sorted into ascending or descending order. The mean is the most frequently used measure of central tendency. The median is not influenced by extreme values and is most useful in the case of skewed distributions. The mode is the only measure of central tendency that can be used with nominal data.

► A portfolio's return is a weighted mean return computed from the returns on the individual assets, where the weight applied to each asset's return is the fraction of the portfolio invested in that asset.

► The geometric mean, $G$, of a set of observations $X_1, X_2, \ldots X_n$ is $G = \sqrt[n]{X_1 X_2 X_3 \ldots X_n}$ with $X_i \geq 0$ for $i = 1, 2, \ldots, n$. The geometric mean is especially important in reporting compound growth rates for time series data.

► Quantiles such as the median, quartiles, quintiles, deciles, and percentiles are location parameters that divide a distribution into halves, quarters, fifths, tenths, and hundredths, respectively.

▶ Dispersion measures such as the variance, standard deviation, and mean absolute deviation (MAD) describe the variability of outcomes around the arithmetic mean.

▶ Range is defined as the maximum value minus the minimum value. Range has only a limited scope because it uses information from only two observations.

▶ MAD for a sample is $\dfrac{\sum\limits_{i=1}^{n}\left|X_i - \overline{X}\right|}{n}$ where $\overline{X}$ is the sample mean and $n$ is the number of observations in the sample.

▶ The variance is the average of the squared deviations around the mean, and the standard deviation is the positive square root of variance. In computing sample variance ($s^2$) and sample standard deviation, the average squared deviation is computed using a divisor equal to the sample size minus 1.

▶ The semivariance is the average squared deviation below the mean; semideviation is the positive square root of semivariance. Target semivariance is the average squared deviation below a target level; target semideviation is its positive square root. All these measures quantify downside risk.

▶ According to Chebyshev's inequality, the proportion of the observations within $k$ standard deviations of the arithmetic mean is at least $1 - 1/k^2$ for all $k > 1$. Chebyshev's inequality permits us to make probabilistic statements about the proportion of observations within various intervals around the mean for any distribution. As a result of Chebyshev's inequality, a two-standard-deviation interval around the mean must contain at least 75 percent of the observations, and a three-standard-deviation interval around the mean must contain at least 89 percent of the observations, no matter how the data are distributed.

▶ The coefficient of variation, CV, is the ratio of the standard deviation of a set of observations to their mean value. A scale-free measure of relative dispersion, by expressing the magnitude of variation among observations relative to their average size, the CV permits direct comparisons of dispersion across different data sets.

▶ The Sharpe ratio for a portfolio, $p$, based on historical returns, is defined as $S_h = \dfrac{\overline{R}_p - \overline{R}_F}{s_p}$, where $\overline{R}_p$ is the mean return to the portfolio, $\overline{R}_F$ is the mean return to a risk-free and asset, and $s_p$ is the standard deviation of return on the portfolio.

▶ Skew describes the degree to which a distribution is not symmetric about its mean. A return distribution with positive skewness has frequent small losses and a few extreme gains. A return distribution with negative skewness has frequent small gains and a few extreme losses. Zero skewness indicates a symmetric distribution of returns.

▶ Kurtosis measures the peakedness of a distribution and provides information about the probability of extreme outcomes. A distribution that is more peaked than the normal distribution is called leptokurtic; a distribution that is less peaked than the normal distribution is called platykurtic; and a distribution identical to the normal distribution in this respect is called mesokurtic. The calculation for kurtosis involves finding the average of deviations from the mean raised to the fourth power and then standardizing that average by the standard deviation raised to the fourth power. Excess kurtosis is kurtosis minus 3, the value of kurtosis for all normal distributions.

## PRACTICE PROBLEMS FOR READING 7

1. Identify each of the following groups as a population or a sample. If the group is a sample, identify the population to which the sample is related.

   A. The S&P MidCap 400 Index viewed as representing U.S. stocks with market capitalization falling within a stated range.

   B. UK shares that traded on 11 August 2003 and that also closed above £100/share as of the close of the London Stock Exchange on that day.

   C. Marsh & McLennan Companies, Inc. (NYSE: MMC) and AON Corporation (NYSE: AON). This group is part of Standard & Poor's Insurance Brokers Index.

   D. The set of 31 estimates for Microsoft EPS for fiscal year 2003, as of the 4 June 2003 date of a First Call/Thomson Financial report.

2. State the type of scale used to measure the following sets of data.

   A. Sales in euros.

   B. The investment style of mutual funds.

   C. An analyst's rating of a stock as *underweight, market weight,* or *overweight,* referring to the analyst's suggested weighting of the stock in a portfolio.

   D. A measure of the risk of portfolios on a scale of whole numbers from 1 (very conservative) to 5 (very risky) where the difference between 1 and 2 represents the same increment in risk as the difference between 4 and 5.

*The table below gives the deviations of a hypothetical portfolio's annual total returns (gross of fees) from its benchmark's annual returns, for a 12-year period ending in 2003. Use this information to answer Problems 3 and 4.*

| Portfolio's Deviations from Benchmark Return, 1992–2003 | |
|---|---|
| 1992 | −7.14% |
| 1993 | 1.62% |
| 1994 | 2.48% |
| 1995 | −2.59% |
| 1996 | 9.37% |
| 1997 | −0.55% |
| 1998 | −0.89% |
| 1999 | −9.19% |
| 2000 | −5.11% |
| 2001 | −0.49% |
| 2002 | 6.84% |
| 2003 | 3.04% |

**3. A.** Calculate the frequency, cumulative frequency, relative frequency, and cumulative relative frequency for the portfolio's deviations from benchmark return, given the set of intervals in the table that follows.

| Return Interval | Frequency | Cumulative Frequency | Relative Frequency | Cumulative Relative Frequency |
|---|---|---|---|---|
| $-9.19 \leq A < -4.55$ | | | | |
| $-4.55 \leq B < 0.09$ | | | | |
| $0.09 \leq C < 4.73$ | | | | |
| $4.73 \leq D \leq 9.37$ | | | | |

  **B.** Construct a histogram using the data.

  **C.** Identify the modal interval of the grouped data.

**4.** Tracking risk (also called tracking error) is the standard deviation of the deviation of a portfolio's gross-of-fees total returns from benchmark return. Calculate the tracking risk of the portfolio, stated in percent (give the answer to two decimal places).

*The table below gives the annual total returns on the MSCI Germany Index from 1993 to 2002. The returns are in the local currency. Use the information in this table to answer Problems 5 through 10.*

| MSCI Germany Index Total Returns, 1993–2002 | |
|---|---|
| **Year** | **Return** |
| 1993 | 46.21% |
| 1994 | −6.18% |
| 1995 | 8.04% |
| 1996 | 22.87% |
| 1997 | 45.90% |
| 1998 | 20.32% |
| 1999 | 41.20% |
| 2000 | −9.53% |
| 2001 | −17.75% |
| 2002 | −43.06% |

*Source*: Ibbotson EnCorr Analyzer™.

**5.** To describe the distribution of observations, perform the following:

    **A.** Create a frequency distribution with five equally spaced classes (round up at the second decimal place in computing the width of class intervals).

    **B.** Calculate the cumulative frequency of the data.

    **C.** Calculate the relative frequency and cumulative relative frequency of the data.

    **D.** State whether the frequency distribution is symmetric or asymmetric. If the distribution is asymmetric, characterize the nature of the asymmetry.

**6.** To describe the central tendency of the distribution, perform the following:

    **A.** Calculate the sample mean return.

    **B.** Calculate the median return.

    **C.** Identify the modal interval (or intervals) of the grouped returns.

**7.** To describe the compound rate of growth of the MSCI Germany Index, calculate the geometric mean return.

**8.** To describe the values at which certain returns fall, calculate the 30th percentile.

**9.** To describe the dispersion of the distribution, perform the following:

    **A.** Calculate the range.

    **B.** Calculate the mean absolute deviation (MAD).

    **C.** Calculate the variance.

    **D.** Calculate the standard deviation.

    **E.** Calculate the semivariance.

    **F.** Calculate the semideviation.

**10.** To describe the degree to which the distribution may depart from normality, perform the following:

    **A.** Calculate the skewness.

    **B.** Explain the finding for skewness in terms of the location of the median and mean returns.

    **C.** Calculate excess kurtosis.

    **D.** Contrast the distribution of annual returns on the MSCI Germany Index to a normal distribution model for returns.

---

**11. A.** Explain the relationship among arithmetic mean return, geometric mean return, and variability of returns.

    **B.** Contrast the use of the arithmetic mean return to the geometric mean return of an investment from the perspective of an investor concerned with the investment's terminal value.

    **C.** Contrast the use of the arithmetic mean return to the geometric mean return of an investment from the perspective of an investor concerned with the investment's average one-year return.

*The following table repeats the annual total returns on the MSCI Germany Index previously given and also gives the annual total returns on the JP Morgan Germany five-to seven-year government bond index (JPM 5–7 Year GBI, for short). During the period given in the table, the International Monetary Fund Germany Money Market Index (IMF Germany MMI, for short) had a mean annual total return of 4.33 percent. Use that information and the information in the table to answer Problems 12 through 14.*

| Year | MSCI Germany Index | JPM Germany 5–7 Year GBI |
|------|--------------------|---------------------------|
| 1993 | 46.21% | 15.74% |
| 1994 | −6.18% | −3.40% |
| 1995 | 8.04% | 18.30% |
| 1996 | 22.87% | 8.35% |
| 1997 | 45.90% | 6.65% |
| 1998 | 20.32% | 12.45% |
| 1999 | 41.20% | −2.19% |
| 2000 | −9.53% | 7.44% |
| 2001 | −17.75% | 5.55% |
| 2002 | −43.06% | 10.27% |

*Source*: Ibbotson EnCorr Analyzer™.

**12.** Calculate the annual returns and the mean annual return on a portfolio 60 percent invested in the MSCI Germany Index and 40 percent invested in the JPM Germany GBI.

**13.** **A.** Calculate the coefficient of variation for
   **i.** the 60/40 equity/bond portfolio described in Problem 12.
   **ii.** the MSCI Germany Index.
   **iii.** the JPM Germany 5–7 Year GBI.

   **B.** Contrast the risk of the 60/40 equity/bond portfolio, the MSCI Germany Index, and the JPM Germany 5–7 Year GBI, as measured by the coefficient of variation.

**14.** **A.** Using the IMF Germany MMI as a proxy for the risk-free return, calculate the Sharpe ratio for
   **i.** the 60/40 equity/bond portfolio described in Problem 12.
   **ii.** the MSCI Germany Index.
   **iii.** the JPM Germany 5–7 Year GBI.

   **B.** Contrast the risk-adjusted performance of the 60/40 equity/bond portfolio, the MSCI Germany Index, and the JPM Germany 5–7 Year GBI, as measured by the Sharpe ratio.

**15.** Suppose a client asks you for a valuation analysis on the eight-stock U.S. common stock portfolio given in the table below. The stocks are equally weighted in the portfolio. You are evaluating the portfolio using three price multiples. The trailing 12 months (TTM) price-to-earnings ratio (P/E) is current price divided by diluted EPS over the past four quarters.[1] The TTM price-to-sales ratio (P/S) is current price divided by sales per share over the last four quarters. The price-to-book ratio (P/B) is the current price divided by book value per share as given in the most recent quarterly statement. The data in the table are as of 12 September 2003.

### Client Portfolio

| Common Stock | TTM P/E | TTM P/S | P/B |
|---|---|---|---|
| Abercrombie & Fitch (NYSE: AFN) | 13.67 | 1.66 | 3.43 |
| Albemarle Corporation (NYSE: ALB) | 14.43 | 1.13 | 1.96 |
| Avon Products, Inc. (NYSE: AVP) | 28.06 | 2.45 | 382.72 |
| Berkshire Hathaway (NYSE: BRK.A) | 18.46 | 2.39 | 1.65 |
| Everest Re Group Ltd (NYSE: RE) | 11.91 | 1.34 | 1.30 |
| FPL Group, Inc. (NYSE: FPL) | 15.80 | 1.04 | 1.70 |
| Johnson Controls, Inc. (NYSE: JCI) | 14.24 | 0.40 | 2.13 |
| Tenneco Automotive, Inc. (NYSE: TEN) | 6.44 | 0.07 | 41.31 |

*Source*: www.multexinvestor.com.

Based only on the information in the above table, calculate the following for the portfolio:

**A.** **i.** Arithmetic mean P/E.
   **ii.** Median P/E.

**B.** **i.** Arithmetic mean P/S.
   **ii.** Median P/S.

**C.** **i.** Arithmetic mean P/B.
   **ii.** Median P/B.

**D.** Based on your answers to Parts A, B, and C, characterize the appropriateness of using the following valuation measures:
   **i.** Mean and median P/E.
   **ii.** Mean and median P/S.
   **iii.** Mean and median P/B.

---

[1] In particular, diluted EPS is for continuing operations and before extraordinary items and accounting changes.

**16.** The table below gives statistics relating to a hypothetical 10-year record of two portfolios.

|  | Mean Annual Return | Standard Deviation of Return | Skewness |
|---|---|---|---|
| Portfolio A | 8.3% | 19.5% | −1.9 |
| Portfolio B | 8.3% | 18.0% | 3.0 |

Based only on the information in the above table, perform the following:

**A.** Contrast the distributions of returns of Portfolios A and B.

**B.** Evaluate the relative attractiveness of Portfolios A and B.

**17.** The table below gives statistics relating to a hypothetical three-year record of two portfolios.

|  | Mean Monthly Return | Standard Deviation | Skewness | Excess Kurtosis |
|---|---|---|---|---|
| Portfolio A | 1.1994% | 5.5461% | −2.2603 | 6.2584 |
| Portfolio B | 1.1994% | 6.4011% | −2.2603 | 8.0497 |

Based only on the information in the above table, perform the following:

**A.** Contrast the distributions of returns of Portfolios A and B.

**B.** Evaluate the relative attractiveness of Portfolios A and B.

**18.** The table below gives statistics relating to a hypothetical five-year record of two portfolios.

|  | Mean Monthly Return | Standard Deviation | Skewness | Excess Kurtosis |
|---|---|---|---|---|
| Portfolio A | 1.6792% | 5.3086% | −0.1395 | −0.0187 |
| Portfolio B | 1.8375% | 5.9047% | 0.4934 | −0.8525 |

Based only on the information in the above table, perform the following:

**A.** Contrast the distributions of returns of Portfolios A and B.

**B.** Evaluate the relative attractiveness of Portfolios A and B.

**19.** At the UXI Foundation, portfolio managers are normally kept on only if their annual rate of return meets or exceeds the mean annual return for portfolio managers of a similar investment style. Recently, the UXI Foundation has also been considering two other evaluation criteria: the median annual return of funds with the same investment style, and two-thirds of the return performance of the top fund with the same investment style.

   The table below gives the returns for nine funds with the same investment style as the UXI Foundation.

| Fund | Return |
|:----:|:------:|
| 1 | 17.8% |
| 2 | 21.0% |
| 3 | 38.0% |
| 4 | 19.2% |
| 5 | 2.5% |
| 6 | 24.3% |
| 7 | 18.7% |
| 8 | 16.9% |
| 9 | 12.6% |

   With the above distribution of fund performance, which of the three evaluation criteria is the most difficult to achieve?

**20.** If the observations in a dataset have different values, is the geometric mean for that dataset less than that dataset's:

|    | harmonic mean? | arithmetic mean? |
|:--:|:--------------:|:----------------:|
| **A.** | No | No |
| **B.** | No | Yes |
| **C.** | Yes | No |

**21.** Is a return distribution characterized by frequent small losses and a few large gains *best* described as having:

|    | negative skew? | a mean that is greater than the median? |
|:--:|:--------------:|:---------------------------------------:|
| **A.** | No | No |
| **B.** | No | Yes |
| **C.** | Yes | No |

**22.** An analyst gathered the following information about the return distributions for two portfolios during the same time period:

| Portfolio | Skewness | Kurtosis |
|-----------|----------|----------|
| A | −1.3 | 2.2 |
| B | 0.5 | 3.5 |

The analyst stated that the distribution for Portfolio A is more peaked than a normal distribution and that the distribution for Portfolio B has a long tail on the left side of the distribution. Which of the following is *most* true?

**A.** The statement is not correct in reference to either portfolio.

**B.** The statement is correct in reference to Portfolio A, but the statement is not correct in reference to portfolio B.

**C.** The statement is not correct in reference to Portfolio A, but the statement is correct in reference to Portfolio B.

**23.** The coefficient of variation is useful in determining the relative degree of variability of different data sets if those data sets have different:

**A.** means or different units of measurement.

**B.** means, but not different units of measurement.

**C.** units of measurement, but not different means.

**24.** An analyst gathered the following information:

| Portfolio | Mean Return | Standard Deviation of Returns |
|-----------|-------------|-------------------------------|
| 1 | 9.8% | 19.9% |
| 2 | 10.5% | 20.3% |
| 3 | 13.3% | 33.9% |

If the risk-free rate of return is 3.0 percent, the portfolio that had the *best* risk-adjusted performance based on the Sharpe ratio is:

**A.** Portfolio 1.

**B.** Portfolio 2.

**C.** Portfolio 3.

**25.** An analyst gathered the following information about a portfolio's performance over the past ten years:

| | |
|---|---|
| Mean annual return | 11.8% |
| Standard deviation of annual returns | 15.7% |
| Portfolio beta | 1.2 |

If the mean return on the risk-free asset over the same period was 5.0%, the coefficient of variation and Sharpe ratio, respectively, for the portfolio are *closest* to:

| | Coefficient of variation | Sharpe ratio |
|---|---|---|
| **A.** | 0.75 | 0.43 |
| **B.** | 1.33 | 0.36 |
| **C.** | 1.33 | 0.43 |

# PROBABILITY CONCEPTS

by Richard A. DeFusco, CFA, Dennis W. McLeavey, CFA, Jerald E. Pinto, CFA, and David E. Runkle, CFA

## LEARNING OUTCOMES

| The candidate should be able to: | Mastery |
|---|:---:|
| **a.** define a random variable, an outcome, an event, mutually exclusive events, and exhaustive events; | ☐ |
| **b.** explain the two defining properties of probability, and distinguish among empirical, subjective, and a priori probabilities; | ☐ |
| **c.** state the probability of an event in terms of odds for or against the event; | ☐ |
| **d.** distinguish between unconditional and conditional probabilities; | ☐ |
| **e.** calculate and interpret 1) the joint probability of two events, 2) the probability that at least one of two events will occur, given the probability of each and the joint probability of the two events, and 3) a joint probability of any number of independent events; | ☐ |
| **f.** distinguish between dependent and independent events; | ☐ |
| **g.** calculate and interpret, using the total probability rule, an unconditional probability; | ☐ |
| **h.** explain the use of conditional expectation in investment applications; | ☐ |
| **i.** diagram an investment problem, using a tree diagram; | ☐ |
| **j.** calculate and interpret covariance and correlation; | ☐ |
| **k.** calculate and interpret the expected value, variance, and standard deviation of a random variable and of returns on a portfolio; | ☐ |
| **l.** calculate and interpret covariance given a joint probability function; | ☐ |
| **m.** calculate and interpret an updated probability, using Bayes' formula; | ☐ |
| **n.** identify the most appropriate method to solve a particular counting problem, and solve counting problems using the factorial, combination, and permutation notations. | ☐ |

# 1

# INTRODUCTION

All investment decisions are made in an environment of risk. The tools that allow us to make decisions with consistency and logic in this setting come under the heading of probability. This reading presents the essential probability tools needed to frame and address many real-world problems involving risk. We illustrate how these tools apply to such issues as predicting investment manager performance, forecasting financial variables, and pricing bonds so that they fairly compensate bondholders for default risk. Our focus is practical. We explore in detail the concepts that are most important to investment research and practice. One such concept is independence, as it relates to the predictability of returns and financial variables. Another is expectation, as analysts continually look to the future in their analyses and decisions. Analysts and investors must also cope with variability. We present variance, or dispersion around expectation, as a risk concept important in investments. The reader will acquire specific skills in using portfolio expected return and variance.

The basic tools of probability, including expected value and variance, are set out in Section 2 of this reading. Section 3 introduces covariance and correlation (measures of relatedness between random quantities) and the principles for calculating portfolio expected return and variance. Two topics end the reading: Bayes' formula and outcome counting. Bayes' formula is a procedure for updating beliefs based on new information. In several areas, including a widely used option-pricing model, the calculation of probabilities involves defining and counting outcomes. The reading ends with a discussion of principles and shortcuts for counting.

# 2

# PROBABILITY, EXPECTED VALUE, AND VARIANCE

The probability concepts and tools necessary for most of an analyst's work are relatively few and simple but require thought to apply. This section presents the essentials for working with probability, expectation, and variance, drawing on examples from equity and fixed income analysis.

An investor's concerns center on returns. The return on a risky asset is an example of a **random variable**, a quantity whose **outcomes** (possible values) are uncertain. For example, a portfolio may have a return objective of 10 percent a year. The portfolio manager's focus at the moment may be on the likelihood of earning a return that is less than 10 percent over the next year. Ten percent is a particular value or outcome of the random variable "portfolio return." Although we may be concerned about a single outcome, frequently our interest may be in a set of outcomes: The concept of "event" covers both.

▶ **Definition of Event.** An **event** is a specified set of outcomes.

We may specify an event to be a single outcome—for example, *the portfolio earns a return of 10 percent.* (We use italics to highlight statements that define events.) We can capture the portfolio manager's concerns by defining the event as *the portfolio earns a return below 10 percent.* This second event, referring as it does to all possible returns greater than or equal to −100 percent (the worst possible return) but less than 10 percent, contains an infinite number of outcomes. To save words, it is common to use a capital letter in italics to represent a defined event. We could define $A$ = *the portfolio earns a return of 10 percent* and $B$ = *the portfolio earns a return below 10 percent.*

To return to the portfolio manager's concern, how likely is it that the portfolio will earn a return below 10 percent?

The answer to this question is a **probability**: a number between 0 and 1 that measures the chance that a stated event will occur. If the probability is 0.40 that the portfolio earns a return below 10 percent, there is a 40 percent chance of that event happening. If an event is impossible, it has a probability of 0. If an event is certain to happen, it has a probability of 1. If an event is impossible or a sure thing, it is not random at all. So, 0 and 1 bracket all the possible values of a probability.

Probability has two properties, which together constitute its definition.

▶ **Definition of Probability.** The two defining properties of a probability are as follows:

**1.** The probability of any event $E$ is a number between 0 and 1: $0 \leq P(E) \leq 1$.

**2.** The sum of the probabilities of any set of mutually exclusive and **exhaustive** events equals 1.

$P$ followed by parentheses stands for "the probability of (the event in parentheses)," as in $P(E)$ for "the probability of event $E$." We can also think of $P$ as a rule or function that assigns numerical values to events consistent with Properties 1 and 2.

In the above definition, the term mutually exclusive means that only one event can occur at a time; **exhaustive** means that the events cover all possible outcomes. The events $A$ = *the portfolio earns a return of 10 percent* and $B$ = *the portfolio earns a return below 10 percent* are mutually exclusive because $A$ and $B$ cannot both occur at the same time. For example, a return of 8.1 percent means that $B$ has occurred and $A$ has not occurred. Although events $A$ and $B$ are mutually exclusive, they are not exhaustive because they do not cover outcomes such as a return of 11 percent. Suppose we define a third event: $C$ = *the portfolio earns a return above 10 percent.* Clearly, $A$, $B$, and $C$ are mutually exclusive and exhaustive events. Each of $P(A)$, $P(B)$, and $P(C)$ is a number between 0 and 1, and $P(A) + P(B) + P(C) = 1$.

The most basic kind of mutually exclusive and exhaustive events is the set of all the distinct possible outcomes of the random variable. If we know both that set and the assignment of probabilities to those outcomes—the probability distribution of the random variable—we have a complete description of the random variable, and we can assign a probability to any event that we might describe.[1] The probability of any event is the sum of the probabilities of the distinct outcomes included in the definition of the event. Suppose the event of interest is $D$ = *the portfolio earns a return above the risk-free rate,* and we know the probability distribution of portfolio returns. Assume the risk-free rate is 4 percent. To calculate $P(D)$, the probability of $D$, we would sum the probabilities of the outcomes that satisfy the definition of the event; that is, we would sum the probabilities of portfolio returns greater than 4 percent.

Earlier, to illustrate a concept, we assumed a probability of 0.40 for a portfolio earning less than 10 percent, without justifying the particular assumption. We

---

[1] In the reading on common probability distributions, we describe some of the probability distributions most frequently used in investment applications.

also talked about using a probability distribution of outcomes to calculate the probability of events, without explaining how a probability distribution might be estimated. Making actual financial decisions using inaccurate probabilities might have grave consequences. How, in practice, do we estimate probabilities? This topic is a field of study in itself, but there are three broad approaches to estimating probabilities. In investments, we often estimate the probability of an event as a relative frequency of occurrence based on historical data. This method produces an **empirical probability**. For example, Amihud and Li (2002) report that of their sample of 16,189 dividend changes for NYSE and Amex stocks during the years 1962 to 2000, 14,911 were increases and 1,278 were decreases. The empirical probability that a dividend change is a dividend decrease for U.S. stocks is thus 1,278/16,189 = 0.08, approximately. We will point out empirical probabilities in several places as they appear in this reading.

Relationships must be stable through time for empirical probabilities to be accurate. We cannot calculate an empirical probability of an event not in the historical record or a reliable empirical probability for a very rare event. There are cases, then, in which we may adjust an empirical probability to account for perceptions of changing relationships. In other cases, we have no empirical probability to use at all. We may also make a personal assessment of probability without reference to any particular data. Each of these three types of probability is a **subjective probability**, one drawing on personal or subjective judgment. Subjective probabilities are of great importance in investments. Investors, in making buy and sell decisions that determine asset prices, often draw on subjective probabilities. Subjective probabilities appear in various places in this reading, notably in our discussion of Bayes' formula.

In a more narrow range of well-defined problems, we can sometimes deduce probabilities by reasoning about the problem. The resulting probability is an **a priori probability**, one based on logical analysis rather than on observation or personal judgment. We will use this type of probability in Example 6. The counting methods we discuss later are particularly important in calculating an a priori probability. Because a priori and empirical probabilities generally do not vary from person to person, they are often grouped as **objective probabilities**.

In business and elsewhere, we often encounter probabilities stated in terms of odds—for instance, "the odds for $E$" or the "odds against $E$." For example, as of mid-2003, analysts' fiscal year 2004 EPS forecasts for one Toronto Stock Exchange-listed company ranged from C\$3.98 to C\$4.25. Nevertheless, one analyst asserts that the odds for the company beating the highest estimate, C\$4.25, are 1 to 7. A second analyst argues that the odds against that happening are 15 to 1. What do those statements imply about the probability of the company's EPS beating the highest estimate? We interpret probabilities stated in terms of odds as follows:

▶ **Probability Stated as Odds.** Given a probability $P(E)$,

   **1.** Odds for $E = P(E)/[1 - P(E)]$. The odds for $E$ are the probability of $E$ divided by 1 minus the probability of $E$. Given odds for $E$ of "$a$ to $b$," the implied probability of $E$ is $a/(a + b)$.

In the example, the statement that the odds for *the company's EPS for FY2004 beating C\$4.25* are 1 to 7 means that the speaker believes the probability of the event is $1/(1 + 7) = 1/8 = 0.125$.

   **2.** Odds against $E = [1 - P(E)]/P(E)$, the reciprocal of odds for $E$. Given odds against $E$ of "$a$ to $b$," the implied probability of $E$ is $b/(a + b)$.

The statement that the odds against *the company's EPS for FY2004 beating C$4.25* are 15 to 1 is consistent with a belief that the probability of the event is $1/(1 + 15) = 1/16 = 0.0625$.

To further explain odds for an event, if $P(E) = 1/8$, the odds for $E$ are $(1/8)/(7/8) = (1/8)(8/7) = 1/7$, or "1 to 7." For each occurrence of $E$, we expect seven cases of non-occurrence; out of eight cases in total, therefore, we expect $E$ to happen once, and the probability of $E$ is $1/8$. In wagering, it is common to speak in terms of the odds against something, as in Statement 2. For odds of "15 to 1" against $E$ (an implied probability of $E$ of $1/16$), a $1 wager on $E$, if successful, returns $15 in profits plus the $1 staked in the wager. We can calculate the bet's anticipated profit as follows:

Win:      Probability = 1/16; Profit = $15
Loss:     Probability = 15/16; Profit = −$1
Anticipated profit = (1/16)($15) + (15/16)(−$1) = $0

Weighting each of the wager's two outcomes by the respective probability of the outcome, if the odds (probabilities) are accurate, the anticipated profit of the bet is $0.

## EXAMPLE 1

### Profiting from Inconsistent Probabilities

You are examining the common stock of two companies in the same industry in which an important antitrust decision will be announced next week. The first company, SmithCo Corporation, will benefit from a governmental decision that there is no antitrust obstacle related to a merger in which it is involved. You believe that SmithCo's share price reflects a 0.85 probability of such a decision. A second company, Selbert Corporation, will equally benefit from a "go ahead" ruling. Surprisingly, you believe Selbert stock reflects only a 0.50 probability of a favorable decision. Assuming your analysis is correct, what investment strategy would profit from this pricing discrepancy?

Consider the logical possibilities. One is that the probability of 0.50 reflected in Selbert's share price is accurate. In that case, Selbert is fairly valued but SmithCo is overvalued, as its current share price overestimates the probability of a "go ahead" decision. The second possibility is that the probability of 0.85 is accurate. In that case, SmithCo shares are fairly valued, but Selbert shares, which build in a lower probability of a favorable decision, are undervalued. You diagram the situation as shown in Table 1.

#### TABLE 1 Worksheet for Investment Problem

| | True Probability of a "Go Ahead" Decision | |
|---|---|---|
| | 0.50 | 0.85 |
| SmithCo | Shares Overvalued | Shares Fairly Valued |
| Selbert | Shares Fairly Valued | Shares Undervalued |

The 0.50 probability column shows that Selbert shares are a better value than SmithCo shares. Selbert shares are also a better value if a

0.85 probability is accurate. Thus SmithCo shares are overvalued relative to Selbert shares.

Your investment actions depend on your confidence in your analysis and on any investment constraints you face (such as constraints on selling stock short).[2] A conservative strategy would be to buy Selbert shares and reduce or eliminate any current position in SmithCo. The most aggressive strategy is to short SmithCo stock (relatively overvalued) and simultaneously buy the stock of Selbert (relatively undervalued). This strategy is known as **pairs arbitrage trade**: a trade in two closely related stocks involving the short sale of one and the purchase of the other.

The prices of SmithCo and Selbert shares reflect probabilities that are not **consistent**. According to one of the most important probability results for investments, the **Dutch Book Theorem**,[3] inconsistent probabilities create profit opportunities. In our example, investors, by their buy and sell decisions to exploit the inconsistent probabilities, should eliminate the profit opportunity and inconsistency.

To understand the meaning of a probability in investment contexts, we need to distinguish between two types of probability: unconditional and conditional. Both unconditional and conditional probabilities satisfy the definition of probability stated earlier, but they are calculated or estimated differently and have different interpretations. They provide answers to different questions.

The probability in answer to the straightforward question "What is the probability of this event A?" is an **unconditional probability**, denoted $P(A)$. Unconditional probabilities are also frequently referred to as **marginal probabilities**.[4]

Suppose the question is "What is the probability that *the stock earns a return above the risk-free rate* (event A)?" The answer is an unconditional probability that can be viewed as the ratio of two quantities. The numerator is the sum of the probabilities of stock returns above the risk-free rate. Suppose that sum is 0.70. The denominator is 1, the sum of the probabilities of all possible returns. The answer to the question is $P(A) = 0.70$.

Contrast the question "What is the probability of A?" with the question "What is the probability of A, given that B has occurred?" The probability in answer to this last question is a **conditional probability**, denoted $P(A \mid B)$ (read: "the probability of A given B").

Suppose we want to know the probability that *the stock earns a return above the risk-free rate* (event A), given that *the stock earns a positive return* (event B). With the words "given that," we are restricting returns to those larger than 0 percent—a new element in contrast to the question that brought forth an unconditional probability. The conditional probability is calculated as the ratio of two quantities. The numerator is the sum of the probabilities of stock returns above the

---

[2] *Selling short* or *shorting stock* means selling borrowed shares in the hope of repurchasing them later at a lower price.

[3] The theorem's name comes from the terminology of wagering. Suppose someone places a $100 bet on X at odds of 10 to 1 against X, and later he is able to place a $600 bet against X at odds of 1 to 1 against X. Whatever the outcome of X, that person makes a riskless profit (equal to $400 if X occurs or $500 if X does not occur) because the implied probabilities are inconsistent. He is said to have made a *Dutch book* in X. Ramsey (1931) presented the problem of inconsistent probabilities. See also Lo (1999).

[4] In analyses of probabilities presented in tables, unconditional probabilities usually appear at the ends or *margins* of the table, hence the term *marginal probability*. Because of possible confusion with the way *marginal* is used in economics (roughly meaning *incremental*), we use the term *unconditional probability* throughout this discussion.

risk-free rate; in this particular case, the numerator is the same as it was in the unconditional case, which we gave as 0.70. The denominator, however, changes from 1 to the sum of the probabilities for all outcomes (returns) above 0 percent. Suppose that number is 0.80, a larger number than 0.70 because returns between 0 and the risk-free rate have some positive probability of occurring. Then $P(A \mid B) = 0.70/0.80 = 0.875$. If we observe that the stock earns a positive return, the probability of a return above the risk-free rate is greater than the unconditional probability, which is the probability of the event given no other information. The result is intuitive.[5] To review, an unconditional probability is the probability of an event without any restriction; it might even be thought of as a stand-alone probability. A conditional probability, in contrast, is a probability of an event given that another event has occurred.

In discussing approaches to calculating probability, we gave one empirical estimate of the probability that a change in dividends is a dividend decrease. That probability was an unconditional probability. Given additional information on company characteristics, could an investor refine that estimate? Investors continually seek an information edge that will help improve their forecasts. In mathematical terms, they are attempting to frame their view of the future using probabilities conditioned on relevant information or events. Investors do not ignore useful information; they adjust their probabilities to reflect it. Thus, the concepts of conditional probability (which we analyze in more detail below), as well as related concepts discussed further on, are extremely important in investment analysis and financial markets.

To state an exact definition of conditional probability, we first need to introduce the concept of joint probability. Suppose we ask the question "What is the probability of both $A$ and $B$ happening?" The answer to this question is a **joint probability**, denoted $P(AB)$ (read: "the probability of $A$ and $B$"). If we think of the probability of $A$ and the probability of $B$ as sets built of the outcomes of one or more random variables, the joint probability of $A$ and $B$ is the sum of the probabilities of the outcomes they have in common. For example, consider two events: *the stock earns a return above the risk-free rate* ($A$) and *the stock earns a positive return* ($B$). The outcomes of $A$ are contained within (a subset of) the outcomes of $B$, so $P(AB)$ equals $P(A)$. We can now state a formal definition of conditional probability that provides a formula for calculating it.

▶ **Definition of Conditional Probability.** The conditional probability of $A$ given that $B$ has occurred is equal to the joint probability of $A$ and $B$ divided by the probability of $B$ (assumed not to equal 0).

$$P(A \mid B) = P(AB)/P(B), P(B) \neq 0 \tag{8-1}$$

Sometimes we know the conditional probability $P(A \mid B)$ and we want to know the joint probability $P(AB)$. We can obtain the joint probability from the following **multiplication rule for probabilities**, which is Equation 8-1 rearranged.

▶ **Multiplication Rule for Probability.** The joint probability of $A$ and $B$ can be expressed as

$$P(AB) = P(A \mid B)P(B) \tag{8-2}$$

---

[5] In this example, the conditional probability is greater than the unconditional probability. The conditional probability of an event may, however, be greater than, equal to, or less than the unconditional probability, depending on the facts. For instance, the probability that *the stock earns a return above the risk-free rate* given that *the stock earns a negative return* is 0.

## EXAMPLE 2

### Conditional Probabilities and Predictability of Mutual Fund Performance (1)

Kahn and Rudd (1995) examined whether historical performance predicts future performance for a sample of mutual funds that included 300 actively managed U.S. domestic equity funds. One approach they used involved calculating each fund's exposure to a set of style indexes (the term "style" captures the distinctions of growth/value and large-capitalization/mid-capitalization/small-capitalization). After establishing a style benchmark (a comparison portfolio matched to the fund's style) for each fund, Kahn and Rudd computed the fund's selection return for two periods. They defined selection return as fund return minus the fund's style-benchmark return. The first period was October 1990 to March 1992. The top 50 percent of funds by selection return for that period were labeled winners; the bottom 50 percent were labeled losers. Based on selection return in the next period, April 1992 to September 1993, the top 50 percent of funds were tagged as winners and the bottom 50 percent as losers for that period. An excerpt from their results is given in Table 2. The winner–winner entry, for example, shows that 79 of the 150 first-period winner funds were also winners in the second period ($52.7\% = 79/150$). Note that the four entries in parentheses in the table can be viewed as conditional probabilities.

### TABLE 2  Equity Selection Returns
#### Period 1: October 1990 to March 1992
#### Period 2: April 1992 to September 1993

Entries are number of funds (percent of row total in parentheses)

|                 | Period 2 Winner | Period 2 Loser |
|-----------------|-----------------|----------------|
| Period 1 winner | 79 (52.7%)      | 71 (47.3%)     |
| Period 1 loser  | 71 (47.3%)      | 79 (52.7%)     |

*Source*: Kahn and Rudd (1995), Table 3.

Based on the data in Table 2, answer the following questions:

1. State the four events needed to define the four conditional probabilities.
2. State the four entries of the table as conditional probabilities using the form $P(\text{this event} \mid \text{that event}) = \text{number}$.
3. Are the conditional probabilities in Part 2 empirical, a priori, or subjective probabilities?
4. Using information in the table, calculate the probability of the event a *fund is a loser in both Period 1 and Period 2*. (Note that because 50 percent of funds are categorized as losers in each period, the unconditional probability that a fund is labeled a loser in either period is 0.5.)

**Solution to 1:** The four events needed to define the conditional probabilities are as follows:

*Fund is a Period 1 winner*

*Fund is a Period 1 loser*

*Fund is a Period 2 loser*

*Fund is a Period 2 winner*

**Solution to 2:**

From Row 1:

P( *fund is a Period 2 winner | fund is a Period 1 winner*) = 0.527

P( *fund is a Period 2 loser | fund is a Period 1 winner*) = 0.473

From Row 2:

P( *fund is a Period 2 winner | fund is a Period 1 loser*) = 0.473

P( *fund is a Period 2 loser | fund is a Period 1 loser*) = 0.527

**Solution to 3:** These probabilities are calculated from data, so they are empirical probabilities.

**Solution to 4:** The estimated probability is 0.264. With *A* the event that a *fund is a Period 2 loser* and *B* the event that a *fund is a Period 1 loser*, *AB* is the event that a *fund is a loser in both Period 1 and Period 2*. From Table 2, $P(A|B) = 0.527$ and $P(B) = 0.50$. Thus, using Equation 8-2, we find that

$$P(AB) = P(A \mid B)P(B) = 0.527(0.50) = 0.2635$$

or a probability of approximately 0.264.

Equation 8-2 states that the joint probability of *A* and *B* equals the probability of *A* given *B* times the probability of *B*. Because $P(AB) = P(BA)$, the expression $P(AB) = P(BA) = P(B \mid A)P(A)$ is equivalent to Equation 8-2.

When we have two events, *A* and *B*, that we are interested in, we often want to know the probability that either *A* or *B* occurs. Here the word "or" is inclusive, meaning that either *A* or *B* occurs or that both *A* and *B* occur. Put another way, the probability of *A* or *B* is the probability that at least one of the two events occurs. Such probabilities are calculated using the **addition rule for probabilities**.

▶ **Addition Rule for Probabilities.** Given events *A* and *B*, the probability that *A* or *B* occurs, or both occur, is equal to the probability that *A* occurs, plus the probability that *B* occurs, minus the probability that both *A* and *B* occur.

$$P(A \text{ or } B) = P(A) + P(B) - P(AB) \qquad \textbf{(8-3)}$$

If we think of the individual probabilities of *A* and *B* as sets built of outcomes of one or more random variables, the first step in calculating the probability of *A* or *B* is to sum the probabilities of the outcomes in *A* to obtain $P(A)$. If *A* and *B* share any outcomes, then if we now added $P(B)$ to $P(A)$, we would count twice the probabilities of those shared outcomes. So we add to $P(A)$ the quantity $[P(B) - P(AB)]$, which is the probability of outcomes in *B* net of the probability of any outcomes already counted when we computed $P(A)$. Figure 1 illustrates this process; we avoid double-counting the outcomes in the intersection of $A$ and $B$ by subtracting $P(AB)$. As an example of the calculation, if $P(A) = 0.50$, $P(B) = 0.40$, and $P(AB) = 0.20$, then $P(A \text{ or } B) = 0.50 + 0.40 - 0.20 = 0.70$. Only if the two events $A$ and $B$ were mutually exclusive, so that $P(AB) = 0$, would it be correct to state that $P(A \text{ or } B) = P(A) + P(B)$.

**FIGURE 1    Addition Rule for Probabilities**

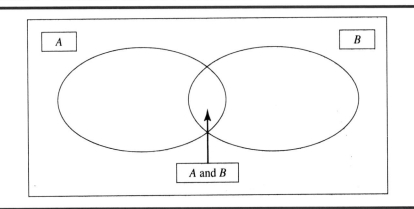

The next example shows how much useful information can be obtained using the few probability rules presented to this point.

### EXAMPLE 3

**Probability of a Limit Order Executing**

You have two buy limit orders outstanding on the same stock. A limit order to buy stock at a stated price is an order to buy at that price or lower. A number of vendors, including an Internet service that you use, supply the estimated probability that a limit order will be filled within a stated time horizon, given the current stock price and the price limit. One buy order (Order 1) was placed at a price limit of $10. The probability that it will execute within one hour is 0.35. The second buy order (Order 2) was placed at a price limit of $9.75; it has a 0.25 probability of executing within the same one-hour time frame.

1. What is the probability that either Order 1 or Order 2 will execute?

2. What is the probability that Order 2 executes, given that Order 1 executes?

**Solution to 1:** The probability is 0.35. The two probabilities that are given are $P(Order\ 1\ executes) = 0.35$ and $P(Order\ 2\ executes) = 0.25$. Note that if Order 2 executes, it is certain that Order 1 also executes because the price must pass through $10 to reach $9.75. Thus,

$$P(Order\ 1\ executes \mid Order\ 2\ executes) = 1$$

and

$$P(Order\ 1\ executes \text{ and } Order\ 2\ executes) = P(Order\ 1\ executes \mid \\ Order\ 2\ executes)P(Order\ 2\ executes) = 1(0.25) = 0.25$$

To answer the question, we use the addition rule for probabilities:

$$P(\text{Order 1 executes or Order 2 executes}) = P(\text{Order 1 executes})$$
$$+ P(\text{Order 2 executes}) - P(\text{Order 1 executes and Order 2 executes})$$
$$= 0.35 + 0.25 - 0.25 = 0.35$$

Note that the outcomes for which Order 2 executes are a subset of the outcomes for which Order 1 executes. After you count the probability that Order 1 executes, you have counted the probability of the outcomes for which Order 2 also executes. Therefore, the answer to the question is the probability that Order 1 executes, 0.35.

**Solution to 2:** If the first order executes, the probability that the second order executes is 0.714. In the solution to Part 1, you found that $P(\text{Order 1 executes and Order 2 executes}) = P(\text{Order 1 executes} \mid \text{Order 2 executes}) P(\text{Order 2 executes}) = 1(0.25) = 0.25$. An equivalent way to state this joint probability is useful here:

$$P(\text{Order 1 executes and Order 2 executes}) = 0.25$$
$$= P(\text{Order 2 executes} \mid \text{Order 1 executes}) P(\text{Order 1 executes})$$

Because $P(\text{Order 1 executes}) = 0.35$ was a given, you have one equation with one unknown:

$$0.25 = P(\text{Order 2 executes} \mid \text{Order 1 executes})(0.35)$$

You conclude that $P(\text{Order 2 executes} \mid \text{Order 1 executes}) = 0.25/0.35 = 5/7$, or about 0.714. You can also use Equation 8-1 to obtain this answer.

Of great interest to investment analysts are the concepts of independence and dependence. These concepts bear on such basic investment questions as which financial variables are useful for investment analysis, whether asset returns can be predicted, and whether superior investment managers can be selected based on their past records.

Two events are independent if the occurrence of one event does not affect the probability of occurrence of the other event.

▶ **Definition of Independent Events.** Two events $A$ and $B$ are **independent** if and only if $P(A \mid B) = P(A)$ or, equivalently, $P(B \mid A) = P(B)$.

When two events are not independent, they are **dependent**: The probability of occurrence of one is related to the occurrence of the other. If we are trying to forecast one event, information about a dependent event may be useful, but information about an independent event will not be useful.

When two events are independent, the multiplication rule for probabilities, Equation 8-2, simplifies because $P(A|B)$ in that equation then equals $P(A)$.

▶ **Multiplication Rule for Independent Events.** When two events are independent, the joint probability of $A$ and $B$ equals the product of the individual probabilities of $A$ and $B$.

$$P(AB) = P(A)P(B) \qquad \textbf{(8-4)}$$

Therefore, if we are interested in two independent events with probabilities of 0.75 and 0.50, respectively, the probability that both will occur is $0.375 = 0.75(0.50)$. The multiplication rule for independent events generalizes to more than two events; for example, if $A$, $B$, and $C$ are independent events, then $P(ABC) = P(A)P(B)P(C)$.

---

### EXAMPLE 4

**BankCorp's Earnings per Share (1)**

As part of your work as a banking industry analyst, you build models for forecasting earnings per share of the banks you cover. Today you are studying BankCorp. The historical record shows that in 55 percent of recent quarters BankCorp's EPS has increased sequentially, and in 45 percent of quarters EPS has decreased or remained unchanged sequentially.[6] At this point in your analysis, you are assuming that changes in sequential EPS are independent.

Earnings per share for 2Q:2004 (that is, EPS for the second quarter of 2004) were larger than EPS for 1Q:2004.

1. What is the probability that 3Q:2004 EPS will be larger than 2Q:2004 EPS (a positive change in sequential EPS)?

2. What is the probability that EPS decreases or remains unchanged in the next two quarters?

**Solution to 1:** Under the assumption of independence, the probability that 3Q:2004 EPS will be larger than 2Q:2004 EPS is the unconditional probability of positive change, 0.55. The fact that 2Q:2004 EPS was larger than 1Q:2004 EPS is not useful information, as the next change in EPS is independent of the prior change.

**Solution to 2:** The probability is $0.2025 = 0.45(0.45)$.

---

The following example illustrates how difficult it is to satisfy a set of independent criteria even when each criterion by itself is not necessarily stringent.

---

### EXAMPLE 5

**Screening Stocks for Investment**

You have developed a stock screen—a set of criteria for selecting stocks. Your investment universe (the set of securities from which you make your choices) is the Russell 1000 Index, an index of 1,000 large-capitalization U.S. equities. Your criteria capture different aspects of the selection problem; you believe that the criteria are independent of each other, to a close approximation.

---

[6] *Sequential* comparisons of quarterly EPS are with the immediate prior quarter. A sequential comparison stands in contrast to a comparison with the same quarter one year ago (another frequent type of comparison).

| Criterion | Fraction of Russell 1000 Stocks Meeting Criterion |
|---|---|
| First valuation criterion | 0.50 |
| Second valuation criterion | 0.50 |
| Analyst coverage criterion | 0.25 |
| Profitability criterion for company | 0.55 |
| Financial strength criterion for company | 0.67 |

How many stocks do you expect to pass your screen?

Only 23 stocks out of 1,000 pass through your screen. If you define five events—*the stock passes the first valuation criterion, the stock passes the second valuation criterion, the stock passes the analyst coverage criterion, the company passes the profitability criterion, the company passes the financial strength criterion* (say events *A*, *B*, *C*, *D*, and *E*, respectively)—then the probability that a stock will pass all five criteria, under independence, is

$$P(ABCDE) = P(A)P(B)P(C)P(D)P(E) = (0.50)(0.50)(0.25)(0.55)(0.67)$$
$$= 0.023031$$

Although only one of the five criteria is even moderately strict (the strictest lets 25 percent of stocks through), the probability that a stock can pass all five is only 0.023031, or about 2 percent. The size of the list of candidate investments is $0.023031(1,000) = 23.031$, or 23 stocks.

An area of intense interest to investment managers and their clients is whether records of past performance are useful in identifying repeat winners and losers. The following example shows how this issue relates to the concept of independence.

## EXAMPLE 6

### Conditional Probabilities and Predictability of Mutual Fund Performance (2)

The purpose of the Kahn and Rudd (1995) study, introduced in Example 2, was to address the question of repeat mutual fund winners and losers. If the status of a fund as a winner or a loser in one period is independent of whether it is a winner in the next period, the practical value of performance ranking is questionable. Using the four events defined in Example 2 as building blocks, we can define the following events to address the issue of predictability of mutual fund performance:

*Fund is a Period 1 winner* and *fund is a Period 2 winner*
*Fund is a Period 1 winner* and *fund is a Period 2 loser*
*Fund is a Period 1 loser* and *fund is a Period 2 winner*
*Fund is a Period 1 loser* and *fund is a Period 2 loser*

In Part 4 of Example 2, you calculated that

*P( fund is a Period 2 loser* and *fund is a Period 1 loser)* = 0.264

If the ranking in one period is independent of the ranking in the next period, what will you expect *P( fund is a Period 2 loser* and *fund is a Period 1 loser)* to be? Interpret the empirical probability 0.264.

By the multiplication rule for independent events, *P( fund is a Period 2 loser* and *fund is a Period 1 loser)* = *P( fund is a Period 2 loser) P( fund is a Period 1 loser)*. Because 50 percent of funds are categorized as losers in each period, the unconditional probability that a fund is labeled a loser in either period is 0.50. Thus *P( fund is a Period 2 loser) P( fund is a Period 1 loser)* = 0.50(0.50) = 0.25. If the status of a fund as a loser in one period is independent of whether it is a loser in the prior period, we conclude that *P( fund is a Period 2 loser* and *fund is a Period 1 loser)* = 0.25. This probability is a priori because it is obtained from reasoning about the problem. You could also reason that the four events described above define categories and that if funds are randomly assigned to the four categories, there is a 1/4 probability of *fund is a Period 1 loser* and *fund is a Period 2 loser.* If the classifications in Period 1 and Period 2 were dependent, then the assignment of funds to categories would not be random. The empirical probability of 0.264 is only slightly above 0.25. Is this apparent slight amount of predictability the result of chance? A test conducted by Kahn and Rudd indicated a 35.6 percent chance of observing the tabled data if the Period 1 and Period 2 rankings were independent.

In investments, the question of whether one event (or characteristic) provides information about another event (or characteristic) arises in both time-series settings (through time) and cross-sectional settings (among units at a given point in time). Examples 4 and 6 illustrated independence in a time-series setting. Example 5 illustrated independence in a cross-sectional setting. Independence/dependence relationships are often also explored in both settings using regression analysis, a technique we discuss in a later reading.

In many practical problems, we logically analyze a problem as follows: We formulate scenarios that we think affect the likelihood of an event that interests us. We then estimate the probability of the event, given the scenario. When the scenarios (conditioning events) are mutually exclusive and exhaustive, no possible outcomes are left out. We can then analyze the event using the **total probability rule**. This rule explains the unconditional probability of the event in terms of probabilities conditional on the scenarios.

The total probability rule is stated below for two cases. Part 1 gives the simplest case, in which we have two scenarios. One new notation is introduced: If we have an event or scenario *S*, the event not-*S*, called the **complement** of *S*, is written $S^C$.[7] Note that $P(S) + P(S^C) = 1$, as either *S* or not-*S* must occur. Part 2 states the rule for the general case of *n* mutually exclusive and exhaustive events or scenarios.

▶ **The Total Probability Rule.**

**1.** $P(A) = P(AS) + P(AS^C)$
$= P(A \mid S)P(S) + P(A \mid S^C)P(S^C)$     **(8-5)**

---

[7] For readers familiar with mathematical treatments of probability, *S*, a notation usually reserved for a concept called the sample space, is being appropriated to stand for *scenario*.

**2.** $P(A) = P(AS_1) + P(AS_2) + \ldots + P(AS_n)$
$= P(A \mid S_1)P(S_1) + P(A \mid S_2)P(S_2) + \ldots + P(A \mid S_n)P(S_n)$ **(8-6)**

where $S_1, S_2, \ldots, S_n$ are mutually exclusive and exhaustive scenarios or events.

Equation 8-6 states the following: The probability of any event $[P(A)]$ can be expressed as a weighted average of the probabilities of the event, given scenarios [terms such $P(A|S_1)$]; the weights applied to these conditional probabilities are the respective probabilities of the scenarios [terms such as $P(S_1)$ multiplying $P(A|S_1)$], and the scenarios must be mutually exclusive and exhaustive. Among other applications, this rule is needed to understand Bayes' formula, which we discuss later in the reading.

In the next example, we use the total probability rule to develop a consistent set of views about BankCorp's earnings per share.

## EXAMPLE 7

### BankCorp's Earnings per Share (2)

You are continuing your investigation into whether you can predict the direction of changes in BankCorp's quarterly EPS. You define four events:

| Event | | | Probability |
|---|---|---|---|
| $A$ | = | change in sequential EPS is positive next quarter | 0.55 |
| $A^C$ | = | change in sequential EPS is 0 or negative next quarter | 0.45 |
| $S$ | = | change in sequential EPS is positive in the prior quarter | 0.55 |
| $S^C$ | = | change in sequential EPS is 0 or negative in the prior quarter | 0.45 |

On inspecting the data, you observe some persistence in EPS changes: Increases tend to be followed by increases, and decreases by decreases. The first probability estimate you develop is $P$(change in sequential EPS is positive next quarter | change in sequential EPS is 0 or negative in the prior quarter) $= P(A|S^C) = 0.40$. The most recent quarter's EPS (2Q:2004) is announced, and the change is a positive sequential change (the event $S$). You are interested in forecasting EPS for 3Q:2004.

**1.** Write this statement in probability notation: "the probability that the change in sequential EPS is positive next quarter, given that the change in sequential EPS is positive the prior quarter."

**2.** Calculate the probability in Part 1. (Calculate the probability that is consistent with your other probabilities or beliefs.)

**Solution to 1:** In probability notation, this statement is written $P(A \mid S)$.

**Solution to 2:** The probability is 0.673 that the change in sequential EPS is positive for 3Q:2004, given the positive change in sequential EPS for 2Q:2004, as shown below.

According to Equation 8-5, $P(A) = P(A \mid S)P(S) + P(A \mid S^C)P(S^C)$. The values of the probabilities needed to calculate $P(A \mid S)$ are already known: $P(A) = 0.55$, $P(S) = 0.55$, $P(S^C) = 0.45$, and $P(A \mid S^C) = 0.40$. Substituting into Equation 8-5,

$$0.55 = P(A \mid S)(0.55) + 0.40(0.45)$$

Solving for the unknown, $P(A \mid S) = [0.55 - 0.40(0.45)]/0.55 = 0.672727$, or $0.673$.

You conclude that $P(\textit{change in sequential EPS is positive next quarter} \mid \textit{change in sequential EPS is positive the prior quarter}) = 0.673$. Any other probability is not consistent with your other estimated probabilities. Reflecting the persistence in EPS changes, this conditional probability of a positive EPS change, 0.673, is greater than the unconditional probability of an EPS increase, 0.55.

In the reading on statistical concepts and market returns, we discussed the concept of a weighted average or weighted mean. The example highlighted in that reading was that portfolio return is a weighted average of the returns on the individual assets in the portfolio, where the weight applied to each asset's return is the fraction of the portfolio invested in that asset. The total probability rule, which is a rule for stating an unconditional probability in terms of conditional probabilities, is also a weighted average. In that formula, probabilities of scenarios are used as weights. Part of the definition of weighted average is that the weights sum to 1. The probabilities of mutually exclusive and exhaustive events do sum to 1 (this is part of the definition of probability). The next weighted average we discuss, the expected value of a random variable, also uses probabilities as weights.

The expected value of a random variable is an essential quantitative concept in investments. Investors continually make use of expected values—in estimating the rewards of alternative investments, in forecasting EPS and other corporate financial variables and ratios, and in assessing any other factor that may affect their financial position. The expected value of a random variable is defined as follows:

▶ **Definition of Expected Value.** The **expected value** of a random variable is the probability-weighted average of the possible outcomes of the random variable. For a random variable $X$, the expected value of $X$ is denoted $E(X)$.

Expected value (for example, expected stock return) looks either to the future, as a forecast, or to the "true" value of the mean (the population mean, discussed in the reading on statistical concepts and market returns). We should distinguish expected value from the concepts of historical or sample mean. The sample mean also summarizes in a single number a central value. However, the sample mean presents a central value for a particular set of observations as an equally weighted average of those observations. To summarize, the contrast is forecast versus historical, or population versus sample.

**EXAMPLE 8**

### BankCorp's Earnings per Share (3)

You continue with your analysis of BankCorp's EPS. In Table 3, you have recorded a probability distribution for BankCorp's EPS for the current fiscal year.

**TABLE 3  Probability Distribution for BankCorp's EPS**

| Probability | EPS |
|---|---|
| 0.15 | $2.60 |
| 0.45 | $2.45 |
| 0.24 | $2.20 |
| 0.16 | $2.00 |
| 1.00 | |

What is the expected value of BankCorp's EPS for the current fiscal year?

Following the definition of expected value, list each outcome, weight it by its probability, and sum the terms.

$$E(\text{EPS}) = 0.15(\$2.60) + 0.45(\$2.45) + 0.24(\$2.20) + 0.16(\$2.00)$$
$$= \$2.3405$$

The expected value of EPS is $2.34.

An equation that summarizes your calculation in Example 8 is

$$E(X) = P(X_1)X_1 + P(X_2)X_2 + \ldots + P(X_n)X_n = \sum_{i=1}^{n} P(X_i)X_i \qquad \textbf{(8-7)}$$

where $X_i$ is one of $n$ possible outcomes of the random variable $X$.[8]

The expected value is our forecast. Because we are discussing random quantities, we cannot count on an individual forecast being realized (although we hope that, on average, forecasts will be accurate). It is important, as a result, to measure the risk we face. Variance and standard deviation measure the dispersion of outcomes around the expected value or forecast.

▶ **Definition of Variance.** The **variance** of a random variable is the expected value (the probability-weighted average) of squared deviations from the random variable's expected value:

$$\sigma^2(X) = E\{[X - E(X)]^2\} \qquad \textbf{(8-8)}$$

The two notations for variance are $\sigma^2(X)$ and $\text{Var}(X)$.

Variance is a number greater than or equal to 0 because it is the sum of squared terms. If variance is 0, there is no dispersion or risk. The outcome is certain, and the quantity $X$ is not random at all. Variance greater than 0 indicates dispersion

---

[8] For simplicity, we model all random variables in this reading as discrete random variables, which have a countable set of outcomes. For continuous random variables, which are discussed along with discrete random variables in the reading on common probability distributions, the operation corresponding to summation is integration.

of outcomes. Increasing variance indicates increasing dispersion, all else equal. Variance of $X$ is a quantity in the squared units of $X$. For example, if the random variable is return in percent, variance of return is in units of percent squared. Standard deviation is easier to interpret than variance, as it is in the same units as the random variable. If the random variable is return in percent, standard deviation of return is also in units of percent.

▶ **Definition of Standard Deviation. Standard deviation** is the positive square root of variance.

The best way to become familiar with these concepts is to work examples.

---

### EXAMPLE 9

**BankCorp's Earnings per Share (4)**

In Example 8, you calculated the expected value of BankCorp's EPS as $2.34, which is your forecast. Now you want to measure the dispersion around your forecast. Table 4 shows your view of the probability distribution of EPS for the current fiscal year.

**TABLE 4  Probability Distribution for BankCorp's EPS**

| Probability | EPS |
|---|---|
| 0.15 | $2.60 |
| 0.45 | $2.45 |
| 0.24 | $2.20 |
| 0.16 | $2.00 |
| 1.00 | |

What are the variance and standard deviation of BankCorp's EPS for the current fiscal year?

The order of calculation is always expected value, then variance, then standard deviation. Expected value has already been calculated. Following the definition of variance above, calculate the deviation of each outcome from the mean or expected value, square each deviation, weight (multiply) each squared deviation by its probability of occurrence, and then sum these terms.

$$
\begin{aligned}
\sigma^2(\text{EPS}) &= P(\$2.60)\,[\$2.60 - E(\text{EPS})]^2 + P(\$2.45)\,[\$2.45 - E(\text{EPS})]^2 \\
&\quad + P(\$2.20)\,[\$2.20 - E(\text{EPS})]^2 + P(\$2.00)\,[\$2.00 - E(\text{EPS})]^2 \\
&= 0.15(2.60 - 2.34)^2 + 0.45(2.45 - 2.34)^2 \\
&\quad + 0.24(2.20 - 2.34)^2 + 0.16(2.00 - 2.34)^2 \\
&= 0.01014 + 0.005445 + 0.004704 + \$0.018496 = \$0.038785
\end{aligned}
$$

Standard deviation is the positive square root of $0.038785:

$$\sigma(\text{EPS}) = \$0.038785^{1/2} = \$0.196939, \text{ or approximately } \$0.20.$$

An equation that summarizes your calculation of variance in Example 9 is

$$\sigma^2(X) = P(X_1)[X_1 - E(X)]^2 + P(X_2)[X_2 - E(X)]^2$$

$$+ \ldots + P(X_n)[X_n - E(X)]^2 = \sum_{i=1}^{n} P(X_i)[X_i - E(X)]^2 \qquad \textbf{(8-9)}$$

where $X_i$ is one of $n$ possible outcomes of the random variable $X$.

In investments, we make use of any relevant information available in making our forecasts. When we refine our expectations or forecasts, we are typically making adjustments based on new information or events; in these cases we are using **conditional expected values**. The expected value of a random variable $X$ given an event or scenario $S$ is denoted $E(X \mid S)$. Suppose the random variable $X$ can take on any one of $n$ distinct outcomes $X_1, X_2, \ldots, X_n$ (these outcomes form a set of mutually exclusive and exhaustive events). The expected value of $X$ conditional on $S$ is the first outcome, $X_1$, times the probability of the first outcome given $S$, $P(X_1 \mid S)$, plus the second outcome, $X_2$, times the probability of the second outcome given $S$, $P(X_2 \mid S)$, and so forth.

$$E(X \mid S) = P(X_1 \mid S)X_1 + P(X_2 \mid S)X_2 + \ldots + P(X_n \mid S)X_n \qquad \textbf{(8-10)}$$

We will illustrate this equation shortly.

Parallel to the total probability rule for stating unconditional probabilities in terms of conditional probabilities, there is a principle for stating (unconditional) expected values in terms of conditional expected values. This principle is the **total probability rule for expected value**.

▶ **The Total Probability Rule for Expected Value.**

**1.** $E(X) = E(X \mid S)P(S) + E(X \mid S^C)P(S^C)$      **(8-11)**

**2.** $E(X) = E(X \mid S_1)P(S_1) + E(X \mid S_2)P(S_2) + \ldots + E(X \mid S_n)P(S_n)$      **(8-12)**

where $S_1, S_2, \ldots, S_n$ are mutually exclusive and exhaustive scenarios or events.

The general case, Equation 8-12, states that the expected value of $X$ equals the expected value of $X$ given Scenario 1, $E(X \mid S_1)$, times the probability of Scenario 1, $P(S_1)$, plus the expected value of $X$ given Scenario 2, $E(X \mid S_2)$, times the probability of Scenario 2, $P(S_2)$, and so forth.

To use this principle, we formulate mutually exclusive and exhaustive scenarios that are useful for understanding the outcomes of the random variable. This approach was employed in developing the probability distribution of BankCorp's EPS in Examples 8 and 9, as we now discuss.

The earnings of BankCorp are interest rate sensitive, benefiting from a declining interest rate environment. Suppose there is a 0.60 probability that BankCorp will operate in a *declining interest rate environment* in the current fiscal year and a 0.40 probability that it will operate in a *stable interest rate environment* (assessing the chance of an increasing interest rate environment as negligible). If a *declining interest rate environment* occurs, the probability that EPS will be $2.60 is estimated at 0.25, and the probability that EPS will be $2.45 is estimated at 0.75. Note that 0.60, the probability of *declining interest rate environment*, times 0.25, the probability of $2.60 EPS given a *declining interest rate environment*, equals 0.15, the (unconditional) probability of $2.60 given in the table in Examples 8 and 9. The probabilities are consistent. Also, $0.60(0.75) = 0.45$, the probability of $2.45 EPS given in Tables 3 and 4. The **tree diagram** in Figure 2 shows the rest of the analysis.

## FIGURE 2    BankCorp's Forecasted EPS

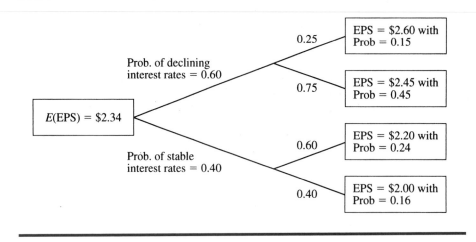

A declining interest rate environment points us to the **node** of the tree that branches off into outcomes of $2.60 and $2.45. We can find expected EPS given a declining interest rate environment as follows, using Equation 8-10:

$$E(EPS \mid \textit{declining interest rate environment}) = 0.25(\$2.60) + 0.75(\$2.45)$$
$$= \$2.4875$$

If interest rates are stable,

$$E(EPS \mid \textit{stable interest rate environment}) = 0.60(\$2.20) + 0.40(\$2.00)$$
$$= \$2.12$$

Once we have the new piece of information that interest rates are stable, for example, we revise our original expectation of EPS from $2.34 downward to $2.12. Now using the total probability rule for expected value,

$$E(EPS) = E(EPS \mid \textit{declining interest rate environment})$$
$$P(\textit{declining interest rate environment})$$
$$+ E(EPS \mid \textit{stable interest rate environment})$$
$$P(\textit{stable interest rate environment})$$

So $E(EPS) = \$2.4875\,(0.60) + \$2.12\,(0.40) = \$2.3405$ or about $2.34.

This amount is identical to the estimate of the expected value of EPS calculated directly from the probability distribution in Example 8. Just as our probabilities must be consistent, so must our expected values, unconditional and conditional; otherwise our investment actions may create profit opportunities for other investors at our expense.

To review, we first developed the factors or scenarios that influence the outcome of the event of interest. After assigning probabilities to these scenarios, we formed expectations conditioned on the different scenarios. Then we worked backward to formulate an expected value as of today. In the problem just worked, EPS was the event of interest, and the interest rate environment was the factor influencing EPS.

We can also calculate the variance of EPS given each scenario:

$\sigma^2$(EPS | *declining interest rate environment*)

$= P(\$2.60 \mid \textit{declining interest rate environment})$
$\times [\$2.60 - E(\text{EPS} \mid \textit{declining interest rate environment})]^2$
$+ P(\$2.45 \mid \textit{declining interest rate environment})$
$\times [\$2.45 - E(\text{EPS} \mid \textit{declining interest rate environment})]^2$
$= 0.25(\$2.60 - \$2.4875)^2 + 0.75(\$2.45 - \$2.4875)^2$
$= 0.004219$

$\sigma^2$(EPS | *stable interest rate environment*)

$= P(\$2.20 \mid \textit{stable interest rate environment})$
$\times [\$2.20 - E(\text{EPS} \mid \textit{stable interest rate environment})]^2$
$+ P(\$2.00 \mid \textit{stable interest rate environment})$
$\times [\$2.00 - E(\text{EPS} \mid \textit{stable interest rate environment})]^2$
$= 0.60(\$2.20 - \$2.12)^2 + 0.40(\$2.00 - \$2.12)^2 = 0.0096$

These are **conditional variances**, the variance of EPS given a *declining interest rate environment* and the variance of EPS given a *stable interest rate environment*. The relationship between unconditional variance and conditional variance is a relatively advanced topic.[9] The main points are 1) that variance, like expected value, has a conditional counterpart to the unconditional concept and 2) that we can use conditional variance to assess risk given a particular scenario.

---

### EXAMPLE 10

#### BankCorp's Earnings per Share (5)

Continuing with BankCorp, you focus now on BankCorp's cost structure. One model you are researching for BankCorp's operating costs is

$$\hat{Y} = a + bX$$

where $\hat{Y}$ is a forecast of operating costs in millions of dollars and $X$ is the number of branch offices. $\hat{Y}$ represents the expected value of $Y$ given $X$, or $E(Y \mid X)$. ($\hat{Y}$ is a notation used in regression analysis, which we discuss in a later reading.) You interpret the intercept $a$ as fixed costs and $b$ as variable costs. You estimate the equation as

$$\hat{Y} = 12.5 + 0.65X$$

BankCorp currently has 66 branch offices, and the equation estimates that $12.5 + 0.65(66) = \$55.4$ million. You have two scenarios for growth, pictured in the tree diagram in Figure 3.

---

[9] The unconditional variance of EPS is the sum of two terms: 1) the expected value (probability-weighted average) of the conditional variances (parallel to the total probability rules) and 2) the variance of conditional expected values of EPS. The second term arises because the variability in conditional expected value is a source of risk. Term 1 is $\sigma^2$(EPS) $= P(\textit{declining interest rate environment}) \, \sigma^2$(EPS | *declining interest rate environment*) $+ P(\textit{stable interest rate environment}) \, \sigma^2$(EPS | *stable interest rate environment*) $= 0.60(0.004219) + 0.40(0.0096) = 0.006371$. Term 2 is $\sigma^2[E(\text{EPS} \mid \textit{interest rate environment})] = 0.60(\$2.4875 - \$2.34)^2 + 0.40(\$2.12 - \$2.34)^2 = 0.032414$. Summing the two terms, unconditional variance equals $0.006371 + 0.032414 = 0.038785$.

**FIGURE 3   BankCorp's Forecasted Operating Costs**

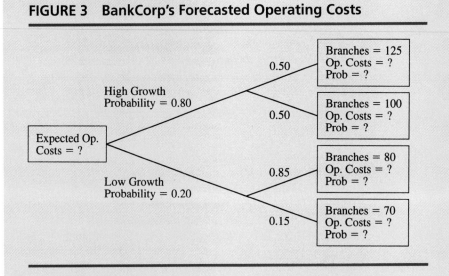

1. Compute the forecasted operating costs given the different levels of operating costs, using $\hat{Y} = 12.5 + 0.65X$. State the probability of each level of the number of branch offices. These are the answers to the questions in the terminal boxes of the tree diagram.

2. Compute the expected value of operating costs under the high growth scenario. Also calculate the expected value of operating costs under the low growth scenario.

3. Answer the question in the initial box of the tree: What are BankCorp's expected operating costs?

**Solution to 1:** Using $\hat{Y} = 12.5 + 0.65X$, from top to bottom, we have

| Operating Costs | Probability |
|---|---|
| $\hat{Y} = 12.5 + 0.65(125) = \$93.75$ million | $0.80(0.50) = 0.40$ |
| $\hat{Y} = 12.5 + 0.65(100) = \$77.50$ million | $0.80(0.50) = 0.40$ |
| $\hat{Y} = 12.5 + 0.65(80) = \$64.50$ million | $0.20(0.85) = 0.17$ |
| $\hat{Y} = 12.5 + 0.65(70) = \$58.00$ million | $0.20(0.15) = 0.03$ |
| | Sum $= 1.00$ |

**Solution to 2:** Dollar amounts are in millions.

$$E(\text{operating costs} \mid high\ growth) = 0.50(\$93.75) + 0.50(\$77.50)$$
$$= \$85.625$$
$$E(\text{operating costs} \mid low\ growth) = 0.85(\$64.50) + 0.15(\$58.00)$$
$$= \$63.525$$

**Solution to 3:** Dollar amounts are in millions.

$$E(\text{operating costs}) = E(\text{operating costs} \mid high\ growth)P(high\ growth)$$
$$+ E(\text{operating costs} \mid low\ growth)P(low\ growth)$$
$$= \$85.625(0.80) + \$63.525(0.20) = \$81.205$$

BankCorp's expected operating costs are \$81.205 million.

We will see conditional probabilities again when we discuss Bayes' formula. This section has introduced a few problems that can be addressed using probability concepts. The following problem draws on these concepts, as well as on analytical skills.

## EXAMPLE 11

### The Default Risk Premium for a One-Period Debt Instrument

As the co-manager of a short-term bond portfolio, you are reviewing the pricing of a speculative-grade, one-year-maturity, zero-coupon bond. For this type of bond, the return is the difference between the amount paid and the principal value received at maturity. Your goal is to estimate an appropriate default risk premium for this bond. You define the default risk premium as the extra return above the risk-free return that will compensate investors for default risk. If $R$ is the promised return (yield-to-maturity) on the debt instrument and $R_F$ is the risk-free rate, the default risk premium is $R - R_F$. You assess the probability that the bond defaults as $P(\text{the bond defaults}) = 0.06$. Looking at current money market yields, you find that one-year U.S. Treasury bills (T-bills) are offering a return of 5.8 percent, an estimate of $R_F$. As a first step, you make the simplifying assumption that bondholders will recover nothing in the event of a default. What is the minimum default risk premium you should require for this instrument?

The challenge in this type of problem is to find a starting point. In many problems, including this one, an effective first step is to divide up the possible outcomes into mutually exclusive and exhaustive events in an economically logical way. Here, from the viewpoint of a bondholder, the two events that affect returns are *the bond defaults* and *the bond does not default*. These two events cover all outcomes. How do these events affect a bondholder's returns? A second step is to compute the value of the bond for the two events. We have no specifics on bond **face value**, but we can compute value per $1 or one unit of currency invested.

|  | *The Bond Defaults* | *The Bond Does Not Default* |
|---|---|---|
| Bond value | $0 | $(1 + R)$ |

The third step is to find the expected value of the bond (per $1 invested).

$$E(\text{bond}) = \$0 \times P(\text{the bond defaults})$$
$$+ \$(1 + R)\,[1 - P(\text{the bond defaults})]$$

So $E(\text{bond}) = \$(1 + R)[1 - P(\text{the bond defaults})]$. The expected value of the T-bill per $1 invested is $(1 + R_F)$. In fact, this value is certain because the T-bill is risk free. The next step requires economic reasoning. You want the default premium to be large enough so that you expect to at least break even compared with investing in the T-bill. This outcome will occur if the expected value of the bond equals the expected value of the T-bill per $1 invested.

| *Expected Value of Bond* | = | *Expected Value of T-Bill* |
|---|---|---|
| $\$(1 + R)[1 - P(\text{the bond defaults})]$ | = | $(1 + R_F)$ |

Solving for the promised return on the bond, you find $R = \{(1 + R_F)/[1 - P(\text{the bond defaults})]\} - 1$. Substituting in the values in the statement of the problem, $R = [1.058/(1 - 0.06)] - 1 = 1.12553 - 1 = 0.12553$ or about 12.55 percent, and default risk premium is $R - R_F = 12.55\% - 5.8\% = 6.75\%$.

You require a default risk premium of at least 675 basis points. You can state the matter as follows: If the bond is priced to yield 12.55 percent, you will earn a 675 basis-point spread and receive the bond principal with 94 percent probability. If the bond defaults, however, you will lose everything. With a premium of 675 basis points, you expect to just break even relative to an investment in T-bills. Because an investment in the zero-coupon bond has variability, if you are risk averse you will demand that the premium be larger than 675 basis points.

This analysis is a starting point. Bondholders usually recover part of their investment after a default. A next step would be to incorporate a recovery rate.

In this section, we have treated random variables such as EPS as stand-alone quantities. We have not explored how descriptors such as expected value and variance of EPS may be functions of other random variables. Portfolio return is one random variable that is clearly a function of other random variables, the random returns on the individual securities in the portfolio. To analyze a portfolio's expected return and variance of return, we must understand these quantities are a function of characteristics of the individual securities' returns. Looking at the dispersion or variance of portfolio return, we see that the way individual security returns move together or covary is important. To understand the significance of these movements, we need to explore some new concepts, covariance and correlation. The next section, which deals with portfolio expected return and variance of return, introduces these concepts.

## 3    PORTFOLIO EXPECTED RETURN AND VARIANCE OF RETURN

Modern portfolio theory makes frequent use of the idea that investment opportunities can be evaluated using expected return as a measure of reward and variance of return as a measure of risk. The calculation and interpretation of portfolio expected return and variance of return are fundamental skills. In this section, we will develop an understanding of portfolio expected return and variance of return.[10] Portfolio return is determined by the returns on the individual holdings. As a result, the calculation of portfolio variance, as a function of the individual asset returns, is more complex than the variance calculations illustrated in the previous section.

We work with an example of a portfolio that is 50 percent invested in an S&P 500 Index fund, 25 percent invested in a U.S. long-term corporate bond fund, and 25 percent invested in a fund indexed to the MSCI EAFE Index (representing equity markets in Europe, Australasia, and the Far East). Table 5 shows these weights.

---

[10] Although we outline a number of basic concepts in this section, we do not present mean–variance analysis per se. For a presentation of mean–variance analysis, see the readings on portfolio concepts, as well as the extended treatments in standard investment textbooks such as Bodie, Kane, and Marcus (2001), Elton, Gruber, Brown, and Goetzmann (2003), Reilly and Brown (2003), and Sharpe, Alexander, and Bailey (1999).

| TABLE 5  Portfolio Weights | |
| --- | --- |
| **Asset Class** | **Weights** |
| S&P 500 | 0.50 |
| U.S. long-term corporate bonds | 0.25 |
| MSCI EAFE | 0.25 |

We first address the calculation of the expected return on the portfolio. In the previous section, we defined the expected value of a random variable as the probability-weighted average of the possible outcomes. Portfolio return, we know, is a weighted average of the returns on the securities in the portfolio. Similarly, the expected return on a portfolio is a weighted average of the expected returns on the securities in the portfolio, using exactly the same weights. When we have estimated the expected returns on the individual securities, we immediately have portfolio expected return. This convenient fact follows from the properties of expected value.

▶ **Properties of Expected Value.** Let $w_i$ be any constant and $R_i$ be a random variable.

**1.** The expected value of a constant times a random variable equals the constant times the expected value of the random variable.

$$E(w_i R_i) = w_i E(R_i)$$

**2.** The expected value of a weighted sum of random variables equals the weighted sum of the expected values, using the same weights.

$$E(w_1 R_1) + w_2 R_2 + \ldots + w_n R_n) = w_1 E(R_1) + w_2 E(R_2) \\ + \ldots + w_n E(R_n)$$

**(8-13)**

Suppose we have a random variable with a given expected value. If we multiply each outcome by 2, for example, the random variable's expected value is multiplied by 2 as well. That is the meaning of Part 1. The second statement is the rule that directly leads to the expression for portfolio expected return. A portfolio with $n$ securities is defined by its portfolio weights, $w_1, w_2, \ldots, w_n$, which sum to 1. So portfolio return, $R_p$, is $R_p = w_1 R_1 + w_2 R_2 + \ldots + w_n R_n$. We can state the following principle:

▶ **Calculation of Portfolio Expected Return.** Given a portfolio with $n$ securities, the expected return on the portfolio is a weighted average of the expected returns on the component securities:

$$E(R_p = E(w_1 R_1 + w_2 R_2 + \ldots + w_n R_n) \\ = w_1 E(R_1) + w_2 E(R_2) + \ldots + w_n E(R_n)$$

Suppose we have estimated expected returns on the assets in the portfolio, as given in Table 6.

| TABLE 6 Weights and Expected Returns | | |
|---|---|---|
| **Asset Class** | **Weight** | **Expected Return (%)** |
| S&P 500 | 0.50 | 13 |
| U.S. long-term corporate bonds | 0.25 | 6 |
| MSCI EAFE | 0.25 | 15 |

We calculate the expected return on the portfolio as 11.75 percent:

$$
\begin{aligned}
E(R_p) &= w_1 E(R_1) + w_2 E(R_2) + w_3 E(R_3) \\
&= 0.50(13\%) + 0.25(6\%) + 0.25(15\%) = 11.75\%
\end{aligned}
$$

In the previous section, we studied variance as a measure of dispersion of outcomes around the expected value. Here we are interested in portfolio variance of return as a measure of investment risk. Letting $R_p$ stand for the return on the portfolio, portfolio variance is $\sigma^2(R_p) = E\{[R_p - E(R_p)]^2\}$ according to Equation 8-8. How do we implement this definition? In the reading on statistical concepts and market returns, we learned how to calculate a historical or sample variance based on a sample of returns. Now we are considering variance in a forward-looking sense. We will use information about the individual assets in the portfolio to obtain portfolio variance of return. To avoid clutter in notation, we write $ER_p$ for $E(R_p)$. We need the concept of covariance.

▶ **Definition of Covariance.** Given two random variables $R_i$ and $R_j$, the covariance between $R_i$ and $R_j$ is

$$
\mathrm{Cov}(R_i, R_j) = E[(R_i - ER_i)(R_j - ER_j)] \tag{8-14}
$$

Alternative notations are $\sigma(R_i, R_j)$ and $\sigma_{ij}$.

Equation 8-14 states that the covariance between two random variables is the probability-weighted average of the cross-products of each random variable's deviation from its own expected value. We will return to discuss covariance after we establish the need for the concept. Working from the definition of variance, we find

$$
\begin{aligned}
\sigma^2(R_p) &= E[(R_p - ER_p)^2] \\
&= E\{[w_1 R_1 + w_2 R_2 + w_3 R_3 - E(w_1 R_1 + w_2 R_2 + w_3 R_3)]^2\} \\
&= E\{[w_1 R_1 + w_2 R_2 + w_3 R_3 - w_1 ER_1 - w_2 ER_2 - w_3 ER_3]^2\} \\
&\qquad \text{(using Equation 8-13)} \\
&= E\{[w_1(R_1 - ER_1) + w_2(R_2 - ER_2) + w_3(R_3 - ER_3)]^2\} \\
&\qquad \text{(rearranging)} \\
&= E\{[w_1(R_1 - ER_1) + w_2(R_2 - ER_2) + w_3(R_3 - ER_3)] \\
&\qquad \times [w_1(R_1 - ER_1) + w_2(R_2 - ER_2) + w_3(R_3 - ER_3)]\} \\
&\qquad \text{(what squaring means)} \\
&= E[w_1 w_1(R_1 - ER_1)(R_1 - ER_1) + w_1 w_2(R_1 - ER_1)(R_2 - ER_2) \\
&\quad + w_1 w_3(R_1 - ER_1)(R_3 - ER_3) + w_2 w_1(R_2 - ER_2)(R_1 - ER_1) \\
&\quad + w_2 w_2(R_2 - ER_2)(R_2 - ER_2) + w_2 w_3(R_2 - ER_2)(R_3 - ER_3) \\
&\quad + w_3 w_1(R_3 - ER_3)(R_1 - ER_1) + w_3 w_2(R_3 - ER_3)(R_2 - ER_2) \\
&\quad + w_3 w_3(R_3 - ER_3)(R_3 - ER_3)] \qquad \text{(doing the multiplication)}
\end{aligned}
$$

$$
\begin{aligned}
= {}& w_1^2 E[(R_1 - ER_1)^2] + w_1 w_2 E[(R_1 - ER_1)(R_2 - ER_2)] \\
& + w_1 w_3 E[(R_1 - ER_1)(R_3 - ER_3)] + w_2 w_1 E[(R_2 - ER_2)(R_1 - ER_1)] \\
& + w_2^2 E[(R_2 - ER_2)^2] + w_2 w_3 E[(R_2 - ER_2)(R_3 - ER_3)] \\
& + w_3 w_1 E[(R_3 - ER_3)(R_1 - ER_1)] + w_3 w_2 E[(R_3 - ER_3)(R_2 - ER_2)] \\
& + w_3^2 E[(R_3 - ER_3)^2] \quad \text{(recalling that the } w_i \text{ terms are constants)} \\
= {}& w_1^2 \sigma^2(R_1) + w_1 w_2 \text{Cov}(R_1, R_2) + w_1 w_3 \text{Cov}(R_1, R_3) \\
& + w_1 w_2 \textit{Cov}(R_1, R_2) + w_2^2 \sigma^2(R_2) + w_2 w_3 \text{Cov}(R_2, R_3) \\
& + w_1 w_3 \textit{Cov}(R_1, R_3) + w_2 w_3 \textit{Cov}(R_2, R_3) + w_3^2 \sigma^2(R_3)
\end{aligned}
\tag{8-15}
$$

The last step follows from the definitions of variance and covariance.[11] For the italicized covariance terms in Equation 8-15, we used the fact that the order of variables in covariance does not matter: $\text{Cov}(R_2, R_1) = \text{Cov}(R_1, R_2)$, for example. As we will show, the diagonal variance terms $\sigma^2(R_1)$, $\sigma^2(R_2)$, and $\sigma^2(R_3)$ can be expressed as $\text{Cov}(R_1, R_1)$, $\text{Cov}(R_2, R_2)$, and $\text{Cov}(R_3, R_3)$, respectively. Using this fact, the most compact way to state Equation 8-15 is $\sigma^2(R_p) = \sum_{i=1}^{3} \sum_{j=1}^{3} w_i w_j \text{Cov}(R_i, R_j)$. The double summation signs say: "Set $i = 1$ and let $j$ run from 1 to 3; then set $i = 2$ and let $j$ run from 1 to 3; next set $i = 3$ and let $j$ run from 1 to 3; finally, add the nine terms." This expression generalizes for a portfolio of any size $n$ to

$$
\sigma^2(R_p) = \sum_{i=1}^{n} \sum_{j=1}^{n} w_i w_j \text{Cov}(R_i, R_j)
\tag{8-16}
$$

We see from Equation 8-15 that individual variances of return (the bolded diagonal terms) constitute part, but not all, of portfolio variance. The three variances are actually outnumbered by the six covariance terms off the diagonal. For three assets, the ratio is 1 to 2, or 50 percent. If there are 20 assets, there are 20 variance terms and $20(20) - 20 = 380$ off-diagonal covariance terms. The ratio of variance terms to off-diagonal covariance terms is less than 6 to 100, or 6 percent. A first observation, then, is that as the number of holdings increases, covariance[12] becomes increasingly important, all else equal.

What exactly is the effect of covariance on portfolio variance? The covariance terms capture how the co-movements of returns affect portfolio variance. For example, consider two stocks: One tends to have high returns (relative to its expected return) when the other has low returns (relative to its expected return). The returns on one stock tend to offset the returns on the other stock, lowering the variability or variance of returns on the portfolio. Like variance, the units of covariance are hard to interpret, and we will introduce a more intuitive concept shortly. Meanwhile, from the definition of covariance, we can establish two essential observations about covariance.

1. We can interpret the sign of covariance as follows:

    Covariance of returns is negative if, when the return on one asset is above its expected value, the return on the other asset tends to be below its expected value (an average inverse relationship between returns).

    Covariance of returns is 0 if returns on the assets are unrelated.

---

[11] Useful facts about variance and covariance include: 1) The variance of a constant *times* a random variable equals the constant squared times the variance of the random variable, or $\sigma^2(wR) = w^2 \sigma^2(R)$; 2) The variance of a constant *plus* a random variable equals the variance of the random variable, or $\sigma^2(w + R) = \sigma^2(R)$ because a constant has zero variance; 3) The covariance between a constant and a random variable is zero.

[12] When the meaning of covariance as "off-diagonal covariance" is obvious, as it is here, we omit the qualifying words. Covariance is usually used in this sense.

Covariance of returns is positive when the returns on both assets tend to be on the same side (above or below) their expected values at the same time (an average positive relationship between returns).

2. The covariance of a random variable with itself (*own covariance*) is its own variance: $\text{Cov}(R, R) = E\{[R - E(R)][R - E(R)]\} = E\{[R - E(R)]^2\} = \sigma^2(R)$.

A complete list of the covariances constitutes all the statistical data needed to compute portfolio variance of return. Covariances are often presented in a square format called a **covariance matrix**. Table 7 summarizes the inputs for portfolio expected return and variance of return.

---

**TABLE 7   Inputs to Portfolio Expected Return and Variance**

**A. Inputs to Portfolio Expected Return**

| Asset | A | B | C |
|---|---|---|---|
| | $E(R_A)$ | $E(R_B)$ | $E(R_C)$ |

**B. Covariance Matrix: The Inputs to Portfolio Variance of Return**

| Asset | A | B | C |
|---|---|---|---|
| A | $\textbf{Cov}(\textbf{R}_\textbf{A}, \textbf{R}_\textbf{A})$ | $\text{Cov}(R_A, R_B)$ | $\text{Cov}(R_A, R_C)$ |
| B | $\text{Cov}(R_B, R_A)$ | $\textbf{Cov}(\textbf{R}_\textbf{B}, \textbf{R}_\textbf{B})$ | $\text{Cov}(R_B, R_C)$ |
| C | $\text{Cov}(R_C, R_A)$ | $\text{Cov}(R_C, R_B)$ | $\textbf{Cov}(\textbf{R}_\textbf{C}, \textbf{R}_\textbf{C})$ |

---

With three assets, the covariance matrix has $3^2 = 3 \times 3 = 9$ entries, but it is customary to treat the diagonal terms, the variances, separately from the off-diagonal terms. These diagonal terms are bolded in Table 7. This distinction is natural, as security variance is a single-variable concept. So there are $9 - 3 = 6$ covariances, excluding variances. But $\text{Cov}(R_B, R_A) = \text{Cov}(R_A, R_B)$, $\text{Cov}(R_C, R_A) = \text{Cov}(R_A, R_C)$, and $\text{Cov}(R_C, R_B) = \text{Cov}(R_B, R_C)$. The covariance matrix below the diagonal is the mirror image of the covariance matrix above the diagonal. As a result, there are only $6/2 = 3$ distinct covariance terms to estimate. In general, for $n$ securities, there are $n(n - 1)/2$ distinct covariances to estimate and $n$ variances to estimate.

Suppose we have the covariance matrix shown in Table 8.

---

**TABLE 8   Covariance Matrix**

| | S&P 500 | U.S. Long-Term Corporate Bonds | MSCI EAFE |
|---|---|---|---|
| S&P 500 | 400 | 45 | 189 |
| U.S. long-term corporate bonds | 45 | 81 | 38 |
| MSCI EAFE | 189 | 38 | 441 |

---

Taking Equation 8-15 and grouping variance terms together produces the following:

$$\sigma^2(R_p) = w_1^2\sigma^2(R_1) + w_2^2\sigma^2(R_2) + w_3^2\sigma^2(R_3) + 2w_1w_2\mathrm{Cov}(R_1, R_2) \quad \textbf{(8-17)}$$
$$+ 2w_1w_3\mathrm{Cov}(R_1, R_3) + 2w_2w_3\mathrm{Cov}(R_2, R_3)$$
$$= (0.50)^2(400) + (0.25)^2(81) + (0.25)^2(441)$$
$$+ 2(0.50)(0.25)(45) + 2(0.50)(0.25)(189)$$
$$+ 2(0.25)(0.25)(38)$$
$$= 100 + 5.0625 + 27.5625 + 11.25 + 47.25 + 4.75 = 195.875$$

The variance is 195.875. Standard deviation of return is $195.875^{1/2} = 14$ percent. To summarize, the portfolio has an expected annual return of 11.75 percent and a standard deviation of return of 14 percent.

Let us look at the first three terms in the calculation above. Their sum, $100 + 5.0625 + 27.5625 = 132.625$, is the contribution of the individual variances to portfolio variance. If the returns on the three assets were independent, covariances would be 0 and the standard deviation of portfolio return would be $132.625^{1/2} = 11.52$ percent as compared to 14 percent before. The portfolio would have less risk. Suppose the covariance terms were negative. Then a negative number would be added to 132.625, so portfolio variance and risk would be even smaller. At the same time, we have not changed expected return. For the same expected portfolio return, the portfolio has less risk. This risk reduction is a diversification benefit, meaning a risk-reduction benefit from holding a portfolio of assets. The diversification benefit increases with decreasing covariance. This observation is a key insight of modern portfolio theory. It is even more intuitively stated when we can use the concept of correlation. Then we can say that as long as security returns are not perfectly positively correlated, diversification benefits are possible. Furthermore, the smaller the correlation between security returns, the greater the cost of not diversifying (in terms of risk-reduction benefits forgone), all else equal.

▶ **Definition of Correlation.** The correlation between two random variables, $R_i$ and $R_j$, is defined as $\rho(R_i, R_j) = \mathrm{Cov}(R_i, R_j)/\sigma(R_i)\sigma(R_j)$. Alternative notations are $\mathrm{Corr}(R_i, R_j)$ and $\rho_{ij}$.

Frequently, covariance is substituted out using the relationship $\mathrm{Cov}(R_i, R_j) = \rho(R_i, R_j)\sigma(R_i)\sigma(R_j)$. The division indicated in the definition makes correlation a pure number (one without a unit of measurement) and places bounds on its largest and smallest possible values. Using the above definition, we can state a correlation matrix from data in the covariance matrix alone. Table 9 shows the correlation matrix.

### TABLE 9  Correlation Matrix of Returns

|  | S&P 500 | U.S. Long-Term Corporate Bonds | MSCI EAFE |
|---|---|---|---|
| S&P 500 | 1.00 | 0.25 | 0.45 |
| U.S. long-term corporate bonds | 0.25 | 1.00 | 0.20 |
| MSCI EAFE | 0.45 | 0.20 | 1.00 |

For example, the covariance between long-term bonds and MSCI EAFE is 38, from Table 8. The standard deviation of long-term bond returns is $81^{1/2} = 9$ percent, that of MSCI EAFE returns is $441^{1/2} = 21$ percent, from diagonal terms in Table 8. The correlation ρ(Return on long-term bonds, Return on EAFE) is $38/(9\%)(21\%) = 0.201$, rounded to 0.20. The correlation of the S&P 500 with itself equals 1: The calculation is its own covariance divided by its standard deviation squared.

► **Properties of Correlation.**

**1.** Correlation is a number between −1 and +1 for two random variables, $X$ and $Y$:

$$-1 \le \rho(X,Y) \le +1$$

**2.** A correlation of 0 (uncorrelated variables) indicates an absence of any linear (straight-line) relationship between the variables.[13] Increasingly positive correlation indicates an increasingly strong positive linear relationship (up to 1, which indicates a perfect linear relationship). Increasingly negative correlation indicates an increasingly strong negative (inverse) linear relationship (down to −1, which indicates a perfect inverse linear relationship).[14]

---

**EXAMPLE 12**

**Portfolio Expected Return and Variance of Return**

You have a portfolio of two mutual funds, A and B, 75 percent invested in A, as shown in Table 10.

**TABLE 10  Mutual Fund Expected Returns, Return Variances, and Covariances**

| Fund | A<br>$E(R_A) = 20\%$ | B<br>$E(R_B) = 12\%$ |
| --- | --- | --- |
| **Covariance Matrix** | | |
| Fund | A | B |
| A | 625 | 120 |
| B | 120 | 196 |

**1.** Calculate the expected return of the portfolio.

**2.** Calculate the correlation matrix for this problem. Carry out the answer to two decimal places.

**3.** Compute portfolio standard deviation of return.

**Solution to 1:** $E(R_p) = w_A E(R_A) + (1 - w_A)E(R_B) = 0.75(20\%) + 0.25(12\%) = 18\%$. Portfolio weights must sum to 1: $w_B = 1 - w_A$.

---

[13] If the correlation is 0, $R_1 = a + bR_2 +$ error, with $b = 0$.

[14] If the correlation is positive, $R_1 = a + bR_2 +$ error, with $b > 0$. If the correlation is negative, $b < 0$.

**Solution to 2:** $\sigma(R_A) = 625^{1/2} = 25$ percent $\sigma(R_B) = 196^{1/2} = 14$ percent. There is one distinct covariance and thus one distinct correlation:
$\rho(R_A, R_B) = \mathrm{Cov}(R_A, R_B)/\sigma(R_A)\sigma(R_B) = 120/25(14) = 0.342857$, or 0.34
Table 11 shows the correlation matrix.

| TABLE 11  Correlation Matrix | | |
|---|---|---|
| | **A** | **B** |
| A | 1.00 | 0.34 |
| B | 0.34 | 1.00 |

Diagonal terms are always equal to 1 in a correlation matrix.

**Solution to 3:**
$$\sigma^2(R_p) = w_A^2\sigma^2(R_A) + w_B^2\sigma^2(R_B) + 2w_A w_B\mathrm{Cov}(R_A, R_B)$$
$$= (0.75)^2(625) + (0.25)^2(196) + 2(0.75)(0.25)(120)$$
$$= 351.5625 + 12.25 + 45 = 408.8125$$
$$\sigma(R_p) = 408.8125^{1/2} = 20.22 \text{ percent}$$

How do we estimate return covariance and correlation? Frequently, we make forecasts on the basis of historical covariance or use other methods based on historical return data, such as a market model regression.[15] We can also calculate covariance using the **joint probability function** of the random variables, if that can be estimated. The joint probability function of two random variables $X$ and $Y$, denoted $P(X, Y)$, gives the probability of joint occurrences of values of $X$ and $Y$. For example, $P(3, 2)$, is the probability that $X$ equals 3 and $Y$ equals 2.

Suppose that the joint probability function of the returns on BankCorp stock $(R_A)$ and the returns on NewBank stock $(R_B)$ has the simple structure given in Table 12.

| TABLE 12  Joint Probability Function of BankCorp and NewBank Returns (Entries Are Joint Probabilities) | | | |
|---|---|---|---|
| | $R_B = 20\%$ | $R_B = 16\%$ | $R_B = 10\%$ |
| $R_A = 25\%$ | 0.20 | 0 | 0 |
| $R_A = 12\%$ | 0 | 0.50 | 0 |
| $R_A = 10\%$ | 0 | 0 | 0.30 |

The expected return on BankCorp stock is $0.20(25\%) + 0.50(12\%) + 0.30(10\%) = 14\%$. The expected return on NewBank stock is $0.20(20\%) + 0.50(16\%) + 0.30(10\%) = 15\%$. The joint probability function above might reflect an analysis based on whether banking industry conditions are good, average, or poor. Table 13 presents the calculation of covariance.

---

[15] See any of the textbooks mentioned in Footnote 10.

**TABLE 13   Covariance Calculations**

| Banking Industry Condition | Deviations BankCorp | Deviations NewBank | Product of Deviations | Probability of Condition | Probability-Weighted Product |
|---|---|---|---|---|---|
| Good | 25–14 | 20–15 | 55 | 0.20 | 11 |
| Average | 12–14 | 16–15 | −2 | 0.50 | −1 |
| Poor | 10–14 | 10–15 | 20 | 0.30 | 6 |
| | | | | | $\text{Cov}(R_A, R_B) = 16$ |

*Note:* Expected return for BankCorp is 14% and for NewBank, 15%.

The first and second columns of numbers show, respectively, the deviations of BankCorp and NewBank returns from their mean or expected value. The next column shows the product of the deviations. For example, for good industry conditions, $(25 - 14)(20 - 15) = 11(5) = 55$. Then 55 is multiplied or weighted by 0.20, the probability that banking industry conditions are good: $55(0.20) = 11$. The calculations for average and poor banking conditions follow the same pattern. Summing up these probability-weighted products, we find that $\text{Cov}(R_A, R_B) = 16$.

A formula for computing the covariance between random variables $R_A$ and $R_B$ is

$$\text{Cov}(R_A, R_B) = \sum_i \sum_j P(R_{A,i}, R_{B,j})(R_{A,i} - ER_A)(R_{B,j} - ER_B) \qquad \textbf{(8-18)}$$

The formula tells us to sum all possible deviation cross-products weighted by the appropriate joint probability. In the example we just worked, as Table 12 shows, only three joint probabilities are nonzero. Therefore, in computing the covariance of returns in this case, we need to consider only three cross-products:

$$
\begin{aligned}
\text{Cov}(R_A, R_B) &= P(25, 20)[(25 - 14)(20 - 15)] + P(12, 16)[(12 - 14) \\
&\quad (16 - 15)] + P(10, 10)[(10 - 14)(10 - 15)] \\
&= 0.20(11)(5) + 0.50(-2)(1) + 0.30(-4)(-5) \\
&= 11 - 1 + 6 = 16
\end{aligned}
$$

One theme of this reading has been independence. Two random variables are independent when every possible pair of events—one event corresponding to a value of $X$ and another event corresponding to a value of $Y$—are independent events. When two random variables are independent, their joint probability function simplifies.

► **Definition of Independence for Random Variables.** Two random variables $X$ and $Y$ are independent if and only if $P(X, Y) = P(X)P(Y)$.

For example, given independence, $P(3, 2) = P(3)P(2)$. We multiply the individual probabilities to get the joint probabilities. *Independence* is a stronger property than *uncorrelatedness* because correlation addresses only linear relationships. The following condition holds for independent random variables and, therefore, also holds for uncorrelated random variables.

▶ **Multiplication Rule for Expected Value of the Product of Uncorrelated Random Variables.** The expected value of the product of uncorrelated random variables is the product of their expected values.

$$E(XY) = E(X)E(Y) \text{ if } X \text{ and } Y \text{ are uncorrelated.}$$

Many financial variables, such as revenue (price times quantity), are the product of random quantities. When applicable, the above rule simplifies calculating expected value of a product of random variables.[16]

# TOPICS IN PROBABILITY      4

In the remainder of the reading we discuss two topics that can be important in solving investment problems. We start with Bayes' formula: what probability theory has to say about learning from experience. Then we move to a discussion of shortcuts and principles for counting.

## 4.1 Bayes' Formula

When we make decisions involving investments, we often start with viewpoints based on our experience and knowledge. These viewpoints may be changed or confirmed by new knowledge and observations. Bayes' formula is a rational method for adjusting our viewpoints as we confront new information.[17] Bayes' formula and related concepts have been applied in many business and investment decision-making contexts, including the evaluation of mutual fund performance.[18]

Bayes' formula makes use of Equation 8-6, the total probability rule. To review, that rule expressed the probability of an event as a weighted average of the probabilities of the event, given a set of scenarios. Bayes' formula works in reverse; more precisely, it reverses the "given that" information. Bayes' formula uses the occurrence of the event to infer the probability of the scenario generating it. For that reason, Bayes' formula is sometimes called an inverse probability. In many applications, including the one illustrating its use in this section, an individual is updating his beliefs concerning the causes that may have produced a new observation.

▶ **Bayes' Formula.** Given a set of prior probabilities for an event of interest, if you receive new information, the rule for updating your probability of the event is

Updated probability of event given the new information

$$= \frac{\text{Probability of the new information given event}}{\text{Unconditional probability of the new information}} \times \text{Prior probability of event}$$

---

[16] Otherwise, the calculation depends on conditional expected value; the calculation can be expressed as $E(XY) = E(X) \, E(Y \mid X)$.

[17] Named after the Reverend Thomas Bayes (1702–61).

[18] See Baks, Metrick, and Wachter (2001).

In probability notation, this formula can be written concisely as:

$$P(\text{Event} \mid \text{Information}) = \frac{P(\text{Information} \mid \text{Event})}{P(\text{Information})} P(\text{Event})$$

To illustrate Bayes' formula, we work through an investment example that can be adapted to any actual problem. Suppose you are an investor in the stock of DriveMed, Inc. Positive earnings surprises relative to consensus EPS estimates often result in positive stock returns, and negative surprises often have the opposite effect. DriveMed is preparing to release last quarter's EPS result, and you are interested in which of these three events happened: *last quarter's EPS exceeded the consensus EPS estimate,* or *last quarter's EPS exactly met the consensus EPS estimate,* or *last quarter's EPS fell short of the consensus EPS estimate.* This list of the alternatives is mutually exclusive and exhaustive.

On the basis of your own research, you write down the following **prior probabilities** (or priors, for short) concerning these three events:

▶ *P(EPS exceeded consensus)* = 0.45

▶ *P(EPS met consensus)* = 0.30

▶ *P(EPS fell short of consensus)* = 0.25

These probabilities are "prior" in the sense that they reflect only what you know now, before the arrival of any new information.

The next day, DriveMed announces that it is expanding factory capacity in Singapore and Ireland to meet increased sales demand. You assess this new information. The decision to expand capacity relates not only to current demand but probably also to the prior quarter's sales demand. You know that sales demand is positively related to EPS. So now it appears more likely that last quarter's EPS will exceed the consensus.

The question you have is, "In light of the new information, what is the updated probability that the prior quarter's EPS exceeded the consensus estimate?"

Bayes' formula provides a rational method for accomplishing this updating. We can abbreviate the new information as *DriveMed expands.* The first step in applying Bayes' formula is to calculate the probability of the new information (here: *DriveMed expands*), given a list of events or scenarios that may have generated it. The list of events should cover all possibilities, as it does here. Formulating these conditional probabilities is the key step in the updating process. Suppose your view is

*P(DriveMed expands | EPS exceeded consensus)* = 0.75
*P(DriveMed expands | EPS met consensus)* = 0.20
*P(DriveMed expands | EPS fell short of consensus)* = 0.05

Conditional probabilities of an observation (here: *DriveMed expands*) are sometimes referred to as **likelihoods.** Again, likelihoods are required for updating the probability.

Next, you combine these conditional probabilities or likelihoods with your prior probabilities to get the unconditional probability for DriveMed expanding, *P(DriveMed expands)*, as follows:

$P(DriveMed\ expands)$

$= P(DriveMed\ expands\ |\ EPS\ exceeded\ consensus)$
$\qquad \times\ P(EPS\ exceeded\ consensus)$
$+\ P(DriveMed\ expands\ |\ EPS\ met\ consensus)$
$\qquad \times\ P(EPS\ met\ consensus)$
$+\ P(DriveMed\ expands\ |\ EPS\ fell\ short\ of\ consensus)$
$\qquad \times\ P(EPS\ fell\ short\ of\ consensus)$
$= 0.75(0.45) + 0.20(0.30) + 0.05(0.25) = 0.41,\ \text{or } 41\%$

This is Equation 8-6, the total probability rule, in action. Now you can answer your question by applying Bayes' formula:

$P(EPS\ exceeded\ consensus\ |\ DriveMed\ expands)$

$= \dfrac{P(DriveMed\ expands\ |\ EPS\ exceeded\ consensus)}{P(DriveMed\ expands)}\ P(EPS\ exceeded\ consensus)$

$= (0.75/0.41)(0.45) = 1.829268(0.45) = 0.823171$

Prior to DriveMed's announcement, you thought the probability that DriveMed would beat consensus expectations was 45 percent. On the basis of your interpretation of the announcement, you update that probability to 82.3 percent. This updated probability is called your **posterior probability** because it reflects or comes after the new information.

The Bayes' calculation takes the prior probability, which was 45 percent, and multiplies it by a ratio—the first term on the right-hand side of the equal sign. The denominator of the ratio is the probability that DriveMed expands, as you view it without considering (conditioning on) anything else. Therefore, this probability is unconditional. The numerator is the probability that DriveMed expands, if last quarter's EPS actually exceeded the consensus estimate. This last probability is larger than unconditional probability in the denominator, so the ratio (1.83 roughly) is greater than 1. As a result, your updated or posterior probability is larger than your prior probability. Thus, the ratio reflects the impact of the new information on your prior beliefs.

## EXAMPLE 13

### Inferring whether DriveMed's EPS Met Consensus EPS

You are still an investor in DriveMed stock. To review the givens, your prior probabilities are $P(EPS\ exceeded\ consensus) = 0.45$, $P(EPS\ met\ consensus) = 0.30$, and $P(EPS\ fell\ short\ of\ consensus) = 0.25$. You also have the following conditional probabilities:

$P(DriveMed\ expands\ |\ EPS\ exceeded\ consensus) = 0.75$

$P(DriveMed\ expands\ |\ EPS\ met\ consensus) = 0.20$

$P(DriveMed\ expands\ |\ EPS\ fell\ short\ of\ consensus) = 0.05$

Recall that you updated your probability that last quarter's EPS exceeded the consensus estimate from 45 percent to 82.3 percent after DriveMed announced it would expand. Now you want to update your other priors.

**1.** Update your prior probability that DriveMed's EPS met consensus.

2. Update your prior probability that DriveMed's EPS fell short of consensus.

3. Show that the three updated probabilities sum to 1. (Carry each probability to four decimal places.)

4. Suppose, because of lack of prior beliefs about whether DriveMed would meet consensus, you updated on the basis of prior probabilities that all three possibilities were equally likely: $P(EPS$ $exceeded\ consensus) = P(EPS\ met\ consensus) = P(EPS\ fell\ short\ of$ $consensus) = 1/3$. What is your estimate of the probability $P(EPS$ $exceeded\ consensus\ |\ DriveMed\ expands)$?

**Solution to 1:** The probability is $P(EPS\ met\ consensus\ |\ DriveMed$ $expands) =$

$$\frac{P(DriveMed\ expands\ |\ EPS\ met\ consensus)}{P(DriveMed\ expands)} P(EPS\ met\ consensus)$$

The probability $P(DriveMed\ expands)$ is found by taking each of the three conditional probabilities in the statement of the problem, such as $P(DriveMed\ expands\ |\ EPS\ exceeded\ consensus)$; multiplying each one by the prior probability of the conditioning event, such as $P(EPS\ exceeded$ $consensus)$; then adding the three products. The calculation is unchanged from the problem in the text above: $P(DriveMed\ expands) =$ $0.75(0.45) + 0.20(0.30) + 0.05(0.25) = 0.41$, or 41 percent. The other probabilities needed, $P(DriveMed\ expands\ |\ EPS\ met\ consensus) = 0.20$ and $P(EPS\ met\ consensus) = 0.30$, are givens. So

$P(EPS\ met\ consensus\ |\ DriveMed\ expands) = [P(DriveMed\ expands\ |\ EPS$ $met\ consensus)/P(DriveMed\ expands)]P(EPS\ met\ consensus)$
$= (0.20/0.41)(0.30) = 0.487805(0.30) = 0.146341$

After taking account of the announcement on expansion, your updated probability that last quarter's EPS for DriveMed just met consensus is 14.6 percent compared with your prior probability of 30 percent.

**Solution to 2:** $P(DriveMed\ expands)$ was already calculated as 41 percent. Recall that $P(DriveMed\ expands\ |\ EPS\ fell\ short\ of\ consensus) =$ 0.05 and $P(EPS\ fell\ short\ of\ consensus) = 0.25$ are givens.

$P(EPS\ fell\ short\ of\ consensus\ |\ DriveMed\ expands)$
$= [P(DriveMed\ expands\ |\ EPS\ fell\ short\ of\ consensus)/$
$\quad P(DriveMed\ expands)]P(EPS\ fell\ short\ of\ consensus)$
$= (0.05/0.41)(0.25) = 0.121951(0.25) = 0.030488$

As a result of the announcement, you have revised your probability that DriveMed's EPS fell short of consensus from 25 percent (your prior probability) to 3 percent.

**Solution to 3:** The sum of the three updated probabilities is

$P(EPS\ exceeded\ consensus\ |\ DriveMed\ expands) + P(EPS\ met\ consensus\ |$ $DriveMed\ expands) + P(EPS\ fell\ short\ of\ consensus\ |\ DriveMed\ expands)$
$= 0.8232 + 0.1463 + 0.0305 = 1.0000$

The three events (*EPS exceeded consensus, EPS met consensus, EPS fell short of consensus*) are mutually exclusive and exhaustive: One of these events or statements must be true, so the conditional probabilities must sum to 1. Whether we are talking about conditional or unconditional probabilities, whenever we have a complete set of the distinct possible events or outcomes, the probabilities must sum to 1. This calculation serves as a check on your work.

**Solution to 4:** Using the probabilities given in the question,

*P(DriveMed expands)*
= *P(DriveMed expands | EPS exceeded consensus)*
*P(EPS exceeded consensus)* +*P(DriveMed expands |*
*EPS met consensus) P(EPS met consensus)* + *P(DriveMed expands |*
*EPS fell short of consensus) P(EPS fell short of consensus)*
= 0.75(1/3) + 0.20(1/3) + 0.05(1/3) = 1/3

Not surprisingly, the probability of DriveMed expanding is 1/3 because the decision maker has no prior beliefs or views regarding how well EPS performed relative to the consensus estimate. Now we can use Bayes' formula to find *P(EPS exceeded consensus | DriveMed expands)* = [*P(DriveMed expands | EPS exceeded consensus)/P(DriveMed expands)*] *P(EPS exceeded consensus)* = [(0.75/(1/3)](1/3) = 0.75 or 75 percent. This probability is identical to your estimate of *P(DriveMed expands | EPS exceeded consensus)*.

When the prior probabilities are equal, the probability of information given an event equals the probability of the event given the information. When a decision-maker has equal prior probabilities (called **diffuse priors**), the probability of an event is determined by the information.

## 4.2 Principles of Counting

The first step in addressing a question often involves determining the different logical possibilities. We may also want to know the number of ways that each of these possibilities can happen. In the back of our mind is often a question about probability. How likely is it that I will observe this particular possibility? Records of success and failure are an example. When we evaluate a market timer's record, one well-known evaluation method uses counting methods presented in this section.[19] An important investment model, the binomial option pricing model, incorporates the combination formula that we will cover shortly. We can also use the methods in this section to calculate what we called a priori probabilities in Section 2. When we can assume that the possible outcomes of a random variable are equally likely, the probability of an event equals the number of possible outcomes favorable for the event divided by the total number of outcomes.

In counting, enumeration (counting the outcomes one by one) is of course the most basic resource. What we discuss in this section are shortcuts and principles. Without these shortcuts and principles, counting the total number of outcomes can be very difficult and prone to error. The first and basic principle of counting is the multiplication rule.

---

[19] Henriksson and Merton (1981).

▶ **Multiplication Rule of Counting.** If one task can be done in $n_1$ ways, and a second task, given the first, can be done in $n_2$ ways, and a third task, given the first two tasks, can be done in $n_3$ ways, and so on for $k$ tasks, then the number of ways the $k$ tasks can be done is $(n_1)(n_2)(n_3) \ldots (n_k)$.

Suppose we have three steps in an investment decision process. The first step can be done in two ways, the second in four ways, and the third in three ways. Following the multiplication rule, there are $(2)(4)(3) = 24$ ways in which we can carry out the three steps.

Another illustration is the assignment of members of a group to an equal number of positions. For example, suppose you want to assign three security analysts to cover three different industries. In how many ways can the assignments be made? The first analyst may be assigned in three different ways. Then two industries remain. The second analyst can be assigned in two different ways. Then one industry remains. The third and last analyst can be assigned in only one way. The total number of different assignments equals $(3)(2)(1) = 6$. The compact notation for the multiplication we have just performed is 3! (read: 3 factorial). If we had $n$ analysts, the number of ways we could assign them to $n$ tasks would be

$$n! = n(n-1)(n-2)(n-3) \ldots 1$$

or *$n$ factorial.* (By convention, 0! = 1.) To review, in this application we repeatedly carry out an operation (here, job assignment) until we use up all members of a group (here, three analysts). With $n$ members in the group, the multiplication formula reduces to $n$ factorial.[20]

The next type of counting problem can be called labeling problems.[21] We want to give each object in a group a label, to place it in a category. The following example illustrates this type of problem.

A mutual fund guide ranked 18 bond mutual funds by total returns for the year 2000. The guide also assigned each fund one of five risk labels: *high risk* (four funds), *above-average risk* (four funds), *average risk* (three funds), *below-average risk* (four funds), and *low risk* (three funds); as $4 + 4 + 3 + 4 + 3 = 18$, all the funds are accounted for. How many different ways can we take 18 mutual funds and label 4 of them high risk, 4 above-average risk, 3 average risk, 4 below-average risk, and 3 low risk, so that each fund is labeled?

The answer is close to 13 billion. We can label any of 18 funds *high risk* (the first slot), then any of 17 remaining funds, then any of 16 remaining funds, then any of 15 remaining funds (now we have 4 funds in the *high risk* group); then we can label any of 14 remaining funds *above-average risk*, then any of 13 remaining funds, and so forth. There are 18! possible sequences. However, order of assignment within a category does not matter. For example, whether a fund occupies the first or third slot of the four funds labeled *high risk*, the fund has the same label (*high risk*). Thus there are 4! ways to assign a given group of four funds to the four *high risk* slots. Making the same argument for the other categories, in total there are $(4!)(4!)(3!)(4!)(3!)$ equivalent sequences. To eliminate such redundancies from the 18! total, we divide 18! by $(4!)(4!)(3!)(4!)(3!)$. We have $18!/(4!)(4!)(3!)(4!)(3!) = 18!/(24)(24)(6)(24)(6) = 12,864,852,000$. This procedure generalizes as follows.

---

[20] The shortest explanation of $n$ factorial is that it is the number of ways to order $n$ objects in a row. In all the problems to which we apply this counting method, we must use up all the members of a group (sampling without replacement).

[21] This discussion follows Kemeny, Schleifer, Snell, and Thompson (1972) in terminology and approach.

▶ **Multinomial Formula (General Formula for Labeling Problems).** The number of ways that $n$ objects can be labeled with $k$ different labels, with $n_1$ of the first type, $n_2$ of the second type, and so on, with $n_1 + n_2 + \ldots + n_k = n$, is given by

$$\frac{n!}{n_1! n_2! \ldots n_k!}$$

The multinomial formula with two different labels ($k = 2$) is especially important. This special case is called the combination formula. A **combination** is a listing in which the order of the listed items does not matter. We state the combination formula in a traditional way, but no new concepts are involved. Using the notation in the formula below, the number of objects with the first label is $r = n_1$ and the number with the second label is $n - r = n_2$ (there are just two categories, so $n_1 + n_2 = n$). Here is the formula.

▶ **Combination Formula (Binomial Formula).** The number of ways that we can choose $r$ objects from a total of $n$ objects, when the order in which the $r$ objects are listed does not matter, is

$$_nC_r = \binom{n}{r} = \frac{n!}{(n - r)! r!}$$

Here $_nC_r$ and $\binom{n}{r}$ are shorthand notations for $n!/(n - r)! r!$ (read: $n$ choose $r$, or $n$ combination $r$).

If we label the $r$ objects as *belongs to the group* and the remaining objects as *does not belong to the group*, whatever the group of interest, the combination formula tells us how many ways we can select a group of size $r$. We can illustrate this formula with the binomial option pricing model. This model describes the movement of the underlying asset as a series of moves, price up (U) or price down (D). For example, two sequences of five moves containing three up moves, such as UUUDD and UDUUD, result in the same final stock price. At least for an option with a payoff dependent on final stock price, the number but not the order of up moves in a sequence matters. How many sequences of five moves *belong to the group with three up moves*? The answer is 10, calculated using the combination formula ("5 choose 3"):

$$\begin{aligned} _5C_3 &= 5!/(5 - 3)! 3! \\ &= (5)(4)(3)(2)(1)/(2)(1)(3)(2)(1) = 120/12 = 10 \text{ ways} \end{aligned}$$

A useful fact can be illustrated as follows: $_5C_3 = 5!/2!3!$ equals $_5C_2 = 5!/3!2!$, as $3 + 2 = 5$; $_5C_4 = 5!/1!4!$ equals $_5C_1 = 5!/4!1!$, as $4 + 1 = 5$. This symmetrical relationship can save work when we need to calculate many possible combinations.

Suppose jurors want to select three companies out of a group of five to receive the first-, second-, and third-place awards for the best annual report. In how many ways can the jurors make the three awards? Order does matter if we want to distinguish among the three awards (the rank within the group of three); clearly the question makes order important. On the other hand, if the question were "In how many ways can the jurors choose three winners, without regard to place of finish?" we would use the combination formula.

To address the first question above, we need to count ordered listings such as *first place, New Company; second place, Fir Company; third place, Well Company.* An ordered listing is known as a **permutation**, and the formula that counts the number of permutations is known as the permutation formula.[22]

▶ **Permutation Formula.** The number of ways that we can choose $r$ objects from a total of $n$ objects, when the order in which the $r$ objects are listed does matter, is

$$_{n}P_{r} = \frac{n!}{(n-r)!}$$

So the jurors have $_{5}P_{3} = 5!/(5-3)! = (5)(4)(3)(2)(1)/(2)(1) = 120/2 = 60$ ways in which they can make their awards. To see why this formula works, note that $(5)(4)(3)(2)(1)/(2)(1)$ reduces to $(5)(4)(3)$, after cancellation of terms. This calculation counts the number of ways to fill three slots choosing from a group of five people, according to the multiplication rule of counting. This number is naturally larger than it would be if order did not matter (compare 60 to the value of 10 for "5 choose 3" that we calculated above). For example, *first place, Well Company; second place, Fir Company; third place, New Company* contains the same three companies as *first place, New Company; second place, Fir Company; third place, Well Company.* If we were concerned only with award winners (without regard to place of finish), the two listings would count as one combination. But when we are concerned with the order of finish, the listings count as two permutations.

Answering the following questions may help you apply the counting methods we have presented in this section.

1. Does the task that I want to measure have a finite number of possible outcomes? If the answer is yes, you may be able to use a tool in this section, and you can go to the second question. If the answer is no, the number of outcomes is infinite, and the tools in this section do not apply.

2. Do I want to assign every member of a group of size $n$ to one of $n$ slots (or tasks)? If the answer is yes, use $n$ factorial. If the answer is no, go to the third question.

3. Do I want to count the number of ways to apply one of three or more labels to each member of a group? If the answer is yes, use the multinomial formula. If the answer is no, go to the fourth question.

4. Do I want to count the number of ways that I can choose $r$ objects from a total of $n$, when the order in which I list the $r$ objects does not matter (can I give the $r$ objects a label)? If the answer to these questions is yes, the combination formula applies. If the answer is no, go to the fifth question.

5. Do I want to count the number of ways I can choose $r$ objects from a total of $n$, when the order in which I list the $r$ objects is important? If the answer is yes, the permutation formula applies. If the answer is no, go to question 6.

6. Can the multiplication rule of counting be used? If it cannot, you may have to count the possibilities one by one, or use more advanced techniques than those presented here.[23]

---

[22] A more formal definition states that a permutation is an ordered subset of $n$ distinct objects.

[23] Feller (1957) contains a very full treatment of counting problems and solution methods.

# SUMMARY

In this reading, we have discussed the essential concepts and tools of probability. We have applied probability, expected value, and variance to a range of investment problems.

- ▶ A random variable is a quantity whose outcome is uncertain.

- ▶ Probability is a number between 0 and 1 that describes the chance that a stated event will occur.

- ▶ An event is a specified set of outcomes of a random variable.

- ▶ Mutually exclusive events can occur only one at a time. Exhaustive events cover or contain all possible outcomes.

- ▶ The two defining properties of a probability are, first, that $0 \leq P(E) \leq 1$ (where $P(E)$ denotes the probability of an event $E$), and second, that the sum of the probabilities of any set of mutually exclusive and exhaustive events equals 1.

- ▶ A probability estimated from data as a relative frequency of occurrence is an empirical probability. A probability drawing on personal or subjective judgment is a subjective probability. A probability obtained based on logical analysis is an a priori probability.

- ▶ A probability of an event $E$, $P(E)$, can be stated as odds for $E = P(E) / [1 - P(E)]$ or odds against $E = [1 - P(E)] / P(E)$.

- ▶ Probabilities that are inconsistent create profit opportunities, according to the Dutch Book Theorem.

- ▶ A probability of an event *not* conditioned on another event is an unconditional probability. The unconditional probability of an event $A$ is denoted $P(A)$. Unconditional probabilities are also called marginal probabilities.

- ▶ A probability of an event given (conditioned on) another event is a conditional probability. The probability of an event $A$ given an event $B$ is denoted $P(A \mid B)$.

- ▶ The probability of both $A$ and $B$ occurring is the joint probability of $A$ and $B$, denoted $P(AB)$.

- ▶ $P(A \mid B) = P(AB) / P(B)$, $P(B) \neq 0$.

- ▶ The multiplication rule for probabilities is $P(AB) = P(A \mid B)P(B)$.

- ▶ The probability that $A$ or $B$ occurs, or both occur, is denoted by $P(A \text{ or } B)$.

- ▶ The addition rule for probabilities is $P(A \text{ or } B) = P(A) + P(B) - P(AB)$.

- ▶ When events are independent, the occurrence of one event does not affect the probability of occurrence of the other event. Otherwise, the events are dependent.

- ▶ The multiplication rule for independent events states that if $A$ and $B$ are independent events, $P(AB) = P(A)P(B)$. The rule generalizes in similar fashion to more than two events.

- ▶ According to the total probability rule, if $S_1, S_2, \ldots, S_n$ are mutually exclusive and exhaustive scenarios or events, then $P(A) = P(A \mid S_1)P(S_1) + P(A \mid S_2)P(S_2) + \ldots + P(A \mid S_n)P(S_n)$.

- ▶ The expected value of a random variable is a probability-weighted average of the possible outcomes of the random variable. For a random variable $X$, the expected value of $X$ is denoted $E(X)$.

▶ The total probability rule for expected value states that $E(X) = E(X \mid S_1)P(S_1) + E(X \mid S_2)P(S_2) + \ldots + E(X \mid S_n)P(S_n)$, where $S_1, S_2, \ldots, S_n$ are mutually exclusive and exhaustive scenarios or events.

▶ The variance of a random variable is the expected value (the probability-weighted average) of squared deviations from the random variable's expected value $E(X)$: $\sigma^2(X) = E\{[X - E(X)]^2\}$, where $\sigma^2(X)$ stands for the variance of $X$.

▶ Variance is a measure of dispersion about the mean. Increasing variance indicates increasing dispersion. Variance is measured in squared units of the original variable.

▶ Standard deviation is the positive square root of variance. Standard deviation measures dispersion (as does variance), but it is measured in the same units as the variable.

▶ Covariance is a measure of the co-movement between random variables.

▶ The covariance between two random variables $R_i$ and $R_j$ is the expected value of the cross-product of the deviations of the two random variables from their respective means: $\text{Cov}(R_i, R_j) = E\{[R_i - E(R_i)][R_j - E(R_j)]\}$. The covariance of a random variable with itself is its own variance.

▶ Correlation is a number between $-1$ and $+1$ that measures the co-movement (linear association) between two random variables: $\rho(R_i, R_j) = \text{Cov}(R_i, R_j)/[\sigma(R_i)\,\sigma(R_j)]$.

▶ To calculate the variance of return on a portfolio of $n$ assets, the inputs needed are the $n$ expected returns on the individual assets, $n$ variances of return on the individual assets, and $n(n-1)/2$ distinct covariances.

▶ Portfolio variance of return is $\sigma^2(R_p) = \sum\limits_{i=1}^{n} \sum\limits_{j=1}^{n} w_i w_j \text{Cov}(R_i, R_j)$.

▶ The calculation of covariance in a forward-looking sense requires the specification of a joint probability function, which gives the probability of joint occurrences of values of the two random variables.

▶ When two random variables are independent, the joint probability function is the product of the individual probability functions of the random variables.

▶ Bayes' formula is a method for updating probabilities based on new information.

▶ Bayes' formula is expressed as follows: Updated probability of event given the new information = [(Probability of the new information given event)/(Unconditional probability of the new information)] × Prior probability of event.

▶ The multiplication rule of counting says, for example, that if the first step in a process can be done in 10 ways, the second step, given the first, can be done in 5 ways, and the third step, given the first two, can be done in 7 ways, then the steps can be carried out in $(10)(5)(7) = 350$ ways.

▶ The number of ways to assign every member of a group of size $n$ to $n$ slots is $n! = n\,(n-1)\,(n-2)(n-3)\ldots 1$. (By convention, $0! = 1$.)

▶ The number of ways that $n$ objects can be labeled with $k$ different labels, with $n_1$ of the first type, $n_2$ of the second type, and so on, with $n_1 + n_2 + \ldots + n_k = n$, is given by $n!/(n_1!n_2! \ldots n_k!)$. This expression is the multinomial formula.

▶ A special case of the multinomial formula is the combination formula. The number of ways to choose $r$ objects from a total of $n$ objects, when the order in which the $r$ objects are listed does not matter, is

$$_nC_r = \binom{n}{r} = \frac{n!}{(n-r)!\,r!}$$

▶ The number of ways to choose $r$ objects from a total of $n$ objects, when the order in which the $r$ objects are listed does matter, is

$$_nP_r = \frac{n!}{(n-r)!}$$

This expression is the permutation formula.

## PRACTICE PROBLEMS FOR READING 8

1. Define the following terms:
   A. Probability.
   B. Conditional probability.
   C. Event.
   D. Independent events.
   E. Variance.

2. State three mutually exclusive and exhaustive events describing the reaction of a company's stock price to a corporate earnings announcement on the day of the announcement.

3. Label each of the following as an empirical, a priori, or subjective probability.
   A. The probability that U.S. stock returns exceed long-term corporate bond returns over a 10-year period, based on Ibbotson Associates data.
   B. An updated (posterior) probability of an event arrived at using Bayes' formula and the perceived prior probability of the event.
   C. The probability of a particular outcome when exactly 12 equally likely possible outcomes exist.
   D. A historical probability of default for double-B rated bonds, adjusted to reflect your perceptions of changes in the quality of double-B rated issuance.

4. You are comparing two companies, BestRest Corporation and Relaxin, Inc. The exports of both companies stand to benefit substantially from the removal of import restrictions on their products in a large export market. The price of BestRest shares reflects a probability of 0.90 that the restrictions will be removed within the year. The price of Relaxin stock, however, reflects a 0.50 probability that the restrictions will be removed within that time frame. By all other information related to valuation, the two stocks appear comparably valued. How would you characterize the implied probabilities reflected in share prices? Which stock is relatively overvalued compared to the other?

5. Suppose you have two limit orders outstanding on two different stocks. The probability that the first limit order executes before the close of trading is 0.45. The probability that the second limit order executes before the close of trading is 0.20. The probability that the two orders both execute before the close of trading is 0.10. What is the probability that at least one of the two limit orders executes before the close of trading?

6. Suppose that 5 percent of the stocks meeting your stock-selection criteria are in the telecommunications (telecom) industry. Also, dividend-paying telecom stocks are 1 percent of the total number of stocks meeting your selection criteria. What is the probability that a stock is dividend paying, given that it is a telecom stock that has met your stock selection criteria?

**7.** You are using the following three criteria to screen potential acquisition targets from a list of 500 companies:

| Criterion | Fraction of the 500 Companies Meeting the Criterion |
|---|---|
| Product lines compatible | 0.20 |
| Company will increase combined sales growth rate | 0.45 |
| Balance sheet impact manageable | 0.78 |

If the criteria are independent, how many companies will pass the screen?

**8.** You apply both valuation criteria and financial strength criteria in choosing stocks. The probability that a randomly selected stock (from your investment universe) meets your valuation criteria is 0.25. Given that a stock meets your valuation criteria, the probability that the stock meets your financial strength criteria is 0.40. What is the probability that a stock meets both your valuation and financial strength criteria?

**9.** A report from Fitch data service states the following two facts:[1]

▶ In 2002, the volume of defaulted U.S. high-yield debt was $109.8 billion. The average market size of the high-yield bond market during 2002 was $669.5 billion.
▶ The average recovery rate for defaulted U.S. high-yield bonds in 2002 (defined as average price one month after default) was $0.22 on the dollar.

Address the following three tasks:

**A.** On the basis of the first fact given above, calculate the default rate on U.S. high-yield debt in 2002. Interpret this default rate as a probability.

**B.** State the probability computed in Part A as an odds against default.

**C.** The quantity 1 minus the recovery rate given in the second fact above is the expected loss per $1 of principal value, given that default has occurred. Suppose you are told that an institution held a diversified high-yield bond portfolio in 2002. Using the information in both facts, what was the institution's expected loss in 2002, per $1 of principal value of the bond portfolio?

[1] "High Yield Defaults 2002: The Perfect Storm," 19 February, 2003.

**10.** You are given the following probability distribution for the annual sales of ElStop Corporation:

**Probability Distribution for ElStop Annual Sales**

| Probability | Sales (Millions) |
|---|---|
| 0.20 | $275 |
| 0.40 | $250 |
| 0.25 | $200 |
| 0.10 | $190 |
| 0.05 | $180 |
| Sum = 1.00 | |

    **A.** Calculate the expected value of ElStop's annual sales.

    **B.** Calculate the variance of ElStop's annual sales.

    **C.** Calculate the standard deviation of ElStop's annual sales.

**11.** Suppose the prospects for recovering principal for a defaulted bond issue depend on which of two economic scenarios prevails. Scenario 1 has probability 0.75 and will result in recovery of $0.90 per $1 principal value with probability 0.45, or in recovery of $0.80 per $1 principal value with probability 0.55. Scenario 2 has probability 0.25 and will result in recovery of $0.50 per $1 principal value with probability 0.85, or in recovery of $0.40 per $1 principal value with probability 0.15.

    **A.** Compute the probability of each of the four possible recovery amounts: $0.90, $0.80, $0.50, and $0.40.

    **B.** Compute the expected recovery, given the first scenario.

    **C.** Compute the expected recovery, given the second scenario.

    **D.** Compute the expected recovery.

    **E.** Graph the information in a tree diagram.

**12.** Suppose we have the expected daily returns (in terms of U.S. dollars), standard deviations, and correlations shown in the table below.

## U.S., German, and Italian Bond Returns

### U.S. Dollar Daily Returns in Percent

|  | U.S. Bonds | German Bonds | Italian Bonds |
|---|---|---|---|
| Expected Return | 0.029 | 0.021 | 0.073 |
| Standard Deviation | 0.409 | 0.606 | 0.635 |

### Correlation Matrix

|  | U.S. Bonds | German Bonds | Italian Bonds |
|---|---|---|---|
| U.S. Bonds | 1 | 0.09 | 0.10 |
| German Bonds |  | 1 | 0.70 |
| Italian Bonds |  |  | 1 |

*Source*: Kool (2000), Table 1 (excerpted and adapted).

**A.** Using the data given above, construct a covariance matrix for the daily returns on U.S., German, and Italian bonds.

**B.** State the expected return and variance of return on a portfolio 70 percent invested in U.S. bonds, 20 percent in German bonds, and 10 percent in Italian bonds.

**C.** Calculate the standard deviation of return for the portfolio in Part B.

**13.** The variance of a stock portfolio depends on the variances of each individual stock in the portfolio and also the covariances among the stocks in the portfolio. If you have five stocks, how many unique covariances (excluding variances) must you use in order to compute the variance of return on your portfolio? (Recall that the covariance of a stock with itself is the stock's variance.)

**14.** Calculate the covariance of the returns on Bedolf Corporation ($R_B$) with the returns on Zedock Corporation ($R_Z$), using the following data.

## Probability Function of Bedolf and Zedock Returns

|  | $R_Z = 15\%$ | $R_Z = 10\%$ | $R_Z = 5\%$ |
|---|---|---|---|
| $R_B = 30\%$ | 0.25 | 0 | 0 |
| $R_B = 15\%$ | 0 | 0.50 | 0 |
| $R_B = 10\%$ | 0 | 0 | 0.25 |

*Note*: Entries are joint probabilities.

**15.** You have developed a set of criteria for evaluating distressed credits. Companies that do not receive a passing score are classed as likely to go bankrupt within 12 months. You gathered the following information when validating the criteria:

- ▶ Forty percent of the companies to which the test is administered will go bankrupt within 12 months: $P(nonsurvivor) = 0.40$.

- ▶ Fifty-five percent of the companies to which the test is administered pass it: $P(pass\ test) = 0.55$.

- ▶ The probability that a company will pass the test given that it will subsequently survive 12 months, is 0.85: $P(pass\ test\ |\ survivor) = 0.85$.

   **A.** What is $P(pass\ test\ |\ nonsurvivor)$?

   **B.** Using Bayes' formula, calculate the probability that a company is a survivor, given that it passes the test; that is, calculate $P(survivor\ |\ pass\ test)$.

   **C.** What is the probability that a company is a *nonsurvivor*, given that it fails the test?

   **D.** Is the test effective?

**16.** On one day in March, 3,292 issues traded on the NYSE: 1,303 advanced, 1,764 declined, and 225 were unchanged. In how many ways could this set of outcomes have happened? (Set up the problem but do not solve it.)

**17.** Your firm intends to select 4 of 10 vice presidents for the investment committee. How many different groups of four are possible?

**18.** As in Example 11, you are reviewing the pricing of a speculative-grade, one-year-maturity, zero-coupon bond. Your goal is to estimate an appropriate default risk premium for this bond. The default risk premium is defined as the extra return above the risk-free return that will compensate investors for default risk. If $R$ is the promised return (yield-to-maturity) on the debt instrument and $R_F$ is the risk-free rate, the default risk premium is $R - R_F$. You assess that the probability that the bond defaults is 0.06: $P(the\ bond\ defaults) = 0.06$. One-year U.S. T-bills are offering a return of 5.8 percent, an estimate of $R_F$. In contrast to your approach in Example 11, you no longer make the simplifying assumption that bondholders will recover nothing in the event of a default. Rather, you now assume that recovery will be $0.35 on the dollar, given default.

   **A.** Denote the fraction of principal and interest recovered in default as $\theta$. Following the model of Example 11, develop a general expression for the promised return $R$ on this bond.

   **B.** Given your expression for $R$ and the estimate of $R_F$, state the minimum default risk premium you should require for this instrument.

**19.** An analyst developed two scenarios with respect to the recovery of $100,000 principal from defaulted loans:

| Scenario | Probability of Scenario | Amount Recovered | Probability of Amount |
|---|---|---|---|
| 1 | 40% | $50,000 | 60% |
| | | $30,000 | 40% |
| 2 | 60% | $80,000 | 90% |
| | | $60,000 | 10% |

The amount of the expected recovery is *closest* to:

A. $36,400.

B. $63,600.

C. $81,600.

**20.** The correlation coefficient that indicates the weakest linear relationship between variables is

A. −0.75.

B. −0.22.

C. 0.35.

# STUDY SESSION 3
## QUANTITATIVE METHODS:
### Application

This study session introduces the discrete and continuous probability distributions that are most commonly used to describe the behavior of random variables. Probability theory and calculations are widely applied in finance, for example, in the field of investment and project valuation and in financial risk management.

Furthermore, this session teaches how to estimate different parameters (e.g., mean and standard deviation) of a population if only a sample, rather than the whole population, can be observed. Hypothesis testing is a closely related topic. This session presents the techniques that can be applied to accept or reject an assumed hypothesis (null hypothesis) about various parameters of a population. Finally, you will also learn about the fundamentals of technical analysis. It is important that analysts properly understand the assumptions and limitations when applying these tools as mis-specified models or improperly used tools can result in misleading conclusions.

## READING ASSIGNMENTS

**Reading 9**  Common Probability Distributions
*Quantitative Methods for Investment Analysis*, Second Edition, by Richard A. DeFusco, CFA, Dennis W. McLeavey, CFA, Jerald E. Pinto, CFA, and David E. Runkle, CFA

**Reading 10**  Sampling and Estimation
*Quantitative Methods for Investment Analysis*, Second Edition, by Richard A. DeFusco, CFA, Dennis W. McLeavey, CFA, Jerald E. Pinto, CFA, and David E. Runkle, CFA

**Reading 11**  Hypothesis Testing
*Quantitative Methods for Investment Analysis*, Second Edition, by Richard A. DeFusco, CFA, Dennis W. McLeavey, CFA, Jerald E. Pinto, CFA, and David E. Runkle, CFA

**Reading 12**  Technical Analysis
*Investment Analysis and Portfolio Management*, Eighth Edition, by Frank K. Reilly, CFA and Keith C. Brown, CFA

369

# COMMON PROBABILITY DISTRIBUTIONS

by Richard A. DeFusco, CFA, Dennis W. McLeavey, CFA,
Jerald E. Pinto, CFA, and David E. Runkle, CFA

## LEARNING OUTCOMES

| The candidate should be able to: | Mastery |
|---|:---:|
| **a.** explain a probability distribution and distinguish between discrete and continuous random variables; | ☐ |
| **b.** describe the set of possible outcomes of a specified discrete random variable; | ☐ |
| **c.** interpret a probability function, a probability density function, and a cumulative distribution function, and calculate and interpret probabilities for a random variable, given its cumulative distribution function; | ☐ |
| **d.** define a discrete uniform random variable and a binomial random variable, calculate and interpret probabilities given the discrete uniform and the binomial distribution functions, and construct a binomial tree to describe stock price movement; | ☐ |
| **e.** describe the continuous uniform distribution, and calculate and interpret probabilities, given a continuous uniform probability distribution; | ☐ |
| **f.** explain the key properties of the normal distribution, distinguish between a univariate and a multivariate distribution, and explain the role of correlation in the multivariate normal distribution; | ☐ |
| **g.** construct and interpret a confidence interval for a normally distributed random variable, and determine the probability that a normally distributed random variable lies inside a given confidence interval; | ☐ |
| **h.** define the standard normal distribution, explain how to standardize a random variable, and calculate and interpret probabilities using the standard normal distribution; | ☐ |
| **i.** define shortfall risk, calculate the safety-first ratio, and select an optimal portfolio using Roy's safety-first criterion; | ☐ |
| **j.** explain the relationship between normal and lognormal distributions and why the lognormal distribution is used to model asset prices; | ☐ |

*Quantitative Methods for Investment Analysis*, Second Edition, by Richard A. DeFusco, CFA, Dennis W. McLeavey, CFA, Jerald E. Pinto, CFA, and David E. Runkle, CFA. Copyright © 2004 by CFA Institute. Reprinted with permission.

| k. | distinguish between discretely and continuously compounded rates of return, and calculate and interpret a continuously compounded rate of return, given a specific holding period return; | ☐ |
| l. | explain Monte Carlo simulation and historical simulation, and describe their major applications and limitations. | ☐ |

## 1    INTRODUCTION TO COMMON PROBABILITY DISTRIBUTIONS

In nearly all investment decisions we work with random variables. The return on a stock and its earnings per share are familiar examples of random variables. To make probability statements about a random variable, we need to understand its probability distribution. A **probability distribution** specifies the probabilities of the possible outcomes of a random variable.

In this reading, we present important facts about four probability distributions and their investment uses. These four distributions—the uniform, binomial, normal, and lognormal—are used extensively in investment analysis. They are used in such basic valuation models as the Black–Scholes–Merton option pricing model, the binomial option pricing model, and the capital asset pricing model. With the working knowledge of probability distributions provided in this reading, you will also be better prepared to study and use other quantitative methods such as hypothesis testing, regression analysis, and time-series analysis.

After discussing probability distributions, we end the reading with an introduction to Monte Carlo simulation, a computer-based tool for obtaining information on complex problems. For example, an investment analyst may want to experiment with an investment idea without actually implementing it. Or she may need to price a complex option for which no simple pricing formula exists. In these cases and many others, Monte Carlo simulation is an important resource. To conduct a Monte Carlo simulation, the analyst must identify risk factors associated with the problem and specify probability distributions for them. Hence, Monte Carlo simulation is a tool that requires an understanding of probability distributions.

Before we discuss specific probability distributions, we define basic concepts and terms. We then illustrate the operation of these concepts through the simplest distribution, the uniform distribution. That done, we address probability distributions that have more applications in investment work but also greater complexity.

# DISCRETE RANDOM VARIABLES                2

A **random variable** is a quantity whose future outcomes are uncertain. The two basic types of random variables are discrete random variables and continuous random variables. A **discrete random variable** can take on at most a countable number of possible values. For example, a discrete random variable $X$ can take on a limited number of outcomes $x_1, x_2, \ldots, x_n$ ($n$ possible outcomes), or a discrete random variable $Y$ can take on an unlimited number of outcomes $y_1, y_2, \ldots$ (without end).[1] Because we can count all the possible outcomes of $X$ and $Y$ (even if we go on forever in the case of $Y$), both $X$ and $Y$ satisfy the definition of a discrete random variable. By contrast, we cannot count the outcomes of a **continuous random variable**. We cannot describe the possible outcomes of a continuous random variable $Z$ with a list $z_1, z_2, \ldots$ because the outcome $(z_1 + z_2)/2$, not in the list, would always be possible. Rate of return is an example of a continuous random variable.

In working with a random variable, we need to understand its possible outcomes. For example, stocks traded on the New York Stock Exchange and Nasdaq are quoted in ticks of $0.01. Quoted stock price is thus a discrete random variable with possible values $0, $0.01, $0.02, \ldots But we can also model stock price as a continuous random variable (as a lognormal random variable, to look ahead). In many applications, we have a choice between using a discrete or a continuous distribution. We are usually guided by which distribution is most efficient for the task we face. This opportunity for choice is not surprising, as many discrete distributions can be approximated with a continuous distribution, and vice versa. In most practical cases, a probability distribution is only a mathematical idealization, or approximate model, of the relative frequencies of a random variable's possible outcomes.

## EXAMPLE 1

### The Distribution of Bond Price

You are researching a probability model for bond price, and you begin by thinking about the characteristics of bonds that affect price. What are the lowest and the highest possible values for bond price? Why? What are some other characteristics of bonds that may affect the distribution of bond price?

The lowest possible value of bond price is 0, when the bond is worthless. Identifying the highest possible value for bond price is more challenging. The promised payments on a coupon bond are the coupons (interest payments) plus the face amount (principal). The price of a bond is the present discounted value of these promised payments. Because investors require a return on their investments, 0 percent is the lower limit on the discount rate that investors would use to discount a bond's promised payments. At a discount rate of 0 percent, the price of a bond is the sum of the face value and the remaining coupons without

---

[1] We follow the convention that an uppercase letter represents a random variable and a lowercase letter represents an outcome or specific value of the random variable. Thus $X$ refers to the random variable, and $x$ refers to an outcome of $X$. We subscript outcomes, as in $x_1$ and $x_2$, when we need to distinguish among different outcomes in a list of outcomes of a random variable.

any discounting. The discount rate thus places the upper limit on bond price. Suppose, for example, that face value is $1,000 and two $40 coupons remain; the interval $0 to $1,080 captures all possible values of the bond's price. This upper limit decreases through time as the number of remaining payments decreases.

Other characteristics of a bond also affect its price distribution. Pull to par value is one such characteristic: As the maturity date approaches, the standard deviation of bond price tends to grow smaller as bond price converges to par value. Embedded options also affect bond price. For example, with bonds that are currently callable, the issuer may retire the bonds at a prespecified premium above par; this option of the issuer cuts off part of the bond's upside. Modeling bond price distribution is a challenging problem.

Every random variable is associated with a probability distribution that describes the variable completely. We can view a probability distribution in two ways. The basic view is the **probability function**, which specifies the probability that the random variable takes on a specific value: $P(X = x)$ is the probability that a random variable $X$ takes on the value $x$. (Note that capital $X$ represents the random variable and lowercase $x$ represents a specific value that the random variable may take.) For a discrete random variable, the shorthand notation for the probability function is $p(x) = P(X = x)$. For continuous random variables, the probability function is denoted $f(x)$ and called the **probability density function** (pdf), or just the density.[2]

A probability function has two key properties (which we state, without loss of generality, using the notation for a discrete random variable):

▶ $0 \leq p(x) \leq 1$, because probability is a number between 0 and 1.

▶ The sum of the probabilities $p(x)$ over all values of $X$ equals 1. If we add up the probabilities of all the distinct possible outcomes of a random variable, that sum must equal 1.

We are often interested in finding the probability of a range of outcomes rather than a specific outcome. In these cases, we take the second view of a probability distribution, the cumulative distribution function (cdf). The **cumulative distribution function**, or distribution function for short, gives the probability that a random variable $X$ is less than or equal to a particular value $x$, $P(X \leq x)$. For both discrete and continuous random variables, the shorthand notation is $F(x) = P(X \leq x)$. How does the cumulative distribution function relate to the probability function? The word "cumulative" tells the story. To find $F(x)$, we sum up, or cumulate, values of the probability function for all outcomes less than or equal to $x$. The function of the cdf is parallel to that of cumulative relative frequency, which we discussed in the reading on statistical concepts and market returns.

Next, we illustrate these concepts with examples and show how we use discrete and continuous distributions. We start with the simplest distribution, the discrete uniform.

---

[2] The technical term for the probability function of a discrete random variable, probability mass function (pmf), is used less frequently.

## 2.1 The Discrete Uniform Distribution

The simplest of all probability distributions is the discrete uniform distribution. Suppose that the possible outcomes are the integers (whole numbers) 1 to 8, inclusive, and the probability that the random variable takes on any of these possible values is the same for all outcomes (that is, it is uniform). With eight outcomes, $p(x) = 1/8$, or 0.125, for all values of $X$ ($X = 1, 2, 3, 4, 5, 6, 7, 8$); the statement just made is a complete description of this discrete uniform random variable. The distribution has a finite number of specified outcomes, and each outcome is equally likely. Table 1 summarizes the two views of this random variable, the probability function and the cumulative distribution function.

**TABLE 1  Probability Function and Cumulative Distribution Function for a Discrete Uniform Random Variable**

| $X = x$ | Probability Function $p(x) = P(X = x)$ | Cumulative Distribution Function $F(x) = P(X \leq x)$ |
|---|---|---|
| 1 | 0.125 | 0.125 |
| 2 | 0.125 | 0.250 |
| 3 | 0.125 | 0.375 |
| 4 | 0.125 | 0.500 |
| 5 | 0.125 | 0.625 |
| 6 | 0.125 | 0.750 |
| 7 | 0.125 | 0.875 |
| 8 | 0.125 | 1.000 |

We can use Table 1 to find three probabilities: $P(X \leq 7)$, $P(4 \leq X \leq 6)$, and $P(4 < X \leq 6)$. The following examples illustrate how to use the cdf to find the probability that a random variable will fall in any interval (for any random variable, not only the uniform).

▶ The probability that $X$ is less than or equal to 7, $P(X \leq 7)$, is the next-to-last entry in the third column, 0.875 or 87.5 percent.

▶ To find $P(4 \leq X \leq 6)$, we need to find the sum of three probabilities: $p(4)$, $p(5)$, and $p(6)$. We can find this sum in two ways. We can add $p(4)$, $p(5)$, and $p(6)$ from the second column. Or we can calculate the probability as the difference between two values of the cumulative distribution function:

$$F(6) = P(X \leq 6) = p(6) + p(5) + p(4) + p(3) + p(2) + p(1)$$
$$F(3) = P(X \leq 3) = p(3) + p(2) + p(1)$$

so

$$P(4 \leq X \leq 6) = F(6) - F(3) = p(6) + p(5) + p(4) = 3/8$$

So we calculate the second probability as $F(6) - F(3) = 3/8$.

▶ The third probability, $P(4 < X \le 6)$, the probability that $X$ is less than or equal to 6 but greater than 4, is $p(5) + p(6)$. We compute it as follows, using the cdf:

$$P(4 < X \le 6) = P(X \le 6) - P(X \le 4) = F(6) - F(4) = p(6) + p(5) = 2/8$$

So we calculate the third probability as $F(6) - F(4) = 2/8$.

Suppose we want to check that the discrete uniform probability function satisfies the general properties of a probability function given earlier. The first property is $0 \le p(x) \le 1$. We see that $p(x) = 1/8$ for all $x$ in the first column of the table. (Note that $p(x)$ equals 0 for numbers $x$ such as $-14$ or $12.215$ that are not in that column.) The first property is satisfied. The second property is that the probabilities sum to 1. The entries in the second column of Table 1 do sum to 1.

The cdf has two other characteristic properties:

▶ The cdf lies between 0 and 1 for any $x$: $0 \le F(x) \le 1$

▶ As we increase $x$, the cdf either increases or remains constant.

Check these statements by looking at the third column in Table 1.

We now have some experience working with probability functions and cdfs for discrete random variables. Later in this reading, we will discuss Monte Carlo simulation, a methodology driven by random numbers. As we will see, the uniform distribution has an important technical use: It is the basis for generating random numbers, which in turn produce random observations for all other probability distributions.[3]

## 2.2 The Binomial Distribution

In many investment contexts, we view a result as either a success or a failure, or as binary (twofold) in some other way. When we make probability statements about a record of successes and failures, or about anything with binary outcomes, we often use the binomial distribution. What is a good model for how a stock price moves through time? Different models are appropriate for different uses. Cox, Ross, and Rubinstein (1979) developed an option pricing model based on binary moves, price up or price down, for the asset underlying the option. Their binomial option pricing model was the first of a class of related option pricing models that have played an important role in the development of the derivatives industry. That fact alone would be sufficient reason for studying the binomial distribution, but the binomial distribution has uses in decision-making as well.

The building block of the binomial distribution is the **Bernoulli random variable**, named after the Swiss probabilist Jakob Bernoulli (1654–1704). Suppose we have a trial (an event that may repeat) that produces one of two outcomes. Such a trial is a **Bernoulli trial**. If we let $Y$ equal 1 when the outcome is

---

[3] See Hillier and Lieberman (2000). Random numbers initially generated by computers are usually random positive integer numbers that are converted to approximate continuous uniform random numbers between 0 and 1. Then the continuous uniform random numbers are used to produce random observations on other distributions, such as the normal, using various techniques. We will discuss random observation generation further in the section on Monte Carlo simulation.

success and $Y$ equal 0 when the outcome is failure, then the probability function of the Bernoulli random variable $Y$ is

$$p(1) = P(Y = 1) = p$$
$$p(0) = P(Y = 0) = 1 - p$$

where $p$ is the probability that the trial is a success. Our next example is the very first step on the road to understanding the binomial option pricing model.

---

### EXAMPLE 2

**One-Period Stock Price Movement as a Bernoulli Random Variable**

Suppose we describe stock price movement in the following way. Stock price today is $S$. Next period stock price can move up or down. The probability of an up move is $p$, and the probability of a down move is $1 - p$. Thus, stock price is a Bernoulli random variable with probability of success (an up move) equal to $p$. When the stock moves up, ending price is $uS$, with $u$ equal to 1 plus the rate of return if the stock moves up. For example, if the stock earns 0.01 or 1 percent on an up move, $u = 1.01$. When the stock moves down, ending price is $dS$, with $d$ equal to 1 plus the rate of return if the stock moves down. For example, if the stock earns $-0.01$ or $-1$ percent on a down move, $d = 0.99$. Figure 1 shows a diagram of this model of stock price dynamics.

**FIGURE 1   One-Period Stock Price as a Bernoulli Random Variable**

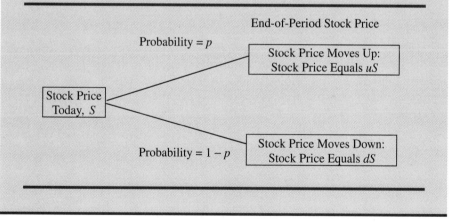

We will continue with the above example later. In the model of stock price movement in Example 2, success and failure at a given trial relate to up moves and down moves, respectively. In the following example, success is a profitable trade and failure is an unprofitable one.

## EXAMPLE 3

### A Trading Desk Evaluates Block Brokers (1)

You work in equities trading at an institutional money manager that regularly trades with a number of block brokers. Blocks are orders to sell or buy that are too large for the liquidity ordinarily available in dealer networks or stock exchanges. Your firm has known interests in certain kinds of stock. Block brokers call your trading desk when they want to sell blocks of stocks that they think your firm may be interested in buying. You know that these transactions have definite risks. For example, if the broker's client (the seller of the shares) has unfavorable information on the stock, or if the total amount he is selling through all channels is not truthfully communicated to you, you may see an immediate loss on the trade. From time to time, your firm audits the performance of block brokers. Your firm calculates the post-trade, market-risk-adjusted dollar returns on stocks purchased from block brokers. On that basis, you classify each trade as unprofitable or profitable. You have summarized the performance of the brokers in a spreadsheet, excerpted in Table 2 for November 2003. (The broker names are coded BB001 and BB002.)

### TABLE 2  Block Trading Gains and Losses

| | November 2003 | |
| --- | --- | --- |
| | Profitable Trades | Losing Trades |
| BB001 | 3 | 9 |
| BB002 | 5 | 3 |

View each trade as a Bernoulli trial. Calculate the percentage of profitable trades with the two block brokers for November 2003. These are estimates of $p$, the underlying probability of a successful (profitable) trade with each broker.

Your firm has logged $3 + 9 = 12$ trades (the row total) with block broker BB001. Because 3 of the 12 trades were profitable, the percentage of profitable trades was $3/12$ or 25 percent. With broker BB002, the percentage of profitable trades was $5/8$ or 62.5 percent. A trade is a Bernoulli trial, and the above calculations provide estimates of the underlying probability of a profitable trade (success) with the two brokers. For broker BB001, your estimate is $\hat{p} = 0.25$; for broker BB002, your estimate is $\hat{p} = 0.625$.[4]

---

[4] The "hat" over $p$ indicates that it is an estimate of $p$, the underlying probability of a profitable trade with the broker.

In $n$ Bernoulli trials, we can have 0 to $n$ successes. If the outcome of an individual trial is random, the total number of successes in $n$ trials is also random. A **binomial random variable** $X$ is defined as the number of successes in $n$ Bernoulli trials. A binomial random variable is the sum of Bernoulli random variables $Y_i$, $i = 1, 2, \ldots, n$:

$$X = Y_1 + Y_2 + \ldots + Y_n$$

where $Y_i$ is the outcome on the $i$th trial (1 if a success, 0 if a failure). We know that a Bernoulli random variable is defined by the parameter $p$. The number of trials, $n$, is the second parameter of a binomial random variable. The binomial distribution makes these assumptions:

▶ The probability, $p$, of success is constant for all trials.

▶ The trials are independent.

The second assumption has great simplifying force. If individual trials were correlated, calculating the probability of a given number of successes in $n$ trials would be much more complicated.

Under the above two assumptions, a binomial random variable is completely described by two parameters, $n$ and $p$. We write

$$X \sim B(n, p)$$

which we read as "$X$ has a binomial distribution with parameters $n$ and $p$." You can see that a Bernoulli random variable is a binomial random variable with $n = 1$: $Y \sim B(1, p)$.

Now we can find the general expression for the probability that a binomial random variable shows $x$ successes in $n$ trials. We can think in terms of a model of stock price dynamics that can be generalized to allow any possible stock price movements if the periods are made extremely small. Each period is a Bernoulli trial: With probability $p$, the stock price moves up; with probability $1 - p$, the price moves down. A success is an up move, and $x$ is the number of up moves or successes in $n$ periods (trials). With each period's moves independent and $p$ constant, the number of up moves in $n$ periods is a binomial random variable. We now develop an expression for $P(X = x)$, the probability function for a binomial random variable.

Any sequence of $n$ periods that shows exactly $x$ up moves must show $n - x$ down moves. We have many different ways to order the up moves and down moves to get a total of $x$ up moves, but given independent trials, any sequence with $x$ up moves must occur with probability $p^x(1 - p)^{n-x}$. Now we need to multiply this probability by the number of different ways we can get a sequence with $x$ up moves. Using a basic result in counting from the reading on probability concepts, there are

$$\frac{n!}{(n - x)!x!}$$

different sequences in $n$ trials that result in $x$ up moves (or successes) and $n - x$ down moves (or failures). Recall from the reading on probability concepts that $n$ factorial ($n!$) is defined as $n(n - 1)(n - 2) \ldots 1$ (and $0! = 1$ by convention). For example, $5! = (5)(4)(3)(2)(1) = 120$. The combination formula $n!/[(n - x)!x!]$ is denoted by

$$\binom{n}{x}$$

(read "$n$ combination $x$" or "$n$ choose $x$"). For example, over three periods, exactly three different sequences have two up moves: UUD, UDU, and DUU. We confirm this by

$$\binom{3}{2} = \frac{3!}{(3-2)!2!} = \frac{(3)(2)(1)}{(1)(2)(1)} = 3$$

If, hypothetically, each sequence with two up moves had a probability of 0.15, then the total probability of two up moves in three periods would be $3 \times 0.15 = 0.45$. This example should persuade you that for $X$ distributed $B(n, p)$, the probability of $x$ successes in $n$ trials is given by

$$p(x) = P(X = x) = \binom{n}{x} p^x (1-p)^{n-x} = \frac{n!}{(n-x)!x!} p^x (1-p)^{n-x} \qquad \textbf{(9-1)}$$

Some distributions are always symmetric, such as the normal, and others are always asymmetric or skewed, such as the lognormal. The binomial distribution is symmetric when the probability of success on a trial is 0.50, but it is asymmetric or skewed otherwise.

We illustrate Equation 9-1 (the probability function) and the cdf through the symmetrical case. Consider a random variable distributed $B(n = 5, p = 0.50)$. Table 3 contains a complete description of this random variable. The fourth column of Table 3 is Column 2, $n$ combination $x$, times Column 3, $p^x(1 - p)^{n-x}$; Column 4 gives the probability for each value of the number of up moves from the first column. The fifth column, cumulating the entries in the fourth column, is the cumulative distribution function.

### TABLE 3   Binomial Probabilities, $p = 0.50$ and $n = 5$

| Number of Up Moves, $x$ (1) | Number of Possible Ways to Reach $x$ Up Moves (2) | Probability for Each Way (3) | Probability for $x$, $p(x)$ (4) = (2) × (3) | $F(x) = P(x \le x)$ (5) |
|---|---|---|---|---|
| 0 | 1 | $0.50^0(1 - 0.50)^5 = 0.03125$ | 0.03125 | 0.03125 |
| 1 | 5 | $0.50^1(1 - 0.50)^4 = 0.03125$ | 0.15625 | 0.18750 |
| 2 | 10 | $0.50^2(1 - 0.50)^3 = 0.03125$ | 0.31250 | 0.50000 |
| 3 | 10 | $0.50^3(1 - 0.50)^2 = 0.03125$ | 0.31250 | 0.81250 |
| 4 | 5 | $0.50^4(1 - 0.50)^1 = 0.03125$ | 0.15625 | 0.96875 |
| 5 | 1 | $0.50^5(1 - 0.50)^0 = 0.03125$ | 0.03125 | 1.00000 |

What would happen if we kept $n = 5$ but sharply lowered the probability of success on a trial to 10 percent? "Probability for Each Way" for $X = 0$ (no up moves) would then be about 59 percent: $0.10^0(1 - 0.10)^5 = 0.59049$. Because zero successes could still happen one way (Column 2), $p(0) = 59$ percent. You may want to check that given $p = 0.10$, $P(X \le 2) = 99.14$ percent: The probability of two or fewer up moves would be more than 99 percent. The random variable's probability would be massed on 0, 1, and 2 up moves, and the probability of larger outcomes would be minute. The outcomes of 3 and larger would be the long right tail, and the distribution would be right skewed. On the other hand, if we set $p = 0.90$, we would have the mirror image of the distribution with $p = 0.10$. The distribution would be left skewed.

With an understanding of the binomial probability function in hand, we can continue with our example of block brokers.

---

### EXAMPLE 4

#### A Trading Desk Evaluates Block Brokers (2)

You now want to evaluate the performance of the block brokers in Example 3. You begin with two questions:

**1.** If you are paying a fair price on average in your trades with a broker, what should be the probability of a profitable trade?

**2.** Did each broker meet or miss that expectation on probability?

You also realize that the brokers' performance has to be evaluated in light of the sample's size, and for that you need to use the binomial probability function (Equation 9-1). You thus address the following (referring to the data in Example 3):

**3.** Under the assumption that the prices of trades were fair,

**A.** calculate the probability of three or fewer profitable trades with broker BB001.

**B.** calculate the probability of five or more profitable trades with broker BB002.

**Solution to 1 and 2:** If the price you trade at is fair, 50 percent of the trades you do with a broker should be profitable.[5] The rate of profitable trades with broker BB001 was 25 percent. Therefore, broker BB001 missed your performance expectation. Broker BB002, at 62.5 percent profitable trades, exceeded your expectation.

**Solution to 3:**

**A.** For broker BB001, the number of trades (the trials) was $n = 12$, and 3 were profitable. You are asked to calculate the probability of three or fewer profitable trades, $F(3) = p(3) + p(2) + p(1) + p(0)$.

Suppose the underlying probability of a profitable trade with BB001 is $p = 0.50$. With $n = 12$ and $p = 0.50$, according to Equation 9-1 the probability of three profitable trades is

$$p(3) = \binom{n}{x} p^x (1-p)^{n-x} = \binom{12}{3} (0.50^3)(0.50^9)$$

$$= \frac{12!}{(12-3)!3!} \, 0.50^{12} = 220(0.000244) = 0.053711$$

---

[5] Of course, you need to adjust for the direction of the overall market after the trade (any broker's record will be helped by a bull market) and perhaps make other risk adjustments. Assume that these adjustments have been made.

The probability of exactly 3 profitable trades out of 12 is 5.4 percent if broker BB001 were giving you fair prices. Now you need to calculate the other probabilities:

$$p(2) = [12!/(12-2)!2!](0.50^2)(0.50^{10}) = 66(0.000244) = 0.016113$$

$$p(1) = [12!/(12-1)!1!](0.50^1)(0.50^{11}) = 12(0.000244) = 0.00293$$

$$p(0) = [12!/(12-0)!0!](0.50^0)(0.50^{12}) = 1(0.000244) = 0.000244$$

Adding all the probabilities, $F(3) = 0.053711 + 0.016113 + 0.00293 + 0.000244 = 0.072998$ or 7.3 percent. The probability of doing 3 or fewer profitable trades out of 12 would be 7.3 percent if your trading desk were getting fair prices from broker BB001.

**B.** For broker BB002, you are assessing the probability that the underlying probability of a profitable trade with this broker was 50 percent, despite the good results. The question was framed as the probability of doing five or more profitable trades if the underlying probability is 50 percent: $1 - F(4) = p(5) + p(6) + p(7) + p(8)$. You could calculate $F(4)$ and subtract it from 1, but you can also calculate $p(5) + p(6) + p(7) + p(8)$ directly.

You begin by calculating the probability that exactly 5 out of 8 trades would be profitable if BB002 were giving you fair prices:

$$p(5) = \binom{8}{5}(0.50^5)(0.50^3)$$

$$= 56(0.003906) = 0.21875$$

The probability is about 21.9 percent. The other probabilities are

$$p(6) = 28(0.003906) = 0.109375$$

$$p(7) = 8(0.003906) = 0.03125$$

$$p(8) = 1(0.003906) = 0.003906$$

So $p(5) + p(6) + p(7) + p(8) = 0.21875 + 0.109375 + 0.03125 + 0.003906 = 0.363281$ or 36.3 percent.[6] A 36.3 percent probability is substantial; the underlying probability of executing a fair trade with BB002 might well have been 0.50 despite your success with BB002 in November 2003. If one of the trades with BB002 had been reclassified from profitable to unprofitable, exactly half the trades would have been profitable. In summary, your trading desk is getting at least fair prices from BB002; you will probably want to accumulate additional evidence before concluding that you are trading at better-than-fair prices.

The magnitude of the profits and losses in these trades is another important consideration. If all profitable trades had small profits but all unprofitable trades had large losses, for example, you might lose money on your trades even if the majority of them were profitable.

---

[6] In this example all calculations were worked through by hand, but binomial probability and cdf functions are also available in computer spreadsheet programs.

In the next example, the binomial distribution helps in evaluating the performance of an investment manager.

## EXAMPLE 5

### Meeting a Tracking Error Objective

You work for a pension fund sponsor. You have assigned a new money manager to manage a $500 million portfolio indexed on the MSCI EAFE (Europe, Australasia, and Far East) Index, which is designed to measure developed-market equity performance excluding the United States and Canada. After research, you believe it is reasonable to expect that the manager will keep tracking error within a band of 75 basis points (bps) of the benchmark's return, on a quarterly basis.[7] **Tracking error** is the total return on the portfolio (gross of fees) minus the total return on the benchmark index—here, the EAFE.[8] To quantify this expectation further, you will be satisfied if tracking error is within the 75 bps band 90 percent of the time. The manager meets the objective in six out of eight quarters. Of course, six out of eight quarters is a 75 percent success rate. But how does the manager's record precisely relate to your expectation of a 90 percent success rate and the sample size, 8 observations? To answer this question, you must find the probability that, given an assumed true or underlying success rate of 90 percent, performance could be as bad as or worse than that delivered. Calculate the probability (by hand or with a spreadsheet).

Specifically, you want to find the probability that tracking error is within the 75 bps band in six or fewer quarters out of the eight in the sample. With $n = 8$ and $p = 0.90$, this probability is $F(6) = p(6) + p(5) + p(4) + p(3) + p(2) + p(1) + p(0)$. Start with

$$p(6) = (8!/6!2!)(0.90^6)(0.10^2) = 28(0.005314) = 0.148803$$

and work through the other probabilities:

$$p(5) = (8!/5!3!)(0.90^5)(0.10^3) = 56(0.00059) = 0.033067$$

$$p(4) = (8!/4!4!)(0.90^4)(0.10^4) = 70(0.000066) = 0.004593$$

$$p(3) = (8!/3!5!)(0.90^3)(0.10^5) = 56(0.000007) = 0.000408$$

$$p(2) = (8!/2!6!)(0.90^2)(0.10^6) = 28(0.000001) = 0.000023$$

$$p(1) = (8!/1!7!)(0.90^1)(0.10^7) = 8(0.00000009) = 0.00000072$$

$$p(0) = (8!/0!8!)(0.90^0)(0.10^8) = 1(0.00000001) = 0.00000001$$

Summing all these probabilities, you conclude that $F(6) = 0.148803 + 0.033067 + 0.004593 + 0.000408 + 0.000023 + 0.00000072 + 0.00000001 = 0.186895$ or 18.7 percent. There is a moderate 18.7 percent probability that the manager would show the record he did (or a worse record) if he had the skill to meet your expectations 90 percent of the time.

[7] A basis point is one-hundredth of 1 percent (0.01 percent).

[8] Some practitioners use tracking error to describe what we later call tracking risk, the standard deviation of the differences between the portfolio's and benchmark's returns.

> You can use other evaluation concepts such as tracking risk, defined as the standard deviation of tracking error, to assess the manager's performance. The calculation above would be only one input into any conclusions that you reach concerning the manager's performance. But to answer problems involving success rates, you need to be skilled in using the binomial distribution.

Two descriptors of a distribution that are often used in investments are the mean and the variance (or the standard deviation, the positive square root of variance).[9] Table 4 gives the expressions for the mean and variance of binomial random variables.

**TABLE 4  Mean and Variance of Binomial Random Variables**

|  | Mean | Variance |
|---|---|---|
| Bernoulli, $B(1, p)$ | $p$ | $p(1 - p)$ |
| Binomial, $B(n, p)$ | $np$ | $np(1 - p)$ |

Because a single Bernoulli random variable, $Y \sim B(1, p)$, takes on the value 1 with probability $p$ and the value 0 with probability $1 - p$, its mean or weighted-average outcome is $p$. Its variance is $p(1 - p)$.[10] A general binomial random variable, $B(n, p)$, is the sum of $n$ Bernoulli random variables, and so the mean of a $B(n, p)$ random variable is $np$. Given that a $B(1, p)$ variable has variance $p(1 - p)$, the variance of a $B(n, p)$ random variable is $n$ times that value, or $np(1 - p)$, assuming that all the trials (Bernoulli random variables) are independent. We can illustrate the calculation for two binomial random variables with differing probabilities as follows:

| Random Variable | Mean | Variance |
|---|---|---|
| $B(n = 5, p = 0.50)$ | $2.50 = 5(0.50)$ | $1.25 = 5(0.50)(0.50)$ |
| $B(n = 5, p = 0.10)$ | $0.50 = 5(0.10)$ | $0.45 = 5(0.10)(0.90)$ |

For a $B(n = 5, p = 0.50)$ random variable, the expected number of successes is 2.5 with a standard deviation of $1.118 = (1.25)^{1/2}$; for a $B(n = 5, p = 0.10)$ random variable, the expected number of successes is 0.50 with a standard deviation of $0.67 = (0.45)^{1/2}$.

---

[9] The mean (or arithmetic mean) is the sum of all values in a distribution or dataset, divided by the number of values summed. The variance is a measure of dispersion about the mean. See the reading on statistical concepts and market returns for further details on these concepts.

[10] We can show that $p(1 - p)$ is the variance of a Bernoulli random variable as follows, noting that a Bernoulli random variable can take on only one of two values, 1 or 0: $\sigma^2(Y) = E[(Y - EY)^2] = E[(Y - p)^2] = (1 - p)^2 p + (0 - p)^2(1 - p) = (1 - p)[(1 - p)p + p^2] = p(1 - p)$.

**EXAMPLE 6**

### The Expected Number of Defaults in a Bond Portfolio

Suppose as a bond analyst you are asked to estimate the number of bond issues expected to default over the next year in an unmanaged high-yield bond portfolio with 25 U.S. issues from distinct issuers. The credit ratings of the bonds in the portfolio are tightly clustered around Moody's B2/Standard & Poor's B, meaning that the bonds are speculative with respect to the capacity to pay interest and repay principal. The estimated annual default rate for B2/B rated bonds is 10.7 percent.

1. Over the next year, what is the expected number of defaults in the portfolio, assuming a **binomial model** for defaults?

2. Estimate the standard deviation of the number of defaults over the coming year.

3. Critique the use of the binomial probability model in this context.

**Solution to 1:** For each bond, we can define a Bernoulli random variable equal to 1 if the bond defaults during the year and zero otherwise. With 25 bonds, the expected number of defaults over the year is $np = 25(0.107) = 2.675$ or approximately 3.

**Solution to 2:** The variance is $np(1 - p) = 25(0.107)(0.893) = 2.388775$. The standard deviation is $(2.388775)^{1/2} = 1.55$. Thus a two standard deviation confidence interval about the expected number of defaults would run from approximately 0 to approximately 6, for example.

**Solution to 3:** An assumption of the binomial model is that the trials are independent. In this context, a trial relates to whether an individual bond issue will default over the next year. Because the issuing companies probably share exposure to common economic factors, the trials may not be independent. Nevertheless, for a quick estimate of the expected number of defaults, the binomial model may be adequate.

Earlier, we looked at a simple one-period model for stock price movement. Now we extend the model to describe stock price movement on three consecutive days. Each day is an independent trial. The stock moves up with constant probability $p$ (the **up transition probability**); if it moves up, $u$ is 1 plus the rate of return for an up move. The stock moves down with constant probability $1 - p$ (the **down transition probability**); if it moves down, $d$ is 1 plus the rate of return for a down move. We graph stock price movement in Figure 2, where we now associate each of the $n = 3$ stock price moves with time indexed by $t$. The shape of the graph suggests why it is a called a **binomial tree**. Each boxed value from which successive moves or outcomes branch in the tree is called a **node**; in this example, a node is potential value for the stock price at a specified time.

## FIGURE 2    A Binomial Model of Stock Price Movement

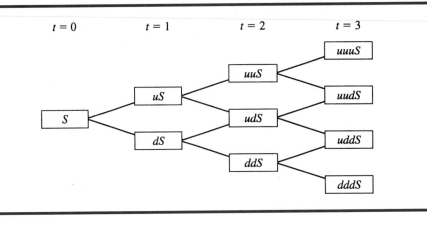

We see from the tree that the stock price at $t = 3$ has four possible values: *uuuS*, *uudS*, *uddS*, and *dddS*. The probability that the stock price equals *any* one of these four values is given by the binomial distribution. For example, three sequences of moves result in a final stock price of *uudS*: These are *uud*, *udu*, and *duu*. These sequences have two up moves out of three moves in total; the combination formula confirms that the number of ways to get two up moves (successes) in three periods (trials) is $3!/(3 - 2)!2! = 3$. Next note that each of these sequences, *uud*, *udu*, and *duu*, has probability $p^2(1 - p)$. So $P(S_3 = uudS) = 3p^2(1 - p)$, where $S_3$ indicates the stock's price after three moves.

The binomial random variable in this application is the number of up moves. Final stock price distribution is a function of the initial stock price, the *number* of up moves, and the *size* of the up moves and down moves. We cannot say that stock price itself is a binomial random variable; rather, it is a function of a binomial random variable, as well as of $u$ and $d$, and initial price. This richness is actually one key to why this way of modeling stock price is useful: It allows us to choose values of these parameters to approximate various distributions for stock price (using a large number of time periods).[11] One distribution that can be approximated is the lognormal, an important continuous distribution model for stock price that we will discuss later. The flexibility extends further. In the tree shown above, the transition probabilities are the same at each node: $p$ for an up move and $1 - p$ for a down move. That standard formula describes a process in which stock return volatility is constant through time. Option experts, however, sometimes model changing volatility through time using a binomial tree in which the probabilities for up and down moves differ at different nodes.

The binomial tree also supplies the possibility of testing a condition or contingency at any node. This flexibility is useful in investment applications such as option pricing. Consider an American call option on a dividend-paying stock. (Recall that an American option can be exercised at any time before expiration,

---

[11] For example, we can split 20 days into 100 subperiods, taking care to use compatible values for $u$ and $d$.

at any node on the tree.) Just before an ex-dividend date, it may be optimal to exercise an American call option on stock to buy the stock and receive the dividend.[12] If we model stock price with a binomial tree, we can test, at each node, whether exercising the option is optimal. Also, if we know the value of the call at the four terminal nodes at $t = 3$ and we have a model for discounting values by one period, we can step backward one period to $t = 2$ to find the call's value at the three nodes there. Continuing back recursively, we can find the call's value today. This type of recursive operation is easily programmed on a computer. As a result, binomial trees can value options even more complex than American calls on stock.[13]

# CONTINUOUS RANDOM VARIABLES     3

In the previous section, we considered discrete random variables (i.e., random variables whose set of possible outcomes is countable). In contrast, the possible outcomes of continuous random variables are never countable. If 1.250 is one possible value of a continuous random variable, for example, we cannot name the next higher or lower possible value. Technically, the range of possible outcomes of a continuous random variable is the real line (all real numbers between $-\infty$ and $+\infty$) or some subset of the real line.

In this section, we focus on the two most important continuous distributions in investment work, the normal and lognormal. As we did with discrete distributions, we introduce the topic through the uniform distribution.

## 3.1 Continuous Uniform Distribution

The continuous uniform distribution is the simplest continuous probability distribution. The uniform distribution has two main uses. As the basis of techniques for generating random numbers, the uniform distribution plays a role in Monte Carlo simulation. As the probability distribution that describes equally likely outcomes, the uniform distribution is an appropriate probability model to represent a particular kind of uncertainty in beliefs in which all outcomes appear equally likely.

The pdf for a uniform random variable is

$$f(x) = \begin{cases} \dfrac{1}{b-a} & \text{for } a < x < b \\ 0 & \text{otherwise} \end{cases}$$

For example, with $a = 0$ and $b = 8$, $f(x) = 1/8$ or 0.125. We graph this density in Figure 3.

---

[12] Cash dividends represent a reduction of a company's assets. Early exercise may be optimal because the exercise price of options is typically not reduced by the amount of cash dividends, so cash dividends negatively affect the position of an American call option holder.

[13] See Chance (2003) for more information on option pricing models.

**FIGURE 3     Continuous Uniform Distribution**

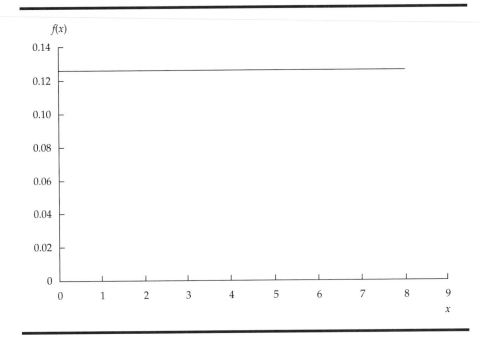

The graph of the density function plots as a horizontal line with a value of 0.125.

What is the probability that a uniform random variable with limits $a = 0$ and $b = 8$ is less than or equal to 3, or $F(3) = P(X \leq 3)$? When we were working with the discrete uniform random variable with possible outcomes 1, 2, . . . , 8, we summed individual probabilities: $p(1) + p(2) + p(3) = 0.375$. In contrast, the probability that a continuous uniform random variable, or any continuous random variable, assumes any given fixed value is 0. To illustrate this point, consider the narrow interval 2.510 to 2.511. Because that interval holds an infinity of possible values, the sum of the probabilities of values in that interval alone would be infinite if each individual value in it had a positive probability. To find the probability $F(3)$, we find the area under the curve graphing the pdf, between 0 to 3 on the $x$ axis. In calculus, this operation is called integrating the probability function $f(x)$ from 0 to 3. This area under the curve is a rectangle with base $3 - 0 = 3$ and height $1/8$. The area of this rectangle equals base times height: $3(1/8) = 3/8$ or 0.375. So $F(3) = 3/8$ or 0.375.

The interval from 0 to 3 is three-eighths of the total length between the limits of 0 and 8, and $F(3)$ is three-eighths of the total probability of 1. The middle line of the expression for the cdf captures this relationship.

$$F(x) = \begin{cases} 0 \text{ for } x \leq a \\ \dfrac{x - a}{b - a} \text{ for } a < x < b \\ 1 \text{ for } x \geq b \end{cases}$$

For our problem, $F(x) = 0$ for $x \leq 0$, $F(x) = x/8$ for $0 < x < 8$, and $F(x) = 1$ for $x \geq 8$. We graph this cdf in Figure 4.

**FIGURE 4   Continuous Uniform Cumulative Distribution**

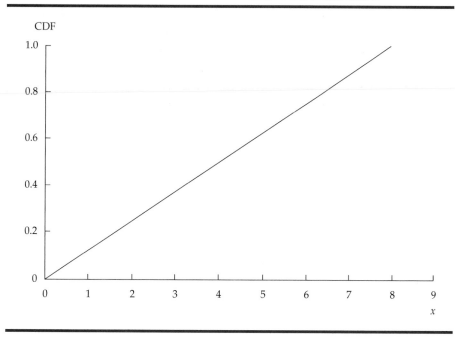

The mathematical operation that corresponds to finding the area under the curve of a pdf $f(x)$ from $a$ to $b$ is the integral of $f(x)$ from $a$ to $b$:

$$P(a \leq X \leq b) = \int_a^b f(x)\,dx \tag{9-2}$$

where $\int dx$ is the symbol for summing $\int$ over small changes $dx$, and the limits of integration ($a$ and $b$) can be any real numbers or $-\infty$ and $+\infty$. All probabilities of continuous random variables can be computed using Equation 9-2. For the uniform distribution example considered above, $F(7)$ is Equation 9-2 with lower limit $a = 0$ and upper limit $b = 7$. The integral corresponding to the cdf of a uniform distribution reduces to the three-line expression given previously. To evaluate Equation 9-2 for nearly all other continuous distributions, including the normal and lognormal, we rely on spreadsheet functions, computer programs, or tables of values to calculate probabilities. Those tools use various numerical methods to evaluate the integral in Equation 9-2.

Recall that the probability of a continuous random variable equaling any fixed point is 0. This fact has an important consequence for working with the cumulative distribution function of a continuous random variable: For any continuous random variable $X$, $P(a \leq X \leq b) = P(a < X \leq b) = P(a \leq X < b) = P(a < X < b)$, because the probabilities at the endpoints $a$ and $b$ are 0. For discrete random variables, these relations of equality are not true, because probability accumulates at points.

## EXAMPLE 7

### Probability That a Lending Facility Covenant Is Breached

You are evaluating the bonds of a below-investment-grade borrower at a low point in its business cycle. You have many factors to consider, including the terms of the company's bank lending facilities. The contract creating a bank lending facility such as an unsecured line of credit typically has clauses known as covenants. These covenants place restrictions on what the borrower can do. The company will be in breach of a covenant in the lending facility if the interest coverage ratio, EBITDA/interest, calculated on EBITDA over the four trailing quarters, falls below 2.0. EBITDA is earnings before interest, taxes, depreciation, and amortization.[14] Compliance with the covenants will be checked at the end of the current quarter. If the covenant is breached, the bank can demand immediate repayment of all borrowings on the facility. That action would probably trigger a liquidity crisis for the company. With a high degree of confidence, you forecast interest charges of $25 million. Your estimate of EBITDA runs from $40 million on the low end to $60 million on the high end.

Address two questions (treating projected interest charges as a constant):

1. If the outcomes for EBITDA are equally likely, what is the probability that EBITDA/interest will fall below 2.0, breaching the covenant?

2. Estimate the mean and standard deviation of EBITDA/interest. For a continuous uniform random variable, the mean is given by $\mu = (a + b)/2$ and the variance is given by $\sigma^2 = (b - a)^2/12$.

**Solution to 1:** EBITDA/interest is a continuous uniform random variable because all outcomes are equally likely. The ratio can take on values between 1.6 = ($40 million)/($25 million) on the low end and 2.4 = ($60 million/$25 million) on the high end. The range of possible values is 2.4 − 1.6 = 0.8. What fraction of the possible values falls below 2.0, the level that triggers default? The distance between 2.0 and 1.6 is 0.40; the value 0.40 is one-half the total length of 0.8, or 0.4/0.8 = 0.50. So the probability that the covenant will be breached is 50 percent.

**Solution to 2:** In Solution 1, we found that the lower limit of EBITDA/interest is 1.6. This lower limit is *a*. We found that the upper limit is 2.4. This upper limit is *b*. Using the formula given above,

$$\mu = (a + b)/2 = (1.6 + 2.4)/2 = 2.0$$

The variance of the interest coverage ratio is

$$\sigma^2 = (b - a)^2/12 = (2.4 - 1.6)^2/12 = 0.053333$$

---

[14] For a detailed discussion on the use and misuse of EBITDA, see Moody's Investors Service Global Credit Research, *Putting EBITDA in Perspective* (June 2000).

The standard deviation is the positive square root of the variance, $0.230940 = (0.053333)^{1/2}$. The standard deviation is not particularly useful as a risk measure for a uniform distribution, however. The probability that lies within various standard deviation bands around the mean is sensitive to different specifications of the upper and lower limits (although Chebyshev's inequality is always satisfied).[15] Here, a one standard deviation interval around the mean of 2.0 runs from 1.769 to 2.231 and captures $0.462/0.80 = 0.5775$ or 57.8 percent of the probability. A two standard deviation interval runs from 1.538 to 2.462, which extends past both the lower and upper limits of the random variable.

## 3.2  The Normal Distribution

The normal distribution may be the most extensively used probability distribution in quantitative work. It plays key roles in modern portfolio theory and in a number of risk management technologies. Because it has so many uses, the normal distribution must be thoroughly understood by investment professionals.

The role of the normal distribution in statistical inference and regression analysis is vastly extended by a crucial result known as the central limit theorem. The central limit theorem states that the sum (and mean) of a large number of independent random variables is approximately normally distributed.[16]

The French mathematician Abraham de Moivre (1667–1754) introduced the normal distribution in 1733 in developing a version of the central limit theorem. As Figure 5 shows, the normal distribution is symmetrical and bell-shaped.

**FIGURE 5    Two Normal Distributions**

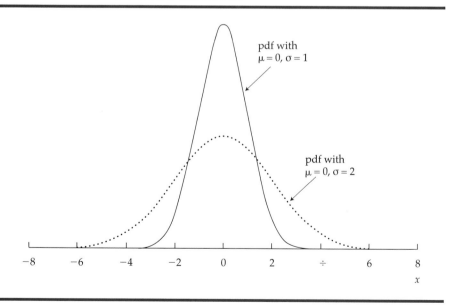

---

[15] Chebyshev's inequality is discussed in the reading on statistical concepts and market returns.

[16] The central limit theorem is discussed further in the reading on sampling.

The range of possible outcomes of the normal distribution is the entire real line: all real numbers lying between $-\infty$ and $+\infty$. The tails of the bell curve extend without limit to the left and to the right.

The defining characteristics of a normal distribution are as follows:

▶ The normal distribution is completely described by two parameters—its mean, $\mu$, and variance, $\sigma^2$. We indicate this as $X \sim N(\mu, \sigma^2)$ (read "$X$ follows a normal distribution with mean $\mu$ and variance $\sigma^2$"). We can also define a normal distribution in terms of the mean and the standard deviation, $\sigma$ (this is often convenient because $\sigma$ is measured in the same units as $X$ and $\mu$). As a consequence, we can answer any probability question about a normal random variable if we know its mean and variance (or standard deviation).

▶ The normal distribution has a skewness of 0 (it is symmetric). The normal distribution has a kurtosis (measure of peakedness) of 3; its excess kurtosis (kurtosis $-$ 3.0) equals 0.[17] As a consequence of symmetry, the mean, median, and the mode are all equal for a normal random variable.

▶ A linear combination of two or more normal random variables is also normally distributed.

These bullet points concern a single variable or univariate normal distribution: the distribution of one normal random variable. A **univariate distribution** describes a single random variable. A **multivariate distribution** specifies the probabilities for a group of related random variables. You will encounter the **multivariate normal distribution** in investment work and reading and should know the following about it.

When we have a group of assets, we can model the distribution of returns on each asset individually, or the distribution of returns on the assets as a group. "As a group" means that we take account of all the statistical interrelationships among the return series. One model that has often been used for security returns is the multivariate normal distribution. A multivariate normal distribution for the returns on $n$ stocks is completely defined by three lists of parameters:

▶ the list of the mean returns on the individual securities ($n$ means in total);

▶ the list of the securities' variances of return ($n$ variances in total); and

▶ the list of all the distinct pairwise return correlations: $n(n-1)/2$ distinct correlations in total.[18]

The need to specify correlations is a distinguishing feature of the multivariate normal distribution in contrast to the univariate normal distribution.

The statement "assume returns are normally distributed" is sometimes used to mean a joint normal distribution. For a portfolio of 30 securities, for example, portfolio return is a weighted average of the returns on the 30 securities. A weighted average is a linear combination. Thus, portfolio return is normally distributed if the individual security returns are (joint) normally distributed. To review, in order to specify the normal distribution for portfolio return, we need the means, variances, and the distinct pairwise correlations of the component securities.

---

[17] If we have a sample of size $n$ from a normal distribution, we may want to know the possible variation in sample skewness and kurtosis. For a normal random variable, the standard deviation of sample skewness is $6/n$ and the standard deviation of sample kurtosis is $24/n$.

[18] For example, a distribution with two stocks (a bivariate normal distribution) has two means, two variances, and one correlation: $2(2-1)/2$. A distribution with 30 stocks has 30 means, 30 variances, and 435 distinct correlations: $30(30-1)/2$. The return correlation of Dow Chemical with American Express stock is the same as the correlation of American Express with Dow Chemical stock, so these are counted as one distinct correlation.

With these concepts in mind, we can return to the normal distribution for one random variable. The curves graphed in Figure 5 are the normal density function:

$$f(x) = \frac{1}{\sigma\sqrt{2\pi}}\exp\left(\frac{-(x-\mu)^2}{2\sigma^2}\right) \text{ for } -\infty < x < +\infty \qquad \textbf{(9-3)}$$

The two densities graphed in Figure 5 correspond to a mean of $\mu = 0$ and standard deviations of $\sigma = 1$ and $\sigma = 2$. The normal density with $\mu = 0$ and $\sigma = 1$ is called the **standard normal distribution** (or **unit normal distribution**). Plotting two normal distributions with the same mean and different standard deviations helps us appreciate why standard deviation is a good measure of dispersion for the normal distribution: Observations are much more concentrated around the mean for the normal distribution with $\sigma = 1$ than for the normal distribution with $\sigma = 2$.

Although not literally accurate, the normal distribution can be considered an approximate model for returns. Nearly all the probability of a normal random variable is contained within three standard deviations of the mean. For realistic values of mean return and return standard deviation for many assets, the normal probability of outcomes below $-100$ percent is very small. Whether the approximation is useful in a given application is an empirical question. For example, the normal distribution is a closer fit for quarterly and yearly holding period returns on a diversified equity portfolio than it is for daily or weekly returns.[19] A persistent departure from normality in most equity return series is kurtosis greater than 3, the fat-tails problem. So when we approximate equity return distributions with the normal distribution, we should be aware that the normal distribution tends to underestimate the probability of extreme returns.[20] Option returns are skewed. Because the normal is a symmetrical distribution, we should be cautious in using the normal distribution to model the returns on portfolios containing significant positions in options.

The normal distribution, however, is less suitable as a model for asset prices than as a model for returns. A normal random variable has no lower limit. This characteristic has several implications for investment applications. An asset price can drop only to 0, at which point the asset becomes worthless. As a result, practitioners generally do not use the normal distribution to model the distribution of asset prices. Also note that moving from any level of asset price to 0 translates into a return of $-100$ percent. Because the normal distribution extends below 0 without limit, it cannot be literally accurate as a model for asset returns.

Having established that the normal distribution is the appropriate model for a variable of interest, we can use it to make the following probability statements:

► Approximately 50 percent of all observations fall in the interval $\mu \pm (2/3)\sigma$.

► Approximately 68 percent of all observations fall in the interval $\mu \pm \sigma$.

► Approximately 95 percent of all observations fall in the interval $\mu \pm 2\sigma$.

► Approximately 99 percent of all observations fall in the interval $\mu \pm 3\sigma$.

One, two, and three standard deviation intervals are illustrated in Figure 6.

---

[19] See Fama (1976) and Campbell, Lo, and MacKinlay (1997).

[20] Fat tails can be modeled by a mixture of normal random variables or by a Student's $t$-distribution with a relatively small number of degrees of freedom. See Kon (1984) and Campbell, Lo, and MacKinlay (1997). We discuss the Student's $t$-distribution in the reading on sampling and estimation.

**FIGURE 6     Units of Standard Deviation**

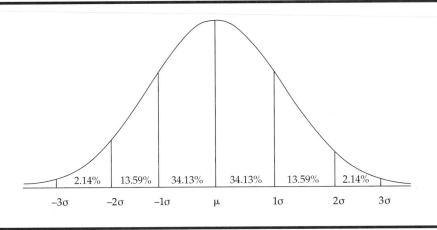

The intervals indicated are easy to remember but are only approximate for the stated probabilities. More-precise intervals are $\mu \pm 1.96\sigma$ for 95 percent of the observations and $\mu \pm 2.58\sigma$ for 99 percent of the observations.

In general, we do not observe the population mean or the population standard deviation of a distribution, so we need to estimate them.[21] We estimate the population mean, $\mu$, using the sample mean, $\overline{X}$ (sometimes denoted as $\hat{\mu}$), and estimate the population standard deviation, $\sigma$, using the sample standard deviation, $s$ (sometimes denoted as $\hat{\sigma}$).

There are as many different normal distributions as there are choices for mean ($\mu$) and variance ($\sigma^2$). We can answer all of the above questions in terms of any normal distribution. Spreadsheets, for example, have functions for the normal cdf for any specification of mean and variance. For the sake of efficiency, however, we would like to refer all probability statements to a single normal distribution. The standard normal distribution (the normal distribution with $\mu = 0$ and $\sigma = 1$) fills that role.

There are two steps in **standardizing** a random variable $X$: Subtract the mean of $X$ from $X$, then divide that result by the standard deviation of $X$. If we have a list of observations on a normal random variable, $X$, we subtract the mean from each observation to get a list of deviations from the mean, then divide each deviation by the standard deviation. The result is the standard normal random variable, $Z$. ($Z$ is the conventional symbol for a standard normal random variable.) If we have $X \sim N(\mu, \sigma^2)$ (read "$X$ follows the normal distribution with parameters $\mu$ and $\sigma^2$"), we standardize it using the formula

$$Z = (X - \mu)/\sigma \qquad \textbf{(9-4)}$$

Suppose we have a normal random variable, $X$, with $\mu = 5$ and $\sigma = 1.5$. We standardize $X$ with $Z = (X - 5)/1.5$. For example, a value $X = 9.5$ corresponds to a standardized value of 3, calculated as $Z = (9.5 - 5)/1.5 = 3$. The probability that we will observe a value as small as or smaller than 9.5 for $X \sim N(5, 1.5)$ is exactly the same as the probability that we will observe a value as small as or smaller than 3 for $Z \sim N(0, 1)$. We can answer all probability questions about $X$ using standardized values and probability tables for $Z$. We generally do not know

---

[21] A population is all members of a specified group, and the population mean is the arithmetic mean computed for the population. A sample is a subset of a population, and the sample mean is the arithmetic mean computed for the sample. For more information on these concepts, see the reading on statistical concepts and market returns.

the population mean and standard deviation, so we often use the sample mean $\overline{X}$ for $\mu$ and the sample standard deviation $s$ for $\sigma$.

Standard normal probabilities can also be computed with spreadsheets, statistical and econometric software, and programming languages. Tables of the cumulative distribution function for the standard normal random variable are in the back of this book. Table 5 shows an excerpt from those tables. $N(x)$ is a conventional notation for the cdf of a standard normal variable.[22]

**TABLE 5** $P(Z \leq x) = N(x)$ for $x \geq 0$ or $P(Z \leq z) = N(z)$ or $z \geq 0$

| x or z | 0 | 0.01 | 0.02 | 0.03 | 0.04 | 0.05 | 0.06 | 0.07 | 0.08 | 0.09 |
|---|---|---|---|---|---|---|---|---|---|---|
| **0.00** | 0.5000 | 0.5040 | 0.5080 | 0.5120 | 0.5160 | 0.5199 | 0.5239 | 0.5279 | 0.5319 | 0.5359 |
| **0.10** | 0.5398 | 0.5438 | 0.5478 | 0.5517 | 0.5557 | 0.5596 | 0.5636 | 0.5675 | 0.5714 | 0.5753 |
| **0.20** | 0.5793 | 0.5832 | 0.5871 | 0.5910 | 0.5948 | 0.5987 | 0.6026 | 0.6064 | 0.6103 | 0.6141 |
| **0.30** | 0.6179 | 0.6217 | 0.6255 | 0.6293 | 0.6331 | 0.6368 | 0.6406 | 0.6443 | 0.6480 | 0.6517 |
| **0.40** | 0.6554 | 0.6591 | 0.6628 | 0.6664 | 0.6700 | 0.6736 | 0.6772 | 0.6808 | 0.6844 | 0.6879 |
| **0.50** | 0.6915 | 0.6950 | 0.6985 | 0.7019 | 0.7054 | 0.7088 | 0.7123 | 0.7157 | 0.7190 | 0.7224 |

To find the probability that a standard normal variable is less than or equal to 0.24, for example, locate the row that contains 0.20, look at the 0.04 column, and find the entry 0.5948. Thus, $P(Z \leq 0.24) = 0.5948$ or 59.48 percent.

The following are some of the most frequently referenced values in the standard normal table:

▶ The 90th percentile point is 1.282: $P(Z \leq 1.282) = N(1.282) = 0.90$ or 90 percent, and 10 percent of values remain in the right tail.

▶ The 95th percentile point is 1.65: $P(Z \leq 1.65) = N(1.65) = 0.95$ or 95 percent, and 5 percent of values remain in the right tail. Note the difference between the use of a percentile point when dealing with one tail rather than two tails. Earlier, we used 1.65 standard deviations for the 90 percent confidence interval, where 5 percent of values lie outside that interval on each of the two sides. Here we use 1.65 because we are concerned with the 5 percent of values that lie only on one side, the right tail.

▶ The 99th percentile point is 2.327: $P(Z \leq 2.327) = N(2.327) = 0.99$ or 99 percent, and 1 percent of values remain in the right tail.

The tables that we give for the normal cdf include probabilities for $x \leq 0$. Many sources, however, give tables only for $x \geq 0$. How would one use such tables to find a normal probability? Because of the symmetry of the normal distribution, we can find all probabilities using tables of the cdf of the standard normal random variable, $P(Z \leq x) = N(x)$, for $x \geq 0$. The relations below are helpful for using tables for $x \geq 0$, as well as in other uses:

▶ For a non-negative number $x$, use $N(x)$ from the table. Note that for the probability to the right of $x$, we have $P(Z \geq x) = 1.0 - N(x)$.

---

[22] Another often-seen notation for the cdf of a standard normal variable is $\Phi(x)$.

▶ For a negative number $-x$, $N(-x) = 1.0 - N(x)$: Find $N(x)$ and subtract it from 1. All the area under the normal curve to the left of $x$ is $N(x)$. The balance, $1.0 - N(x)$, is the area and probability to the right of $x$. By the symmetry of the normal distribution around its mean, the area and the probability to the right of $x$ are equal to the area and the probability to the left of $-x$, $N(-x)$.

▶ For the probability to the right of $-x$, $P(Z \geq -x) = N(x)$.

## EXAMPLE 8

### Probabilities for a Common Stock Portfolio (2)

Assume the portfolio mean return is 12 percent and the standard deviation of return estimate is 22 percent per year.

You want to calculate the following probabilities, assuming that a normal distribution describes returns. (You can use the excerpt from the table of normal probabilities to answer these questions.)

1. What is the probability that portfolio return will exceed 20 percent?
2. What is the probability that portfolio return will be between 12 percent and 20 percent? In other words, what is $P(12\% \leq \text{Portfolio return} \leq 20\%)$?
3. You can buy a one-year T-bill that yields 5.5 percent. This yield is effectively a one-year risk-free interest rate. What is the probability that your portfolio's return will be equal to or less than the risk-free rate?

If $X$ is portfolio return, standardized portfolio return is $Z = (X - \overline{X})/s = (X - 12\%)/22\%$. We use this expression throughout the solutions.

**Solution to 1:** For $X = 20\%$, $Z = (20\% - 12\%)/22\% = 0.363636$. You want to find $P(Z > 0.363636)$. First note that $P(Z > x) = P(Z \geq x)$ because the normal is a continuous distribution. Recall that $P(Z \geq x) = 1.0 - P(Z \leq x)$ or $1 - N(x)$. Rounding 0.363636 to 0.36, according to the table, $N(0.36) = 0.6406$. Thus, $1 - 0.6406 = 0.3594$. The probability that portfolio return will exceed 20 percent is about 36 percent if your normality assumption is accurate.

**Solution to 2:** $P(12\% \leq \text{Portfolio return} \leq 20\%) = N(Z$ corresponding to 20%) $- N(Z$ corresponding to 12%). For the first term, $Z = (20\% - 12\%)/22\% = 0.36$ approximately, and $N(0.36) = 0.6406$ (as in Solution 1). To get the second term immediately, note that 12 percent is the mean, and for the normal distribution 50 percent of the probability lies on either side of the mean. Therefore, $N(Z$ corresponding to 12%) must equal 50 percent. So $P(12\% \leq \text{Portfolio return} \leq 20\%) = 0.6406 - 0.50 = 0.1406$ or approximately 14 percent.

**Solution to 3:** If $X$ is portfolio return, then we want to find $P(\text{Portfolio return} \leq 5.5\%)$. This question is more challenging than Parts 1 or 2, but when you have studied the solution below you will have a useful pattern for calculating other shortfall probabilities.

There are three steps, which involve standardizing the portfolio return: First, subtract the portfolio mean return from each side of the inequality: $P$(Portfolio return $- 12\% \le 5.5\% - 12\%$). Second, divide each side of the inequality by the standard deviation of portfolio return: $P$[(Portfolio return $- 12\%)/22\% \le (5.5\% - 12\%)/22\%$] = $P(Z \le -0.295455) = N(-0.295455)$. Third, recognize that on the left-hand side we have a standard normal variable, denoted by $Z$. As we pointed out above, $N(-x) = 1 - N(x)$. Rounding $-0.29545$ to $-0.30$ for use with the excerpted table, we have $N(-0.30) = 1 - N(0.30) = 1 - 0.6179 = 0.3821$, roughly 38 percent. The probability that your portfolio will underperform the one-year risk-free rate is about 38 percent.

We can get the answer above quickly by subtracting the mean portfolio return from 5.5 percent, dividing by the standard deviation of portfolio return, and evaluating the result ($-0.295455$) with the standard normal cdf.

## 3.3 Applications of the Normal Distribution

Modern portfolio theory (MPT) makes wide use of the idea that the value of investment opportunities can be meaningfully measured in terms of mean return and variance of return. In economic theory, **mean–variance analysis** holds exactly when investors are risk averse; when they choose investments so as to maximize expected utility, or satisfaction; and when either (1) returns are normally distributed, or (2) investors have quadratic utility functions.[23] Mean–variance analysis can still be useful, however—that is, it can hold approximately—when either assumption (1) or (2) is violated. Because practitioners prefer to work with observables such as returns, the proposition that returns are at least approximately normally distributed has played a key role in much of MPT.

Mean–variance analysis generally considers risk symmetrically in the sense that standard deviation captures variability both above and below the mean.[24] An alternative approach evaluates only downside risk. We discuss one such approach, safety-first rules, as it provides an excellent illustration of the application of normal distribution theory to practical investment problems. **Safety-first rules** focus on **shortfall risk**, the risk that portfolio value will fall below some minimum acceptable level over some time horizon. The risk that the assets in a defined benefit plan will fall below plan liabilities is an example of a shortfall risk.

Suppose an investor views any return below a level of $R_L$ as unacceptable. Roy's safety-first criterion states that the optimal portfolio minimizes the probability that portfolio return, $R_P$, falls below the threshold level, $R_L$.[25] In symbols, the investor's objective is to choose a portfolio that minimizes $P(R_P < R_L)$. When portfolio returns are normally distributed, we can calculate $P(R_P < R_L)$ using the number of standard deviations that $R_L$ lies below the expected portfolio return, $E(R_P)$. The portfolio for which $E(R_P) - R_L$ is largest relative to standard

---

[23] Utility functions are mathematical representations of attitudes toward risk and return.

[24] We shall discuss mean–variance analysis in detail in the readings on portfolio concepts.

[25] A. D. Roy (1952) introduced this criterion.

deviation minimizes $P(R_P < R_L)$. Therefore, if returns are normally distributed, the safety-first optimal portfolio *maximizes* the safety-first ratio (SFRatio):

$$\text{SFRatio} = [E(R_P) - R_L]/\sigma_P$$

The quantity $E(R_P) - R_L$ is the distance from the mean return to the shortfall level. Dividing this distance by $\sigma_P$ gives the distance in units of standard deviation. There are two steps in choosing among portfolios using Roy's criterion (assuming normality):[26]

1. Calculate each portfolio's SFRatio.
2. Choose the portfolio with the highest SFRatio.

For a portfolio with a given safety-first ratio, the probability that its return will be less than $R_L$ is $N(-\text{SFRatio})$, and the safety-first optimal portfolio has the lowest such probability. For example, suppose an investor's threshold return, $R_L$, is 2 percent. He is presented with two portfolios. Portfolio 1 has an expected return of 12 percent with a standard deviation of 15 percent. Portfolio 2 has an expected return of 14 percent with a standard deviation of 16 percent. The SFRatios are $0.667 = (12 - 2)/15$ and $0.75 = (14 - 2)/16$ for Portfolios 1 and 2, respectively. For the superior Portfolio 2, the probability that portfolio return will be less than 2 percent is $N(-0.75) = 1 - N(0.75) = 1 - 0.7734 = 0.227$ or about 23 percent, assuming that portfolio returns are normally distributed.

You may have noticed the similarity of SFRatio to the Sharpe ratio. If we substitute the risk-free rate, $R_F$, for the critical level $R_L$, the SFRatio becomes the Sharpe ratio. The safety-first approach provides a new perspective on the Sharpe ratio: When we evaluate portfolios using the Sharpe ratio, the portfolio with the highest Sharpe ratio is the one that minimizes the probability that portfolio return will be less than the risk-free rate (given a normality assumption).

### EXAMPLE 9

**The Safety-First Optimal Portfolio for a Client**

You are researching asset allocations for a client with an $800,000 portfolio. Although her investment objective is long-term growth, at the end of a year she may want to liquidate $30,000 of the portfolio to fund educational expenses. If that need arises, she would like to be able to take out the $30,000 without invading the initial capital of $800,000. Table 6 shows three alternative allocations.

**TABLE 6  Mean and Standard Deviation for Three Allocations (in Percent)**

|                              | A  | B  | C  |
|------------------------------|----|----|----|
| Expected annual return       | 25 | 11 | 14 |
| Standard deviation of return | 27 | 8  | 20 |

---

[26] If there is an asset offering a risk-free return over the time horizon being considered, and if $R_L$ is less than or equal to that risk-free rate, then it is optimal to be fully invested in the risk-free asset. Holding the risk-free asset in this case eliminates the chance that the threshold return is not met.

Address these questions (assume normality for Parts 2 and 3):

1. Given the client's desire not to invade the $800,000 principal, what is the shortfall level, $R_L$? Use this shortfall level to answer Part 2.

2. According to the safety-first criterion, which of the three allocations is the best?

3. What is the probability that the return on the safety-first optimal portfolio will be less than the shortfall level?

**Solution to 1:** Because $30,000/$800,000 is 3.75 percent, for any return less than 3.75 percent the client will need to invade principal if she takes out $30,000. So $R_L$ = 3.75 percent.

**Solution to 2:** To decide which of the three allocations is safety-first optimal, select the alternative with the highest ratio $[E(R_P) - R_L]/\sigma_P$:

    Allocation A: $0.787037 = (25 - 3.75)/27$

    Allocation B: $0.90625 = (11 - 3.75)/8$

    Allocation C: $0.5125 = (14 - 3.75)/20$

Allocation B, with the largest ratio (0.90625), is the best alternative according to the safety-first criterion.

**Solution to 3:** To answer this question, note that $P(R_B < 3.75) = N(-0.90625)$. We can round 0.90625 to 0.91 for use with tables of the standard normal cdf. First, we calculate $N(-0.91) = 1 - N(0.91) = 1 - 0.8186 = 0.1814$ or about 18.1 percent. Using a spreadsheet function for the standard normal cdf on $-0.90625$ without rounding, we get 18.24 percent or about 18.2 percent. The safety-first optimal portfolio has a roughly 18 percent chance of not meeting a 3.75 percent return threshold.

    Several points are worth noting. First, if the inputs were even slightly different, we could get a different ranking. For example, if the mean return on B were 10 rather than 11 percent, A would be superior to B. Second, if meeting the 3.75 percent return threshold were a necessity rather than a wish, $830,000 in one year could be modeled as a liability. Fixed income strategies such as cash flow matching could be used to offset or immunize the $830,000 quasi-liability.

    Roy's safety-first rule was the earliest approach to addressing shortfall risk. The standard mean–variance portfolio selection process can also accommodate a shortfall risk constraint.[27]

---

[27] See Leibowitz and Henriksson (1989), for example.

In many investment contexts besides Roy's safety-first criterion, we use the normal distribution to estimate a probability. For example, Kolb, Gay, and Hunter (1985) developed an expression based on the standard normal distribution for the probability that a futures trader will exhaust his liquidity because of losses in a futures contract. Another arena in which the normal distribution plays an important role is financial risk management. Financial institutions such as investment banks, security dealers, and commercial banks have formal systems to measure and control financial risk at various levels, from trading positions to the overall risk for the firm.[28] Two mainstays in managing financial risk are Value at Risk (VAR) and stress testing/scenario analysis. **Stress testing/scenario analysis**, a complement to VAR, refers to a set of techniques for estimating losses in extremely unfavorable combinations of events or scenarios. **Value at Risk (VAR)** is a money measure of the minimum value of losses expected over a specified time period (for example, a day, a quarter, or a year) at a given level of probability (often 0.05 or 0.01). Suppose we specify a one-day time horizon and a level of probability of 0.05, which would be called a 95 percent one-day VAR.[29] If this VAR equaled €5 million for a portfolio, there would be a 0.05 probability that the portfolio would lose €5 million or more in a single day (assuming our assumptions were correct). One of the basic approaches to estimating VAR, the variance–covariance or analytical method, assumes that returns follow a normal distribution. For more information on VAR, see Chance (2003).

## 3.4 The Lognormal Distribution

Closely related to the normal distribution, the lognormal distribution is widely used for modeling the probability distribution of share and other asset prices. For example, the lognormal appears in the Black–Scholes–Merton option pricing model. The Black–Scholes–Merton model assumes that the price of the asset underlying the option is lognormally distributed.

A random variable $Y$ follows a lognormal distribution if its natural logarithm, $\ln Y$, is normally distributed. The reverse is also true: If the natural logarithm of random variable $Y$, $\ln Y$, is normally distributed, then $Y$ follows a lognormal distribution. If you think of the term lognormal as "the log is normal," you will have no trouble remembering this relationship.

The two most noteworthy observations about the lognormal distribution are that it is bounded below by 0 and it is skewed to the right (it has a long right tail). Note these two properties in the graphs of the pdfs of two lognormal distributions in Figure 7. Asset prices are bounded from below by 0. In practice, the lognormal distribution has been found to be a usefully accurate description of the distribution of prices for many financial assets. On the other hand, the normal distribution is often a good approximation for returns. For this reason, both distributions are very important for finance professionals.

Like the normal distribution, the lognormal distribution is completely described by two parameters. Unlike the other distributions we have considered, a

---

[28] **Financial risk** is risk relating to asset prices and other financial variables. The contrast is to other, nonfinancial risks (for example, relating to operations and technology), which require different tools to manage.

[29] In 95 percent one-day VAR, the 95 percent refers to the confidence in the value of VAR and is equal to $1 - 0.05$; this is a traditional way to state VAR.

**FIGURE 7   Two Lognormal Distributions**

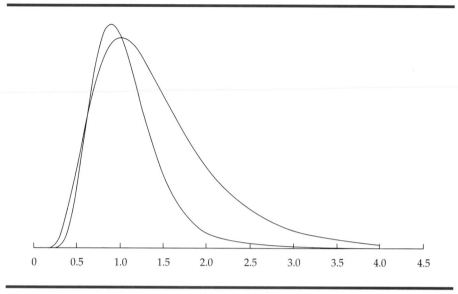

lognormal distribution is defined in terms of the parameters of a *different* distribution. The two parameters of a lognormal distribution are the mean and standard deviation (or variance) of its associated normal distribution: the mean and variance of ln $Y$, given that $Y$ is lognormal. Remember, we must keep track of two sets of means and standard deviations (or variances): the mean and standard deviation (or variance) of the associated normal distribution (these are the parameters), and the mean and standard deviation (or variance) of the lognormal variable itself.

The expressions for the mean and variance of the lognormal variable itself are challenging. Suppose a normal random variable $X$ has expected value $\mu$ and variance $\sigma^2$. Define $Y = \exp(X)$. Remember that the operation indicated by $\exp(X)$ or $e^X$ is the opposite operation from taking logs.[30] Because ln $Y =$ ln $[\exp(X)] = X$ is normal (we assume $X$ is normal), $Y$ is lognormal. What is the expected value of $Y = \exp(X)$? A guess might be that the expected value of $Y$ is $\exp(\mu)$. The expected value is actually $\exp(\mu + 0.50\sigma^2)$, which is larger than $\exp(\mu)$ by a factor of $\exp(0.50\sigma^2) > 1$.[31] To get some insight into this concept, think of what happens if we increase $\sigma^2$. The distribution spreads out; it can spread upward, but it cannot spread downward past 0. As a result, the center of its distribution is pushed to the right—the distribution's mean increases.[32]

The expressions for the mean and variance of a lognormal variable are summarized below, where $\mu$ and $\sigma^2$ are the mean and variance of the associated normal distribution (refer to these expressions as needed, rather than memorizing them):

▶ Mean ($\mu_L$) of a lognormal random variable $= \exp(\mu + 0.50\sigma^2)$

▶ Variance ($\sigma_L^2$) of a lognormal random variable $= \exp(2\mu + \sigma^2) \times [\exp(\sigma^2) - 1]$

---

[30] The quantity $e \approx 2.7182818$.

[31] Note that $\exp(0.50\sigma^2) > 1$ because $\sigma^2 > 0$.

[32] Luenberger (1998) is the source of this explanation.

We now explore the relationship between the distribution of stock return and stock price. In the following we show that if a stock's continuously compounded return is normally distributed, then future stock price is necessarily lognormally distributed.[33] Furthermore, we show that stock price may be well described by the lognormal distribution even when continuously compounded returns do not follow a normal distribution. These results provide the theoretical foundation for using the lognormal distribution to model prices.

To outline the presentation that follows, we first show that the stock price at some future time $T$, $S_T$, equals the current stock price, $S_0$, multiplied by $e$ raised to power $r_{0,T}$, the continuously compounded return from 0 to $T$; this relationship is expressed as $S_T = S_0 \exp(r_{0,T})$. We then show that we can write $r_{0,T}$ as the sum of shorter-term continuously compounded returns and that if these shorter-period returns are normally distributed, then $r_{0,T}$ is normally distributed (given certain assumptions) or approximately normally distributed (not making those assumptions). As $S_T$ is proportional to the log of a normal random variable, $S_T$ is lognormal.

To supply a framework for our discussion, suppose we have a series of equally spaced observations on stock price: $S_0, S_1, S_2, \ldots, S_T$. Current stock price, $S_0$, is a known quantity and so is nonrandom. The future prices (such as $S_1$), however, are random variables. The **price relative**, $S_1/S_0$, is an ending price, $S_1$, over a beginning price, $S_0$; it is equal to 1 plus the holding period return on the stock from $t = 0$ to $t = 1$:

$$S_1/S_0 = 1 + R_{0,1}$$

For example, if $S_0 = \$30$ and $S_1 = \$34.50$, then $S_1/S_0 = \$34.50/\$30 = 1.15$. Therefore, $R_{0,1} = 0.15$ or 15 percent. In general, price relatives have the form

$$S_{t+1}/S_t = 1 + R_{t,t+1}$$

where $R_{t,t+1}$ is the rate of return from $t$ to $t + 1$.

An important concept is the continuously compounded return associated with a holding period return such as $R_{0,1}$. The **continuously compounded return** associated with a holding period is the natural logarithm of 1 plus that holding period return, or equivalently, the natural logarithm of the ending price over the beginning price (the price relative).[34] For example, if we observe a one-week holding period return of 0.04, the equivalent continuously compounded return, called the one-week continuously compounded return, is $\ln(1.04) = 0.039221$; €1.00 invested for one week at 0.039221 continuously compounded gives €1.04, equivalent to a 4 percent one-week holding period return. The continuously compounded return from $t$ to $t + 1$ is

$$r_{t,t+1} = \ln(S_{t+1}/S_t) = \ln(1 + R_{t,t+1}) \tag{9-5}$$

For our example, $r_{0,1} = \ln(S_1/S_0) = \ln(1 + R_{0,1}) = \ln(\$34.50/\$30) = \ln(1.15) = 0.139762$. Thus, 13.98 percent is the continuously compounded return from $t = 0$ to $t = 1$. The continuously compounded return is smaller than the

---

[33] Continuous compounding treats time as essentially continuous or unbroken, in contrast to discrete compounding, which treats time as advancing in discrete finite intervals. Continuously compounded returns are the model for returns in so-called **continuous time** finance models such as the Black–Scholes–Merton option pricing model. See the reading on the time value of money for more information on compounding.

[34] In this reading we use lowercase $r$ to refer specifically to continuously compounded returns.

associated holding period return. If our investment horizon extends from $t = 0$ to $t = T$, then the continuously compounded return to $T$ is

$$r_{0,T} = \ln (S_T/S_0)$$

Applying the function exp to both sides of the equation, we have $\exp(r_{0,T}) = \exp[\ln (S_T/S_0)] = S_T/S_0$, so

$$S_T = S_0 \exp(r_{0,T})$$

We can also express $S_T/S_0$ as the product of price relatives:

$$S_T/S_0 = (S_T/S_{T-1})(S_{T-1}/S_{T-2}) \ldots (S_1/S_0)$$

Taking logs of both sides of this equation, we find that continuously compounded return to time $T$ is the sum of the one-period continuously compounded returns:

$$r_{0,T} = r_{T-1,T} + r_{T-2,T-1} + \ldots + r_{0,1} \qquad \textbf{(9-6)}$$

Using holding period returns to find the ending value of a \$1 investment involves the multiplication of quantities (1 + holding period return). Using continuously compounded returns involves addition.

A key assumption in many investment applications is that returns are **independently and identically distributed (IID)**. Independence captures the proposition that investors cannot predict future returns using past returns (i.e., weak-form market efficiency). Identical distribution captures the assumption of stationarity.[35]

Assume that the one-period continuously compounded returns (such as $r_{0,1}$) are IID random variables with mean $\mu$ and variance $\sigma^2$ (but making no normality or other distributional assumption). Then

$$E(r_{0,T}) = E(r_{T-1,T}) + E(r_{T-2,T-1}) + \ldots + E(r_{0,1}) = \mu T \qquad \textbf{(9-7)}$$

(we add up $\mu$ for a total of $T$ times) and

$$\sigma^2(r_{0,T}) = \sigma^2 T \qquad \textbf{(9-8)}$$

(as a consequence of the independence assumption). The variance of the $T$ holding period continuously compounded return is $T$ multiplied by the variance of the one-period continuously compounded return; also, $\sigma(r_{0,T}) = \sigma\sqrt{T}$. If the one-period continuously compounded returns on the right-hand side of Equation 9-6 are normally distributed, then the $T$ holding period continuously compounded return, $r_{0,T}$, is also normally distributed with mean $\mu T$ and variance $\sigma^2 T$. This relationship is so because a linear combination of normal random variables is also normal. But even if the one-period continuously compounded returns are not normal, their sum, $r_{0,T}$, is approximately normal according to a result in statistics known as the central limit theorem.[36] Now compare $S_T = S_0\exp(r_{0,T})$ to $Y = \exp(X)$, where $X$ is normal and $Y$ is lognormal (as we discussed above).

---

[35] Stationarity implies that the mean and variance of return do not change from period to period.

[36] We mentioned the central limit theorem earlier in our discussion of the normal distribution. To give a somewhat fuller statement of it, according to the central limit theorem the sum (as well as the mean) of a set of independent, identically distributed random variables with finite variances is normally distributed, whatever distribution the random variables follow. We discuss the central limit theorem in the reading on sampling.

Clearly, we can model future stock price $S_T$ as a lognormal random variable because $r_{0,T}$ should be at least approximately normal. This assumption of normally distributed returns is the basis in theory for the lognormal distribution as a model for the distribution of prices of shares and other assets.

Continuously compounded returns play a role in many option pricing models, as mentioned earlier. An estimate of volatility is crucial for using option pricing models such as the Black–Scholes–Merton model. **Volatility** measures the standard deviation of the continuously compounded returns on the underlying asset.[37] In practice, we very often estimate volatility using a historical series of continuously compounded daily returns. We gather a set of daily holding period returns and then use Equation 9-5 to convert them into continuously compounded daily returns. We then compute the standard deviation of the continuously compounded daily returns and annualize that number using Equation 9-8.[38] (By convention, volatility is stated as an annualized measure.)[39] Example 10 illustrates the estimation of volatility for the shares of Michelin.

### EXAMPLE 10

#### Volatility as Used in Option Pricing Models

Suppose you are researching Michelin (Euronext: MICP.PA) and are interested in Michelin's price action in a week in which a number of international events affected stock markets. You decide to use volatility as a measure of the variability of Michelin shares during that week. Table 7 shows closing prices during that week.

| TABLE 7 Michelin Daily Closing Prices | |
| --- | --- |
| **Date** | **Closing Price** |
| 31 March 2003 | €25.20 |
| 01 April 2003 | €25.21 |
| 02 April 2003 | €25.52 |
| 03 April 2003 | €26.10 |
| 04 April 2003 | €26.14 |

*Source*: fr.finance.yahoo.com.

---

[37] Volatility is also called the instantaneous standard deviation, and as such is denoted $\sigma$. The underlying asset, or simply the underlying, is the asset underlying the option. For more information on these concepts, see Chance (2003).

[38] To compute the standard deviation of a set or sample of $n$ returns, we sum the squared deviation of each return from the mean return and then divide that sum by $n - 1$. The result is the sample variance. Taking the square root of the sample variance gives the sample standard deviation. To review the calculation of standard deviation, see the reading on statistical concepts and market returns.

[39] Annualizing is often done on the basis of 250 days in a year, the approximate number of days markets are open for trading. The 250-day number may lead to a better estimate of volatility than the 365-day number. Thus if daily volatility were 0.01, we would state volatility (on an annual basis) as $0.01\sqrt{250} = 0.1581$.

Use the data in Table 7 to do the following:

1. Estimate the volatility of Michelin shares. (Annualize volatility based on 250 days in a year.)

2. Identify the probability distribution for Michelin share prices if continuously compounded daily returns follow the normal distribution.

**Solution to 1:** First, use Equation 9-5 to calculate the continuously compounded daily returns; then find their standard deviation in the usual way. (In the calculation of sample variance to get sample standard deviation, use a divisor of 1 less than the sample size.)

$\ln(25.21/25.20) = 0.000397$, $\ln(25.52/25.21) = 0.012222$

$\ln(26.10/25.52) = 0.022473$, $\ln(26.14/26.10) = 0.001531$

Sum = 0.036623, Mean = 0.009156, Variance = 0.000107, Standard Deviation = 0.010354

The standard deviation of continuously compounded daily returns is 0.010354. Equation 9-8 states that $\hat{\sigma}(r_{0,T}) = \hat{\sigma}\sqrt{T}$. In this example, $\hat{\sigma}$ is the sample standard deviation of one-period continuously compounded returns. Thus, $\hat{\sigma}$ refers to 0.010354. We want to annualize, so the horizon $T$ corresponds to one year. As $\hat{\sigma}$ is in days, we set $T$ equal to the number of trading days in a year (250).

We find that annualized volatility for Michelin stock that week was 16.4 percent, calculated as $0.010354\sqrt{250} = 0.163711$.

Note that the sample mean, 0.009156, is a possible estimate of the mean, $\mu$, of the continuously compounded one-period or daily returns. The sample mean can be translated into an estimate of the expected continuously compounded annual return using Equation 9-7: $\hat{\mu}T = 0.009156(250)$ (using 250 to be consistent with the calculation of volatility). But four observations are far too few to estimate expected returns. The variability in the daily returns overwhelms any information about expected return in a series this short.

**Solution to 2:** Michelin share prices should follow the lognormal distribution if the continuously compounded daily returns on Michelin shares follow the normal distribution.

We have shown that the distribution of stock price is lognormal, given certain assumptions. What are the mean and variance of $S_T$ if $S_T$ follows the lognormal distribution? Earlier in this section, we gave bullet-point expressions for the mean and variance of a lognormal random variable. In the bullet-point expressions, the $\hat{\mu}$ and $\hat{\sigma}^2$ would refer, in the context of this discussion, to the mean and variance of the $T$ horizon (not the one-period) continuously compounded returns (assumed to follow a normal distribution), compatible with the horizon of $S_T$.[40] Related to the use of mean and variance (or standard deviation), earlier in this reading we

---

[40] The expression for the mean is $E(S_T) = S_0 \exp[E(r_{0,T}) + 0.5\sigma^2(r_{0,T})]$, for example.

used those quantities to construct intervals in which we expect to find a certain percentage of the observations of a normally distributed random variable. Those intervals were symmetric about the mean. Can we state similar, symmetric intervals for a lognormal random variable? Unfortunately, we cannot. Because the lognormal distribution is not symmetric, such intervals are more complicated than for the normal distribution, and we will not discuss this specialist topic here.[41]

Finally, we have presented the relation between the mean and variance of continuously compounded returns associated with different time horizons (see Equations 9-7 and 9-8), but how are the means and variances of holding period returns and continuously compounded returns related? As analysts, we typically think in terms of holding period returns rather than continuously compounded returns, and we may desire to convert means and standard deviations of holding period returns to means and standard deviations of continuously compounded returns for an option application, for example. To effect such conversions (and those in the other direction, from a continuous compounding to a holding period basis), we can use the expressions in Ferguson (1993).

## 4     MONTE CARLO SIMULATION

With an understanding of probability distributions, we are now prepared to learn about a computer-based technique in which probability distributions play an integral role. The technique is called Monte Carlo simulation. **Monte Carlo simulation** in finance involves the use of a computer to represent the operation of a complex financial system. A characteristic feature of Monte Carlo simulation is the generation of a large number of random samples from a specified probability distribution or distributions to represent the role of risk in the system.

Monte Carlo simulation has several quite distinct uses. One use is in planning. Stanford University researcher Sam Savage provided the following neat picture of that role: "What is the last thing you do before you climb on a ladder? You shake it, and that is Monte Carlo simulation."[42] Just as shaking a ladder helps us assess the risks in climbing it, Monte Carlo simulation allows us to experiment with a proposed policy before actually implementing it. For example, investment performance can be evaluated with reference to a benchmark or a liability. Defined benefit pension plans often invest assets with reference to plan liabilities. Pension liabilities are a complex random process. In a Monte Carlo asset–liability financial planning study, the functioning of pension assets and liabilities is simulated over time, given assumptions about how assets are invested, the work force, and other variables. A key specification in this and all Monte Carlo simulations is the probability distributions of the various sources of risk (including interest rates and security market returns, in this case). The implications of different investment policy decisions on the plan's funded status can be assessed through simulated time. The experiment can be repeated for another set of assumptions. We can view Example 11 below as coming under this heading. In that example, market return series are not long enough to address researchers' questions on stock market timing, so the researchers simulate market returns to find answers to their questions.

Monte Carlo simulation is also widely used to develop estimates of VAR. In this application, we simulate the portfolio's profit and loss performance for a

---

[41] See Hull (2003) for a discussion of lognormal confidence intervals.

[42] *Business Week,* 22 January 2001.

specified time horizon. Repeated trials within the simulation (each trial involving a draw of random observations from a probability distribution) produce a frequency distribution for changes in portfolio value. The point that defines the cutoff for the least favorable 5 percent of simulated changes is an estimate of 95 percent VAR, for example.

In an extremely important use, Monte Carlo simulation is a tool for valuing complex securities, particularly European-style options, for which no analytic pricing formula is available.[43] For other securities, such as mortgage-backed securities with complex embedded options, Monte Carlo simulation is also an important modeling resource.

Researchers use Monte Carlo simulation to test their models and tools. How critical is a particular assumption to the performance of a model? Because we control the assumptions when we do a simulation, we can run the model through a Monte Carlo simulation to examine a model's sensitivity to a change in our assumptions.

To understand the technique of Monte Carlo simulation, let us present the process as a series of steps.[44] To illustrate the steps, we take the case of using Monte Carlo simulation to value a type of option for which no analytic pricing formula is available, an Asian call option on a stock. An **Asian call option** is a European-style option with a value at maturity equal to the difference between the stock price at maturity and the average stock price during the life of the option, or $0, whichever is greater. For instance, if the final stock price is $34 with an average value of $31 over the life of the option, the value of the option at maturity is $3 (the greater of $34 − $31 = $3 and $0). Steps 1 through 3 of the process describe specifying the simulation; Steps 4 through 7 describe running the simulation.

1. Specify the quantities of interest (option value, for example, or the funded status of a pension plan) in terms of underlying variables. The underlying variable or variables could be stock price for an equity option, the market value of pension assets, or other variables relating to the pension benefit obligation for a pension plan. Specify the starting values of the underlying variables.

   To illustrate the steps, we are using the case of valuing an Asian call option on stock. We use $C_{iT}$ to represent the value of the option at maturity $T$. The subscript $i$ in $C_{iT}$ indicates that $C_{iT}$ is a value resulting from the $i$th **simulation trial**, each simulation trial involving a drawing of random values (an iteration of Step 4).

2. Specify a time grid. Take the horizon in terms of calendar time and split it into a number of subperiods, say $K$ in total. Calendar time divided by the number of subperiods, $K$, is the time increment, $\Delta t$.

3. Specify distributional assumptions for the risk factors that drive the underlying variables. For example, stock price is the underlying variable for the Asian call, so we need a model for stock price movement. Say we choose the following model for changes in stock price, where $Z_k$ stands for the standard normal random variable:

$$\Delta \text{ (Stock price)} = (\mu \times \text{Prior stock price} \times \Delta t) + (\sigma \times \text{Prior stock price} \times Z_k)$$

---

[43] A **European-style option** or **European option** is an option exercisable only at maturity.

[44] The steps should be viewed as providing an overview of Monte Carlo simulation rather than as a detailed recipe for implementing a Monte Carlo simulation in its many varied applications.

In the way that we are using the term, $Z_k$ is a risk factor in the simulation. Through our choice of $\mu$ and $\sigma$, we control the distribution of stock price. Although this example has one risk factor, a given simulation may have multiple risk factors.

4. Using a computer program or spreadsheet function, draw $K$ random values of each risk factor. In our example, the spreadsheet function would produce a draw of $K$ values of the standard normal variable $Z_k$: $Z_1, Z_2, Z_3, \ldots, Z_K$.

5. Calculate the underlying variables using the random observations generated in Step 4. Using the above model of stock price dynamics, the result is $K$ observations on changes in stock price. An additional calculation is needed to convert those changes into $K$ stock prices (using initial stock price, which is given). Another calculation produces the average stock price during the life of the option (the sum of $K$ stock prices divided by $K$).

6. Compute the quantities of interest. In our example, the first calculation is the value of an Asian call at maturity, $C_{iT}$. A second calculation discounts this terminal value back to the present to get the call value as of today, $C_{i0}$. We have completed one simulation trial. (The subscript $i$ in $C_{i0}$ stands for the $i$th simulation trial, as it does in $C_{iT}$.) In a Monte Carlo simulation, a running tabulation is kept of statistics relating to the distribution of the quantities of interest, including their mean value and standard deviation, over the simulation trials to that point.

7. Iteratively go back to Step 4 until a specified number of trials, $I$, is completed. Finally, produce statistics for the simulation. The key value for our example is the mean value of $C_{i0}$ for the total number of simulation trials. This mean value is the Monte Carlo estimate of the value of the Asian call.

How many simulation trials should be specified? In general, we need to increase the number of trials by a factor of 100 to get each extra digit of accuracy. Depending on the problem, tens of thousands of trials may be needed to obtain accuracy to two decimal places (as required for option value, for example). Conducting a large number of trials is not necessarily a problem, given today's computing power. The number of trials needed can be reduced using variance reduction procedures, a topic outside the scope of this reading.[45]

In Step 4 of our example, a computer function produced a set of random observations on a standard normal random variable. Recall that for a uniform distribution, all possible numbers are equally likely. The term **random number generator** refers to an algorithm that produces uniformly distributed random numbers between 0 and 1. In the context of computer simulations, the term **random number** refers to an observation drawn from a uniform distribution.[46] For other distributions, the term "random observation" is used in this context.

It is a remarkable fact that random observations from any distribution can be produced using the uniform random variable with endpoints 0 and 1. To see why this is so, consider the inverse transformation method of producing random

---

[45] For details on this and other technical aspects of Monte Carlo simulation, see Hillier and Lieberman (2000).

[46] The numbers that random number generators produce depend on a seed or initial value. If the same seed is fed to the same generator, it will produce the same sequence. All sequences eventually repeat. Because of this predictability, the technically correct name for the numbers produced by random number generators is **pseudo-random numbers**. Pseudo-random numbers have sufficient qualities of randomness for most practical purposes.

observations. Suppose we are interested in obtaining random observations for a random variable, $X$, with cumulative distribution function $F(x)$. Recall that $F(x)$ evaluated at $x$ is a number between 0 and 1. Suppose a random outcome of this random variable is 3.21 and that $F(3.21) = 0.25$ or 25 percent. Define an inverse of $F$, call it $F^{-1}$, that can do the following: Substitute the probability 0.25 into $F^{-1}$ and it returns the random outcome 3.21. In other words, $F^{-1}(0.25) = 3.21$. To generate random observations on $X$, the steps are (1) generate a uniform random number, $r$, between 0 and 1 using the random number generator and (2) evaluate $F^{-1}(r)$ to obtain a random observation on $X$. Random observation generation is a field of study in itself, and we have briefly discussed the inverse transformation method here just to illustrate a point. As a generalist you do not need to address the technical details of converting random numbers into random observations, but you do need to know that random observations from any distribution can be generated using a uniform random variable.

In Examples 11 and 12, we give an application of Monte Carlo simulation to a question of great interest to investment practice: the potential gains from market timing.

## EXAMPLE 11

### Potential Gains from Market Timing: A Monte Carlo Simulation (1)

All active investors want to achieve superior performance. One possible source of superior performance is market timing ability. How accurate does an investor need to be as a bull- and bear-market forecaster for market timing to be profitable? What size gains compared with a buy-and-hold strategy accrue to a given level of accuracy? Because of the variability in asset returns, a huge amount of return data is needed to find statistically reliable answers to these questions. Chua, Woodward, and To (1987) thus selected Monte Carlo simulation to address the potential gains from market timing. They were interested in the perspective of a Canadian investor.

To understand their study, suppose that at the beginning of a year, an investor predicts that the next year will see either a bull market or bear market. If the prediction is *bull market*, the investor puts all her money in stocks and earns the market return for that year. On the other hand, if the prediction is *bear market*, the investor holds T-bills and earns the T-bill return. After the fact, a market is categorized as *bull market* if the stock market return, $R_{Mt}$, minus T-bill return, $R_{Ft}$, is positive for the year; otherwise, the market is classed as *bear market*. The investment results of a market timer can be compared with those of a buy-and-hold investor. A buy-and-hold investor earns the market return every year. For Chua et al., one quantity of interest was the gain from market timing. They defined this quantity as the market timer's average return minus the average return to a buy-and-hold investor.

To simulate market returns, Chua et al. generated 10,000 random standard normal observations, $Z_t$. At the time of the study, Canadian stocks had a historical mean annual return of 12.95 percent with a standard deviation of 18.30 percent. To reflect these parameters, the simulated market returns are $R_{Mt} = 0.1830Z_t + 0.1295$, $t = 1, 2, \ldots, 10,000$.

Using a second set of 10,000 random standard normal observations, historical return parameters for Canadian T-bills, as well as the historical correlation of T-bill and stock returns, the authors generated 10,000 T-bill returns.

An investor can have different skills in forecasting bull and bear markets. Chua et al. characterized market timers by accuracy in forecasting bull markets and accuracy in forecasting bear markets. For example, bull market forecasting accuracy of 50 percent means that when the timer forecasts *bull market* for the next year, she is right just half the time, indicating no skill. Suppose an investor has 60 percent accuracy in forecasting *bull market* and 80 percent accuracy in forecasting *bear market* (a 60–80 timer). We can simulate how an investor would fare. After generating the first observation on $R_{Mt} - R_{Ft}$, we know whether that observation is a bull or bear market. If the observation is *bull market,* then 0.60 (forecast accuracy for bull markets) is compared with a random number (between 0 and 1). If the random number is less than 0.60, which occurs with a 60 percent probability, then the market timer is assumed to have correctly predicted *bull market* and her return for that first observation is the market return. If the random number is greater than 0.60, then the market timer is assumed to have made an error and predicted *bear market;* her return for that observation is the risk-free rate. In a similar fashion, if that first observation is *bear market,* the timer has an 80 percent chance of being right in forecasting *bear market* based on a random number draw. In either case, her return is compared with the market return to record her gain versus a buy-and-hold strategy. That process is one simulation trial. The simulated mean return earned by the timer is the average return earned by the timer over all trials in the simulation.

To increase our understanding of the process, consider a hypothetical Monte Carlo simulation with four trials for the 60–80 timer (who, to reiterate, has 60 percent accuracy in forecasting bull markets and 80 percent accuracy in forecasting bear markets). Table 8 gives data for the simulation. Let us look at Trials 1 and 2. In Trial 1, the first random number drawn leads to a market return of 0.121. Because the market return, 0.121, exceeded the T-bill return, 0.050, we have a bull market. We generate a random number, 0.531, which we then compare with the timer's bull market accuracy, 0.60. Because 0.531 is less than 0.60, the timer is assumed to have made a correct bull market forecast and thus to have invested in stocks. Thus the timer earns the stock market return, 0.121, for that trial. In the second trial we observe another bull market, but because the random number 0.725 is greater than 0.60, the timer is assumed to have made an error and predicted a bear market; therefore, the timer earned the T-bill return, 0.081, rather than higher stock market return.

| TABLE 8 | Hypothetical Simulation for a 60–80 Market Timer | | | | | |
|---|---|---|---|---|---|---|

| | After Draws for $Z_t$ and for the T-bill Return | | | Simulation Results | | |
|---|---|---|---|---|---|---|
| Trial | $R_{Mt}$ | $R_{Ft}$ | Bull or Bear Market? | Value of $X$ | Timer's Prediction Correct? | Return Earned by Timer |
| 1 | 0.121 | 0.050 | Bull | 0.531 | Yes | 0.121 |
| 2 | 0.092 | 0.081 | Bull | 0.725 | No | 0.081 |
| 3 | −0.020 | 0.034 | Bear | 0.786 | Yes | 0.034 |
| 4 | 0.052 | 0.055 | *A* | 0.901 | *B* | *C* |
| | | | | | | $\bar{R} = D$ |

*Note*: $\bar{R}$ is the mean return earned by the timer over the four simulation trials.

Using the data in Table 8, determine the values of *A*, *B*, *C*, and *D*.

**Solution:** The value of *A* is *Bear* because the stock market return was less than the T-bill return in Trial 4. The value of *B* is *No*. Because we observe a bear market, we compare the random number 0.901 with 0.80, the timer's bear-market forecasting accuracy. Because 0.901 is greater than 0.8, the timer is assumed to have made an error. The value of *C* is 0.052, the return on the stock market, because the timer made an error and invested in the stock market and earned 0.052 rather than the higher T-bill return of 0.055. The value of *D* is $\bar{R} = (0.121 + 0.081 + 0.034 + 0.052) = 0.288/4 = 0.072$. Note that we could calculate other statistics besides the mean, such as the standard deviation of the returns earned by the timer over the four trials in the simulation.

## EXAMPLE 12

### Potential Gains from Market Timing: A Monte Carlo Simulation (2)

Having discussed the plan of the Chua et al. study and illustrated the method for a hypothetical Monte Carlo simulation with four trials, we conclude our presentation of the study.

The hypothetical simulation in Example 11 had four trials, far too few to reach statistically precise conclusions. The simulation of Chua et al. incorporated 10,000 trials. Chua et al. specified bull- and bear-market prediction skill levels of 50, 60, 70, 80, 90, and 100 percent. Table 9 presents a very small excerpt from their simulation results for the no transaction costs case (transaction costs were also examined). Reading across the row, the timer with 60 percent bull market and 80 percent bear market forecasting accuracy had a mean annual gain from market timing of −1.12 percent per year. On average, the buy-and-hold investor out-earned this skillful timer by 1.12 percentage points. There was substantial variability in gains across the simulation trials, however: The standard deviation of the gain was 14.77 percent, so in many trials (but not on average) the gain was positive. Row 3 (win/loss) is the ratio of profitable switches between stocks and T-bills to unprofitable switches. This ratio was a favorable 1.2070 for the 60–80 timer. (When transaction costs were considered, however, fewer switches are profitable: The win–loss ratio was 0.5832 for the 60–80 timer.)

**TABLE 9  Gains from Stock Market Timing (No Transaction Costs)**

| Bull Market Accuracy (%) | | Bear Market Accuracy (%) | | | | | |
| --- | --- | --- | --- | --- | --- | --- | --- |
| | | 50 | 60 | 70 | 80 | 90 | 100 |
| 60 | Mean (%) | −2.50 | −1.99 | −1.57 | −1.12 | −0.68 | −0.22 |
| | S.D. (%) | 13.65 | 14.11 | 14.45 | 14.77 | 15.08 | 15.42 |
| | Win/Loss | 0.7418 | 0.9062 | 1.0503 | 1.2070 | 1.3496 | 1.4986 |

*Source*: Chua, Woodward, and To (1987), Table II (excerpt).

The authors concluded that the cost of not being invested in the market during bull market years is high. Because a buy-and-hold investor never misses a bull market year, she has 100 percent forecast accuracy for bull markets (at the cost of 0 percent accuracy for bear markets). Given their definitions and assumptions, the authors also concluded that successful market timing requires a minimum accuracy of 80 percent in forecasting both bull and bear markets. Market timing is a continuing area of interest and study, and other perspectives exist. However, this example illustrates how Monte Carlo simulation is used to address important investment issues.

The analyst chooses the probability distributions in Monte Carlo simulation. By contrast, **historical simulation** samples from a historical record of returns (or other underlying variables) to simulate a process. The concept underlying historical simulation (also called **back simulation**) is that the historical record provides the most direct evidence on distributions (and that the past applies to the future). For example, refer back to Step 2 in the outline of Monte Carlo simulation above and suppose the time increment is one day. Further, suppose we base the simulation on the record of daily stock returns over the last five years. In one type of historical simulation, we randomly draw $K$ returns from that record to generate one simulation trial. We put back the observations into the sample, and in the next trial we again randomly sample with replacement. The simulation results directly reflect frequencies in the data. A drawback of this approach is that any risk not represented in the time period selected (for example, a stock market crash) will not be reflected in the simulation. Compared with Monte Carlo simulation, historical simulation does not lend itself to "what if" analyses. Nevertheless, historic simulation is an established alternative simulation methodology.

Monte Carlo simulation is a complement to analytical methods. It provides only statistical estimates, not exact results. Analytical methods, where available, provide more insight into cause-and-effect relationships. For example, the Black–Scholes–Merton option pricing model for the value of a European call option is an analytical method, expressed as a formula. It is a much more efficient method for valuing such a call than is Monte Carlo simulation. As an analytical expression, the Black–Scholes–Merton model permits the analyst to quickly gauge the sensitivity of call value to changes in current stock price and the other variables that determine call value. In contrast, Monte Carlo simulations do not directly provide such precise insights. However, only some types of options can be priced with analytical expressions. As financial product innovations proceed, the field of applications for Monte Carlo simulation continues to grow.

# SUMMARY

In this reading, we have presented the most frequently used probability distributions in investment analysis and the Monte Carlo simulation.

▶ A probability distribution specifies the probabilities of the possible outcomes of a random variable.

▶ The two basic types of random variables are discrete random variables and continuous random variables. Discrete random variables take on at most a countable number of possible outcomes that we can list as $x_1, x_2, \ldots$ In contrast, we cannot describe the possible outcomes of a continuous random variable $Z$ with a list $z_1, z_2, \ldots$ because the outcome $(z_1 + z_2)/2$, not in the list, would always be possible.

▶ The probability function specifies the probability that the random variable will take on a specific value. The probability function is denoted $p(x)$ for a discrete random variable and $f(x)$ for a continuous random variable. For any probability function $p(x)$, $0 \leq p(x) \leq 1$, and the sum of $p(x)$ over all values of $X$ equals 1.

▶ The cumulative distribution function, denoted $F(x)$ for both continuous and discrete random variables, gives the probability that the random variable is less than or equal to $x$.

▶ The discrete uniform and the continuous uniform distributions are the distributions of equally likely outcomes.

▶ The binomial random variable is defined as the number of successes in $n$ Bernoulli trials, where the probability of success, $p$, is constant for all trials and the trials are independent. A Bernoulli trial is an experiment with two outcomes, which can represent success or failure, an up move or a down move, or another binary (two-fold) outcome.

▶ A binomial random variable has an expected value or mean equal to $np$ and variance equal to $np(1 - p)$.

▶ A binomial tree is the graphical representation of a model of asset price dynamics in which, at each period, the asset moves up with probability $p$ or down with probability $(1 - p)$. The binomial tree is a flexible method for modeling asset price movement and is widely used in pricing options.

▶ The normal distribution is a continuous symmetric probability distribution that is completely described by two parameters: its mean, $\mu$, and its variance, $\sigma^2$.

▶ A univariate distribution specifies the probabilities for a single random variable. A multivariate distribution specifies the probabilities for a group of related random variables.

▶ To specify the normal distribution for a portfolio when its component securities are normally distributed, we need the means, standard deviations, and all the distinct pairwise correlations of the securities. When we have those statistics, we have also specified a multivariate normal distribution for the securities.

▶ For a normal random variable, approximately 68 percent of all possible outcomes are within a one standard deviation interval about the mean, approximately 95 percent are within a two standard deviation interval about the mean, and approximately 99 percent are within a three standard deviation interval about the mean.

▶ A normal random variable, $X$, is standardized using the expression $Z = (X - \mu)/\sigma$, where $\mu$ and $\sigma$ are the mean and standard deviation of $X$. Generally, we use the sample mean $\overline{X}$ as an estimate of $\mu$ and the sample standard deviation $s$ as an estimate of $\sigma$ in this expression.

▶ The standard normal random variable, denoted $Z$, has a mean equal to 0 and variance equal to 1. All questions about any normal random variable can be answered by referring to the cumulative distribution function of a standard normal random variable, denoted $N(x)$ or $N(z)$.

▶ Shortfall risk is the risk that portfolio value will fall below some minimum acceptable level over some time horizon.

▶ Roy's safety-first criterion, addressing shortfall risk, asserts that the optimal portfolio is the one that minimizes the probability that portfolio return falls below a threshold level. According to Roy's safety-first criterion, if returns are normally distributed, the safety-first optimal portfolio $P$ is the one that maximizes the quantity $[E(R_P) - R_L]/\sigma_P$, where $R_L$ is the minimum acceptable level of return.

▶ A random variable follows a lognormal distribution if the natural logarithm of the random variable is normally distributed. The lognormal distribution is defined in terms of the mean and variance of its associated normal distribution. The lognormal distribution is bounded below by 0 and skewed to the right (it has a long right tail).

▶ The lognormal distribution is frequently used to model the probability distribution of asset prices because it is bounded below by zero.

▶ Continuous compounding views time as essentially continuous or unbroken; discrete compounding views time as advancing in discrete finite intervals.

▶ The continuously compounded return associated with a holding period is the natural log of 1 plus the holding period return, or equivalently, the natural log of ending price over beginning price.

▶ If continuously compounded returns are normally distributed, asset prices are lognormally distributed. This relationship is used to move back and forth between the distributions for return and price. Because of the central limit theorem, continuously compounded returns need not be normally distributed for asset prices to be reasonably well described by a lognormal distribution.

▶ Monte Carlo simulation involves the use of a computer to represent the operation of a complex financial system. A characteristic feature of Monte Carlo simulation is the generation of a large number of random samples from specified probability distribution(s) to represent the operation of risk in the system. Monte Carlo simulation is used in planning, in financial risk management, and in valuing complex securities. Monte Carlo simulation is a complement to analytical methods but provides only statistical estimates, not exact results.

▶ Historical simulation is an established alternative to Monte Carlo simulation that in one implementation involves repeated sampling from a historical data series. Historical simulation is grounded in actual data but can reflect only risks represented in the sample historical data. Compared with Monte Carlo simulation, historical simulation does not lend itself to "what if" analyses.

## PRACTICE PROBLEMS FOR READING 9

1. A European put option on stock conveys the right to sell the stock at a prespecified price, called the exercise price, at the maturity date of the option. The value of this put at maturity is (Exercise price – Stock price) or $0, whichever is greater. Suppose the exercise price is $100 and the underlying stock trades in ticks of $0.01. At any time before maturity, the terminal value of the put is a random variable.

   A. Describe the distinct possible outcomes for terminal put value. (Think of the put's maximum and minimum values and its minimum price increments.)

   B. Is terminal put value, at a time before maturity, a discrete or continuous random variable?

   C. Letting $Y$ stand for terminal put value, express in standard notation the probability that terminal put value is less than or equal to $24. No calculations or formulas are necessary.

2. Suppose $X$, $Y$, and $Z$ are discrete random variables with these sets of possible outcomes: $X = \{2, 2.5, 3\}$, $Y = \{0, 1, 2, 3\}$, and $Z = \{10, 11, 12\}$. For each of the functions $f(X)$, $g(Y)$, and $h(Z)$, state whether the function satisfies the conditions for a probability function.

   A. $f(2) = -0.01$     $f(2.5) = -0.50$     $f(3) = -0.51$

   B. $g(0) = 0.25$     $g(1) = 0.50$     $g(2) = 0.125$     $g(3) = 0.125$

   C. $h(10) = 0.35$     $h(11) = 0.15$     $h(12) = 0.52$

3. Define the term "binomial random variable." Describe the types of problems for which the binomial distribution is used.

4. Over the last 10 years, a company's annual earnings increased year over year seven times and decreased year over year three times. You decide to model the number of earnings increases for the next decade as a binomial random variable.

   A. What is your estimate of the probability of success, defined as an increase in annual earnings?

   For Parts B, C, and D of this problem, assume the estimated probability is the actual probability for the next decade.

   B. What is the probability that earnings will increase in exactly 5 of the next 10 years?

   C. Calculate the expected number of yearly earnings increases during the next 10 years.

   D. Calculate the variance and standard deviation of the number of yearly earnings increases during the next 10 years.

   E. The expression for the probability function of a binomial random variable depends on two major assumptions. In the context of this problem, what must you assume about annual earnings increases to apply the binomial distribution in Part B? What reservations might you have about the validity of these assumptions?

5. You are examining the record of an investment newsletter writer who claims a 70 percent success rate in making investment recommendations that are profitable over a one-year time horizon. You have the one-year record of the newsletter's seven most recent recommendations. Four of those recommendations were profitable. If all the recommendations are independent and the newsletter writer's skill is as claimed, what is the probability of observing four or fewer profitable recommendations out of seven in total?

6. By definition, a down-and-out call option on stock becomes worthless and terminates if the price of the underlying stock moves down and touches a prespecified point during the life of the call. If the prespecified level is $75, for example, the call expires worthless if and when the stock price falls to $75. Describe, without a diagram, how a binomial tree can be used to value a down-and-out call option.

7. You are forecasting sales for a company in the fourth quarter of its fiscal year. Your low-end estimate of sales is €14 million, and your high-end estimate is €15 million. You decide to treat all outcomes for sales between these two values as equally likely, using a continuous uniform distribution.

   **A.** What is the expected value of sales for the fourth quarter?

   **B.** What is the probability that fourth-quarter sales will be less than or equal to €14,125,000?

8. State the approximate probability that a normal random variable will fall within the following intervals:

   **A.** Mean plus or minus one standard deviation.

   **B.** Mean plus or minus two standard deviations.

   **C.** Mean plus or minus three standard deviations.

9. Find the area under the normal curve up to $z = 0.36$; that is, find $P(Z \leq 0.36)$. Interpret this value.

10. In futures markets, profits or losses on contracts are settled at the end of each trading day. This procedure is called marking to market or daily resettlement. By preventing a trader's losses from accumulating over many days, marking to market reduces the risk that traders will default on their obligations. A futures markets trader needs a liquidity pool to meet the daily mark to market. If liquidity is exhausted, the trader may be forced to his position at an unfavorable time.

   Suppose you are using financial futures contracts to hedge a risk in your portfolio. You have a liquidity pool (cash and cash equivalents) of $\lambda$ dollars per contract and a time horizon of $T$ trading days. For a given size liquidity pool, $\lambda$, Kolb, Gay, and Hunter (1985) developed an expression for the probability stating that you will exhaust your liquidity pool within a $T$-day horizon as a result of the daily mark to market. Kolb et al. assumed that the expected change in futures price is 0 and that futures price changes are normally distributed. With $\sigma$ representing the standard deviation of daily futures price changes, the standard deviation of price changes over a time horizon to day $T$ is $\sigma\sqrt{T}$, given continuous compounding. With that background, the Kolb et al. expression is

   $$\text{Probability of exhausting liquidity pool} = 2[1 - N(x)]$$

   where $x = \lambda/(\sigma\sqrt{T})$. Here $x$ is a standardized value of $\lambda$. $N(x)$ is the standard normal cumulative distribution function. For some intuition about $1 - N(x)$

in the expression, note that the liquidity pool is exhausted if losses exceed the size of the liquidity pool at any time up to and including $T$; the probability of that event happening can be shown to be proportional to an area in the right tail of a standard normal distribution, $1 - N(x)$.

Using the Kolb et al. expression, answer the following questions:

**A.** Your hedging horizon is five days, and your liquidity pool is $2,000 per contract. You estimate that the standard deviation of daily price changes for the contract is $450. What is the probability that you will exhaust your liquidity pool in the five-day period?

**B.** Suppose your hedging horizon is 20 days, but all the other facts given in Part A remain the same. What is the probability that you will exhaust your liquidity pool in the 20-day period?

## Use the information and table below to solve Questions 11–13

As reported by Liang (1999), U.S. equity funds in three style categories had the following mean monthly returns, standard deviations of return, and Sharpe ratios during the period January 1994 to December 1996:

| Strategy | January 1994 to December 1996 | | |
| --- | --- | --- | --- |
| | **Mean Return** | **Standard Deviation** | **Sharpe Ratio** |
| Large-cap growth | 1.15% | 2.89% | 0.26 |
| Large-cap value | 1.08% | 2.20% | 0.31 |
| Large-cap blend | 1.07% | 2.38% | 0.28 |

*Source*: Liang (1999), Table 5 (excerpt).

**11.** Basing your estimate of future-period monthly return parameters on the sample mean and standard deviation for the period January 1994 to December 1996, construct a 90 percent confidence interval for the monthly return on a large-cap blend fund. Assume fund returns are normally distributed.

**12.** Basing your estimate of future-period monthly return parameters on the sample mean and standard deviation for the period January 1994 to December 1996, calculate the probability that a large-cap growth fund will earn a monthly return of 0 percent or less. Assume fund returns are normally distributed.

**13.** Assuming fund returns are normally distributed, which fund category minimized the probability of earning less than the risk-free rate for the period January 1994 to December 1996?

**14.** A client has a portfolio of common stocks and fixed-income instruments with a current value of £1,350,000. She intends to liquidate £50,000 from the portfolio at the end of the year to purchase a partnership share in a business. Furthermore, the client would like to be able to withdraw the £50,000 without reducing the initial capital of £1,350,000. The following table shows four alternative asset allocations.

**Mean and Standard Deviation for Four Allocations (in Percent)**

|                             | A  | B  | C  | D  |
|-----------------------------|----|----|----|----|
| Expected annual return      | 16 | 12 | 10 | 9  |
| Standard deviation of return| 24 | 17 | 12 | 11 |

Address the following questions (assume normality for Parts B and C):

**A.** Given the client's desire not to invade the £1,350,000 principal, what is the shortfall level, $R_L$? Use this shortfall level to answer Part B.

**B.** According to the safety-first criterion, which of the three allocations is the best?

**C.** What is the probability that the return on the safety-first optimal portfolio will be less than the shortfall level, $R_L$?

**15. A.** Describe two important characteristics of the lognormal distribution.

**B.** Compared with the normal distribution, why is the lognormal distribution a more reasonable model for the distribution of asset prices?

**C.** What are the two parameters of a lognormal distribution?

**16.** The basic calculation for volatility (denoted $\sigma$) as used in option pricing is the annualized standard deviation of continuously compounded daily returns. Calculate volatility for Dollar General Corporation (NYSE: DG) based on its closing prices for two weeks, given in the table below. (Annualize based on 250 days in a year.)

**Dollar General Corporation
Daily Closing Stock Price**

| Date             | Closing Price |
|------------------|---------------|
| 27 January 2003  | $10.68        |
| 28 January 2003  | $10.87        |
| 29 January 2003  | $11.00        |
| 30 January 2003  | $10.95        |
| 31 January 2003  | $11.26        |
| 3 February 2003  | $11.31        |
| 4 February 2003  | $11.23        |
| 5 February 2003  | $10.91        |
| 6 February 2003  | $10.80        |
| 7 February 2003  | $10.47        |

*Source*: finance.yahoo.com.

**17. A.** Define Monte Carlo simulation and explain its use in finance.

**B.** Compared with analytical methods, what are the strengths and weaknesses of Monte Carlo simulation for use in valuing securities?

**18.** A standard lookback call option on stock has a value at maturity equal to (Value of the stock at maturity − Minimum value of stock during the life of the option prior to maturity) or $0, whichever is greater. If the minimum value reached prior to maturity was $20.11 and the value of the stock at maturity is $23, for example, the call is worth $23 − $20.11 = $2.89. Briefly discuss how you might use Monte Carlo simulation in valuing a lookback call option.

**19.** At the end of the current year, an investor wants to make a donation of $20,000 to charity but does not want the year-end market value of her portfolio to fall below $600,000. If the shortfall level is equal to the risk-free rate of return and returns from all portfolios considered are normally distributed, will the portfolio that minimizes the probability of failing to achieve the investor's objective *most likely* have the:

| | highest safety-first ratio? | highest Sharpe ratio? |
|---|---|---|
| **A.** | No | Yes |
| **B.** | Yes | No |
| **C.** | Yes | Yes |

**20.** An analyst stated that normal distributions are suitable for describing asset returns and that lognormal distributions are suitable for describing distributions of asset prices. The analyst's statement is correct in regard to

**A.** both normal distributions and log-normal distributions.

**B.** normal distributions, but incorrect in regard to lognormal distributions.

**C.** lognormal distributions, but incorrect in regard to normal distributions.

# SAMPLING AND ESTIMATION

by Richard A. DeFusco, CFA, Dennis W. McLeavey, CFA,
Jerald E. Pinto, CFA, and David E. Runkle, CFA

## LEARNING OUTCOMES

| The candidate should be able to: | Mastery |
|---|:---:|
| **a.** define simple random sampling, sampling error, and a sampling distribution, and interpret sampling error; | ☐ |
| **b.** distinguish between simple random and stratified random sampling; | ☐ |
| **c.** distinguish between time-series and cross-sectional data; | ☐ |
| **d.** interpret the central limit theorem and describe its importance; | ☐ |
| **e.** calculate and interpret the standard error of the sample mean; | ☐ |
| **f.** distinguish between a point estimate and a confidence interval estimate of a population parameter; | ☐ |
| **g.** identify and describe the desirable properties of an estimator; | ☐ |
| **h.** explain the construction of confidence intervals; | ☐ |
| **i.** describe the properties of Student's *t*-distribution, and calculate and interpret its degrees of freedom; | ☐ |
| **j.** calculate and interpret a confidence interval for a population mean, given a normal distribution with 1) a known population variance, 2) an unknown population variance, or 3) with an unknown variance and the sample size is large; | ☐ |
| **k.** discuss the issues regarding selection of the appropriate sample size, data-mining bias, sample selection bias, survivorship bias, look-ahead bias, and time-period bias. | ☐ |

## INTRODUCTION 1

Each day, we observe the high, low, and close of stock market indexes from around the world. Indexes such as the S&P 500 Index and the Nikkei–Dow Jones Average are samples of stocks. Although the S&P 500 and the Nikkei do not represent the populations of U.S. or Japanese stocks, we view them as valid indicators of the whole population's behavior. As analysts, we are accustomed to using this sample information to assess how various markets from around the world are performing. Any statistics that we compute with sample information, however, are only estimates of the underlying population parameters. A sample, then, is a subset of the population—a subset studied to infer conclusions about the population itself.

This reading explores how we sample and use sample information to estimate population parameters. In the next section, we discuss **sampling**—the process of obtaining a sample. In investments, we continually make use of the mean as a measure of central tendency of random variables, such as return and earnings per share. Even when the probability distribution of the random variable is unknown, we can make probability statements about the population mean using the central limit theorem. In Section 3, we discuss and illustrate this key result. Following that discussion, we turn to statistical estimation. Estimation seeks precise answers to the question "What is this parameter's value?"

The central limit theorem and estimation are the core of the body of methods presented in this reading. In investments, we apply these and other statistical techniques to financial data; we often interpret the results for the purpose of deciding what works and what does not work in investments. We end this reading with a discussion of the interpretation of statistical results based on financial data and the possible pitfalls in this process.

## 2    SAMPLING

In this section, we present the various methods for obtaining information on a population (all members of a specified group) through samples (part of the population). The information on a population that we try to obtain usually concerns the value of a **parameter**, a quantity computed from or used to describe a population of data. When we use a sample to estimate a parameter, we make use of sample statistics (statistics, for short). A **statistic** is a quantity computed from or used to describe a sample of data.

We take samples for one of two reasons. In some cases, we cannot possibly examine every member of the population. In other cases, examining every member of the population would not be economically efficient. Thus, savings of time and money are two primary factors that cause an analyst to use sampling to answer a question about a population. In this section, we discuss two methods of random sampling: simple random sampling and stratified random sampling. We then define and illustrate the two types of data an analyst uses: cross-sectional data and time-series data.

### 2.1  Simple Random Sampling

Suppose a telecommunications equipment analyst wants to know how much major customers will spend on average for equipment during the coming year. One strategy is to survey the population of telecom equipment customers and inquire what their purchasing plans are. In statistical terms, the characteristics of the population of customers' planned expenditures would then usually be expressed by descriptive measures such as the mean and variance. Surveying all companies, however, would be very costly in terms of time and money.

Alternatively, the analyst can collect a representative sample of companies and survey them about upcoming telecom equipment expenditures. In this case, the analyst will compute the sample mean expenditure, $\bar{X}$, a statistic. This strategy has a substantial advantage over polling the whole population because it can be accomplished more quickly and at lower cost.

Sampling, however, introduces error. The error arises because not all the companies in the population are surveyed. The analyst who decides to sample is trading time and money for sampling error.

When an analyst chooses to sample, he must formulate a sampling plan. A **sampling plan** is the set of rules used to select a sample. The basic type of sample from which we can draw statistically sound conclusions about a population is the **simple random sample** (random sample, for short).

▶ **Definition of Simple Random Sample.** A simple random sample is a subset of a larger population created in such a way that each element of the population has an equal probability of being selected to the subset.

The procedure of drawing a sample to satisfy the definition of a simple random sample is called **simple random sampling**. How is simple random sampling carried out? We need a method that ensures randomness—the lack of any pattern—in the selection of the sample. For a finite (limited) population, the most common method for obtaining a random sample involves the use of random numbers (numbers with assured properties of randomness). First, we number the members of the population in sequence. For example, if the population contains 500 members, we number them in sequence with three digits, starting with 001 and ending with 500. Suppose we want a simple random sample of size 50. In that case, using a computer random-number generator or a table of random numbers, we generate a series of three-digit random numbers. We then match these random numbers with the number codes of the population members until we have selected a sample of size 50.

Sometimes we cannot code (or even identify) all the members of a population. We often use **systematic sampling** in such cases. With systematic sampling, we select every $k$th member until we have a sample of the desired size. The sample that results from this procedure should be approximately random. Real sampling situations may require that we take an approximately random sample.

Suppose the telecommunications equipment analyst polls a random sample of telecom equipment customers to determine the average equipment expenditure. The sample mean will provide the analyst with an estimate of the population mean expenditure. Any difference between the sample mean and the population mean is called **sampling error**.

▶ **Definition of Sampling Error.** Sampling error is the difference between the observed value of a statistic and the quantity it is intended to estimate.

A random sample reflects the properties of the population in an unbiased way, and sample statistics, such as the sample mean, computed on the basis of a random sample are valid estimates of the underlying population parameters.

A sample statistic is a random variable. In other words, not only do the original data from the population have a distribution but so does the sample statistic. This distribution is the statistic's **sampling distribution**.

▶ **Definition of Sampling Distribution of a Statistic.** The sampling distribution of a statistic is the distribution of all the distinct possible values that the statistic can assume when computed from samples of the same size randomly drawn from the same population.

In the case of the sample mean, for example, we refer to the "sampling distribution of the sample mean" or the distribution of the sample mean. We will have more to say about sampling distributions later in this reading. Next, however, we look at another sampling method that is useful in investment analysis.

## 2.2 Stratified Random Sampling

The simple random sampling method just discussed may not be the best approach in all situations. One frequently used alternative is stratified random sampling.

▶ **Definition of Stratified Random Sampling.** In stratified random sampling, the population is divided into subpopulations (strata) based on one or more classification criteria. Simple random samples are then drawn from each stratum in sizes proportional to the relative size of each stratum in the population. These samples are then pooled to form a stratified random sample.

In contrast to simple random sampling, stratified random sampling guarantees that population subdivisions of interest are represented in the sample. Another advantage is that estimates of parameters produced from stratified sampling have greater precision—that is, smaller variance or dispersion—than estimates obtained from simple random sampling.

Bond indexing is one area in which stratified sampling is frequently applied. **Indexing** is an investment strategy in which an investor constructs a portfolio to mirror the performance of a specified index. In pure bond indexing, also called the full-replication approach, the investor attempts to fully replicate an index by owning all the bonds in the index in proportion to their market value weights. Many bond indexes consist of thousands of issues, however, so pure bond indexing is difficult to implement. In addition, transaction costs would be high because many bonds do not have liquid markets. Although a simple random sample could be a solution to the cost problem, the sample would probably not match the index's major risk factors—interest rate sensitivity, for example. Because the major risk factors of fixed-income portfolios are well known and quantifiable, stratified sampling offers a more effective approach. In this approach, we divide the population of index bonds into groups of similar duration (interest rate sensitivity), cash flow distribution, sector, credit quality, and call exposure. We refer to each group as a stratum or cell (a term frequently used in this context).[1] Then, we choose a sample from each stratum proportional to the relative market weighting of the stratum in the index to be replicated.

---

**EXAMPLE 1**

**Bond Indexes and Stratified Sampling**

Suppose you are the manager of a mutual fund indexed to the Lehman Brothers Government Index. You are exploring several approaches to indexing, including a stratified sampling approach. You first distinguish

---

[1] See Fabozzi (2004b).

agency bonds from U.S. Treasury bonds. For each of these two groups, you define 10 maturity intervals—1 to 2 years, 2 to 3 years, 3 to 4 years, 4 to 6 years, 6 to 8 years, 8 to 10 years, 10 to 12 years, 12 to 15 years, 15 to 20 years, and 20 to 30 years—and also separate the bonds with coupons (annual interest rates) of 6 percent or less from the bonds with coupons of more than 6 percent.

**1.** How many cells or strata does this sampling plan entail?

**2.** If you use this sampling plan, what is the minimum number of issues the indexed portfolio can have?

**3.** Suppose that in selecting among the securities that qualify for selection within each cell, you apply a criterion concerning the liquidity of the security's market. Is the sample obtained random? Explain your answer.

**Solution to 1:** We have 2 issuer classifications, 10 maturity classifications, and 2 coupon classifications. So, in total, this plan entails $2(10)(2) = 40$ different strata or cells. (This answer is an application of the multiplication rule of counting discussed in the reading on probability concepts.)

**Solution to 2:** You cannot have fewer than one issue for each cell, so the portfolio must include at least 40 issues.

**Solution to 3:** If you apply any additional criteria to the selection of securities for the cells, not every security that might be included has an equal probability of being selected. As a result, the sampling is not random. In practice, indexing using stratified sampling usually does not strictly involve random sampling because the selection of bond issues within cells is subject to various additional criteria. Because the purpose of sampling in this application is not to make an inference about a population parameter but rather to index a portfolio, lack of randomness is not in itself a problem in this application of stratified sampling.

In the next section, we discuss the kinds of data used by financial analysts in sampling and practical issues that arise in selecting samples.

## 2.3 Time-Series and Cross-Sectional Data

Investment analysts commonly work with both time-series and cross-sectional data. A time series is a sequence of returns collected at discrete and equally spaced intervals of time (such as a historical series of monthly stock returns). Cross-sectional data are data on some characteristic of individuals, groups, geographical regions, or companies at a single point in time. The 2003 year-end book value per share for all New York Stock Exchange-listed companies is an example of cross-sectional data.

Economic or financial theory offers no basis for determining whether a long or short time period should be selected to collect a sample. As analysts, we might have to look for subtle clues. For example, combining data from a period of fixed exchange rates with data from a period of floating exchange rates would be inappropriate. The variance of exchange rates when exchange rates were fixed would certainly be less than when rates were allowed to float. As a consequence, we would not be sampling from a population described by a single set of parameters.[2] Tight versus loose **monetary policy** also influences the distribution of returns to stocks; thus, combining data from tight-money and loose-money periods would be inappropriate. Example 2 illustrates the problems that can arise when sampling from more than one distribution.

---

**EXAMPLE 2**

### Calculating Sharpe Ratios: One or Two Years of Quarterly Data

Analysts often use the Sharpe ratio to evaluate the performance of a managed portfolio. The **Sharpe ratio** is the average return in excess of the risk-free rate divided by the standard deviation of returns. This ratio measures the excess return earned per unit of standard deviation of return.

To compute the Sharpe ratio, suppose that an analyst collects eight quarterly excess returns (i.e., total return in excess of the risk-free rate). During the first year, the investment manager of the portfolio followed a low-risk strategy, and during the second year, the manager followed a high-risk strategy. For each of these years, the analyst also tracks the quarterly excess returns of some benchmark against which the manager will be evaluated. For each of the two years, the Sharpe ratio for the benchmark is 0.21. Table 1 gives the calculation of the Sharpe ratio of the portfolio.

**TABLE 1    Calculation of Sharpe Ratios: Low-Risk and High-Risk Strategies**

| Quarter/Measure | Year 1 Excess Returns | Year 2 Excess Returns |
|---|---|---|
| Quarter 1 | −3% | −12% |
| Quarter 2 | 5 | 20 |
| Quarter 3 | −3 | −12 |
| Quarter 4 | 5 | 20 |
| Quarterly average | 1% | 4% |
| Quarterly standard deviation | −4.62% | −18.48% |
| Sharpe ratio = 0.22 = 1/4.62 = 4/18.48 | | |

For the first year, during which the manager followed a low-risk strategy, the average quarterly return in excess of the risk-free rate was 1 percent with a standard deviation of 4.62 percent. The Sharpe ratio is thus $1/4.62 = 0.22$. The second year's results mirror the first year except for the higher average return and volatility. The Sharpe ratio for the second year is $4/18.48 = 0.22$. The Sharpe ratio for the benchmark is 0.21 during the first and second years. Because larger Sharpe ratios are better than smaller ones (providing more return per unit of risk), the manager appears to have outperformed the benchmark.

Now, suppose the analyst believes a larger sample to be superior to a small one. She thus decides to pool the two years together and

---

[2] When the mean or variance of a time series is not constant through time, the time series is not stationary.

calculate a Sharpe ratio based on eight quarterly observations. The average quarterly excess return for the two years is the average of each year's average excess return. For the two-year period, the average excess return is $(1 + 4)/2 = 2.5$ percent per quarter. The standard deviation for all eight quarters measured from the sample mean of 2.5 percent is 12.57 percent. The portfolio's Sharpe ratio for the two-year period is now $2.5/12.57 = 0.199$; the Sharpe ratio for the benchmark remains 0.21. Thus, when returns for the two-year period are pooled, the manager appears to have provided less return per unit of risk than the benchmark and less when compared with the separate yearly results.

The problem with using eight quarters of return data is that the analyst has violated the assumption that the sampled returns come from the same population. As a result of the change in the manager's investment strategy, returns in Year 2 followed a different distribution than returns in Year 1. Clearly, during Year 1, returns were generated by an underlying population with lower mean and variance than the population of the second year. Combining the results for the first and second years yielded a sample that was representative of no population. Because the larger sample did not satisfy model assumptions, any conclusions the analyst reached based on the larger sample are incorrect. For this example, she was better off using a smaller sample than a larger sample because the smaller sample represented a more homogeneous distribution of returns.

The second basic type of data is cross-sectional data.[3] With cross-sectional data, the observations in the sample represent a characteristic of individuals, groups, geographical regions, or companies at a single point in time. The telecommunications analyst discussed previously is essentially collecting a cross-section of planned capital expenditures for the coming year.

Whenever we sample cross-sectionally, certain assumptions must be met if we wish to summarize the data in a meaningful way. Again, a useful approach is to think of the observation of interest as a random variable that comes from some underlying population with a given mean and variance. As we collect our sample and begin to summarize the data, we must be sure that all the data do, in fact, come from the same underlying population. For example, an analyst might be interested in how efficiently companies use their inventory assets. Some companies, however, turn over their inventory more quickly than others because of differences in their operating environments (e.g., grocery stores turn over inventory more quickly than automobile manufacturers, in general). So the distribution of inventory turnover rates may not be characterized by a single distribution with a given mean and variance. Therefore, summarizing inventory turnover across all companies might be inappropriate. If random variables are generated by different underlying distributions, the sample statistics computed from combined samples are not related to one underlying population parameter. The size of the sampling error in such cases is unknown.

In instances such as these, analysts often summarize company-level data by industry. Attempting to summarize by industry partially addresses the problem

---

[3] The reader may also encounter two types of datasets that have both time-series and cross-sectional aspects. **Panel data** consist of observations through time on a single characteristic of multiple observational units. For example, the annual inflation rate of the Eurozone countries over a five-year period would represent panel data. **Longitudinal data** consist of observations on characteristic(s) of the same observational unit through time. Observations on a set of financial ratios for a single company over a 10-year period would be an example of longitudinal data. Both panel and longitudinal data may be represented by arrays (matrixes) in which successive rows represent the observations for successive time periods.

of differing underlying distributions, but large corporations are likely to be in more than one industrial sector, so analysts should be sure they understand how companies are assigned to the industry groups.

Whether we deal with time-series data or cross-sectional data, we must be sure to have a random sample that is representative of the population we wish to study. With the objective of inferring information from representative samples, we now turn to the next part of this reading, which focuses on the central limit theorem as well as point and interval estimates of the population mean.

# 3    DISTRIBUTION OF THE SAMPLE MEAN

Earlier in this reading, we presented a telecommunications equipment analyst who decided to sample in order to estimate mean planned capital expenditures by his customers. Supposing that the sample is representative of the underlying population, how can the analyst assess the sampling error in estimating the population mean? Viewed as a formula that takes a function of the random outcomes of a random variable, the sample mean is itself a random variable with a probability distribution. That probability distribution is called the statistic's sampling distribution.[4] To estimate how closely the sample mean can be expected to match the underlying population mean, the analyst needs to understand the sampling distribution of the mean. Fortunately, we have a result, the central limit theorem, that helps us understand the sampling distribution of the mean for many of the estimation problems we face.

## 3.1  The Central Limit Theorem

One of the most practically useful theorems in probability theory, the central limit theorem has important implications for how we construct confidence intervals and test hypotheses. Formally, it is stated as follows:

▶ **The Central Limit Theorem.** Given a population described by any probability distribution having mean $\mu$ and finite variance $\sigma^2$, the sampling distribution of the sample mean $\overline{X}$ computed from samples of size $n$ from this population will be approximately normal with mean $\mu$ (the population mean) and variance $\sigma^2/n$ (the population variance divided by $n$) when the sample size $n$ is large.

The central limit theorem allows us to make quite precise probability statements about the population mean by using the sample mean, *whatever the distribution* of *the population*, because the sample mean follows an approximate normal distribution for large-size samples. The obvious question is, "When is a sample's size large enough that we can assume the sample mean is normally distributed?" In general, when sample size $n$ is greater than or equal to 30, we can assume that the sample mean is approximately normally distributed.[5]

---

[4] Sometimes confusion arises because "sample mean" is also used in another sense. When we calculate the sample mean for a particular sample, we obtain a definite number, say 8. If we state that "the sample mean is 8" we are using "sample mean" in the sense of a particular outcome of sample mean as a random variable. The number 8 is of course a constant and does not have a probability distribution. In this discussion, we are not referring to "sample mean" in the sense of a constant number related to a particular sample.

[5] When the underlying population is very nonnormal, a sample size well in excess of 30 may be required for the normal distribution to be a good description of the sampling distribution of the mean.

The central limit theorem states that the variance of the distribution of the sample mean is $\sigma^2/n$. The positive square root of variance is standard deviation. The standard deviation of a sample statistic is known as the standard error of the statistic. The standard error of the sample mean is an important quantity in applying the central limit theorem in practice.

▶ **Definition of the Standard Error of the Sample Mean.** For sample mean $\overline{X}$ calculated from a sample generated by a population with standard deviation $\sigma$, the standard error of the sample mean is given by one of two expressions:

$$\sigma_{\overline{X}} = \frac{\sigma}{\sqrt{n}} \qquad\qquad \textbf{(10-1)}$$

when we know $\sigma$, the population standard deviation, or by

$$s_{\overline{X}} = \frac{s}{\sqrt{n}} \qquad\qquad \textbf{(10-2)}$$

when we do not know the population standard deviation and need to use the sample standard deviation, $s$, to estimate it.[6]

In practice, we almost always need to use Equation 10-2. The estimate of $s$ is given by the square root of the sample variance, $s^2$, calculated as follows:

$$s^2 = \frac{\sum_{i=1}^{n}(X_i - \overline{X})^2}{n-1} \qquad\qquad \textbf{(10-3)}$$

We will soon see how we can use the sample mean and its standard error to make probability statements about the population mean by using the technique of confidence intervals. First, however, we provide an illustration of the central limit theorem's force.

## EXAMPLE 3

### The Central Limit Theorem

It is remarkable that the sample mean for large sample sizes will be distributed normally regardless of the distribution of the underlying population. To illustrate the central limit theorem in action, we specify in this example a distinctly nonnormal distribution and use it to generate a large number of random samples of size 100. We then calculate the sample mean for each sample. The frequency distribution of the calculated sample means is an approximation of the sampling distribution of the sample mean for that sample size. Does that sampling distribution look like a normal distribution?

We return to the telecommunications analyst studying the capital expenditure plans of telecom businesses. Suppose that capital expenditures

---

[6] We need to note a technical point: When we take a sample of size $n$ from a finite population of size $N$, we apply a shrinkage factor to the estimate of the standard error of the sample mean that is called the finite population correction factor (fpc). The fpc is equal to $[(N-n)/(N-1)]^{1/2}$. Thus, if $N = 100$ and $n = 20$, $[(100 - 20)/(100 - 1)]^{1/2} = 0.898933$. If we have estimated a standard error of, say, 20, according to Equation 10-1 or Equation 10-2, the new estimate is $20(0.898933) = 17.978663$. The fpc applies only when we sample from a finite population without replacement; most practitioners also do not apply the fpc if sample size $n$ is very small relative to $N$ (say, less than 5 percent of $N$). For more information on the finite population correction factor, see Daniel and Terrell (1995).

for communications equipment form a continuous uniform random variable with a **lower bound** equal to $0 and an upper bound equal to $100—for short, call this a uniform (0, 100) random variable. The probability function of this continuous uniform random variable has a rather simple shape that is anything but normal. It is a horizontal line with a vertical intercept equal to 1/100. Unlike a normal random variable, for which outcomes close to the mean are most likely, all possible outcomes are equally likely for a uniform random variable.

To illustrate the power of the central limit theorem, we conduct a Monte Carlo simulation to study the capital expenditure plans of telecom businesses.[7] In this simulation, we collect 200 random samples of the capital expenditures of 100 companies (200 random draws, each consisting of the capital expenditures of 100 companies with $n = 100$). In each simulation trial, 100 values for capital expenditure are generated from the uniform (0, 100) distribution. For each random sample, we then compute the sample mean. We conduct 200 simulation trials in total. Because we have specified the distribution generating the samples, we know that the population mean capital expenditure is equal to ($0 + $100 million)/2 = $50 million; the population variance of capital expenditures is equal to $(100 - 0)^2/12 = 833.33$; thus, the standard deviation is $28.87 million and the standard error is $28.87/\sqrt{100} = 2.887$ under the central limit theorem.[8]

The results of this Monte Carlo experiment are tabulated in Table 2 in the form of a frequency distribution. This distribution is the estimated sampling distribution of the sample mean.

### TABLE 2  Frequency Distribution: 200 Random Samples of a Uniform (0,100) Random Variable

| Range of Sample Means ($ Million) | Absolute Frequency |
|---|---|
| $42.5 \leq \overline{X} < 44$ | 1 |
| $44 \leq \overline{X} < 45.5$ | 6 |
| $45.5 \leq \overline{X} < 47$ | 22 |
| $47 \leq \overline{X} < 48.5$ | 39 |
| $48.5 \leq \overline{X} < 50$ | 41 |
| $50 \leq \overline{X} < 51.5$ | 39 |
| $51.5 \leq \overline{X} < 53$ | 23 |
| $53 \leq \overline{X} < 54.5$ | 12 |
| $54.5 \leq \overline{X} < 56$ | 12 |
| $56 \leq \overline{X} < 57.5$ | 5 |

*Note*: $\overline{X}$ is the mean capital expenditure for each sample.

---

[7] Monte Carlo simulation involves the use of a computer to represent the operation of a system subject to risk. An integral part of Monte Carlo simulation is the generation of a large number of random samples from a specified probability distribution or distributions.

[8] If $a$ is the lower limit of a uniform random variable and $b$ is the upper limit, then the random variable's mean is given by $(a + b)/2$ and its variance is given by $(b - a)^2/12$. The reading on common probability distributions fully describes continuous uniform random variables.

The frequency distribution can be described as bell-shaped and centered close to the population mean of 50. The most frequent, or modal, range, with 41 observations, is 48.5 to 50. The overall average of the sample means is $49.92, with a standard error equal to $2.80. The calculated standard error is close to the value of 2.887 given by the central limit theorem. The discrepancy between calculated and expected values of the mean and standard deviation under the central limit theorem is a result of random chance (sampling error).

In summary, although the distribution of the underlying population is very nonnormal, the simulation has shown that a normal distribution well describes the estimated sampling distribution of the sample mean, with mean and standard error consistent with the values predicted by the central limit theorem.

To summarize, according to the central limit theorem, when we sample from any distribution, the distribution of the sample mean will have the following properties as long as our sample size is large:

▶ The distribution of the sample mean $\overline{X}$ will be approximately normal.

▶ The mean of the distribution of $\overline{X}$ will be equal to the mean of the population from which the samples are drawn.

▶ The variance of the distribution of $\overline{X}$ will be equal to the variance of the population divided by the sample size.

With the central limit theorem in hand, we next discuss the concepts and tools related to estimating the population parameters, with a special focus on the population mean. We focus on the population because analysts are more likely to meet interval estimates for the population mean than any other type of interval estimate.

# POINT AND INTERVAL ESTIMATES OF THE POPULATION MEAN

4

Statistical inference traditionally consists of two branches, hypothesis testing and estimation. Hypothesis testing addresses the question "Is the value of this parameter (say, a population mean) equal to some specific value (0, for example)?" In this process, we have a hypothesis concerning the value of a parameter, and we seek to determine whether the evidence from a sample supports or does not support that hypothesis. We discuss hypothesis testing in detail in the reading on hypothesis testing.

The second branch of statistical inference, and the focus of this reading, is estimation. Estimation seeks an answer to the question "What is this parameter's (for example, the population mean's) value?" In estimating, unlike in hypothesis testing, we do not start with a hypothesis about a parameter's value and seek to test it. Rather, we try to make the best use of the information in a sample to form one of several types of estimates of the parameter's value. With estimation, we are interested in arriving at a rule for best calculating a single number to estimate the unknown population parameter (a point estimate). Together with calculating a point estimate, we may also be interested in calculating a range of values that brackets the unknown population parameter with some specified level of probability (a confidence interval). In Section 4.1 we discuss point estimates of parameters and then, in Section 4.2, the formulation of confidence intervals for the population mean.

## 4.1 Point Estimators

An important concept introduced in this reading is that sample statistics viewed as formulas involving random outcomes are random variables. The formulas that we use to compute the sample mean and all the other sample statistics are examples of estimation formulas or **estimators**. The particular value that we calculate from sample observations using an estimator is called an **estimate**. An estimator has a sampling distribution; an estimate is a fixed number pertaining to a given sample and thus has no sampling distribution. To take the example of the mean, the calculated value of the sample mean in a given sample, used as an estimate of the population mean, is called a **point estimate** of the population mean. As Example 3 illustrated, the formula for the sample mean can and will yield different results in repeated samples as different samples are drawn from the population.

In many applications, we have a choice among a number of possible estimators for estimating a given parameter. How do we make our choice? We often select estimators because they have one or more desirable statistical properties. Following is a brief description of three desirable properties of estimators: unbiasedness (lack of bias), efficiency, and consistency.[9]

▶ **Definition of Unbiasedness.** An unbiased estimator is one whose expected value (the mean of its sampling distribution) equals the parameter it is intended to estimate.

For example, the expected value of the sample mean, $\overline{X}$, equals $\mu$, the population mean, so we say that the sample mean is an unbiased estimator (of the population mean). The sample variance, $s^2$, which is calculated using a divisor of $n - 1$ (Equation 10-3), is an unbiased estimator of the population variance, $\sigma^2$. If we were to calculate the sample variance using a divisor of $n$, the estimator would be biased: Its expected value would be smaller than the population variance. We would say that sample variance calculated with a divisor of $n$ is a biased estimator of the population variance.

Whenever one unbiased estimator of a parameter can be found, we can usually find a large number of other unbiased estimators. How do we choose among alternative unbiased estimators? The criterion of efficiency provides a way to select from among unbiased estimators of a parameter.

▶ **Definition of Efficiency.** An unbiased estimator is efficient if no other unbiased estimator of the same parameter has a sampling distribution with smaller variance.

To explain the definition, in repeated samples we expect the estimates from an efficient estimator to be more tightly grouped around the mean than estimates from other unbiased estimators. Efficiency is an important property of an estimator.[10] Sample mean $\overline{X}$ is an efficient estimator of the population mean; sample variance $s^2$ is an efficient estimator of $\sigma^2$.

---

[9] See Daniel and Terrell (1995) or Greene (2003) for a thorough treatment of the properties of estimators.

[10] An efficient estimator is sometimes referred to as the best unbiased estimator.

Recall that a statistic's sampling distribution is defined for a given sample size. Different sample sizes define different sampling distributions. For example, the variance of sampling distribution of the sample mean is smaller for larger sample sizes. Unbiasedness and efficiency are properties of an estimator's sampling distribution that hold for any size sample. An unbiased estimator is unbiased equally in a sample of size 10 and in a sample of size 1,000. In some problems, however, we cannot find estimators that have such desirable properties as unbiasedness in small samples.[11] In this case, statisticians may justify the choice of an estimator based on the properties of the estimator's sampling distribution in extremely large samples, the estimator's so-called asymptotic properties. Among such properties, the most important is consistency.

▶ **Definition of Consistency.** A consistent estimator is one for which the probability of estimates close to the value of the population parameter increases as sample size increases.

Somewhat more technically, we can define a consistent estimator as an estimator whose sampling distribution becomes concentrated on the value of the parameter it is intended to estimate as the sample size approaches infinity. The sample mean, in addition to being an efficient estimator, is also a consistent estimator of the population mean: As sample size $n$ goes to infinity, its standard error, $\sigma/\sqrt{n}$, goes to 0 and its sampling distribution becomes concentrated right over the value of population mean, $\mu$. To summarize, we can think of a consistent estimator as one that tends to produce more and more accurate estimates of the population parameter as we increase the sample's size. If an estimator is consistent, we may attempt to increase the accuracy of estimates of a population parameter by calculating estimates using a larger sample. For an inconsistent estimator, however, increasing sample size does not help to increase the probability of accurate estimates.

## 4.2 Confidence Intervals for the Population Mean

When we need a single number as an estimate of a population parameter, we make use of a point estimate. However, because of sampling error, the point estimate is not likely to equal the population parameter in any given sample. Often, a more useful approach than finding a point estimate is to find a range of values that we expect to bracket the parameter with a specified level of probability—an interval estimate of the parameter. A confidence interval fulfills this role.

▶ **Definition of Confidence Interval.** A confidence interval is a range for which one can assert with a given probability $1 - \alpha$, called the **degree of confidence**, that it will contain the parameter it is intended to estimate. This interval is often referred to as the $(1 - \alpha)\%$ confidence interval for the parameter.

The endpoints of a confidence limit are referred to as the lower and upper confidence limits. In this reading, we are concerned only with two-sided confidence intervals—confidence intervals for which we calculate both lower and upper limits.[12]

---

[11] Such problems frequently arise in regression and time-series analyses.

[12] It is also possible to define two types of one-sided confidence intervals for a population parameter. A lower one-sided confidence interval establishes a lower limit only. Associated with such an interval is an assertion that with a specified degree of confidence the population parameter equals or exceeds the lower limit. An upper one-sided confidence interval establishes an upper limit only; the related assertion is that the population parameter is less than or equal to that upper limit, with a specified degree of confidence. Investment researchers rarely present one-sided confidence intervals, however.

Confidence intervals are frequently given either a probabilistic interpretation or a practical interpretation. In the probabilistic interpretation, we interpret a 95 percent confidence interval for the population mean as follows. In repeated sampling, 95 percent of such confidence intervals will, in the long run, include or bracket the population mean. For example, suppose we sample from the population 1,000 times, and based on each sample, we construct a 95 percent confidence interval using the calculated sample mean. Because of random chance, these confidence intervals will vary from each other, but we expect 95 percent, or 950, of these intervals to include the unknown value of the population mean. In practice, we generally do not carry out such repeated sampling. Therefore, in the practical interpretation, we assert that we are 95 percent confident that a single 95 percent confidence interval contains the population mean. We are justified in making this statement because we know that 95 percent of all possible confidence intervals constructed in the same manner will contain the population mean. The confidence intervals that we discuss in this reading have structures similar to the following basic structure.

▶ **Construction of Confidence Intervals.** A $(1 - \alpha)\%$ confidence interval for a parameter has the following structure.

Point estimate $\pm$ Reliability factor $\times$ Standard error
where

Point estimate $=$ a point estimate of the parameter (a value of a sample statistic)

Reliability factor $=$ a number based on the assumed distribution of the point estimate and the degree of confidence $(1 - \alpha)$ for the confidence interval

Standard error $=$ the standard error of the sample statistic providing the point estimate[13]

The most basic confidence interval for the population mean arises when we are sampling from a normal distribution with known variance. The reliability factor in this case is based on the standard normal distribution, which has a mean of 0 and a variance of 1. A standard normal random variable is conventionally denoted by $Z$. The notation $z_\alpha$ denotes the point of the standard normal distribution such that $\alpha$ of the probability remains in the right tail. For example, 0.05 or 5 percent of the possible values of a standard normal random variable are larger than $z_{0.05} = 1.65$.

Suppose we want to construct a 95 percent confidence interval for the population mean and, for this purpose, we have taken a sample of size 100 from a normally distributed population with known variance of $\sigma^2 = 400$ (so, $\sigma = 20$). We calculate a sample mean of $\overline{X} = 25$. Our point estimate of the population mean is, therefore, 25. If we move 1.96 standard deviations above the mean of a normal distribution, 0.025 or 2.5 percent of the probability remains in the right tail; by symmetry of the normal distribution, if we move 1.96 standard deviations below the mean, 0.025 or 2.5 percent of the probability remains in the left tail. In total, 0.05 or 5 percent of the probability is in the two tails and 0.95 or 95 percent lies in between. So, $z_{0.025} = 1.96$ is the reliability factor for this 95 percent confidence interval. Note the relationship $(1 - \alpha)\%$ for the confidence interval and the $z_{\alpha/2}$ for the reliability factor. The standard error of the sample mean, given by

---

[13] The quantity (Reliability factor) $\times$ (Standard error) is sometimes called the precision of the estimator; larger values of the product imply lower precision in estimating the population parameter.

Equation 10-1, is $\sigma_{\overline{X}} = 20/\sqrt{100} = 2$. The confidence interval, therefore, has a lower limit of $\overline{X} - 1.96\sigma_{\overline{X}} = 25 - 1.96(2) = 25 - 3.92 = 21.08$. The upper limit of the confidence interval is $\overline{X} + 1.96\sigma_{\overline{X}} = 25 + 1.96(2) = 25 + 3.92 = 28.92$. The 95 percent confidence interval for the population mean spans 21.08 to 28.92.

▶ **Confidence Intervals for the Population Mean (Normally Distributed Population with Known Variance).** A $(1 - \alpha)\%$ confidence interval for population mean $\mu$ when we are sampling from a normal distribution with known variance $\sigma^2$ is given by

$$\overline{X} \pm z_{\alpha/2} \frac{\sigma}{\sqrt{n}} \qquad \textbf{(10-4)}$$

The reliability factors for the most frequently used confidence intervals are as follows.

▶ **Reliability Factors for Confidence Intervals Based on the Standard Normal Distribution.** We use the following reliability factors when we construct confidence intervals based on the standard normal distribution:[14]

- ▶ 90 percent confidence intervals: Use $z_{0.05} = 1.65$
- ▶ 95 percent confidence intervals: Use $z_{0.025} = 1.96$
- ▶ 99 percent confidence intervals: Use $z_{0.005} = 2.58$

These reliability factors highlight an important fact about all confidence intervals. As we increase the degree of confidence, the confidence interval becomes wider and gives us less precise information about the quantity we want to estimate. "The surer we want to be, the less we have to be sure of."[15]

In practice, the assumption that the sampling distribution of the sample mean is at least approximately normal is frequently reasonable, either because the underlying distribution is approximately normal or because we have a large sample and the central limit theorem applies. However, rarely do we know the population variance in practice. When the population variance is unknown but the sample mean is at least approximately normally distributed, we have two acceptable ways to calculate the confidence interval for the population mean. We will soon discuss the more conservative approach, which is based on Student's $t$-distribution (the $t$-distribution, for short).[16] In investment literature, it is the most frequently used approach in both estimation and hypothesis tests concerning the mean when the population variance is not known, whether sample size is small or large.

A second approach to confidence intervals for the population mean, based on the standard normal distribution, is the $z$-alternative. It can be used only when sample size is large. (In general, a sample size of 30 or larger may be considered large.) In contrast to the confidence interval given in Equation 10-4, this confidence interval uses the sample standard deviation, $s$, in computing the standard error of the sample mean (Equation 10-2).

---

[14] Most practitioners use values for $z_{0.05}$ and $z_{0.005}$ that are carried to two decimal places. For reference, more exact values for $z_{0.05}$ and $z_{0.005}$ are 1.645 and 2.575, respectively. For a quick calculation of a 95 percent confidence interval, $z_{0.025}$ is sometimes rounded from 1.96 to 2.

[15] Freund and Williams (1977), p. 266.

[16] The distribution of the statistic $t$ is called Student's $t$-distribution after the pen name "Student" used by W. S. Gosset, who published his work in 1908.

▶ **Confidence Intervals for the Population Mean—The *z*-Alternative (Large Sample, Population Variance Unknown).** A $(1 - \alpha)\%$ confidence interval for population mean $\mu$ when sampling from any distribution with unknown variance and when sample size is large is given by

$$\overline{X} \pm z_{\alpha/2} \frac{s}{\sqrt{n}} \qquad\qquad \textbf{(10-5)}$$

Because this type of confidence interval appears quite often, we illustrate its calculation in Example 4.

---

### EXAMPLE 4

**Confidence Interval for the Population Mean of Sharpe Ratios—*z*-Statistic**

Suppose an investment analyst takes a random sample of U.S. equity mutual funds and calculates the average Sharpe ratio. The sample size is 100, and the average Sharpe ratio is 0.45. The sample has a standard deviation of 0.30. Calculate and interpret the 90 percent confidence interval for the population mean of all U.S. equity mutual funds by using a reliability factor based on the standard normal distribution.

The reliability factor for a 90 percent confidence interval, as given earlier, is $z_{0.05} = 1.65$. The confidence interval will be

$$\overline{X} \pm z_{0.05} \frac{s}{\sqrt{n}} = 0.45 \pm 1.65 \frac{0.30}{\sqrt{100}} = 0.45 \pm 1.65(0.03) = 0.45 \pm 0.0495$$

The confidence interval spans 0.4005 to 0.4995, or 0.40 to 0.50, carrying two decimal places. The analyst can say with 90 percent confidence that the interval includes the population mean.

In this example, the analyst makes no specific assumption about the probability distribution describing the population. Rather, the analyst relies on the central limit theorem to produce an approximate normal distribution for the sample mean.

---

As Example 4 shows, even if we are unsure of the underlying population distribution, we can still construct confidence intervals for the population mean as long as the sample size is large because we can apply the central limit theorem.

We now turn to the conservative alternative, using the *t*-distribution, for constructing confidence intervals for the population mean when the population variance is not known. For confidence intervals based on samples from normally distributed populations with unknown variance, the theoretically correct reliability factor is based on the *t*-distribution. Using a reliability factor based on the *t*-distribution is essential for a small sample size. Using a *t* reliability factor is appropriate when the population variance is unknown, even when we have a large sample and could use the central limit theorem to justify using a *z* reliability factor. In this large sample case, the *t*-distribution provides more-conservative (wider) confidence intervals.

The *t*-distribution is a symmetrical probability distribution defined by a single parameter known as **degrees of freedom (df)**. Each value for the number of degrees of freedom defines one distribution in this family of distributions. We will shortly compare *t*-distributions with the standard normal distribution, but first we need to understand the concept of degrees of freedom. We can do so by examining the calculation of the sample variance.

Equation 10-3 gives the unbiased estimator of the sample variance that we use. The term in the denominator, $n - 1$, which is the sample size minus 1, is the number of degrees of freedom in estimating the population variance when using Equation 10-3. We also use $n - 1$ as the number of degrees of freedom for determining reliability factors based on the $t$-distribution. The term "degrees of freedom" is used because in a random sample, we assume that observations are selected independently of each other. The numerator of the sample variance, however, uses the sample mean. How does the use of the sample mean affect the number of observations collected independently for the sample variance formula? With a sample of size 10 and a mean of 10 percent, for example, we can freely select only 9 observations. Regardless of the 9 observations selected, we can always find the value for the 10th observation that gives a mean equal to 10 percent. From the standpoint of the sample variance formula, then, there are 9 degrees of freedom. Given that we must first compute the sample mean from the total of $n$ independent observations, only $n - 1$ observations can be chosen independently for the calculation of the sample variance. The concept of degrees of freedom comes up frequently in statistics, and you will see it often in later readings.

Suppose we sample from a normal distribution. The ratio $z = (\overline{X} - \mu)/(\sigma/\sqrt{n})$ is distributed normally with a mean of 0 and standard deviation of 1; however, the ratio $t = (\overline{X} - \mu)/(s/\sqrt{n})$ follows the $t$-distribution with a mean of 0 and $n - 1$ degrees of freedom. The ratio represented by $t$ is not normal because $t$ is the ratio of two random variables, the sample mean and the sample standard deviation. The definition of the standard normal random variable involves only one random variable, the sample mean. As degrees of freedom increase, however, the $t$-distribution approaches the standard normal distribution. Figure 1 shows the standard normal distribution and two $t$-distributions, one with df = 2 and one with df = 8.

Of the three distributions shown in Figure 1, the standard normal distribution has tails that approach zero faster than the tails of the two $t$-distributions. The $t$-distribution is also symmetrically distributed around its mean value of zero, just

**FIGURE 1    Student's $t$-Distribution versus the Standard Normal Distribution**

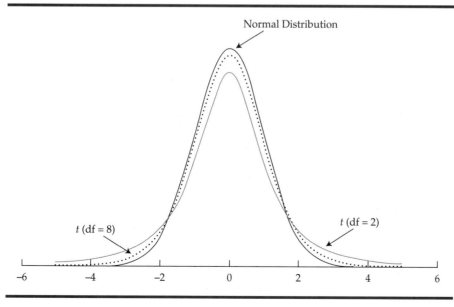

like the normal distribution. As the degrees of freedom increase, the *t*-distribution approaches the standard normal. The *t*-distribution with df = 8 is closer to the standard normal than the *t*-distribution with df = 2.

Beyond plus and minus four standard deviations from the mean, the area under the standard normal distribution appears to approach 0; both *t*-distributions continue to show some area under each curve beyond four standard deviations, however. The *t*-distributions have fatter tails, but the tails of the *t*-distribution with df = 8 more closely resemble the normal distribution's tails. As the degrees of freedom increase, the tails of the *t*-distribution become less fat.

Frequently referred to values for the *t*-distribution are presented in tables at the end of the book. For each degree of freedom, five values are given: $t_{0.10}$, $t_{0.05}$, $t_{0.025}$, $t_{0.01}$, and $t_{0.005}$. The values for $t_{0.10}$, $t_{0.05}$, $t_{0.025}$, $t_{0.01}$, and $t_{0.005}$ are such that, respectively, 0.10, 0.05, 0.025, 0.01, and 0.005 of the probability remains in the right tail, for the specified number of degrees of freedom.[17] For example, for df = 30, $t_{0.10}$ = 1.310, $t_{0.05}$ = 1.697, $t_{0.025}$ = 2.042, $t_{0.01}$ = 2.457, and $t_{0.005}$ = 2.750.

We now give the form of confidence intervals for the population mean using the *t*-distribution.

▶ **Confidence Intervals for the Population Mean (Population Variance Unknown)—*t*-Distribution.** If we are sampling from a population with unknown variance and either of the conditions below holds:

▶ the sample is large, or

▶ the sample is small but the population is normally distributed, or approximately normally distributed,

then a $(1 - \alpha)\%$ confidence interval for the population mean $\mu$ is given by

$$\overline{X} \pm t_{\alpha/2} \frac{s}{\sqrt{n}} \qquad \textbf{(10-6)}$$

where the number of degrees of freedom for $t_{\alpha/2}$ is $n - 1$ and $n$ is the sample size.

Example 5 reprises the data of Example 4 but uses the *t*-statistic rather than the *z*-statistic to calculate a confidence interval for the population mean of Sharpe ratios.

## EXAMPLE 5

### Confidence Interval for the Population Mean of Sharpe Ratios—*t*-Statistic

As in Example 4, an investment analyst seeks to calculate a 90 percent confidence interval for the population mean Sharpe ratio of U.S. equity mutual funds based on a random sample of 100 U.S. equity mutual funds. The sample mean Sharpe ratio is 0.45, and the sample standard

---

[17] The values $t_{0.10}$, $t_{0.05}$, $t_{0.025}$, $t_{0.01}$, and $t_{0.005}$ are also referred to as one-sided critical values of *t* at the 0.10, 0.05, 0.025, 0.01, and 0.005 significance levels, for the specified number of degrees of freedom.

deviation of the Sharpe ratios is 0.30. Now recognizing that the population variance of the distribution of Sharpe ratios is unknown, the analyst decides to calculate the confidence interval using the theoretically correct $t$-statistic.

Because the sample size is 100, df = 99. In the tables in the back of the book, the closest value is df = 100. Using df = 100 and reading down the 0.05 column, we find that $t_{0.05} = 1.66$. This reliability factor is slightly larger than the reliability factor $z_{0.05} = 1.65$ that was used in Example 4. The confidence interval will be

$$\overline{X} \pm t_{0.05}\frac{s}{\sqrt{n}} = 0.45 \pm 1.66\frac{0.30}{\sqrt{100}} = 0.45 \pm 1.66(0.03) = 0.45 \pm 0.0498$$

The confidence interval spans 0.4002 to 0.4998, or 0.40 to 0.50, carrying two decimal places. To two decimal places, the confidence interval is unchanged from the one computed in Example 4.

Table 3 summarizes the various reliability factors that we have used.

### TABLE 3  Basis of Computing Reliability Factors

| Sampling from: | Statistic for Small Sample Size | Statistic for Large Sample Size |
|---|---|---|
| Normal distribution with known variance | $z$ | $z$ |
| Normal distribution with unknown variance | $t$ | $t^*$ |
| Nonnormal distribution with known variance | not available | $z$ |
| Nonnormal distribution with unknown variance | not available | $t^*$ |

*Use of $z$ also acceptable.

## 4.3  Selection of Sample Size

What choices affect the width of a confidence interval? To this point we have discussed two factors that affect width: the choice of statistic ($t$ or $z$) and the choice of degree of confidence (affecting which specific value of $t$ or $z$ we use). These two choices determine the reliability factor. (Recall that a confidence interval has the structure Point estimate $\pm$ Reliability factor $\times$ Standard error.)

The choice of sample size also affects the width of a confidence interval. All else equal, a larger sample size decreases the width of a confidence interval. Recall the expression for the standard error of the sample mean:

$$\text{Standard error of the sample mean} = \frac{\text{Sample standard deviation}}{\sqrt{\text{Sample size}}}$$

We see that the standard error varies inversely with the square root of sample size. As we increase sample size, the standard error decreases and consequently the width of the confidence interval also decreases. The larger the sample size, the greater precision with which we can estimate the population parameter.[18] All else equal, larger samples are good, in that sense. In practice, however, two considerations may operate against increasing sample size. First, as we saw in Example 2 concerning the Sharpe ratio, increasing the size of a sample may result in sampling from more than one population. Second, increasing sample size may involve additional expenses that outweigh the value of additional precision. Thus three issues that the analyst should weigh in selecting sample size are the need for precision, the risk of sampling from more than one population, and the expenses of different sample sizes.

---

### EXAMPLE 6

#### A Money Manager Estimates Net Client Inflows

A money manager wants to obtain a 95 percent confidence interval for fund inflows and outflows over the next six months for his existing clients. He begins by calling a random sample of 10 clients and inquiring about their planned additions to and withdrawals from the fund. The manager then computes the change in cash flow for each client sampled as a percentage change in total funds placed with the manager. A positive percentage change indicates a net cash inflow to the client's account, and a negative percentage change indicates a net cash outflow from the client's account. The manager weights each response by the relative size of the account within the sample and then computes a weighted average.

As a result of this process, the money manager computes a weighted average of 5.5 percent. Thus, a point estimate is that the total amount of funds under management will increase by 5.5 percent in the next six months. The standard deviation of the observations in the sample is 10 percent. A histogram of past data looks fairly close to normal, so the manager assumes the population is normal.

1. Calculate a 95 percent confidence interval for the population mean and interpret your findings.

The manager decides to see what the confidence interval would look like if he had used a sample size of 20 or 30 and found the same mean (5.5 percent) and standard deviation (10 percent).

2. Using the sample mean of 5.5 percent and standard deviation of 10 percent, compute the confidence interval for sample sizes of 20 and 30. For the sample size of 30, use Equation 10-6.

3. Interpret your results from Parts 1 and 2.

**Solution to 1:** Because the population is unknown and the sample size is small, the manager must use the *t*-statistic in Equation 10-6 to calculate the confidence interval. Based on the sample size of 10,

---

[18] A formula exists for determining the sample size needed to obtain a desired width for a confidence interval. Define $E$ = Reliability factor × Standard error. The smaller $E$ is, the smaller the width of the confidence interval, because $2E$ is the confidence interval's width. The sample size to obtain a desired value of $E$ at a given degree of confidence $(1 - \alpha)$ is $n = [(t\alpha/2s)/E]^2$.

df = $n - 1 = 10 - 1 = 9$. For a 95 percent confidence interval, he needs to use the value of $t_{0.025}$ for df = 9. According to the tables in the back of the book, this value is 2.262. Therefore, a 95 percent confidence interval for the population mean is

$$\overline{X} \pm t_{0.025} \frac{s}{\sqrt{n}} = 5.5\% \pm 2.262 \frac{10\%}{\sqrt{10}}$$

$$= 5.5\% \pm 2.262(3.162)$$

$$= 5.5\% \pm 7.15\%$$

The confidence interval for the population mean spans −1.65 percent to +12.65 percent.[19] The manager can be confident at the 95 percent level that this range includes the population mean.

**Solution to 2:** Table 4 gives the calculations for the three sample sizes.

### TABLE 4  The 95 Percent Confidence Interval for Three Sample Sizes

| Distribution | 95% Confidence Interval | Lower Bound | Upper Bound | Relative Size |
|---|---|---|---|---|
| $t(n = 10)$ | 5.5% ± 2.262(3.162) | −1.65% | 12.65% | 100.0% |
| $t(n = 20)$ | 5.5% ± 2.093(2.236) | 0.82 | 10.18 | 65.5 |
| $t(n = 30)$ | 5.5% ± 2.045(1.826) | 1.77 | 9.23 | 52.2 |

**Solution to 3:** The width of the confidence interval decreases as we increase the sample size. This decrease is a function of the standard error becoming smaller as $n$ increases. The reliability factor also becomes smaller as the number of degrees of freedom increases. The last column of Table 4 shows the relative size of the width of confidence intervals based on $n = 10$ to be 100 percent. Using a sample size of 20 reduces the confidence interval's width to 65.5 percent of the interval width for a sample size of 10. Using a sample size of 30 cuts the width of the interval almost in half. Comparing these choices, the money manager would obtain the most precise results using a sample of 30.

Having covered many of the fundamental concepts of sampling and estimation, we are in a good position to focus on sampling issues of special concern to analysts. The quality of inferences depends on the quality of the data as well as on the quality of the sampling plan used. Financial data pose special problems, and sampling plans frequently reflect one or more biases. The next section of this reading discusses these issues.

---

[19] We assumed in this example that sample size is sufficiently small compared with the size of the client base that we can disregard the finite population correction factor (mentioned in Footnote 6).

# 5

# MORE ON SAMPLING

We have already seen that the selection of sample period length may raise the issue of sampling from more than one population. There are, in fact, a range of challenges to valid sampling that arise in working with financial data. In this section we discuss four such sampling-related issues: data-mining bias, sample selection bias, look-ahead bias, and time-period bias. All of these issues are important for point and interval estimation and hypothesis testing. As we will see, if the sample is biased in any way, then point and interval estimates and any other conclusions that we draw from the sample will be in error.

## 5.1 Data-Mining Bias

Data mining relates to overuse of the same or related data in ways that we shall describe shortly. Data-mining bias refers to the errors that arise from such misuse of data. Investment strategies that reflect data-mining biases are often not successful in the future. Nevertheless, both investment practitioners and researchers have frequently engaged in data mining. Analysts thus need to understand and guard against this problem.

**Data-mining** is the practice of determining a model by extensive searching through a dataset for statistically significant patterns (that is, repeatedly "drilling" in the same data until finding something that appears to work).[20] In exercises involving statistical significance we set a significance level, which is the probability of rejecting the hypothesis we are testing when the hypothesis is in fact correct.[21] Because rejecting a true hypothesis is undesirable, the investigator often sets the significance level at a relatively small number such as 0.05 or 5 percent.[22] Suppose we test the hypothesis that a variable does not predict stock returns, and we test in turn 100 different variables. Let us also suppose that in truth none of the 100 variables has the ability to predict stock returns. Using a 5 percent significance level in our tests, we would still expect that 5 out of 100 variables would appear to be significant predictors of stock returns because of random chance alone. We have mined the data to find some apparently significant variables. In essence, we have explored the same data again and again until we found some after-the-fact pattern or patterns in the dataset. This is the sense in which data mining involves overuse of data. If we were to just report the significant variables, without also reporting the total number of variables that we tested that were unsuccessful as predictors, we would be presenting a very misleading picture of our findings. Our results would appear to be far more significant than they actually were, because a series of tests such as the one just described invalidates the conventional interpretation of a given significance level (such as 5 percent), according to the theory of inference.

How can we investigate the presence of data-mining bias? With most financial data, the most ready means is to conduct out-of-sample tests of the proposed variable or strategy. An **out-of-sample test** uses a sample that does not overlap the time period(s) of the sample(s) on which a variable, strategy, or model, was developed. If a variable or investment strategy is the result of data mining, it should

---

[20] Some researchers use the term "data snooping" instead of data mining.

[21] To convey an understanding of data mining, it is very helpful to introduce some basic concepts related to hypothesis testing. The reading on hypothesis testing contains further discussion of significance levels and tests of significance.

[22] In terms of our previous discussion of confidence intervals, significance at the 5 percent level corresponds to a hypothesized value for a population statistic falling outside a 95 percent confidence interval based on an appropriate sample statistic (e.g., the sample mean, when the hypothesis concerns the population mean).

generally not be significant in out-of-sample tests. A variable or investment strategy that is statistically and economically significant in out-of-sample tests, and that has a plausible economic basis, may be the basis for a valid investment strategy. Caution is still warranted, however. The most crucial out-of-sample test is future investment success. If the strategy becomes known to other investors, prices may adjust so that the strategy, however well tested, does not work in the future. To summarize, the analyst should be aware that many apparently profitable investment strategies may reflect data-mining bias and thus be cautious about the future applicability of published investment research results.

Untangling the extent of data mining can be complex. To assess the significance of an investment strategy, we need to know how many unsuccessful strategies were tried not only by the current investigator but also by *previous* investigators using the same or related datasets. Much research, in practice, closely builds on what other investigators have done, and so reflects intergenerational data mining, to use the terminology of McQueen and Thorley (1999). **Intergenerational data mining** involves using information developed by previous researchers using a dataset to guide current research using the same or a related dataset.[23] Analysts have accumulated many observations about the peculiarities of many financial datasets, and other analysts may develop models or investment strategies that will tend to be supported within a dataset based on their familiarity with the prior experience of other analysts. As a consequence, the importance of those new results may be overstated. Research has suggested that the magnitude of this type of data-mining bias may be considerable.[24]

With the background of the above definitions and explanations, we can understand McQueen and Thorley's (1999) cogent exploration of data mining in the context of the popular Motley Fool "Foolish Four" investment strategy. The Foolish Four strategy, first presented in 1996, was a version of the Dow Dividend Strategy that was tuned by its developers to exhibit an even higher arithmetic mean return than the Dow Dividend Strategy over 1973 to 1993.[25] From 1973 to 1993, the Foolish Four portfolio had an average annual return of 25 percent, and the claim was made in print that the strategy should have similar returns in the future. As McQueen and Thorley discussed, however, the Foolish Four strategy was very much subject to data-mining bias, including bias from intergenerational data mining, as the strategy's developers exploited observations about the dataset made by earlier workers. McQueen and Thorley highlighted the data-mining issues by taking the Foolish Four portfolio one step further. They mined the data to create a "Fractured Four" portfolio that earned nearly 35 percent over 1973 to 1996, beating the Foolish Four strategy by almost 8 percentage points. Observing that all of the Foolish Four stocks did well in even years but not odd years and that the second-to-lowest-priced high-yielding stock was relatively the best performing stock in odd years, the strategy of the Fractured Four portfolio was to hold the Foolish Four stocks with equal weights in even years and hold only the second-to-lowest-priced stock in odd years.

---

[23] The term "intergenerational" comes from viewing each round of researchers as a generation. Campbell, Lo, and MacKinlay (1997) have called intergenerational data mining "data snooping." The latter phrase, however, is commonly used as a synonym of data mining; thus McQueen and Thorley's terminology is less ambiguous. The term "intragenerational data mining" is available when we want to highlight that the reference is to an investigator's new or independent data mining.

[24] For example, Lo and MacKinlay (1990) concluded that the magnitude of this type of bias on tests of the capital asset pricing model was considerable.

[25] The Dow Dividend Strategy, also known as Dogs of the Dow Strategy, consists of holding an equally weighted portfolio of the 10 highest-yielding DJIA stocks as of the beginning of a year. At the time of McQueen and Thorley's research, the Foolish Four strategy was as follows: At the beginning of each year, the Foolish Four portfolio purchases a 4-stock portfolio from the 5 lowest-priced stocks of the 10 highest-yielding DJIA stocks. The lowest-priced stock of the five is excluded, and 40 percent is invested in the second-to-lowest-priced stock, with 20 percent weights in the remaining three.

How likely is it that a performance difference between even and odd years reflected underlying economic forces, rather than a chance pattern of the data over the particular time period? Probably, very unlikely. Unless an investment strategy reflected underlying economic forces, we would not expect it to have any value in a forward-looking sense. Because the Foolish Four strategy also partook of data mining, the same issues applied to it. McQueen and Thorley found that in an out-of-sample test over the 1949–72 period, the Foolish Four strategy had about the same mean return as buying and holding the DJIA, but with higher risk. If the higher taxes and transaction costs of the Foolish Four strategy were accounted for, the comparison would have been even more unfavorable.

McQueen and Thorley presented two signs that can warn analysts about the potential existence of data mining:

▶ *Too much digging/too little confidence.* The testing of many variables by the researcher is the "too much digging" warning sign of a data-mining problem. Unfortunately, many researchers do not disclose the number of variables examined in developing a model. Although the number of variables examined may not be reported, we should look closely for verbal hints that the researcher searched over many variables. The use of terms such as "we noticed (or noted) that" or "someone noticed (or noted) that," with respect to a pattern in a dataset, should raise suspicions that the researchers were trying out variables based on their own or others' observations of the data.

▶ *No story/no future.* The absence of an explicit economic rationale for a variable or trading strategy is the "no story" warning sign of a data-mining problem. Without a plausible economic rationale or story for why a variable should work, the variable is unlikely to have predictive power. In a demonstration exercise using an extensive search of variables in an international financial database, Leinweber (1997) found that butter production in a particular country remote from the United States explained 75 percent of the variation in U.S. stock returns as represented by the S&P 500. Such a pattern, with no plausible economic rationale, is highly likely to be a random pattern particular to a specific time period.[26] What if we do have a plausible economic explanation for a significant variable? McQueen and Thorley caution that a plausible economic rationale is a necessary but not a sufficient condition for a trading strategy to have value. As we mentioned earlier, if the strategy is publicized, market prices may adjust to reflect the new information as traders seek to exploit it; as a result, the strategy may no longer work.

## 5.2 Sample Selection Bias

When researchers look into questions of interest to analysts or portfolio managers, they may exclude certain stocks, bonds, portfolios, or time periods from the analysis for various reasons—perhaps because of data availability. When data availability leads to certain assets being excluded from the analysis, we call the resulting problem **sample selection bias**. For example, you might sample from a database that tracks only companies currently in existence. Many mutual fund databases, for instance, provide historical information about only those funds that currently exist. Databases that report historical balance sheet

---

[26] In the finance literature, such a random but irrelevant-to-the-future pattern is sometimes called an artifact of the dataset.

and income statement information suffer from the same sort of bias as the mutual fund databases: Funds or companies that are no longer in business do not appear there. So, a study that uses these types of databases suffers from a type of sample selection bias known as **survivorship bias**.

Dimson, Marsh, and Staunton (2002) raised the issue of survivorship bias in international indexes:

> An issue that has achieved prominence is the impact of market survival on estimated long-run returns. Markets can experience not only disappointing performance but also total loss of value through confiscation, hyperinflation, nationalization, and market failure. By measuring the performance of markets that survive over long intervals, we draw inferences that are conditioned on survival. Yet, as pointed out by Brown, Goetzmann, and Ross (1995) and Jorion and Goetzmann (1999), one cannot determine in advance which markets will survive and which will perish. (p. 41)

Survivorship bias sometimes appears when we use both stock price and accounting data. For example, many studies in finance have used the ratio of a company's market price to book equity per share (i.e., the price-to-book ratio, P/B) and found that P/B is inversely related to a company's returns (see Fama and French 1992, 1993). P/B is also used to create many popular value and growth indexes. If the database that we use to collect accounting data excludes failing companies, however, a survivorship bias might result. Kothari, Shanken, and Sloan (1995) investigated just this question and argued that failing stocks would be expected to have low returns and low P/Bs. If we exclude failing stocks, then those stocks with low P/Bs that are included will have returns that are higher on average than if all stocks with low P/Bs were included. Kothari, Shanken, and Sloan suggested that this bias is responsible for the previous findings of an inverse relationship between average return and P/B.[27] The only advice we can offer at this point is to be aware of any biases potentially inherent in a sample. Clearly, sample selection biases can cloud the results of any study.

A sample can also be biased because of the removal (or delisting) of a company's stock from an exchange.[28] For example, the Center for Research in Security Prices at the University of Chicago is a major provider of return data used in academic research. When a delisting occurs, CRSP attempts to collect returns for the delisted company, but many times, it cannot do so because of the difficulty involved; CRSP must simply list delisted company returns as missing. A study in the *Journal of Finance* by Shumway and Warther (1999) documented the bias caused by delisting for CRSP Nasdaq return data. The authors showed that delistings associated with poor company performance (e.g., bankruptcy) are missed more often than delistings associated with good or neutral company performance (e.g., merger or moving to another exchange). In addition, delistings occur more frequently for small companies.

Sample selection bias occurs even in markets where the quality and consistency of the data are quite high. Newer asset classes such as hedge funds may present even greater problems of sample selection bias. Hedge funds are a heterogeneous group of investment vehicles typically organized so as to be free from regulatory oversight. In general, hedge funds are not required to publicly disclose performance (in contrast to, say, mutual funds). Hedge funds themselves

---

[27] See Fama and French (1996, p. 80) for discussion of data snooping and survivorship bias in their tests.

[28] Delistings occur for a variety of reasons: merger, bankruptcy, liquidation, or migration to another exchange.

decide whether they want to be included in one of the various databases of hedge fund performance. Hedge funds with poor track records clearly may not wish to make their records public, creating a problem of self-selection bias in hedge fund databases. Further, as pointed out by Fung and Hsieh (2002), because only hedge funds with good records will volunteer to enter a database, in general, overall past hedge fund industry performance will tend to appear better than it really is. Furthermore, many hedge fund databases drop funds that go out of business, creating survivorship bias in the database. Even if the database does not drop defunct hedge funds, in the attempt to eliminate survivorship bias, the problem remains of hedge funds that stop reporting performance because of poor results.[29]

## 5.3 Look-Ahead Bias

A test design is subject to **look-ahead bias** if it uses information that was not available on the test date. For example, tests of trading rules that use stock market returns and accounting balance sheet data must account for look-ahead bias. In such tests, a company's book value per share is commonly used to construct the P/B variable. Although the market price of a stock is available for all market participants at the same point in time, fiscal year-end book equity per share might not become publicly available until sometime in the following quarter.

## 5.4 Time-Period Bias

A test design is subject to **time-period bias** if it is based on a time period that may make the results time-period specific. A short time series is likely to give period specific results that may not reflect a longer period. A long time series may give a more accurate picture of true investment performance; its disadvantage lies in the potential for a structural change occurring during the time frame that would result in two different return distributions. In this situation, the distribution that would reflect conditions before the change differs from the distribution that would describe conditions after the change.

---

### EXAMPLE 7

**Biases in Investment Research**

An analyst is reviewing the empirical evidence on historical U.S. equity returns. She finds that value stocks (i.e., those with low P/Bs) outperformed growth stocks (i.e., those with high P/Bs) in some recent time periods. After reviewing the U.S. market, the analyst wonders whether value stocks might be attractive in the United Kingdom. She investigates the performance of value and growth stocks in the U.K. market from January 1990 to December 2003. To conduct this research, the analyst does the following:

---

[29] See Ackerman, McEnally, and Ravenscraft (1999) and Fung and Hsieh (2002) for more details on the problems of interpreting hedge fund performance. Note that an offsetting type of bias may occur if successful funds stop reporting performance because they no longer want new cash inflows.

▶ obtains the current composition of the Financial Times Stock Exchange (FTSE) All Share Index, which is a market-capitalization-weighted index;

▶ eliminates the few companies that do not have December fiscal year-ends;

▶ uses year-end book values and market prices to rank the remaining universe of companies by P/Bs at the end of the year;

▶ based on these rankings, divides the universe into 10 portfolios, each of which contains an equal number of stocks;

▶ calculates the equal-weighted return of each portfolio and the return for the FTSE All Share Index for the 12 months following the date each ranking was made; and

▶ subtracts the FTSE returns from each portfolio's returns to derive excess returns for each portfolio.

Describe and discuss each of the following biases introduced by the analyst's research design:

▶ survivorship bias,
▶ look-ahead bias, and
▶ time-period bias.

*Survivorship Bias.* A test design is subject to survivorship bias if it fails to account for companies that have gone bankrupt, merged, or otherwise departed the database. In this example, the analyst used the current list of FTSE stocks rather than the actual list of stocks that existed at the start of each year. To the extent that the computation of returns excluded companies removed from the index, the performance of the portfolios with the lowest P/B is subject to survivorship bias and may be overstated. At some time during the testing period, those companies not currently in existence were eliminated from testing. They would probably have had low prices (and low P/Bs) and poor returns.

*Look-Ahead Bias.* A test design is subject to look-ahead bias if it uses information unavailable on the test date. In this example, the analyst conducted the test under the assumption that the necessary accounting information was available at the end of the fiscal year. For example, the analyst assumed that book value per share for fiscal 1990 was available on 31 December 1990. Because this information is not released until several months after the close of a fiscal year, the test may have contained look-ahead bias. This bias would make a strategy based on the information appear successful, but it assumes perfect forecasting ability.

*Time-Period Bias.* A test design is subject to time-period bias if it is based on a time period that may make the results time-period specific. Although the test covered a period extending more than 10 years, that period may be too short for testing an anomaly. Ideally, an analyst should test market anomalies over several business cycles to ensure that results are not period specific. This bias can favor a proposed strategy if the time period chosen was favorable to the strategy.

# SUMMARY

In this reading, we have presented basic concepts and results in sampling and estimation. We have also emphasized the challenges faced by analysts in appropriately using and interpreting financial data. As analysts, we should always use a critical eye when evaluating the results from any study. The quality of the sample is of the utmost importance: If the sample is biased, the conclusions drawn from the sample will be in error.

▶ To draw valid inferences from a sample, the sample should be random.

▶ In simple random sampling, each observation has an equal chance of being selected. In stratified random sampling, the population is divided into subpopulations, called strata or cells, based on one or more classification criteria; simple random samples are then drawn from each stratum.

▶ Stratified random sampling ensures that population subdivisions of interest are represented in the sample. Stratified random sampling also produces more-precise parameter estimates than simple random sampling.

▶ Time-series data are a collection of observations at equally spaced intervals of time. Cross-sectional data are observations that represent individuals, groups, geographical regions, or companies at a single point in time.

▶ The central limit theorem states that for large sample sizes, for any underlying distribution for a random variable, the sampling distribution of the sample mean for that variable will be approximately normal, with mean equal to the population mean for that random variable and variance equal to the population variance of the variable divided by sample size.

▶ Based on the central limit theorem, when the sample size is large, we can compute confidence intervals for the population mean based on the normal distribution regardless of the distribution of the underlying population. In general, a sample size of 30 or larger can be considered large.

▶ An estimator is a formula for estimating a parameter. An estimate is a particular value that we calculate from a sample by using an estimator.

▶ Because an estimator or statistic is a random variable, it is described by some probability distribution. We refer to the distribution of an estimator as its sampling distribution. The standard deviation of the sampling distribution of the sample mean is called the standard error of the sample mean.

▶ The desirable properties of an estimator are unbiasedness (the expected value of the estimator equals the population parameter), efficiency (the estimator has the smallest variance), and consistency (the probability of accurate estimates increases as sample size increases).

▶ The two types of estimates of a parameter are point estimates and interval estimates. A point estimate is a single number that we use to estimate a parameter. An interval estimate is a range of values that brackets the population parameter with some probability.

▶ A confidence interval is an interval for which we can assert with a given probability $1 - \alpha$, called the degree of confidence, that it will contain the parameter it is intended to estimate. This measure is often referred to as the $(1 - \alpha)\%$ confidence interval for the parameter.

▶ A $(1 - \alpha)\%$ confidence interval for a parameter has the following structure: Point estimate ± Reliability factor × Standard error, where the reliability factor is a number based on the assumed distribution of the point estimate and the degree of confidence $(1 - \alpha)$ for the confidence interval and where standard error is the standard error of the sample statistic providing the point estimate.

▶ A $(1 - \alpha)\%$ confidence interval for population mean $\mu$ when sampling from a normal distribution with known variance $\sigma^2$ is given by $\overline{X} \pm z_{\alpha/2} (\sigma / \sqrt{n})$, where $z_{\alpha/2}$ is the point of the standard normal distribution such that $\alpha/2$ remains in the right tail.

▶ Student's $t$-distribution is a family of symmetrical distributions defined by a single parameter, degrees of freedom.

▶ A random sample of size $n$ is said to have $n - 1$ degrees of freedom for estimating the population variance, in the sense that there are only $n - 1$ independent deviations from the mean on which to base the estimate.

▶ The degrees of freedom number for use with the $t$-distribution is also $n - 1$.

▶ The $t$-distribution has fatter tails than the standard normal distribution but converges to the standard normal distribution as degrees of freedom go to infinity.

▶ A $(1 - \alpha)\%$ confidence interval for the population mean $\mu$ when sampling from a normal distribution with unknown variance (a $t$-distribution confidence interval) is given by $\overline{X} \pm t_{\alpha/2} (s / \sqrt{n})$, where $t_{\alpha/2}$ is the point of the $t$-distribution such that $\alpha/2$ remains in the right tail and $s$ is the sample standard deviation. This confidence interval can also be used, because of the central limit theorem, when dealing with a large sample from a population with unknown variance that may not be normal.

▶ We may use the confidence interval $\overline{X} \pm z_{\alpha/2} (s / \sqrt{n})$ as an alternative to the $t$-distribution confidence interval for the population mean when using a large sample from a population with unknown variance. The confidence interval based on the $z$-statistic is less conservative (narrower) than the corresponding confidence interval based on a $t$-distribution.

▶ Three issues in the selection of sample size are the need for precision, the risk of sampling from more than one population, and the expenses of different sample sizes.

▶ Sample data in investments can have a variety of problems. Survivorship bias occurs if companies are excluded from the analysis because they have gone out of business or because of reasons related to poor performance. Data-mining bias comes from finding models by repeatedly searching through databases for patterns. Look-ahead bias exists if the model uses data not available to market participants at the time the market participants act in the model. Finally, time-period bias is present if the time period used makes the results time-period specific or if the time period used includes a point of structural change.

## PRACTICE PROBLEMS FOR READING 10

1. Peter Biggs wants to know how growth managers performed last year. Biggs assumes that the population cross-sectional standard deviation of growth manager returns is 6 percent and that the returns are independent across managers.

   A. How large a random sample does Biggs need if he wants the standard deviation of the sample means to be 1 percent?

   B. How large a random sample does Biggs need if he wants the standard deviation of the sample means to be 0.25 percent?

2. Petra Munzi wants to know how value managers performed last year. Munzi assumes that the population cross-sectional standard deviation of value manager returns is 4 percent and that the returns are independent across managers.

   A. Munzi wants to build a 95 percent confidence interval for the mean return. How large a random sample does Munzi need if she wants the 95 percent confidence interval to have a total width of 1 percent?

   B. Munzi expects a cost of about $10 to collect each observation. If she has a $1,000 budget, will she be able to construct the confidence interval she wants?

3. Assume that the equity risk premium is normally distributed with a population mean of 6 percent and a population standard deviation of 18 percent. Over the last four years, equity returns (relative to the risk-free rate) have averaged −2.0 percent. You have a large client who is very upset and claims that results this poor should *never* occur. Evaluate your client's concerns.

   A. Construct a 95 percent confidence interval around the population mean for a sample of four-year returns.

   B. What is the probability of a −2.0 percent or lower average return over a four-year period?

4. Compare the standard normal distribution and Student's *t*-distribution.

5. Find the reliability factors based on the *t*-distribution for the following confidence intervals for the population mean (df = degrees of freedom, *n* = sample size):

   A. A 99 percent confidence interval, df = 20.

   B. A 90 percent confidence interval, df = 20.

   C. A 95 percent confidence interval, *n* = 25.

   D. A 95 percent confidence interval, *n* = 16.

6. Assume that monthly returns are normally distributed with a mean of 1 percent and a sample standard deviation of 4 percent. The population standard deviation is unknown. Construct a 95 percent confidence interval for the sample mean of monthly returns if the sample size is 24.

**7.** Ten analysts have given the following fiscal year earnings forecasts for a stock:

| Forecast ($X_i$) | Number of Analysts ($n_i$) |
|---|---|
| 1.40 | 1 |
| 1.43 | 1 |
| 1.44 | 3 |
| 1.45 | 2 |
| 1.47 | 1 |
| 1.48 | 1 |
| 1.50 | 1 |

Because the sample is a small fraction of the number of analysts who follow this stock, assume that we can ignore the finite population correction factor. Assume that the analyst forecasts are normally distributed.

**A.** What are the mean forecast and standard deviation of forecasts?

**B.** Provide a 95 percent confidence interval for the population mean of the forecasts.

**8.** Thirteen analysts have given the following fiscal-year earnings forecasts for a stock:

| Forecast ($X_i$) | Number of Analysts ($n_i$) |
|---|---|
| 0.70 | 2 |
| 0.72 | 4 |
| 0.74 | 1 |
| 0.75 | 3 |
| 0.76 | 1 |
| 0.77 | 1 |
| 0.82 | 1 |

Because the sample is a small fraction of the number of analysts who follow this stock, assume that we can ignore the finite population correction factor.

**A.** What are the mean forecast and standard deviation of forecasts?

**B.** What aspect of the data makes us uncomfortable about using $t$-tables to construct confidence intervals for the population mean forecast?

**9.** Explain the differences between constructing a confidence interval when sampling from a normal population with a known population variance and sampling from a normal population with an unknown variance.

10. An exchange rate has a given expected future value and standard deviation.

   A. Assuming that the exchange rate is normally distributed, what are the probabilities that the exchange rate will be at least 1, 2, or 3 standard deviations away from its mean?

   B. Assume that you do not know the distribution of exchange rates. Use Chebyshev's inequality (that at least $1 - 1/k^2$ proportion of the observations will be within $k$ standard deviations of the mean for any positive integer $k$ greater than 1) to calculate the maximum probabilities that the exchange rate will be at least 1, 2, or 3 standard deviations away from its mean.

11. Although he knows security returns are not independent, a colleague makes the claim that because of the central limit theorem, if we diversify across a large number of investments, the portfolio standard deviation will eventually approach zero as $n$ becomes large. Is he correct?

12. Why is the central limit theorem important?

13. What is wrong with the following statement of the central limit theorem?

> ***Central Limit Theorem.*** "If the random variables $X_1, X_2, X_3, \ldots, X_n$ are a random sample of size $n$ from any distribution with finite mean $\mu$ and variance $\sigma^2$, then the distribution of $\overline{X}$ will be approximately normal, with a standard deviation of $\sigma/\sqrt{n}$."

14. Suppose we take a random sample of 30 companies in an industry with 200 companies. We calculate the sample mean of the ratio of cash flow to total debt for the prior year. We find that this ratio is 23 percent. Subsequently, we learn that the population cash flow to total debt ratio (taking account of all 200 companies) is 26 percent. What is the explanation for the discrepancy between the sample mean of 23 percent and the population mean of 26 percent?

   A. Sampling error.

   B. Bias.

   C. A lack of consistency.

15. Alcorn Mutual Funds is placing large advertisements in several financial publications. The advertisements prominently display the returns of 5 of Alcorn's 30 funds for the past 1-, 3-, 5-, and 10-year periods. The results are indeed impressive, with all of the funds beating the major market indexes and a few beating them by a large margin. Is the Alcorn family of funds superior to its competitors?

16. A pension plan executive says, "One hundred percent of our portfolio managers are hired because they have above-average performance records relative to their benchmarks. We do not keep portfolio managers who have below-average records. And yet, each year about half of our managers beat their benchmarks and about half do not. What is going on?" Give a possible statistical explanation.

**17.** Julius Spence has tested several predictive models in order to identify undervalued stocks. Spence used about 30 company-specific variables and 10 market-related variables to predict returns for about 5,000 North American and European stocks. He found that a final model using eight variables applied to telecommunications and computer stocks yields spectacular results. Spence wants you to use the model to select investments. Should you? What steps would you take to evaluate the model?

**18.** Hand Associates manages two portfolios that are meant to closely track the returns of two stock indexes. One index is a value-weighted index of 500 stocks in which the weight for each stock depends on the stock's total market value. The other index is an equal-weighted index of 500 stocks in which the weight for each stock is 1/500. Hand Associates invests in only about 50 to 100 stocks in each portfolio in order to control transactions costs. Should Hand use simple random sampling or stratified random sampling to choose the stocks in each portfolio?

**19.** Give an example of each of the following:

**A.** Sample-selection bias.

**B.** Look-ahead bias.

**C.** Time-period bias.

**20.** What are some of the desirable statistical properties of an estimator, such as a sample mean?

**21.** An analyst performed a regression using one independent variable. If the *F*-statistic is equal to zero, the *most* accurate statement about the regression is that the

**A.** intercept is equal to one.

**B.** intercept is equal to zero.

**C.** slope coefficient is equal to zero.

**22.** An analyst stated that as degrees of freedom increase, a *t*-distribution will become more peaked and the tails of the *t*-distribution will become less fat. Is the analyst's statement correct with respect to the *t*-distribution:

|  | becoming more peaked? | tails becoming less fat? |
|---|---|---|
| **A.** | No | Yes |
| **B.** | Yes | No |
| **C.** | Yes | Yes |

**23.** An analyst stated that, all else equal, increasing sample size will decrease both the standard error and the width of the confidence interval. The analyst's statement is correct in regard to

**A.** both the standard error and the confidence interval.

**B.** the standard error, but incorrect in regard to the confidence interval.

**C.** the confidence interval, but incorrect in regard to the standard error.

# HYPOTHESIS TESTING

by Richard A. DeFusco, CFA, Dennis W. McLeavey, CFA,
Jerald E. Pinto, CFA, and David E. Runkle, CFA

## LEARNING OUTCOMES

| The candidate should be able to: | Mastery |
|---|---|
| **a.** define a hypothesis, describe the steps of hypothesis testing, interpret and discuss the choice of the null hypothesis and alternative hypothesis, and distinguish between one-tailed and two-tailed tests of hypotheses; | ☐ |
| **b.** define and interpret a test statistic, a Type I and a Type II error, and a significance level, and explain how significance levels are used in hypothesis testing; | ☐ |
| **c.** define and interpret a decision rule and the power of a test, and explain the relation between confidence intervals and hypothesis tests; | ☐ |
| **d.** distinguish between a statistical result and an economically meaningful result; | ☐ |
| **e.** identify the appropriate test statistic and interpret the results for a hypothesis test concerning 1) the population mean of a normally distributed population with a) known or b) unknown variance, 2) the equality of the population means of two normally distributed populations, based on independent random samples with a) equal or b) unequal assumed variances, and 3) the mean difference of two normally distributed populations (paired comparisons test); | ☐ |
| **f.** identify the appropriate test statistic and interpret the results for a hypothesis test concerning 1) the variance of a normally distributed population, and 2) the equality of the variances of two normally distributed populations, based on two independent random samples; | ☐ |
| **g.** distinguish between parametric and nonparametric tests and describe the situations in which the use of nonparametric tests may be appropriate. | ☐ |

## INTRODUCTION     1

Analysts often confront competing ideas about how financial markets work. Some of these ideas develop through personal research or experience with markets; others come from interactions with colleagues; and many others appear

*Quantitative Methods for Investment Analysis*, Second Edition, by Richard A. DeFusco, CFA, Dennis W. McLeavey, CFA, Jerald E. Pinto, CFA, and David E. Runkle, CFA. Copyright © 2004 by CFA Institute. Reprinted with permission.

in the professional literature on finance and investments. In general, how can an analyst decide whether statements about the financial world are probably true or probably false?

When we can reduce an idea or assertion to a definite statement about the value of a quantity, such as an underlying or population mean, the idea becomes a statistically testable statement or hypothesis. The analyst may want to explore questions such as the following:

▶ Is the underlying mean return on this mutual fund different from the underlying mean return on its benchmark?

▶ Did the volatility of returns on this stock change after the stock was added to a stock market index?

▶ Are a security's bid–ask spreads related to the number of dealers making a market in the security?

▶ Do data from a national bond market support a prediction of an economic theory about the term structure of interest rates (the relationship between yield and maturity)?

To address these questions, we use the concepts and tools of hypothesis testing. Hypothesis testing is part of statistical inference, the process of making judgments about a larger group (a population) on the basis of a smaller group actually observed (a sample). The concepts and tools of hypothesis testing provide an objective means to gauge whether the available evidence supports the hypothesis. After a statistical test of a hypothesis we should have a clearer idea of the probability that a hypothesis is true or not, although our conclusion always stops short of certainty. Hypothesis testing has been a powerful tool in the advancement of investment knowledge and science. As Robert L. Kahn of the Institute for Social Research (Ann Arbor, Michigan) has written, "The mill of science grinds only when hypothesis and data are in continuous and abrasive contact."

The main emphases of this reading are the framework of hypothesis testing and tests concerning mean and variance, two quantities frequently used in investments. We give an overview of the procedure of hypothesis testing in the next section. We then address testing hypotheses about the mean and hypotheses about the differences between means. In the fourth section of this reading, we address testing hypotheses about a single variance and hypotheses about the differences between variances. We end the reading with an overview of some other important issues and techniques in statistical inference.

## 2     HYPOTHESIS TESTING

Hypothesis testing, as we have mentioned, is part of the branch of statistics known as statistical inference. Traditionally, the field of statistical inference has two subdivisions: **estimation** and **hypothesis testing**. Estimation addresses the question "What is this parameter's (e.g., the population mean's) value?" The answer is in the form of a confidence interval built around a point estimate. Take the case of the mean: We build a confidence interval for the population mean around the sample mean as a point estimate. For the sake of specificity, suppose the sample mean is 50 and a 95 percent confidence interval for the population mean is $50 \pm 10$ (the confidence interval runs from 40 to 60). If this confidence interval has been properly constructed, there is a 95 percent probability that the interval from 40 to 60 contains the population mean's value.[1] The second branch of statistical inference, hypothesis testing, has a somewhat different focus. A hypothesis testing question is "Is the value of the parameter (say, the population mean) 45 (or some other specific value)?" The assertion "the population mean is 45" is a hypothesis. A **hypothesis** is defined as a statement about one or more populations.

This section focuses on the concepts of hypothesis testing. The process of hypothesis testing is part of a rigorous approach to acquiring knowledge known as the scientific method. The scientific method starts with observation and the formulation of a theory to organize and explain observations. We judge the correctness of the theory by its ability to make accurate predictions—for example, to predict the results of new observations.[2] If the predictions are correct, we continue to maintain the theory as a possibly correct explanation of our observations. When risk plays a role in the outcomes of observations, as in finance, we can only try to make unbiased, probability-based judgments about whether the new data support the predictions. Statistical hypothesis testing fills that key role of testing hypotheses when chance plays a role. In an analyst's day-to-day work, he may address questions to which he might give answers of varying quality. When an analyst correctly formulates the question into a testable hypothesis and carries out and reports on a hypothesis test, he has provided an element of support to his answer consistent with the standards of the scientific method. Of course, the analyst's logic, economic reasoning, information sources, and perhaps other factors also play a role in our assessment of the answer's quality.[3]

We organize this introduction to hypothesis testing around the following list of seven steps.

> ► **Steps in Hypothesis Testing.** The steps in testing a hypothesis are as follows:[4]
>
>   **1.** Stating the hypotheses.
>   **2.** Identifying the appropriate test statistic and its probability distribution.
>   **3.** Specifying the significance level.
>   **4.** Stating the decision rule.
>   **5.** Collecting the data and calculating the test statistic.
>   **6.** Making the statistical decision.
>   **7.** Making the economic or investment decision.

We will explain each of these steps using as illustration a hypothesis test concerning the sign of the risk premium on Canadian stocks. The steps above constitute a traditional approach to hypothesis testing. We will end the section with a frequently used alternative to those steps, the $p$-value approach.

---

[1] We discussed the construction and interpretation of confidence intervals in the reading on sampling and estimation.

[2] To be testable, a theory must be capable of making predictions that can be shown to be wrong.

[3] See Freeley and Steinberg (1999) for a discussion of critical thinking applied to reasoned decision making.

[4] This list is based on one in Daniel and Terrell (1986).

*The first step in hypothesis testing is stating the hypotheses.* We always state two hypotheses: the null hypothesis (or null), designated $H_0$, and the alternative hypothesis, designated $H_a$.

▶ **Definition of Null Hypothesis.** The null hypothesis is the hypothesis to be tested. For example, we could hypothesize that the population mean risk premium for Canadian equities is less than or equal to zero.

The null hypothesis is a proposition that is considered true unless the sample we use to conduct the hypothesis test gives convincing evidence that the null hypothesis is false. When such evidence is present, we are led to the alternative hypothesis.

▶ **Definition of Alternative Hypothesis.** The alternative hypothesis is the hypothesis accepted when the null hypothesis is rejected. Our alternative hypothesis is that the population mean risk premium for Canadian equities is greater than zero.

Suppose our question concerns the value of a population parameter, $\theta$, in relation to one possible value of the parameter, $\theta_0$ (these are read, respectively, "theta" and "theta sub zero").[5] Examples of a population parameter include the population mean, $\mu$, and the population variance, $\sigma^2$. We can formulate three different sets of hypotheses, which we label according to the assertion made by the alternative hypothesis.

▶ **Formulations of Hypotheses.** We can formulate the null and alternative hypotheses in three different ways:
   **1.** $H_0: \theta = \theta_0$ versus $H_a: \theta \neq \theta_0$   (a "not equal to" alternative hypothesis)
   **2.** $H_0: \theta \leq \theta_0$ versus $H_a: \theta > \theta_0$   (a "greater than" alternative hypothesis)
   **3.** $H_0: \theta \geq \theta_0$ versus $H_a: \theta < \theta_0$   (a "less than" alternative hypothesis)

In our Canadian example, $\theta = \mu_{RP}$ and represents the population mean risk premium on Canadian equities. Also, $\theta_0 = 0$ and we are using the second of the above three formulations.

The first formulation is a **two-sided hypothesis test** (or **two-tailed hypothesis test**): We reject the null in favor of the alternative if the evidence indicates that the population parameter is either smaller or larger than $\theta_0$. In contrast, Formulations 2 and 3 are each a **one-sided hypothesis test** (or **one-tailed hypothesis test**). For Formulations 2 and 3, we reject the null only if the evidence indicates that the population parameter is respectively greater than or less than $\theta_0$. The alternative hypothesis has one side.

Notice that in each case above, we state the null and alternative hypotheses such that they account for all possible values of the parameter. With Formulation 1, for example, the parameter is either equal to the hypothesized value $\theta_0$ (under the null hypothesis) or not equal to the hypothesized value $\theta_0$ (under the alternative hypothesis). Those two statements logically exhaust all possible values of the parameter.

Despite the different ways to formulate hypotheses, we always conduct a test of the null hypothesis at the point of equality, $\theta = \theta_0$. Whether the null is $H_0: \theta = \theta_0$, $H_0: \theta \leq \theta_0$, or $H_0: \theta \geq \theta_0$, we actually test $\theta = \theta_0$. The reasoning is straightforward. Suppose the hypothesized value of the parameter is 5. Consider $H_0: \theta \leq 5$, with a "greater than" alternative hypothesis, $H_a: \theta > 5$. If we have enough evidence to reject $H_0: \theta = 5$ in favor of $H_a: \theta > 5$, we definitely also have enough

---

[5] Greek letters, such as $\sigma$, are reserved for population parameters; Roman letters in italics, such as $s$, are used for sample statistics.

evidence to reject the hypothesis that the parameter, $\theta$, is some smaller value, such as 4.5 or 4. To review, the calculation to test the null hypothesis is the same for all three formulations. What is different for the three formulations, we will see shortly, is how the calculation is evaluated to decide whether or not to reject the null.

How do we choose the null and alternative hypotheses? Probably most common are "not equal to" alternative hypotheses. We reject the null because the evidence indicates that the parameter is either larger or smaller than $\theta_0$. Sometimes, however, we may have a "suspected" or "hoped for" condition for which we want to find supportive evidence.[6] In that case, we can formulate the alternative hypothesis as the statement that this condition is true; the null hypothesis that we test is the statement that this condition is not true. If the evidence supports rejecting the null and accepting the alternative, we have statistically confirmed what we thought was true. For example, economic theory suggests that investors require a positive risk premium on stocks (the **risk premium** is defined as the expected return on stocks minus the risk-free rate). Following the principle of stating the alternative as the "hoped for" condition, we formulate the following hypotheses:

$H_0$: The population mean risk premium on Canadian stocks is less than or equal to 0.

$H_a$: The population mean risk premium on Canadian stocks is positive.

Note that "greater than" and "less than" alternative hypotheses reflect the beliefs of the researcher more strongly than a "not equal to" alternative hypothesis. To emphasize an attitude of neutrality, the researcher may sometimes select a "not equal to" alternative hypothesis when a one-sided alternative hypothesis is also reasonable.

*The second step in hypothesis testing is identifying the appropriate test statistic and its probability distribution.*

▶ **Definition of Test Statistic.** A test statistic is a quantity, calculated based on a sample, whose value is the basis for deciding whether or not to reject the null hypothesis.

The focal point of our statistical decision is the value of the test statistic. Frequently (in all the cases that we examine in this reading), the test statistic has the form

$$\text{Test statistic} = \frac{\text{Sample statistic} - \text{Value of the population parameter under } H_0}{\text{Standard error of the sample statistic}} \qquad \textbf{(11-1)}$$

For our risk premium example, the population parameter of interest is the population mean risk premium, $\mu_{RP}$. We label the hypothesized value of the population mean under $H_0$ as $\mu_0$. Restating the hypotheses using symbols, we test $H_0$: $\mu_{RP} \le \mu_0$ versus $H_a$: $\mu_{RP} > \mu_0$. However, because under the null we are testing $\mu_0 = 0$, we write $H_0$: $\mu_{RP} \le 0$ versus $H_a$: $\mu_{RP} > 0$.

The sample mean provides an estimate of the population mean. Therefore, we can use the sample mean risk premium calculated from historical data, $\overline{X}_{RP}$, as the sample statistic in Equation 11-1. The standard deviation of the sample statistic, known as the "standard error" of the statistic, is the denominator in Equation 11-1. For this example, the sample statistic is a sample mean. For a sample mean, $\overline{X}$, calculated from a sample generated by a population with standard deviation $\sigma$, the standard error is given by one of two expressions:

---

[6] Part of this discussion of the selection of hypotheses follows Bowerman and O'Connell (1997, p. 386).

$$\sigma_{\overline{X}} = \frac{\sigma}{\sqrt{n}}$$

(11-2)

when we know $\sigma$ (the population standard deviation), or

$$s_{\overline{X}} = \frac{s}{\sqrt{n}}$$

(11-3)

when we do not know the population standard deviation and need to use the sample standard deviation $s$ to estimate it. For this example, because we do not know the population standard deviation of the process generating the return, we use Equation 11-3. The test statistic is thus

$$\frac{\overline{X}_{RP} - \mu_0}{s_{\overline{X}}} = \frac{\overline{X}_{RP} - 0}{s/\sqrt{n}}$$

In making the substitution of 0 for $\mu_0$, we use the fact already highlighted that we test any null hypothesis at the point of equality, as well as the fact that $\mu_0 = 0$ here.

We have identified a test statistic to test the null hypothesis. What probability distribution does it follow? We will encounter four distributions for test statistics in this reading:

▶ the $t$-distribution (for a $t$-test),

▶ the standard normal or $z$-distribution (for a $z$-test),

▶ the chi-square ($\chi^2$) distribution (for a chi-square test), and

▶ the $F$-distribution (for an $F$-test).

We will discuss the details later, but assume we can conduct a $z$-test based on the central limit theorem because our Canadian sample has many observations.[7] To summarize, the test statistic for the hypothesis test concerning the mean risk premium is $\overline{X}_{RP}/s_{\overline{X}}$. We can conduct a $z$-test because we can plausibly assume that the test statistic follows a standard normal distribution.

*The third step in hypothesis testing is specifying the significance level.* When the test statistic has been calculated, two actions are possible: (1) We reject the null hypothesis or (2) we do not reject the null hypothesis. The action we take is based on comparing the calculated test statistic to a specified possible value or values. The comparison values we choose are based on the level of significance selected. The level of significance reflects how much sample evidence we require to reject the null. Analogous to its counterpart in a court of law, the required standard of proof can change according to the nature of the hypotheses and the seriousness of the consequences of making a mistake. There are four possible outcomes when we test a null hypothesis:

1. We reject a false null hypothesis. This is a correct decision.

2. We reject a true null hypothesis. This is called a **Type I error.**

---

[7] The central limit theorem says that the sampling distribution of the sample mean will be approximately normal with mean $\mu$ and variance $\sigma^2/n$ when the sample size is large. The sample we will use for this example has 103 observations.

**3.** We do not reject a false null hypothesis. This is called a **Type II error**.

**4.** We do not reject a true null hypothesis. This is a correct decision.

We illustrate these outcomes in Table 1.

**TABLE 1  Type I and Type II Errors in Hypothesis Testing**

|  | True Situation | |
|---|---|---|
| Decision | $H_0$ True | $H_0$ False |
| Do not reject $H_0$ | Correct Decision | Type II Error |
| Reject $H_0$ (accept $H_a$) | Type I Error | Correct Decision |

When we make a decision in a hypothesis test, we run the risk of making either a Type I or a Type II error. These are mutually exclusive errors: If we mistakenly reject the null, we can only be making a Type I error; if we mistakenly fail to reject the null, we can only be making a Type II error.

The probability of a Type I error in testing a hypothesis is denoted by the Greek letter alpha, $\alpha$. This probability is also known as the **level of significance** of the test. For example, a level of significance of 0.05 for a test means that there is a 5 percent probability of rejecting a true null hypothesis. The probability of a Type II error is denoted by the Greek letter beta, $\beta$.

Controlling the probabilities of the two types of errors involves a trade-off. All else equal, if we decrease the probability of a Type I error by specifying a smaller significance level (say 0.01 rather than 0.05), we increase the probability of making a Type II error because we will reject the null less frequently, including when it is false. The only way to reduce the probabilities of both types of errors simultaneously is to increase the sample size, $n$.

Quantifying the trade-off between the two types of error in practice is usually impossible because the probability of a Type II error is itself hard to quantify. Consider $H_0: \theta \leq 5$ versus $H_a: \theta > 5$. Because every true value of $\theta$ greater than 5 makes the null hypothesis false, each value of $\theta$ greater than 5 has a different $\beta$ (Type II error probability). In contrast, it is sufficient to state a Type I error probability for $\theta = 5$, the point at which we conduct the test of the null hypothesis. Thus, in general, we specify only $\alpha$, the probability of a Type I error, when we conduct a hypothesis test. Whereas the significance level of a test is the probability of incorrectly rejecting the null, the **power of a test** is the probability of *correctly* rejecting the null—that is, the probability of rejecting the null when it is false.[8] When more than one test statistic is available to conduct a hypothesis test, we should prefer the most powerful, all else equal.[9]

To summarize, the standard approach to hypothesis testing involves specifying a level of significance (probability of Type I error) only. It is most appropriate to specify this significance level prior to calculating the test statistic. If we specify it after calculating the test statistic, we may be influenced by the result of the calculation, which detracts from the objectivity of the test.

We can use three conventional significance levels to conduct hypothesis tests: 0.10, 0.05, and 0.01. Qualitatively, if we can reject a null hypothesis at the

---

[8] The power of a test is, in fact, 1 minus the probability of a Type II error.

[9] We do not always have information on the relative power of the test for competing test statistics, however.

0.10 level of significance, we have *some evidence* that the null hypothesis is false. If we can reject a null hypothesis at the 0.05 level, we have *strong evidence* that the null hypothesis is false. And if we can reject a null hypothesis at the 0.01 level, we have *very strong evidence* that the null hypothesis is false. For the risk premium example, we will specify a 0.05 significance level.

*The fourth step in hypothesis testing is stating the decision rule.* The general principle is simply stated. When we test the null hypothesis, if we find that the calculated value of the test statistic is as extreme or more extreme than a given value or values determined by the specified level of significance, $\alpha$, we reject the null hypothesis. We say the result is **statistically significant**. Otherwise, we do not reject the null hypothesis and we say the result is not statistically significant. The value or values with which we compare the calculated test statistic to make our decision are the rejection points (critical values) for the test.[10]

► **Definition of a Rejection Point (Critical Value) for the Test Statistic.** A rejection point (critical value) for a test statistic is a value with which the computed test statistic is compared to decide whether to reject or not reject the null hypothesis.

For a one-tailed test, we indicate a rejection point using the symbol for the test statistic with a subscript indicating the specified probability of a Type I error, $\alpha$; for example, $z_\alpha$. For a two-tailed test, we indicate $z_{\alpha/2}$. To illustrate the use of rejection points, suppose we are using a $z$-test and have chosen a 0.05 level of significance.

► For a test of $H_0$: $\theta = \theta_0$ versus $H_a$: $\theta \neq \theta_0$, two rejection points exist, one negative and one positive. For a two-sided test at the 0.05 level, the total probability of a Type I error must sum to 0.05. Thus, $0.05/2 = 0.025$ of the probability should be in each tail of the distribution of the test statistic under the null. Consequently, the two rejection points are $z_{0.025} = 1.96$ and $-z_{0.025} = -1.96$. Let $z$ represent the calculated value of the test statistic. We reject the null if we find that $z < -1.96$ or $z > 1.96$. We do not reject if $-1.96 \leq z \leq 1.96$.

► For a test of $H_0$: $\theta \leq \theta_0$ versus $H_a$: $\theta > \theta_0$ at the 0.05 level of significance, the rejection point is $z_{0.05} = 1.645$. We reject the null hypothesis if $z > 1.645$. The value of the standard normal distribution such that 5 percent of the outcomes lie to the right is $z_{0.05} = 1.645$.

► For a test of $H_0$: $\theta \geq \theta_0$ versus $H_a$: $\theta < \theta_0$, the rejection point is $-z_{0.05} = -1.645$. We reject the null hypothesis if $z < -1.645$.

Figure 1 illustrates a test $H_0$: $\mu = \mu_0$ versus $H_a$: $\mu \neq \mu_0$ at the 0.05 significance level using a $z$-test. The "acceptance region" is the traditional name for the set of values of the test statistic for which we do not reject the null hypothesis. (The traditional name, however, is inaccurate. We should avoid using phrases such as "accept the null hypothesis" because such a statement implies a greater degree of conviction about the null than is warranted when we fail to reject it.)[11] On either side of the acceptance region is a rejection region (or critical region). If the null hypothesis that $\mu = \mu_0$ is true, the test statistic has a 2.5 percent chance of falling in the left rejection region and a 2.5 percent chance of falling in the right rejection region. Any calculated value of the test statistic that falls in either of these

---

[10] "Rejection point" is a descriptive synonym for the more traditional term "critical value."

[11] The analogy in some courts of law (for example, in the United States) is that if a jury does not return a verdict of guilty (the alternative hypothesis), it is most accurate to say that the jury has failed to reject the null hypothesis, namely, that the defendant is innocent.

**FIGURE 1**  **Rejection Points (Critical Values), 0.05 Significance Level, Two-Sided Test of the Population Mean Using a *z*-Test**

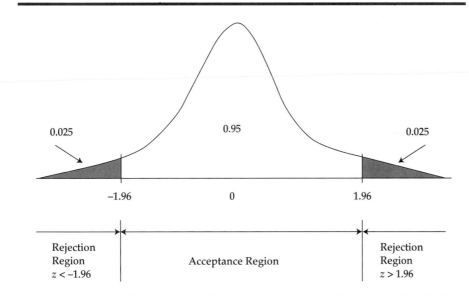

two regions causes us to reject the null hypothesis at the 0.05 significance level. The rejection points of 1.96 and −1.96 are seen to be the dividing lines between the acceptance and rejection regions.

Figure 1 affords a good opportunity to highlight the relationship between confidence intervals and hypothesis tests. A 95 percent confidence interval for the population mean, $\mu$, based on sample mean, $\overline{X}$, is given by $\overline{X} - 1.96\ s_{\overline{X}}$ to $\overline{X} + 1.96\ s_{\overline{X}}$, where $s_{\overline{X}}$ is the standard error of the sample mean (Equation 11-3).[12]

Now consider one of the conditions for rejecting the null hypothesis:

$$\frac{\overline{X} - \mu_0}{s_{\overline{X}}} > 1.96$$

Here, $\mu_0$ is the hypothesized value of the population mean. The condition states that rejection is warranted if the test statistic exceeds 1.96. Multiplying both sides by $s_{\overline{X}}$, we have $\overline{X} - \mu_0 > 1.96\ s_{\overline{X}}$, or after rearranging, $\overline{X} - 1.96\ s_{\overline{X}} > \mu_0$, which we can also write as $\mu_0 < \overline{X} - 1.96\ s_{\overline{X}}$. This expression says that if the hypothesized population mean, $\mu_0$, is less than the lower limit of the 95 percent confidence interval based on the sample mean, we must reject the null hypothesis at the 5 percent significance level (the test statistic falls in the rejection region to the right).

Now, we can take the other condition for rejecting the null hypothesis:

$$\frac{\overline{X} - \mu_0}{s_{\overline{X}}} < -1.96$$

and, using algebra as before, rewrite it as $\mu_0 > \overline{X} + 1.96\ s_{\overline{X}}$. If the hypothesized population mean is larger than the upper limit of the 95 percent confidence

---

[12] Just as with the hypothesis test, we can use this confidence interval, based on the standard normal distribution, when we have large samples. An alternative hypothesis test and confidence interval uses the *t*-distribution, which requires concepts that we introduce in the next section.

interval, we reject the null hypothesis at the 5 percent level (the test statistic falls in the rejection region to the left). Thus, an α significance level in a two-sided hypothesis test can be interpreted in exactly the same way as a $(1 - \alpha)$ confidence interval.

In summary, when the hypothesized value of the population parameter under the null is outside the corresponding confidence interval, the null hypothesis is rejected. We could use confidence intervals to test hypotheses; practitioners, however, usually do not. Computing a test statistic (one number, versus two numbers for the usual confidence interval) is more efficient. Also, analysts encounter actual cases of one-sided confidence intervals only rarely. Furthermore, only when we compute a test statistic can we obtain a $p$-value, a useful quantity relating to the significance of our results (we will discuss $p$-values shortly).

To return to our risk premium test, we stated hypotheses $H_0$: $\mu_{RP} \leq 0$ versus $H_a$: $\mu_{RP} > 0$. We identified the test statistic as $\overline{X}_{RP} / s_{\overline{X}}$ and stated that it follows a standard normal distribution. We are, therefore, conducting a one-sided $z$-test. We specified a 0.05 significance level. For this one-sided $z$-test, the rejection point at the 0.05 level of significance is 1.645. We will reject the null if the calculated $z$-statistic is larger than 1.645. Figure 2 illustrates this test.

**FIGURE 2     Rejection Point (Critical Value), 0.05 Significance Level, One-Sided Test of the Population Mean Using a $z$-Test**

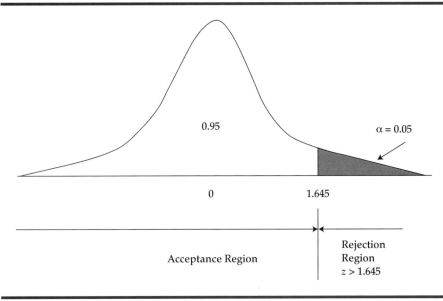

*The fifth step in hypothesis testing is collecting the data and calculating the test statistic.* The quality of our conclusions depends not only on the appropriateness of the statistical model but also on the quality of the data we use in conducting the test. We first need to check for measurement errors in the recorded data. Some other issues to be aware of include sample selection bias and time-period bias. Sample selection bias refers to bias introduced by systematically excluding some members of the population according to a particular attribute. One type of sample selection bias is survivorship bias. For example, if we define our sample as U.S. bond mutual funds currently operating and we collect returns for just these funds, we will systematically exclude funds that have not survived to the present date. Nonsurviving funds are likely to have underperformed surviving funds, on average; as a result the performance reflected in the sample may be biased upward. Time-period bias refers to the possibility that when we use a time-series sample, our statistical conclusion may be sensitive to the starting and ending dates of the sample.[13]

To continue with the risk premium hypothesis, we focus on Canadian equities. According to Dimson, Marsh, and Staunton (2002) as updated to the end of 2002,[14] for the period 1900 to 2002 inclusive (103 annual observations), the arithmetic mean equity risk premium for Canadian stocks relative to bond returns, $\overline{X}_{RP}$, was 5.1 percent per year. The sample standard deviation of the annual risk premiums was 18.6 percent. Using Equation 11-3, the standard error of the sample mean is $s_{\overline{X}} = s/\sqrt{n} = 18.6\%/\sqrt{103} = 1.833\%$. The test statistic is $z = \overline{X}_{RP}/s_{\overline{X}} = 5.1\%/1.833\% = 2.78$.

*The sixth step in hypothesis testing is making the statistical decision.* For our example, because the test statistic $z = 2.78$ is larger than the rejection point of 1.645, we reject the null hypothesis in favor of the alternative hypothesis that the risk premium on Canadian stocks is positive. The first six steps are the statistical steps. The final decision concerns our use of the statistical decision.

*The seventh and final step in hypothesis testing is making the economic or investment decision.* The economic or investment decision takes into consideration not only the statistical decision but also all pertinent economic issues. In the sixth step, we found strong statistical evidence that the Canadian risk premium is positive. The magnitude of the estimated risk premium, 5.1 percent a year, is economically very meaningful as well. Based on these considerations, an investor might decide to commit funds to Canadian equities. A range of nonstatistical considerations, such as the investor's tolerance for risk and financial position, might also enter the decision-making process.

The preceding discussion raises an issue that often arises in this decision-making step. We frequently find that slight differences between a variable and its hypothesized value are statistically significant but not economically meaningful. For example, we may be testing an investment strategy and reject a null hypothesis that the mean return to the strategy is zero based on a large sample. Equation 11-1 shows that the smaller the standard error of the sample statistic (the divisor in the formula), the larger the value of the test statistic and the greater the chance the null will be rejected, all else equal. The standard error decreases as the sample size, $n$, increases, so that for very large samples, we can reject the null for small departures from it. We may find that although a strategy provides a statistically significant positive mean return, the results are not economically significant when we account for transaction costs, taxes, and risk. Even if we conclude that a strategy's results are economically meaningful, we should explore the logic of why the strategy might work in the future before actually implementing it. Such considerations cannot be incorporated into a hypothesis test.

Before leaving the subject of the process of hypothesis testing, we should discuss an important alternative approach called the *p*-value approach to hypothesis testing. Analysts and researchers often report the *p*-value (also called the marginal significance level) associated with hypothesis tests.

> ▶ **Definition of *p*-Value.** The *p*-value is the smallest level of significance at which the null hypothesis can be rejected.

For the value of the test statistic of 2.78 in the risk premium hypothesis test, using a spreadsheet function for the standard normal distribution, we calculate a *p*-value of 0.002718. We can reject the null hypothesis at that level of significance. The smaller the *p*-value, the stronger the evidence against the null hypothesis and in favor of the alternative hypothesis. The *p*-value for a two-sided

---

[13] These issues are discussed further in the reading on sampling.

[14] Updated by communication dated 19 May 2003 to the authors.

test that a parameter equals zero is frequently generated automatically by statistical and econometric software programs.[15]

We can use $p$-values in the hypothesis testing framework presented above as an alternative to using rejection points. If the $p$-value is less than our specified level of significance, we reject the null hypothesis. Otherwise, we do not reject the null hypothesis. Using the $p$-value in this fashion, we reach the same conclusion as we do using rejection points. For example, because 0.002718 is less than 0.05, we would reject the null hypothesis in the risk premium test. The $p$-value, however, provides more precise information on the strength of the evidence than does the rejection points approach. The $p$-value of 0.002718 indicates that the null is rejected at a far smaller level of significance than 0.05.

If one researcher examines a question using a 0.05 significance level and another researcher uses a 0.01 significance level, the reader may have trouble comparing the findings. This concern has given rise to an approach to presenting the results of hypothesis tests that features $p$-values and omits specification of the significance level (Step 3). The interpretation of the statistical results is left to the consumer of the research. This has sometimes been called the $p$-value approach to hypothesis testing.[16]

## 3    HYPOTHESIS TESTS CONCERNING THE MEAN

Hypothesis tests concerning the mean are among the most common in practice. In this section we discuss such tests for several distinct types of problems. In one type (discussed in Section 3.1), we test whether the population mean of a single population is equal to (or greater or less than) some hypothesized value. Then, in Sections 3.2 and 3.3, we address inference on means based on two samples. Is an observed difference between two sample means due to chance or different underlying (population) means? When we have two random samples that are independent of each other—no relationship exists between the measurements in one sample and the measurements in the other—the techniques of Section 3.2 apply. When the samples are dependent, the methods of Section 3.3 are appropriate.[17]

### 3.1 Tests Concerning a Single Mean

An analyst who wants to test a hypothesis concerning the value of an underlying or population mean will conduct a $t$-test in the great majority of cases. A **$t$-test** is a hypothesis test using a statistic ($t$-statistic) that follows a $t$-distribution. The $t$-distribution is a probability distribution defined by a single parameter known as degrees of freedom (df). Each value of degrees of freedom defines one distribution in this family of distributions. The $t$-distribution is closely related to the standard normal distribution. Like the standard normal distribution, a $t$-distribution is symmetrical with a mean of zero. However, the $t$-distribution is

---

[15] We can use spreadsheets to calculate $p$-values as well. In Microsoft Excel, for example, we may use the worksheet functions TTEST, NORMSDIST, CHIDIST, and FDIST to calculate $p$-values for $t$-tests, $z$-tests, chi-square tests, and $F$-tests, respectively.

[16] Davidson and MacKinnon (1993) argued the merits of this approach: "The P value approach does not necessarily force us to make a decision about the null hypothesis. If we obtain a P value of, say, 0.000001, we will almost certainly want to reject the null. But if we obtain a P value of, say, 0.04, or even 0.004, we are not *obliged* to reject it. We may simply file the result away as information that casts some doubt on the null hypothesis, but that is not, by itself, conclusive. We believe that this somewhat agnostic attitude toward test statistics, in which they are merely regarded as pieces of information that we may or may not want to act upon, is usually the most sensible one to take." (p. 80)

[17] When we want to test whether the population means of more than two populations are equal, we use analysis of variance (ANOVA). We introduce ANOVA in its most common application, regression analysis, in the reading on correlation and regression analysis.

more spread out: It has a standard deviation greater than 1 (compared to 1 for the standard normal)[18] and more probability for outcomes distant from the mean (it has fatter tails than the standard normal distribution). As the number of degrees of freedom increases with sample size, the spread decreases and the $t$-distribution approaches the standard normal distribution as a limit.

Why is the $t$-distribution the focus for the hypothesis tests of this section? In practice, investment analysts need to estimate the population standard deviation by calculating a sample standard deviation. That is, the population variance (or standard deviation) is unknown. For hypothesis tests concerning the population mean of a normally distributed population with unknown variance, the theoretically correct test statistic is the $t$-statistic. What if a normal distribution does not describe the population? The $t$-test is **robust** to moderate departures from normality, except for outliers and strong skewness.[19] When we have large samples, departures of the underlying distribution from the normal are of increasingly less concern. The sample mean is approximately normally distributed in large samples according to the central limit theorem, whatever the distribution describing the population. In general, a sample size of 30 or more usually can be treated as a large sample and a sample size of 29 or less is treated as a small sample.[20]

▶ **Test Statistic for Hypothesis Tests of the Population Mean (Practical Case—Population Variance Unknown).** If the population sampled has unknown variance and either of the conditions below holds:

**1.** the sample is large, or

**2.** the sample is small but the population sampled is normally distributed, or approximately normally distributed,

then the test statistic for hypothesis tests concerning a single population mean, $\mu$, is

$$t_{n-1} = \frac{\overline{X} - \mu_0}{s/\sqrt{n}}$$

(11-4)

where

$t_{n-1}$ = $t$-statistic with $n - 1$ degrees of freedom ($n$ is the sample size)
$\overline{X}$ = the sample mean
$\mu_0$ = the hypothesized value of the population mean
$s$ = the sample standard deviation

The denominator of the $t$-statistic is an estimate of the sample mean standard error, $s_{\overline{X}} = s/\sqrt{n}$.[21]

In Example 1, because the sample size is small, the test is called a small sample test concerning the population mean.

---

[18] The formula for the variance of a $t$-distribution is $df/(df - 2)$.

[19] See Moore and McCabe (1998). A statistic is robust if the required probability calculations are insensitive to violations of the assumptions.

[20] Although this generalization is useful, we caution that the sample size needed to obtain an approximately normal sampling distribution for the sample mean depends on how non-normal the original population is. For some populations, "large" may be a sample size well in excess of 30.

[21] A technical note, for reference, is required. When the sample comes from a finite population, estimates of the standard error of the mean, whether from Equation 11-2 or Equation 11-3, overestimate the true standard error. To address this, the computed standard error is multiplied by a shrinkage factor called the finite population correction factor (fpc), equal to $\sqrt{(N - n)/(N - 1)}$, where $N$ is the population size and $n$ is the sample size. When the sample size is small relative to the population size (less than 5 percent of the population size), the fpc is usually ignored. The overestimation problem arises only in the usual situation of sampling without replacement (after an item is selected, it cannot be picked again) as opposed to sampling with replacement.

**EXAMPLE 1**

### Risk and Return Characteristics of an Equity Mutual Fund (1)

You are analyzing Sendar Equity Fund, a midcap growth fund that has been in existence for 24 months. During this period, it has achieved a mean monthly return of 1.50 percent with a sample standard deviation of monthly returns of 3.60 percent. Given its level of systematic (market) risk and according to a pricing model, this mutual fund was expected to have earned a 1.10 percent mean monthly return during that time period. Assuming returns are normally distributed, are the actual results consistent with an underlying or population mean monthly return of 1.10 percent?

1. Formulate null and alternative hypotheses consistent with the verbal description of the research goal.

2. Identify the test statistic for conducting a test of the hypotheses in Part 1.

3. Identify the rejection point or points for the hypothesis tested in Part 1 at the 0.10 level of significance.

4. Determine whether the null hypothesis is rejected or not rejected at the 0.10 level of significance. (Use the tables in the back of this book.)

**Solution to 1:** We have a "not equal to" alternative hypothesis, where $\mu$ is the underlying mean return on Sendar Equity Fund—$H_0$: $\mu = 1.10$ versus $H_a$: $\mu \neq 1.10$.

**Solution to 2:** Because the population variance is not known, we use a $t$-test with $24 - 1 = 23$ degrees of freedom.

**Solution to 3:** Because this is a two-tailed test, we have the rejection point $t_{\alpha/2, n-1} = t_{0.05,23}$. In the table for the $t$-distribution, we look across the row for 23 degrees of freedom to the 0.05 column, to find 1.714. The two rejection points for this two-sided test are 1.714 and $-1.714$. We will reject the null if we find that $t > 1.714$ or $t < -1.714$.

**Solution to 4:**

$$t_{23} = \frac{1.50 - 1.10}{3.60/\sqrt{24}} = \frac{0.40}{0.734847} = 0.544331 \text{ or } 0.544$$

Because 0.544 does not satisfy either $t > 1.714$ or $t < -1.714$, we do not reject the null hypothesis.

The confidence interval approach provides another perspective on this hypothesis test. The theoretically correct $100(1 - \alpha)\%$ confidence interval for the population mean of a normal distribution with unknown variance, based on a sample of size $n$, is

$$\overline{X} - t_{\alpha/2} s_{\overline{X}} \quad \text{to} \quad \overline{X} + t_{\alpha/2} s_{\overline{X}}$$

where $t_{\alpha/2}$ is the value of $t$ such that $\alpha/2$ of the probability remains in the right tail and where $-t_{\alpha/2}$ is the value of $t$ such that $\alpha/2$ of the probability remains in the left tail, for $n-1$ degrees of freedom. Here, the 90 percent confidence interval runs from $1.5 - (1.714)(0.734847) = 0.240$ to $1.5 + (1.714)(0.734847) = 2.760$, compactly $[0.240, 2.760]$. The hypothesized value of mean return, 1.10, falls within this confidence interval, and we see from this perspective also that the null hypothesis is not rejected. At a 10 percent level of significance, we conclude that a population mean monthly return of 1.10 percent is consistent with the 24-month observed data series. Note that 10 percent is a relatively high probability of rejecting the hypothesis of a 1.10 percent population mean monthly return when it is true.

## EXAMPLE 2

### A Slowdown in Payments of Receivables

FashionDesigns, a supplier of casual clothing to retail chains, is concerned about a possible slowdown in payments from its customers. The controller's office measures the rate of payment by the average number of days in receivables.[22] FashionDesigns has generally maintained an average of 45 days in receivables. Because it would be too costly to analyze all of the company's receivables frequently, the controller's office uses sampling to track customers' payment rates. A random sample of 50 accounts shows a mean number of days in receivables of 49 with a standard deviation of 8 days.

**1.** Formulate null and alternative hypotheses consistent with determining whether the evidence supports the suspected condition that customer payments have slowed.

**2.** Identify the test statistic for conducting a test of the hypotheses in Part 1.

**3.** Identify the rejection point or points for the hypothesis tested in Part 1 at the 0.05 and 0.01 levels of significance.

**4.** Determine whether the null hypothesis is rejected or not rejected at the 0.05 and 0.01 levels of significance.

**Solution to 1:** The suspected condition is that the number of days in receivables has increased relative to the historical rate of 45 days, which suggests a "greater than" alternative hypothesis. With $\mu$ as the population mean number of days in receivables, the hypotheses are $H_0$: $\mu \leq 45$ versus $H_a$: $\mu > 45$.

**Solution to 2:** Because the population variance is not known, we use a $t$-test with $50 - 1 = 49$ degrees of freedom.

---

[22] This measure represents the average length of time that the business must wait after making a sale before receiving payment. The calculation is (Accounts receivable)/(Average sales per day).

**Solution to 3:** The rejection point is found across the row for degrees of freedom of 49. To find the one-tailed rejection point for a 0.05 significance level, we use the 0.05 column: The value is 1.677. To find the one-tailed rejection point for a 0.01 level of significance, we use the 0.01 column: The value is 2.405. To summarize, at a 0.05 significance level, we reject the null if we find that $t > 1.677$; at a 0.01 significance level, we reject the null if we find that $t > 2.405$.

**Solution to 4:**

$$t_{49} = \frac{49 - 45}{8/\sqrt{50}} = \frac{4}{1.131371} = 3.536$$

Because $3.536 > 1.677$, the null hypothesis is rejected at the 0.05 level. Because $3.536 > 2.405$, the null hypothesis is also rejected at the 0.01 level. We can say with a high level of confidence that FashionDesigns has experienced a slowdown in customer payments. The level of significance, 0.01, is a relatively low probability of rejecting the hypothesized mean of 45 days or less. Rejection gives us confidence that the mean has increased above 45 days.

We stated above that when population variance is not known, we use a $t$-test for tests concerning a single population mean. Given at least approximate normality, the $t$-test is always called for when we deal with small samples and do not know the population variance. For large samples, the central limit theorem states that the sample mean is approximately normally distributed, whatever the distribution of the population. So the $t$-test is still appropriate, but an alternative test may be more useful when sample size is large.

For large samples, practitioners sometimes use a $z$-test in place of a $t$-test for tests concerning a mean.[23] The justification for using the $z$-test in this context is twofold. First, in large samples, the sample mean should follow the normal distribution at least approximately, as we have already stated, fulfilling the normality assumption of the $z$-test. Second, the difference between the rejection points for the $t$-test and $z$-test becomes quite small when sample size is large. For a two-sided test at the 0.05 level of significance, the rejection points for a $z$-test are 1.96 and $-1.96$. For a $t$-test, the rejection points are 2.045 and $-2.045$ for df = 29 (about a 4 percent difference between the $z$ and $t$ rejection points) and 2.009 and $-2.009$ for df = 50 (about a 2.5 percent difference between the $z$ and $t$ rejection points). Because the $t$-test is readily available as statistical program output and theoretically correct for unknown population variance, we present it as the test of choice.

In a very limited number of cases, we may know the population variance; in such cases, the $z$-test is theoretically correct.[24]

---

[23] These practitioners choose between $t$-tests and $z$-tests based on sample size. For small samples ($n < 30$), they use a $t$-test, and for large samples, a $z$-test.

[24] For example, in Monte Carlo simulation, we prespecify the probability distributions for the risk factors. If we use a normal distribution, we know the true values of mean and variance. Monte Carlo simulation involves the use of a computer to represent the operation of a system subject to risk; we discuss Monte Carlo simulation in the reading on common probability distributions.

▶ **The $z$-Test Alternative.**

1. If the population sampled is normally distributed with known variance $\sigma^2$, then the test statistic for a hypothesis test concerning a single population mean, $\mu$, is

$$z = \frac{\overline{X} - \mu_0}{\sigma/\sqrt{n}} \qquad \textbf{(11-5)}$$

2. If the population sampled has unknown variance and the sample is large, in place of a $t$-test, an alternative test statistic (relying on the central limit theorem) is

$$z = \frac{\overline{X} - \mu_0}{s/\sqrt{n}} \qquad \textbf{(11-6)}$$

In the above equations,

$\sigma$ = the known population standard deviation

$s$ = the sample standard deviation

$\mu_0$ = the hypothesized value of the population mean

When we use a $z$-test, we most frequently refer to a rejection point in the list below.

▶ **Rejection Points for a $z$-Test.**

**A.** Significance level of $\alpha = 0.10$.

1. $H_0: \theta = \theta_0$ versus $H_a: \theta \neq \theta_0$. The rejection points are $z_{0.05} = 1.645$ and $-z_{0.05} = -1.645$.
   Reject the null hypothesis if $z > 1.645$ or if $z < -1.645$.
2. $H_0: \theta \leq \theta_0$ versus $H_a: \theta > \theta_0$. The rejection point is $z_{0.10} = 1.28$.
   Reject the null hypothesis if $z > 1.28$.
3. $H_0: \theta \geq \theta_0$ versus $H_a: \theta < \theta_0$. The rejection point is $-z_{0.10} = -1.28$.
   Reject the null hypothesis if $z < -1.28$.

**B.** Significance level of $\alpha = 0.05$.

1. $H_0: \theta = \theta_0$ versus $H_a: \theta \neq \theta_0$. The rejection points are $z_{0.025} = 1.96$ and $-z_{0.025} = -1.96$.
   Reject the null hypothesis if $z > 1.96$ or if $z < -1.96$.
2. $H_0: \theta \leq \theta_0$ versus $H_a: \theta > \theta_0$. The rejection point is $z_{0.05} = 1.645$.
   Reject the null hypothesis if $z > 1.645$.
3. $H_0: \theta \geq \theta_0$ versus $H_a: \theta < \theta_0$. The rejection point is $-z_{0.05} = -1.645$.
   Reject the null hypothesis if $z < -1.645$.

**C.** Significance level of $\alpha = 0.01$.

1. $H_0: \theta = \theta_0$ versus $H_a: \theta \neq \theta_0$. The rejection points are $z_{0.005} = 2.575$ and $-z_{0.005} = -2.575$.
   Reject the null hypothesis if $z > 2.575$ or if $z < -2.575$.
2. $H_0: \theta \leq \theta_0$ versus $H_a: \theta > \theta_0$. The rejection point is $z_{0.01} = 2.33$.
   Reject the null hypothesis if $z > 2.33$.
3. $H_0: \theta \geq \theta_0$ versus $H_a: \theta < \theta_0$. The rejection point is $-z_{0.01} = -2.33$.
   Reject the null hypothesis if $z < -2.33$.

## EXAMPLE 3

### The Effect of Commercial Paper Issuance on Stock Prices

Commercial paper (CP) is unsecured short-term corporate debt that, like U.S. Treasury bills, is characterized by a single payment at maturity. When a company enters the CP market for the first time, how do stock market participants react to the announcement of the CP ratings?

Nayar and Rozeff (1994) addressed this question using data for the period October 1981 to December 1985. During this period, 132 CP issues (96 industrial and 36 non-industrial) received an initial rating in Standard & Poor's *CreditWeek* or Moody's Investors Service *Bond Survey*. Nayar and Rozeff categorized ratings as superior or inferior. Superior CP ratings were A1+ or A1 from Standard & Poor's and Prime-1 (P1) from Moody's. Inferior CP ratings were A2 or lower from Standard & Poor's and Prime-2 (P2) or lower from Moody's. The publication day of the initial ratings was designated $t = 0$. The researchers found, however, that companies themselves often disseminate the rating information prior to publication in *CreditWeek* or the *Bond Survey*. The reaction of stock price was studied on the day before publication, $t - 1$, because that date was closer to the actual date of information release.

If CP ratings provide *new* information useful for equity valuation, the information should cause a change in stock prices and returns once it is available. Only one component of stock returns is of interest: the return in excess of that predicted given a stock's market risk or beta, called the abnormal return. Positive (negative) abnormal returns indicate that investors perceive favorable (unfavorable) corporate news in the ratings announcement. Although Nayar and Rozeff examined abnormal returns for various time horizons or event windows, we report a selection of their findings for the day prior to rating publication $(t - 1)$.

*All CP Issues* ($n = 132$ issues). The null hypothesis was that the average abnormal stock return on day $t - 1$ was 0. The null would be true if stock investors did not find either positive or negative information in the announcement.

Mean abnormal return = 0.39 percent.

Sample standard error of the mean of abnormal returns = 0.1336 percent.[25]

*Industrial CP Issues with Superior Ratings* ($n = 72$ issues). The null hypothesis was that the average abnormal stock return on day $t - 1$ was 0. The null would be true if stock investors did not find either positive or negative information in the announcement.

Mean abnormal return = 0.79 percent.

Sample standard error of the mean of abnormal returns = 0.197 percent.

*Industrial CP Issues with Inferior Ratings* ($n = 24$ issues). The null hypothesis was that the average abnormal stock return on day $t - 1$ was 0. The null would be true if stock investors did not find either positive or negative information in the announcement.

Mean abnormal return = −0.57 percent.

---

[25] This standard error was calculated as a sample standard deviation over the 132 issues (a cross-sectional standard deviation) divided by the square root of 132. Other standard errors were calculated similarly.

Sample standard error of the mean of abnormal returns = 0.38 percent.

The researchers chose to use z-tests.

1. With respect to each of the three cases, suppose that the null hypothesis reflects the belief that investors do not, on average, perceive either positive or negative information in initial ratings. State one set of hypotheses (a null hypothesis and an alternative hypothesis) that covers all three cases.

2. Determine whether the null hypothesis formulated in Part 1 is rejected or not rejected at the 0.05 and 0.01 levels of significance for the *All CP Issues* case. Interpret the results.

3. Determine whether the null hypothesis formulated in Part 1 is rejected or not rejected at the 0.05 and 0.01 levels of significance for the *Industrial CP Issues with Superior Ratings* case. Interpret the results.

4. Determine whether the null hypothesis formulated in Part 1 is rejected or not rejected at the 0.05 and 0.01 levels of significance for the *Industrial CP Issues with Inferior Ratings* case. Interpret the results.

**Solution to 1:** A set of hypotheses consistent with no information in CP credit ratings relevant to stock investors is

$H_0$: The population mean abnormal return on day $t - 1$ equals 0.

$H_a$: The population mean abnormal return on day $t - 1$ does not equal 0.

**Solution to 2:** From the information on rejection points for z-tests, we know that we reject the null hypothesis at the 0.05 significance level if $z > 1.96$ or if $z < -1.96$, and at the 0.01 significance level if $z > 2.575$ or if $z < -2.575$. Using the z-test, $z = (0.39\% - 0\%)/0.1336\% = 2.92$ is significant at the 0.05 and 0.01 levels. The null is rejected. The fact of CP issuance itself appears to be viewed as favorable news.

Because it is possible that significant results could be due to outliers, the researchers also reported the number of cases of positive and negative abnormal returns. The ratio of cases of positive to negative abnormal returns was 80:52, which tends to support the conclusion of positive abnormal returns from the z-test.

**Solution to 3:** Using the z-test, $z = (0.79\% - 0\%)/0.197\% = 4.01$ is significant at the 0.05 and 0.01 levels. Stocks earned clearly positive abnormal returns in response to the news of a superior initial CP rating. Investors may view rating agencies as certifying through a superior rating that a company's future prospects are strong.

The ratio of cases of positive to negative abnormal returns was 48:24, which tends to support the conclusion of positive abnormal returns from the z-test.

**Solution to 4:** Using the z-test, $z = (-0.57\% - 0\%)/0.38\% = -1.50$ is not significant at either the 0.01 or 0.05 levels. In the case of inferior ratings, we cannot conclude that investors found either positive or negative information in the announcements of initial CP ratings.

The ratio of cases of positive to negative abnormal returns was 11:13 and tends to support the conclusion of the z-test, which did not reject the null hypothesis.

Nearly all practical situations involve an unknown population variance. Table 2 summarizes our discussion for tests concerning the population mean when the population variance is unknown.

| TABLE 2  Test Concerning the Population Mean (Population Variance Unknown) | | |
|---|---|---|
| | **Large Sample** ($n \geq 30$) | **Small Sample** ($n < 30$) |
| Population normal | $t$-Test ($z$-Test alternative) | $t$-Test |
| Population non-normal | $t$-Test ($z$-Test alternative) | Not Available |

## 3.2 Tests Concerning Differences between Means

We often want to know whether a mean value—for example, a mean return—differs between two groups. Is an observed difference due to chance or to different underlying values for the mean? We have two samples, one for each group. When it is reasonable to believe that the samples are from populations at least approximately normally distributed and that the samples are also independent of each other, the techniques of this section apply. We discuss two $t$-tests for a test concerning differences between the means of two populations. In one case, the population variances, although unknown, can be assumed to be equal. Then, we efficiently combine the observations from both samples to obtain a pooled estimate of the common but unknown population variance. A pooled estimate is an estimate drawn from the combination of two different samples. In the second case, we do not assume that the unknown population variances are equal, and an approximate $t$-test is then available. Letting $\mu_1$ and $\mu_2$ stand, respectively, for the population means of the first and second populations, we most often want to test whether the population means are equal or whether one is larger than the other. Thus we usually formulate the following hypotheses:

1. $H_0: \mu_1 - \mu_2 = 0$ versus $H_a: \mu_1 - \mu_2 \neq 0$ (the alternative is that $\mu_1 \neq \mu_2$)

2. $H_0: \mu_1 - \mu_2 \leq 0$ versus $H_a: \mu_1 - \mu_2 > 0$ (the alternative is that $\mu_1 > \mu_2$)

3. $H_0: \mu_1 - \mu_2 \geq 0$ versus $H_a: \mu_1 - \mu_2 < 0$ (the alternative is that $\mu_1 < \mu_2$)

We can, however, formulate other hypotheses, such as $H_0: \mu_1 - \mu_2 = 2$ versus $H_a: \mu_1 - \mu_2 \neq 2$. The procedure is the same.

The definition of the $t$-test follows.

▶ **Test Statistic for a Test of the Difference between Two Population Means (Normally Distributed Populations, Population Variances Unknown but Assumed Equal).** When we can assume that the two populations are normally distributed and that the unknown population variances are equal, a $t$-test based on independent random samples is given by

$$t = \frac{(\overline{X}_1 - \overline{X}_2) - (\mu_1 - \mu_2)}{\left(\dfrac{s_p^2}{n_1} + \dfrac{s_p^2}{n_2}\right)^{1/2}} \tag{11-7}$$

where $s_p^2 = \dfrac{(n_1 - 1)s_1^2 + (n_2 - 1)s_2^2}{n_1 + n_2 - 2}$ is a pooled estimator of the common variance.

The number of degrees of freedom is $n_1 + n_2 - 2$.

## EXAMPLE 4

### Mean Returns on the S&P 500: A Test of Equality across Decades

The realized mean monthly return on the S&P 500 Index in the 1980s appears to have been substantially different than the mean return in the 1970s. Was the difference statistically significant? The data, shown in Table 3, indicate that assuming equal population variances for returns in the two decades is not unreasonable.

#### TABLE 3  S&P 500 Monthly Return and Standard Deviation for Two Decades

| Decade | Number of Months (n) | Mean Monthly Return (%) | Standard Deviation |
|--------|----------------------|-------------------------|--------------------|
| 1970s  | 120                  | 0.580                   | 4.598              |
| 1980s  | 120                  | 1.470                   | 4.738              |

1. Formulate null and alternative hypotheses consistent with a two-sided hypothesis test.
2. Identify the test statistic for conducting a test of the hypotheses in Part 1.
3. Identify the rejection point or points for the hypothesis tested in Part 1 at the 0.10, 0.05, and 0.01 levels of significance.
4. Determine whether the null hypothesis is rejected or not rejected at the 0.10, 0.05, and 0.01 levels of significance.

**Solution to 1:** Letting $\mu_1$ stand for the population mean return for the 1970s and $\mu_2$ stand for the population mean return for the 1980s, we formulate the following hypotheses:

$$H_0: \mu_1 - \mu_2 = 0 \text{ versus } H_a: \mu_1 - \mu_2 \neq 0$$

**Solution to 2:** Because the two samples are drawn from different decades, they are independent samples. The population variances are not known but can be assumed to be equal. Given all these considerations, the $t$-test given in Equation 11-7 has $120 + 120 - 2 = 238$ degrees of freedom.

**Solution to 3:** In the tables (Appendix C), the closest degrees of freedom to 238 is 200. For a two-sided test, the rejection points are $\pm 1.653$, $\pm 1.972$, and $\pm 2.601$ for, respectively, the 0.10, 0.05, and 0.01 levels for df = 200. To summarize, at the 0.10 level, we will reject the null if $t < -1.653$ or $t > 1.653$; at the 0.05 level, we will reject the null if $t < -1.972$ or $t > 1.972$; and at the 0.01 level, we will reject the null if $t < -2.601$ or $t > 2.601$.

**Solution to 4:** In calculating the test statistic, the first step is to calculate the pooled estimate of variance:

$$s_p^2 = \frac{(n_1 - 1)s_1^2 + (n_2 - 1)s_2^2}{n_1 + n_2 - 2} = \frac{(120 - 1)(4.598)^2 + (120 - 1)(4.738)^2}{120 + 120 - 2}$$

$$= \frac{5{,}187.239512}{238} = 21.795124$$

$$t = \frac{(\overline{X}_1 - \overline{X}_2) - (\mu_1 - \mu_2)}{\left(\frac{s_p^2}{n_1} + \frac{s_p^2}{n_2}\right)^{1/2}} = \frac{(0.580 - 1.470) - 0}{\left(\frac{21.795124}{120} + \frac{21.795124}{120}\right)^{1/2}}$$

$$= \frac{-0.89}{0.602704} = -1.477$$

The $t$ value of $-1.477$ is not significant at the 0.10 level, so it is also not significant at the 0.05 and 0.01 levels. Therefore, we do not reject the null hypothesis at any of the three levels.

In many cases of practical interest, we cannot assume that population variances are equal. The following test statistic is often used in the investment literature in such cases:

▶ **Test Statistic for a Test of the Difference between Two Population Means (Normally Distributed Populations, Unequal and Unknown Population Variances).** When we can assume that the two populations are normally distributed but do not know the population variances and cannot assume that they are equal, an approximate $t$-test based on independent random samples is given by

$$t = \frac{(\overline{X}_1 - \overline{X}_2) - (\mu_1 - \mu_2)}{\left(\frac{s_1^2}{n_1} + \frac{s_2^2}{n_2}\right)^{1/2}} \qquad \textbf{(11-8)}$$

where we use tables of the $t$-distribution using "modified" degrees of freedom computed with the formula

$$\mathrm{df} = \frac{\left(\frac{s_1^2}{n_1} + \frac{s_2^2}{n_2}\right)^2}{\frac{(s_1^2/n_1)^2}{n_1} + \frac{(s_2^2/n_2)^2}{n_2}} \qquad \textbf{(11-9)}$$

A practical tip is to compute the $t$-statistic before computing the degrees of freedom. Whether or not the $t$-statistic is significant will sometimes be obvious.

## EXAMPLE 5

### Recovery Rates on Defaulted Bonds: A Hypothesis Test

How are the required yields on risky corporate bonds determined? Two key factors are the expected probability of default and the expected amount that will be recovered in the event of default, or the recovery rate. Altman and Kishore (1996) documented for the first time the average recovery rates on defaulted bonds stratified by industry and seniority. For their study period, 1971 to 1995, Altman and Kishore discovered that defaulted bonds of public utilities and chemicals, petroleum, and plastics manufacturers experienced much higher recovery rates than did other industrial sectors. Could the differences be explained by a greater preponderance of senior debt in the higher-recovery sectors? They studied this by examining recovery rates stratified by seniority. We discuss their results for senior secured bonds. With $\mu_1$ denoting the population mean recovery rate for the senior secured bonds of utilities and $\mu_2$ denoting the population mean recovery rate for the senior secured bonds of other sectors (non-utilities), the hypotheses are $H_0$: $\mu_1 - \mu_2 = 0$ versus $H_a$: $\mu_1 - \mu_2 \neq 0$.

Table 4 excerpts from their findings.

### TABLE 4  Recovery Rates by Seniority

| Industry Group/ Seniority | Industry Group | | | Ex-Utilities Sample | | |
| --- | --- | --- | --- | --- | --- | --- |
| | Number of Observations | Average Price[a] | Standard Deviation | Number of Observations | Average Price[a] | Standard Deviation |
| Public Utilities | | | | | | |
| Senior Secured | 21 | $64.42 | $14.03 | 64 | $55.75 | $25.17 |

[a] This is the average price at default and is a measure of recovery rate.
*Source*: Altman and Kishore (1996), Table 5.

Following the researchers, assume that the populations (recovery rates of utilities, recovery rates of non-utilities) are normally distributed and that the samples are independent. Based on the data in the table, address the following:

1. Discuss why Altman and Kishore would choose a test based on Equation 11-8 rather than Equation 11-7.

2. Calculate the test statistic to test the null hypothesis given above.

3. What is the value of the test's modified degrees of freedom?

4. Determine whether to reject the null hypothesis at the 0.10 level.

**Solution to 1:** The sample standard deviation for the recovery rate on the senior secured bonds of utilities ($14.03) appears much smaller than the sample standard deviation of the comparable bonds for non-utilities ($25.17). Properly choosing not to assume equal variances, Altman and Kishore employed the approximate *t*-test given in Equation 11-8.

**Solution to 2:** The test statistic is

$$t = \frac{(\overline{X}_1 - \overline{X}_2)}{\left(\dfrac{s_1^2}{n_1} + \dfrac{s_2^2}{n_2}\right)^{1/2}}$$

where

$\overline{X}_1$ = sample mean recovery rate for utilities = 64.42
$\overline{X}_2$ = sample mean recovery rate for non-utility sectors = 55.75
$s_1^2$ = sample variance for utilities = $14.03^2$ = 196.8409
$s_2^2$ = sample variance for non-utilities = $25.17^2$ = 633.5289
$n_1$ = sample size of the utility sample = 21
$n_2$ = sample size of the non-utility sample = 64

Thus, $t = (64.42 - 55.75)/[(196.8409/21) + (633.5289/64)]^{1/2}$ = $8.67/(9.373376 + 9.898889)^{1/2}$ = $8.67/4.390019 = 1.975$. The calculated $t$-statistic is thus 1.975.

**Solution to 3:**

$$df = \frac{\left(\dfrac{s_1^2}{n_1} + \dfrac{s_2^2}{n_2}\right)^2}{\dfrac{(s_1^2/n_1)^2}{n_1} + \dfrac{(s_2^2/n_2)^2}{n_2}} = \frac{\left(\dfrac{196.8409}{21} + \dfrac{633.5289}{64}\right)^2}{\dfrac{(196.8409/21)^2}{21} + \dfrac{(633.5289/64)^2}{64}}$$

$$= \frac{371.420208}{5.714881} = 64.99 \text{ or } 65 \text{ degrees of freedom}$$

**Solution to 4:** The closest entry to df = 65 in the tables for the $t$-distribution is df = 60. For $\alpha = 0.10$, we find $t_{\alpha/2} = 1.671$. Thus, we reject the null if $t < -1.671$ or $t > 1.671$. Based on the computed value of 1.975, we reject the null hypothesis at the 0.10 level. Some evidence exists that recovery rates differ between utilities and other industries. Why? Altman and Kishore suggest that the differing nature of the companies' assets and industry competitive structures may explain the different recovery rates.

## 3.3 Tests Concerning Mean Differences

In the previous section, we presented two $t$-tests for discerning differences between population means. The tests were based on two samples. An assumption for those tests' validity was that the samples were independent—i.e., unrelated to each other. When we want to conduct tests on two means based on samples that we believe are dependent, the methods of this section apply.

The $t$-test in this section is based on data arranged in **paired observations**, and the test itself is sometimes called a **paired comparisons test**. Paired observations are observations that are dependent because they have something in common. A paired comparisons test is a statistical test for differences in dependent items. For example, we may be concerned with the dividend policy of companies before and after a change in the tax law affecting the taxation of dividends. We then have pairs of "before" and "after" observations for the same companies. We may test a hypothesis about the mean of the differences (mean differences) that we observe across companies. In other cases, the paired observations are not on the same units. For example, we may be testing whether the mean returns earned by two investment strategies were equal over a study period. The observations here are dependent in the sense that there is one observation for each strategy in each month, and both observations depend on underlying market risk factors. Because the returns to both strategies are likely to be related to some common risk factors, such as the market return, the samples are dependent. By calculating a standard error based on differences, the *t*-test presented below takes account of correlation between the observations.

Letting A represent "after" and B "before," suppose we have observations for the random variables $X_A$ and $X_B$ and that the samples are dependent. We arrange the observations in pairs. Let $d_i$ denote the difference between two paired observations. We can use the notation $d_i = x_{Ai} - x_{Bi}$, where $x_{Ai}$ and $x_{Bi}$ are the *i*th pair of observations, $i = 1, 2, \ldots, n$ on the two variables. Let $\mu_d$ stand for the population mean difference. We can formulate the following hypotheses, where $\mu_{d0}$ is a hypothesized value for the population mean difference:

1.  $H_0$: $\mu_d = \mu_{d0}$ versus $H_a$: $\mu_d \neq \mu_{d0}$
2.  $H_0$: $\mu_d \leq \mu_{d0}$ versus $H_a$: $\mu_d > \mu_{d0}$
3.  $H_0$: $\mu_d \geq \mu_{d0}$ versus $H_a$: $\mu_d < \mu_{d0}$

In practice, the most commonly used value for $\mu_{d0}$ is 0.

As usual, we are concerned with the case of normally distributed populations with unknown population variances, and we will formulate a *t*-test. To calculate the *t*-statistic, we first need to find the sample mean difference:

$$\bar{d} = \frac{1}{n} \sum_{i=1}^{n} d_i \qquad \text{(11-10)}$$

where $n$ is the number of pairs of observations. The sample variance, denoted by $s_d^2$, is

$$s_d^2 = \frac{\sum_{i=1}^{n} (d_i - \bar{d})^2}{n - 1} \qquad \text{(11-11)}$$

Taking the square root of this quantity, we have the sample standard deviation, $s_d$, which then allows us to calculate the standard error of the mean difference as follows:[26]

$$s_{\bar{d}} = \frac{s_d}{\sqrt{n}} \qquad \text{(11-12)}$$

▶ **Test Statistic for a Test of Mean Differences (Normally Distributed Populations, Unknown Population Variances).** When we have data consisting of paired observations from samples generated by normally distributed populations with unknown variances, a *t*-test is based on

$$t = \frac{\bar{d} - \mu_{d0}}{s_{\bar{d}}} \qquad \text{(11-13)}$$

with $n - 1$ degrees of freedom, where $n$ is the number of paired observations, $\bar{d}$ is the sample mean difference (as given by Equation 11-10), and $s_{\bar{d}}$ is the standard error of $\bar{d}$ (as given by Equation 11-12).

---

[26] We can also use the following equivalent expression, which makes use of the correlation between the two variables: $s_{\bar{d}} = \sqrt{s_A^2 + s_B^2 - 2r(X_A, X_B) s_A s_B}$ where $s_A^2$ is the sample variance of $X_A$, $s_B^2$ is the sample variance of $X_B$, and $r(X_A, X_B)$ is the sample correlation between $X_A$ and $X_B$.

Table 5 reports the quarterly returns from 1997 to 2002 for two managed portfolios specializing in precious metals. The two portfolios were closely similar in risk (as measured by standard deviation of return and other measures) and had nearly identical expense ratios. A major investment services company rated Portfolio B more highly than Portfolio A in early 2003. In investigating the portfolios' relative performance, suppose we want to test the hypothesis that the mean quarterly return on Portfolio A equaled the mean quarterly return on Portfolio B from 1997 to 2002. Because the two portfolios shared essentially the same set of risk factors, their returns were not independent, so a paired comparisons test is appropriate. Let $\mu_d$ stand for the population mean value of difference between the returns on the two portfolios during this period. We test $H_0$: $\mu_d = 0$ versus $H_a$: $\mu_d \neq 0$ at a 0.05 significance level.

**TABLE 5  Quarterly Returns on Two Managed Portfolios: 1997–2002**

| Quarter | Portfolio A (%) | Portfolio B (%) | Difference (Portfolio A – Portfolio B) |
|---------|-----------------|-----------------|----------------------------------------|
| 4Q:2002 | 11.40 | 14.64 | −3.24 |
| 3Q:2002 | −2.17 | 0.44 | −2.61 |
| 2Q:2002 | 10.72 | 19.51 | −8.79 |
| 1Q:2002 | 38.91 | 50.40 | −11.49 |
| 4Q:2001 | 4.36 | 1.01 | 3.35 |
| 3Q:2001 | 5.13 | 10.18 | −5.05 |
| 2Q:2001 | 26.36 | 17.77 | 8.59 |
| 1Q:2001 | −5.53 | 4.76 | −10.29 |
| 4Q:2000 | 5.27 | −5.36 | 10.63 |
| 3Q:2000 | −7.82 | −1.54 | −6.28 |
| 2Q:2000 | 2.34 | 0.19 | 2.15 |
| 1Q:2000 | −14.38 | −12.07 | −2.31 |
| 4Q:1999 | −9.80 | −9.98 | 0.18 |
| 3Q:1999 | 19.03 | 26.18 | −7.15 |
| 2Q:1999 | 4.11 | −2.39 | 6.50 |
| 1Q:1999 | −4.12 | −2.51 | −1.61 |
| 4Q:1998 | −0.53 | −11.32 | 10.79 |
| 3Q:1998 | 5.06 | 0.46 | 4.60 |
| 2Q:1998 | −14.01 | −11.56 | −2.45 |
| 1Q:1998 | 12.50 | 3.52 | 8.98 |
| 4Q:1997 | −29.05 | −22.45 | −6.60 |
| 3Q:1997 | 3.60 | 0.10 | 3.50 |
| 2Q:1997 | −7.97 | −8.96 | 0.99 |
| 1Q:1997 | −8.62 | −0.66 | −7.96 |
| Mean | 1.87 | 2.52 | −0.65 |

Sample standard deviation of differences = 6.71

The sample mean difference, $\bar{d}$, between Portfolio A and Portfolio B is −0.65 percent per quarter. The standard error of the sample mean difference is $s_{\bar{d}} = 6.71/\sqrt{24} = 1.369673$. The calculated test statistic is $t = (-0.65 - 0)/1.369673 = -0.475$ with $n - 1 = 24 - 1 = 23$ degrees of freedom. At the 0.05 significance level, we reject the null if $t > 2.069$ or if $t < -2.069$. Because −0.475 is not less than −2.069, we fail to reject the null. At the 0.10 significance level, we reject the null if $t > 1.714$ or if $t < 1.714$. Thus the difference in mean quarterly returns is not significant at any conventional significance level.

The following example illustrates the application of this test to evaluate two competing investment strategies.

## EXAMPLE 6

### The Dow-10 Investment Strategy

McQueen, Shields, and Thorley (1997) examined the popular investment strategy of investing in the 10 stocks with the highest yields (rebalancing annually) in the Dow Jones Industrial Average, compared with a buy-and-hold strategy in all 30 stocks of the DJIA. Their study period was the 50 years from 1946 to 1995.

### TABLE 6  Annual Return Summary for Dow-10 and Dow-30 Portfolios: 1946 to 1995 ($n = 50$)

| Strategy | Mean Return | Standard Deviation |
|---|---|---|
| Dow-10 | 16.77% | 19.10% |
| Dow-30 | 13.71 | 16.64 |
| Difference | 3.06 | 6.62[a] |

[a] Sample standard deviation of differences.
*Source*: McQueen, Shields, and Thorley (1997, Table 1).

From Table 6 we have $\overline{d} = 3.06\%$ and $s_d = 6.62\%$.

1. Formulate null and alternative hypotheses consistent with a two-sided test that the mean difference between the Dow-10 and Dow-30 strategies equals 0.

2. Identify the test statistic for conducting a test of the hypotheses in Part 1.

3. Identify the rejection point or points for the hypothesis tested in Part 1 at the 0.01 level of significance.

4. Determine whether the null hypothesis is rejected or not rejected at the 0.01 level of significance. (Use the tables in the back of this book.)

5. Discuss the choice of a paired comparisons test.

**Solution to 1:** With $\mu_d$ as the underlying mean difference between the Dow-10 and Dow-30 strategies, we have $H_0$: $\mu_d = 0$ versus $H_a$: $\mu_d \neq 0$.

**Solution to 2:** Because the population variance is unknown, the test statistic is a $t$-test with $50 - 1 = 49$ degrees of freedom.

**Solution to 3:** In the table for the $t$-distribution, we look across the row for 49 degrees of freedom to the 0.005 column, to find 2.68. We will reject the null if we find that $t > 2.68$ or $t < -2.68$.

**Solution to 4:**

$$t_{49} = \frac{3.06}{6.62/\sqrt{50}} = \frac{3.06}{0.936209} = 3.2685 \text{ or } 3.27$$

Because $3.27 > 2.68$, we reject the null hypothesis. The authors concluded that the difference in mean returns was clearly statistically significant. However, after adjusting for the Dow-10's higher risk, extra transaction costs, and unfavorable tax treatment, they found that the Dow-10 portfolio did not beat the Dow-30 economically.

**Solution to 5:** The Dow-30 includes the Dow-10. As a result, they are not independent samples; in general, the correlation of returns on the Dow-10 and Dow-30 should be positive. Because the samples are dependent, a paired comparisons test was appropriate.

## 4    HYPOTHESIS TESTS CONCERNING VARIANCE

Because variance and standard deviation are widely used quantitative measures of risk in investments, analysts should be familiar with hypothesis tests concerning variance. The tests discussed in this section make regular appearances in investment literature. We examine two types: tests concerning the value of a single population variance and tests concerning the differences between two population variances.

### 4.1 Tests Concerning a Single Variance

In this section, we discuss testing hypotheses about the value of the variance, $\sigma^2$, of a single population. We use $\sigma_0^2$ to denote the hypothesized value of $\sigma^2$. We can formulate hypotheses as follows:

1.  $H_0$: $\sigma^2 = \sigma_0^2$ versus $H_a$: $\sigma^2 \neq \sigma_0^2$    (a "not equal to" alternative hypothesis)

2.  $H_0$: $\sigma^2 \leq \sigma_0^2$ versus $H_a$: $\sigma^2 > \sigma_0^2$    (a "greater than" alternative hypothesis)

3.  $H_0$: $\sigma^2 \geq \sigma_0^2$ versus $H_a$: $\sigma^2 < \sigma_0^2$    (a "less than" alternative hypothesis)

In tests concerning the variance of a single normally distributed population, we make use of a chi-square test statistic, denoted $\chi^2$. The chi-square distribution, unlike the normal and $t$-distributions, is asymmetrical. Like the $t$-distribution, the chi-square distribution is a family of distributions. A different distribution exists for each possible value of degrees of freedom, $n - 1$ ($n$ is sample size). Unlike the $t$-distribution, the chi-square distribution is bounded below by 0; $\chi^2$ does not take on negative values.

▶  **Test Statistic for Tests Concerning the Value of a Population Variance (Normal Population).** If we have $n$ independent observations from a normally distributed population, the appropriate test statistic is

$$\chi^2 = \frac{(n-1)s^2}{\sigma_0^2} \tag{11-14}$$

with $n - 1$ degrees of freedom. In the numerator of the expression is the sample variance, calculated as

$$s^2 = \frac{\sum_{i=1}^{n} (X_i - \overline{X})^2}{n - 1}$$    **(11-15)**

In contrast to the $t$-test, for example, the chi-square test is sensitive to violations of its assumptions. If the sample is not actually random or if it does not come from a normally distributed population, inferences based on a chi-square test are likely to be faulty.

If we choose a level of significance, $\alpha$, the rejection points for the three kinds of hypotheses are as follows:

▶ **Rejection Points for Hypothesis Tests on the Population Variance.**

1. "Not equal to" $H_a$: Reject the null hypothesis if the test statistic is greater than the upper $\alpha/2$ point (denoted $\chi^2_{\alpha/2}$) or less than the lower $\alpha/2$ point (denoted $\chi^2_{1-\alpha/2}$) of the chi-square distribution with df $= n - 1$.[27]

2. "Greater than" $H_a$: Reject the null hypothesis if the test statistic is greater than the upper $\alpha$ point of the chi-square distribution with df $= n - 1$.

3. "Less than" $H_a$: Reject the null hypothesis if the test statistic is less than the lower $\alpha$ point of the chi-square distribution with df $= n - 1$.

## EXAMPLE 7

### Risk and Return Characteristics of an Equity Mutual Fund (2)

You continue with your analysis of Sendar Equity Fund, a midcap growth fund that has been in existence for only 24 months. Recall that during this period, Sendar Equity achieved a sample standard deviation of monthly returns of 3.60 percent. You now want to test a claim that the particular investment disciplines followed by Sendar result in a standard deviation of monthly returns of less than 4 percent.

1. Formulate null and alternative hypotheses consistent with the verbal description of the research goal.

2. Identify the test statistic for conducting a test of the hypotheses in Part 1.

3. Identify the rejection point or points for the hypothesis tested in Part 1 at the 0.05 level of significance.

4. Determine whether the null hypothesis is rejected or not rejected at the 0.05 level of significance. (Use the tables in the back of this book.)

---

[27] Just as with other hypothesis tests, the chi-square test can be given a confidence interval interpretation. Unlike confidence intervals based on $z$- or $t$-statistics, however, chi-square confidence intervals for variance are asymmetric. A two-sided confidence interval for population variance, based on a sample of size $n$, has a lower limit L $= (n - 1)s^2/\chi^2_{\alpha/2}$ and an upper limit U $= (n - 1)s^2/\chi^2_{1-\alpha/2}$. Under the null hypothesis, the hypothesized value of the population variance should fall within these two limits.

**Solution to 1:** We have a "less than" alternative hypothesis, where $\sigma$ is the underlying standard deviation of return on Sendar Equity Fund. Being careful to square standard deviation to obtain a test in terms of variance, the hypotheses are $H_0$: $\sigma^2 \geq 16.0$ versus $H_a$: $\sigma^2 < 16.0$.

**Solution to 2:** The test statistic is chi-square with $24 - 1 = 23$ degrees of freedom.

**Solution to 3:** The lower 0.05 rejection point is found on the line for df = 23, under the 0.95 column (95 percent probability in the right tail, to give 0.95 probability of getting a test statistic this large or larger). The rejection point is 13.091. We will reject the null if we find that chi-square is less than 13.091.

**Solution to 4:**

$$\chi^2 = \frac{(n-1)s^2}{\sigma_0^2} = \frac{23 \times 3.60^2}{4^2} = \frac{298.08}{16} = 18.63$$

Because 18.63 (the calculated value of the test statistic) is not less than 13.091, we do not reject the null hypothesis. We cannot conclude that Sendar's investment disciplines result in a standard deviation of monthly returns of less than 4 percent.

## 4.2 Tests Concerning the Equality (Inequality) of Two Variances

Suppose we have a hypothesis about the relative values of the variances of two normally distributed populations with means $\mu_1$ and $\mu_2$ and variances $\sigma_1^2$ and $\sigma_2^2$. We can formulate all hypotheses as one of the choices below:

**1.** $H_0$: $\sigma_1^2 = \sigma_2^2$ versus $H_a$: $\sigma_1^2 \neq \sigma_2^2$

**2.** $H_0$: $\sigma_1^2 \leq \sigma_2^2$ versus $H_a$: $\sigma_1^2 > \sigma_2^2$

**3.** $H_0$: $\sigma_1^2 \geq \sigma_2^2$ versus $H_a$: $\sigma_1^2 < \sigma_2^2$

Note that at the point of equality, the null hypothesis $\sigma_1^2 = \sigma_2^2$ implies that the ratio of population variances equals 1: $\sigma_1^2 / \sigma_2^2 = 1$. Given independent random samples from these populations, tests related to these hypotheses are based on an $F$-test, which is the ratio of sample variances. Suppose we use $n_1$ observations in calculating the sample variance $s_1^2$ and $n_2$ observations in calculating the sample variance $s_2^2$. Tests concerning the difference between the variances of two populations make use of the $F$-distribution. Like the chi-square distribution, the $F$-distribution is a family of asymmetrical distributions bounded from below by 0. Each $F$-distribution is defined by two values of degrees of freedom, called the numerator and denominator degrees of freedom.[28] The $F$-test, like the chi-square test, is not robust to violations of its assumptions.

---

[28] The relationship between the chi-square and $F$-distributions is as follows: If $\chi_1^2$ is one chi-square random variable with $m$ degrees of freedom and $\chi_2^2$ is another chi-square random variable with $n$ degrees of freedom, then $F = (\chi_1^2/m)/(\chi_2^2/n)$ follows an $F$-distribution with $m$ numerator and $n$ denominator degrees of freedom.

▶ **Test Statistic for Tests Concerning Differences between the Variances of Two Populations (Normally Distributed Populations).** Suppose we have two samples, the first with $n_1$ observations and sample variance $s_1^2$, the second with $n_2$ observations and sample variance $s_2^2$. The samples are random, independent of each other, and generated by normally distributed populations. A test concerning differences between the variances of the two populations is based on the ratio of sample variances

$$F = \frac{s_1^2}{s_2^2}$$

**(11-16)**

with $df_1 = n_1 - 1$ numerator degrees of freedom and $df_2 = n_2 - 1$ denominator degrees of freedom. Note that $df_1$ and $df_2$ are the divisors used in calculating $s_1^2$ and $s_2^2$, respectively.

A convention, or usual practice, is to use the larger of the two ratios $s_1^2/s_2^2$ or $s_2^2/s_1^2$ as the actual test statistic. When we follow this convention, the value of the test statistic is always greater than or equal to 1; tables of critical values of $F$ then need include only values greater than or equal to 1. Under this convention, the rejection point for any formulation of hypotheses is a single value in the right-hand side of the relevant $F$-distribution. Note that the labeling of populations as "1" or "2" is arbitrary in any case.

▶ **Rejection Points for Hypothesis Tests on the Relative Values of Two Population Variances.** Follow the convention of using the larger of the two ratios $s_1^2/s_2^2$ and $s_2^2/s_1^2$ and consider two cases:

1. A "not equal to" alternative hypothesis: Reject the null hypothesis at the $\alpha$ significance level if the test statistic is greater than the upper $\alpha/2$ point of the $F$-distribution with the specified numerator and denominator degrees of freedom.

2. A "greater than" or "less than" alternative hypothesis: Reject the null hypothesis at the $\alpha$ significance level if the test statistic is greater than the upper $\alpha$ point of the $F$-distribution with the specified number of numerator and denominator degrees of freedom.

Thus, if we conduct a two-sided test at the $\alpha = 0.01$ level of significance, we need to find the rejection point in $F$-tables at the $\alpha/2 = 0.01/2 = 0.005$ significance level for a one-sided test (Case 1). But a one-sided test at 0.01 uses rejection points in $F$-tables for $\alpha = 0.01$ (Case 2). As an example, suppose we are conducting a two-sided test at the 0.05 significance level. We calculate a value of $F$ of 2.77 with 12 numerator and 19 denominator degrees of freedom. Using the $F$-tables for $0.05/2 = 0.025$ in the back of the book, we find that the rejection point is 2.72. Because the value 2.77 is greater than 2.72, we reject the null hypothesis at the 0.05 significance level.

If the convention stated above is not followed and we are given a calculated value of $F$ less than 1, can we still use $F$-tables? The answer is yes; using a reciprocal property of $F$-statistics, we can calculate the needed value. The easiest way to present this property is to show a calculation. Suppose our chosen level of significance is 0.05 for a two-tailed test and we have a value of $F$ of 0.11, with 7 numerator degrees of freedom and 9 denominator degrees of freedom. We take the reciprocal, $1/0.11 = 9.09$. Then we look up this value in the $F$-tables for 0.025 (because it is a two-tailed test) with degrees of freedom reversed: $F$ for 9 numerator and 7 denominator degrees of freedom. In other words, $F_{9,7} = 1/F_{7,9}$ and 9.09 exceeds the critical value of 4.82, so $F_{7,9} = 0.11$ is significant at the 0.05 level.

**EXAMPLE 8**

### Volatility and the Crash of 1987

You are investigating whether the population variance of returns on the S&P 500 changed subsequent to the October 1987 market crash. You gather the data in Table 7 for 120 months of returns before October 1987 and 120 months of returns after October 1987. You have specified a 0.01 level of significance.

**TABLE 7  S&P 500 Returns and Variance before and after October 1987**

|  | n | Mean Monthly Return (%) | Variance of Returns |
|---|---|---|---|
| Before October 1987 | 120 | 1.498 | 18.776 |
| After October 1987 | 120 | 1.392 | 13.097 |

1. Formulate null and alternative hypotheses consistent with the verbal description of the research goal.

2. Identify the test statistic for conducting a test of the hypotheses in Part 1.

3. Determine whether or not to reject the null hypothesis at the 0.01 level of significance. (Use the $F$-tables in the back of this book.)

**Solution to 1:** We have a "not equal to" alternative hypothesis:

$$H_0: \sigma^2_{Before} = \sigma^2_{After} \text{ versus } H_a: \sigma^2_{Before} \neq \sigma^2_{After}$$

**Solution to 2:** To test a null hypothesis of the equality of two variances, we use $F = s_1^2/s_2^2$ with $120 - 1 = 119$ numerator and denominator degrees of freedom.

**Solution to 3:** The "before" sample variance is larger, so following a convention for calculating $F$-statistics, the "before" sample variance goes in the numerator: $F = 18.776/13.097 = 1.434$. Because this is a two-tailed test, we use $F$-tables for the 0.005 level ($= 0.01/2$) to give a 0.01 significance level. In the tables in the back of the book, the closest value to 119 degrees of freedom is 120 degrees of freedom. At the 0.01 level, the rejection point is 1.61. Because 1.434 is less than the critical value 1.61, we cannot reject the null hypothesis that the population variance of returns is the same in the pre- and postcrash periods.

## EXAMPLE 9

### The Volatility of Derivatives Expiration Days

In the 1980s concern arose in the United States about the triple occurrence of stock option, index option, and futures expirations on the same day during four months of the year. Such days were known as "triple witching days." Table 8 presents evidence on the daily standard deviation of return for normal days and options/futures expiration days during the period 1 July 1983 to 24 October 1986. The tabled data refer to options and futures on the S&P 100, a subset of the S&P 500 that includes 100 of the most liquid S&P 500 stocks on which there are traded options.

**TABLE 8  Standard Deviation of Return:**
**1 July 1983 to 24 October 1986**

| Type of Day | n | Standard Deviation (%) |
|---|---|---|
| Normal trading | 115 | 0.786 |
| Options/futures expiration | 12 | 1.178 |

*Source*: Based on Edwards (1988), Table I.

1. Formulate null and alternative hypotheses consistent with the belief that triple witching days displayed above-normal volatility.
2. Identify the test statistic for conducting a test of the hypotheses in Part 1.
3. Determine whether or not to reject the null hypothesis at the 0.05 level of significance. (Use the $F$-tables in the back of this book.)

**Solution to 1:** We have a "greater than" alternative hypothesis:

$$H_0: \sigma^2_{\text{Expirations}} \leq \sigma^2_{\text{Normal}} \text{ versus } H_a: \sigma^2_{\text{Expirations}} > \sigma^2_{\text{Normal}}$$

**Solution to 2:** Let $\sigma^2_1$ represent the variance of triple witching days, and $\sigma^2_2$ represent the variance of normal days, following the convention for the selection of the numerator and the denominator stated earlier. To test the null hypothesis, we use $F = s^2_1/s^2_2$ with $12 - 1 = 11$ numerator and $115 - 1 = 114$ denominator degrees of freedom.

**Solution to 3:** $F = (1.178)^2/(0.786)^2 = 1.388/0.618 = 2.25$. Because this is a one-tailed test at the 0.05 significance level, we use $F$-tables for the 0.05 level directly. In the tables in the back of the book, the closest value to 114 degrees of freedom is 120 degrees of freedom. At the 0.05 level, the rejection point is 1.87. Because 2.25 is greater than 1.87, we reject the null hypothesis. It appears that triple witching days had above-normal volatility.

**5** # OTHER ISSUES: NONPARAMETRIC INFERENCE

The hypothesis-testing procedures we have discussed to this point have two characteristics in common. First, they are concerned with parameters, and second, their validity depends on a definite set of assumptions. Mean and variance, for example, are two parameters, or defining quantities, of a normal distribution. The tests also make specific assumptions—in particular, assumptions about the distribution of the population producing the sample. Any test or procedure with either of the above two characteristics is a **parametric test** or procedure. In some cases, however, we are concerned about quantities other than parameters of distributions. In other cases, we may believe that the assumptions of parametric tests do not hold for the particular data we have. In such cases, a nonparametric test or procedure can be useful. A **nonparametric test** is a test that is not concerned with a parameter, or a test that makes minimal assumptions about the population from which the sample comes.[29]

We primarily use nonparametric procedures in three situations: when the data we use do not meet distributional assumptions, when the data are given in ranks, or when the hypothesis we are addressing does not concern a parameter.

The first situation occurs when the data available for analysis suggest that the distributional assumptions of the parametric test are not satisfied. For example, we may want to test a hypothesis concerning the mean of a population but believe that neither a $t$-test nor a $z$-test is appropriate because the sample is small and may come from a markedly non-normally distributed population. In that case, we may use a nonparametric test. The nonparametric test will frequently involve the conversion of observations (or a function of observations) into ranks according to magnitude, and sometimes it will involve working with only "greater than" or "less than" relationships (using the signs + and − to denote those relationships). Characteristically, one must refer to specialized statistical tables to determine the rejection points of the test statistic, at least for small samples.[30] Such tests, then, typically interpret the null hypothesis as a thesis about ranks or signs. In Table 9, we give examples of nonparametric alternatives to the parametric tests we have discussed in this reading.[31] The reader should consult a comprehensive business statistics textbook for an introduction to such tests, and a specialist textbook for details.[32]

**TABLE 9  Nonparametric Alternatives to Parametric Tests**

|  | Parametric | Nonparametric |
|---|---|---|
| Tests concerning a single mean | $t$-test <br> $z$-test | Wilcoxon signed-rank test |
| Tests concerning differences between means | $t$-test <br> Approximate $t$-test | Mann–Whitney U test |
| Tests concerning mean differences (paired comparisons tests) | $t$-test | Wilcoxon signed-rank test <br> Sign test |

[29] Some writers make a distinction between "nonparametric" and "distribution-free" tests. They refer to procedures that do not concern the parameters of a distribution as nonparametric and to procedures that make minimal assumptions about the underlying distribution as distribution free. We follow a commonly accepted, inclusive usage of the term nonparametric.

[30] For large samples, there is often a transformation of the test statistic that permits the use of tables for the standard normal or $t$-distribution.

[31] In some cases, there are several nonparametric alternatives to a parametric test.

[32] See, for example, Hettmansperger and McKean (1998) or Siegel (1956).

We pointed out that when we use nonparametric tests, we often convert the original data into ranks. In some cases, the original data are already ranked. In those cases, we also use nonparametric tests because parametric tests generally require a stronger measurement scale than ranks. For example, if our data were the rankings of investment managers, hypotheses concerning those rankings would be tested using nonparametric procedures. Ranked data also appear in many other finance contexts. For example, Heaney, Koga, Oliver, and Tran (1999) studied the relationship between the size of Japanese companies (as measured by revenue) and their use of derivatives. The companies studied used derivatives to hedge one or more of five types of risk exposure: interest rate risk, foreign exchange risk, commodity price risk, marketable security price risk, and credit risk. The researchers gave a "perceived scope of risk exposure" score to each company that was equal to the number of types of risk exposure that the company reported hedging. Although revenue is measured on a strong scale (a ratio scale), scope of risk exposure is measured on only an ordinal scale.[33] The researchers thus employed nonparametric statistics to explore the relationship between derivatives usage and size.

A third situation in which we use nonparametric procedures occurs when our question does not concern a parameter. For example, if the question concerns whether a sample is random or not, we use the appropriate nonparametric test (a so-called runs test). Another type of question nonparametrics can address is whether a sample came from a population following a particular probability distribution (using the Kolmogorov–Smirnov test, for example).

We end this reading by describing in some detail a nonparametric statistic that has often been used in investment research, the Spearman rank correlation.

## 5.1 Tests Concerning Correlation: The Spearman Rank Correlation Coefficient

In many contexts in investments, we want to assess the strength of the linear relationship between two variables—the correlation between them. In a majority of cases, we use the correlation coefficient described in the readings on probability concepts and correlation and regression. However, the $t$-test of the hypothesis that two variables are uncorrelated, based on the correlation coefficient, relies on fairly stringent assumptions.[34] When we believe that the population under consideration meaningfully departs from those assumptions, we can employ a test based on the **Spearman rank correlation coefficient**, $r_S$. The Spearman rank correlation coefficient is essentially equivalent to the usual correlation coefficient calculated on the *ranks* of the two variables (say $X$ and $Y$) within their respective samples. Thus it is a number between $-1$ and $+1$, where $-1$ ($+1$) denotes a perfect inverse (positive) straight-line relationship between the variables and 0 represents the absence of any straight-line relationship (no correlation). The calculation of $r_S$ requires the following steps:

**1.** Rank the observations on $X$ from largest to smallest. Assign the number 1 to the observation with the largest value, the number 2 to the observation with second-largest value, and so on. In case of ties, we assign to each tied observation the average of the ranks that they jointly occupy. For example,

---

[33] We discussed scales of measurement in the reading on statistical concepts and market returns.

[34] The $t$-test is described in the reading on correlation and regression. The assumption of the test is that each observation $(x, y)$ on the two variables $(X, Y)$ is a random observation from a bivariate normal distribution. Informally, in a bivariate or two-variable normal distribution, each individual variable is normally distributed and their joint relationship is completely described by the correlation, $\rho$, between them. For more details, see, for example, Daniel and Terrell (1986).

if the third- and fourth-largest values are tied, we assign both observations the rank of 3.5 (the average of 3 and 4). Perform the same procedure for the observations on $Y$.

2. Calculate the difference, $d_i$, between the ranks of each pair of observations on $X$ and $Y$.

3. Then, with $n$ the sample size, the Spearman rank correlation is given by[35]

$$r_S = 1 - \frac{6\sum\limits_{i=1}^{n} d_i^2}{n(n^2 - 1)}$$

**(11-17)**

Suppose an investor wants to invest in a U.S. large-cap growth mutual fund. He has narrowed the field to 10 funds. In examining the funds, a question arises as to whether the funds' reported three-year Sharpe ratios are related to their most recent reported expense ratios. Because the assumptions of the $t$-test on the correlation coefficient may not be met, it is appropriate to conduct a test on the rank correlation coefficient.[36] Table 10 presents the calculation of $r_S$.[37] The first two rows contain the original data. The row of $X$ ranks converts the Sharpe ratios to ranks; the row of $Y$ ranks converts the expense ratios to ranks. We want to test $H_0$: $\rho = 0$ versus $H_a$: $\rho \neq 0$, where $\rho$ is defined in this context as

**TABLE 10  The Spearman Rank Correlation: An Example**

| | | | | | Mutual Fund | | | | | |
|---|---|---|---|---|---|---|---|---|---|---|
| | **1** | **2** | **3** | **4** | **5** | **6** | **7** | **8** | **9** | **10** |
| Sharpe Ratio ($X$) | $-1.08$ | $-0.96$ | $-1.13$ | $-1.16$ | $-0.91$ | $-1.08$ | $-1.18$ | $-1.00$ | $-1.06$ | $-1.00$ |
| Expense Ratio ($Y$) | 1.34 | 0.92 | 1.02 | 1.45 | 1.35 | 0.50 | 1.00 | 1.50 | 1.45 | 1.50 |
| $X$ Rank | 6.5 | 2 | 8 | 9 | 1 | 6.5 | 10 | 3.5 | 5 | 3.5 |
| $Y$ Rank | 6 | 9 | 7 | 3.5 | 5 | 10 | 8 | 1.5 | 3.5 | 1.5 |
| $d_i$ | 0.5 | $-7$ | 1 | 5.5 | $-4$ | $-3.5$ | 2 | 2 | 1.5 | 2 |
| $d_i^2$ | 0.25 | 49 | 1 | 30.25 | 16 | 12.25 | 4 | 4 | 2.25 | 4 |

$$r_S = 1 - \frac{6\Sigma d_i^2}{n(n^2 - 1)} = 1 - \frac{6(123)}{10(100 - 1)} = 0.2545$$

---

[35] Calculating the usual correlation coefficient on the ranks would yield approximately the same result as Equation 11-17.

[36] The expense ratio (the ratio of a fund's operating expenses to average net assets) is bounded both from below (by zero) and from above. The Sharpe ratio is also observed within a limited range, in practice. Thus neither variable can be normally distributed, and hence jointly they cannot follow a bivariate normal distribution. In short, the assumptions of a $t$-test are not met.

[37] The data for the table are based on statistics reported in Standard & Poor's Mutual Fund Reports for actual large-cap growth funds for the three-year period ending in the first quarter of 2003. The negative Sharpe ratios reflect in part declining U.S. equity markets during this period.

the population correlation of $X$ and $Y$ after ranking. For small samples, the rejection points for the test based on $r_S$ must be looked up in Table 11. For large samples (say $n > 30$), we can conduct a $t$-test using

$$t = \frac{(n - 2)^{1/2} r_S}{(1 - r_S^2)^{1/2}}$$

**(11-18)**

based on $n - 2$ degrees of freedom.

In the example at hand, a two-tailed test with a 0.05 significance level, Table 11 gives the upper-tail rejection point for $n = 10$ as 0.6364 (we use the 0.025 column for a two-tailed test at a 0.05 significance level). Accordingly, we reject the null hypothesis if $r_S$ is less than $-0.6364$ or greater than 0.6364. With $r_S$ equal to 0.2545, we do not reject the null hypothesis.

## TABLE 11  Spearman Rank Correlation Distribution Approximate Upper-Tail Rejection Points

| Sample Size: $n$ | $\alpha = 0.05$ | $\alpha = 0.025$ | $\alpha = 0.01$ |
|:---:|:---:|:---:|:---:|
| 5 | 0.8000 | 0.9000 | 0.9000 |
| 6 | 0.7714 | 0.8286 | 0.8857 |
| 7 | 0.6786 | 0.7450 | 0.8571 |
| 8 | 0.6190 | 0.7143 | 0.8095 |
| 9 | 0.5833 | 0.6833 | 0.7667 |
| 10 | 0.5515 | 0.6364 | 0.7333 |
| 11 | 0.5273 | 0.6091 | 0.7000 |
| 12 | 0.4965 | 0.5804 | 0.6713 |
| 13 | 0.4780 | 0.5549 | 0.6429 |
| 14 | 0.4593 | 0.5341 | 0.6220 |
| 15 | 0.4429 | 0.5179 | 0.6000 |
| 16 | 0.4265 | 0.5000 | 0.5824 |
| 17 | 0.4118 | 0.4853 | 0.5637 |
| 18 | 0.3994 | 0.4716 | 0.5480 |
| 19 | 0.3895 | 0.4579 | 0.5333 |
| 20 | 0.3789 | 0.4451 | 0.5203 |
| 21 | 0.3688 | 0.4351 | 0.5078 |
| 22 | 0.3597 | 0.4241 | 0.4963 |
| 23 | 0.3518 | 0.4150 | 0.4852 |
| 24 | 0.3435 | 0.4061 | 0.4748 |
| 25 | 0.3362 | 0.3977 | 0.4654 |
| 26 | 0.3299 | 0.3894 | 0.4564 |
| 27 | 0.3236 | 0.3822 | 0.4481 |
| 28 | 0.3175 | 0.3749 | 0.4401 |
| 29 | 0.3113 | 0.3685 | 0.4320 |
| 30 | 0.3059 | 0.3620 | 0.4251 |

*Note*: The corresponding lower tail critical value is obtained by changing the sign of the upper-tail critical value.

In the mutual fund example, we converted observations on two variables into ranks. If one or both of the original variables were in the form of ranks, we would need to use $r_S$ to investigate correlation.

## 5.2 Nonparametric Inference: Summary

Nonparametric statistical procedures extend the reach of inference because they make few assumptions, can be used on ranked data, and may address questions unrelated to parameters. Quite frequently, nonparametric tests are reported alongside parametric tests. The reader can then assess how sensitive the statistical conclusion is to the assumptions underlying the parametric test. However, if the assumptions of the parametric test are met, the parametric test (where available) is generally preferred to the nonparametric test because the parametric test usually permits us to draw sharper conclusions.[38] For complete coverage of all the nonparametric procedures that may be encountered in the finance and investment literature, it is best to consult a specialist textbook.[39]

---

[38] To use a concept introduced in an earlier section, the parametric test is often more powerful.

[39] See, for example, Hettmansperger and McKean (1998) or Siegel (1956).

# SUMMARY

In this reading, we have presented the concepts and methods of statistical inference and hypothesis testing.

▶ A hypothesis is a statement about one or more populations.

▶ The steps in testing a hypothesis are as follows:
  1. Stating the hypotheses.
  2. Identifying the appropriate test statistic and its probability distribution.
  3. Specifying the significance level.
  4. Stating the decision rule.
  5. Collecting the data and calculating the test statistic.
  6. Making the statistical decision.
  7. Making the economic or investment decision.

▶ We state two hypotheses: The null hypothesis is the hypothesis to be tested; the alternative hypothesis is the hypothesis accepted when the null hypothesis is rejected.

▶ There are three ways to formulate hypotheses:
  1. $H_0: \theta = \theta_0$ versus $H_a: \theta \neq \theta_0$
  2. $H_0: \theta \leq \theta_0$ versus $H_a: \theta > \theta_0$
  3. $H_0: \theta \geq \theta_0$ versus $H_a: \theta < \theta_0$

  where $\theta_0$ is a hypothesized value of the population parameter and $\theta$ is the true value of the population parameter. In the above, Formulation 1 is a two-sided test and Formulations 2 and 3 are one-sided tests.

▶ When we have a "suspected" or "hoped for" condition for which we want to find supportive evidence, we frequently set up that condition as the alternative hypothesis and use a one-sided test. To emphasize a neutral attitude, however, the researcher may select a "not equal to" alternative hypothesis and conduct a two-sided test.

▶ A test statistic is a quantity, calculated on the basis of a sample, whose value is the basis for deciding whether to reject or not reject the null hypothesis. To decide whether to reject, or not to reject, the null hypothesis, we compare the computed value of the test statistic to a critical value (rejection point) for the same test statistic.

▶ In reaching a statistical decision, we can make two possible errors: We may reject a true null hypothesis (a Type I error), or we may fail to reject a false null hypothesis (a Type II error).

▶ The level of significance of a test is the probability of a Type I error that we accept in conducting a hypothesis test. The probability of a Type I error is denoted by the Greek letter alpha, $\alpha$. The standard approach to hypothesis testing involves specifying a level of significance (probability of Type I error) only.

▶ The power of a test is the probability of correctly rejecting the null (rejecting the null when it is false).

▶ A decision rule consists of determining the rejection points (critical values) with which to compare the test statistic to decide whether to reject or not to reject the null hypothesis. When we reject the null hypothesis, the result is said to be statistically significant.

▶ The $(1 - \alpha)$ confidence interval represents the range of values of the test statistic for which the null hypothesis will not be rejected at an $\alpha$ significance level.

▶ The statistical decision consists of rejecting or not rejecting the null hypothesis. The economic decision takes into consideration all economic issues pertinent to the decision.

▶ The $p$-value is the smallest level of significance at which the null hypothesis can be rejected. The smaller the $p$-value, the stronger the evidence against the null hypothesis and in favor of the alternative hypothesis. The $p$-value approach to hypothesis testing does not involve setting a significance level; rather it involves computing a $p$-value for the test statistic and allowing the consumer of the research to interpret its significance.

▶ For hypothesis tests concerning the population mean of a normally distributed population with unknown (known) variance, the theoretically correct test statistic is the $t$-statistic ($z$-statistic). In the unknown variance case, given large samples (generally, samples of 30 or more observations), the $z$-statistic may be used in place of the $t$-statistic because of the force of the central limit theorem.

▶ The $t$-distribution is a symmetrical distribution defined by a single parameter: degrees of freedom. Compared to the standard normal distribution, the $t$-distribution has fatter tails.

▶ When we want to test whether the observed difference between two means is statistically significant, we must first decide whether the samples are independent or dependent (related). If the samples are independent, we conduct tests concerning differences between means. If the samples are dependent, we conduct tests of mean differences (paired comparisons tests).

▶ When we conduct a test of the difference between two population means from normally distributed populations with unknown variances, if we can assume the variances are equal, we use a $t$-test based on pooling the observations of the two samples to estimate the common (but unknown) variance. This test is based on an assumption of independent samples.

▶ When we conduct a test of the difference between two population means from normally distributed populations with unknown variances, if we cannot assume that the variances are equal, we use an approximate $t$-test using modified degrees of freedom given by a formula. This test is based on an assumption of independent samples.

▶ In tests concerning two means based on two samples that are not independent, we often can arrange the data in paired observations and conduct a test of mean differences (a paired comparisons test). When the samples are from normally distributed populations with unknown variances, the appropriate test statistic is a $t$-statistic. The denominator of the $t$-statistic, the standard error of the mean differences, takes account of correlation between the samples.

▶ In tests concerning the variance of a single, normally distributed population, the test statistic is chi-square ($\chi^2$) with $n - 1$ degrees of freedom, where $n$ is sample size.

▶ For tests concerning differences between the variances of two normally distributed populations based on two random, independent samples, the appropriate test statistic is based on an $F$-test (the ratio of the sample variances).

▶ The *F*-statistic is defined by the numerator and denominator degrees of freedom. The numerator degrees of freedom (number of observations in the sample minus 1) is the divisor used in calculating the sample variance in the numerator. The denominator degrees of freedom (number of observations in the sample minus 1) is the divisor used in calculating the sample variance in the denominator. In forming an *F*-test, a convention is to use the larger of the two ratios, $s_1^2 / s_2^2$ or $s_2^2 / s_1^2$, as the actual test statistic.

▶ A parametric test is a hypothesis test concerning a parameter or a hypothesis test based on specific distributional assumptions. In contrast, a nonparametric test either is not concerned with a parameter or makes minimal assumptions about the population from which the sample comes.

▶ A nonparametric test is primarily used in three situations: when data do not meet distributional assumptions, when data are given in ranks, or when the hypothesis we are addressing does not concern a parameter.

▶ The Spearman rank correlation coefficient is calculated on the ranks of two variables within their respective samples.

## PRACTICE PROBLEMS FOR READING 11

1. Define the following terms:
   A. Null hypothesis.
   B. Alternative hypothesis.
   C. Test statistic.
   D. Type I error.
   E. Type II error.
   F. Power of a test.
   G. Rejection point (critical value).

2. Suppose that, on the basis of a sample, we want to test the hypothesis that the mean debt-to-total-assets ratio of companies that become takeover targets is the same as the mean debt-to-total-assets ratio of companies in the same industry that do not become takeover targets. Explain under what conditions we would commit a Type I error and under what conditions we would commit a Type II error.

3. Suppose we are testing a null hypothesis, $H_0$, versus an alternative hypothesis, $H_a$, and the $p$-value for the test statistic is 0.031. At which of the following levels of significance—$\alpha = 0.10$, $\alpha = 0.05$, and/or $\alpha = 0.01$—would we reject the null hypothesis?

4. Identify the appropriate test statistic or statistics for conducting the following hypothesis tests. (Clearly identify the test statistic and, if applicable, the number of degrees of freedom. For example, "We conduct the test using an $x$-statistic with $y$ degrees of freedom.")

   A. $H_0$: $\mu = 0$ versus $H_a$: $\mu \neq 0$, where $\mu$ is the mean of a normally distributed population with unknown variance. The test is based on a sample of 15 observations.

   B. $H_0$: $\mu = 0$ versus $H_a$: $\mu \neq 0$, where $\mu$ is the mean of a normally distributed population with unknown variance. The test is based on a sample of 40 observations.

   C. $H_0$: $\mu \leq 0$ versus $H_a$: $\mu > 0$, where $\mu$ is the mean of a normally distributed population with known variance $\sigma^2$. The sample size is 45.

   D. $H_0$: $\sigma^2 = 200$ versus $H_a$: $\sigma^2 \neq 200$, where $\sigma^2$ is the variance of a normally distributed population. The sample size is 50.

   E. $H_0$: $\sigma_1^2 = \sigma_2^2$ versus $H_a$: $\sigma_1^2 \neq \sigma_2^2$, where $\sigma_1^2$ is the variance of one normally distributed population and $\sigma_2^2$ is the variance of a second normally distributed population. The test is based on two independent random samples.

   F. $H_0$: (Population mean 1) − (Population mean 2) = 0 versus $H_a$: (Population mean 1) − (Population mean 2) ≠ 0, where the samples are drawn from normally distributed populations with unknown variances. The observations in the two samples are correlated.

   G. $H_0$: (Population mean 1) − (Population mean 2) = 0 versus $H_a$: (Population mean 1) − (Population mean 2) ≠ 0, where the samples are drawn from normally distributed populations with unknown but assumed equal variances. The observations in the two samples (of size 25 and 30, respectively) are independent.

**5.** For each of the following hypothesis tests concerning the population mean, $\mu$, state the rejection point condition or conditions for the test statistic (e.g., $t > 1.25$); $n$ denotes sample size.

**A.** $H_0$: $\mu = 10$ versus $H_a$: $\mu \neq 10$, using a $t$-test with $n = 26$ and $\alpha = 0.05$

**B.** $H_0$: $\mu = 10$ versus $H_a$: $\mu \neq 10$, using a $t$-test with $n = 40$ and $\alpha = 0.01$

**C.** $H_0$: $\mu \leq 10$ versus $H_a$: $\mu > 10$, using a $t$-test with $n = 40$ and $\alpha = 0.01$

**D.** $H_0$: $\mu \leq 10$ versus $H_a$: $\mu > 10$, using a $t$-test with $n = 21$ and $\alpha = 0.05$

**E.** $H_0$: $\mu \geq 10$ versus $H_a$: $\mu < 10$, using a $t$-test with $n = 19$ and $\alpha = 0.10$

**F.** $H_0$: $\mu \geq 10$ versus $H_a$: $\mu < 10$, using a $t$-test with $n = 50$ and $\alpha = 0.05$

**6.** For each of the following hypothesis tests concerning the population mean, $\mu$, state the rejection point condition or conditions for the test statistic (e.g., $z > 1.25$); $n$ denotes sample size.

**A.** $H_0$: $\mu = 10$ versus $H_a$: $\mu \neq 10$, using a $z$-test with $n = 50$ and $\alpha = 0.01$

**B.** $H_0$: $\mu = 10$ versus $H_a$: $\mu \neq 10$, using a $z$-test with $n = 50$ and $\alpha = 0.05$

**C.** $H_0$: $\mu = 10$ versus $H_a$: $\mu \neq 10$, using a $z$-test with $n = 50$ and $\alpha = 0.10$

**D.** $H_0$: $\mu \leq 10$ versus $H_a$: $\mu > 10$, using a $z$-test with $n = 50$ and $\alpha = 0.05$

**7.** Identify the theoretically correct test statistic to use for a hypothesis test concerning the mean of a single population under the following conditions:

**A.** The sample comes from a normally distributed population with known variance.

**B.** The sample comes from a normally distributed population with unknown variance.

**C.** The sample comes from a population following a non-normal distribution with unknown variance. The sample size is large.

**8.** Willco is a manufacturer in a mature cyclical industry. During the most recent industry cycle, its net income averaged $30 million per year with a standard deviation of $10 million ($n = 6$ observations). Management claims that Willco's performance during the most recent cycle results from new approaches and that we can dismiss profitability expectations based on its average or normalized earnings of $24 million per year in prior cycles.

**A.** With $\mu$ as the population value of mean annual net income, formulate null and alternative hypotheses consistent with testing Willco management's claim.

**B.** Assuming that Willco's net income is at least approximately normally distributed, identify the appropriate test statistic.

**C.** Identify the rejection point or points at the 0.05 level of significance for the hypothesis tested in Part A.

**D.** Determine whether or not to reject the null hypothesis at the 0.05 significance level.

# Use the following table to answer Questions 9–10

## Performance in Forecasting Quarterly Earnings per Share

|  | Number of Forecasts | Mean Forecast Error (Predicted – Actual) | Standard Deviations of Forecast Errors |
|---|---|---|---|
| Analyst A | 101 | 0.05 | 0.10 |
| Analyst B | 121 | 0.02 | 0.09 |

9.  Investment analysts often use earnings per share (EPS) forecasts. One test of forecasting quality is the zero-mean test, which states that optimal forecasts should have a mean forecasting error of 0. (Forecasting error = Predicted value of variable − Actual value of variable.)

    You have collected data (shown in the table above) for two analysts who cover two different industries: Analyst A covers the telecom industry; Analyst B covers automotive parts and suppliers.

    A. With $\mu$ as the population mean forecasting error, formulate null and alternative hypotheses for a zero-mean test of forecasting quality.

    B. For Analyst A, using both a $t$-test and a $z$-test, determine whether to reject the null at the 0.05 and 0.01 levels of significance.

    C. For Analyst B, using both a $t$-test and a $z$-test, determine whether to reject the null at the 0.05 and 0.01 levels of significance.

10. Reviewing the EPS forecasting performance data for Analysts A and B, you want to investigate whether the larger average forecast errors of Analyst A are due to chance or to a higher underlying mean value for Analyst B. Assume that the forecast errors of both analysts are normally distributed and that the samples are independent.

    A. Formulate null and alternative hypotheses consistent with determining whether the population mean value of Analyst A's forecast errors $(\mu_1)$ are larger than Analyst B's $(\mu_2)$.

    B. Identify the test statistic for conducting a test of the null hypothesis formulated in Part A.

    C. Identify the rejection point or points for the hypothesis tested in Part A, at the 0.05 level of significance.

    D. Determine whether or not to reject the null hypothesis at the 0.05 level of significance.

**11.** Altman and Kishore (1996), in the course of a study on the recovery rates on defaulted bonds, investigated the recovery of utility bonds versus other bonds, stratified by seniority. The following table excerpts their findings.

**Recovery Rates by Seniority**

| Industry Group/ Seniority | Industry Group | | | Ex-Utilities Sample | | |
|---|---|---|---|---|---|---|
| | Number of Observations | Average Price[a] | Standard Deviation | Number of Observations | Average Price[a] | Standard Deviation |
| *Public Utilities* | | | | | | |
| Senior Unsecured | 32 | $77.74 | $18.06 | 189 | $42.56 | $24.89 |

[a] This is the average price at default and is a measure of recovery rate.

*Source*: Altman and Kishore (1996, Table 5).

Assume that the populations (recovery rates of utilities, recovery rates of non-utilities) are normally distributed and that the samples are independent. The population variances are unknown; do not assume they are equal. The test hypotheses are $H_0: \mu_1 - \mu_2 = 0$ versus $H_a: \mu_1 - \mu_2 \neq 0$, where $\mu_1$ is the population mean recovery rate for utilities and $\mu_2$ is the population mean recovery rate for non-utilities.

**A.** Calculate the test statistic.

**B.** Determine whether to reject the null hypothesis at the 0.01 significance level without reference to degrees of freedom.

**C.** Calculate the degrees of freedom.

**12.** The table below gives data on the monthly returns on the S&P 500 and small-cap stocks for the period January 1960 through December 1999 and provides statistics relating to their mean differences.

| Measure | S&P 500 Return (%) | Small-Cap Stock Return (%) | Differences (S&P 500 – Small-Cap Stock) |
|---|---|---|---|
| *January 1960–December 1999, 480 months* | | | |
| Mean | 1.0542 | 1.3117 | −0.258 |
| Standard deviation | 4.2185 | 5.9570 | 3.752 |
| *January 1960–December 1979, 240 months* | | | |
| Mean | 0.6345 | 1.2741 | −0.640 |
| Standard deviation | 4.0807 | 6.5829 | 4.096 |
| *January 1980–December 1999, 240 months* | | | |
| Mean | 1.4739 | 1.3492 | 0.125 |
| Standard deviation | 4.3197 | 5.2709 | 3.339 |

Let $\mu_d$ stand for the population mean value of difference between S&P 500 returns and small-cap stock returns. Use a significance level of 0.05 and suppose that mean differences are approximately normally distributed.

**A.** Formulate null and alternative hypotheses consistent with testing whether any difference exists between the mean returns on the S&P 500 and small-cap stocks.

**B.** Determine whether or not to reject the null hypothesis at the 0.05 significance level for the January 1960 to December 1999 period.

**C.** Determine whether or not to reject the null hypothesis at the 0.05 significance level for the January 1960 to December 1979 subperiod.

**D.** Determine whether or not to reject the null hypothesis at the 0.05 significance level for the January 1980 to December 1999 subperiod.

**13.** During a 10-year period, the standard deviation of annual returns on a portfolio you are analyzing was 15 percent a year. You want to see whether this record is sufficient evidence to support the conclusion that the portfolio's underlying variance of return was less than 400, the return variance of the portfolio's benchmark.

**A.** Formulate null and alternative hypotheses consistent with the verbal description of your objective.

**B.** Identify the test statistic for conducting a test of the hypotheses in Part A.

**C.** Identify the rejection point or points at the 0.05 significance level for the hypothesis tested in Part A.

**D.** Determine whether the null hypothesis is rejected or not rejected at the 0.05 level of significance.

**14.** You are investigating whether the population variance of returns on the S&P 500/BARRA Growth Index changed subsequent to the October 1987 market crash. You gather the following data for 120 months of returns before October 1987 and for 120 months of returns after October 1987. You have specified a 0.05 level of significance.

| Time Period | n | Mean Monthly Return (%) | Variance of Returns |
|---|---|---|---|
| Before October 1987 | 120 | 1.416 | 22.367 |
| After October 1987 | 120 | 1.436 | 15.795 |

**A.** Formulate null and alternative hypotheses consistent with the verbal description of the research goal.

**B.** Identify the test statistic for conducting a test of the hypotheses in Part A.

**C.** Determine whether or not to reject the null hypothesis at the 0.05 level of significance. (Use the $F$-tables in the back of this volume.)

**15.** You are interested in whether excess risk-adjusted return (alpha) is correlated with mutual fund expense ratios for U.S. large-cap growth funds. The following table presents the sample.

| Mutual Fund | 1 | 2 | 3 | 4 | 5 | 6 | 7 | 8 | 9 |
|---|---|---|---|---|---|---|---|---|---|
| Alpha ($X$) | −0.52 | −0.13 | −0.60 | −1.01 | −0.26 | −0.89 | −0.42 | −0.23 | −0.60 |
| Expense Ratio ($Y$) | 1.34 | 0.92 | 1.02 | 1.45 | 1.35 | 0.50 | 1.00 | 1.50 | 1.45 |

**A.** Formulate null and alternative hypotheses consistent with the verbal description of the research goal.

**B.** Identify the test statistic for conducting a test of the hypotheses in Part A.

**C.** Justify your selection in Part B.

**D.** Determine whether or not to reject the null hypothesis at the 0.05 level of significance.

**16.** All else equal, is specifying a smaller significance level in a hypothesis test likely to increase the probability of a:

| | Type I error? | Type II error? |
|---|---|---|
| **A.** | No | No |
| **B.** | No | Yes |
| **C.** | Yes | No |

**17.** All else equal, is increasing the sample size for a hypothesis test likely to decrease the probability of a:

| | Type I error? | Type II error? |
|---|---|---|
| **A.** | No | Yes |
| **B.** | Yes | No |
| **C.** | Yes | Yes |

# TECHNICAL ANALYSIS

by Frank K. Reilly, CFA and Keith C. Brown, CFA

## LEARNING OUTCOMES

| The candidate should be able to: | Mastery |
|---|---|
| **a.** explain the underlying assumptions of technical analysis; | ☐ |
| **b.** discuss the advantages of and challenges to technical analysis; | ☐ |
| **c.** list and describe examples of each major category of technical trading rules and indicators. | ☐ |

# INTRODUCTION 1

► The market reacted yesterday to the report of a large increase in the short interest on the NYSE.

► Although the market declined today, it was not considered bearish because of the light volume.

► The market declined today after three days of increases due to profit taking by investors.

These and similar statements appear daily in the financial news. All of them have as their rationale one of numerous technical trading rules. *Technical analysts,* or *technicians,* develop technical trading rules from observations of past price movements of the stock market and individual stocks. The philosophy behind technical analysis is in sharp contrast to the efficient market hypothesis that we studied, which contends that past performance has no influence on future performance or market values. It also differs from what we learned about

---

Richard T. McCabe, Chief Market Analyst at Merrill Lynch Capital Markets, provided helpful comments and material for this reading.

*Investment Analysis and Portfolio Management,* Eighth Edition, by Frank K. Reilly, CFA and Keith C. Brown, CFA. Copyright © 2005 by Thomson South-Western. Reprinted with permission of South-Western, a division of Thomson Learning.

fundamental analysis, which involves making investment decisions based on the examination of the economy, an industry, and company variables that lead to an estimate of intrinsic value for an investment, which is then compared to its prevailing market price. In contrast to the efficient market hypothesis or fundamental analysis, **technical analysis** involves the examination of past market data such as prices and the volume of trading, which leads to an estimate of future price trends and, therefore, an investment decision. Whereas fundamental analysts use economic data that are usually separate from the stock or bond market, the technical analyst uses data *from the market itself* because the market is its own best predictor. Therefore, technical analysis is an alternative method of making the investment decision and answering the questions: What securities should an investor buy or sell? When should these investments be made?

Technical analysts see no need to study the multitude of economic, industry, and company variables to arrive at an estimate of future value because they believe that past price movements will signal future price movements. Technicians also believe that a change in the price trend may predict a forthcoming change in the fundamental variables such as earnings and risk before the change is perceived by most fundamental analysis. Are technicians correct? Many investors using these techniques claim to have experienced superior rates of return on many investments. In addition, many newsletter writers base their recommendations on technical analysis. Finally, even the major investment firms that employ many fundamental analysts also employ technical analysts to provide investment advice. Numerous investment professionals and individual investors believe in and use technical trading rules to make their investment decisions. Therefore, whether a fan of technical analysis or an advocate of the efficient market hypothesis, investors should still have an understanding of the basic philosophy and reasoning behind technical approaches. Thus, we begin this reading with an examination of the basic philosophy underlying technical analysis. Subsequently, we consider the advantages and potential problems with the technical approach. Finally, we present alternative technical trading rules applicable to both the U.S. and foreign securities markets.

## 2  UNDERLYING ASSUMPTIONS OF TECHNICAL ANALYSIS

Technical analysts base trading decisions on examinations of prior price and volume data to determine past market trends from which they predict future behavior for the market as a whole and for individual securities. Several assumptions summarized in Levy (1966) lead to this view of price movements. Certain aspects of these assumptions are controversial, leading fundamental analysts and advocates of efficient markets to question their validity. We have italicized those aspects in our list.

1. The market value of any good or service is determined solely by the interaction of supply and demand.

| EXHIBIT 1 | Technicians' View of Price Adjustment to New Information |
|-----------|--------------------------------------------------------|

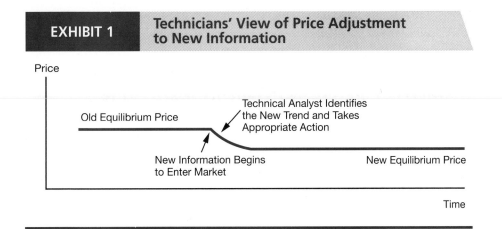

2. Supply and demand are governed by numerous rational and irrational factors. Included in these factors are those economic variables relied on by the fundamental analyst as well as opinions, moods, and guesses. The market weighs all these factors continually and automatically.

3. Disregarding minor fluctuations, *the prices for individual securities and the overall value of the market tend to move in trends, which persist for appreciable lengths of time.*

4. Prevailing trends change in reaction to shifts in supply and demand relationships. These shifts, no matter why they occur, *can be detected sooner or later in the action of the market itself.*

The first two assumptions are almost universally accepted by technicians and nontechnicians alike. Almost anyone who has had a basic course in economics would agree that, at any point in time, the price of a security (or any good or service) is determined by the interaction of supply and demand. In addition, most observers would acknowledge that supply and demand are governed by many variables. The only difference in opinion might concern the influence of the irrational factors. Certainly, everyone would agree that the market continually weighs all these factors.

In contrast, there is a significant difference of opinion regarding the assumption about the *speed of adjustment* of stock prices to changes in supply and demand. Technical analysts expect stock prices to move in trends that persist for long periods because they believe that new information does *not* come to the market at one point in time but rather enters the market *over a period of time.* This pattern of information access occurs because of different sources of information or because certain investors receive the information or perceive fundamental changes earlier than others. As various groups—ranging from insiders to well-informed professionals to the average investor—receive the information and buy or sell a security accordingly, its price moves gradually toward the new equilibrium. Therefore, technicians do not expect the price adjustment to be as abrupt as fundamental analysts and efficient market supporters do; rather, they expect a *gradual price adjustment* to reflect the gradual flow of information.

Exhibit 1 shows this process wherein new information causes a decrease in the equilibrium price for a security but the price adjustment is not rapid. It occurs as a trend that persists until the stock reaches its new equilibrium. Technical analysts look for the beginning of a movement from one equilibrium value to a new equilibrium value but do not attempt to predict the new equilibrium value. They look for the start of a change so that they can get on the bandwagon early and benefit from the move to the new equilibrium price by buying if the trend is up or selling if the trend is down. Obviously, if there is a rapid adjustment of prices to the new information (as expected by those who espouse an efficient market), the ride on the bandwagon would be so short that investors could not benefit.

## 3 ADVANTAGES OF TECHNICAL ANALYSIS

Although technicians understand the logic of fundamental analysis, they see several benefits in their approach. Most technical analysts admit that a fundamental analyst with good information, good analytical ability, and a keen sense of information's impact on the market should achieve above-average returns. However, this statement requires qualification. According to technical analysts, it is important to recognize that the fundamental analysts can experience superior returns *only* if they obtain new information before other investors and process it *correctly* and *quickly*. Technical analysts do not believe the majority of investors can consistently get new information before other investors and consistently process it correctly and quickly.

In addition, technical analysts claim that a major advantage of their method is that *it is not heavily dependent on financial accounting statements*—the major source of information about the past performance of a firm or industry. As we know, the fundamental analyst evaluates such statements to help project future return and risk characteristics for industries and individual securities. The technician contends that there are several major problems with accounting statements:

1. They lack a great deal of information needed by security analysts, such as information related to sales, earnings, and capital utilized by product line and customers.

2. According to GAAP (Generally Accepted Accounting Principles), corporations may choose among several procedures for reporting expenses, assets, or liabilities. Notably, these alternative procedures can produce vastly different values for expenses, income, return on assets, and return on equity, depending on whether the firm is conservative or aggressive. As a result, an investor can have trouble comparing the statements of two firms within the same industry, much less firms across industries.

3. Many psychological factors and other nonquantifiable variables do not appear in financial statements. Examples include employee training and loyalty, customer goodwill, and general investor attitude toward an industry. Investor attitudes could be important when investors become concerned about the risk from restrictions or taxes on products such as tobacco or alcohol or when firms do business in countries that have significant political risk.

Therefore, because technicians are suspicious of financial statements, they consider it advantageous not to depend on them. As we will show, most of the data used by technicians, such as security prices, volume of trading, and other trading information, are derived from the stock market itself.

Also, a fundamental analyst must process new information correctly and *quickly* to derive a new intrinsic value for the stock or bond before the other investors can. Technicians, on the other hand, only need to quickly recognize a movement to a new equilibrium value *for whatever reason*—that is, they do not need to know about a specific event and determine the effect of the event on the value of the firm and its stock.

Finally, assume a fundamental analyst determines that a given security is under- or overvalued a long time before other investors. He or she still must determine when to make the purchase or sale. Ideally, the highest rate of return would come from making the transaction just before the change in market value occurs. For example, assume that based on your analysis in February, you expect a firm to report substantially higher earnings in June. Although you could buy the stock in February, you would be better off waiting until about May to buy the stock so your funds would not be tied up for an extra three months, but you may be reticent to wait that long. Because most technicians do not invest until the move to the new equilibrium is under way, they contend that they are more likely than a fundamental analyst to experience ideal timing.

# CHALLENGES TO TECHNICAL ANALYSIS                     4

Those who doubt the value of technical analysis for investment decisions question the usefulness of this technique in two areas. First, they challenge some of its basic assumptions. Second, they challenge some specific technical trading rules and their long-run usefulness. In this section we consider these challenges.

## Challenges to Technical Analysis Assumptions

The major challenge to technical analysis is based on the results of empirical tests of the efficient market hypothesis (EMH). For technical trading rules to generate superior risk-adjusted returns after taking account of transaction costs, the market would have to be slow to adjust prices to the arrival of new information; that is, it would have to be inefficient. That current stock prices fully reflect security market information such as past prices and returns is referred to as the weak-form efficient market hypothesis. The two sets of tests of the weak-form EMH are (1) the statistical analysis of prices to determine if prices moved in trends or were a random walk, and (2) the analysis of specific trading rules to determine if their use could beat a buy-and-hold policy after considering transactions costs and risk. Almost all the studies testing the weak-form EMH using statistical analysis have found that prices do not move in trends based on statistical tests of auto-correlation and runs. These results support the EMH.

Regarding the analysis of specific trading rules, numerous technical trading rules exist that have not been or cannot be tested. Still, the vast majority of the results for the trading rules that have been tested support the EMH.

## Challenges to Technical Trading Rules

An obvious challenge to technical analysis is that the past price patterns or relationships between specific market variables and stock prices may not be repeated. As a result, a technique that previously worked might miss subsequent market turns. This possibility leads most technicians to follow several trading rules and to seek a consensus of all of them to predict the future market pattern.

Other critics contend that many price patterns become self-fulfilling prophecies. For example, assume that many analysts expect a stock selling at $40 a share to go to $50 or more if it should rise above its current pattern and break through its channel at $45. As soon as it reaches $45, enough technicians will buy to cause the price to rise to $50, exactly as predicted. In fact, some technicians may place a buy-stop order to buy the stock at such a breakout point. Under such conditions, the increase will probably be only temporary and the price will return to its true equilibrium.

Another problem with technical analysis is that the success of a particular trading rule will encourage many investors to adopt it. It is contended that this popularity and the resulting competition will eventually neutralize the technique. If numerous investors focus on a specific technical trading rule, some of them will attempt to anticipate the price pattern and either ruin the expected historical price pattern or eliminate profits for most traders by causing the price to change faster than expected. For example, suppose it becomes known that technicians who employ short-selling data have been enjoying high rates of return. Based on this knowledge, other technicians will likely start using these data and thus accelerate the stock price pattern following changes in short selling. As a result, this profitable trading rule may no longer be profitable after the first few investors react.

Further, as we will see when we examine specific trading rules, *they all require a great deal of subjective judgment.* Two technical analysts looking at the same price pattern may arrive at widely different interpretations of what has happened and, therefore, will come to different investment decisions. This implies that the use of various techniques is neither completely mechanical nor obvious. Finally, as we will discuss in connection with several trading rules, *the standard values that signal investment decisions can change over time.* Therefore, in some instances technical analysts adjust the specified values that trigger investment decisions to conform to the new environment. In other cases, trading rules have been abandoned because they no longer work.

## 5    TECHNICAL TRADING RULES AND INDICATORS

To illustrate the specific technical trading rules, Exhibit 2 shows a typical stock price cycle that could be an example for the overall stock market or for an individual stock. The graph shows a peak and trough, along with a rising trend channel, a flat trend channel, a declining trend channel, and indications of when a technical analyst would ideally want to trade.

The graph begins with the end of a declining (bear) market that finishes in a **trough**, followed by an upward trend that breaks through the **declining trend channel**. Confirmation that the declining trend has reversed would be a buy signal. The technical analyst would buy stocks that showed this pattern.

| EXHIBIT 2 | Typical Stock-Market Cycle |
| --- | --- |

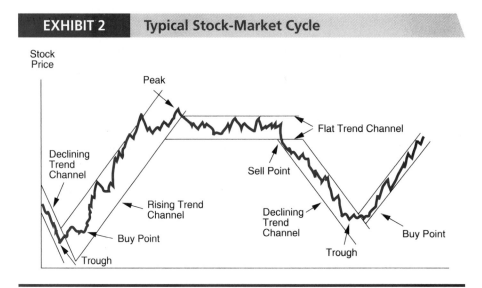

The analyst would then expect the development of a **rising trend channel**. As long as the stock price stayed in this rising channel, the technician would hold the stock(s). Ideally, they want to sell at the **peak** of the cycle, but they cannot identify a peak until after the trend changes.

If the stock (or the market) begins trading in a flat pattern, it will necessarily break out of its rising trend channel. At this point, some technical analysts would sell, but most would hold to see if the stock experiences a period of consolidation and then breaks out of the **flat trend channel** on the upside and begins rising again. Alternatively, if the stock were to break out of the channel on the downside, the technician would take this as a sell signal and would expect a declining trend channel. The next buy signal would come after the trough when the price breaks out of the declining channel and establishes a rising trend. We will consider strategies to detect these changes in trend and the importance of volume in this analysis shortly.

There are numerous technical trading rules and a range of interpretations for each of them. Almost all technical analysts watch many alternative rules and decide on a buy or sell decision based on a *consensus* of the signals because complete agreement of all the rules is rare. In the following discussion of several well-known techniques, we have divided the rules into four groups based on the attitudes of technical analysts. The first group includes trading rules used by analysts who like to trade against the crowd using contrary-opinion signals. The second group attempts to emulate astute investors, that is, the smart money. The third group includes popular technical indicators that are not easily classified. Finally, the fourth group includes pure price and volume techniques, including the famous Dow Theory.

## Contrary-Opinion Rules

Many technical analysts rely on technical trading rules that assume that the majority of investors are wrong as the market approaches peaks and troughs. Therefore, these technicians try to determine when the majority of investors is either strongly bullish or bearish and then trade in the opposite direction.

**Mutual Fund Cash Positions**  Mutual funds hold some part of their portfolio in cash for one of several reasons. One is that they need cash to liquidate shares submitted by fundholders. Another is that new investments in the mutual fund may not have been invested. Third, the portfolio manager might be bearish on the market and want to increase the fund's defensive cash position.

Mutual funds' ratios of cash as a percentage of the total assets in their portfolios (the cash ratio or *liquid asset ratio*) are reported in the press, including monthly figures in *Barron's*.[1] This percentage of cash has varied in recent years from a low point of about 4 percent to a high point near 11 percent, although there appears to be a declining trend to the series.

Contrary-opinion technicians believe that mutual funds usually are wrong at peaks and troughs. Thus, they expect mutual funds to have a high percentage of cash near a market trough—the time when they should be fully invested to take advantage of the impending market rise. At the market peak, these technicians expect mutual funds to be almost fully invested with a low percentage of cash when they should be selling stocks and realizing gains. Therefore, contrary-opinion technicians watch for the mutual fund cash position to approach one of the extremes and act contrary to the mutual funds. Specifically, they would tend to buy when the cash ratio approaches 11 percent and to sell when the cash ratio approaches 4 percent.

---

[1] *Barron's* is a prime source for numerous technical indicators. For a readable discussion of relevant data and their use, see Martin E. Zweig (1987).

An alternative rationale is that a high cash position is a bullish indicator because of potential buying power. Irrespective of the reason for a large cash balance, these technicians believe the cash funds held will eventually be invested and will cause stock prices to increase. Alternatively, a low cash ratio would mean that the institutions have bought heavily and are left with little potential buying power.

**Credit Balances in Brokerage Accounts**   Credit balances result when investors sell stocks and leave the proceeds with their brokers, expecting to reinvest them shortly. The amounts are reported by the SEC and the NYSE in *Barron's*. Because technical analysts view these credit balances as potential purchasing power, a decline in these balances is considered bearish because it indicates lower purchasing power as the market approaches a peak. Alternatively, a buildup of credit balances indicates an increase in buying power and is a bullish signal.

**Investment Advisory Opinions**   Many technicians believe that if a large proportion of investment advisory services are bearish, this signals the approach of a market trough and the onset of a bull market. Because most advisory services tend to be trend followers, the number of bears usually is greatest when market bottoms are approaching. This trading rule is specified in terms of the percent of advisory services that are bearish/bullish given the number of services expressing an opinion.[2] A 60 percent bearish or 20 percent bullish reading indicates a major market bottom (a bullish indicator), while a 60 percent bullish or 20 percent bearish reading suggests a major market top (a bearish signal). Exhibit 3 shows a time-series plot of the DJIA and both the bearish sentiment index and the bullish sentiment index. As of mid-2005, both indexes are near the bearish boundary values.

**OTC versus NYSE Volume**   This ratio of trading volume is considered a measure of speculative activity. Speculative trading typically peaks at market peaks. Notably, the interpretation of the ratio has changed—that is, the decision rules have changed. Specifically, during the mid-1990s, the decision rule was in terms of specific percentages—112 percent was considered heavy speculative trading and an overbought market while 87 percent was considered low speculative trading and an oversold market. The problem was that the percentages kept increasing because of faster growth in OTC trading volume and dominance of the OTC market by a few large-cap stocks. It was subsequently decided to detect excess speculative activity by using the *direction* of the volume ratio as a guide. For example, if this ratio is increasing, it would indicate a bearish speculative environment.

**Chicago Board Options Exchange (CBOE) Put-Call Ratio**   Contrary-opinion technicians use put options, which give the holder the right to sell stock at a specified price for a given time period, as signals of a bearish attitude. A higher put-call ratio indicates a pervasive bearish attitude for investors, which technicians consider a bullish indicator.

This ratio fluctuates between 0.60 and 0.40 and has typically been substantially less than 1 because investors tend to be bullish and avoid selling short or buying puts. The current decision rule states that a put-call ratio above 0.60—that is, sixty puts are traded for every one hundred calls—indicates that investors are generally bearish, so it is considered bullish, while a relatively low put-call ratio of 0.40 or less is considered bearish.

**Futures Traders Bullish on Stock-Index Futures**   Another relatively new contrary-opinion measure is the percentage of speculators in stock-index futures

---

[2] This ratio is compiled by Investors Intelligence, Larchmont, NY 10538. Richard McCabe at Merrill Lynch uses this series as one of his "Investor Sentiment Indicators."

| EXHIBIT 3 | Time-Series Plot of Dow Jones Industrial Average and the Bullish and Bearish Advisory Services |

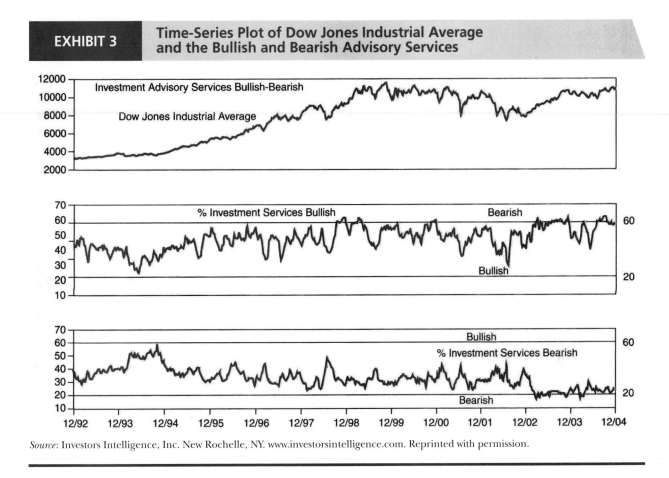

*Source*: Investors Intelligence, Inc. New Rochelle, NY. www.investorsintelligence.com. Reprinted with permission.

who are bullish regarding stocks based on a survey of individual futures traders. These technicians would consider it a bearish sign when more than 70 percent of the speculators are bullish, and a bullish sign when this ratio declines to 30 percent or lower. The plot in Exhibit 4 shows that as of mid-2005 this indicator was slightly less than 70 percent, so it is officially neutral but toward a bearish zone.

As we have shown, contrary-opinion technicians have several measures of how the majority of investors are investing that prompt them to take the opposite action. They generally employ several of these series to provide a consensus regarding investors' attitudes.

## Follow the Smart Money

Some technical analysts have created a set of indicators and corresponding rules that they believe indicate the behavior of smart, sophisticated investors. We discuss three such indicators in this section.

**Confidence Index** Published by *Barron's*, the Confidence Index is the ratio of *Barron's* average yield on 10 top-grade corporate bonds to the yield on the Dow Jones average of forty bonds.[3] This index measures the difference in yield spread between high-grade bonds and a large cross section of bonds. Because the yields

---

[3] Historical data for this index are contained in the *Dow Jones Investor's Handbook*, Princeton, NJ (Dow Jones Books, annual). Current figures appear in *Barron's*.

**EXHIBIT 4** **Time-Series Plot of Dow Jones Industrial Average and the Market Vane Percentage of Futures Traders Bullish and Bearish on Stock-Index Futures**

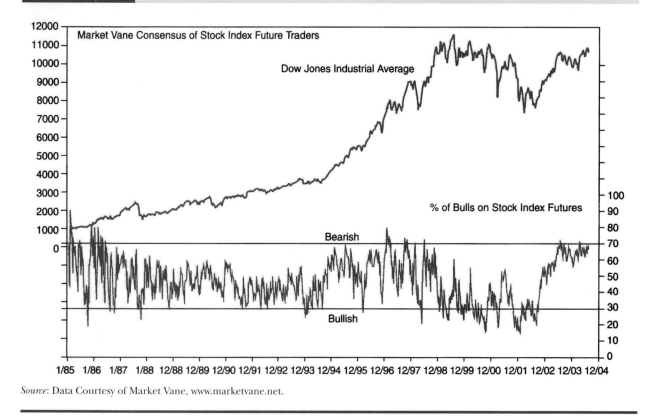

*Source*: Data Courtesy of Market Vane, www.marketvane.net.

on high-grade bonds always should be lower than those on a large cross section of bonds, this ratio should approach 100 as the spread between the two sets of bonds gets smaller.

Technicians believe the ratio is a bullish indicator because, during periods of high confidence, investors are willing to invest in lower-quality bonds for the added yield, which causes a decrease in the average yield for the large cross section of bonds relative to the yield on high-grade bonds. Therefore, this ratio of yields—the Confidence Index—will increase. In contrast, when investors are pessimistic, they avoid investing in low-quality bonds, which increases the yield spread between high-grade and average bonds, which in turn causes the Confidence Index to decline.

Unfortunately, this interpretation assumes that changes in the yield spread are caused almost exclusively by changes in investor demand for different quality bonds. In fact, the yield differences have frequently changed because of changes in the supply of bonds. For example, a large issue of high-grade AT&T bonds could cause a temporary increase in yields on all high-grade bonds, which would reduce the yield spread, and increase the Confidence Index without any change in investors' attitudes. Such a change can generate a false signal of a change in confidence.

**T-Bill-Eurodollar Yield Spread**   A popular measure of investor attitude or confidence on a global basis is the spread between T-bill yields and Eurodollar rates. It is reasoned that, at times of international crisis, this spread widens as the smart money flows to safe-haven U.S. T-bills, which causes a decline in this ratio. It is contended that the stock market typically experiences a trough shortly thereafter.

**Debit Balances in Brokerage Accounts (Margin Debt)**   Debit balances in brokerage accounts represent borrowing (margin debt) by knowledgeable investors from their brokers. Hence, these balances indicate the attitude of sophisticated investors who engage in margin transactions. Therefore, an increase in debit balances implies buying by these sophisticated investors and is considered a bullish sign, while a decline in debit balances would indicate selling and would be a bearish indicator.

Monthly data on margin debt is reported in *Barron's*. Unfortunately, this index does not include borrowing by investors from other sources such as banks. Also, because it is an absolute value, technicians would look for changes in the trend of borrowing—that is, increases are bullish, declines are bearish.

## Momentum Indicators

In addition to contrary-opinion and smart money signals, several indicators of overall market momentum are used to make aggregate market decisions.

**Breadth of Market**   Breadth of market measures the number of issues that have increased each day and the number of issues that have declined. It helps explain the cause of a change of direction in a composite market index such as the S&P 500 Index. Most stock-market indexes are heavily influenced by the stocks of large firms because they are value weighted. Therefore, a stock-market index can experience an increase while the majority of the individual issues do not, which means that most stocks are not participating in the rising market. Such a divergence can be detected by examining the advance-decline figures for all stocks on the exchange, along with the overall market index.

The advance–decline index is typically a cumulative index of net advances or net declines. Specifically, each day major newspapers publish figures on the number of issues on the NYSE that advanced, declined, or were unchanged. The figures for a five-day sample, as would be reported in *Barron's*, are shown in Exhibit 5. These figures, along with changes in the DJIA at the bottom of the table, indicate a strong market advance because the DJIA was increasing and the net advance figure was strong, indicating that the market increase was broadly

| EXHIBIT 5 | Daily Advances and Declines on the New York Stock Exchange | | | | |
|---|---|---|---|---|---|
| **Day** | **1** | **2** | **3** | **4** | **5** |
| Issues traded | 3,608 | 3,641 | 3,659 | 3,651 | 3,612 |
| Advances | 2,310 | 2,350 | 1,558 | 2,261 | 2,325 |
| Declines | 909 | 912 | 1,649 | 933 | 894 |
| Unchanged | 389 | 379 | 452 | 457 | 393 |
| Net advances (advances minus declines) | +1,401 | +1,438 | −91 | +1,328 | +1,431 |
| Cumulative net advances | +1,401 | +2,839 | +2,748 | +4,076 | +5,507 |
| Changes in DJIA | +40.47 | +95.75 | −15.25 | +108.42 | +140.63 |

*Sources*: New York Stock Exchange and *Barron's*.

based. Even the results on Day 3, when the market declined 15 points, were encouraging since it was a small overall decline and the individual stock issues were split just about 50-50, which points toward a fairly even environment.

**Stocks above Their 200-Day Moving Average**   Technicians often compute moving averages of an index to determine its general trend. To examine individual stocks, the 200-day **moving average** of prices has been fairly popular. From these moving-average indexes for numerous stocks, Media General Financial Services calculates how many stocks currently are trading above their 200-day moving-average index, and this is used as an indicator of general investor sentiment. The market is considered to be *overbought* and subject to a negative correction when more than 80 percent of the stocks are trading above their 200-day moving average. In contrast, if less than 20 percent of the stocks are selling above their 200-day moving average, the market is considered to be *oversold*, which means investors should expect a positive correction. As shown in Exhibit 6, as of mid-2005 the percent of stocks selling above their 200-day moving average has been above 80 percent, which indicates an overbought, bearish signal, but recently went below the 80 percent line.

## Stock Price and Volume Techniques

In the introduction to this reading, we examined a hypothetical stock price chart that demonstrated market peaks and troughs along with rising and declining trend channels and breakouts from channels that signal new price trends or reversals of the price trends. While price patterns alone are important, most technical trading rules consider both stock price and corresponding volume movements.

**Dow Theory**   Any discussion of technical analysis using price and volume data should begin with a consideration of the Dow Theory because it was among the earliest work on this topic and remains the basis for many technical indicators.[4] Dow described stock prices as moving in trends analogous to the movement of water. He postulated three types of price movements over time: (1) major trends that are like tides in the ocean, (2) intermediate trends that resemble waves, and (3) short-run movements that are like ripples. Followers of the Dow Theory attempt to detect the direction of the major price trend (tide), recognizing that

|  | Percentage of NYSE Common Stocks Trading above Their 200-Day Moving Average Price |
| --- | --- |

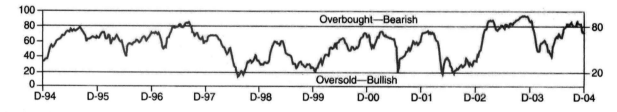

*Source*: Walter G. Murphy, Research Analyst, Merrill Lynch. Reprinted by permission. Copyright © 2005 Merrill Lynch, Pierce, Fenner & Smith Incorporated. Further reproduction or distribution is strictly prohibited.

---

[4] A study that discusses and provides support for the Dow Theory is David A. Glickstein and Rolf E. Wubbels (1983).

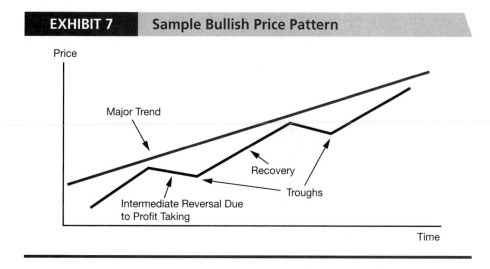

**EXHIBIT 7** | **Sample Bullish Price Pattern**

Price

Major Trend

Recovery

Troughs

Intermediate Reversal Due
to Profit Taking

Time

intermediate movements (waves) may occasionally move in the opposite direction. They recognize that a major market advance does not go straight up, but rather includes small price declines as some investors decide to take profits.

Exhibit 7 shows the typical bullish pattern. The technician would look for every recovery to reach a new peak above the prior peak, and this price rise should be accompanied by heavy trading volume. Alternatively, each profit-taking reversal that follows an increase to a new peak should have a trough above the prior trough, with relatively light trading volume during the profit-taking reversals. When this pattern of price and volume movements changes, the major trend may be entering a period of consolidation (a flat trend) or a major reversal.

**Importance of Volume**   As noted, technicians watch volume changes along with price movements as an indicator of changes in supply and demand. A price movement in one direction means that the net effect on price is in that direction, but the price change alone does not indicate the breadth of the excess demand or supply. Therefore, the technician looks for a price increase on heavy volume relative to the stock's normal trading volume as an indication of bullish activity. Conversely, a price decline with heavy volume is considered bearish. A generally bullish pattern would be when price increases are accompanied by heavy volume and small price reversals occur with light trading volume.

Technicians also use a ratio of upside-downside volume as an indicator of short-term momentum for the aggregate stock market. Each day the stock exchanges announce the volume of trading in stocks that experienced an increase divided by the volume of trading in stocks that declined. These data are reported daily in *The Wall Street Journal* and weekly in *Barron's*. This ratio is used as an indicator of market momentum. Specifically, technicians believe that an upside-downside volume value of 1.75 or more indicates an overbought position that is bearish. Alternatively, a value of 0.75 and lower supposedly reflects an oversold position and is considered bullish.

**Support and Resistance Levels**   A **support level** is the price range at which the technician would expect a substantial increase in the demand for a stock. Generally, a support level will develop after a stock has enjoyed a meaningful price increase and the stock experiences profit taking. Technicians reason that at some price below the recent peak other investors who did not buy during the first price increase (waiting for a small reversal) will get into the stock. When the price reaches this support price, demand surges and price and volume begin to increase again.

A **resistance level** is the price range at which the technician would expect an increase in the supply of stock and a price reversal. A resistance level develops after a significant decline from a higher price level. After the decline, the stock begins to recover, but the prior decline in price leads some investors who acquired the stock at a higher price to look for an opportunity to sell it near their breakeven points. Therefore, the supply of stock owned by these nervous investors is *overhanging* the market. When the price rebounds to the target price set by these investors, this overhanging supply of stock comes to the market and there is a price decline on heavy volume. It is also possible to envision a rising trend of support and resistance levels for a stock. For example, the rising support prices would be a set of higher prices where investors over time would see the price increase and would take the opportunity to buy when there is profit taking. In this latter case, there would be a succession of higher support levels over time.

Exhibit 8 contains the daily stock prices for Gillette (G), with support and resistance lines. The graphs show a rising pattern since Gillette has experienced strong price increases during this period. At present, the resistance level is at about $44 and is rising, while the support level is about $40 and is also rising. The bullish technician would look for future prices to rise in line with this channel. If prices fell significantly below the support line on strong volume, it would be considered a bearish signal, while an increase above the $44 resistance price would be bullish.

**Moving-Average Lines**   Earlier, we discussed how technicians use a moving average of past stock prices as an indicator of the long-run trend and how they examine current prices relative to this trend for signals of a change. We also noted that a 200-day moving average is a relatively popular measure for individual stocks and the aggregate market. In this discussion, we add a 50-day moving-average price line (short-term trend) and consider large volume.

Exhibit 9 is a daily stock price chart from Yahoo! Inc. for Pfizer, Inc. (PFE) for the year ending June 4, 2004. It also contains 50-day and 200-day moving-average (MA) lines. As noted, MA lines are meant to reflect the overall trend for the price series with the shorter MA line (the 50-day versus 200-day) reflecting shorter trends. Two comparisons involving the MA lines are considered impor-

| EXHIBIT 8 | Daily Stock Prices and Volume for Gillette with Indications of Support and Resistance Levels |

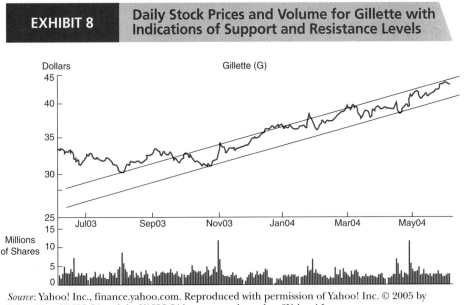

*Source*: Yahoo! Inc., finance.yahoo.com. Reproduced with permission of Yahoo! Inc. © 2005 by Yahoo! Inc. YAHOO! and the YAHOO! logo are trademarks of Yahoo! Inc.

| EXHIBIT 9 | Daily Stock Prices for Pfizer, Inc. with 50-Day and 200-Day Moving-Average Lines |

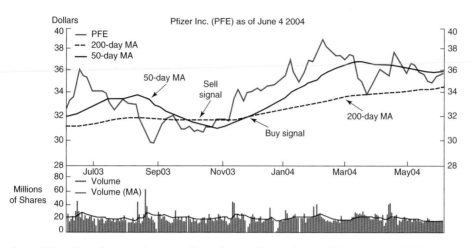

*Source*: Yahoo! Inc., finance.yahoo.com. Reproduced with permission of Yahoo! Inc. © 2005 by Yahoo! Inc. YAHOO! and the YAHOO! logo are trademarks of YAHOO! Inc.

tant. The first comparison is the specific prices to the shorter-run 50-day MA line. If the overall price trend of a stock or the market has been down, the moving-average price line generally would lie above current prices. If prices reverse and break through the moving-average line *from below* accompanied by heavy trading volume, most technicians would consider this a *positive* change and speculate that this breakthrough could signal a reversal of the declining trend. In contrast, if the price of a stock had been rising, the moving-average line would also be rising, but it would be below current prices. If current prices declined and broke through the moving-average line *from above* accompanied by heavy trading volume, this would be considered a bearish pattern that would possibly signal a reversal of the long-run rising trend.

The second comparison is between the 50- and 200-day MA lines. Specifically, when these two lines cross, it signals a change in the overall trend. Specifically, if the 50-day MA line crosses the 200-day MA line from below on good volume, this would be a bullish indicator (buy signal) because it confirms a reversal in trend from negative to positive. In contrast, when the 50-day line crosses the 200-day line from above, it confirms a change to a negative trend and would be a sell signal. As shown in Exhibit 9, in the case of Pfizer (PFE) there was a bearish crossing in late September 2003, but it was reversed in December 2003 when there was a bullish crossing. Following this bullish crossing, the 50-day line has been consistently above the 200-day line as prices reached a peak of about $38 and were at about $36 at the end of the period. There is a cautionary signal to this chart, since the price line has broken through the 50-day line from above several times and is slightly below this MA line at the end of the graph.

Overall, for a *bullish* trend the 50-day MA line should be above the 200-day MA line, as it has been for Pfizer since December 2003. Notably, if this positive gap between the 50-day and 200-day lines gets too large (which happens with a fast run-up in price), a technician might consider this an indication that the stock is temporarily overbought, which is bearish in the short run. A *bearish* trend is when the 50-day MA line is always below the 200-day MA line. Still, if the gap gets large on the downside, it might be considered a signal of an oversold stock, which is bullish for the short run.

**Relative Strength**   Technicians believe that once a trend begins, it will continue until some major event causes a change in direction. They believe this is also true of *relative* performance. If an individual stock or an industry group is outperforming the market, technicians believe it will continue to do so.

Therefore, technicians compute weekly or monthly **relative-strength (RS) ratios** for individual stocks and industry groups. The RS ratio is equal to the price of a stock or an industry index divided by the value for some stock-market index such as the S&P 500. If this ratio increases over time, it shows that the stock or industry is outperforming the overall stock market, and a technician would expect this superior performance to continue. Relative-strength ratios work during declining as well as rising markets. In a declining market, if a stock's price declines less than the market does, the stock's relative-strength ratio will continue to rise. Technicians believe that if this ratio is stable or increases during a bear market, the stock should do well during the subsequent bull market.

Merrill Lynch publishes relative-strength charts for industry groups. Exhibit 10 describes how to read the charts. Further, some technicians construct graphs of stocks relative to the stock's industry index in addition to the comparison relative to the market.

| EXHIBIT 10 | How to Read Industry Group Charts |
| --- | --- |

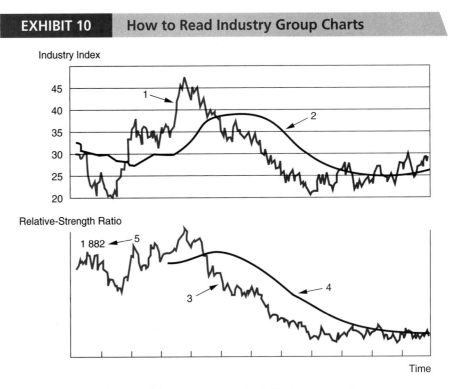

The industry group charts in this report display the following elements:

1. A line chart of the weekly close of the Standard & Poor's Industry Group Index for the past nine and one-half years, with the index range indicated to the left.
2. A line of the seventy-five-week moving average of the Standard & Poor's Industry Group Index.
3. A relative-strength line of the Standard & Poor's Industry Group Index compared with the New York Stock Exchange Composite Index.
4. A seventy-five-week moving average of relative strength.

*(Exhibit continued on next page …)*

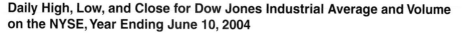

**EXHIBIT 10**    (continued)

**5.** A volatility reading that measures the maximum amount by which the index has outperformed (or underperformed) the NYSE Composite Index during the time period displayed.

*Source*: Walter G. Murphy, Research Analyst, Merrill Lynch. Reprinted by permission. Copyright © 2002 Merrill Lynch, Pierce, Fenner & Smith Incorporated. Further reproduction or distribution is strictly prohibited.

**Bar Charting**    Technicians use charts that show daily, weekly, or monthly time series of stock prices. For a given interval, the technical analyst plots the high and low prices and connects the two points vertically to form a bar. Typically, he or she will also draw a small horizontal line across this vertical bar to indicate the closing price. Finally, almost all bar charts include the volume of trading at the bottom of the chart so that the technical analyst can relate the price and volume movements. A typical bar chart in Exhibit 11 shows data for the DJIA from *The Wall Street Journal* along with volume figures for the NYSE.

**Multiple-Indicator Charts**    Thus far we have presented charts that deal with only one trading technique such as moving-average lines or relative-strength rules. In the real world, it is fairly typical for technical charts to contain several indicators that can be used together like the two MA lines (50- and 200-day) and the RS

**EXHIBIT 11**    A Typical Bar Chart

**Daily High, Low, and Close for Dow Jones Industrial Average and Volume on the NYSE, Year Ending June 10, 2004**

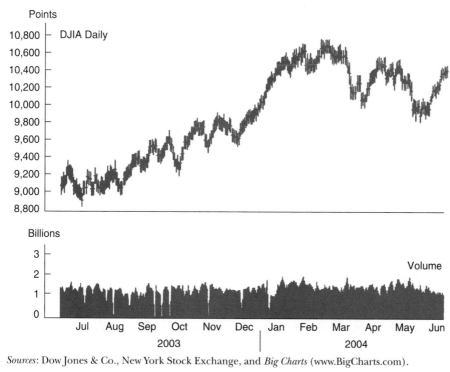

*Sources*: Dow Jones & Co., New York Stock Exchange, and *Big Charts* (www.BigCharts.com).

| EXHIBIT 12 | Sample Point-and-Figure Chart |
|---|---|

```
50  |  |   |   |   |   |   |   |   |
48  |  |   |   |   |   |   |   |   |
46  |  |   | X |   |   |   |   |   |
44  |  |   | X |   |   |   |   |   |
42  |  X | X | X |   |   |   |   |   |
40  |  X | X | X |   |   |   |   |   |
38  |  |  X | X |   |   |   |   |   |
36  |  |  X | X |   |   |   |   |   |
34  |  |  X | X |   |   |   |   |   |
32  |  |   |   |   |   |   |   |   |
30  |  |   |   |   |   |   |   |   |
```

line, because they can provide added support to the analysis. Technicians include as many price and volume indicators as are reasonable on one chart and then, based on the performance of *several* technical indicators, try to arrive at a consensus about the future movement for the stock.

**Point-and-Figure Charts**    Another graph that is popular with technicians is the point-and-figure chart. Unlike the bar chart, which typically includes all ending prices and volumes to show a trend, the point-and-figure chart includes only significant price changes, regardless of their timing. The technician determines what price interval to record as significant (one point, two points, and so on) and when to note price reversals.

To demonstrate how a technical analyst would use such a chart, suppose we want to chart a volatile stock that is currently selling for $40 a share. Because of its volatility, we believe that anything less than a two-point price change is not significant. Also, we consider anything less than a four-point reversal, meaning a movement in the opposite direction, quite minor. Therefore, we would set up a chart similar to the one in Exhibit 12, but our new chart would start at 40; it would also progress in two-point increments. If the stock moved to $42, we would place an *X* in the box above 40 and do nothing else until the stock rose to $44 or dropped to $38 (a four-point reversal from its high of $42). If it dropped to $38, we would move a column to the right, which indicates a reversal in direction, and begin again at 38 (fill in boxes at 42 and 40). If the stock price dropped to $34, we would enter an *X* at 36 and another at 34. If the stock then rose to $38 (another four-point reversal), we would move to the next column and begin at 38, going up (fill in 34 and 36). If the stock then went to $46, we would fill in more *X*s as shown and wait for further increases or a reversal.

Depending on how fast the prices rise and fall, this process might take anywhere from two to six months. Given these figures, the technician would attempt to determine trends just as with the bar chart. As always, the technician would look for breakouts to either higher or lower price levels. A long horizontal movement with many reversals but no major trends up or down would be considered a *period of consolidation* wherein the stock is moving from buyers to sellers and back again with no strong consensus about its direction. Once the stock breaks out and moves up or down after a period of consolidation, technical analysts anticipate a major move because previous trading set the stage for it. In other words, the longer the period of consolidation, the larger the subsequent move when there is finally a breakout.

Point-and-figure charts provide a compact record of movements because they only consider significant price changes for the stock being analyzed. Therefore, some technicians contend they are easier to work with and give more vivid pictures of price movements.

# TECHNICAL ANALYSIS OF FOREIGN MARKETS 6

Our discussion thus far has concentrated on U.S. markets, but analysts have discovered that these techniques apply to foreign markets as well. Merrill Lynch, for instance, prepares separate technical analysis publications for individual countries such as Japan, Germany, and the United Kingdom as well as a summary of all world markets. The examples that follow show that when analyzing non-U.S. markets, many techniques are limited to price and volume data rather than the more detailed U.S. market information. The reason is that the detailed information available on the U.S. market through the SEC, the stock exchanges, the Nasdaq system, and various investment services is not always available for other countries.

## Foreign Stock-Market Indexes

Exhibit 13 contains the daily time-series plot for the Japanese Nikkei Index. This chart shows the generally declining trend by the Japanese stock market during the period from May 2000 to April 2003, followed by rising stock prices through May 2004 and generally flat performance into May 2005. In the written analysis, the market analyst at Merrill Lynch estimated support and resistance levels for the Japanese Stock Exchange index and commented on the medium-term outlook for this market. Merrill Lynch publishes similar charts for 10 other countries and compares the countries and ranks them by stock and currency performance.

| **EXHIBIT 13** | **Graph and Summary Comments on the Japanese Stock Market** |

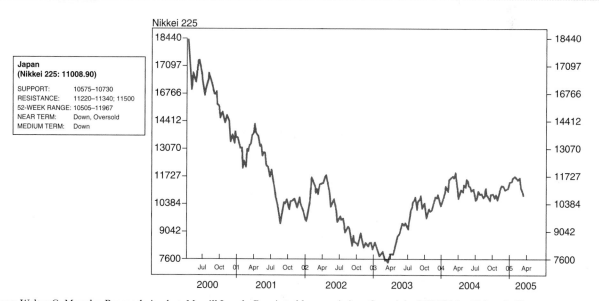

*Source*: Walter G. Murphy, Research Analyst, Merrill Lynch. Reprinted by permission. Copyright © 2005 Merrill Lynch, Pierce, Fenner & Smith Incorporated. Further reproduction or distribution is strictly prohibited.

## Technical Analysis of Foreign Exchange Rates

On numerous occasions, we have discussed the importance of changes in foreign exchange rates on the rates of return on foreign securities. Because of the importance of these relationships, bond-and-stock traders in world markets examine the time-series data of various currencies such as the British pound and the Euro. They also analyze the spread between currencies, such as the difference between the Japanese yen and the British pound. Finally, they would typically examine the time series for the U.S. dollar trade-weighted exchange rate that experienced significant weakness during 2003–2005.

## 7    TECHNICAL ANALYSIS OF BOND MARKETS

Thus far, we have emphasized the use of technical analysis in stock markets. These techniques can also be applied to the bond market. The theory and rationale for technical analysis of bonds is the same as for stocks, and many of the same trading rules are used. A major difference is that it was generally not possible to consider the volume of trading of bonds because most bonds are traded OTC, where volume was not reported until 2004.

Exhibit 14 demonstrates the use of technical analysis techniques applied to bond-yield series. Specifically, the graph contains a time-series plot of world bond yields based on a seven-country composite. As shown, yields declined steadily until a trough in June 2003, followed by a sharp recovery and a roller-coaster pattern between late 2003 and mid-2005. Notably, the outlook by the analyst is for lower yields medium and longer term. Such a technical graph provides important insights to a global bond-portfolio manager interested in adjusting his or her bond portfolio.

---

**EXHIBIT 14    Time-Series Plot of Global Bond Yields (Seven-Country Composite)**

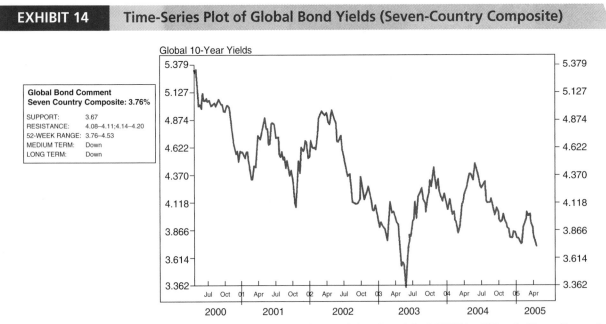

*Source*: Walter G. Murphy, Research Analyst, Merrill Lynch. Reprinted by permission. Copyright © 2005 Merrill Lynch, Pierce, Fenner & Smith Incorporated. Further reproduction or distribution is strictly prohibited.

---

## THE INTERNET

### Investments Online

By its nature, technical analysis uses charts and graphs, and many Web sites offer them for use by investors and analysts; some are free, but some of the sites for more sophisticated users require payment for access. Here are several interesting sites:

*www.mta.org/* The home page of the Market Technicians Association, a professional group of chartists whose goal is to enhance technical analysis and educate investors about its role. The group sponsors the Chartered Market Technician (CMT) designation. This site features news groups, investment links, training and education sources, a journal, and a variety of technical analysis charts. Its "members" tab includes links to Web sites of its members' firms.

*http://bigcharts.marketwatch.com/* This site offers free intraday and historical charts and price quotes. Its database includes stocks, mutual funds, and indexes. Users can learn which stocks have the largest percentage gain (loss) in price and volume and which stocks are hitting new 52-week highs (lows). Other features include momentum charts, stocks with the largest short interest, and a variety of other items of interest to technicians.

*http://stockcharts.com/* This site offers a variety of charting options, including point-and-figure charts. It offers a "chart school," which offers summaries of different charting techniques and uses.

# SUMMARY

► Numerous investors believe in and use the principles of technical analysis. The fact is, the large investment houses provide extensive support for technical analysis, and a large proportion of the discussion related to securities markets in the media is based on a technical view of the market.

► Their answers to two main questions separate technical analysts and efficient market advocates. First, in the information dissemination process does everybody get the information at about the same time? Second, how quickly do investors adjust security prices to reflect new information? Technical analysts believe that news takes time to travel from the insider and expert to the individual investor. They also believe that price adjustments are not instantaneous. As a result, they contend that security prices move in trends that persist and, therefore, they can use past price trends and volume information along with other market indicators to determine future price trends.

► Technical trading rules fall into four general categories: contrary-opinion rules, follow-the-smart-money tactics, momentum indicators, and stock price and volume techniques. These techniques and trading rules can be applied to both domestic and foreign markets. They can also be used to analyze currency exchange rates and determine the prevailing sentiment in the bond market.

► Most technicians employ several indicators and attempt to derive a consensus to guide their decision to buy, sell, or do nothing.[5]

---

[5] An analysis using numerous indicators is the study by Jerome Baesel, George Shows, and Edward Thorp (1982).

# APPENDICES

# SOLUTIONS FOR READING 2

1. **B is correct.** This question involves Standard III(B)—Fair Dealing. Smith disseminated a change in the stock recommendation to his clients but then received a request contrary to that recommendation from a client who likely had not yet received the recommendation. Prior to executing the order, Smith should take additional steps to ensure that the customer has received the change of recommendation. Answer A is incorrect because the client placed the order prior to receiving the recommendation and, therefore, does not have the benefit of Smith's most recent recommendation. Answer C is incorrect because it would result in a delay in executing an order requested by the client. Answer D is also incorrect; simply because the client request is contrary to the firm's recommendation does not mean a member can override a direct request by a client. After Smith contacts the client to ensure that the client received the changed recommendation, if the client still wants to place a buy order for the shares, Smith is obligated to comply with the client's directive.

2. **D is correct.** This question involves Standard III(A)—Loyalty, Prudence, and Care and the specific topic of soft dollars or soft commissions. Answer D is the correct choice because client brokerage commissions may not be directed to pay for the investment manager's operating expenses. Answer B would be an incorrect choice because brokerage commissions may be directed to pay for securities research used in managing a client's portfolio. Answer C describes how members and candidates should determine how to use brokerage commissions: if the use is in the best interests of clients and is commensurate with the value of the services provided. Answer A describes a practice that is commonly referred to as "directed brokerage." Because brokerage is an asset of the client and is used to benefit the client, not the manager, such practice does not violate a duty of loyalty to the client. Members and candidates are obligated in all situations to disclose to clients their practices in the use of client brokerage commissions.

3. **C is correct.** This question involves Standard VI(A)—Disclosure of Conflicts. The question establishes a conflict of interest whereby an analyst, Jamison, is asked to write a research report on a company that is a client of Jamison's employer. In addition, two directors of the company are senior officers of Jamison's employer. Both facts are conflicts of interest and must be disclosed by Jamison in her research report. Answer D would be incorrect because an analyst is not prevented from writing a report because of the special relationship the analyst's employer has with the company so long as that relationship is disclosed. Whether or not Jamison expresses any opinions in the report is irrelevant to her duty to disclose a conflict of interest. Not expressing opinions does not relieve the analyst of the responsibility to disclose the special relationships between the two companies. Therefore, answer A is incorrect. Answer B is also incorrect; although an employer should not put pressure on an analyst to alter a report in any way and Jamison cannot change the report based on her employer's influence, the relationships between the two companies posing the conflict of interest must be disclosed.

4. **C is correct.** This question asks about compliance procedures relating to personal investments of members and candidates. The statement in answer C clearly conflicts with the recommended procedures in the *Handbook*.

Employers should compare personal transactions of employees with those of clients on a regular basis regardless of the existence of a requirement by a regulatory organization. Such comparisons ensure that employees' personal trades do not conflict with their duty to their clients, and the comparisons can be conducted in a confidential manner. The statement in answer A does not conflict with the procedures in the *Handbook*. Disclosure of such policies will give full information to clients regarding potential conflicts of interest on the part of those entrusted to manage their money. Answer B is incorrect because firms are encouraged to establish policies whereby employees clear personal holdings and transactions. Answer D describes the categories of securities that compliance procedures designed to monitor personal transactions should cover.

5. B is correct. This question relates to Standard III(A)—Loyalty, Prudence, and Care and Standard III(E)—Preservation of Confidentiality. In this case, the member manages funds of a private endowment. Members and candidates owe a fiduciary duty to their clients, who are in this case the trustees of the fund. Bronson cannot disclose confidential financial information to anyone without the permission of the fund, regardless of whether the disclosure may benefit the fund. Therefore, answer A is incorrect. Answer C is also incorrect because Bronson must notify the fund and obtain the fund's permission before publicizing the information. Answer D is incorrect because, even if the information is nonmaterial, the member cannot disclose the information because it is confidential. Only if Bronson receives permission from the trustees can he disclose the information to the alumnus.

6. C is correct. Under Standard IV(C)—Responsibilities of Supervisors, members and candidates may delegate supervisory duties to subordinates but such delegation does not relieve members or candidates of their supervisory responsibilities. As a result, answers B and D are incorrect. Moreover, whether or not Miller's subordinates are subject to the CFA Institute Code and Standards is irrelevant to her supervisory responsibilities. Therefore, answer A is incorrect.

7. D is correct. This question relates to Standard V(A)—Diligence and Reasonable Basis. Willier's action in changing the recommendation based on the opinion of another financial analyst is not an adequate basis for the recommendation. Answer A is thus incorrect. So is answer B because, although it is true that members and candidates must distinguish between facts and opinions in recommendations, the question does not illustrate a violation of that nature. Answer C is incorrect; whether or not a member or candidate has to seek approval from the firm of a change in a recommendation is a matter of policy set by the firm; the Standards do not require that members and candidates seek such approval. If the opinion overheard by Willier had sparked him to conduct additional research and investigation that justified a change of opinion, then a changed recommendation would be appropriate.

8. B is correct. This question relates to Standard I(B)—Independence and Objectivity. When asked to change a recommendation on a company stock to gain business for the firm, the head of the brokerage unit must refuse in order to maintain his independence and objectivity in making the recommendation. He must not yield to pressure by the firm's investment banking department. To avoid the appearance of a conflict of interest, the firm should discontinue issuing recommendations about the company. Answer A is incorrect; changing the recommendation in any manner that is contrary to the analyst's opinion violates the duty to maintain

independence and objectivity. Answer C is incorrect because merely assigning a new analyst to decide if the stock deserves a higher rating will not address the conflict of interest. Answer D would actually exacerbate the conflict of interest.

**9.** A is correct. Standard VII(B)—Reference to CFA Institute, the CFA Designation, and the CFA Program is the subject of this question. The reference on Albert's business card implies that there is a "CFA Level II" designation; Tye merely indicates in promotional material that he is participating in the CFA Program and has completed Levels I and II. Candidates may not imply that there is some sort of partial designation earned after passing a level of the CFA examination. Therefore, Albert has violated Standard VII(B). Candidates may communicate that they are participating in the CFA Program, however, and may state the levels that they have completed. Therefore, Tye has not violated Standard VII(B).

**10.** B is correct. This question relates to Standard V(B)—Communication with Clients and Prospective Clients. Scott has issued a research report stating that he expects the price of Walkton Industries stock to rise by $8 a share "because the dividend will increase" by $1.50 per share. He has made this statement knowing that the dividend will increase only if Congress enacts certain legislation, an uncertain prospect. By stating that the dividend will increase, Scott failed to separate fact from opinion. Therefore, B is correct. The information regarding passage of legislation is not material nonpublic information because it is conjecture, and it is not clear that the U.S. Representative gave Scott her opinion on the passage of the legislation in confidence. She could be offering this opinion to anyone who asks. Therefore, statement A is incorrect. It may be acceptable to base a recommendation, in part, on an expectation of future events, even though they may be uncertain. Therefore, answer C is incorrect. Answer D is incorrect because there is a violation of the Standards as indicated in answer B.

**11.** B is correct. This question, which relates to Standard III(B)—Fair Dealing, tests the knowledge of the procedures that will assist members and candidates to treat clients fairly when making investment recommendations. The steps listed in A, C, and D will all help ensure the fair treatment of clients. Answer B, distributing recommendations to institutional clients before distributing them to individual accounts, discriminates among clients based on size and class of assets and is a violation of Standard III(B).

**12.** B is correct. This question deals with Standard II(A)—Material Nonpublic Information. The mosaic theory states that an analyst may use material public information or nonmaterial nonpublic information in creating a larger picture than shown by any individual piece of information and the conclusions the analyst reaches become material only after the pieces are assembled. Answers A, C, and D are accurate statements relating to the Code and Standards but do not describe the mosaic theory.

**13.** C is correct. This question involves Standard IV(B)—Additional Compensation Arrangements. The arrangement described in the question, whereby Jurgens would be compensated beyond that provided by her firm, based on the account's performance is not a violation of the Standards so long as Jurgens discloses the arrangement in writing to her employer and obtains permission from her employer prior to entering into the arrangement. Answer A is incorrect; although the private compensation arrangement could conflict with the interests of other clients, members and candidates may enter into such agreements so long as they have disclosed the arrangements to their employer and obtained permission for the arrangement from their employer. Answer D is also incorrect; this potential conflict can be managed through disclosure. Answer B is incorrect because members and candidates are not required to receive permission from CFA Institute for such arrangements.

**14.** B is correct. This question relates to Standard III(A)—Loyalty, Prudence, and Care—specifically, a member or candidate's responsibility for voting proxies and the use of client brokerage. According to the facts stated in the question, Farnsworth did not violate Standard III(A). Although the company president asked Farnsworth to vote the shares of the Jones Corporation profit-sharing plan a certain way, Farnsworth investigated the issue and concluded, independently, the best way to vote. Therefore, even though his decision coincided with the wishes of the company president, Farnsworth is not in violation of his fiduciary responsibility to his clients. In this case, the participants and the beneficiaries of the profit-sharing plan are the clients, not the company's management. Had Farnsworth not investigated the issue or had he yielded to the president's wishes and voted for a slate of directors that he had determined was not in the best interest of the company, Farnsworth would have violated his fiduciary responsibility to the beneficiaries of the plan. In addition, because the brokerage firm provides the lowest commissions and best execution for securities transactions, Farnsworth has met his fiduciary duties to the client in using this brokerage firm. It does not matter that the brokerage firm also provides research information that is not useful for the account generating the commission, because Farnsworth is not paying extra money of the client's for that information.

**15.** A is correct. In this question, Brown is providing investment recommendations before making inquiries about the client's financial situation, investment experience, or investment objectives. Brown is thus violating Standard III(C)—Suitability. As for answer B, why the client changed investment firms might be useful information, but it is not the only information the member needs to provide suitable investment recommendations, and Brown is under no obligation to notify CFA Institute of any violation of the Code and Standards other than her own. Answers C and D provide examples of information members and candidates should discuss with their clients at the outset of the relationship, but these answers do not constitute a complete list of those factors. Answer A is the best answer.

**16.** B is correct. This question involves Standard I(C)—Misrepresentation. Statement I is a factual statement that discloses to clients and prospects accurate information about the terms of the investment instrument. Statement II, which guarantees a specific rate of return for a mutual fund, is an opinion stated as a fact and, therefore, violates Standard I(C). If Statement II were rephrased to include a qualifying statement, such as "in my opinion, investors may earn . . . ," it would not be in violation of the Standards.

**17.** D is correct. This question involves three Standards. Anderb, the portfolio manager, has been obtaining lower prices for her personal securities transactions than she gets for her clients, which is a breach of Standard III(A)—Loyalty, Prudence, and Care. In addition, she violated Standard I(D)—Misconduct, by failing to adhere to company policy and hiding her personal transactions from her firm. Anderb's supervisor, Bates, violated Standard IV(C)—Responsibilities of Supervisors; although the company had requirements for reporting personal trading, Bates failed to adequately enforce those procedures. There is no indication that the company has a prohibition against employees using the same broker they use for their personal accounts that they also use for their client accounts. There is also no such prohibition in the Code and Standards. Therefore, statements A, B, and C are all consistent with the Standards and answer D is inconsistent with the Standards.

18. A is correct. This question relates to Standard I(A)—Knowledge of the Law—specifically, global application of the Code and Standards. Members and candidates who practice in multiple jurisdictions may be subject to various securities laws and regulations. If applicable law is more strict than the requirements of the Code and Standards, members and candidates must adhere to applicable law; otherwise, members and candidates must adhere to the Code and Standards. Therefore, answer A is correct. Answer B is incorrect because members and candidates must adhere to the higher standard set by the Code and Standards if local applicable law is less strict. Statement C is incorrect because when no applicable law exists, members and candidates are required to adhere to the Code and Standards, and the Code and Standards prohibit the use of material nonpublic information. Answer D is incorrect because members and candidates must always comply with applicable law.

19. B is correct. The best course of action under Standard I(B)—Independence and Objectivity is to avoid a conflict of interest whenever possible. Therefore, paying for all expenses is the correct answer. Answer C details a course of action in which the conflict would be disclosed, but the solution is not as appropriate as avoiding the conflict of interest. Answer A would not be the best course because it would not remove the appearance of a conflict of interest; even though the report would not be affected by the reimbursement of expenses, it could appear to be. Answer D is not appropriate because, by failing to take advantage of close inspection of the company, Ward would not be using all the information available in completing his report.

20. A is correct. Under Standard IV(A)—Duties to Employer: Loyalty, members and candidates may undertake independent practice that may result in compensation or other benefit in competition with their employer so long as they obtain consent from their employer. Answers B and C are consistent with Standard IV(A). Answer D is also consistent with the Standards because the Standards allow members and candidates to make arrangements or preparations to go into competitive business so long as those arrangements do not interfere with their duty to their current employer. Answer A is not consistent with the Standards because the Standards do not include a complete prohibition against undertaking independent practice.

21. D is correct. This question involves Standard VI(A)—Disclosure of Conflicts. Answers A, B, and C describe conflicts of interest for Smithers or her firm that would have to be disclosed. Answer A describes an employment relationship between the analyst and the company that is the subject of the recommendation. Answer B describes the beneficial interest of the analyst's employer in the company's stock, and answer C describes the analyst's own beneficial interest in the company stock. In answer D, the relationship between the analyst and the company through a relative is so tangential that it does not create a conflict of interest necessitating disclosure.

**22.** D is correct. This question relates to Standard I(C)—Misrepresentation. Although Michelieu's statement regarding the total return of his client's accounts on average may be technically true, it is misleading because the majority of the gain resulted from one client's large position taken against Michelieu's advice. Therefore, this statement misrepresents the investment performance the member is responsible for. He has not taken steps to present a fair, accurate, and complete presentation of performance. Answer C is thus incorrect. Answer B is incorrect because although Michelieu is not guaranteeing future results, his words are still a misrepresentation of his performance history. Answer A is incorrect because failing to disclose the risk preferences of clients does not make a statement misleading and is not a violation of the Standards in this context.

**23.** B is correct. The best policy to prevent violation of Standard II(A)—Material Nonpublic Information is the establishment of "firewalls" within a firm to prevent exchange of insider information. The physical and informational barrier of a firewall between the investment banking department and the brokerage operation prevents the investment banking department from providing information to analysts on the brokerage side who may be writing recommendations regarding a company stock. Prohibiting recommendations of the stock of companies that are clients of the investment banking department is an alternative, but answer A states that this prohibition would be permanent, which is not the best answer. Once an offering is complete and the material nonpublic information obtained by the investment banking department becomes public, resuming publishing recommendations on the stock is not a violation of the Code and Standards because the information of the investment banking department no longer gives the brokerage operation an advantage in writing the report. Answer C is incorrect; whether or not a fiduciary duty is owed to clients does not override the prohibition against use of material nonpublic information. Answer D is incorrect because no exchange of information should be occurring between the investment banking department and the brokerage operation, so monitoring of such exchanges is not an effective compliance procedure for preventing the use of material nonpublic information.

**24.** C is correct. Under Standard III(A)—Loyalty, Prudence, and Care, members and candidates who manage a company's pension funds owe a fiduciary duty to the participants and beneficiaries of the plan, not the management of the company or the company shareholders.

**25.** C is correct. Answers A and B give the two primary reasons listed in the *Standards of Practice Handbook* for disclosing referral fees to clients under Standard VI(C)—Disclosure of Referral Fees. Answer D describes the type of disclosure that must be made according to the guidance in the *Standards of Practice Handbook*. Answer C is inconsistent with Standard VI(C) because disclosure of referral fees, to be effective, should be made to prospective clients before entering into a formal client relationship.

**26.** C is correct. Bogwell distinguished between fact and opinion about the manufacturing company after conducting a thorough analysis of the company. The CEO can disagree with his opinion, and Bogwell can remain in compliance with CFA Institute Standards.

**27.** C is correct. Members should consider the Professional Conduct Program as an extension of themselves when requested to provide information about a client in support of a PCP investigation into their own conduct.

**28.** A is correct. A member must keep information about clients confidential unless the information concerns illegal activities on the part of the client. The Standard relating to knowledge of the law does not require members to become experts in compliance. When in doubt, members should consult with their employer's compliance personnel or outside counsel before disclosing confidential information about clients. B and C are incorrect because there are no violations of these Standards.

**29.** B is correct. If a member has reasonable ground to believe that ongoing employee activities are illegal or unethical, the member must dissociate from the activity. A is incorrect because while a member may want to consider directly confronting the person committing the violation, it is not required by the Standards. C is incorrect because while such actions are encouraged, they are not required.

**30.** C is correct. In presenting a similar scenario the SOPH states, "Best practice would be to avoid the conflict by asking his employer to assign another analyst to draft the follow-up report." A is incorrect because recommending or requiring this action would be burdensome and discriminatory for members. B is incorrect because this action is unnecessary, especially given the number of other analysts covering the technology sector at the firm.

**31.** A is correct. There is no violation; the Standards do not prohibit former employees from contacting clients from their former employer so long as the contact information does not come from the records of the former employer or violate an applicable non-compete agreement. B is incorrect because he did not contact Creek clients while still employed by Creek. C is incorrect because there is nothing in the question to suggest he used privileged information; it is reasonable to assume that Cavanagh would have the contact information for any personal friends.

**32.** C is correct because the SOPH states, "Standalone codes of ethics should be written in plain language and address general fiduciary concepts, unencumbered by numerous detailed procedures directed to the day-to-day operations of the firm." A and B are incorrect because these actions and qualities are specifically supported in the SOPH.

**33.** A is correct. The SOPH states that family accounts in which the member has a beneficial interest should not undertake transactions until client accounts and the employer have had an opportunity to act. Brenner discloses to his employer that he has beneficial ownership in his parents' account and follows the pre-clearance and reporting requirements of his employer. B and C are incorrect because there are no violations.

**34.** A is correct. Standard III(E) protects the confidentiality of client information even if the person is no longer a client. The SOPH states that members must keep information about current, former, and prospective clients confidential *unless* the information concerns illegal activities on the part of the client and provided such disclosure is not specifically prohibited by applicable law. The requirements of the Standard are not intended to prevent members from cooperating with an investigation by the Professional Conduct Program.

**35.** B is correct. The SOPH states, "If a member or candidate determines that information is material, the member or candidate should make reasonable efforts to achieve public dissemination of the information. This usually entails encouraging the issuer company to make the information public." A is incorrect because LeMay should make reasonable efforts to achieve public dissemination of the information. C is incorrect because the action should be taken only after attempts to achieve public dissemination have failed.

## SOLUTION FOR READING 4

**1.** A is correct. Real Estate is one of the eight major sections of GIPS.
Answers B and C are not included in the eight major sections of GIPS.

## SOLUTIONS FOR READING 5

**1. A.** Investment 2 is identical to Investment 1 except that Investment 2 has low liquidity. The difference between the interest rate on Investment 2 and Investment 1 is 0.5 percentage point. This amount represents the liquidity premium, which represents compensation for the risk of loss relative to an investment's fair value if the investment needs to be converted to cash quickly.

**B.** To estimate the default risk premium, find the two investments that have the same maturity but different levels of default risk. Both Investments 4 and 5 have a maturity of eight years. Investment 5, however, has low liquidity and thus bears a liquidity premium. The difference between the interest rates of Investments 5 and 4 is 2.5 percentage points. The liquidity premium is 0.5 percentage point (from Part A). This leaves $2.5 - 0.5 = 2.0$ percentage points that must represent a default risk premium reflecting Investment 5's high default risk.

**C.** Investment 3 has liquidity risk and default risk comparable to Investment 2, but with its longer time to maturity, Investment 3 should have a higher maturity premium. The interest rate on Investment 3, $r_3$, should thus be above 2.5 percent (the interest rate on Investment 2). If the liquidity of Investment 3 were high, Investment 3 would match Investment 4 except for Investment 3's shorter maturity. We would then conclude that Investment 3's interest rate should be less than the interest rate on Investment 4, which is 4 percent. In contrast to Investment 4, however, Investment 3 has low liquidity. It is possible that the interest rate on Investment 3 exceeds that of Investment 4 despite 3's shorter maturity, depending on the relative size of the liquidity and maturity premiums. However, we expect $r_3$ to be less than 4.5 percent, the expected interest rate on Investment 4 if it had low liquidity. Thus 2.5 percent $< r_3 <$ 4.5 percent.

**2. i.** Draw a time line.

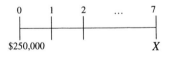

**ii.** Identify the problem as the future value of a lump sum.
**iii.** Use the formula for the future value of a lump sum.

$$PV = 0.05 \times \$5,000,000 = \$250,000$$
$$FV_N = PV(1 + r)^N$$
$$= \$250,000(1.03)^7$$
$$= \$307,468.47$$

Solutions to 1–20 taken from *Quantitative Methods for Investment Analysis*, Second Edition, by Richard A. DeFusco, CFA, Dennis W. McLeavey, CFA, Jerald E. Pinto, CFA, and David E. Runkle, CFA. Copyright © 2004 by CFA Institute. Reprinted with permission. All other solutions copyright © CFA Institute.

The future value in seven years of $250,000 received today is $307,468.47 if the interest rate is 3 percent compounded annually.

**3.** **i.** Draw a time line.

**ii.** Identify the problem as the future value of a lump sum.

**iii.** Use the formula for the future value of a lump sum.

$$FV_N = PV(1 + r)^N$$
$$= \$500,000(1.07)^{10}$$

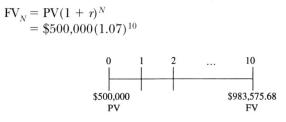

$$= \$983,575.68$$

Your client will have $983,575.68 in 10 years if she invests $500,000 today and earns 7 percent annually.

**4. A.** To solve this problem, take the following steps:

**i.** Draw a time line and recognize that a year consists of four quarterly periods.

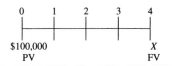

**ii.** Recognize the problem as the future value of a lump sum with quarterly compounding.

**iii.** Use the formula for the future value of a lump sum with periodic compounding, where $m$ is the frequency of compounding within a year and $N$ is the number of years.

$$FV_N = PV\left(1 + \frac{r_s}{m}\right)^{mN}$$

$$= \$100,000\left(1 + \frac{0.07}{4}\right)^{4(1)}$$

$$= \$107,185.90$$

**iv.** As an alternative to Step iii, use a financial calculator. Most of the equations in this reading can be solved using a financial calculator. Calculators vary in the exact keystrokes required (see your calculator's manual for the appropriate keystrokes), but the following table illustrates the basic variables and algorithms.

| Time Value of Money Variable | Notation Used on Most Calculators | Numerical Value for This Problem |
|---|---|---|
| Number of periods or payments | $N$ | 4 |
| Interest rate per period | $\%i$ | 7/4 |
| Present value | PV | $100,000 |
| Future value | **FV compute** | $X$ |
| Payment size | PMT | n/a (= 0) |

Remember, however, that a financial calculator is only a shortcut way of performing the mechanics and is not a substitute for setting up the problem or knowing which equation is appropriate.

In summary, your client will have $107,185.90 in one year if he deposits $100,000 today in a bank account paying a stated interest rate of 7 percent compounded quarterly.

**B.** To solve this problem, take the following steps:

    **i.** Draw a time line and recognize that with monthly compounding, we need to express all values in monthly terms. Therefore, we have 12 periods.

    **ii.** Recognize the problem as the future value of a lump sum with monthly compounding.

    **iii.** Use the formula for the future value of a lump sum with periodic compounding, where $m$ is the frequency of compounding within a year and $N$ is the number of years.

$$\text{FV}_N = \text{PV}\left(1 + \frac{r_s}{m}\right)^{mN}$$

$$= \$100,000\left(1 + \frac{0.07}{12}\right)^{12(1)}$$

$$= \$107,229.01$$

```
   0    1    2   ...   12
   |----|----|---------|
$100,000              $107,229.01
   PV                    FV
```

    **iv.** As an alternative to Step iii, use a financial calculator.

| Notation Used on Most Calculators | Numerical Value for This Problem |
|---|---|
| $N$ | 12 |
| $\%i$ | 7/12 |
| PV | $100,000 |
| **FV compute** | $X$ |
| PMT | n/a (= 0) |

Using your calculator's financial functions, verify that the future value, $X$, equals $107,229.01.

In summary, your client will have $107,229.01 at the end of one year if he deposits $100,000 today in his bank account paying a stated interest rate of 7 percent compounded monthly.

**C.** To solve this problem, take the following steps:

   **i.** Draw a time line and recognize that with continuous compounding, we need to use the formula for the future value with continuous compounding.

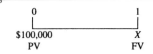

   **ii.** Use the formula for the future value with continuous compounding ($N$ is the number of years in the expression).

$$FV_N = PV\, e^{r_sN}$$
$$= \$100{,}000 e^{0.07(1)}$$
$$= \$107{,}250.82$$

The notation $e^{0.07(1)}$ is the exponential function, where $e$ is a number approximately equal to 2.718282. On most calculators, this function is on the key marked $e^x$. First calculate the value of $X$. In this problem, $X$ is $0.07(1) = 0.07$. Key 0.07 into the calculator. Next press the $e^x$ key. You should get 1.072508. If you cannot get this figure, check your calculator's manual.

In summary, your client will have $107,250.82 at the end of one year if he deposits $100,000 today in his bank account paying a stated interest rate of 7 percent compounded continuously.

**5.** Stated annual interest rate = 5.89 percent.
Effective annual rate on bank deposits = 6.05 percent.

$$1 + EAR = \left(1 + \frac{\text{Stated interest rate}}{m}\right)^m$$
$$1.0605 = \left(1 + \frac{0.0589}{m}\right)^m$$

For annual compounding, with $m = 1$, $1.0605 \neq 1.0589$.
For quarterly compounding, with $m = 4$, $1.0605 \neq 1.060214$.
For monthly compounding, with $m = 12$, $1.0605 \approx 1.060516$.
Hence, the bank uses monthly compounding.

**6. A.** Use the formula for the effective annual rate.
Effective annual rate = $(1 + \text{Periodic interest rate})^m - 1$

$$\left(1 + \frac{0.08}{4}\right)^{4(1)} - 1 = 0.0824 \text{ or } 8.24\%$$

**B.** Use the formula for the effective annual rate.
Effective annual rate = $(1 + \text{Periodic interest rate})^m - 1$

$$\left(1 + \frac{0.08}{12}\right)^{12(1)} - 1 = 0.0830 \text{ or } 8.30\%$$

**C.** Use the formula for the effective annual rate with continuous compounding.
Effective annual rate = $e^{r_s} - 1$
$e^{0.08} - 1 = 0.0833$ or 8.33%

**7.** **i.** Draw a time line.

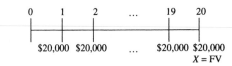

**ii.** Identify the problem as the future value of an annuity.
**iii.** Use the formula for the future value of an annuity.

$$FV_N = A\left[\frac{(1 + r)^N - 1}{r}\right]$$

$$= \$20{,}000\left[\frac{(1 + 0.07)^{20} - 1}{0.07}\right]$$

$$= \$819{,}909.85$$

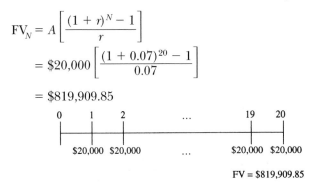

**iv.** Alternatively, use a financial calculator.

| Notation Used on Most Calculators | Numerical Value for This Problem |
|---|---|
| $N$ | 20 |
| $\%i$ | 7 |
| PV | n/a (=0) |
| FV **compute** | $X$ |
| PMT | $20,000 |

Enter 20 for $N$, the number of periods. Enter 7 for the interest rate and 20,000 for the payment size. The present value is not needed, so enter 0. Calculate the future value. Verify that you get $819,909.85 to make sure you have mastered your calculator's keystrokes.

   In summary, if the couple sets aside $20,000 each year (starting next year), they will have $819,909.85 in 20 years if they earn 7 percent annually.

**8.** **i.** Draw a time line.

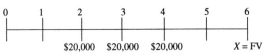

**ii.** Recognize the problem as the future value of a delayed annuity. Delaying the payments requires two calculations.
**iii.** Use the formula for the future value of an annuity (Equation 5-7).

$$FV_N = A\left[\frac{(1 + r)^N - 1}{r}\right]$$

to bring the three $20,000 payments to an equivalent lump sum of
$65,562.00 four years from today.

| Notation Used on Most Calculators | Numerical Value for This Problem |
|---|---|
| $N$ | 3 |
| $\%i$ | 9 |
| PV | n/a (=0) |
| FV **compute** | $X$ |
| PMT | $20,000 |

**iv.** Use the formula for the future value of a lump sum (Equation 5-2), $FV_N = PV(1 + r)^N$, to bring the single lump sum of $65,562.00 to an equivalent lump sum of $77,894.21 six years from today.

| Notation Used on Most Calculators | Numerical Value for This Problem |
|---|---|
| $N$ | 2 |
| $\%i$ | 9 |
| PV | $65,562.00 |
| FV **compute** | $X$ |
| PMT | n/a (=0) |

In summary, your client will have $77,894.21 in six years if she receives three yearly payments of $20,000 starting in Year 2 and can earn 9 percent annually on her investments.

**9. i.** Draw a time line.

**ii.** Identify the problem as the present value of a lump sum.

**iii.** Use the formula for the present value of a lump sum.

$$\begin{aligned}PV &= FV_N(1 + r)^{-N} \\ &= \$75,000(1 + 0.06)^{-5} \\ &= \$56,044.36\end{aligned}$$

In summary, the father will need to invest $56,044.36 today in order to have $75,000 in five years if his investments earn 6 percent annually.

**10. i.** Draw a time line and recognize that a year consists of four quarterly periods.

**ii.** Recognize the problem as the present value of a lump sum with quarterly compounding.

**iii.** Use the formula for the present value of a lump sum with periodic compounding, where $m$ is the frequency of compounding within a year and $N$ is the number of years.

$$PV = FV_N\left(1 + \frac{r_s}{m}\right)^{-mN}$$

$$= €100,000\left(1 + \frac{0.07}{4}\right)^{-4(1)}$$

$$= €93,295.85$$

**iv.** Alternatively, use a financial calculator.

| Notation Used on Most Calculators | Numerical Value for This Problem |
|---|---|
| $N$ | 4 |
| $\%i$ | 7/4 |
| PV **compute** | $X$ |
| FV | €100,000 |
| PMT | n/a (=0) |

Use your calculator's financial functions to verify that the present value, $X$, equals €93,295.85.

In summary, your client will have to deposit €93,295.85 today to have €100,000 in one year if her bank account pays 7 percent compounded quarterly.

**11. i.** Draw a time line for the 10 annual payments.

   **ii.**  Identify the problem as the present value of an annuity.

  **iii.**  Use the formula for the present value of an annuity.

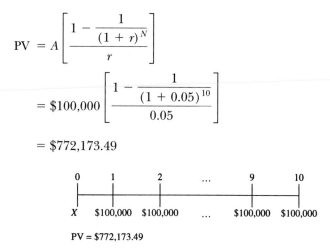

$$PV = A\left[\frac{1 - \frac{1}{(1 + r)^N}}{r}\right]$$

$$= \$100{,}000\left[\frac{1 - \frac{1}{(1 + 0.05)^{10}}}{0.05}\right]$$

$$= \$772{,}173.49$$

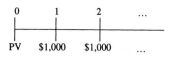

PV = $772,173.49

  **iv.**  Alternatively, use a financial calculator.

| Notation Used on Most Calculators | Numerical Value for This Problem |
|---|---|
| $N$ | 10 |
| $\%i$ | 5 |
| PV **compute** | $X$ |
| FV | n/a (=0) |
| PMT | $100,000 |

     In summary, the present value of 10 payments of $100,000 is $772,173.49 if the first payment is received in one year and the rate is 5 percent compounded annually. Your client should accept no less than this amount for his lump sum payment.

**12. i.**  Draw a time line.

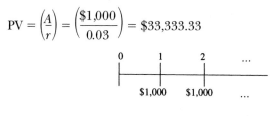

  **ii.**  Recognize the problem as the present value of a perpetuity.

  **iii.**  Use the formula for the present value of a perpetuity.

$$PV = \left(\frac{A}{r}\right) = \left(\frac{\$1{,}000}{0.03}\right) = \$33{,}333.33$$

PV = $33,333.33

The investor will have to pay $33,333.33 today to receive $1,000 per quarter forever if his required rate of return is 3 percent per quarter (12 percent per year).

**13. i.** Draw a time line to compare the lump sum and the annuity.

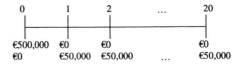

  **ii.** Recognize that we have to compare the present values of a lump sum and an annuity.

  **iii.** Use the formula for the present value of an annuity (Equation 5-11).

$$PV = €50,000 \left[ \frac{1 - \dfrac{1}{(1.06)^{20}}}{0.06} \right] = €573,496$$

| Notation Used on Most Calculators | Numerical Value for This Problem |
| --- | --- |
| $N$ | 20 |
| $\%i$ | 6 |
| PV **compute** | $X$ |
| FV | n/a (=0) |
| PMT | $50,000 |

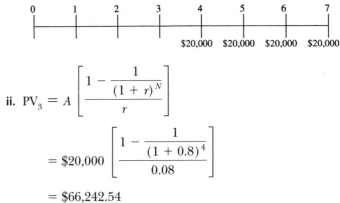

Equation 5-11

The annuity plan is better by €73,496 in present value terms (€573,496 − €500,000).

**14. A.** To evaluate the first instrument, take the following steps:

  **i.** Draw a time line.

| 0 | 1 | 2 | 3 | 4 | 5 | 6 | 7 |
|---|---|---|---|---|---|---|---|
|   |   |   |   | $20,000 | $20,000 | $20,000 | $20,000 |

  **ii.** $PV_3 = A \left[ \dfrac{1 - \dfrac{1}{(1 + r)^N}}{r} \right]$

$$= \$20,000 \left[ \frac{1 - \dfrac{1}{(1 + 0.8)^4}}{0.08} \right]$$

$$= \$66,242.54$$

**iii.** $PV_0 = \dfrac{PV_3}{(1 + r)^N} = \dfrac{\$66,242.54}{1.08^3} = \$52,585.46$

You should be willing to pay \$52,585.46 for this instrument.

**B.** To evaluate the second instrument, take the following steps:

**i.** Draw a time line.

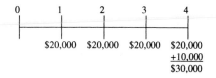

The time line shows that this instrument can be analyzed as an ordinary annuity of \$20,000 with four payments (valued in Step ii below) and a \$10,000 payment to be received at $t = 4$ (valued in Step iii below).

**ii.** $PV = A \left[ \dfrac{1 - \dfrac{1}{(1 + r)^N}}{r} \right]$

$= \$20,000 \left[ \dfrac{1 - \dfrac{1}{(1 + 0.08)^4}}{0.08} \right]$

$= \$66,242.54$

**iii.** $PV = \dfrac{FV_4}{(1 + r)^N} = \dfrac{\$10,000}{(1 + 0.08)^4} = \$7,350.30$

**iv.** Total $= \$66,242.54 + \$7,350.30 = \$73,592.84$

You should be willing to pay \$73,592.84 for this instrument.

**15. i.** Draw a time line.

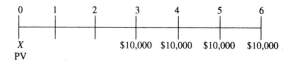

**ii.** Recognize the problem as a delayed annuity. Delaying the payments requires two calculations.

**iii.** Use the formula for the present value of an annuity (Equation 5-11).

$PV = A \left[ \dfrac{1 - \dfrac{1}{(1 + r)^N}}{r} \right]$

to bring the four payments of \$10,000 back to a single equivalent lump sum of \$33,121.27 at $t = 2$. Note that we use $t = 2$ because the first annuity payment is then one period away, giving an ordinary annuity.

| Notation Used on Most Calculators | Numerical Value for This Problem |
| --- | --- |
| $N$ | 4 |
| $\%i$ | 8 |
| PV **compute** | $X$ |
| PMT | \$10,000 |

iv. Then use the formula for the present value of a lump sum (Equation 5-8), $PV = FV_N(1 + r)^{-N}$, to bring back the single payment of $33,121.27 (at $t = 2$) to an equivalent single payment of $28,396.15 (at $t = 0$).

| Notation Used on Most Calculators | Numerical Value for This Problem |
|---|---|
| $N$ | 2 |
| $\%i$ | 8 |
| PV **compute** | $X$ |
| FV | $33,121.27 |
| PMT | n/a ($=0$) |

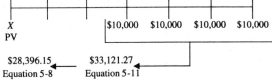

In summary, you should set aside $28,396.15 today to cover four payments of $10,000 starting in three years if your investments earn a rate of 8 percent annually.

**16. i.** Draw a time line.

ii. Recognize the problem as the future value of a lump sum with monthly compounding.

iii. Use the formula for the future value of a lump sum with periodic compounding

$$FV_N = PV[1 + (r_s/m)]^{mN}$$

and solve for $r_s$, the stated annual interest rate:

$1,061.68 = 1,000 [1 + (r_s/12)]^{12(1)}$ so $r_s = 0.06$

iv. Alternatively, use a financial calculator to solve for $r$.

| Notation Used on Most Calculators | Numerical Value for This Problem |
|---|---|
| $N$ | 12 |
| $\%i$ **compute** | $X$ |
| PV | $1,000 |
| FV | $1,061.68 |
| PMT | n/a ($=0$) |

Use your calculator's financial functions to verify that the stated interest rate of the savings account is 6 percent with monthly compounding.

**17. i.** Draw a time line.

**ii.** Recognize the problem as the future value of a lump sum with monthly compounding.

**iii.** Use the formula for the future value of a lump sum, $FV_N =$ $PV[1 + (r_s/m)]^{mN}$, where $m$ is the frequency of compounding within a year and $N$ is the number of years. Solve for $mN$, the number of months.

€100,000 = €35,000 $[1 + (0.05/12)]^{12N}$ so $12N = 252.48$ months

**iv.** Alternatively, use a financial calculator.

| Notation Used on Most Calculators | Numerical Value for This Problem |
|---|---|
| $N$ compute | $X$ |
| $\%i$ | 5/12 |
| PV | €35,000 |
| FV | €100,000 |
| PMT | n/a (=0) |

Use your calculator's financial functions to verify that your client will have to wait 252.48 months to have €100,000 if he deposits €35,000 today in a bank account paying 5 percent compounded monthly. (Some calculators will give 253 months.)

**18. i.** Draw a time line.

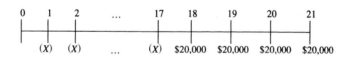

**ii.** Recognize that you need to equate the values of two annuities.

**iii.** Equate the value of the four $20,000 payments to a single payment in Period 17 using the formula for the present value of an annuity (Equation 5-11), with $r = 0.05$. The present value of the college costs as of $t = 17$ is $70,919.

$$PV = \$20,000 \left[ \frac{1 - \dfrac{1}{(1.05)^4}}{0.05} \right] = \$70,919$$

| Notation Used on Most Calculators | Numerical Value for This Problem |
|---|---|
| $N$ | 4 |
| $\%i$ | 5 |
| PV compute | $X$ |
| FV | n/a (=0) |
| PMT | $20,000 |

iv. Equate the value of the 17 investments of $X$ to the amount calculated in Step iii, college costs as of $t = 17$, using the formula for the future value of an annuity (Equation 5-7). Then solve for $X$.

$$\$70{,}919 = \left[ \frac{(1.05)^{17} - 1}{0.05} \right] = 25.840366X$$

$$X = \$2{,}744.50$$

| Notation Used on Most Calculators | Numerical Value for This Problem |
|---|---|
| $N$ | 17 |
| $\%i$ | 5 |
| PV | n/a (=0) |
| FV | $70,919 |
| PMT **compute** | $X$ |

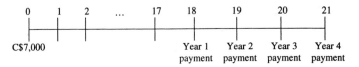

In summary, your client will have to save $2,744.50 each year if she starts next year and makes 17 payments into a savings account paying 5 percent annually.

**19. i.** Draw a time line.

ii. Recognize that the payments in Years 18, 19, 20, and 21 are the future values of a lump sum of C$7,000 in Year 0.

iii. With $r = 5\%$, use the formula for the future value of a lump sum (Equation 5-2), $FV_N = PV (1 + r)^N$, four times to find the payments. These future values are shown on the time line below.

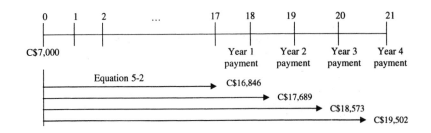

**iv.** Using the formula for the present value of a lump sum ($r = 6\%$), equate the four college payments to single payments as of $t = 17$ and add them together. C\$16,846$(1.06)^{-1}$ + C\$17,689$(1.06)^{-2}$ + C\$18,573$(1.06)^{-3}$ + C\$19,502$(1.06)^{-4}$ = C\$62,677

**v.** Equate the sum of C\$62,677 at $t = 17$ to the 17 payments of $X$, using the formula for the future value of an annuity (Equation 5-7). Then solve for $X$.

$$C\$62{,}677 = X\left[\frac{(1.06)^{17} - 1}{0.06}\right] = 28.21288X$$

$$X = C\$2{,}221.58$$

| Notation Used on Most Calculators | Numerical Value for This Problem |
|---|---|
| $N$ | 17 |
| $\%i$ | 6 |
| PV | n/a (=0) |
| FV | C\$62,677 |
| PMT **compute** | $X$ |

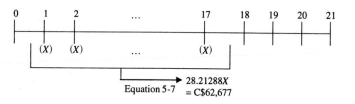

In summary, the couple will need to put aside C\$2,221.58 each year if they start next year and make 17 equal payments.

**20.** To compute the compound growth rate, we only need the beginning and ending EPS values of \$4.00 and \$7.00 respectively, and use the following equation:

$$FV_N = PV(1 + r)^N$$

$$7 = 4(1 + r)^4$$

$$1 + r = (7/4)^{1/4}$$

$$r = (7/4)^{1/4} - 1$$

$$= 0.1502 = 15.02\%$$

EPS grew at an annual rate of 15.02 percent during the four years.

**21.** A is correct. Using the general time value of money formula, for sales, solve for $r$ in the equation $2 = 1 \times (1 + r)^5$. For income, solve $3 = 1 \times (1 + r)^5$. Alternatively, using a financial calculator, for sales, enter $N=5$, PV$=1$, PMT$=0$, FV$=-2$ and compute I/Y. For income, change the FV to $-3$ and again solve for I/Y. The solution for sales is 14.87%; and for income is 24.57%.

## SOLUTIONS FOR READING 6

1. We can calculate the present value of the cash inflows in several ways. We can discount each cash inflow separately at the required rate of return of 12 percent and then sum the present values. We can also find the present value of a four-year annuity of C$3 million, add to it the present value of the $t = 5$ cash flow of C$10 million, and subtract the $t = 0$ outflow of C$13 million. Or we can compute the present value of a five-year annuity of C$3 million, add to it the present value of a cash inflow of C$7 million = C$10 million − C$3 million dated $t = 5$, and subtract the $t = 0$ outflow of C$13 million. For this last approach, we illustrate the keystrokes for many financial calculators.

| Notation Used on Most Calculators | Numerical Value for This Problem |
|---|---|
| $N$ | 5 |
| $\%i$ | 12 |
| PV **compute** | $X$ |
| PMT | 3,000,000 |
| FV | 7,000,000 |

We find that the PV of the inflows is C$14,786,317.

   **A.** Therefore, NPV = C$14,786,317 − C$13,000,000 = C$1,786,317.

   **B.** Waldrup should undertake this project because it has a positive NPV.

2. **A.** The internal rate of return is the discount rate that makes the NPV equal zero:

$$NPV = CF_0 + \frac{CF_1}{(1 + IRR)^1} + \frac{CF_2}{(1 + IRR)^2} + \ldots + \frac{CF_N}{(1 + IRR)^N} = 0$$

   To show that the investment project has an IRR of 13.51 percent we need to show that its NPV equals zero, ignoring rounding errors. Substituting the project's cash flows and IRR = 0.1351 into the above equation,

$$NPV = -C\$5,500,000 + \frac{C\$1,000,000}{(1.1351)^1} + \frac{C\$1,500,000}{(1.1351)^4} + \frac{C\$7,000,000}{(1.1351)^5}$$

$$= -C\$5,500,000 + C\$5,499,266 = -C\$734$$

   Given that the cash flows were of the magnitude of millions, the amount C$734 differs negligibly from 0.

   **B.** The internal rate of return is unaffected by any change in any external rate, including the increase in Waldrup's opportunity cost of capital.

3. **A.** NPV is the sum of the present values of all the cash flows associated with the investment, where inflows are signed positive and outflows are signed negative. This problem has only one outflow, an initial expenditure of $10 million at $t = 0$. The projected cash inflows from this advertising project form a perpetuity. We calculate the present value of a

*Quantitative Methods for Investment Analysis*, Second Edition, by Richard A. DeFusco, CFA, Dennis W. McLeavey, CFA, Jerald E. Pinto, CFA, and David E. Runkle, CFA. Copyright © 2004 by CFA Institute. Reprinted with permission.

perpetuity as $\overline{CF}/r$, where $\overline{CF}$ is the level annual cash flow and $r$ is the discount rate. Using the opportunity cost of capital of 12.5 percent as the discount rate, we have

$$NPV = -\$10,000,000 + 1,600,000/0.125 = -\$10,000,000 + 12,800,000$$
$$= \$2,800,000$$

**B.** In this case, the cash inflows are a perpetuity. Therefore, we can solve for the internal rate of return as follows:

$$\text{Initial investment} = (\text{Annual cash inflow})/\text{IRR}$$
$$10,000,000 = 1,600,000/\text{IRR}$$
$$\text{IRR} = 16 \text{ percent}$$

**C.** Yes, Bestfoods should spend $10 million on advertising. The NPV of $2.8 million is positive. The IRR of 16 percent is also in excess of the 12.5 percent opportunity cost of capital.

4. Using the IRR function in a spreadsheet or an IRR-enabled financial calculator, we enter the individual cash flows and apply the IRR function. We illustrate how we can solve for IRR in this particular problem using a financial calculator without a dedicated IRR function. The cash flows from $t = 1$ through $t = 6$ can be treated as a six-year, $4 million annuity with $7 million − $4 million = $3 million, entered as a future amount at $t = 6$.

| Notation Used on Most Calculators | Numerical Value for This Problem |
|---|---|
| $N$ | 6 |
| $\%i$ **compute** | $X$ |
| PV | $-15,000,000$ |
| PMT | 4,000,000 |
| FV | 3,000,000 |

**A.** The IRR of the project is 18.25 percent.

**B.** Because the project's IRR is less than the hurdle rate of 19 percent, the company should not undertake the project.

5. **A.** *Company A.* Let $\overline{CF} = £300,000$ be the amount of the perpetuity. Then with $r = 0.12$, the NPV in acquiring Company A would be

$$NPV = CF_0 + \overline{CF}/r = -£2,000,000 + £300,000/0.12 = £500,000$$

*Company B.* Let $\overline{CF} = £435,000$ be the amount of the perpetuity. Then with $r = 0.12$, the NPV in acquiring Company B would be

$$NPV = CF_0 + \overline{CF}/r = -£3,000,000 + £435,000/0.12 = £625,000$$

Both Company A and Company B would be positive NPV acquisitions, but Westcott–Smith cannot purchase both because the total purchase price of £5 million exceeds its budgeted amount of £4 million. Because Company B's NPV of £625,000 is higher than Company A's NPV of £500,000, Westcott–Smith should purchase Company B according to the NPV rule.

**B.** *Company A.* Using the notation from Part A, IRR is defined by the expression NPV = −Investment + $\overline{CF}$/IRR = 0. Thus −£2,000,000 + £300,000/IRR = 0 and solving for IRR,

IRR = £300,000/£2,000,000 = 0.15 or 15 percent

*Company B.*

IRR = £435,000/£3,000,000 = 0.145 or 14.5 percent

Both Company A and Company B have IRRs that exceed Westcott–Smith's opportunity cost of 12 percent, but Westcott–Smith cannot purchase both because of its budget constraint. According to the IRR rule, Westcott–Smith should purchase Company A because its IRR of 15 percent is higher than Company B's IRR of 14.5 percent.

**C.** Westcott–Smith should purchase Company B. When the NPV and IRR rules conflict in ranking mutually exclusive investments, we should follow the NPV rule because it directly relates to shareholder wealth maximization.

**6. A.** The money-weighted rate of return is the discount rate that equates the present value of inflows to the present value of outflows.

*Outflows:*

At $t = 0$ (1 January 2002):

150 shares purchased × $156.30 per share = $23,445

*Inflows:*

At $t = 1$ (1 January 2003):

150 shares × $10 dividend per share = $1,500

100 shares sold × $165 per share = $16,500

At $t = 2$ (1 January 2004):

50 shares remaining × $15 dividend per share = $750

50 shares sold × $170 per share = $8,500

PV (Outflows) = PV (Inflows)

$$23,445 = \frac{1,500 + 16,500}{1 + r} + \frac{750 + 8,500}{(1 + r)^2}$$

$$= \frac{18,000}{1 + r} + \frac{9,250}{(1 + r)^2}$$

The last line is the equation for calculating the money-weighted rate of return on Wilson's portfolio.

**B.** We can solve for the money-weighted return by entering −23,445, 18,000, and 9,250 in a spreadsheet or calculator with an IRR function. In this case, we can also solve for money-weighted rate of return as the real root of the quadratic equation $18,000x + 9,250x^2 − 23,445 = 0$, where $x = 1/(1 + r)$. By any method, the solution is $r = 0.120017$ or approximately 12 percent.

**C.** The time-weighted rate of return is the solution to $(1 + \text{Time-weighted rate of return})^2 = (1 + r_1)(1 + r_2)$, where $r_1$ and $r_2$ are the holding period returns in the first and second years, respectively. The value of the portfolio at $t = 0$ is $23,445. At $t = 1$, there are inflows of sale proceeds of $16,500 and $1,500 in dividends, or $18,000 in total. The balance of 50 shares is worth $8,250 = 50 shares × $165 per share. So at $t = 1$ the valuation is $26,250 = $18,000 + $8,250. Thus

$$r_1 = (\$26,250 - \$23,445)/\$23,445 = 0.119642 \text{ for the first year}$$

The amount invested at $t = 1$ is $8,250 = (50 shares)($165 per share). At $t = 2$, $750 in dividends are received, as well as sale proceeds of $8,500 (50 shares sold × $170 per share). So at $t = 2$, the valuation is $9,250 = $750 + $8,500. Thus

$$r_2 = (\$9,250 - \$8,250)/\$8,250 = 0.121212 \text{ for the second year}$$

Time-weighted rate of return $= \sqrt{(1.119642)(1.121212)} - 1 = 0.1204$ or approximately 12 percent.

**D.** If Wilson is a private investor with full discretionary control over the timing and amount of withdrawals and additions to his portfolios, then the money-weighted rate of return is an appropriate measure of portfolio returns.

**E.** If Wilson is an investment manager whose clients exercise discretionary control over the timing and amount of withdrawals and additions to the portfolio, then the time-weighted rate of return is the appropriate measure of portfolio returns. Time-weighted rate of return is standard in the investment management industry.

**7.** *Similarities.* The time-weighted returns for Luongo's and Weaver's investments will be equal, because the time-weighted return is not sensitive to additions or withdrawals of funds. Even though Weaver purchased another share at €110, the return earned by Luongo and Weaver each year for the time-weighted return calculation is the same.

*Differences.* The money-weighted returns for Luongo and Weaver will differ because they take into account the timing of additions and withdrawals. During the two-year period, Weaver owned more shares of the stock during the year that it did poorly (the stock return for Year 1 is $(110 + 5 - 100)/100 = 15$ percent and for Year 2 it is $(100 + 5 - 110)/110 = -4.55$ percent). As a consequence, the money-weighted return for Weaver (1.63 percent) is less than that of Luongo (5.00 percent). The money-weighted return reflects the timing of additions and withdrawals. Note, the cash flows for the money-weighted returns for Luongo and Weaver are (for $t = 0, 1,$ and 2) Luongo: $-100, +5, +105$; Weaver: $-100, -105, +210$.

**8.** In this solution, $F$ stands for face value, $P$ stands for price, and $D$ stands for the discount from face value ($D = F - P$).

**A.** Use the discount yield formula (Equation 6-3), $r_{BD} = D/F \times 360/t$:

$$r_{BD} = (\$1,500/\$100,000) \times (360/120) = 0.0150 \times 3 = 0.045$$

The T-bill's bank discount yield is 4.5 percent a year.

**B.** Use your answer from Part A and the money market yield formula (Equation 6-6), $r_{MM} = (360 \times r_{BD})/(360 - t \times r_{BD})$:

$$r_{MM} = (360 \times 0.045)/(360 - 120 \times 0.045) = 0.04568$$

The T-bill's bank discount yield is 4.57 percent a year.

**C.** Calculate the holding period yield (using Equation 6-4), then compound it forward to one year. First, the holding period yield (HPY) is

$$\text{HPY} = \frac{P_1 - P + D_1}{P_0} = (100{,}000 - 98{,}500)/98{,}500 = 0.015228$$

Next, compound the 120-day holding period yield, a periodic rate, forward to one year using Equation 6-5:

Effective annual yield $= (1 + \text{HPY})^{365/t} - 1$

Effective annual yield $= (1.015228)^{365/120} - 1 = 0.047044$

The T-bill's effective annual yield is 4.7 percent a year.

**9. A.** In the United States, T-bill yields are quoted on a bank discount basis. The bank discount yield is not a meaningful measure of the return for three reasons: First, the yield is based on the face value of the bond, not on its purchase price. Returns from investments should be evaluated relative to the amount that is invested. Second, the yield is annualized based on a 360-day year rather than a 365-day year. Third, the bank discount yield annualizes with simple interest, which ignores the opportunity to earn interest on interest (compound interest).

**B.** The money market yield is superior to the bank discount yield because the money market yield is computed relative to the purchase price (not the face value).

**C.** The T-bill yield can be restated on a money market basis by multiplying the bank discount yield by the ratio of the face value to the purchase price. Cavell could divide the annualized yield by 4 to compute the 90-day holding period yield. This is a more meaningful measure of the return that she will actually earn over 90 days (assuming that she holds the T-bill until it matures).

# SOLUTIONS FOR READING 7

1. **A.** The S&P MidCap 400 Index represents a sample of all U.S. stocks in the mid-cap or medium capitalization range. The related population is "all U.S. mid-cap stocks."

   **B.** The statement tells us to enumerate all members of a group and is sufficiently precise to allow us to do that. The statement defines a population.

   **C.** The two companies constitute a sample of U.S. insurance brokers. The related population is "U.S. insurance brokers."

   **D.** The statement defines a population. The 31 estimates for Microsoft EPS are the population of publicly available U.S. analyst estimates of Microsoft's FY2003 EPS, as of the report's date.

2. **A.** Sales in euros are measured on a ratio scale.

   **B.** Mutual fund investment styles are measured on a nominal scale. We can count the number of funds following a particular style, but whatever classification scheme we use, we cannot order styles into "greater than" or "less than" relationships.

   **C.** The ratings are measured on an ordinal scale. An analyst's rating of a stock as underweight, market weight, or overweight orders the rated securities in terms of levels of expected investment performance.

   **D.** The risk measurements are measured on an interval scale because not only do the measurements involve a ranking, but differences between adjacent values represent equal differences in risk. Because the measurement scale does not have a true zero, they are not measured on a ratio scale.

3. **A.** The entries in the table are as follows.

| Return Interval | Frequency | Cumulative Frequency | Relative Frequency | Cumulative Relative Frequency |
|---|---|---|---|---|
| $-9.19\% \leq A < -4.55\%$ | 3 | 3 | 25.00% | 25.00% |
| $-4.55\% \leq B < 0.09\%$ | 4 | 7 | 33.33% | 58.33% |
| $0.09\% \leq C < 4.73\%$ | 3 | 10 | 25.00% | 83.33% |
| $4.73\% \leq D \leq 9.37\%$ | 2 | 12 | 16.67% | 100.00% |

The frequency column provides the count of the observations falling in each return interval. The cumulative frequency adds up (cumulates) the frequencies. For example, the cumulative frequency of 7 for Interval B is the sum of the frequency of 3 for Interval A and the frequency of 4 for Interval B. The cumulative frequency for the last interval, D, equals the total number of observations, 12. The relative frequency column gives the frequency of an interval as a percentage of the total number of observations. The relative frequency for Interval B, for example, is 4/12 = 33.33 percent. The cumulative relative frequency column cumulates the relative frequencies. After reaching the last interval, the cumulative relative frequency should be 100 percent, ignoring rounding errors.

Solutions to 1–19 taken from *Quantitative Methods for Investment Analysis*, Second Edition, by Richard A. DeFusco, CFA, Dennis W. McLeavey, CFA, Jerald E. Pinto, CFA, and David E. Runkle, CFA. Copyright © 2004 by CFA Institute. Reprinted with permission. All other solutions copyright © CFA Institute.

**B.** The histogram for these data is shown below.

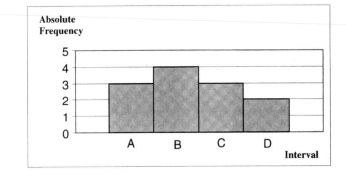

**C.** From the frequency distribution in Part A or the histogram in Part B, we can see that Interval B (−4.55 to 0.09) has the most members, 4. Interval B is thus the modal interval.

**4.** To calculate tracking risk of the portfolio, we use the sample standard deviation of the data in the table. We use the expression for sample standard deviation rather than population standard deviation because we are estimating the portfolio's tracking risk based on a sample. We use Equation 7-14,

$$s = \sqrt{\frac{\sum_{i=1}^{n}(X_i - \overline{X})^2}{n-1}}$$

where $X_i$ is the $i$th entry in the table of return deviations. The calculation in detail is as follows:

i. $\overline{X} = (−7.14 + 1.62 + 2.48 − 2.59 + 9.37 − 0.55 − 0.89 − 9.19 − 5.11 − 0.49 + 6.84 + 3.04)/12 = −2.61/12 = −0.2175$ percent.

ii. Having established that the mean deviation from the benchmark was $\overline{X} = −0.2175$, we calculate the squared deviations from the mean as follows:

$[−7.14 − (−0.2175)]^2 = (−6.9225)^2 = 47.921006$
$[1.62 − (−0.2175)]^2 = (1.8375)^2 = 3.376406$
$[2.48 − (−0.2175)]^2 = (2.6975)^2 = 7.276506$
$[−2.59 − (−0.2175)]^2 = (−2.3725)^2 = 5.628756$
$[9.37 − (−0.2175)]^2 = (9.5875)^2 = 91.920156$
$[−0.55 − (−0.2175)]^2 = (−0.3325)^2 = 0.110556$
$[−0.89 − (−0.2175)]^2 = (−0.6725)^2 = 0.452256$
$[−9.19 − (−0.2175)]^2 = (−8.9725)^2 = 80.505756$
$[−5.11 − (−0.2175)]^2 = (−4.8925)^2 = 23.936556$
$[−0.49 − (−0.2175)]^2 = (−0.2725)^2 = 0.074256$
$[6.84 − (−0.2175)]^2 = (7.0575)^2 = 49.808306$
$[3.04 − (−0.2175)]^2 = (3.2575)^2 = 10.611306$

iii. The sum of the squared deviations from the mean is

$$\sum_{i=1}^{12}(X_i - \overline{X})^2 = 321.621825$$

Note that the sum is given with full precision. You may also get 321.621822, adding the terms rounded at the sixth decimal place. The solution is not affected.

   **iv.** Divide the sum of the squared deviations from the mean by $n - 1$:

$$321.621825/(12 - 1) = 321.621825/11 = 29.238347$$

   **v.** Take the square root: $s = \sqrt{29.238347} = 5.41$ percent. Thus the portfolio's tracking risk was 5.41 percent a year.

**5. A.** A frequency distribution is a tabular display of data summarized into a relatively small number of equally sized intervals. In this example, we want five equally sized intervals. To make the frequency distribution table, we take the following seven steps.
   **i.** Sort the data in ascending order.

| |
|---:|
| $-43.06\%$ |
| $-17.75\%$ |
| $-9.53\%$ |
| $-6.18\%$ |
| $8.04\%$ |
| $20.32\%$ |
| $22.87\%$ |
| $41.20\%$ |
| $45.90\%$ |
| $46.21\%$ |

   **ii.** Calculate the range. Recall that the range formula is

     Range = Maximum value − Minimum value.

   In this case, the range is $46.21 - (-43.06) = 89.27$.

  **iii.** Decide on the number of intervals in the frequency distribution, $k$. This number was specified as $k = 5$ in the statement of the problem.

  **iv.** Determine the interval width as Range$/k = 89.27/5 = 17.854$ or 17.86, rounding up at the second decimal place as instructed in the statement of the problem. Note that if we rounded down to 17.85, the final class would terminate at 46.19 and not capture the largest return, 46.21.

   **v.** Determine the intervals by successively adding the interval width to the minimum value, to determine the ending points of intervals, stopping after we reach an interval that includes the maximum value.

| |
|---:|
| $-43.06 + 17.86 = -25.20$ |
| $-25.20 + 17.86 = \phantom{0}-7.34$ |
| $-7.34 + 17.86 = \phantom{0}10.52$ |
| $10.52 + 17.86 = \phantom{0}28.38$ |
| $28.38 + 17.86 = \phantom{0}46.24$ |

   Thus the intervals are from $-43.06$ up to (but not including) $-25.20$, $-25.20$ to $-7.34$, $-7.34$ to 10.52, 10.52 to 28.38, and 28.38 to (including) 46.24.

**vi.** Count the number of observations falling in each interval. The count is one observation in −43.06 to −25.20, two observations in −25.20 to −7.34, two observations in −7.34 to 10.52, two observations in 10.52 to 28.38, and three observations in 28.38 to 46.24.

**vii.** Construct a table of the intervals listed from smallest to largest that shows the number of observations falling in each interval. The heading of the last column may be "frequency" or "absolute frequency."

| Interval | | Frequency |
|---|---|---|
| A | $-43.06 \leq$ observation $< -25.20$ | 1 |
| B | $-25.20 \leq$ observation $< -7.34$ | 2 |
| C | $-7.34 \leq$ observation $< 10.52$ | 2 |
| D | $10.52 \leq$ observation $< 28.38$ | 2 |
| E | $28.38 \leq$ observation $\leq 46.24$ | 3 |

**B.** We find the cumulative frequencies by adding the absolute frequencies as we move from the first interval to the last interval.

| Interval | Absolute Frequency | Calculations for Cumulative Frequency | Cumulative Frequency |
|---|---|---|---|
| A $-43.06 \leq$ observation $< -25.20$ | 1 | | 1 |
| B $-25.20 \leq$ observation $< -7.34$ | 2 | $1 + 2 =$ | 3 |
| C $\ -7.34 \leq$ observation $< 10.52$ | 2 | $3 + 2 =$ | 5 |
| D $\ \ 10.52 \leq$ observation $< 28.38$ | 2 | $5 + 2 =$ | 7 |
| E $\ \ 28.38 \leq$ observation $\leq 46.24$ | 3 | $7 + 3 =$ | 10 |

The cumulative frequency is a running total of the absolute frequency, and the cumulative frequency for the last interval equals the total number of observations, 10.

**C.** The relative frequency of an interval is the frequency of the interval divided by the total number of observations. The cumulative relative frequency sums the relative frequencies. The cumulative relative frequency for the last interval is 100 percent.

| Intervals | Absolute Frequency | Relative Frequency | Calculations for Cumulative Frequency | Cumulative Relative Frequency |
|---|---|---|---|---|
| A $-43.06 \leq$ observation $< -25.20$ | 1 | $1/10 = 10\%$ | | 10% |
| B $-25.20 \leq$ observation $< -7.34$ | 2 | $2/10 = 20\%$ | $10\% + 20\% =$ | 30% |
| C $\ -7.34 \leq$ observation $< 10.52$ | 2 | $2/10 = 20\%$ | $30\% + 20\% =$ | 50% |
| D $\ \ 10.52 \leq$ observation $< 28.38$ | 2 | $2/10 = 20\%$ | $50\% + 20\% =$ | 70% |
| E $\ \ 28.38 \leq$ observation $\leq 46.24$ | $\underline{3}$ <br> 10 | $3/10 = 30\%$ | $70\% + 30\% =$ | 100% |

**D.** The last interval in the frequency distribution contains 30 percent of the observations, whereas the first interval contains 10 percent of the observations. The middle three intervals each contain 20 percent of the observations. The last two intervals thus contain 50 percent of the observations. The distribution is asymmetric. With most observations somewhat concentrated to the right but with one extreme negative observation (in the first interval), we conclude that the distribution is negatively skewed.

**6. A.** We calculate the sample mean by finding the sum of the 10 values in the table and then dividing by 10. According to Equation 7-3, the sample mean return, $\bar{R}$, is

$$\bar{R} = \frac{\sum_{i=1}^{10} R_i}{10}$$

using a common notation for returns, $R_i$. Thus $\bar{R} = (46.21 - 6.18 + 8.04 + 22.87 + 45.90 + 20.32 + 41.20 - 9.53 - 17.75 - 43.06)/10 = 108.02/10 = 10.802$ or 10.80 percent.

**B.** The median is defined as the value of the middle item of a group that has been sorted into ascending or descending order. In a sample of $n$ items, where $n$ is an odd number, the median is the value of the item in the sorted data set occupying the $(n + 1)/2$ position. When the data set has an even number of observations (as in this example), the median is the mean of the values of the items occupying the $n/2$ and $(n + 2)/2$ positions (the two middle items). With $n = 10$, these are the fifth and sixth positions.

To find the median, the first step is to rank the data. We previously sorted the returns in ascending order in Solution 5A(i).

| Returns | Position |
|---------|----------|
| −43.06% | 1 |
| −17.75% | 2 |
| −9.53% | 3 |
| −6.18% | 4 |
| 8.04% | 5 |
| 20.32% | 6 |
| 22.87% | 7 |
| 41.20% | 8 |
| 45.90% | 9 |
| 46.21% | 10 |

The value of the item in the fifth position is 8.04, and the value of the item in the sixth position is 20.32. The median return is then $(8.04 + 20.32)/2 = 28.36/2 = 14.18$ percent.

**C.** The modal return interval, as noted in Solution 5A, is Interval E, running from 28.38 percent to 46.24 percent.

**7.** The geometric mean requires that all the numbers be greater than or equal to 0. To ensure that the returns satisfy this requirement, after converting the returns to decimal form we add 1 to each return. We then use Equation 7-6 for the geometric mean return, $R_G$:

$$R_G = \left[ \prod_{t=1}^{10} (1 + R_t) \right]^{(1/10)} - 1$$

which can also be written as

$$R_G = \sqrt[10]{(1 + R_1)(1 + R_2)\ldots(1 + R_{10})} - 1$$

To find the geometric mean in this example, we take the following five steps:

  **i.** Divide each figure in the table by 100 to put the returns into decimal representation.

  **ii.** Add 1 to each return to obtain the terms $1 + R_t$.

| Return | Return in Decimal Form | 1 + Return |
|--------|------------------------|------------|
| 46.21% | 0.4621 | 1.4621 |
| −6.18% | −0.0618 | 0.9382 |
| 8.04% | 0.0804 | 1.0804 |
| 22.87% | 0.2287 | 1.2287 |
| 45.90% | 0.4590 | 1.4590 |
| 20.32% | 0.2032 | 1.2032 |
| 41.20% | 0.4120 | 1.4120 |
| −9.53% | −0.0953 | 0.9047 |
| −17.75% | −0.1775 | 0.8225 |
| −43.06% | −0.4306 | 0.5694 |

  **iii.** Multiply together all the numbers in the third column to get 1.9124.

  **iv.** Take the 10th root of 1.9124 to get $\sqrt[10]{1.9124} = 1.0670$. On most calculators, we evaluate $\sqrt[10]{1.9124}$ using the $y^x$ key. Enter 1.9124 with the $y^x$ key. Next, enter $1/10 = 0.10$. Then press the = key to get 1.0670.

  **v.** Subtract 1 to get 0.0670, or 6.70 percent a year. The geometric mean return is 6.70 percent. This result means that the compound annual rate of growth of the MSCI Germany Index was 6.7 percent annually during the 1993–2002 period. Note that this value is much less than the arithmetic mean of 10.80 percent that we calculated in the solution to Problem 6A.

**8.** Recall the formula for the location of the percentile (Equation 7-8):

$$L_y = (n + 1) \frac{y}{100}$$

where $Ly$ is the location or position of the $y$th percentile, $P_y$, and $y$ is the percentage point at which we want to divide the distribution.

  If we apply the percentile location formula, we find $L_{30} = (10 + 1) \frac{30}{100} =$

3.3, which is not a whole number. To find the 30th percentile from the sorted data, we interpolate by taking the value in the third position, $-9.53$, and adding 30 percent of the difference between the items in fourth and third position. The estimate of the 30th percentile is $P_{30} \approx -9.53 + 0.3[-6.18 - (-9.53)] = -9.53 + 0.3(3.35) = -9.53 + 1.005 = -8.53$.

   Therefore, the 30th percentile is $-8.53$. By definition, the 30th percentile is that value at or below which 30 percent of the observations lie. In this problem, 3 observations out of 10 lie below $-8.53$.

9. **A.** In the solution to Problem 5A, we calculated the range as
   Maximum value $-$ Minimum value $= 46.21 - (-43.06) = 89.27$.

   **B.** The mean absolute deviation is defined in Equation 7-10 as

$$\text{MAD} = \frac{\sum_{i=1}^{10} \left| R_i - \bar{R} \right|}{10}$$

To find the MAD for this example, we take the following four steps:

   **i.** Calculate the arithmetic mean of the original values.
   **ii.** Subtract the arithmetic mean from each value.
   **iii.** Take the absolute value of each deviation from the mean.
   **iv.** Sum the absolute values of the deviations and divide by the total number of observations. The mean absolute deviation in this case is 24.50 percent.

| Original Data $R_i$ | Deviation from Mean $R_i - \bar{R}$ | Absolute Value of Deviation from Mean $|R_i - \bar{R}|$ |
|---|---|---|
| 46.21 | 35.41 | 35.41 |
| $-6.18$ | $-16.98$ | 16.98 |
| 8.04 | $-2.76$ | 2.76 |
| 22.87 | 12.07 | 12.07 |
| 45.90 | 35.10 | 35.10 |
| 20.32 | 9.52 | 9.52 |
| 41.20 | 30.40 | 30.40 |
| $-9.53$ | $-20.33$ | 20.33 |
| $-17.75$ | $-28.55$ | 28.55 |
| $-43.06$ | $-53.86$ | 53.86 |
| $\bar{R} = 10.8$ | | |

$$\sum_{i=1}^{10} \left| R_i - \bar{R} \right| = 244.98$$

$$\text{MAD} = \frac{\sum_{i=1}^{10} \left| R_i - \bar{R} \right|}{10} = 24.50$$

C. Variance is defined as the mean of the squared deviations around the mean. We find the sample variance with Equation 7-13:

$$s^2 = \frac{\sum\limits_{i=1}^{10}(R_i - \bar{R})^2}{10 - 1}$$

To calculate the variance, we take the following four steps:

  i. Calculate the arithmetic mean of the original values.

 ii. Subtract the arithmetic mean from each value.

iii. Square each deviation from the mean.

 iv. Sum the squared deviations and divide by the total number of observations minus 1. The variance, in this case, is 896.844711.

The following table summarizes the calculation.

| Original Data $R_i$ | Deviation from Mean $R_i - \bar{R}$ | Squared Value of Deviation from Mean $(R_i - \bar{R})^2$ |
|---|---|---|
| 46.21 | 35.41 | 1253.8681 |
| −6.18 | −16.98 | 288.3204 |
| 8.04 | −2.76 | 7.6176 |
| 22.87 | 12.07 | 145.6849 |
| 45.90 | 35.10 | 1232.0100 |
| 20.32 | 9.52 | 90.6304 |
| 41.20 | 30.40 | 924.1600 |
| −9.53 | −20.33 | 413.3089 |
| −17.75 | −28.55 | 815.1025 |
| −43.06 | −53.86 | 2900.8996 |

$\bar{R} = 10.8$

$$\sum_{i=1}^{10}(R_i - \bar{R})^2 = 8{,}071.6024$$

$$s^2 = \frac{\sum\limits_{i=1}^{10}(R_i - \bar{R})^2}{9} = 896.844711$$

Recall that the units of variance are the squared units of the underlying variable, so to be precise we say that the sample variance is 896.844711 percent squared. To have a result in the original units of measurement, we calculate the standard deviation.

D. The standard deviation is the positive square root of the variance. We calculate the standard deviation with Equation 7-14:

$$s = \sqrt{896.844711} = 29.9474 \text{ or } 29.95\%$$

The standard deviation is thus 29.95 percent.

**E.** Semivariance is the average squared deviation below the mean. Five observations ($-43.06$, $-17.75$, $-9.53$, $-6.18$, and $8.04$) lie below the mean return of $10.8$. We compute the sum of the squared deviations from the mean as $(-43.06 - 10.8)^2 + (-17.75 - 10.8)^2 + (-9.53 - 10.8)^2 + (-6.18 - 10.8)^2 + (8.04 - 10.8)^2 = 4,425.2490$. Semivariance equals $4,425.2490/(10 - 1) = 491.6943$.

**F.** Semideviation equals $\sqrt{491.6943} = 22.174$ or $22.17\%$.

**10. A.** According to Equation 7-17, sample skewness $S_K$ is

$$S_K = \left[ \frac{n}{(n-1)(n-2)} \right] \frac{\sum_{i=1}^{n}(R_i - \bar{R})^3}{s^3}$$

The sample size, $n$, is 10. We previously calculated $\bar{R} = 10.8$ and deviations from the mean (see the tables in the solution to Problems 9B and 9C). We also calculated $s = 29.9474$ (showing four decimal places) in the solution to 9D. Thus $s^3 = 26,858.2289$. Using these results, we calculate the sum of the cubed deviations from the mean as follows:

$$\begin{aligned}
\sum_{i=1}^{10}(R_i - \bar{R})^3 &= \sum_{i=1}^{10}(R_i - 10.8)^3 = 35.41^3 + (-16.98)^3 + (-2.76)^3 + 12.07^3 \\
&\quad + 35.1^3 + 9.52^3 + 30.4^3 + (-20.33)^3 + (-28.55)^3 + (-53.86)^3 \\
&= 44,399.4694 - 4,895.6804 - 21.0246 + 1,758.4167 \\
&\quad + 43,243.551 + 862.8014 + 28,094.464 - 8,402.5699 \\
&\quad - 23,271.1764 - 156,242.4525 \\
&= -74,474.2012
\end{aligned}$$

So finally we have

$$S_K = \frac{10}{(9)(8)} \frac{-74,474.2012}{26,858.2289} = -0.39$$

In the sample period, the returns on the MSCI Germany Index were slightly negatively skewed.

**B.** For a negatively skewed distribution, the median is greater than the arithmetic mean. In our sample, the median return of 14.18 percent is greater than the mean return of 10.80.

**C.** According to Equation 7-18 sample excess kurtosis, $K_E$, is

$$K_E = \left\{ \left[ \frac{n(n+1)}{(n-1)(n-2)(n-3)} \right] \frac{\sum_{i=1}^{n}(R_i - \bar{R})^4}{s^4} \right\} - \frac{3(n-1)^2}{(n-2)(n-3)}$$

The sample size, $n$, is 10. We previously calculated $\bar{R} = 10.8$ and deviations from the mean (see the tables in the solution to Problems 9B and 9C). We also calculated $s = 29.9474$ (showing four decimal places) in the answer to 9D. Thus $s^4 = 804,334.1230$. Using these results, we calculate the sum of the deviations from the mean raised to the fourth power as follows:

$$\begin{aligned}
\sum_{i=1}^{10}(R_i - \bar{R})^4 &= \sum_{i=1}^{10}(R_i - 10.8)^4 = 35.41^4 + (-16.98)^4 + (-2.76)^4 + 12.07^4 \\
&\quad + 35.1^4 + 9.52^4 + 30.4^4 + (-20.33)^4 + (-28.55)^4 + (-53.86)^4 \\
&= 1,572,185.212 + 83,128.6531 + 58.0278 + 21,224.0901 \\
&\quad + 1,517,848.64 + 8,213.8694 + 854,071.7056 + 170,824.2468 \\
&\quad + 664,392.0855 + 8,415,218.489 \\
&= 13,307,165.02
\end{aligned}$$

Thus we have

$$\left\{\left[\frac{10(11)}{(9)(8)(7)}\right]\frac{13,307,165.02}{804,334.123}\right\} - \frac{3(9)^2}{(8)(7)} = 3.6109 - 4.3393 = -0.73$$

In the sample period, the returns on the MSCI Germany Index were slightly platykurtic. This means that there were fewer observations in the tails of the distribution than we would expect based on a normal distribution model for returns.

**D.** In contrast to a normal distribution, the distribution of returns on the MSCI Germany Index is somewhat asymmetric in direction of negative skew and is somewhat platykurtic (less peaked).

**11. A.** So long as a return series has any variability, the geometric mean return must be less than the arithmetic mean return. As one illustration of this relationship, in the solution to Problem 6A, we computed the arithmetic mean annual return on the MSCI Germany Index as 10.80 percent. In the solution to Problem 7, we computed the geometric mean annual return as 6.7 percent. In general, the difference between the geometric and arithmetic means increases with the variability of the period-by-period observations.

**B.** The geometric mean return is more meaningful than the arithmetic mean return for an investor concerned with the terminal value of an investment. The geometric mean return is the compound rate of growth, so it directly relates to the terminal value of an investment. By contrast, a higher arithmetic mean return does not necessarily imply a higher terminal value for an investment.

**C.** The arithmetic mean return is more meaningful than the geometric mean return for an investor concerned with the average one-period performance of an investment. The arithmetic mean return is a direct representation of the average one-period return. In contrast, the geometric mean return, as a compound rate of growth, aims to summarize what a return series means for the growth rate of an investment over many periods.

**12.** The following table shows the calculation of the portfolio's annual returns, and the mean annual return.

| Year | Weighted Mean Calculation | Portfolio Return |
|------|---------------------------|------------------|
| 1993 | 0.60(46.21) + 0.40(15.74) = | 34.02% |
| 1994 | 0.60(−6.18) + 0.40(−3.40) = | −5.07% |
| 1995 | 0.60(8.04) + 0.40(18.30) = | 12.14% |
| 1996 | 0.60(22.87) + 0.40(8.35) = | 17.06% |
| 1997 | 0.60(45.90) + 0.40(6.65) = | 30.20% |
| 1998 | 0.60(20.32) + 0.40(12.45) = | 17.17% |
| 1999 | 0.60(41.20) + 0.40(−2.19) = | 23.84% |
| 2000 | 0.60(−9.53) + 0.40(7.44) = | −2.74% |
| 2001 | 0.60(−17.75) + 0.40(5.55) = | −8.43% |
| 2002 | 0.60(−43.06) + 0.40(10.27) = | −21.73% |
| | Sum = | 96.46% |
| | Mean Annual Return = | 9.65% |

*Note*: The sum of the portfolio returns carried without rounding is 96.48.

**13. A.**  **i.** For the 60/40 equity/bond portfolio, the mean return (as computed in Problem 12) was 9.65 percent. We can compute the sample standard deviation of returns as $s = 18.31$ percent using Equation 7-14. The coefficient of variation for the 60/40 portfolio was $CV = s/\overline{R} = 18.31/9.65 = 1.90$.

**ii.** For the MSCI Germany Index, $CV = s/\overline{R} = 29.95/10.80 = 2.77$.

**iii.** For the JPM Germany 5–7 Year GBI, $CV = s/\overline{R} = 6.94/7.92 = 0.88$.

**B.** The coefficient of variation is a measure of relative dispersion. For returns, it measures the amount of risk per unit of mean return. The MSCI Germany Index portfolio, the JPM Germany GBI, and the 60/40 equity/bond portfolio, were respectively most risky, least risky, and intermediate in risk, based on their values of CV.

| Portfolio | CV | Risk |
|---|---|---|
| MSCI Germany Index | 2.77 | Highest |
| 60/40 Equity/bond portfolio | 1.90 | |
| JPM Germany GBI | 0.88 | Lowest |

**14. A.**  **i.** For the 60/40 equity/bond portfolio, we earlier computed a mean return and standard deviation of return of 9.65 percent and 18.31, respectively. The statement of the problem gave the mean annual return on the proxy for the risk-free rate, the IMF Germany MMI, as 4.33 percent. We compute the Sharpe ratio as

$$S_h = \frac{\overline{R}_p - \overline{R}_F}{s_p} = \frac{9.65 - 4.33}{18.31} = 0.29$$

**ii.** For the MSCI Germany Index,

$$S_h = \frac{\overline{R}_p - \overline{R}_F}{s_p} = \frac{10.80 - 4.33}{29.95} = 0.22$$

**iii.** For the JPM Germany 5–7 Year GBI,

$$S_h = \frac{\overline{R}_p - \overline{R}_F}{s_p} = \frac{7.92 - 4.33}{6.94} = 0.52$$

**B.** The Sharpe ratio measures excess return per unit of risk as measured by standard deviation. Because we are comparing positive Sharpe ratios, a larger Sharpe ratio reflects better risk-adjusted performance. During the period, the JPM Germany GBI had the best risk-adjusted performance and the MSCI Germany Index had the worst risk-adjusted performance, as measured by the Sharpe ratio. The 60/40 equity/bond portfolio was intermediate in risk-adjusted performance.

| Portfolio | Sharpe Ratio | Performance |
|---|---|---|
| JPM Germany GBI | 0.52 | Best |
| 60/40 Equity/bond portfolio | 0.29 | |
| MSCI Germany Index | 0.22 | Worst |

**15. A.  i.** The arithmetic mean P/E is (13.67 + 14.43 + 28.06 + 18.46 + 11.91 + 15.80 + 14.24 + 6.44)/8 = 15.38.

   **ii.** Because the portfolio has an even number of stocks (eight), the median P/E is the mean of the P/Es in the $n/2 = 8/2 = $ 4th and $(n + 2)/2 = 10/2 = $ 5th positions in the data sorted in ascending order. (These are the middle two P/Es.) The fourth position P/E is 14.24, and the fifth position P/E is 14.43. The median P/E is (14.24 + 14.43)/2 = 14.34.

**B.  i.** The arithmetic mean P/S is (1.66 + 1.13 + 2.45 + 2.39 + 1.34 + 1.04 + 0.40 + 0.07)/8 = 1.31.

   **ii.** The median P/S is the mean of the P/Ss in the fourth and fifth positions in the data sorted in ascending order. The fourth position P/S is 1.13, and the fifth position P/S is 1.34. The median P/S is (1.13 + 1.34)/2 = 1.24.

**C.  i.** The arithmetic mean P/B is (3.43 + 1.96 + 382.72 + 1.65 + 1.30 + 1.70 + 2.13 + 41.31)/8 = 54.53.

   **ii.** The median P/B is the mean of the P/Bs in the fourth and fifth positions in the data sorted in ascending order. The fourth position P/B is 1.96, and the fifth position P/B is 2.13. The median P/B is (1.96 + 2.13)/2 = 2.05.

**D.  i.** The distribution of P/Es is not characterized by outliers (extreme values) and the mean P/E and median P/E at 15.38 and 14.34, respectively, are similar in magnitude. Both the mean P/E and the median P/E are appropriate measures of central tendency. Because the mean P/E uses all the information in the sample and is mathematically simpler than the median, however, we might give it preference.

   **ii.** Both the mean P/S and the median P/S are appropriate measures of central tendency. The mean P/S and median P/S at 1.31 and 1.24, respectively, are similar in magnitude. The P/S of 0.07 for Tenneco Automotive, Inc. is very small, yet it has only a moderate influence on the mean. As price is bounded from below at zero and sales are non-negative, the lowest possible P/S is 0. By contrast, there is no upper limit in theory on any price ratio. It is extremely high rather than extremely low P/Ss that would be the greater concern in using an arithmetic mean P/S. Note, too, that the P/E of about 6.4 for Tenneco, the lowest P/E observation, is not inconsistent with the P/S of 0.07 as long as the P/S is a valid observation (rather than a recording error).

   **iii.** The median P/B, but not the mean P/B, is an appropriate measure of central tendency. The mean P/B of 54.53 is unduly influenced by the extreme P/Bs of roughly 383 for Avon Products and roughly 41 for Tenneco Automotive. The case of Tenneco is interesting. The P/E and the P/S in particular appear to indicate that the stock is cheap in terms of the earnings and sales that a dollar buys; the P/B appears to indicate the reverse. Because book value is an accounting number subject to such decisions as write-downs, we might investigate whether book value per share for Tenneco and Avon reflects such actions.

**16. A.** With identical means, the two return distributions are similarly centered. Portfolio B's distribution has somewhat less dispersion, as measured by standard deviation. Both return distributions are asymmetric but in different ways. The return distribution for Portfolio A is negatively skewed; Portfolio B's distribution is positively skewed.

**B.** Most investors would prefer the return distribution of Portfolio B, which has the same mean return as Portfolio A but less risk as measured by standard deviation of return. Furthermore, Portfolio B's returns are positively skewed, indicating a higher frequency of very large positive returns relative to Portfolio A. In contrast, Portfolio A's returns are negatively skewed.

**17. A.** With identical means, the two return distributions are similarly centered. Portfolio B's distribution has somewhat more dispersion, as measured by standard deviation. Both return distributions are negatively skewed to the same degree. Both portfolios have very large excess kurtosis, indicating much more frequent returns at the extremes, both positive and negative, than for a normal distribution.

**B.** With identical mean returns and skewness, the comparison reduces to risk. Portfolio B is riskier as measured by standard deviation. Furthermore, risk–averse investors might view Portfolio B's more frequent extreme returns (both negative and positive), as indicated by greater kurtosis, as an additional risk element. Consequently, Portfolio A has the better risk–reward profile.

**18. A.** Portfolio B's returns are centered to the right of Portfolio A's, as indicated by mean return. Portfolio B's distribution has somewhat more dispersion than A's. Both return distributions are asymmetric but in different ways. The return distribution for Portfolio A is slightly negatively skewed. Portfolio B's distribution is moderately positively skewed. Portfolio A's return distribution is mesokurtic, and Portfolio B's return distribution is slightly platykurtic.

**B.** We cannot know which portfolio particular investors would prefer without knowing their exact preferences for risk and return. Portfolio B has a higher mean return and moderately positive skewness, but it also has more risk as measured by standard deviation of return.

**19.** To determine which evaluation criterion is the most difficult to achieve, we need to (i) calculate the mean return of the nine funds, (ii) calculate the median return of the nine funds, (iii) calculate two-thirds of the return of the best-performing fund, and (iv) compare the results.

  **i.** Calculate the mean return of the nine funds.
    Find the sum of the values in the table and divide by 9.

$$\overline{X} = (17.8 + 21.0 + 38.0 + 19.2 + 2.5 + 24.3 + 18.7 + 16.9 + 12.6)/9$$
$$= 171/9 = 19.0$$

  **ii.** Calculate the median return of the nine funds. The first step is to sort the returns from largest to smallest.

| Return | Ranking |
|--------|---------|
| 38.0%  | 9 |
| 24.3%  | 8 |
| 21.0%  | 7 |
| 19.2%  | 6 |
| 18.7%  | 5 |
| 17.8%  | 4 |
| 16.9%  | 3 |
| 12.6%  | 2 |
| 2.5%   | 1 |

The median is the middle item, which occupies the $(n + 1)/2 = 5$th position in this odd-numbered sample. We conclude that the median is 18.7.

iii. Calculate two-thirds of the return of the best-performing fund. The top return is 38.0; therefore, two-thirds of the top return is $(2/3)38.0 = 25.33$.

iv. The following table summarizes what we have learned about these funds.

| Criterion 1 | Criterion 2 | Criterion 3 |
|---|---|---|
| 19.0 | 18.7 | 25.3 |

Criterion 3, two-thirds of the return on the top fund, is the most difficult to meet.

In analyzing this problem, note that Criterion 3 is very sensitive to the value of the maximum observation. For example, if we were to subtract 10 from the maximum (to make it 28) and add 10 to the minimum (to make it 12.5), the mean and median would be unchanged. Criterion 3 would fall to two-thirds of 28, or 18.67. In this case, the mean, at 19.0, would be the most difficult criterion to achieve.

**20.** B is correct. Unless all the values of the observations in a data set have the same value, the harmonic mean is less than the corresponding geometric mean, which in turn is less than the corresponding arithmetic mean. In other words, regarding means, typically harmonic mean < geometric mean < arithmetic mean.

**21.** B is correct. A distribution with frequent small losses and a few large gains has positive skew (long tail on the right side) and the mean is greater than the median.

**22.** A is correct. The analyst's statement is not correct in reference to either portfolio. Portfolio A has a kurtosis of less than 3 meaning that it is less peaked than a normal distribution (platykurtic). Portfolio B is positively skewed (long tail on the right side of the distribution).

**23.** A is correct. The coefficient of variation is a relative measure of risk (dispersion) and is useful for both data sets that have different means and for data sets that do not have the same unit of measurement.

**24.** B is correct. The Sharpe ratio is the mean excess return (mean return less risk-free rate of 3.0 percent) divided by the standard deviation of the portfolio. It is highest for portfolio 2 with a Sharpe ratio of $7.5/20.3 = 0.3695$. For portfolio 1, the Sharpe ratio is $6.8/19.9 = 0.3417$ and for portfolio 3 the Sharpe ratio is $10.3/33.9 = 0.3038$.

**25.** C is correct. The coefficient of variation measures total risk per unit of return or standard deviation/mean return, or $15.7/11.8 = 1.33$. The Sharpe ratio is excess return per unit of risk or excess return/standard deviation. The mean excess return is $11.8\% - 5.0\% = 6.8\%$, so the Sharpe ratio is $6.8/15.7 = 0.43$.

# SOLUTIONS FOR READING 8

1. **A.** Probability is defined by the following two properties: (1) the probability of any event is a number between 0 and 1 inclusive, and (2) the sum of the probabilities of any set of mutually exclusive and exhaustive events equals 1.

   **B.** Conditional probability is the probability of a stated event, given that another event has occurred. For example $P(A \mid B)$ is the probability of $A$, given that $B$ has occurred.

   **C.** An event is any specified outcome or set of outcomes of a random variable.

   **D.** Two events are independent if the occurrence of one event does not affect the probability of occurrence of the other event. In symbols, two events $A$ and $B$ are independent if and only if $P(A \mid B) = P(A)$ or, equivalently, $P(B \mid A) = P(B)$.

   **E.** The variance of a random variable is the expected value (the probability-weighted average) of squared deviations from the random variable's expected value. In symbols, $\sigma^2(X) = E\{[X - E(X)]^2\}$.

2. One logical set of three mutually exclusive and exhaustive events for the reaction of a company's stock price on the day of a corporate earnings announcement is as follows (wording may vary):

   ▶ Stock price increases on the day of the announcement.

   ▶ Stock price does not change on the day of the announcement.

   ▶ Stock price decreases on the day of the announcement.

   In fact, there is an unlimited number of ways to split up the possible outcomes into three mutually exclusive and exhaustive events. For example, the following list also answers this question satisfactorily:

   ▶ Stock price increases by more than 4 percent on the day of the announcement.

   ▶ Stock price increases by 0 percent to 4 percent on the day of the announcement.

   ▶ Stock price decreases on the day of the announcement.

3. **A.** The probability is an empirical probability.

   **B.** The probability is a subjective probability.

   **C.** The probability is an a priori probability.

   **D.** The probability is a subjective probability.

4. The implied probabilities of 0.90 and 0.50 are inconsistent in that they create a potential profit opportunity. Compared with Relaxin shares, the shares of BestRest are relatively overvalued because their price incorporates a much higher probability of the favorable event (lifting of the trade restriction) than the shares of Relaxin.

5. The probability that at least one of the two orders executes is given by the addition rule for probabilities. Let $A$ stand for the event that *the first limit order executes before the close of trading* $[P(A) = 0.45]$ and let $B$ stand for the event that *the second limit order executes before the close of trading* $[P(B) = 0.20]$.

$P(AB)$ is given as 0.10. Therefore, $P(A \text{ or } B) = P(A) + P(B) - P(AB) = 0.45 + 0.20 - 0.10 = 0.55$. The probability that at least one of the two orders executes before the close of trading is 0.55.

6. Use Equation 8-1 to find this conditional probability: $P(\textit{stock is dividend paying} \mid \textit{telecom stock that meets criteria}) = P(\textit{stock is dividend paying and telecom stock that meets criteria}) / P(\textit{telecom stock that meets criteria}) = 0.01/0.05 = 0.20$.

7. According to the multiplication rule for independent events, the probability of a company meeting all three criteria is the product of the three probabilities. Labeling the event that a company passes the first, second, and third criteria, $A$, $B$, and $C$, respectively $P(ABC) = P(A)P(B)P(C) = (0.20)(0.45)(0.78) = 0.0702$. As a consequence, $(0.0702)(500) = 35.10$, so 35 companies pass the screen.

8. Use Equation 8-2, the multiplication rule for probabilities $P(AB) = P(A \mid B)P(B)$, defining $A$ as the event that *a stock meets the financial strength criteria* and defining $B$ as the event that *a stock meets the valuation criteria*. Then $P(AB) = P(A \mid B)P(B) = 0.40 \times 0.25 = 0.10$. The probability that a stock meets both the financial and valuation criteria is 0.10.

9. **A.** The default rate was ($\$109.8$ billion)/($\$669.5$ billion) $= 0.164$ or 16.4 percent. This result can be interpreted as the probability that $\$1$ invested in a market-value-weighted portfolio of U.S. high-yield bonds was subject to default in 2002.

   **B.** The odds against an event are denoted $E = [1 - P(E)]/P(E)$. In this case, the odds against default are $(1 - 0.164)/0.164 = 5.098$, or "5.1 to 1."

   **C.** First, note that $E(\textit{loss} \mid \textit{bond defaults}) = 1 - \$0.22 = \$0.78$. According to the total probability rule for expected value, $E(\textit{loss}) = E(\textit{loss} \mid \textit{bond defaults})P(\textit{bond defaults}) + E(\textit{loss} \mid \textit{bond does not default})P(\textit{bond does not default}) = (\$0.78)(0.164) + (\$0.0)(0.836) = 0.128$, or $\$0.128$. Thus, the institution's expected loss was approximately 13 cents per dollar of principal value invested.

10. **A.** Using Equation 8-7 for the expected value of a random variable (dollar amounts are in millions),

$$E(\text{Sales}) = 0.20(\$275) + 0.40(\$250) + 0.25(\$200) + 0.10(\$190) + 0.05(\$180) = \$233$$

   **B.** Using Equation 8-9 for variance,

$$\begin{aligned}\sigma^2(\text{Sales}) &= P(\$275)[\$275 - E(\text{Sales})]^2 + P(\$250)[\$250 - E(\text{Sales})]^2 \\ &\quad + P(\$200)[\$200 - E(\text{Sales})]^2 + P(\$190) \\ &\quad [\$190 - E(\text{Sales})]^2 + P(\$180)[\$180 - E(\text{Sales})]^2 \\ &= 0.20\,(\$275 - \$233)^2 + 0.40(\$250 - \$233)^2 \\ &\quad + 0.25(\$200 - \$233)^2 + 0.10(\$190 - \$233)^2 \\ &\quad + 0.05(\$180 - \$233)^2 \\ &= \$352.80 + \$115.60 + \$272.25 + \$184.90 + \$140.45 \\ &= \$1{,}066\ (\text{million})^2\end{aligned}$$

   **C.** The standard deviation of annual sales is $[\$1{,}066\ (\text{million})^2]^{1/2} = \$32.649655$ million, or $\$32.65$ million.

11. **A.** *Outcomes associated with Scenario 1:* With a 0.45 probability of a $\$0.90$ recovery per $\$1$ principal value, given Scenario 1, and with the probability of Scenario 1 equal to 0.75, the probability of recovering $\$0.90$ is $0.45\,(0.75) = 0.3375$. By a similar calculation, the probability of recovering $\$0.80$ is $0.55(0.75) = 0.4125$.

*Outcomes associated with Scenario 2:* With a 0.85 probability of a $0.50 recovery per $1 principal value, given Scenario 2, and with the probability of Scenario 2 equal to 0.25, the probability of recovering $0.50 is 0.85(0.25) = 0.2125. By a similar calculation, the probability of recovering $0.40 is 0.15(0.25) = 0.0375.

**B.** $E(recovery \mid Scenario\ 1) = 0.45(\$0.90) + 0.55(\$0.80) = \$0.845$

**C.** $E(recovery \mid Scenario\ 2) = 0.85(\$0.50) + 0.15(\$0.40) = \$0.485$

**D.** $E(recovery) = 0.75(\$0.845) + 0.25(\$0.485) = \$0.755$

**E.**

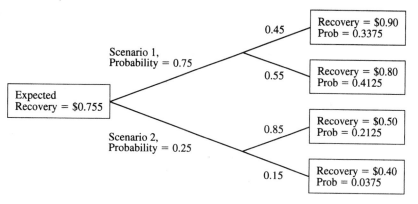

**12. A.** The diagonal entries in the covariance matrix are the variances, found by squaring the standard deviations.

Var(U.S. bond returns) = $0.409^2$ = 0.167281
Var(German bond returns) = $0.606^2$ = 0.367236
Var(Italian bond returns) = $0.635^2$ = 0.403225

The covariances are found using the relationship $\text{Cov}(R_i, R_j) = \rho(R_i, R_j)\sigma(R_i)\sigma(R_j)$.
There are three distinct covariances:

▶ Cov(U.S. bond returns, German bond returns) = ρ(U.S. bond returns, German bond returns)σ(U.S. bond returns)σ(German bond returns) = 0.09 × 0.409 × 0.606 = 0.022307

▶ Cov(U.S. bond returns, Italian bond returns) = ρ(U.S. bond returns, Italian bond returns)σ(U.S. bond returns)σ(Italian bond returns) = 0.10 × 0.409 × 0.635 = 0.025972

▶ Cov(German bond returns, Italian bond returns) = ρ(German bond returns, Italian bond returns)σ(German bond returns)σ(Italian bond returns) = 0.70 × 0.606 × 0.635 = 0.269367

### Covariance Matrix of Returns

|  | U.S. Bonds | German Bonds | Italian Bonds |
|---|---|---|---|
| U.S. Bonds | 0.167281 | 0.022307 | 0.025972 |
| German Bonds | 0.022307 | 0.367236 | 0.269367 |
| Italian Bonds | 0.025972 | 0.269367 | 0.403225 |

**B.** Using Equations 8-13 and 8-16, we find

$E(R_p)$ = 0.70 × 0.029 + 0.20 × 0.021 + 0.10 × 0.073 = 0.0318, or 3.2 percent

$$\sigma^2(R_p) = w_1^2\,\sigma^2(R_1) + w_2^2\,\sigma^2(R_2) + w_3^2\sigma^2(R_3) + 2w_1w_2\mathrm{Cov}(R_1, R_2)$$
$$+\ 2w_1w_3\mathrm{Cov}(R_1, R_3) + 2w_2w_3\,\mathrm{Cov}(R_2, R_3)$$
$$= (0.70)^2(0.167281) + (0.20)^2(0.367236) + (0.10)^2(0.403225)$$
$$+\ 2(0.70)(0.20)(0.022307) + 2(0.70)(0.10)(0.025972)$$
$$+\ 2(0.20)(0.10)(0.269367)$$
$$= (0.081968 + 0.014689 + 0.004032 + 0.006246 + 0.003636$$
$$+\ 0.010775$$
$$= 0.121346$$

**C.** The standard deviation of this portfolio is $\sqrt{\sigma^2(R_p)} = (0.121346)^{1/2} =$ 0.348348, or 34.8 percent.

**13.** A covariance matrix for five assets has $5 \times 5 = 25$ entries. Subtracting the five diagonal variance terms, we have $25 - 5 = 20$ off-diagonal entries. Because the covariance matrix is symmetric, only 10 entries are unique ($10 = 20/2$). Hence, you must use 10 unique covariances in your five-stock portfolio variance calculation.

**14.** The covariance is 25, computed as follows. First, we calculate expected values:

$$E(R_B) = (0.25 \times 30\%) + (0.50 \times 15\%) + (0.25 \times 10\%) = 17.5\%$$
$$E(R_Z) = (0.25 \times 15\%) + (0.50 \times 10\%) + (0.25 \times 5\%) = 10\%$$

Then we find the covariance as follows:

$$\mathrm{Cov}\ (R_B, R_Z) = P(30, 15) \times [(30 - 17.5) \times (15 - 10)] + P(15, 10)$$
$$\times\ [(15 - 17.5) \times (10 - 10)] + P(10, 5) \times [(10 - 17.5)$$
$$\times\ (5 - 10)]$$
$$= (0.25 \times 12.5 \times 5) + [0.50 \times (-2.5) \times 0] + [0.25$$
$$\times\ (-7.5) \times (-5)]$$
$$= 15.625 + 0 + 9.375 = 25$$

**15. A.** We can set up the equation using the total probability rule:

$$P(pass\ test) = P(pass\ test \mid survivor)P(survivor)$$
$$+\ P(pass\ test \mid nonsurvivor)P(nonsurvivor)$$

We know that $P(survivor) = 1 - P(nonsurvivor) = 1 - 0.40 = 0.60$. Therefore, $P(pass\ test) = 0.55 = 0.85(0.60) + P(pass\ test \mid nonsurvivor)(0.40)$. Thus $P(pass\ test \mid nonsurvivor) = [0.55 - 0.85(0.60)]/0.40 = 0.10$.

**B.** $P(survivor \mid pass\ test) = [P(pass\ test \mid survivor)/P(pass\ test)]P(survivor)$
$$= (0.85/0.55)0.60 = 0.927273$$

The information that a company passes the test causes you to update your probability that it is a survivor from 0.60 to approximately 0.927.

**C.** According to Bayes' formula, $P(nonsurvivor \mid fail\ test) = [P(fail\ test \mid nonsurvivor)/P(fail\ test)]P(nonsurvivor) = [P(fail\ test \mid nonsurvivor)/0.45]0.40$.
We can set up the following equation to obtain $P(fail\ test \mid nonsurvivor)$:

$$P(fail\ test) = P(fail\ test \mid nonsurvivor)P(nonsurvivor)$$
$$+\ P(fail\ test \mid survivor)P(survivor)$$
$$0.45 = P(fail\ test \mid nonsurvivor)0.40 + 0.15(0.60)$$

where $P(\textit{fail test} \mid \textit{survivor}) = 1 - P(\textit{pass test} \mid \textit{survivor}) = 1 - 0.85 = 0.15$. So $P(\textit{fail test} \mid \textit{nonsurvivor}) = [0.45 - 0.15(0.60)]/0.40 = 0.90$. Using this result with the formula above, we find $P(\textit{nonsurvivor} \mid \textit{fail test}) = (0.90/0.45)0.40 = 0.80$. Seeing that a company fails the test causes us to update the probability that it is a nonsurvivor from 0.40 to 0.80.

**D.** A company passing the test greatly increases our confidence that it is a survivor. A company failing the test doubles the probability that it is a nonsurvivor. Therefore, the test appears to be useful.

**16.** This is a labeling problem in which we assign each NYSE issue a label: advanced, declined, or unchanged. The expression to count the number of ways 3,292 issues can be assigned to these three categories such that 1,303 advanced, 1,764 declined, and 225 remained unchanged is $3{,}292!/(1{,}303!)(1{,}764!)(225!)$.

**17.** We find the answer using the combination formula $\binom{n}{r} = n!/[(n-r)!r!]$.

Here, $n = 10$ and $r = 4$, so the answer is $10!/[(10-4)!4!] = 3{,}628{,}800/(720)(24) = 210$.

**18. A.** The two events that affect a bondholder's returns are *the bond defaults* and *the bond does not default*. First, compute the value of the bond for the two events per \$1 invested.

|  | *The Bond Defaults* | *The Bond Does Not Default* |
|---|---|---|
| Bond value | $\theta \times \$(1 + R)$ | $\$(1 + R)$ |

Second, find the expected value of the bond (per \$1 invested):

$$E(\text{bond}) = \theta \times \$(1 + R) \times P(\textit{the bond defaults}) + \$(1 + R) \times [1 - P(\textit{the bond defaults})]$$

On the other hand, the expected value of the T-bill is the certain value $(1 + R_F)$. Setting the expected value of the bond to the expected value of the T-bill permits us to find the promised return on the bond such that bondholders expect to break even.

$$\theta \times \$(1 + R) \times P(\textit{the bond defaults}) + \$(1 + R) \times [1 - P(\textit{the bond defaults})] = \$(1 + R_F)$$

Rearranging the left-hand side,
$$(1 + R) \times \{\theta \times P(\textit{the bond defaults}) + [1 - P(\textit{the bond defaults})]\} = (1 + R_F)$$
$$R = (1 + R_F)/\{\theta \times P(\textit{the bond defaults}) + [1 - P(\textit{the bond defaults})]\} - 1$$

**B.** For this problem, $R_F = 0.058$, $P(\textit{the bond defaults}) = 0.06$, $1 - P(\textit{the bond defaults}) = 0.94$, and $\theta = 0.35$.

$$R = [1.058/(0.35(0.06) + 0.94)] - 1 = 0.100937, \text{ or } 10.1 \text{ percent}$$

With a recovery rate of 35 cents on the dollar, a minimum default risk premium of about 430 basis points is required, calculated as $4.3\% = 10.1\% - 5.8\%$.

**19.** B is correct. If scenario 1 occurs the expected recovery is 60%($50,000) + 40%($30,000) = $42,000 and if scenario 2 occurs the expected recovery is 90%($80,000) + 10%($60,000) = $78,000. Weighting by the probability of each scenario, the expected recovery is 40%($42,000) + 60%($78,000) = $63,600. Alternatively, first calculating the probability of each amount occurring, the expected recovery is (40%)(60%)($50,000) + (40%)(40%)($30,000) + (60%)(90%)($80,000) + (60%)(10%)($60,000) = $63,600.

**20.** B is correct. Correlations near positive 1.00 exhibit strong positive linearity; correlations near negative 1.00 exhibit strong negative linearity. Correlations of zero indicate no linear relation between variables. The closer the correlation is to zero, the weaker is the linear relationship.

# SOLUTIONS FOR READING 9

1. **A.** The put's minimum value is $0. The put's value is $0 when the stock price is at or above $100 at the maturity date of the option. The put's maximum value is $100 = $100 (the exercise price) − $0 (the lowest possible stock price). The put's value is $100 when the stock is worthless at the option's maturity date. The put's minimum price increments are $0.01. The possible outcomes of terminal put value are thus $0.00, $0.01, $0.02, . . . , $100.

   **B.** The price of the underlying has minimum price fluctuations of $0.01: These are the minimum price fluctuations for terminal put value. For example, if the stock finishes at $98.20, the payoff on the put is $100 − $98.20 = $1.80. We can specify that the nearest values to $1.80 are $1.79 and $1.81. With a continuous random variable, we cannot specify the nearest values. So, we must characterize terminal put value as a discrete random variable.

   **C.** The probability that terminal put value is less than or equal to $24 is $P(Y \le 24)$ or $F(24)$, in standard notation, where $F$ is the cumulative distribution function for terminal put value.

2. **A.** Because $f(2) = -0.01$ is negative, $f(X)$ cannot be a probability function. Probabilities are numbers between 0 and 1.

   **B.** The function $g(Y)$ does satisfy the conditions of a probability function: All the values of $g(Y)$ are between 0 and 1, and the values of $g(Y)$ sum to 1.

   **C.** The function $h(Z)$ cannot be a probability function: The values of $h(Z)$ sum to 1.02, which is more than 1.

3. A binomial random variable is defined as the number of successes in $n$ Bernoulli trials (a trial that produces one of two outcomes). The binomial distribution is used to make probability statements about a record of successes and failures or about anything with binary (twofold) outcomes.

4. **A.** The probability of an earnings increase (success) in a year is estimated as $7/10 = 0.70$ or 70 percent, based on the record of the past 10 years.

   **B.** The probability that earnings will increase in 5 out of the next 10 years is about 10.3 percent. Define a binomial random variable $X$, counting the number of earnings increases over the next 10 years. From Part A, the probability of an earnings increase in a given year is $p = 0.70$ and the number of trials (years) is $n = 10$. Equation 9-1 gives the probability that a binomial random variable has $x$ successes in $n$ trials, with the probability of success on a trial equal to $p$.

$$P(X = x) = \binom{n}{x} p^x (1 - p)^{n-x} = \frac{n!}{(n-x)! \, x!} p^x (1 - p)^{n-x}$$

For this example,

$$\binom{10}{5} 0.7^5 0.3^{10-5} = \frac{10!}{(10-5)! \, 5!} 0.7^5 0.3^{10-5}$$

$$= 252 \times 0.16807 \times 0.00243 = 0.102919$$

We conclude that the probability that earnings will increase in exactly 5 of the next 10 years is 0.1029, or approximately 10.3 percent.

Solutions to 1–19 taken from *Quantitative Methods for Investment Analysis*, Second Edition, by Richard A. DeFusco, CFA, Dennis W. McLeavey, CFA, Jerald E. Pinto, CFA, and David E. Runkle, CFA. Copyright © 2004 by CFA Institute. Reprinted with permission. All other solutions copyright © CFA Institute.

   **C.** The expected number of yearly increases is $E(X) = np = 10 \times 0.70 = 7$.

   **D.** The variance of the number of yearly increases over the next 10 years is $\sigma^2 = np\,(1 - p) = 10 \times 0.70 \times 0.30 = 2.1$. The standard deviation is 1.449 (the positive square root of 2.1).

   **E.** You must assume that (1) the probability of an earnings increase (success) is constant from year to year and (2) earnings increases are independent trials. If current and past earnings help forecast next year's earnings, Assumption 2 is violated. If the company's business is subject to economic or industry cycles, neither assumption is likely to hold.

**5.** The observed success rate is $4/7 = 0.571$, or 57.1 percent. The probability of four or fewer successes is $F(4) = p(4) + p(3) + p(2) + p(1) + p(0)$, where $p(4)$, $p(3)$, $p(2)$, $p(1)$, and $p(0)$ are respectively the probabilities of 4, 3, 2, 1, and 0 successes, according to the binomial distribution with $n = 7$ and $p = 0.70$. We have

$$p(4) = (7!/4!3!)(0.70^4)(0.30^3) = 35(0.006483) = 0.226895$$
$$p(3) = (7!/3!4!)(0.70^3)(0.30^4) = 35(0.002778) = 0.097241$$
$$p(2) = (7!/2!5!)(0.70^2)(0.30^5) = 21(0.001191) = 0.025005$$
$$p(1) = (7!/1!6!)(0.70^1)(0.30^6) = 7(0.000510) = 0.003572$$
$$p(0) = (7!/0!7!)(0.70^0)(0.30^7) = 1(0.000219) = 0.003572$$

Summing all these probabilities, you conclude that $F(4) = 0.226895 + 0.097241 + 0.025005 + 0.003572 + 0.000219 = 0.352931$, or 35.3 percent.

**6.** At each node of a binomial tree, we can test the condition that stock price is at or below the prespecified level. As in Figure 2, we calculate stock price at all nodes of the tree. We calculate the value of the call at the terminal nodes as a function of the terminal price of the stock. Using a model for discounting values by one period, we calculate call value one period earlier, and so forth, to reach $t = 0$. But at any node at which stock price is at or below the prespecified level, we automatically set call value to \$0.

**7.** **A.** The expected value of fourth-quarter sales is €14,500,000, calculated as (€14,000,000 + €15,000,000)/2. With a continuous uniform random variable, the mean or expected value is the midpoint between the smallest and largest values. (See Example 7.)

   **B.** The probability that fourth-quarter sales will be less than €14,125,000 is 0.125 or 12.5 percent, calculated as (€14,125,000 − €14,000,000)/(€15,000,000 − €14,000,000).

**8.** **A.** Approximately 68 percent of all outcomes of a normal random variable fall within plus or minus one standard deviation of the mean.

   **B.** Approximately 95 percent of all outcomes of a normal random variable fall within plus or minus two standard deviations of the mean.

   **C.** Approximately 99 percent of all outcomes of a normal random variable fall within plus or minus three standard deviations of the mean.

**9.** The area under the normal curve for $z = 0.36$ is 0.6406 or 64.06 percent. The table below presents an excerpt from the tables of the standard normal cumulative distribution function in the back of this book. To locate $z = 0.36$, find 0.30 in the fourth row of numbers, then look at the column for 0.06 (the second decimal place of 0.36). The entry is 0.6406.

| | | | | $P(Z \leq x) = N(x)$ for $x \geq 0$ or $P(Z \leq z) = N(z)$ for $z \geq 0$ | | | | | |
|---|---|---|---|---|---|---|---|---|---|
| *x* or *z* | 0 | 0.01 | 0.02 | 0.03 | 0.04 | 0.05 | 0.06 | 0.07 | 0.08 | 0.09 |
| **0.00** | 0.5000 | 0.5040 | 0.5080 | 0.5120 | 0.5160 | 0.5199 | 0.5239 | 0.5279 | 0.5319 | 0.5359 |
| **0.10** | 0.5398 | 0.5438 | 0.5478 | 0.5517 | 0.5557 | 0.5596 | 0.5636 | 0.5675 | 0.5714 | 0.5753 |
| **0.20** | 0.5793 | 0.5832 | 0.5871 | 0.5910 | 0.5948 | 0.5987 | 0.6026 | 0.6064 | 0.6103 | 0.6141 |
| **0.30** | 0.6179 | 0.6217 | 0.6255 | 0.6293 | 0.6331 | 0.6368 | **0.6406** | 0.6443 | 0.6480 | 0.6517 |
| **0.40** | 0.6554 | 0.6591 | 0.6628 | 0.6664 | 0.6700 | 0.6736 | 0.6772 | 0.6808 | 0.6844 | 0.6879 |
| **0.50** | 0.6915 | 0.6950 | 0.6985 | 0.7019 | 0.7054 | 0.7088 | 0.7123 | 0.7157 | 0.7190 | 0.7224 |

The interpretation of 64.06 percent for $z = 0.36$ is that 64.06 percent of observations on a standard normal random variable are smaller than or equal to the value 0.36. (So $100\% - 64.06\% = 35.94\%$ of the values are greater than 0.36.)

**10. A.** The probability of exhausting the liquidity pool is 4.7 percent. First calculate $x = \lambda/(\sigma\sqrt{T}) = \$2,000/(\$450\sqrt{5}) = 1.987616$. We can round this value to 1.99 to use the standard normal tables in the back of this book. Using those tables, we find that $N(1.99) = 0.9767$. Thus, the probability of exhausting the liquidity pool is $2[1 - N(1.99)] = 2(1 - 0.9767) = 0.0466$ or about 4.7 percent.

**B.** The probability of exhausting the liquidity pool is now 32.2 percent. The calculation follows the same steps as those in Part A. We calculate $x = \lambda/(\sigma\sqrt{T}) = \$2,000/(\$450\sqrt{20}) = 0.993808$. We can round this value to 0.99 to use the standard normal tables in the back of this book. Using those tables, we find that $N(0.99) = 0.8389$. Thus, the probability of exhausting the liquidity pool is $2[1 - N(0.99)] = 2(1 - 0.8389) = 0.3222$ or about 32.2 percent. This is a substantial probability that you will run out of funds to meet mark to market.

In their paper, Kolb et al. call the probability of exhausting the liquidity pool the probability of ruin, a traditional name for this type of calculation.

**11.** A 90 percent confidence interval for returns on large-cap blend funds is the interval $[-2.857\%, 4.997\%]$. An exact 90 percent confidence interval is equal to the mean plus and minus 1.65 standard deviations. The lower limit is $1.07\% - 1.65(2.38\%) = -2.857\%$. The upper limit is $1.07\% + 1.65(2.38\%) = 4.997\%$.

**12.** Under a normality assumption, the probability that the average large-cap growth fund will earn a negative monthly return is 34.5 percent. We calculate the standardized value as $(0\% - 1.15\%)/2.89\% = -0.397924$. Rounding this value to $-0.40$ to use the standard normal tables in the back of the book, we find that $N(-0.40) = 0.3446$. If you use a spreadsheet function on $-0.397924$, you will find $N(-0.397924) = 0.345343$.

**13.** The large-cap value fund category minimized the probability of earning a return less than the risk-free rate of return for the period. Large-cap value funds achieved the highest Sharpe ratio during the period. Recall from our discussion of Roy's safety-first criterion that the Sharpe ratio is equivalent to using the risk-free rate as the shortfall level in SFRatio, and the alternative with the largest SFRatio minimizes the probability of earning a return less than the shortfall level (under a normality assumption). Therefore, to answer the question, we select the alternative with the highest Sharpe ratio, the large-cap value fund.

**14. A.** Because £50,000/£1,350,000 is 3.7 percent, for any return less than 3.7 percent the client will need to invade principal if she takes out £50,000. So $R_L$ = 3.7 percent.

**B.** To decide which of the three allocations is safety-first optimal, select the alternative with the highest ratio $[E(R_P) - R_L]/\sigma_P$:

Allocation A: $0.5125 = (16 - 3.7)/24$

Allocation B: $0.488235 = (12 - 3.7)/17$

Allocation C: $0.525 = (10 - 3.7)/12$

Allocation D: $0.481818 = (9 - 3.7)/11$

Allocation C, with the largest ratio (0.525), is the best alternative according to the safety-first criterion.

**C.** To answer this question, note that $P(R_C < 3.7) = N(-0.525)$. We can round 0.525 to 0.53 for use with tables of the standard normal cdf. First, we calculate $N(-0.53) = 1 - N(0.53) = 1 - 0.7019 = 0.2981$ or about 30 percent. The safety-first optimal portfolio has a roughly 30 percent chance of not meeting a 3.7 percent return threshold.

**15. A.** Two important features of the lognormal distribution are that it is bounded below by 0 and it is right-skewed.

**B.** Normal random variables can be negative (the bell curve extends to the left without limit). In contrast, lognormal random variables cannot be negative. Asset prices also cannot be negative. So the lognormal distribution is superior to the normal as a probability model for asset prices.

**C.** The two parameters of a lognormal distribution are the mean and variance (or standard deviation) of the associated normal distribution. If $Y$ is lognormal and $Y = \ln X$, the two parameters of the distribution of $Y$ are the mean and variance (or standard deviation) of $X$.

**16.** To compute volatility for Dollar General Corporation, we begin by calculating the continuously compounded daily returns using Equation 9-5:

$$r_{t,t+1} = \ln(S_{t+1}/S_t) = \ln(1 + R_{t,t+1})$$

Then we find the variance of those continuously compounded returns, the sum of the squared deviations from the mean divided by 8 (the sample size of 9 continuously compounded returns minus 1). We take the square root of the variance to find the standard deviation. Finally, we multiply the standard deviation by $\sqrt{250}$ to annualize it.

The continuously compounded daily returns are (reading across the line, then down):

$\ln(10.87/10.68) = 0.017634$, $\ln(11.00/10.87) = 0.011889$,
$\ln(10.95/11.00) = -0.004556$, $\ln(11.26/10.95) = 0.027917$,
$\ln(11.31/11.26) = 0.004431$, $\ln(11.23/11.31) = -0.007099$,
$\ln(10.91/11.23) = -0.028909$, $\ln(10.80/10.91) = -0.010134$,
$\ln(10.47/10.80) = -0.031032$.

Sum = -0.019859, Mean = -0.002207, Variance = 0.000398, Standard deviation = 0.019937

The standard deviation of continuously compounded daily returns is 0.019937. Then $\sigma\sqrt{T} = 0.019937\sqrt{250} = 0.315232$ or 31.5 percent.

**17. A.** Elements that should appear in a definition of Monte Carlo simulation are that it makes use of a computer; that it is used to represent the operation of a complex system, or in some applications, to find an approximate solution to a problem; and that it involves the generation of a large number of random samples from a specified probability distribution. The exact wording can vary, but one definition follows:

Monte Carlo simulation in finance involves the use of a computer to represent the operation of a complex financial system. In some important applications, Monte Carlo simulation is used to find an approximate solution to a complex financial problem. An integral part of Monte Carlo simulation is the generation of a large number of random samples from a probability distribution.

**B.** *Strengths.* Monte Carlo simulation can be used to price complex securities for which no analytic expression is available, particularly European-style options.

*Weaknesses.* Monte Carlo simulation provides only statistical estimates, not exact results. Analytic methods, when available, provide more insight into cause-and-effect relationships than does Monte Carlo simulation.

**18.** In the text, we described how we could use Monte Carlo simulation to value an Asian option, a complex European-style option. Just as we can calculate the average value of the stock over a simulation trial to value an Asian option, we can also calculate the minimum value of the stock over a simulation trial. Then, for a given simulation trial, we can calculate the terminal value of the call, given the minimum value of the stock for the simulation trial. We can then discount back this terminal value to the present to get the value of the call today ($t = 0$). The average of these $t = 0$ values over all simulation trials is the Monte Carlo simulated value of the lookback call option.

**19.** C is correct. The portfolio with the highest safety-first ratio minimizes the probability that the portfolio return will be less than the shortfall level (given normality). In this problem, the shortfall level is equal to the risk-free rate of return and thus the highest safety-first ratio portfolio will be the same as the highest Sharpe ratio portfolio.

**20.** A is correct. A normal distribution is suitable for describing asset returns. However, the normal distribution is not suitable for asset prices because asset prices cannot be negative. The lognormal distribution is bounded by zero (skewed to the right) and is suitable for describing distributions of asset prices.

## SOLUTIONS FOR READING 10

1. **A.** The standard deviation or standard error of the sample mean is $\sigma_{\overline{X}} = \sigma/\sqrt{n}$. Substituting in the values for $\sigma_{\overline{X}}$ and $\sigma$, we have $1\% = 6\%/\sqrt{n}$, or $\sqrt{n} = 6$. Squaring this value, we get a random sample of $n = 36$.

   **B.** As in Part A, the standard deviation of sample mean is $\sigma_{\overline{X}} = \sigma/\sqrt{n}$. Substituting in the values for $\sigma_{\overline{X}}$ and $\sigma$, we have $0.25\% = 6\%/\sqrt{n}$, or $\sqrt{n} = 24$. Squaring this value, we get a random sample of $n = 576$, which is substantially larger than for Part A of this question.

2. **A.** Assume the sample size will be large and thus the 95 percent confidence interval for the mean of a sample of manager returns is $\overline{X} \pm 1.96s_{\overline{X}}$, where $s_{\overline{X}} = s/\sqrt{n}$. Munzi wants the distance between the upper limit and lower limit in the confidence interval to be 1 percent, which is

   $$(\overline{X} + 1.96s_{\overline{X}}) - (\overline{X} - 1.96s_{\overline{X}}) = 1\%$$

   Simplifying this equation, we get $2(1.96s_{\overline{X}}) = 1\%$. Finally, we have $3.92s_{\overline{X}} = 1\%$, which gives us the standard deviation of the sample mean, $s_{\overline{X}} = 0.255\%$. The distribution of sample means is $s_{\overline{X}} = s/\sqrt{n}$. Substituting in the values for $s_{\overline{X}}$ and $s$, we have $0.255\% = 4\%/\sqrt{n}$, or $\sqrt{n} = 15.69$. Squaring this value, we get a random sample of $n = 246$.

   **B.** With her budget, Munzi can pay for a sample of up to 100 observations, which is far short of the 246 observations needed. Munzi can either proceed with her current budget and settle for a wider confidence interval or she can raise her budget (to around $2,460) to get the sample size for a 1 percent width in her confidence interval.

3. **A.** This is a small-sample problem in which the sample comes from a normal population with a known standard deviation; thus we use the $z$-distribution in the solution. For a 95 percent confidence interval (and 2.5 percent in each tail), the critical $z$-value is 1.96. For returns that are normally distributed, a 95 percent confidence interval is of the form

   $$\mu + 1.96 \frac{\sigma}{\sqrt{n}}$$

   The lower limit is $X_l = \mu - 1.96 \dfrac{\sigma}{\sqrt{n}} = 6\% - 1.96 \dfrac{18\%}{\sqrt{4}} = 6\% - 1.96(9\%) = -11.64\%$.

   The upper limit is $X_u = \mu + 1.96 \dfrac{\sigma}{\sqrt{n}} = 6\% + 1.96 \dfrac{18\%}{\sqrt{4}} = 6\% + 1.96(9\%) = 23.64\%$.

   There is a 95 percent probability that four-year average returns will be between $-11.64$ percent and $+23.64$ percent.

   **B.** The critical $z$-value associated with the $-2.0$ percent return is

   $$Z = \frac{\overline{X} - \mu}{\sigma/\sqrt{n}} = \frac{-2\% - 6\%}{18\%/\sqrt{4}} = \frac{-8\%}{9\%} = -0.89$$

   Using a normal table, the probability of a $z$-value less than $-0.89$ is $P(Z < -0.89) = 0.1867$. Unfortunately, although your client is unhappy with the investment result, a four-year average return of $-2.0$ percent or lower should occur 18.67 percent of the time.

4. (Refer to Figure 1 to help visualize the answer to this question.) Basically, only one standard normal distribution exists, but many $t$-distributions exist—one for every different number of degrees of freedom. The normal distribution and the $t$-distribution for a large number of degrees of freedom are practically the same. The lower the degrees of freedom, the flatter the $t$-distribution becomes. The $t$-distribution has less mass (lower probabilities) in the center of the distribution and more mass (higher probabilities) out in both tails. Therefore, the confidence intervals based on $t$-values will be wider than those based on the normal distribution. Stated differently, the probability of being within a given number of standard deviations (such as within $\pm 1$ standard deviation or $\pm 2$ standard deviations) is lower for the $t$-distribution than for the normal distribution.

5. **A.** For a 99 percent confidence interval, the reliability factor we use is $t_{0.005}$; for df $= 20$, this factor is 2.845.

   **B.** For a 90 percent confidence interval, the reliability factor we use is $t_{0.05}$; for df $= 20$, this factor is 1.725.

   **C.** Degrees of freedom equals $n - 1$, or in this case $25 - 1 = 24$. For a 95 percent confidence interval, the reliability factor we use is $t_{0.025}$; for df $= 24$, this factor is 2.064.

   **D.** Degrees of freedom equals $16 - 1 = 15$. For a 95 percent confidence interval, the reliability factor we use is $t_{0.025}$; for df $= 15$, this factor is 2.131.

6. Because this is a small sample from a normal population and we have only the sample standard deviation, we use the following model to solve for the confidence interval of the population mean:

$$\overline{X} \pm t_{\alpha/2} \frac{s}{\sqrt{n}}$$

where we find $t_{0.025}$ (for a 95 percent confidence interval) for df $= n - 1 = 24 - 1 = 23$; this value is 2.069. Our solution is $1\% \pm 2.069(4\%)/\sqrt{24} = 1\% \pm 2.069(0.8165) = 1\% \pm 1.69$. The 95 percent confidence interval spans the range from $-0.69$ percent to $+2.69$ percent.

7. The following table summarizes the calculations used in the answers.

| Forecast $(X_i)$ | Number of Analysts $(n_i)$ | $X_i n_i$ | $(X_i - \overline{X})$ | $(X_i - \overline{X})^2$ | $(X_i - \overline{X})^2 n_i$ |
|---|---|---|---|---|---|
| 1.40 | 1 | 1.40 | $-0.05$ | 0.0025 | 0.0025 |
| 1.43 | 1 | 1.43 | $-0.02$ | 0.0004 | 0.0004 |
| 1.44 | 3 | 4.32 | $-0.01$ | 0.0001 | 0.0003 |
| 1.45 | 2 | 2.90 | 0.00 | 0.0000 | 0.0000 |
| 1.47 | 1 | 1.47 | 0.02 | 0.0004 | 0.0004 |
| 1.48 | 1 | 1.48 | 0.03 | 0.0009 | 0.0009 |
| 1.50 | 1 | 1.50 | 0.05 | 0.0025 | 0.0025 |
| Sums | 10 | 14.50 | | | 0.0070 |

**A.** With $n = 10$, $\overline{X} = \sum\limits_{i=1}^{10} X_i/n = 14.50/10 = 1.45$. The variance is

$$s^2 = \left[\sum_{i=1}^{10}(X_i - \overline{X})^2\right] / (n-1) = 0.0070/9 = 0.0007778.$$ The sample

standard deviation is $s = \sqrt{0.0007778} = 0.02789$.

**B.** The confidence interval for the mean can be estimated by using $\overline{X} \pm t_{\alpha/2}(s/\sqrt{n})$. For 9 degrees of freedom, the reliability factor, $t_{0.025}$, equals 2.262 and the confidence interval is $1.45 \pm 2.262 \times 0.02789/\sqrt{10} = 1.45 \pm 2.262(0.00882) = 1.45 \pm 0.02$. The confidence interval for the population mean ranges from 1.43 to 1.47.

**8.** The following table summarizes the calculations used in the answers.

| Forecast $(X_i)$ | Number of Analysts $(n_i)$ | $X_i n_i$ | $(X_i - \overline{X})$ | $(X_i - \overline{X})^2$ | $(X_i - \overline{X})^2 n_i$ |
|---|---|---|---|---|---|
| 0.70 | 2 | 1.40 | −0.04 | 0.0016 | 0.0032 |
| 0.72 | 4 | 2.88 | −0.02 | 0.0004 | 0.0016 |
| 0.74 | 1 | 0.74 | 0.00 | 0.0000 | 0.0000 |
| 0.75 | 3 | 2.25 | 0.01 | 0.0001 | 0.0003 |
| 0.76 | 1 | 0.76 | 0.02 | 0.0004 | 0.0004 |
| 0.77 | 1 | 0.77 | 0.03 | 0.0009 | 0.0009 |
| 0.82 | 1 | 0.82 | 0.08 | 0.0064 | 0.0064 |
| Sums | 13 | 9.62 | | | 0.0128 |

**A.** With $n = 13$, $\overline{X} = \sum\limits_{i=1}^{13} X_i/n = 9.62/13 = 0.74$. The variance is $s^2 =$

$$\left[\sum_{i=1}^{13}(X_i - \overline{X})^2\right] / (n-1) = 0.0128/12 = 0.001067.$$ The sample standard

deviation is $s^2 = \sqrt{0.001067} = 0.03266$.

**B.** The sample is small, and the distribution appears to be bimodal. We cannot compute a confidence interval for the population mean because we have probably sampled from a distribution that is not normal.

**9.** If the population variance is known, the confidence interval is

$$\overline{X} \pm z_{\alpha/2}\frac{\sigma}{\sqrt{n}}$$

The confidence interval for the population mean is centered at the sample mean, $\overline{X}$. The population standard deviation is $\sigma$, and the sample size is $n$. The population standard deviation divided by the square root of $n$ is the standard error of the estimate of the mean. The value of $z$ depends on the desired degree of confidence. For a 95 percent confidence interval, $z_{0.025} = 1.96$ and the confidence interval estimate is

$$\overline{X} \pm 1.96\frac{\sigma}{\sqrt{n}}$$

If the population variance is not known, we make two changes to the technique used when the population variance is known. First, we must use the sample standard deviation instead of the population standard deviation. Second, we use the *t*-distribution instead of the normal distribution. The critical *t*-value will depend on degrees of freedom $n - 1$. If the sample size is large, we have the alternative of using the *z*-distribution with the sample standard deviation.

**10. A.** The probabilities can be taken from a normal table, in which the critical *z*-values are 1.00, 2.00, or 3.00 and we are including the probabilities in both tails. The probabilities that the exchange rate will be at least 1, 2, or 3 standard deviations away from the mean are

$$P(\,|\,X - \mu\,| \geq 1\sigma) = 0.3174$$
$$P(\,|\,X - \mu\,| \geq 2\sigma) = 0.0456$$
$$P(\,|\,X - \mu\,| \geq 3\sigma) = 0.0026$$

**B.** With Chebyshev's inequality, the maximum probability of the exchange rate being at least *k* standard deviations from the mean is $P(\,|\,X - \mu\,| \geq k\sigma) \leq (1/k)^2$. The maximum probabilities of the rate being at least 1, 2, or 3 standard deviations away from the mean are

$$P(\,|\,X - \mu\,| \geq 1\sigma) \leq (1/1)^2 = 1.0000$$
$$P(\,|\,X - \mu\,| \geq 2\sigma) \leq (1/2)^2 = 0.2500$$
$$P(\,|\,X - \mu\,| \geq 3\sigma) \leq (1/3)^2 = 0.1111$$

The probability of the rate being outside 1, 2, or 3 standard deviations of the mean is much smaller with a known normal distribution than when the distribution is unknown and we are relying on Chebyshev's inequality.

**11.** No. If security returns were independent of each other, your colleague would be correct. We could diversify across a large number of investments and make the portfolio standard deviation very small, approaching zero. The returns of investments, however, are not independent; they are correlated with each other and with common market factors. Diversifying across many investments reduces *unsystematic* (stock-specific) risk, but it does not remove *systematic* (market) risk.

**12.** In many instances, the distribution that describes the underlying population is not normal or the distribution is not known. The central limit theorem states that if the sample size is large, regardless of the shape of the underlying population, the distribution of the sample mean is approximately normal. Therefore, even in these instances, we can still construct confidence intervals (and conduct tests of inference) as long as the sample size is large (generally $n \geq 30$).

**13.** The statement makes the following mistakes:

▶ Given the conditions in the statement, the distribution of $\overline{X}$ will be approximately normal only for large sample sizes.
▶ The statement omits the important element of the central limit theorem that the distribution of $\overline{X}$ will have mean $\mu$.

**14.** A is correct. The discrepancy arises from sampling error. Sampling error exists whenever one fails to observe every element of the population, because a sample statistic can vary from sample to sample. As stated in the reading, the sample mean is an unbiased estimator, a consistent estimator, and an efficient estimator of the population mean. Although the sample mean is an unbiased estimator of the population mean—the expected value of the sample mean equals the population mean—because of sampling error, we do not expect the sample mean to exactly equal the population mean in any one sample we may take.

15. No, we cannot say that Alcorn Mutual Funds as a group is superior to competitors. Alcorn Mutual Funds' advertisement may easily mislead readers because the advertisement does not show the performance of all its funds. In particular, Alcorn Mutual Funds is engaging in sample selection bias by presenting the investment results from its best-performing funds only.

16. The question raises the issue of whether above-average money management performance is the result of skill or luck. Assembling a group of above-average portfolio managers can be an attempt to exploit survivorship bias. We attempt it by hiring only managers with above-average records and by firing any managers that have below-average records. If past successful performance is a function of skill that can be repeated, then managers with above-average records will perform better than average in the future. An explanation for what is going on in the statement may be that past superior performance has resulted not from skill but from luck.

    Say we assume that performance is a matter of luck. Suppose there is a 0.5 chance for a manager to beat his or her benchmark. If we start out with 100 managers and define success as two benchmark-beating years in a row, we will have about 25 successful managers. Their successful track records will not predict future success if performance is random. If performance is random, no matter how we pick our managers, future performance will be above average about half the time and below average about half the time. If we wish to appraise skill, we must discount results that would happen by chance.

17. Spence may be guilty of data mining. He has used so many possible combinations of variables on so many stocks, it is not surprising that he found some instances in which a model worked. In fact, it would have been more surprising if he had not found any. To decide whether to use his model, you should do two things: First, ask that the model be tested on out-of-sample data—that is, data that were not used in building the model. The model may not be successful with out-of-sample data. Second, examine his model to make sure that the relationships in the model make economic sense, have a story, and have a future.

18. Hand Associates should use stratified random sampling for its portfolio that tracks the value-weighted index. Using 50–100 stocks to track 500 means that Hand will invest in all or almost all of the largest stocks in the index and few of the smallest. In addition to size, the stocks may be grouped by industry, riskiness, and other traits, and Hand Associates may select stocks to represent each of these groups or strata. For the equal-weighted index, Hand can use simple random sampling, in which each stock is equally likely to be chosen. Even in this case, however, Hand could use stratified random sampling to make sure it is choosing stocks that represent the various factors underlying stock performance.

19. A. An example of sample-selection bias is the failure to include the returns of delisted stocks in reporting portfolio returns. Because delisted stocks frequently are troubled stocks with poor returns, ignoring their returns will bias upwards the returns of portfolios that do not include them.

    B. An example of look-ahead bias is a statistician using data that were not yet available at the time a decision was being made. If you are building portfolios on January 1 of each year, you do not yet have the financial results for fiscal years ending on December 31. So, you do not know this information when you make investment decisions. Suppose a statistician is studying historical portfolio returns and has used annual accounting results to make portfolio selections at the beginning of each year. She is using a statistical model that assumes information is available several weeks before it is actually available. The results of such a model are biased.

**C.** One kind of time-period bias is an investment manager reporting the results from a short time period that give an inaccurate picture of the investment performance that might be expected over a longer time period. Time-period bias exists when a test is carried out for a time period that may make the results time-period specific. Another type of time-period bias arises with long time series. Long time series may give a more accurate picture of true investment performance than short time series, but they have the potential of including structural changes that would result in two different return distributions within the long period.

**20.** An estimator should have several desirable properties, including the following.

▶ Unbiasedness: The expected value of the estimator is equal to the population parameter.

▶ Efficiency: An efficient estimator is unbiased and has a smaller variance than all other unbiased estimators.

▶ Consistency: A consistent estimator tends to produce more accurate estimates of the population parameter as sample size increases.

**21.** C is correct. The *F*-statistic indicates that the regression results are statistically insignificant. Statistically, none of the variation in the dependent variable is explained by the independent variable, thus, the slope coefficient is equal to zero.

**22.** C is correct. As degrees of freedom increase, the *t*-distribution will more closely resemble a normal distribution, becoming more peaked and having less fat tails.

**23.** A is correct. All else equal, a larger sample size will decrease both the standard error and the width of the confidence interval. In other words, the precision of the estimate of the population parameter is increased.

## SOLUTIONS FOR READING 11

1. **A.** The null hypothesis is the hypothesis to be tested.

   **B.** The alternative hypothesis is the hypothesis accepted when the null hypothesis is rejected.

   **C.** A test statistic is a quantity, calculated on the basis of a sample, whose value is the basis for deciding whether to reject or not reject the null hypothesis.

   **D.** A Type I error, also called alpha, occurs when we reject a true null hypothesis.

   **E.** A Type II error, also called beta, occurs when we do not reject a false null hypothesis.

   **F.** The power of a test is the probability of correctly rejecting the null hypothesis (rejecting the null hypothesis when it is false).

   **G.** The rejection point (critical value) is a value against which a computed test statistic is compared to decide whether to reject or not reject the null hypothesis.

2. If we rejected the hypothesis of the equality of the mean debt-to-total-assets ratios of takeover target companies and non-takeover-target companies when, in fact, the means were equal, we would be committing a Type I error.

   On the other hand, if we failed to reject the equality of the mean debt-to-total-assets ratios of takeover target companies and non-takeover-target companies when the means were different, we would be committing a Type II error.

3. By the definition of $p$-value, 0.031 is the smallest level of significance at which we can reject the null hypothesis. Because 0.031 is smaller than 0.10 and 0.05, we can reject the null hypothesis at the 0.10 and 0.05 significance levels. Because 0.031 is larger than 0.01, however, we cannot reject the null hypothesis at the 0.01 significance level.

4. **A.** The appropriate test statistic is a $t$-statistic with $n - 1 = 15 - 1 = 14$ degrees of freedom. A $t$-statistic is theoretically correct when the sample comes from a normally distributed population with unknown variance. When the sample size is also small, there is no practical alternative.

   **B.** The appropriate test statistic is a $t$-statistic with $40 - 1 = 39$ degrees of freedom. A $t$-statistic is theoretically correct when the sample comes from a normally distributed population with unknown variance. When the sample size is large (generally, 30 or more is a "large" sample), it is also possible to use a $z$-statistic, whether the population is normally distributed or not. A test based on a $t$-statistic is more conservative than a $z$-statistic test.

   **C.** The appropriate test statistic is a $z$-statistic because the sample comes from a normally distributed population with known variance. (The known population standard deviation is used to compute the standard error of the mean using Equation 11-2 in the text.)

   **D.** The appropriate test statistic is chi-square ($\chi^2$) with $50 - 1 = 49$ degrees of freedom.

   **E.** The appropriate test statistic is the $F$-statistic (the ratio of the sample variances).

   **F.** The appropriate test statistic is a $t$-statistic for a paired observations test (a paired comparisons test), because the samples are correlated.

**G.** The appropriate test statistic is a $t$-statistic using a pooled estimate of the population variance. The $t$-statistic has $25 + 30 - 2 = 53$ degrees of freedom. This statistic is appropriate because the populations are normally distributed with unknown variances; because the variances are assumed equal, the observations can be pooled to estimate the common variance. The requirement of independent samples for using this statistic has been met.

**5. A.** With degrees of freedom (df) $n - 1 = 26 - 1 = 25$, the rejection point conditions for this two-sided test are $t > 2.060$ and $t < -2.060$. Because the significance level is 0.05, $0.05/2 = 0.025$ of the probability is in each tail. The tables give one-sided (one-tailed) probabilities, so we used the 0.025 column. Read across df $= 25$ to the $\alpha = 0.025$ column to find 2.060, the rejection point for the right tail. By symmetry, $-2.060$ is the rejection point for the left tail.

**B.** With df $= 39$, the rejection point conditions for this two-sided test are $t > 2.708$ and $t < -2.708$. This is a two-sided test, so we use the $0.01/2 = 0.005$ column. Read across df $= 39$ to the $\alpha = 0.005$ column to find 2.708, the rejection point for the right tail. By symmetry, $-2.708$ is the rejection point for the left tail.

**C.** With df $= 39$, the rejection point condition for this one-sided test is $t > 2.426$. Read across df $= 39$ to the $\alpha = 0.01$ column to find 2.426, the rejection point for the right tail. Because we have a "greater than" alternative, we are concerned with only the right tail.

**D.** With df $= 20$, the rejection point condition for this one-sided test is $t > 1.725$. Read across df $= 20$ to the $\alpha = 0.05$ column to find 1.725, the rejection point for the right tail. Because we have a "greater than" alternative, we are concerned with only the right tail.

**E.** With df $= 18$, the rejection point condition for this one-sided test is $t < -1.330$. Read across df $= 18$ to the $\alpha = 0.10$ column to find 1.330, the rejection point for the right tail. By symmetry, the rejection point for the left tail is $-1.330$.

**F.** With df $= 49$, the rejection point condition for this one-sided test is $t < -1.677$. Read across df $= 49$ to the $\alpha = 0.05$ column to find 1.677, the rejection point for the right tail. By symmetry, the rejection point for the left tail is $-1.677$.

**6.** Recall that with a $z$-test (in contrast to the $t$-test), we do not employ degrees of freedom. The standard normal distribution is a single distribution applicable to all $z$-tests. You should refer to "Rejection Points for a $z$-Test" in Section 3.1 to answer these questions.

**A.** This is a two-sided test at a 0.01 significance level. In Part C of "Rejection Points for a $z$-Test," we find that the rejection point conditions are $z > 2.575$ and $z < -2.575$.

**B.** This is a two-sided test at a 0.05 significance level. In Part B of "Rejection Points for a $z$-Test," we find that the rejection point conditions are $z > 1.96$ and $z < -1.96$.

**C.** This is a two-sided test at a 0.10 significance level. In Part A of "Rejection Points for a $z$-Test," we find that the rejection point conditions are $z > 1.645$ and $z < -1.645$.

**D.** This is a one-sided test at a 0.05 significance level. In Part B of "Rejection Points for a $z$-Test," we find that the rejection point condition for a test with a "greater than" alternative hypothesis is $z > 1.645$.

7. **A.** When sampling from a normally distributed population with known variance, the correct test statistic for hypothesis tests concerning the mean is the $z$-statistic.

   **B.** When sampling from a normally distributed population with unknown variance, the theoretically correct test statistic for hypothesis tests concerning the mean is the $t$-statistic.

   **C.** When the sample size is large, the central limit theorem applies. Consequently, the sample mean will be approximately normally distributed. When the population variance is not known, a test using the $t$-statistic is theoretically preferred. A test using the $z$-statistic is also sufficient when the sample size is large, as in this case.

8. **A.** As stated in the text, we often set up the "hoped for" or "suspected" condition as the alternative hypothesis. Here, that condition is that the population value of Willco's mean annual net income exceeds $24 million. Thus we have $H_0: \mu \le 24$ versus $H_a: \mu > 24$.

   **B.** Given that net income is normally distributed with unknown variance, the appropriate test statistic is $t$ with $n - 1 = 6 - 1 = 5$ degrees of freedom.

   **C.** In the $t$-distribution table in the back of the book, in the row for df $= 5$ under $\alpha = 0.05$, we read the rejection point (critical value) of 2.015. We will reject the null if $t > 2.015$.

   **D.** The $t$-test is given by Equation 11-4:

   $$t_5 = \frac{\overline{X} - \mu_0}{s/\sqrt{n}} = \frac{30 - 24}{10/\sqrt{6}} = \frac{6}{4.082483} = 1.469694$$

   or 1.47. Because 1.47 does not exceed 2.015, we do not reject the null hypothesis. The difference between the sample mean of $30 million and the hypothesized value of $24 million under the null is not statistically significant.

9. **A.** $H_0: \mu = 0$ versus $H_a: \mu \ne 0$.

   **B.** The $t$-test is based on $t = \dfrac{\overline{X} - \mu_0}{s/\sqrt{n}}$ with $n - 1 = 101 - 1 = 100$ degrees of freedom. At the 0.05 significance level, we reject the null if $t > 1.984$ or if $t < -1.984$. At the 0.01 significance level, we reject the null if $t > 2.626$ or if $t < -2.626$. For Analyst A, we have $t = (0.05 - 0)/(0.10/\sqrt{101}) = 0.05/0.00995 = 5.024938$ or 5.025. We clearly reject the null hypothesis at both the 0.05 and 0.01 levels.

   The calculation of the $z$-statistic with unknown variance, as in this case, is the same as the calculation of the $t$-statistic. The rejection point conditions for a two-tailed test are as follows: $z > 1.96$ and $z < -1.96$ at the 0.05 level; and $z > 2.575$ and $z < -2.575$ at the 0.01 level. Note that the $z$-test is a less conservative test than the $t$-test, so when the $z$-test is used, the null is easier to reject. Because $z = 5.025$ is greater than 2.575, we reject the null at the 0.01 level; we also reject the null at the 0.05 level.

   In summary, Analyst A's EPS forecasts appear to be biased upward—they tend to be too high.

   **C.** For Analyst B, the $t$-test is based on $t$ with $121 - 1 = 120$ degrees of freedom. At the 0.05 significance level, we reject the null if $t > 1.980$ or if $t < -1.980$. At the 0.01 significance level, we reject the null if $t > 2.617$ or if $t < -2.617$. We calculate $t = (0.02 - 0)/(0.09/\sqrt{121}) = 0.02/0.008182 = 2.444444$ or 2.44. Because $2.44 > 1.98$, we reject the null at the 0.05 level. However, 2.44 is not larger than 2.617, so we do not reject the null at the 0.01 level.

For a $z$-test, the rejection point conditions are the same as given in Part B, and we come to the same conclusions as with the $t$-test. Because $2.44 > 1.96$, we reject the null at the 0.05 significance level; however, because 2.44 is not greater than 2.575, we do not reject the null at the 0.01 level.

The mean forecast error of Analyst B is only $0.02; but because the test is based on a large number of observations, it is sufficient evidence to reject the null of mean zero forecast errors at the 0.05 level.

**10. A.** Stating the suspected condition as the alternative hypothesis, we have

$$H_0: \mu_1 - \mu_2 \le 0 \text{ versus } H_a: \mu_1 - \mu_2 > 0$$

where

$\mu_1$ = the population mean value of Analyst A's forecast errors
$\mu_2$ = the population mean value of Analyst B's forecast errors

**B.** We have two normally distributed populations with unknown variances. Based on the samples, it is reasonable to assume that the population variances are equal. The samples are assumed to be independent; this assumption is reasonable because the analysts cover quite different industries. The appropriate test statistic is $t$ using a pooled estimate of the common variance. The number of degrees of freedom is $n_1 + n_2 - 2 = 101 + 121 - 2 = 222 - 2 = 220$.

**C.** For df = 200 (the closest value to 220), the rejection point for a one-sided test at the 0.05 significance level is 1.653.

**D.** We first calculate the pooled estimate of variance:

$$s_p^2 = \frac{(n_1 - 1)s_1^2 + (n_2 - 1)s_2^2}{n_1 + n_2 - 2} = \frac{(101 - 1)(0.10)^2 + (121 - 1)(0.09)^2}{101 + 121 - 2}$$

$$= \frac{1.972}{220} = 0.008964$$

Then

$$t = \frac{(\overline{X}_1 - \overline{X}_2) - (\mu_1 - \mu_2)}{\left(\frac{s_p^2}{n_1} + \frac{s_p^2}{n_2}\right)^{1/2}} = \frac{(0.05 - 0.02) - 0}{\left(\frac{0.008964}{101} + \frac{0.008964}{121}\right)^{1/2}}$$

$$= \frac{0.03}{0.01276} = 2.351018$$

or 2.35. Because $2.35 > 1.653$, we reject the null hypothesis in favor of the alternative hypothesis that the population mean forecast error of Analyst A is greater than that of Analyst B.

**11. A.** The test statistic is

$$t = \frac{\overline{X}_1 - \overline{X}_2}{\left(\dfrac{s_1^2}{n_1} + \dfrac{s_2^2}{n_2}\right)^{1/2}}$$

where

$\overline{X}_1$ = sample mean recovery rate for utilities = 77.74

$\overline{X}_2$ = sample mean recovery rate for non-utility sectors = 42.56

$s_1^2$ = sample variance for utilities = $18.06^2$ = 326.1636

$s_2^2$ = sample variance for non-utilities = $24.89^2$ = 619.5121

$n_1$ = sample size of the utility sample = 32

$n_2$ = sample size of the non-utility sample = 189

Therefore, $t = (77.74 - 42.56)/[(326.1636/32) + (619.5121/189)]^{1/2} = 35.18/(10.192613 + 3.277842)^{1/2} = 35.18/3.670212 = 9.585$. The calculated $t$-statistic is thus 9.585.

**B.** Usually, we need to know degrees of freedom to determine whether a $t$-statistic is significant. The magnitude of the $t$-statistic is so large that in this case, there is actually no doubt about its significance even at the 0.01 level. For a two-sided test at the 0.01 level of significance, we look under the 0.005 column (0.01/2 = 0.005). For all but the very first two entries, for 1 and 2 degrees of freedom, the calculated test statistic is larger than the indicated rejection point (critical value). Clearly, with samples of size 32 and 189, there are more than 2 degrees of freedom.

**C.** This question confirms that we can calculate the degrees of freedom for the test, if needed:

$$\text{df} = \frac{\left(\dfrac{s_1^2}{n_1} + \dfrac{s_2^2}{n_2}\right)^2}{\dfrac{(s_1^2/n_1)^2}{n_1} + \dfrac{(s_2^2/n_2)^2}{n_2}} = \frac{\left(\dfrac{326.1636}{32} + \dfrac{619.5121}{189}\right)^2}{\dfrac{(326.1636/32)^2}{32} + \dfrac{(619.5121/189)^2}{189}}$$

$$= \frac{181.453139}{3.30339} = 54.93 \text{ or } 55 \text{ degrees of freedom.}$$

**12. A.** We test $H_0: \mu_d = 0$ versus $H_a: \mu_d \neq 0$.

**B.** This is a paired comparisons $t$-test with $n - 1 = 480 - 1 = 479$ degrees of freedom. At the 0.05 significance level, we reject the null hypothesis if either $t > 1.96$ or $t < -1.96$. We use df = $\infty$ in the $t$-distribution table under $\alpha = 0.025$ because we have a very large sample and a two-sided test.

$$t = \frac{\overline{d} - \mu_{d0}}{s_{\overline{d}}} = \frac{-0.258 - 0}{3.752/\sqrt{480}} = \frac{-0.258}{0.171255} = -1.506529 \text{ or } -1.51$$

At the 0.05 significance level, because neither rejection point condition is met, we do not reject the null hypothesis that the mean difference between the returns on the S&P 500 and small-cap stocks during the entire sample period was 0.

**C.** This $t$-test now has $n - 1 = 240 - 1 = 239$ degrees of freedom. At the 0.05 significance level, we reject the null hypothesis if either if $t > 1.972$ or $t < -1.972$, using df = 200 in the $t$-distribution tables.

$$t = \frac{\bar{d} - \mu_{d0}}{s_{\bar{d}}} = \frac{-0.640 - 0}{4.096/\sqrt{240}} = \frac{-0.640}{0.264396} = -2.420615 \text{ or } -2.42$$

Because $-2.42 < -1.972$, we reject the null hypothesis at the 0.05 significance level. During this subperiod, small-cap stocks significantly outperformed the S&P 500.

**D.** This $t$-test has $n - 1 = 240 - 1 = 239$ degrees of freedom. At the 0.05 significance level, we reject the null hypothesis if either if $t > 1.972$ or $t < -1.972$, using df = 200 in the $t$-distribution tables.

$$t = \frac{\bar{d} - \mu_{d0}}{s_{\bar{d}}} = \frac{0.125 - 0}{3.339/\sqrt{240}} = \frac{0.125}{0.215532} = 0.579962 \text{ or } 0.58$$

At the 0.05 significance level, because neither rejection point condition is met, we do not reject the null hypothesis that for the January 1980–December 1999 period, the mean difference between the returns on the S&P 500 and small-cap stocks was zero.

**13. A.** We have a "less than" alternative hypothesis, where $\sigma^2$ is the variance of return on the portfolio. The hypotheses are $H_0: \sigma^2 \geq 400$ versus $H_a: \sigma^2 < 400$, where 400 is the hypothesized value of variance, $\sigma_0^2$.

**B.** The test statistic is chi-square with $10 - 1 = 9$ degrees of freedom.

**C.** The rejection point is found across degrees of freedom of 9, under the 0.95 column (95 percent of probability above the value). It is 3.325. We will reject the null hypothesis if we find that $\chi^2 < 3.325$.

**D.** The test statistic is calculated as

$$\chi^2 = \frac{(n-1)s^2}{\sigma_0^2} = \frac{9 \times 15^2}{400} = \frac{2,025}{400} = 5.0625 \text{ or } 5.06$$

Because 5.06 is not less than 3.325, we do not reject the null hypothesis.

**14. A.** We have a "not equal to" alternative hypothesis:

$$H_0: \sigma^2_{Before} = \sigma^2_{After} \text{ versus } H_a: \sigma^2_{Before} \neq \sigma^2_{After}$$

**B.** To test a null hypothesis of the equality of two variances, we use an $F$-test:

$$F = \frac{s_1^2}{s_2^2}$$

**C.** The "before" sample variance is larger, so following a convention for calculating $F$-statistics, the "before" sample variance goes in the numerator. $F = 22.367/15.795 = 1.416$, with $120 - 1 = 119$ numerator and denominator degrees of freedom. Because this is a two-tailed test, we use $F$-tables for the 0.025 level (df = 0.05/2). Using the tables in the back of the book, the closest value to 119 is 120 degrees of freedom. At the 0.05 level, the rejection point is 1.43. (Using the Insert/Function/Statistical feature on a Microsoft Excel spreadsheet, we would find FINV(0.025, 119, 119) = 1.434859 as the critical $F$-value.) Because 1.416 is not greater than 1.43, we do not reject the null hypothesis that the "before" and "after" variances are equal.

**15. A.** We have a "not equal to" alternative hypothesis:

$$H_0: \rho = 0 \text{ versus } H_a: \rho \neq 0$$

**B.** We would use the nonparametric Spearman rank correlation coefficient to conduct the test.
**C.** Mutual fund expense ratios are bounded from above and below, and in practice there is at least a lower bound on alpha (as any return cannot be less than −100 percent). These variables are markedly non-normally distributed, and the assumptions of a parametric test are not likely to be fulfilled. Thus a nonparametric test appears to be appropriate.
**D.** The calculation of the Spearman rank correlation coefficient is given in the following table.

| Mutual Fund | 1 | 2 | 3 | 4 | 5 | 6 | 7 | 8 | 9 |
|---|---|---|---|---|---|---|---|---|---|
| Alpha ($X$) | −0.52 | −0.13 | −0.60 | −1.01 | −0.26 | −0.89 | −0.42 | −0.23 | −0.60 |
| Expense Ratio ($Y$) | 1.34 | 0.92 | 1.02 | 1.45 | 1.35 | 0.50 | 1.00 | 1.50 | 1.45 |
| $X$ Rank | 5 | 1 | 6.5 | 9 | 3 | 8 | 4 | 2 | 6.5 |
| $Y$ Rank | 5 | 8 | 6 | 2.5 | 4 | 9 | 7 | 1 | 2.5 |
| $d_i$ | 0 | −7 | 0.5 | 6.5 | −1 | −1 | −3 | 1 | 4 |
| $d_i^2$ | 0 | 49 | 0.25 | 42.25 | 1 | 1 | 9 | 1 | 16 |

$$r_S = 1 - \frac{6\Sigma d_i^2}{n(n^2 - 1)} = 1 - \frac{6(119.50)}{9(81 - 1)} = 0.0042$$

We use Table 11 to tabulate the rejection points for a test on the Spearman rank correlation. Given a sample size of 9 in a two-tailed test at a 0.05 significance level, the upper-tail rejection point is 0.6833 (we use the 0.025 column). Thus we reject the null hypothesis if the Spearman rank correlation coefficient is less than −0.6833 or greater than 0.6833. Because $r_S$ is equal to 0.0042, we do not reject the null hypothesis.

**16.** B is correct. Specifying a smaller significance level decreases the probability of a Type I error (rejecting a true null hypothesis), but increases the probability of a Type II error (not rejecting a false null hypothesis). As the level of significance decreases, the null hypothesis is less frequently rejected.

**17.** C is correct. The only way to avoid the trade-off between the two types of errors is to increase the sample size; increasing sample size (all else equal) reduces the probability of both types of errors. From the reading on sampling and estimations, all else equal, a larger sample size will decrease both the standard error and the width of the confidence interval. In other words, the precision of the estimate of the population parameter is increased.

## Appendix B    Cumulative Probabilities for a Standard Normal Distribution

$$P(Z \leq x) = N(x) \text{ for } x \geq 0 \text{ or } P(Z \leq z) = N(z) \text{ for } z \geq 0$$

| x or z | 0 | 0.01 | 0.02 | 0.03 | 0.04 | 0.05 | 0.06 | 0.07 | 0.08 | 0.09 |
|---|---|---|---|---|---|---|---|---|---|---|
| 0.00 | 0.5000 | 0.5040 | 0.5080 | 0.5120 | 0.5160 | 0.5199 | 0.5239 | 0.5279 | 0.5319 | 0.5359 |
| 0.10 | 0.5398 | 0.5438 | 0.5478 | 0.5517 | 0.5557 | 0.5596 | 0.5636 | 0.5675 | 0.5714 | 0.5753 |
| 0.20 | 0.5793 | 0.5832 | 0.5871 | 0.5910 | 0.5948 | 0.5987 | 0.6026 | 0.6064 | 0.6103 | 0.6141 |
| 0.30 | 0.6179 | 0.6217 | 0.6255 | 0.6293 | 0.6331 | 0.6368 | 0.6406 | 0.6443 | 0.6480 | 0.6517 |
| 0.40 | 0.6554 | 0.6591 | 0.6628 | 0.6664 | 0.6700 | 0.6736 | 0.6772 | 0.6808 | 0.6844 | 0.6879 |
| 0.50 | 0.6915 | 0.6950 | 0.6985 | 0.7019 | 0.7054 | 0.7088 | 0.7123 | 0.7157 | 0.7190 | 0.7224 |
| 0.60 | 0.7257 | 0.7291 | 0.7324 | 0.7357 | 0.7389 | 0.7422 | 0.7454 | 0.7486 | 0.7517 | 0.7549 |
| 0.70 | 0.7580 | 0.7611 | 0.7642 | 0.7673 | 0.7704 | 0.7734 | 0.7764 | 0.7794 | 0.7823 | 0.7852 |
| 0.80 | 0.7881 | 0.7910 | 0.7939 | 0.7967 | 0.7995 | 0.8023 | 0.8051 | 0.8078 | 0.8106 | 0.8133 |
| 0.90 | 0.8159 | 0.8186 | 0.8212 | 0.8238 | 0.8264 | 0.8289 | 0.8315 | 0.8340 | 0.8365 | 0.8389 |
| 1.00 | 0.8413 | 0.8438 | 0.8461 | 0.8485 | 0.8508 | 0.8531 | 0.8554 | 0.8577 | 0.8599 | 0.8621 |
| 1.10 | 0.8643 | 0.8665 | 0.8686 | 0.8708 | 0.8729 | 0.8749 | 0.8770 | 0.8790 | 0.8810 | 0.8830 |
| 1.20 | 0.8849 | 0.8869 | 0.8888 | 0.8907 | 0.8925 | 0.8944 | 0.8962 | 0.8980 | 0.8997 | 0.9015 |
| 1.30 | 0.9032 | 0.9049 | 0.9066 | 0.9082 | 0.9099 | 0.9115 | 0.9131 | 0.9147 | 0.9162 | 0.9177 |
| 1.40 | 0.9192 | 0.9207 | 0.9222 | 0.9236 | 0.9251 | 0.9265 | 0.9279 | 0.9292 | 0.9306 | 0.9319 |
| 1.50 | 0.9332 | 0.9345 | 0.9357 | 0.9370 | 0.9382 | 0.9394 | 0.9406 | 0.9418 | 0.9429 | 0.9441 |
| 1.60 | 0.9452 | 0.9463 | 0.9474 | 0.9484 | 0.9495 | 0.9505 | 0.9515 | 0.9525 | 0.9535 | 0.9545 |
| 1.70 | 0.9554 | 0.9564 | 0.9573 | 0.9582 | 0.9591 | 0.9599 | 0.9608 | 0.9616 | 0.9625 | 0.9633 |
| 1.80 | 0.9641 | 0.9649 | 0.9656 | 0.9664 | 0.9671 | 0.9678 | 0.9686 | 0.9693 | 0.9699 | 0.9706 |
| 1.90 | 0.9713 | 0.9719 | 0.9726 | 0.9732 | 0.9738 | 0.9744 | 0.9750 | 0.9756 | 0.9761 | 0.9767 |
| 2.00 | 0.9772 | 0.9778 | 0.9783 | 0.9788 | 0.9793 | 0.9798 | 0.9803 | 0.9808 | 0.9812 | 0.9817 |
| 2.10 | 0.9821 | 0.9826 | 0.9830 | 0.9834 | 0.9838 | 0.9842 | 0.9846 | 0.9850 | 0.9854 | 0.9857 |
| 2.20 | 0.9861 | 0.9864 | 0.9868 | 0.9871 | 0.9875 | 0.9878 | 0.9881 | 0.9884 | 0.9887 | 0.9890 |
| 2.30 | 0.9893 | 0.9896 | 0.9898 | 0.9901 | 0.9904 | 0.9906 | 0.9909 | 0.9911 | 0.9913 | 0.9916 |
| 2.40 | 0.9918 | 0.9920 | 0.9922 | 0.9925 | 0.9927 | 0.9929 | 0.9931 | 0.9932 | 0.9934 | 0.9936 |
| 2.50 | 0.9938 | 0.9940 | 0.9941 | 0.9943 | 0.9945 | 0.9946 | 0.9948 | 0.9949 | 0.9951 | 0.9952 |
| 2.60 | 0.9953 | 0.9955 | 0.9956 | 0.9957 | 0.9959 | 0.9960 | 0.9961 | 0.9962 | 0.9963 | 0.9964 |
| 2.70 | 0.9965 | 0.9966 | 0.9967 | 0.9968 | 0.9969 | 0.9970 | 0.9971 | 0.9972 | 0.9973 | 0.9974 |
| 2.80 | 0.9974 | 0.9975 | 0.9976 | 0.9977 | 0.9977 | 0.9978 | 0.9979 | 0.9979 | 0.9980 | 0.9981 |
| 2.90 | 0.9981 | 0.9982 | 0.9982 | 0.9983 | 0.9984 | 0.9984 | 0.9985 | 0.9985 | 0.9986 | 0.9986 |
| 3.00 | 0.9987 | 0.9987 | 0.9987 | 0.9988 | 0.9988 | 0.9989 | 0.9989 | 0.9989 | 0.9990 | 0.9990 |
| 3.10 | 0.9990 | 0.9991 | 0.9991 | 0.9991 | 0.9992 | 0.9992 | 0.9992 | 0.9992 | 0.9993 | 0.9993 |
| 3.20 | 0.9993 | 0.9993 | 0.9994 | 0.9994 | 0.9994 | 0.9994 | 0.9994 | 0.9995 | 0.9995 | 0.9995 |
| 3.30 | 0.9995 | 0.9995 | 0.9995 | 0.9996 | 0.9996 | 0.9996 | 0.9996 | 0.9996 | 0.9996 | 0.9997 |
| 3.40 | 0.9997 | 0.9997 | 0.9997 | 0.9997 | 0.9997 | 0.9997 | 0.9997 | 0.9997 | 0.9997 | 0.9998 |
| 3.50 | 0.9998 | 0.9998 | 0.9998 | 0.9998 | 0.9998 | 0.9998 | 0.9998 | 0.9998 | 0.9998 | 0.9998 |
| 3.60 | 0.9998 | 0.9998 | 0.9999 | 0.9999 | 0.9999 | 0.9999 | 0.9999 | 0.9999 | 0.9999 | 0.9999 |
| 3.70 | 0.9999 | 0.9999 | 0.9999 | 0.9999 | 0.9999 | 0.9999 | 0.9999 | 0.9999 | 0.9999 | 0.9999 |
| 3.80 | 0.9999 | 0.9999 | 0.9999 | 0.9999 | 0.9999 | 0.9999 | 0.9999 | 0.9999 | 0.9999 | 0.9999 |
| 3.90 | 1.0000 | 1.0000 | 1.0000 | 1.0000 | 1.0000 | 1.0000 | 1.0000 | 1.0000 | 1.0000 | 1.0000 |
| 4.00 | 1.0000 | 1.0000 | 1.0000 | 1.0000 | 1.0000 | 1.0000 | 1.0000 | 1.0000 | 1.0000 | 1.0000 |

For example, to find the z-value leaving 2.5 percent of the area/probability in the upper tail, find the element 0.9750 in the body of the table. Read 1.90 at the left end of the element's row and 0.06 at the top of the element's column, to give 1.90 + 0.06 = 1.96. *Table generated with Excel.*

*Quantitative Methods for Investment Analysis*, Second Edition, by Richard A. DeFusco, CFA, Dennis W. McLeavey, CFA, Jerald E. Pinto, CFA, and David E. Runkle, CFA. Copyright © 2004 by CFA Institute. Reprinted with permission.

## Appendix B (continued)
## Cumulative Probabilities for a Standard Normal Distribution
$P(Z \leq x) = N(x)$ for $x \leq 0$ or $P(Z \leq z) = N(z)$ for $z \leq 0$

| x or z | 0 | 0.01 | 0.02 | 0.03 | 0.04 | 0.05 | 0.06 | 0.07 | 0.08 | 0.09 |
|---|---|---|---|---|---|---|---|---|---|---|
| 0.00 | 0.5000 | 0.4960 | 0.4920 | 0.4880 | 0.4840 | 0.4801 | 0.4761 | 0.4721 | 0.4681 | 0.4641 |
| −0.10 | 0.4602 | 0.4562 | 0.4522 | 0.4483 | 0.4443 | 0.4404 | 0.4364 | 0.4325 | 0.4286 | 0.4247 |
| −0.20 | 0.4207 | 0.4168 | 0.4129 | 0.4090 | 0.4052 | 0.4013 | 0.3974 | 0.3936 | 0.3897 | 0.3859 |
| −0.30 | 0.3821 | 0.3783 | 0.3745 | 0.3707 | 0.3669 | 0.3632 | 0.3594 | 0.3557 | 0.3520 | 0.3483 |
| −0.40 | 0.3446 | 0.3409 | 0.3372 | 0.3336 | 0.3300 | 0.3264 | 0.3228 | 0.3192 | 0.3156 | 0.3121 |
| −0.50 | 0.3085 | 0.3050 | 0.3015 | 0.2981 | 0.2946 | 0.2912 | 0.2877 | 0.2843 | 0.2810 | 0.2776 |
| −0.60 | 0.2743 | 0.2709 | 0.2676 | 0.2643 | 0.2611 | 0.2578 | 0.2546 | 0.2514 | 0.2483 | 0.2451 |
| −0.70 | 0.2420 | 0.2389 | 0.2358 | 0.2327 | 0.2296 | 0.2266 | 0.2236 | 0.2206 | 0.2177 | 0.2148 |
| −0.80 | 0.2119 | 0.2090 | 0.2061 | 0.2033 | 0.2005 | 0.1977 | 0.1949 | 0.1922 | 0.1894 | 0.1867 |
| −0.90 | 0.1841 | 0.1814 | 0.1788 | 0.1762 | 0.1736 | 0.1711 | 0.1685 | 0.1660 | 0.1635 | 0.1611 |
| −1.00 | 0.1587 | 0.1562 | 0.1539 | 0.1515 | 0.1492 | 0.1469 | 0.1446 | 0.1423 | 0.1401 | 0.1379 |
| −1.10 | 0.1357 | 0.1335 | 0.1314 | 0.1292 | 0.1271 | 0.1251 | 0.1230 | 0.1210 | 0.1190 | 0.1170 |
| −1.20 | 0.1151 | 0.1131 | 0.1112 | 0.1093 | 0.1075 | 0.1056 | 0.1038 | 0.1020 | 0.1003 | 0.0985 |
| −1.30 | 0.0968 | 0.0951 | 0.0934 | 0.0918 | 0.0901 | 0.0885 | 0.0869 | 0.0853 | 0.0838 | 0.0823 |
| −1.40 | 0.0808 | 0.0793 | 0.0778 | 0.0764 | 0.0749 | 0.0735 | 0.0721 | 0.0708 | 0.0694 | 0.0681 |
| −1.50 | 0.0668 | 0.0655 | 0.0643 | 0.0630 | 0.0618 | 0.0606 | 0.0594 | 0.0582 | 0.0571 | 0.0559 |
| −1.60 | 0.0548 | 0.0537 | 0.0526 | 0.0516 | 0.0505 | 0.0495 | 0.0485 | 0.0475 | 0.0465 | 0.0455 |
| −1.70 | 0.0446 | 0.0436 | 0.0427 | 0.0418 | 0.0409 | 0.0401 | 0.0392 | 0.0384 | 0.0375 | 0.0367 |
| −1.80 | 0.0359 | 0.0351 | 0.0344 | 0.0336 | 0.0329 | 0.0322 | 0.0314 | 0.0307 | 0.0301 | 0.0294 |
| −1.90 | 0.0287 | 0.0281 | 0.0274 | 0.0268 | 0.0262 | 0.0256 | 0.0250 | 0.0244 | 0.0239 | 0.0233 |
| −2.00 | 0.0228 | 0.0222 | 0.0217 | 0.0212 | 0.0207 | 0.0202 | 0.0197 | 0.0192 | 0.0188 | 0.0183 |
| −2.10 | 0.0179 | 0.0174 | 0.0170 | 0.0166 | 0.0162 | 0.0158 | 0.0154 | 0.0150 | 0.0146 | 0.0143 |
| −2.20 | 0.0139 | 0.0136 | 0.0132 | 0.0129 | 0.0125 | 0.0122 | 0.0119 | 0.0116 | 0.0113 | 0.0110 |
| −2.30 | 0.0107 | 0.0104 | 0.0102 | 0.0099 | 0.0096 | 0.0094 | 0.0091 | 0.0089 | 0.0087 | 0.0084 |
| −2.40 | 0.0082 | 0.0080 | 0.0078 | 0.0075 | 0.0073 | 0.0071 | 0.0069 | 0.0068 | 0.0066 | 0.0064 |
| −2.50 | 0.0062 | 0.0060 | 0.0059 | 0.0057 | 0.0055 | 0.0054 | 0.0052 | 0.0051 | 0.0049 | 0.0048 |
| −2.60 | 0.0047 | 0.0045 | 0.0044 | 0.0043 | 0.0041 | 0.0040 | 0.0039 | 0.0038 | 0.0037 | 0.0036 |
| −2.70 | 0.0035 | 0.0034 | 0.0033 | 0.0032 | 0.0031 | 0.0030 | 0.0029 | 0.0028 | 0.0027 | 0.0026 |
| −2.80 | 0.0026 | 0.0025 | 0.0024 | 0.0023 | 0.0023 | 0.0022 | 0.0021 | 0.0021 | 0.0020 | 0.0019 |
| −2.90 | 0.0019 | 0.0018 | 0.0018 | 0.0017 | 0.0016 | 0.0016 | 0.0015 | 0.0015 | 0.0014 | 0.0014 |
| −3.00 | 0.0013 | 0.0013 | 0.0013 | 0.0012 | 0.0012 | 0.0011 | 0.0011 | 0.0011 | 0.0010 | 0.0010 |
| −3.10 | 0.0010 | 0.0009 | 0.0009 | 0.0009 | 0.0008 | 0.0008 | 0.0008 | 0.0008 | 0.0007 | 0.0007 |
| −3.20 | 0.0007 | 0.0007 | 0.0006 | 0.0006 | 0.0006 | 0.0006 | 0.0006 | 0.0005 | 0.0005 | 0.0005 |
| −3.30 | 0.0005 | 0.0005 | 0.0005 | 0.0004 | 0.0004 | 0.0004 | 0.0004 | 0.0004 | 0.0004 | 0.0003 |
| −3.40 | 0.0003 | 0.0003 | 0.0003 | 0.0003 | 0.0003 | 0.0003 | 0.0003 | 0.0003 | 0.0003 | 0.0002 |
| −3.50 | 0.0002 | 0.0002 | 0.0002 | 0.0002 | 0.0002 | 0.0002 | 0.0002 | 0.0002 | 0.0002 | 0.0002 |
| −3.60 | 0.0002 | 0.0002 | 0.0001 | 0.0001 | 0.0001 | 0.0001 | 0.0001 | 0.0001 | 0.0001 | 0.0001 |
| −3.70 | 0.0001 | 0.0001 | 0.0001 | 0.0001 | 0.0001 | 0.0001 | 0.0001 | 0.0001 | 0.0001 | 0.0001 |
| −3.80 | 0.0001 | 0.0001 | 0.0001 | 0.0001 | 0.0001 | 0.0001 | 0.0001 | 0.0001 | 0.0001 | 0.0001 |
| −3.90 | 0.0000 | 0.0000 | 0.0000 | 0.0000 | 0.0000 | 0.0000 | 0.0000 | 0.0000 | 0.0000 | 0.0000 |
| −4.00 | 0.0000 | 0.0000 | 0.0000 | 0.0000 | 0.0000 | 0.0000 | 0.0000 | 0.0000 | 0.0000 | 0.0000 |

For example, to find the z-value leaving 2.5 percent of the area/probability in the lower tail, find the element 0.0250 in the body of the table. Read −1.90 at the left end of the element's row and 0.06 at the top of the element's column, to give −1.90 − 0.06 = −1.96. *Table generated with Excel.*

## Appendix C    Table of the Student's t-Distribution (One-Tailed Probabilities)

| df | p = 0.10 | p = 0.05 | p = 0.025 | p = 0.01 | p = 0.005 |
|---|---|---|---|---|---|
| 1 | 3.078 | 6.314 | 12.706 | 31.821 | 63.657 |
| 2 | 1.886 | 2.920 | 4.303 | 6.965 | 9.925 |
| 3 | 1.638 | 2.353 | 3.182 | 4.541 | 5.841 |
| 4 | 1.533 | 2.132 | 2.776 | 3.747 | 4.604 |
| 5 | 1.476 | 2.015 | 2.571 | 3.365 | 4.032 |
| 6 | 1.440 | 1.943 | 2.447 | 3.143 | 3.707 |
| 7 | 1.415 | 1.895 | 2.365 | 2.998 | 3.499 |
| 8 | 1.397 | 1.860 | 2.306 | 2.896 | 3.355 |
| 9 | 1.383 | 1.833 | 2.262 | 2.821 | 3.250 |
| 10 | 1.372 | 1.812 | 2.228 | 2.764 | 3.169 |
| 11 | 1.363 | 1.796 | 2.201 | 2.718 | 3.106 |
| 12 | 1.356 | 1.782 | 2.179 | 2.681 | 3.055 |
| 13 | 1.350 | 1.771 | 2.160 | 2.650 | 3.012 |
| 14 | 1.345 | 1.761 | 2.145 | 2.624 | 2.977 |
| 15 | 1.341 | 1.753 | 2.131 | 2.602 | 2.947 |
| 16 | 1.337 | 1.746 | 2.120 | 2.583 | 2.921 |
| 17 | 1.333 | 1.740 | 2.110 | 2.567 | 2.898 |
| 18 | 1.330 | 1.734 | 2.101 | 2.552 | 2.878 |
| 19 | 1.328 | 1.729 | 2.093 | 2.539 | 2.861 |
| 20 | 1.325 | 1.725 | 2.086 | 2.528 | 2.845 |
| 21 | 1.323 | 1.721 | 2.080 | 2.518 | 2.831 |
| 22 | 1.321 | 1.717 | 2.074 | 2.508 | 2.819 |
| 23 | 1.319 | 1.714 | 2.069 | 2.500 | 2.807 |
| 24 | 1.318 | 1.711 | 2.064 | 2.492 | 2.797 |
| 25 | 1.316 | 1.708 | 2.060 | 2.485 | 2.787 |
| 26 | 1.315 | 1.706 | 2.056 | 2.479 | 2.779 |
| 27 | 1.314 | 1.703 | 2.052 | 2.473 | 2.771 |
| 28 | 1.313 | 1.701 | 2.048 | 2.467 | 2.763 |
| 29 | 1.311 | 1.699 | 2.045 | 2.462 | 2.756 |
| 30 | 1.310 | 1.697 | 2.042 | 2.457 | 2.750 |

| df | p = 0.10 | p = 0.05 | p = 0.025 | p = 0.01 | p = 0.005 |
|---|---|---|---|---|---|
| 31 | 1.309 | 1.696 | 2.040 | 2.453 | 2.744 |
| 32 | 1.309 | 1.694 | 2.037 | 2.449 | 2.738 |
| 33 | 1.308 | 1.692 | 2.035 | 2.445 | 2.733 |
| 34 | 1.307 | 1.691 | 2.032 | 2.441 | 2.728 |
| 35 | 1.306 | 1.690 | 2.030 | 2.438 | 2.724 |
| 36 | 1.306 | 1.688 | 2.028 | 2.434 | 2.719 |
| 37 | 1.305 | 1.687 | 2.026 | 2.431 | 2.715 |
| 38 | 1.304 | 1.686 | 2.024 | 2.429 | 2.712 |
| 39 | 1.304 | 1.685 | 2.023 | 2.426 | 2.708 |
| 40 | 1.303 | 1.684 | 2.021 | 2.423 | 2.704 |
| 41 | 1.303 | 1.683 | 2.020 | 2.421 | 2.701 |
| 42 | 1.302 | 1.682 | 2.018 | 2.418 | 2.698 |
| 43 | 1.302 | 1.681 | 2.017 | 2.416 | 2.695 |
| 44 | 1.301 | 1.680 | 2.015 | 2.414 | 2.692 |
| 45 | 1.301 | 1.679 | 2.014 | 2.412 | 2.690 |
| 46 | 1.300 | 1.679 | 2.013 | 2.410 | 2.687 |
| 47 | 1.300 | 1.678 | 2.012 | 2.408 | 2.685 |
| 48 | 1.299 | 1.677 | 2.011 | 2.407 | 2.682 |
| 49 | 1.299 | 1.677 | 2.010 | 2.405 | 2.680 |
| 50 | 1.299 | 1.676 | 2.009 | 2.403 | 2.678 |
| 60 | 1.296 | 1.671 | 2.000 | 2.390 | 2.660 |
| 70 | 1.294 | 1.667 | 1.994 | 2.381 | 2.648 |
| 80 | 1.292 | 1.664 | 1.990 | 2.374 | 2.639 |
| 90 | 1.291 | 1.662 | 1.987 | 2.368 | 2.632 |
| 100 | 1.290 | 1.660 | 1.984 | 2.364 | 2.626 |
| 110 | 1.289 | 1.659 | 1.982 | 2.361 | 2.621 |
| 120 | 1.289 | 1.658 | 1.980 | 2.358 | 2.617 |
| 200 | 1.286 | 1.653 | 1.972 | 2.345 | 2.601 |
| ∞ | 1.282 | 1.645 | 1.960 | 2.326 | 2.576 |

To find a critical t-value, enter the table with df and a specified value for $\alpha$, the significance level. For example, with 5 df, $\alpha = 0.05$ and a one-tailed test, the desired probability in the tail would be $p = 0.05$ and the critical t-value would be $t(5, 0.05) = 2.015$. With $\alpha = 0.05$ and a two-tailed test, the desired probability in each tail would be $p = 0.025 = \alpha/2$, giving $t(0.025) = 2.571$. Table generated using Excel.

*Quantitative Methods for Investment Analysis*, Second Edition, by Richard A. DeFusco, CFA, Dennis W. McLeavey, CFA, Jerald E. Pinto, CFA, and David E. Runkle, CFA. Copyright © 2004 by CFA Institute. Reprinted with permission.

## Appendix D  Values of $\chi^2$ (Degrees of Freedom, Level of Significance)

| Degrees of Freedom | Probability in Right Tail | | | | | | | | |
|---|---|---|---|---|---|---|---|---|---|
|  | 0.99 | 0.975 | 0.95 | 0.9 | 0.1 | 0.05 | 0.025 | 0.01 | 0.005 |
| 1 | 0.000157 | 0.000982 | 0.003932 | 0.0158 | 2.706 | 3.841 | 5.024 | 6.635 | 7.879 |
| 2 | 0.020100 | 0.050636 | 0.102586 | 0.2107 | 4.605 | 5.991 | 7.378 | 9.210 | 10.597 |
| 3 | 0.1148 | 0.2158 | 0.3518 | 0.5844 | 6.251 | 7.815 | 9.348 | 11.345 | 12.838 |
| 4 | 0.297 | 0.484 | 0.711 | 1.064 | 7.779 | 9.488 | 11.143 | 13.277 | 14.860 |
| 5 | 0.554 | 0.831 | 1.145 | 1.610 | 9.236 | 11.070 | 12.832 | 15.086 | 16.750 |
| 6 | 0.872 | 1.237 | 1.635 | 2.204 | 10.645 | 12.592 | 14.449 | 16.812 | 18.548 |
| 7 | 1.239 | 1.690 | 2.167 | 2.833 | 12.017 | 14.067 | 16.013 | 18.475 | 20.278 |
| 8 | 1.647 | 2.180 | 2.733 | 3.490 | 13.362 | 15.507 | 17.535 | 20.090 | 21.955 |
| 9 | 2.088 | 2.700 | 3.325 | 4.168 | 14.684 | 16.919 | 19.023 | 21.666 | 23.589 |
| 10 | 2.558 | 3.247 | 3.940 | 4.865 | 15.987 | 18.307 | 20.483 | 23.209 | 25.188 |
| 11 | 3.053 | 3.816 | 4.575 | 5.578 | 17.275 | 19.675 | 21.920 | 24.725 | 26.757 |
| 12 | 3.571 | 4.404 | 5.226 | 6.304 | 18.549 | 21.026 | 23.337 | 26.217 | 28.300 |
| 13 | 4.107 | 5.009 | 5.892 | 7.041 | 19.812 | 22.362 | 24.736 | 27.688 | 29.819 |
| 14 | 4.660 | 5.629 | 6.571 | 7.790 | 21.064 | 23.685 | 26.119 | 29.141 | 31.319 |
| 15 | 5.229 | 6.262 | 7.261 | 8.547 | 22.307 | 24.996 | 27.488 | 30.578 | 32.801 |
| 16 | 5.812 | 6.908 | 7.962 | 9.312 | 23.542 | 26.296 | 28.845 | 32.000 | 34.267 |
| 17 | 6.408 | 7.564 | 8.672 | 10.085 | 24.769 | 27.587 | 30.191 | 33.409 | 35.718 |
| 18 | 7.015 | 8.231 | 9.390 | 10.865 | 25.989 | 28.869 | 31.526 | 34.805 | 37.156 |
| 19 | 7.633 | 8.907 | 10.117 | 11.651 | 27.204 | 30.144 | 32.852 | 36.191 | 38.582 |
| 20 | 8.260 | 9.591 | 10.851 | 12.443 | 28.412 | 31.410 | 34.170 | 37.566 | 39.997 |
| 21 | 8.897 | 10.283 | 11.591 | 13.240 | 29.615 | 32.671 | 35.479 | 38.932 | 41.401 |
| 22 | 9.542 | 10.982 | 12.338 | 14.041 | 30.813 | 33.924 | 36.781 | 40.289 | 42.796 |
| 23 | 10.196 | 11.689 | 13.091 | 14.848 | 32.007 | 35.172 | 38.076 | 41.638 | 44.181 |
| 24 | 10.856 | 12.401 | 13.848 | 15.659 | 33.196 | 36.415 | 39.364 | 42.980 | 45.558 |
| 25 | 11.524 | 13.120 | 14.611 | 16.473 | 34.382 | 37.652 | 40.646 | 44.314 | 46.928 |
| 26 | 12.198 | 13.844 | 15.379 | 17.292 | 35.563 | 38.885 | 41.923 | 45.642 | 48.290 |
| 27 | 12.878 | 14.573 | 16.151 | 18.114 | 36.741 | 40.113 | 43.195 | 46.963 | 49.645 |
| 28 | 13.565 | 15.308 | 16.928 | 18.939 | 37.916 | 41.337 | 44.461 | 48.278 | 50.994 |
| 29 | 14.256 | 16.047 | 17.708 | 19.768 | 39.087 | 42.557 | 45.722 | 49.588 | 52.335 |
| 30 | 14.953 | 16.791 | 18.493 | 20.599 | 40.256 | 43.773 | 46.979 | 50.892 | 53.672 |
| 50 | 29.707 | 32.357 | 34.764 | 37.689 | 63.167 | 67.505 | 71.420 | 76.154 | 79.490 |
| 60 | 37.485 | 40.482 | 43.188 | 46.459 | 74.397 | 79.082 | 83.298 | 88.379 | 91.952 |
| 80 | 53.540 | 57.153 | 60.391 | 64.278 | 96.578 | 101.879 | 106.629 | 112.329 | 116.321 |
| 100 | 70.065 | 74.222 | 77.929 | 82.358 | 118.498 | 124.342 | 129.561 | 135.807 | 140.170 |

To have a probability of 0.05 in the right tail when df = 5, the tabled value is $\chi^2(5, 0.05) = 11.070$.

*Quantitative Methods for Investment Analysis*, Second Edition, by Richard A. DeFusco, CFA, Dennis W. McLeavey, CFA, Jerald E. Pinto, CFA, and David E. Runkle, CFA. Copyright © 2004 by CFA Institute. Reprinted with permission.

## Appendix E    Table of the F-Distribution

**Panel A.** Critical values for right-hand tail area equal to 0.05

Numerator: $df_1$ and Denominator: $df_2$

| df2: \ df1: | 1 | 2 | 3 | 4 | 5 | 6 | 7 | 8 | 9 | 10 | 11 | 12 | 15 | 20 | 21 | 22 | 23 | 24 | 25 | 30 | 40 | 60 | 120 | ∞ |
|---|---|---|---|---|---|---|---|---|---|---|---|---|---|---|---|---|---|---|---|---|---|---|---|---|
| 1 | 161 | 200 | 216 | 225 | 230 | 234 | 237 | 239 | 241 | 242 | 243 | 244 | 246 | 248 | 248 | 249 | 249 | 249 | 249 | 250 | 251 | 252 | 253 | 254 |
| 2 | 18.5 | 19.0 | 19.2 | 19.2 | 19.3 | 19.3 | 19.4 | 19.4 | 19.4 | 19.4 | 19.4 | 19.4 | 19.4 | 19.4 | 19.4 | 19.5 | 19.5 | 19.5 | 19.5 | 19.5 | 19.5 | 19.5 | 19.5 | 19.5 |
| 3 | 10.1 | 9.55 | 9.28 | 9.12 | 9.01 | 8.94 | 8.89 | 8.85 | 8.81 | 8.79 | 8.76 | 8.74 | 8.70 | 8.66 | 8.65 | 8.65 | 8.64 | 8.64 | 8.63 | 8.62 | 8.59 | 8.57 | 8.55 | 8.53 |
| 4 | 7.71 | 6.94 | 6.59 | 6.39 | 6.26 | 6.16 | 6.09 | 6.04 | 6.00 | 5.96 | 5.94 | 5.91 | 5.86 | 5.80 | 5.79 | 5.79 | 5.78 | 5.77 | 5.77 | 5.75 | 5.72 | 5.69 | 5.66 | 5.63 |
| 5 | 6.61 | 5.79 | 5.41 | 5.19 | 5.05 | 4.95 | 4.88 | 4.82 | 4.77 | 4.74 | 4.70 | 4.68 | 4.62 | 4.56 | 4.55 | 4.54 | 4.53 | 4.53 | 4.52 | 4.50 | 4.46 | 4.43 | 4.40 | 4.37 |
| 6 | 5.99 | 5.14 | 4.76 | 4.53 | 4.39 | 4.28 | 4.21 | 4.15 | 4.10 | 4.06 | 4.03 | 4.00 | 3.94 | 3.87 | 3.86 | 3.86 | 3.85 | 3.84 | 3.83 | 3.81 | 3.77 | 3.74 | 3.70 | 3.67 |
| 7 | 5.59 | 4.74 | 4.35 | 4.12 | 3.97 | 3.87 | 3.79 | 3.73 | 3.68 | 3.64 | 3.60 | 3.57 | 3.51 | 3.44 | 3.43 | 3.43 | 3.42 | 3.41 | 3.40 | 3.38 | 3.34 | 3.30 | 3.27 | 3.23 |
| 8 | 5.32 | 4.46 | 4.07 | 3.84 | 3.69 | 3.58 | 3.50 | 3.44 | 3.39 | 3.35 | 3.31 | 3.28 | 3.22 | 3.15 | 3.14 | 3.13 | 3.12 | 3.12 | 3.11 | 3.08 | 3.04 | 3.01 | 2.97 | 2.93 |
| 9 | 5.12 | 4.26 | 3.86 | 3.63 | 3.48 | 3.37 | 3.29 | 3.23 | 3.18 | 3.14 | 3.10 | 3.07 | 3.01 | 2.94 | 2.93 | 2.92 | 2.91 | 2.90 | 2.89 | 2.86 | 2.83 | 2.79 | 2.75 | 2.71 |
| 10 | 4.96 | 4.10 | 3.71 | 3.48 | 3.33 | 3.22 | 3.14 | 3.07 | 3.02 | 2.98 | 2.94 | 2.91 | 2.85 | 2.77 | 2.76 | 2.75 | 2.75 | 2.74 | 2.73 | 2.70 | 2.66 | 2.62 | 2.58 | 2.54 |
| 11 | 4.84 | 3.98 | 3.59 | 3.36 | 3.20 | 3.09 | 3.01 | 2.95 | 2.90 | 2.85 | 2.82 | 2.79 | 2.72 | 2.65 | 2.64 | 2.63 | 2.62 | 2.61 | 2.60 | 2.57 | 2.53 | 2.49 | 2.45 | 2.40 |
| 12 | 4.75 | 3.89 | 3.49 | 3.26 | 3.11 | 3.00 | 2.91 | 2.85 | 2.80 | 2.75 | 2.72 | 2.69 | 2.62 | 2.54 | 2.53 | 2.52 | 2.51 | 2.51 | 2.50 | 2.47 | 2.43 | 2.38 | 2.34 | 2.30 |
| 13 | 4.67 | 3.81 | 3.41 | 3.18 | 3.03 | 2.92 | 2.83 | 2.77 | 2.71 | 2.67 | 2.63 | 2.60 | 2.53 | 2.46 | 2.45 | 2.44 | 2.43 | 2.42 | 2.41 | 2.38 | 2.34 | 2.30 | 2.25 | 2.21 |
| 14 | 4.60 | 3.74 | 3.34 | 3.11 | 2.96 | 2.85 | 2.76 | 2.70 | 2.65 | 2.60 | 2.57 | 2.53 | 2.46 | 2.39 | 2.38 | 2.37 | 2.36 | 2.35 | 2.34 | 2.31 | 2.27 | 2.22 | 2.18 | 2.13 |
| 15 | 4.54 | 3.68 | 3.29 | 3.06 | 2.90 | 2.79 | 2.71 | 2.64 | 2.59 | 2.54 | 2.51 | 2.48 | 2.40 | 2.33 | 2.32 | 2.31 | 2.30 | 2.29 | 2.28 | 2.25 | 2.20 | 2.16 | 2.11 | 2.07 |
| 16 | 4.49 | 3.63 | 3.24 | 3.01 | 2.85 | 2.74 | 2.66 | 2.59 | 2.54 | 2.49 | 2.46 | 2.42 | 2.35 | 2.28 | 2.26 | 2.25 | 2.24 | 2.24 | 2.23 | 2.19 | 2.15 | 2.11 | 2.06 | 2.01 |
| 17 | 4.45 | 3.59 | 3.20 | 2.96 | 2.81 | 2.70 | 2.61 | 2.55 | 2.49 | 2.45 | 2.41 | 2.38 | 2.31 | 2.23 | 2.22 | 2.21 | 2.20 | 2.19 | 2.18 | 2.15 | 2.10 | 2.06 | 2.01 | 1.96 |
| 18 | 4.41 | 3.55 | 3.16 | 2.93 | 2.77 | 2.66 | 2.58 | 2.51 | 2.46 | 2.41 | 2.37 | 2.34 | 2.27 | 2.19 | 2.18 | 2.17 | 2.16 | 2.15 | 2.14 | 2.11 | 2.06 | 2.02 | 1.97 | 1.92 |
| 19 | 4.38 | 3.52 | 3.13 | 2.90 | 2.74 | 2.63 | 2.54 | 2.48 | 2.42 | 2.38 | 2.34 | 2.31 | 2.23 | 2.16 | 2.14 | 2.13 | 2.12 | 2.11 | 2.11 | 2.07 | 2.03 | 1.98 | 1.93 | 1.88 |
| 20 | 4.35 | 3.49 | 3.10 | 2.87 | 2.71 | 2.60 | 2.51 | 2.45 | 2.39 | 2.35 | 2.31 | 2.28 | 2.20 | 2.12 | 2.11 | 2.10 | 2.09 | 2.08 | 2.07 | 2.04 | 1.99 | 1.95 | 1.90 | 1.84 |
| 21 | 4.32 | 3.47 | 3.07 | 2.84 | 2.68 | 2.57 | 2.49 | 2.42 | 2.37 | 2.32 | 2.28 | 2.25 | 2.18 | 2.10 | 2.08 | 2.07 | 2.06 | 2.05 | 2.05 | 2.01 | 1.96 | 1.92 | 1.87 | 1.81 |
| 22 | 4.30 | 3.44 | 3.05 | 2.82 | 2.66 | 2.55 | 2.46 | 2.40 | 2.34 | 2.30 | 2.26 | 2.23 | 2.15 | 2.07 | 2.06 | 2.05 | 2.04 | 2.03 | 2.02 | 1.98 | 1.94 | 1.89 | 1.84 | 1.78 |
| 23 | 4.28 | 3.42 | 3.03 | 2.80 | 2.64 | 2.53 | 2.44 | 2.37 | 2.32 | 2.27 | 2.24 | 2.20 | 2.13 | 2.05 | 2.04 | 2.02 | 2.01 | 2.01 | 2.00 | 1.96 | 1.91 | 1.86 | 1.81 | 1.76 |
| 24 | 4.26 | 3.40 | 3.01 | 2.78 | 2.62 | 2.51 | 2.42 | 2.36 | 2.30 | 2.25 | 2.22 | 2.18 | 2.11 | 2.03 | 2.01 | 2.00 | 1.99 | 1.98 | 1.97 | 1.94 | 1.89 | 1.84 | 1.79 | 1.73 |
| 25 | 4.24 | 3.39 | 2.99 | 2.76 | 2.60 | 2.49 | 2.40 | 2.34 | 2.28 | 2.24 | 2.20 | 2.16 | 2.09 | 2.01 | 2.00 | 1.98 | 1.97 | 1.96 | 1.96 | 1.92 | 1.87 | 1.82 | 1.77 | 1.71 |
| 30 | 4.17 | 3.32 | 2.92 | 2.69 | 2.53 | 2.42 | 2.33 | 2.27 | 2.21 | 2.16 | 2.13 | 2.09 | 2.01 | 1.93 | 1.92 | 1.91 | 1.90 | 1.89 | 1.88 | 1.84 | 1.79 | 1.74 | 1.68 | 1.62 |
| 40 | 4.08 | 3.23 | 2.84 | 2.61 | 2.45 | 2.34 | 2.25 | 2.18 | 2.12 | 2.08 | 2.04 | 2.00 | 1.92 | 1.84 | 1.83 | 1.81 | 1.80 | 1.79 | 1.78 | 1.74 | 1.69 | 1.64 | 1.58 | 1.51 |
| 60 | 4.00 | 3.15 | 2.76 | 2.53 | 2.37 | 2.25 | 2.17 | 2.10 | 2.04 | 1.99 | 1.95 | 1.92 | 1.84 | 1.75 | 1.73 | 1.72 | 1.71 | 1.70 | 1.69 | 1.65 | 1.59 | 1.53 | 1.47 | 1.39 |
| 120 | 3.92 | 3.07 | 2.68 | 2.45 | 2.29 | 2.18 | 2.09 | 2.02 | 1.96 | 1.91 | 1.87 | 1.83 | 1.75 | 1.66 | 1.64 | 1.63 | 1.62 | 1.61 | 1.60 | 1.55 | 1.50 | 1.43 | 1.35 | 1.25 |
| Infinity | 3.84 | 3.00 | 2.60 | 2.37 | 2.21 | 2.10 | 2.01 | 1.94 | 1.88 | 1.83 | 1.79 | 1.75 | 1.67 | 1.57 | 1.56 | 1.54 | 1.53 | 1.52 | 1.51 | 1.46 | 1.39 | 1.32 | 1.22 | 1.00 |

With 1 degree of freedom (df) in the numerator and 3 df in the denominator, the critical F-value is 10.1 for a right-hand tail area equal to 0.05.

*Quantitative Methods for Investment Analysis*, Second Edition, by Richard A. DeFusco, CFA, Dennis W. McLeavey, CFA, Jerald E. Pinto, CFA, and David E. Runkle, CFA. Copyright © 2004 by CFA Institute. Reprinted with permission.

# Appendix E    Table of the F-Distribution

Panel B. Critical values for right-hand tail area equal to 0.025

| df2: \ df1: | 1 | 2 | 3 | 4 | 5 | 6 | 7 | 8 | 9 | 10 | 11 | 12 | 15 | 20 | 21 | 22 | 23 | 24 | 25 | 30 | 40 | 60 | 120 | ∞ |
|---|---|---|---|---|---|---|---|---|---|---|---|---|---|---|---|---|---|---|---|---|---|---|---|---|
| 1 | 648 | 799 | 864 | 900 | 922 | 937 | 948 | 957 | 963 | 969 | 973 | 977 | 985 | 993 | 994 | 995 | 996 | 997 | 998 | 1001 | 1006 | 1010 | 1014 | 1018 |
| 2 | 38.51 | 39.00 | 39.17 | 39.25 | 39.30 | 39.33 | 39.36 | 39.37 | 39.39 | 39.40 | 39.41 | 39.41 | 39.43 | 39.45 | 39.45 | 39.45 | 39.45 | 39.46 | 39.46 | 39.46 | 39.47 | 39.48 | 39.49 | 39.50 |
| 3 | 17.44 | 16.04 | 15.44 | 15.10 | 14.88 | 14.73 | 14.62 | 14.54 | 14.47 | 14.42 | 14.37 | 14.34 | 14.25 | 14.17 | 14.16 | 14.14 | 14.13 | 14.12 | 14.12 | 14.08 | 14.04 | 13.99 | 13.95 | 13.90 |
| 4 | 12.22 | 10.65 | 9.98 | 9.60 | 9.36 | 9.20 | 9.07 | 8.98 | 8.90 | 8.84 | 8.79 | 8.75 | 8.66 | 8.56 | 8.55 | 8.53 | 8.52 | 8.51 | 8.50 | 8.46 | 8.41 | 8.36 | 8.31 | 8.26 |
| 5 | 10.01 | 8.43 | 7.76 | 7.39 | 7.15 | 6.98 | 6.85 | 6.76 | 6.68 | 6.62 | 6.57 | 6.52 | 6.43 | 6.33 | 6.31 | 6.30 | 6.29 | 6.28 | 6.27 | 6.23 | 6.18 | 6.12 | 6.07 | 6.02 |
| 6 | 8.81 | 7.26 | 6.60 | 6.23 | 5.99 | 5.82 | 5.70 | 5.60 | 5.52 | 5.46 | 5.41 | 5.37 | 5.27 | 5.17 | 5.15 | 5.14 | 5.13 | 5.12 | 5.11 | 5.07 | 5.01 | 4.96 | 4.90 | 4.85 |
| 7 | 8.07 | 6.54 | 5.89 | 5.52 | 5.29 | 5.12 | 4.99 | 4.90 | 4.82 | 4.76 | 4.71 | 4.67 | 4.57 | 4.47 | 4.45 | 4.44 | 4.43 | 4.41 | 4.40 | 4.36 | 4.31 | 4.25 | 4.20 | 4.14 |
| 8 | 7.57 | 6.06 | 5.42 | 5.05 | 4.82 | 4.65 | 4.53 | 4.43 | 4.36 | 4.30 | 4.24 | 4.20 | 4.10 | 4.00 | 3.98 | 3.97 | 3.96 | 3.95 | 3.94 | 3.89 | 3.84 | 3.78 | 3.73 | 3.67 |
| 9 | 7.21 | 5.71 | 5.08 | 4.72 | 4.48 | 4.32 | 4.20 | 4.10 | 4.03 | 3.96 | 3.91 | 3.87 | 3.77 | 3.67 | 3.65 | 3.64 | 3.63 | 3.61 | 3.60 | 3.56 | 3.51 | 3.45 | 3.39 | 3.33 |
| 10 | 6.94 | 5.46 | 4.83 | 4.47 | 4.24 | 4.07 | 3.95 | 3.85 | 3.78 | 3.72 | 3.66 | 3.62 | 3.52 | 3.42 | 3.40 | 3.39 | 3.38 | 3.37 | 3.35 | 3.31 | 3.26 | 3.20 | 3.14 | 3.08 |
| 11 | 6.72 | 5.26 | 4.63 | 4.28 | 4.04 | 3.88 | 3.76 | 3.66 | 3.59 | 3.53 | 3.47 | 3.43 | 3.33 | 3.23 | 3.21 | 3.20 | 3.18 | 3.17 | 3.16 | 3.12 | 3.06 | 3.00 | 2.94 | 2.88 |
| 12 | 6.55 | 5.10 | 4.47 | 4.12 | 3.89 | 3.73 | 3.61 | 3.51 | 3.44 | 3.37 | 3.32 | 3.28 | 3.18 | 3.07 | 3.06 | 3.04 | 3.03 | 3.02 | 3.01 | 2.96 | 2.91 | 2.85 | 2.79 | 2.72 |
| 13 | 6.41 | 4.97 | 4.35 | 4.00 | 3.77 | 3.60 | 3.48 | 3.39 | 3.31 | 3.25 | 3.20 | 3.15 | 3.05 | 2.95 | 2.93 | 2.92 | 2.91 | 2.89 | 2.88 | 2.84 | 2.78 | 2.72 | 2.66 | 2.60 |
| 14 | 6.30 | 4.86 | 4.24 | 3.89 | 3.66 | 3.50 | 3.38 | 3.29 | 3.21 | 3.15 | 3.09 | 3.05 | 2.95 | 2.84 | 2.83 | 2.81 | 2.80 | 2.79 | 2.78 | 2.73 | 2.67 | 2.61 | 2.55 | 2.49 |
| 15 | 6.20 | 4.77 | 4.15 | 3.80 | 3.58 | 3.41 | 3.29 | 3.20 | 3.12 | 3.06 | 3.01 | 2.96 | 2.86 | 2.76 | 2.74 | 2.73 | 2.71 | 2.70 | 2.69 | 2.64 | 2.59 | 2.52 | 2.46 | 2.40 |
| 16 | 6.12 | 4.69 | 4.08 | 3.73 | 3.50 | 3.34 | 3.22 | 3.12 | 3.05 | 2.99 | 2.93 | 2.89 | 2.79 | 2.68 | 2.67 | 2.65 | 2.64 | 2.63 | 2.61 | 2.57 | 2.51 | 2.45 | 2.38 | 2.32 |
| 17 | 6.04 | 4.62 | 4.01 | 3.66 | 3.44 | 3.28 | 3.16 | 3.06 | 2.98 | 2.92 | 2.87 | 2.82 | 2.72 | 2.62 | 2.60 | 2.59 | 2.57 | 2.56 | 2.55 | 2.50 | 2.44 | 2.38 | 2.32 | 2.25 |
| 18 | 5.98 | 4.56 | 3.95 | 3.61 | 3.38 | 3.22 | 3.10 | 3.01 | 2.93 | 2.87 | 2.81 | 2.77 | 2.67 | 2.56 | 2.54 | 2.53 | 2.52 | 2.50 | 2.49 | 2.44 | 2.38 | 2.32 | 2.26 | 2.19 |
| 19 | 5.92 | 4.51 | 3.90 | 3.56 | 3.33 | 3.17 | 3.05 | 2.96 | 2.88 | 2.82 | 2.76 | 2.72 | 2.62 | 2.51 | 2.49 | 2.48 | 2.46 | 2.45 | 2.44 | 2.39 | 2.33 | 2.27 | 2.20 | 2.13 |
| 20 | 5.87 | 4.46 | 3.86 | 3.51 | 3.29 | 3.13 | 3.01 | 2.91 | 2.84 | 2.77 | 2.72 | 2.68 | 2.57 | 2.46 | 2.45 | 2.43 | 2.42 | 2.41 | 2.40 | 2.35 | 2.29 | 2.22 | 2.16 | 2.09 |
| 21 | 5.83 | 4.42 | 3.82 | 3.48 | 3.25 | 3.09 | 2.97 | 2.87 | 2.80 | 2.73 | 2.68 | 2.64 | 2.53 | 2.42 | 2.41 | 2.39 | 2.38 | 2.37 | 2.36 | 2.31 | 2.25 | 2.18 | 2.11 | 2.04 |
| 22 | 5.79 | 4.38 | 3.78 | 3.44 | 3.22 | 3.05 | 2.93 | 2.84 | 2.76 | 2.70 | 2.65 | 2.60 | 2.50 | 2.39 | 2.37 | 2.36 | 2.34 | 2.33 | 2.32 | 2.27 | 2.21 | 2.14 | 2.08 | 2.00 |
| 23 | 5.75 | 4.35 | 3.75 | 3.41 | 3.18 | 3.02 | 2.90 | 2.81 | 2.73 | 2.67 | 2.62 | 2.57 | 2.47 | 2.36 | 2.34 | 2.33 | 2.31 | 2.30 | 2.29 | 2.24 | 2.18 | 2.11 | 2.04 | 1.97 |
| 24 | 5.72 | 4.32 | 3.72 | 3.38 | 3.15 | 2.99 | 2.87 | 2.78 | 2.70 | 2.64 | 2.59 | 2.54 | 2.44 | 2.33 | 2.31 | 2.30 | 2.28 | 2.27 | 2.26 | 2.21 | 2.15 | 2.08 | 2.01 | 1.94 |
| 25 | 5.69 | 4.29 | 3.69 | 3.35 | 3.13 | 2.97 | 2.85 | 2.75 | 2.68 | 2.61 | 2.56 | 2.51 | 2.41 | 2.30 | 2.28 | 2.27 | 2.26 | 2.24 | 2.23 | 2.18 | 2.12 | 2.05 | 1.98 | 1.91 |
| 30 | 5.57 | 4.18 | 3.59 | 3.25 | 3.03 | 2.87 | 2.75 | 2.65 | 2.57 | 2.51 | 2.46 | 2.41 | 2.31 | 2.20 | 2.18 | 2.16 | 2.15 | 2.14 | 2.12 | 2.07 | 2.01 | 1.94 | 1.87 | 1.79 |
| 40 | 5.42 | 4.05 | 3.46 | 3.13 | 2.90 | 2.74 | 2.62 | 2.53 | 2.45 | 2.39 | 2.33 | 2.29 | 2.18 | 2.07 | 2.05 | 2.03 | 2.02 | 2.01 | 1.99 | 1.94 | 1.88 | 1.80 | 1.72 | 1.64 |
| 60 | 5.29 | 3.93 | 3.34 | 3.01 | 2.79 | 2.63 | 2.51 | 2.41 | 2.33 | 2.27 | 2.22 | 2.17 | 2.06 | 1.94 | 1.93 | 1.91 | 1.90 | 1.88 | 1.87 | 1.82 | 1.74 | 1.67 | 1.58 | 1.48 |
| 120 | 5.15 | 3.80 | 3.23 | 2.89 | 2.67 | 2.52 | 2.39 | 2.30 | 2.22 | 2.16 | 2.10 | 2.05 | 1.94 | 1.82 | 1.81 | 1.79 | 1.77 | 1.76 | 1.75 | 1.69 | 1.61 | 1.53 | 1.43 | 1.31 |
| Infinity | 5.02 | 3.69 | 3.12 | 2.79 | 2.57 | 2.41 | 2.29 | 2.19 | 2.11 | 2.05 | 1.99 | 1.94 | 1.83 | 1.71 | 1.69 | 1.67 | 1.66 | 1.64 | 1.63 | 1.57 | 1.48 | 1.39 | 1.27 | 1.00 |

Numerator: $df_1$ and Denominator: $df_2$

# Appendix E        Table of the F-Distribution

Panel C.  Critical values for right-hand tail area equal to 0.01

Numerator: $df_1$ and Denominator: $df_2$

| $df_2$: | $df_1$: 1 | 2 | 3 | 4 | 5 | 6 | 7 | 8 | 9 | 10 | 11 | 12 | 15 | 20 | 21 | 22 | 23 | 24 | 25 | 30 | 40 | 60 | 120 | ∞ |
|---|---|---|---|---|---|---|---|---|---|---|---|---|---|---|---|---|---|---|---|---|---|---|---|---|
| 1 | 4052 | 5000 | 5403 | 5625 | 5764 | 5859 | 5928 | 5982 | 6023 | 6056 | 6083 | 6106 | 6157 | 6209 | 6216 | 6223 | 6229 | 6235 | 6240 | 6261 | 6287 | 6313 | 6339 | 6366 |
| 2 | 98.5 | 99.0 | 99.2 | 99.2 | 99.3 | 99.3 | 99.4 | 99.4 | 99.4 | 99.4 | 99.4 | 99.4 | 99.4 | 99.4 | 99.5 | 99.5 | 99.5 | 99.5 | 99.5 | 99.5 | 99.5 | 99.5 | 99.5 | 99.5 |
| 3 | 34.1 | 30.8 | 29.5 | 28.7 | 28.2 | 27.9 | 27.7 | 27.5 | 27.3 | 27.2 | 27.1 | 27.1 | 26.9 | 26.7 | 26.7 | 26.6 | 26.6 | 26.6 | 26.6 | 26.5 | 26.4 | 26.3 | 26.2 | 26.1 |
| 4 | 21.2 | 18.0 | 16.7 | 16.0 | 15.5 | 15.2 | 15.0 | 14.8 | 14.7 | 14.5 | 14.5 | 14.4 | 14.2 | 14.0 | 14.0 | 14.0 | 13.9 | 13.9 | 13.9 | 13.8 | 13.7 | 13.7 | 13.6 | 13.5 |
| 5 | 16.3 | 13.3 | 12.1 | 11.4 | 11.0 | 10.7 | 10.5 | 10.3 | 10.2 | 10.1 | 10.0 | 9.89 | 9.72 | 9.55 | 9.53 | 9.51 | 9.49 | 9.47 | 9.45 | 9.38 | 9.29 | 9.20 | 9.11 | 9.02 |
| 6 | 13.7 | 10.9 | 9.78 | 9.15 | 8.75 | 8.47 | 8.26 | 8.10 | 7.98 | 7.87 | 7.79 | 7.72 | 7.56 | 7.40 | 7.37 | 7.35 | 7.33 | 7.31 | 7.30 | 7.23 | 7.14 | 7.06 | 6.97 | 6.88 |
| 7 | 12.2 | 9.55 | 8.45 | 7.85 | 7.46 | 7.19 | 6.99 | 6.84 | 6.72 | 6.62 | 6.54 | 6.47 | 6.31 | 6.16 | 6.13 | 6.11 | 6.09 | 6.07 | 6.06 | 5.99 | 5.91 | 5.82 | 5.74 | 5.65 |
| 8 | 11.3 | 8.65 | 7.59 | 7.01 | 6.63 | 6.37 | 6.18 | 6.03 | 5.91 | 5.81 | 5.73 | 5.67 | 5.52 | 5.36 | 5.34 | 5.32 | 5.30 | 5.28 | 5.26 | 5.20 | 5.12 | 5.03 | 4.95 | 4.86 |
| 9 | 10.6 | 8.02 | 6.99 | 6.42 | 6.06 | 5.80 | 5.61 | 5.47 | 5.35 | 5.26 | 5.18 | 5.11 | 4.96 | 4.81 | 4.79 | 4.77 | 4.75 | 4.73 | 4.71 | 4.65 | 4.57 | 4.48 | 4.40 | 4.31 |
| 10 | 10.0 | 7.56 | 6.55 | 5.99 | 5.64 | 5.39 | 5.20 | 5.06 | 4.94 | 4.85 | 4.77 | 4.71 | 4.56 | 4.41 | 4.38 | 4.36 | 4.34 | 4.33 | 4.31 | 4.25 | 4.17 | 4.08 | 4.00 | 3.91 |
| 11 | 9.65 | 7.21 | 6.22 | 5.67 | 5.32 | 5.07 | 4.89 | 4.74 | 4.63 | 4.54 | 4.46 | 4.40 | 4.25 | 4.10 | 4.08 | 4.06 | 4.04 | 4.02 | 4.01 | 3.94 | 3.86 | 3.78 | 3.69 | 3.60 |
| 12 | 9.33 | 6.93 | 5.95 | 5.41 | 5.06 | 4.82 | 4.64 | 4.50 | 4.39 | 4.30 | 4.22 | 4.16 | 4.01 | 3.86 | 3.84 | 3.82 | 3.80 | 3.78 | 3.76 | 3.70 | 3.62 | 3.54 | 3.45 | 3.36 |
| 13 | 9.07 | 6.70 | 5.74 | 5.21 | 4.86 | 4.62 | 4.44 | 4.30 | 4.19 | 4.10 | 4.02 | 3.96 | 3.82 | 3.66 | 3.64 | 3.62 | 3.60 | 3.59 | 3.57 | 3.51 | 3.43 | 3.34 | 3.25 | 3.17 |
| 14 | 8.86 | 6.51 | 5.56 | 5.04 | 4.70 | 4.46 | 4.28 | 4.14 | 4.03 | 3.94 | 3.86 | 3.80 | 3.66 | 3.51 | 3.48 | 3.46 | 3.44 | 3.43 | 3.41 | 3.35 | 3.27 | 3.18 | 3.09 | 3.00 |
| 15 | 8.68 | 6.36 | 5.42 | 4.89 | 4.56 | 4.32 | 4.14 | 4.00 | 3.89 | 3.80 | 3.73 | 3.67 | 3.52 | 3.37 | 3.35 | 3.33 | 3.31 | 3.29 | 3.28 | 3.21 | 3.13 | 3.05 | 2.96 | 2.87 |
| 16 | 8.53 | 6.23 | 5.29 | 4.77 | 4.44 | 4.20 | 4.03 | 3.89 | 3.78 | 3.69 | 3.62 | 3.55 | 3.41 | 3.26 | 3.24 | 3.22 | 3.20 | 3.18 | 3.16 | 3.10 | 3.02 | 2.93 | 2.84 | 2.75 |
| 17 | 8.40 | 6.11 | 5.19 | 4.67 | 4.34 | 4.10 | 3.93 | 3.79 | 3.68 | 3.59 | 3.52 | 3.46 | 3.31 | 3.16 | 3.14 | 3.12 | 3.10 | 3.08 | 3.07 | 3.00 | 2.92 | 2.83 | 2.75 | 2.65 |
| 18 | 8.29 | 6.01 | 5.09 | 4.58 | 4.25 | 4.01 | 3.84 | 3.71 | 3.60 | 3.51 | 3.43 | 3.37 | 3.23 | 3.08 | 3.05 | 3.03 | 3.02 | 3.00 | 2.98 | 2.92 | 2.84 | 2.75 | 2.66 | 2.57 |
| 19 | 8.19 | 5.93 | 5.01 | 4.50 | 4.17 | 3.94 | 3.77 | 3.63 | 3.52 | 3.43 | 3.36 | 3.30 | 3.15 | 3.00 | 2.98 | 2.96 | 2.94 | 2.92 | 2.91 | 2.84 | 2.76 | 2.67 | 2.58 | 2.49 |
| 20 | 8.10 | 5.85 | 4.94 | 4.43 | 4.10 | 3.87 | 3.70 | 3.56 | 3.46 | 3.37 | 3.29 | 3.23 | 3.09 | 2.94 | 2.92 | 2.90 | 2.88 | 2.86 | 2.84 | 2.78 | 2.69 | 2.61 | 2.52 | 2.42 |
| 21 | 8.02 | 5.78 | 4.87 | 4.37 | 4.04 | 3.81 | 3.64 | 3.51 | 3.40 | 3.31 | 3.24 | 3.17 | 3.03 | 2.88 | 2.86 | 2.84 | 2.82 | 2.80 | 2.79 | 2.72 | 2.64 | 2.55 | 2.46 | 2.36 |
| 22 | 7.95 | 5.72 | 4.82 | 4.31 | 3.99 | 3.76 | 3.59 | 3.45 | 3.35 | 3.26 | 3.18 | 3.12 | 2.98 | 2.83 | 2.81 | 2.78 | 2.77 | 2.75 | 2.73 | 2.67 | 2.58 | 2.50 | 2.40 | 2.31 |
| 23 | 7.88 | 5.66 | 4.76 | 4.26 | 3.94 | 3.71 | 3.54 | 3.41 | 3.30 | 3.21 | 3.14 | 3.07 | 2.93 | 2.78 | 2.76 | 2.74 | 2.72 | 2.70 | 2.69 | 2.62 | 2.54 | 2.45 | 2.35 | 2.26 |
| 24 | 7.82 | 5.61 | 4.72 | 4.22 | 3.90 | 3.67 | 3.50 | 3.36 | 3.26 | 3.17 | 3.09 | 3.03 | 2.89 | 2.74 | 2.72 | 2.70 | 2.68 | 2.66 | 2.64 | 2.58 | 2.49 | 2.40 | 2.31 | 2.21 |
| 25 | 7.77 | 5.57 | 4.68 | 4.18 | 3.86 | 3.63 | 3.46 | 3.32 | 3.22 | 3.13 | 3.06 | 2.99 | 2.85 | 2.70 | 2.68 | 2.66 | 2.64 | 2.62 | 2.60 | 2.53 | 2.45 | 2.36 | 2.27 | 2.17 |
| 30 | 7.56 | 5.39 | 4.51 | 4.02 | 3.70 | 3.47 | 3.30 | 3.17 | 3.07 | 2.98 | 2.91 | 2.84 | 2.70 | 2.55 | 2.53 | 2.51 | 2.49 | 2.47 | 2.45 | 2.39 | 2.30 | 2.21 | 2.11 | 2.01 |
| 40 | 7.31 | 5.18 | 4.31 | 3.83 | 3.51 | 3.29 | 3.12 | 2.99 | 2.89 | 2.80 | 2.73 | 2.66 | 2.52 | 2.37 | 2.35 | 2.33 | 2.31 | 2.29 | 2.27 | 2.20 | 2.11 | 2.02 | 1.92 | 1.80 |
| 60 | 7.08 | 4.98 | 4.13 | 3.65 | 3.34 | 3.12 | 2.95 | 2.82 | 2.72 | 2.63 | 2.56 | 2.50 | 2.35 | 2.20 | 2.17 | 2.15 | 2.13 | 2.12 | 2.10 | 2.03 | 1.94 | 1.84 | 1.73 | 1.60 |
| 120 | 6.85 | 4.79 | 3.95 | 3.48 | 3.17 | 2.96 | 2.79 | 2.66 | 2.56 | 2.47 | 2.40 | 2.34 | 2.19 | 2.03 | 2.01 | 1.99 | 1.97 | 1.95 | 1.93 | 1.86 | 1.76 | 1.66 | 1.53 | 1.38 |
| Infinity | 6.63 | 4.61 | 3.78 | 3.32 | 3.02 | 2.80 | 2.64 | 2.51 | 2.41 | 2.32 | 2.25 | 2.18 | 2.04 | 1.88 | 1.85 | 1.83 | 1.81 | 1.79 | 1.77 | 1.70 | 1.59 | 1.47 | 1.32 | 1.00 |

# Appendix E    Table of the F-Distribution

Panel D. Critical values for right-hand tail area equal to 0.005

Numerator: $df_1$ and Denominator: $df_2$

| df2: / df1: | 1 | 2 | 3 | 4 | 5 | 6 | 7 | 8 | 9 | 10 | 11 | 12 | 15 | 20 | 21 | 22 | 23 | 24 | 25 | 30 | 40 | 60 | 120 | ∞ |
|---|---|---|---|---|---|---|---|---|---|---|---|---|---|---|---|---|---|---|---|---|---|---|---|---|
| 1 | 16211 | 20000 | 21615 | 22500 | 23056 | 23437 | 23715 | 23925 | 24091 | 24222 | 24334 | 24426 | 24630 | 24836 | 24863 | 24892 | 24915 | 24940 | 24959 | 25044 | 25146 | 25253 | 25359 | 25464 |
| 2 | 198.5 | 199.0 | 199.2 | 199.2 | 199.3 | 199.3 | 199.4 | 199.4 | 199.4 | 199.4 | 199.4 | 199.4 | 199.4 | 199.4 | 199.4 | 199.4 | 199.4 | 199.4 | 199.4 | 199.5 | 199.5 | 199.5 | 199.5 | 200 |
| 3 | 55.55 | 49.80 | 47.47 | 46.20 | 45.39 | 44.84 | 44.43 | 44.13 | 43.88 | 43.68 | 43.52 | 43.39 | 43.08 | 42.78 | 42.73 | 42.69 | 42.66 | 42.62 | 42.59 | 42.47 | 42.31 | 42.15 | 41.99 | 41.83 |
| 4 | 31.33 | 26.28 | 24.26 | 23.15 | 22.46 | 21.98 | 21.62 | 21.35 | 21.14 | 20.97 | 20.82 | 20.70 | 20.44 | 20.17 | 20.13 | 20.09 | 20.06 | 20.03 | 20.00 | 19.89 | 19.75 | 19.61 | 19.47 | 19.32 |
| 5 | 22.78 | 18.31 | 16.53 | 15.56 | 14.94 | 14.51 | 14.20 | 13.96 | 13.77 | 13.62 | 13.49 | 13.38 | 13.15 | 12.90 | 12.87 | 12.84 | 12.81 | 12.78 | 12.76 | 12.66 | 12.53 | 12.40 | 12.27 | 12.14 |
| 6 | 18.63 | 14.54 | 12.92 | 12.03 | 11.46 | 11.07 | 10.79 | 10.57 | 10.39 | 10.25 | 10.13 | 10.03 | 9.81 | 9.59 | 9.56 | 9.53 | 9.50 | 9.47 | 9.45 | 9.36 | 9.24 | 9.12 | 9.00 | 8.88 |
| 7 | 16.24 | 12.40 | 10.88 | 10.05 | 9.52 | 9.16 | 8.89 | 8.68 | 8.51 | 8.38 | 8.27 | 8.18 | 7.97 | 7.75 | 7.72 | 7.69 | 7.67 | 7.64 | 7.62 | 7.53 | 7.42 | 7.31 | 7.19 | 7.08 |
| 8 | 14.69 | 11.04 | 9.60 | 8.81 | 8.30 | 7.95 | 7.69 | 7.50 | 7.34 | 7.21 | 7.10 | 7.01 | 6.81 | 6.61 | 6.58 | 6.55 | 6.53 | 6.50 | 6.48 | 6.40 | 6.29 | 6.18 | 6.06 | 5.95 |
| 9 | 13.61 | 10.11 | 8.72 | 7.96 | 7.47 | 7.13 | 6.88 | 6.69 | 6.54 | 6.42 | 6.31 | 6.23 | 6.03 | 5.83 | 5.80 | 5.78 | 5.75 | 5.73 | 5.71 | 5.62 | 5.52 | 5.41 | 5.30 | 5.19 |
| 10 | 12.83 | 9.43 | 8.08 | 7.34 | 6.87 | 6.54 | 6.30 | 6.12 | 5.97 | 5.85 | 5.75 | 5.66 | 5.47 | 5.27 | 5.25 | 5.22 | 5.20 | 5.17 | 5.15 | 5.07 | 4.97 | 4.86 | 4.75 | 4.64 |
| 11 | 12.23 | 8.91 | 7.60 | 6.88 | 6.42 | 6.10 | 5.86 | 5.68 | 5.54 | 5.42 | 5.32 | 5.24 | 5.05 | 4.86 | 4.83 | 4.80 | 4.78 | 4.76 | 4.74 | 4.65 | 4.55 | 4.45 | 4.34 | 4.23 |
| 12 | 11.75 | 8.51 | 7.23 | 6.52 | 6.07 | 5.76 | 5.52 | 5.35 | 5.20 | 5.09 | 4.99 | 4.91 | 4.72 | 4.53 | 4.50 | 4.48 | 4.45 | 4.43 | 4.41 | 4.33 | 4.23 | 4.12 | 4.01 | 3.90 |
| 13 | 11.37 | 8.19 | 6.93 | 6.23 | 5.79 | 5.48 | 5.25 | 5.08 | 4.94 | 4.82 | 4.72 | 4.64 | 4.46 | 4.27 | 4.24 | 4.22 | 4.19 | 4.17 | 4.15 | 4.07 | 3.97 | 3.87 | 3.76 | 3.65 |
| 14 | 11.06 | 7.92 | 6.68 | 6.00 | 5.56 | 5.26 | 5.03 | 4.86 | 4.72 | 4.60 | 4.51 | 4.43 | 4.25 | 4.06 | 4.03 | 4.01 | 3.98 | 3.96 | 3.94 | 3.86 | 3.76 | 3.66 | 3.55 | 3.44 |
| 15 | 10.80 | 7.70 | 6.48 | 5.80 | 5.37 | 5.07 | 4.85 | 4.67 | 4.54 | 4.42 | 4.33 | 4.25 | 4.07 | 3.88 | 3.86 | 3.83 | 3.81 | 3.79 | 3.77 | 3.69 | 3.59 | 3.48 | 3.37 | 3.26 |
| 16 | 10.58 | 7.51 | 6.30 | 5.64 | 5.21 | 4.91 | 4.69 | 4.52 | 4.38 | 4.27 | 4.18 | 4.10 | 3.92 | 3.73 | 3.71 | 3.68 | 3.66 | 3.64 | 3.62 | 3.54 | 3.44 | 3.33 | 3.22 | 3.11 |
| 17 | 10.38 | 7.35 | 6.16 | 5.50 | 5.07 | 4.78 | 4.56 | 4.39 | 4.25 | 4.14 | 4.05 | 3.97 | 3.79 | 3.61 | 3.58 | 3.56 | 3.53 | 3.51 | 3.49 | 3.41 | 3.31 | 3.21 | 3.10 | 2.98 |
| 18 | 10.22 | 7.21 | 6.03 | 5.37 | 4.96 | 4.66 | 4.44 | 4.28 | 4.14 | 4.03 | 3.94 | 3.86 | 3.68 | 3.50 | 3.47 | 3.45 | 3.42 | 3.40 | 3.38 | 3.30 | 3.20 | 3.10 | 2.99 | 2.87 |
| 19 | 10.07 | 7.09 | 5.92 | 5.27 | 4.85 | 4.56 | 4.34 | 4.18 | 4.04 | 3.93 | 3.84 | 3.76 | 3.59 | 3.40 | 3.37 | 3.35 | 3.33 | 3.31 | 3.29 | 3.21 | 3.11 | 3.00 | 2.89 | 2.78 |
| 20 | 9.94 | 6.99 | 5.82 | 5.17 | 4.76 | 4.47 | 4.26 | 4.09 | 3.96 | 3.85 | 3.76 | 3.68 | 3.50 | 3.32 | 3.29 | 3.27 | 3.24 | 3.22 | 3.20 | 3.12 | 3.02 | 2.92 | 2.81 | 2.69 |
| 21 | 9.83 | 6.89 | 5.73 | 5.09 | 4.68 | 4.39 | 4.18 | 4.01 | 3.88 | 3.77 | 3.68 | 3.60 | 3.43 | 3.24 | 3.22 | 3.19 | 3.17 | 3.15 | 3.13 | 3.05 | 2.95 | 2.84 | 2.73 | 2.61 |
| 22 | 9.73 | 6.81 | 5.65 | 5.02 | 4.61 | 4.32 | 4.11 | 3.94 | 3.81 | 3.70 | 3.61 | 3.54 | 3.36 | 3.18 | 3.15 | 3.12 | 3.10 | 3.08 | 3.06 | 2.98 | 2.88 | 2.77 | 2.66 | 2.55 |
| 23 | 9.63 | 6.73 | 5.58 | 4.95 | 4.54 | 4.26 | 4.05 | 3.88 | 3.75 | 3.64 | 3.55 | 3.47 | 3.30 | 3.12 | 3.09 | 3.06 | 3.04 | 3.02 | 3.00 | 2.92 | 2.82 | 2.71 | 2.60 | 2.48 |
| 24 | 9.55 | 6.66 | 5.52 | 4.89 | 4.49 | 4.20 | 3.99 | 3.83 | 3.69 | 3.59 | 3.50 | 3.42 | 3.25 | 3.06 | 3.04 | 3.01 | 2.99 | 2.97 | 2.95 | 2.87 | 2.77 | 2.66 | 2.55 | 2.43 |
| 25 | 9.48 | 6.60 | 5.46 | 4.84 | 4.43 | 4.15 | 3.94 | 3.78 | 3.64 | 3.54 | 3.45 | 3.37 | 3.20 | 3.01 | 2.99 | 2.96 | 2.94 | 2.92 | 2.90 | 2.82 | 2.72 | 2.61 | 2.50 | 2.38 |
| 30 | 9.18 | 6.35 | 5.24 | 4.62 | 4.23 | 3.95 | 3.74 | 3.58 | 3.45 | 3.34 | 3.25 | 3.18 | 3.01 | 2.82 | 2.80 | 2.77 | 2.75 | 2.73 | 2.71 | 2.63 | 2.52 | 2.42 | 2.30 | 2.18 |
| 40 | 8.83 | 6.07 | 4.98 | 4.37 | 3.99 | 3.71 | 3.51 | 3.35 | 3.22 | 3.12 | 3.03 | 2.95 | 2.78 | 2.60 | 2.57 | 2.55 | 2.52 | 2.50 | 2.48 | 2.40 | 2.30 | 2.18 | 2.06 | 1.93 |
| 60 | 8.49 | 5.79 | 4.73 | 4.14 | 3.76 | 3.49 | 3.29 | 3.13 | 3.01 | 2.90 | 2.82 | 2.74 | 2.57 | 2.39 | 2.36 | 2.33 | 2.31 | 2.29 | 2.27 | 2.19 | 2.08 | 1.96 | 1.83 | 1.69 |
| 120 | 8.18 | 5.54 | 4.50 | 3.92 | 3.55 | 3.28 | 3.09 | 2.93 | 2.81 | 2.71 | 2.62 | 2.54 | 2.37 | 2.19 | 2.16 | 2.13 | 2.11 | 2.09 | 2.07 | 1.98 | 1.87 | 1.75 | 1.61 | 1.43 |
| Infinity | 7.88 | 5.30 | 4.28 | 3.72 | 3.35 | 3.09 | 2.90 | 2.74 | 2.62 | 2.52 | 2.43 | 2.36 | 2.19 | 2.00 | 1.97 | 1.95 | 1.92 | 1.90 | 1.88 | 1.79 | 1.67 | 1.53 | 1.36 | 1.00 |

## Appendix F        Critical Values for the Durbin-Watson Statistic ($\alpha$ = .05)

| n | $d_l$ | $d_u$ | $d_l$ | $d_u$ | $d_l$ | $d_u$ | $d_l$ | $d_u$ | $d_l$ | $d_u$ |
|---|---|---|---|---|---|---|---|---|---|---|
| | **K = 1** | | **K = 2** | | **K = 3** | | **K = 4** | | **K = 5** | |
| 15 | 1.08 | 1.36 | 0.95 | 1.54 | 0.82 | 1.75 | 0.69 | 1.97 | 0.56 | 2.21 |
| 16 | 1.10 | 1.37 | 0.98 | 1.54 | 0.86 | 1.73 | 0.74 | 1.93 | 0.62 | 2.15 |
| 17 | 1.13 | 1.38 | 1.02 | 1.54 | 0.90 | 1.71 | 0.78 | 1.90 | 0.67 | 2.10 |
| 18 | 1.16 | 1.39 | 1.05 | 1.53 | 0.93 | 1.69 | 0.82 | 1.87 | 0.71 | 2.06 |
| 19 | 1.18 | 1.40 | 1.08 | 1.53 | 0.97 | 1.68 | 0.86 | 1.85 | 0.75 | 2.02 |
| 20 | 1.20 | 1.41 | 1.10 | 1.54 | 1.00 | 1.68 | 0.90 | 1.83 | 0.79 | 1.99 |
| 21 | 1.22 | 1.42 | 1.13 | 1.54 | 1.03 | 1.67 | 0.93 | 1.81 | 0.83 | 1.96 |
| 22 | 1.24 | 1.43 | 1.15 | 1.54 | 1.05 | 1.66 | 0.96 | 1.80 | 0.86 | 1.94 |
| 23 | 1.26 | 1.44 | 1.17 | 1.54 | 1.08 | 1.66 | 0.99 | 1.79 | 0.90 | 1.92 |
| 24 | 1.27 | 1.45 | 1.19 | 1.55 | 1.10 | 1.66 | 1.01 | 1.78 | 0.93 | 1.90 |
| 25 | 1.29 | 1.45 | 1.21 | 1.55 | 1.12 | 1.66 | 1.04 | 1.77 | 0.95 | 1.89 |
| 26 | 1.30 | 1.46 | 1.22 | 1.55 | 1.14 | 1.65 | 1.06 | 1.76 | 0.98 | 1.88 |
| 27 | 1.32 | 1.47 | 1.24 | 1.56 | 1.16 | 1.65 | 1.08 | 1.76 | 1.01 | 1.86 |
| 28 | 1.33 | 1.48 | 1.26 | 1.56 | 1.18 | 1.65 | 1.10 | 1.75 | 1.03 | 1.85 |
| 29 | 1.34 | 1.48 | 1.27 | 1.56 | 1.20 | 1.65 | 1.12 | 1.74 | 1.05 | 1.84 |
| 30 | 1.35 | 1.49 | 1.28 | 1.57 | 1.21 | 1.65 | 1.14 | 1.74 | 1.07 | 1.83 |
| 31 | 1.36 | 1.50 | 1.30 | 1.57 | 1.23 | 1.65 | 1.16 | 1.74 | 1.09 | 1.83 |
| 32 | 1.37 | 1.50 | 1.31 | 1.57 | 1.24 | 1.65 | 1.18 | 1.73 | 1.11 | 1.82 |
| 33 | 1.38 | 1.51 | 1.32 | 1.58 | 1.26 | 1.65 | 1.19 | 1.73 | 1.13 | 1.81 |
| 34 | 1.39 | 1.51 | 1.33 | 1.58 | 1.27 | 1.65 | 1.21 | 1.73 | 1.15 | 1.81 |
| 35 | 1.40 | 1.52 | 1.34 | 1.58 | 1.28 | 1.65 | 1.22 | 1.73 | 1.16 | 1.80 |
| 36 | 1.41 | 1.52 | 1.35 | 1.59 | 1.29 | 1.65 | 1.24 | 1.73 | 1.18 | 1.80 |
| 37 | 1.42 | 1.53 | 1.36 | 1.59 | 1.31 | 1.66 | 1.25 | 1.72 | 1.19 | 1.80 |
| 38 | 1.43 | 1.54 | 1.37 | 1.59 | 1.32 | 1.66 | 1.26 | 1.72 | 1.21 | 1.79 |
| 39 | 1.43 | 1.54 | 1.38 | 1.60 | 1.33 | 1.66 | 1.27 | 1.72 | 1.22 | 1.79 |
| 40 | 1.44 | 1.54 | 1.39 | 1.60 | 1.34 | 1.66 | 1.29 | 1.72 | 1.23 | 1.79 |
| 45 | 1.48 | 1.57 | 1.43 | 1.62 | 1.38 | 1.67 | 1.34 | 1.72 | 1.29 | 1.78 |
| 50 | 1.50 | 1.59 | 1.46 | 1.63 | 1.42 | 1.67 | 1.38 | 1.72 | 1.34 | 1.77 |
| 55 | 1.53 | 1.60 | 1.49 | 1.64 | 1.45 | 1.68 | 1.41 | 1.72 | 1.38 | 1.77 |
| 60 | 1.55 | 1.62 | 1.51 | 1.65 | 1.48 | 1.69 | 1.44 | 1.73 | 1.41 | 1.77 |
| 65 | 1.57 | 1.63 | 1.54 | 1.66 | 1.50 | 1.70 | 1.47 | 1.73 | 1.44 | 1.77 |
| 70 | 1.58 | 1.64 | 1.55 | 1.67 | 1.52 | 1.70 | 1.49 | 1.74 | 1.46 | 1.77 |
| 75 | 1.60 | 1.65 | 1.57 | 1.68 | 1.54 | 1.71 | 1.51 | 1.74 | 1.49 | 1.77 |
| 80 | 1.61 | 1.66 | 1.59 | 1.69 | 1.56 | 1.72 | 1.53 | 1.74 | 1.51 | 1.77 |
| 85 | 1.62 | 1.67 | 1.60 | 1.70 | 1.57 | 1.72 | 1.55 | 1.75 | 1.52 | 1.77 |
| 90 | 1.63 | 1.68 | 1.61 | 1.70 | 1.59 | 1.73 | 1.57 | 1.75 | 1.54 | 1.78 |
| 95 | 1.64 | 1.69 | 1.62 | 1.71 | 1.60 | 1.73 | 1.58 | 1.75 | 1.56 | 1.78 |
| 100 | 1.65 | 1.69 | 1.63 | 1.72 | 1.61 | 1.74 | 1.59 | 1.76 | 1.57 | 1.78 |

*Note*: K = the number of slope parameters in the model.

*Source*: From J. Durbin and G.S. Watson, "Testing for Serial Correlation in Least Squares Regression, II." *Biometrika* 38 (1951): 159–178. Reproduced by permission of Oxford University Press.

**A priori probability** A probability based on logical analysis rather than on observation or personal judgment.

**Abandonment option** The ability to terminate a project at some future time if the financial results are disappointing.

**Abnormal rate of return** The amount by which a security's actual return differs from its expected rate of return which is based on the market's rate of return and the security's relationship with the market.

**Above full-employment equilibrium** A macroeconomic equilibrium in which real GDP exceeds potential GDP.

**Absolute dispersion** The amount of variability present without comparison to any reference point or benchmark.

**Absolute frequency** The number of observations in a given interval (for grouped data).

**Accelerated methods of depreciation** Depreciation methods that allocate a relatively large proportion of the cost of an asset to the early years of the asset's useful life.

**Account** With the accounting systems, a formal record of increases and decreases in a specific asset, liability, component of owners' equity, revenue, or expense.

**Account format** A method of presentation of accounting transactions in which effects on assets appear at the left and effects on liabilities and equity appear at the right of a central dividing line; also known as T-account format.

**Accounting profit (income before taxes or pretax income)** Income as reported on the income statement, in accordance with prevailing accounting standards, before the provisions for income tax expense.

**Accounting risk** The risk associated with accounting standards that vary from country to country or with any uncertainty about how certain transactions should be recorded.

**Accounts payable** Amounts that a business owes to its vendors for goods and services that were purchased from them but which have not yet been paid.

**Accounts receivable turnover** Ratio of sales on credit to the average balance in accounts receivable.

**Accrual basis** Method of accounting in which the effect of transactions on financial condition and income are recorded when they occur, not when they are settled in cash.

**Accrued expenses (accrued liabilities)** Liabilities related to expenses that have been incurred but not yet paid as of the end of an accounting period—an example of an accrued expense is rent that has been incurred but not yet paid, resulting in a liability "rent payable."

**Accrued interest** Interest earned but not yet paid.

**Accumulated benefit obligation** Under U.S. GAAP, a measure used in estimating a defined-benefit pension plan's liabilities, defined as "the actuarial present value of benefits (whether vested or non-vested) attributed by the pension benefit formula to employee service rendered before a specified date and based on employee service and compensation (if applicable) prior to that date."

**Accumulated depreciation** An offset to property, plant, and equipment (PPE) reflecting the amount of the cost of PPE that has been allocated to current and previous accounting periods.

**Accumulation phase** Phase in the investment life cycle during which individuals in the early-to-middle years of their working career attempt to accumulate assets to satisfy short-term needs and longer-term goals.

**Acquiring company, or acquirer** The company in a merger or acquisition that is acquiring the target.

**Acquisition** The purchase of some portion of one company by another; the purchase may be for assets, a definable segment of another entity, or the purchase of an entire company.

**Acquisition method** A method of accounting for a business combination where the acquirer is required to measure each identifiable asset and liability at fair value. This method was the result of a joint project of the IASB and FASB aiming at convergence in standards for the accounting of business combinations.

**Active factor risk** The contribution to active risk squared resulting from the portfolio's different-than-benchmark exposures relative to factors specified in the risk model.

**Active return** The return on a portfolio minus the return on the portfolio's benchmark.

**Active risk** The standard deviation of active returns.

**Active risk squared** The variance of active returns; active risk raised to the second power.

**Active specific risk or asset selection risk** The contribution to active risk squared resulting from the portfolio's active weights on individual assets as those weights interact with assets' residual risk.

**G-1**

**Active strategy** In reference to short-term cash management, an investment strategy characterized by monitoring and attempting to capitalize on market conditions to optimize the risk and return relationship of short-term investments.

**Activity ratios (asset utilization or operating efficiency ratios)** Ratios that measure how efficiently a company performs day-to-day tasks, such as the collection of receivables and management of inventory.

**Addition rule for probabilities** A principle stating that the probability that $A$ or $B$ occurs (both occur) equals the probability that $A$ occurs, plus the probability that $B$ occurs, minus the probability that both $A$ and $B$ occur.

**Add-on interest** A procedure for determining the interest on a bond or loan in which the interest is added onto the face value of a contract.

**Adjusted beta** Historical beta adjusted to reflect the tendency of beta to be mean reverting.

**Adjusted $R^2$** A measure of goodness-of-fit of a regression that is adjusted for degrees of freedom and hence does not automatically increase when another independent variable is added to a regression.

**Agency costs** Costs associated with the conflict of interest present when a company is managed by non-owners. Agency costs result from the inherent conflicts of interest between managers and equity owners.

**Agency costs of equity** The smaller the stake that managers have in the company, the less is their share in bearing the cost of excessive perquisite consumption or not giving their best efforts in running the company.

**Agency problem, or principal-agent problem** A conflict of interest that arises when the agent in an agency relationship has goals and incentives that differ from the principal to whom the agent owes a fiduciary duty.

**Agency relationships** An arrangement whereby someone, an agent, acts on behalf of another person, the principal.

**Aggregate demand** The relationship between the quantity of real GDP demanded and the price level.

**Aggregate hours** The total number of hours worked by all the people employed, both full time and part time, during a year.

**Aging schedule** A breakdown of accounts into categories of days outstanding.

**Allowance for bad debts** An offset to accounts receivable for the amount of accounts receivable that are estimated to be uncollectible.

**Alternative hypothesis** The hypothesis accepted when the null hypothesis is rejected.

**American option** An option contract that can be exercised at any time until its expiration date.

**Amortization** The process of allocating the cost of intangible long-term assets having a finite useful life to accounting periods; the allocation of the amount of a bond premium or discount to the periods remaining until bond maturity.

**Amortizing and accreting swaps** A swap in which the notional principal changes according to a formula related to changes in the underlying.

**Analysis of variance (ANOVA)** The analysis of the total variability of a dataset (such as observations on the dependent variable in a regression) into components representing different sources of variation; with reference to regression, ANOVA provides the inputs for an $F$-test of the significance of the regression as a whole.

**Annual percentage rate** The cost of borrowing expressed as a yearly rate.

**Annuity** A finite set of level sequential cash flows.

**Annuity due** An annuity having a first cash flow that is paid immediately.

**Anomalies** Security price relationships that appear to contradict a well-regarded hypothesis; in this case, the efficient market hypothesis.

**Anticipation stock** Excess inventory that is held in anticipation of increased demand, often because of seasonal patterns of demand.

**Antidilutive** With reference to a transaction or a security, one that would increase earnings per share (EPS) or result in EPS higher than the company's basic EPS—antidilutive securities are not included in the calculation of diluted EPS.

**Arbitrage** (1) The simultaneous purchase of an undervalued asset or portfolio and sale of an overvalued but equivalent asset or portfolio, in order to obtain a riskless profit on the price differential. Taking advantage of a market inefficiency in a risk-free manner. (2) A trading strategy designed to generate a guaranteed profit from a transaction that requires no capital commitment or risk bearing on the part of the trader. A simple example of an arbitrage trade would be the simultaneous purchase and sale of the same security in different markets at different prices. (3) The condition in a financial market in which equivalent assets or combinations of assets sell for two different prices, creating an opportunity to profit at no risk with no commitment of money. In a well-functioning financial market, few arbitrage opportunities are possible. (4) A risk-free operation that earns an expected positive net profit but requires no net investment of money.

**Arbitrage opportunity**  An opportunity to conduct an arbitrage; an opportunity to earn an expected positive net profit without risk and with no net investment of money.

**Arbitrage portfolio**  The portfolio that exploits an arbitrage opportunity.

**Arithmetic mean**  The sum of the observations divided by the number of observations.

**Arrears swap**  A type of interest rate swap in which the floating payment is set at the end of the period and the interest is paid at that same time.

**Asian call option**  A European-style option with a value at maturity equal to the difference between the stock price at maturity and the average stock price during the life of the option, or $0, whichever is greater.

**Asset allocation**  The process of deciding how to distribute an investor's wealth among different asset classes for investment purposes.

**Asset beta**  The unlevered beta; reflects the business risk of the assets; the asset's systematic risk.

**Asset class**  Securities that have similar characteristics, attributes, and risk/return relationships.

**Asset purchase**  An acquisition in which the acquirer purchases the target company's assets and payment is made directly to the target company.

**Asset retirement obligations (AROs)**  The fair value of the estimated costs to be incurred at the end of a tangible asset's service life. The fair value of the liability is determined on the basis of discounted cash flows.

**Asset-based loan**  A loan that is secured with company assets.

**Assets**  Resources controlled by an enterprise as a result of past events and from which future economic benefits to the enterprise are expected to flow.

**Assignment of accounts receivable**  The use of accounts receivable as collateral for a loan.

**Asymmetric information**  The differential of information between corporate insiders and outsiders regarding the company's performance and prospects. Managers typically have more information about the company's performance and prospects than owners and creditors.

**At the money**  An option in which the underlying value equals the exercise price.

**Autocorrelation**  The correlation of a time series with its own past values.

**Autocorrelation test**  A test of the efficient market hypothesis that compares security price changes over time to check for predictable correlation patterns.

**Automated Clearing House**  An electronic payment network available to businesses, individuals, and financial institutions in the United States, U.S. Territories, and Canada.

**Automatic fiscal policy**  A fiscal policy action that is triggered by the state of the economy.

**Automatic stabilizers**  Mechanisms that stabilize real GDP without explicit action by the government.

**Autonomous tax multiplier**  The magnification effect of a change in taxes on aggregate demand.

**Autoregressive (AR) model**  A time series regressed on its own past values, in which the independent variable is a lagged value of the dependent variable.

**Available-for-sale investments**  Debt and equity securities not classified as either held-to-maturity or held-for-trading securities. The investor is willing to sell but not actively planning to sell. In general, available-for-sale securities are reported at fair value on the balance sheet.

**Average cost pricing rule**  A rule that sets price to cover cost including normal profit, which means setting the price equal to average total cost.

**Average fixed cost**  Total fixed cost per unit of output.

**Average product**  The average product of a factor of production. It equals total product divided by the quantity of the factor employed.

**Average tax rate**  A person's total tax payment divided by his or her total income.

**Average total cost**  Total cost per unit of output.

**Average variable cost**  Total variable cost per unit of output.

**Backtesting**  With reference to portfolio strategies, the application of a strategy's portfolio selection rules to historical data to assess what would have been the strategy's historical performance.

**Backward integration**  A merger involving the purchase of a target ahead of the acquirer in the value or production chain; for example, to acquire a supplier.

**Backwardation**  A condition in the futures markets in which the benefits of holding an asset exceed the costs, leaving the futures price less than the spot price.

**Balance sheet (statement of financial position or statement of financial condition)**  The financial statement that presents an entity's current financial position by disclosing resources the entity controls (its assets) and the claims on those resources (its liabilities and equity claims), as of a particular point in time (the date of the balance sheet).

**Balance sheet ratios**   Financial ratios involving balance sheet items only.

**Balanced budget**   A government budget in which tax revenues and outlays are equal.

**Balanced budget multiplier**   The magnification effect on aggregate demand of a simultaneous change in government expenditure and taxes that leaves the budget balanced.

**Balance-sheet-based accruals ratio**   The difference between net operating assets at the end and the beginning of the period compared to the average net operating assets over the period.

**Balance-sheet-based aggregate accruals**   The difference between net operating assets at the end and the beginning of the period.

**Bank discount basis**   A quoting convention that annualizes, on a 360-day year, the discount as a percentage of face value.

**Bargain purchase**   When a company is acquired and the purchase price is less than the fair value of the net assets. The current treatment of the excess of fair value over the purchase price is different under IFRS and U.S. GAAP. The excess is never accounted for as negative goodwill.

**Barriers to entry**   Legal or natural constraints that protect a firm from potential competitors.

**Barter**   The direct exchange of one good or service for other goods and services.

**Basic EPS**   Net earnings available to common shareholders (i.e., net income minus preferred dividends) divided by the weighted average number of common shares outstanding.

**Basis**   The difference between the spot price of the underlying asset and the futures contract price at any point in time (e.g., the *initial* basis at the time of contract origination, the *cover* basis at the time of contract termination).

**Basis point value (BPV)**   Also called *present value of a basis point* or *price value of a basis point* (PVBP), the change in the bond price for a 1 basis point change in yield.

**Basis swap**   (1) An interest rate swap involving two floating rates. (2) A swap in which both parties pay a floating rate.

**Bayes' formula**   A method for updating probabilities based on new information.

**Bear hug**   A tactic used by acquirers to circumvent target management's objections to a proposed merger by submitting the proposal directly to the target company's board of directors.

**Bear spread**   An option strategy that involves selling a put with a lower exercise price and buying a put with a higher exercise price. It can also be executed with calls.

**Behavioral finance**   Involves the analysis of various psychological traits of individuals and how these traits affect how they act as investors, analysts, and portfolio managers.

**Below full-employment equilibrium**   A macroeconomic equilibrium in which potential GDP exceeds real GDP.

**Benchmark**   A comparison portfolio; a point of reference or comparison.

**Benchmark error**   Situation where an inappropriate or incorrect benchmark is used to compare and assess portfolio returns and management.

**Benchmark portfolio**   A comparison standard of risk and assets included in the policy statement and similar to the investor's risk preference and investment needs, which can be used to evaluate the investment performance of the portfolio manager.

**Bernoulli random variable**   A random variable having the outcomes 0 and 1.

**Bernoulli trial**   An experiment that can produce one of two outcomes.

**Beta**   A standardized measure of systematic risk based upon an asset's covariance with the market portfolio.

**Big tradeoff**   The conflict between equality and efficiency.

**Bilateral monopoly**   A situation in which a single seller (a monopoly) faces a single buyer (a monopsony).

**Binomial model**   A model for pricing options in which the underlying price can move to only one of two possible new prices.

**Binomial random variable**   The number of successes in $n$ Bernoulli trials for which the probability of success is constant for all trials and the trials are independent.

**Binomial tree**   The graphical representation of a model of asset price dynamics in which, at each period, the asset moves up with probability $p$ or down with probability $(1 - p)$.

**Black market**   An illegal market in which the price exceeds the legally imposed price ceiling.

**Block**   Orders to buy or sell that are too large for the liquidity ordinarily available in dealer networks or stock exchanges.

**Bond equivalent yield**   A calculation of yield that is annualized using the ratio of 365 to the number of days to maturity. Bond equivalent yield allows for the restatement and comparison of securities with different compounding periods.

**Bond option**   An option in which the underlying is a bond; primarily traded in over-the-counter markets.

**Bond yield plus risk premium approach** An estimate of the cost of common equity that is produced by summing the before-tax cost of debt and a risk premium that captures the additional yield on a company's stock relative to its bonds. The additional yield is often estimated using historical spreads between bond yields and stock yields.

**Bond-equivalent basis** A basis for stating an annual yield that annualizes a semiannual yield by doubling it.

**Bond-equivalent yield** The yield to maturity on a basis that ignores compounding.

**Bonding costs** Costs borne by management to assure owners that they are working in the owners' best interest (e.g., implicit cost of non-compete agreements).

**Book value equity per share** The amount of book value (also called carrying value) of common equity per share of common stock, calculated by dividing the book value of shareholders' equity by the number of shares of common stock outstanding.

**Bootstrapping earnings** An increase in a company's earnings that results as a consequence of the idiosyncrasies of a merger transaction itself rather than because of resulting economic benefits of the combination.

**Bottom-up analysis** With reference to investment selection processes, an approach that involves selection from all securities within a specified investment universe, i.e., without prior narrowing of the universe on the basis of macroeconomic or overall market considerations.

**Box spread** An option strategy that combines a bull spread and a bear spread having two different exercise prices, which produces a risk-free payoff of the difference in the exercise prices.

**Break point** In the context of the weighted average cost of capital (WACC), a break point is the amount of capital at which the cost of one or more of the sources of capital changes, leading to a change in the WACC.

**Breakeven point** The number of units produced and sold at which the company's net income is zero (revenues = total costs).

**Breakup value** The value that can be achieved if a company's assets are divided and sold separately.

**Breusch–Pagan test** A test for conditional heteroskedasticity in the error term of a regression.

**Broker** (1) An agent who executes orders to buy or sell securities on behalf of a client in exchange for a commission. (2) *See* Futures commission merchants.

**Budget deficit** A government's budget balance that is negative—outlays exceed tax revenues.

**Budget surplus** A government's budget balance that is positive—tax revenues exceed outlays.

**Bull spread** An option strategy that involves buying a call with a lower exercise price and selling a call with a higher exercise price. It can also be executed with puts.

**Business risk** The risk associated with operating earnings. Operating earnings are uncertain because total revenues and many of the expenditures contributed to produce those revenues are uncertain.

**Butterfly spread** An option strategy that combines two bull or bear spreads and has three exercise prices.

**Call** An option that gives the holder the right to buy an underlying asset from another party at a fixed price over a specific period of time.

**Call market** A market in which trading for individual stocks only takes place at specified times. All the bids and asks available at the time are combined and the market administrators specify a single price that will possibly clear the market at that time.

**Cannibalization** Cannibalization occurs when an investment takes customers and sales away from another part of the company.

**Cap** (1) A contract on an interest rate, whereby at periodic payment dates, the writer of the cap pays the difference between the market interest rate and a specified cap rate if, and only if, this difference is positive. This is equivalent to a stream of call options on the interest rate. (2) A combination of interest rate call options designed to hedge a borrower against rate increases on a floating-rate loan.

**Capital allocation line (CAL)** A graph line that describes the combinations of expected return and standard deviation of return available to an investor from combining the optimal portfolio of risky assets with the risk-free asset.

**Capital appreciation** A return objective in which the investor seeks to increase the portfolio value, primarily through capital gains, over time to meet a future need rather than dividend yield.

**Capital asset pricing model (CAPM)** An equation describing the expected return on any asset (or portfolio) as a linear function of its beta relative to the market portfolio.

**Capital budgeting** The allocation of funds to relatively long-range projects or investments.

**Capital market line (CML)** The line with an intercept point equal to the risk-free rate that is tangent to the efficient frontier of risky assets; represents the efficient frontier when a risk-free asset is available for investment.

**Capital preservation** A return objective in which the investor seeks to minimize the risk of loss; generally a goal of the risk-averse investor.

**Capital rationing** A capital rationing environment assumes that the company has a fixed amount of funds to invest.

**Capital structure** The mix of debt and equity that a company uses to finance its business; a company's specific mixture of long-term financing.

**Capitalized inventory costs** Costs of inventories including costs of purchase, costs of conversion, other costs to bring the inventories to their present location and condition, and the allocated portion of fixed production overhead costs.

**Caplet** Each component call option in a cap.

**Capped swap** A swap in which the floating payments have an upper limit.

**Captive finance subsidiary** A wholly-owned subsidiary of a company that is established to provide financing of the sales of the parent company.

**Carrying amount (book value)** The amount at which an asset or liability is valued according to accounting principles.

**Cartel** A group of firms that has entered into a collusive agreement to restrict output and increase prices and profits.

**Cash** In accounting contexts, cash on hand (e.g., petty cash and cash not yet deposited to the bank) and demand deposits held in banks and similar accounts that can be used in payment of obligations.

**Cash basis** Accounting method in which the only relevant transactions for the financial statements are those that involve cash.

**Cash conversion cycle (net operating cycle)** A financial metric that measures the length of time required for a company to convert cash invested in its operations to cash received as a result of its operations; equal to days of inventory on hand + days of sales outstanding – number of days of payables.

**Cash equivalents** Very liquid short-term investments, usually maturing in 90 days or less.

**Cash flow additivity principle** The principle that dollar amounts indexed at the same point in time are additive.

**Cash flow at risk (CFAR)** A variation of VAR that reflects the risk of a company's cash flow instead of its market value.

**Cash flow from operations (cash flow from operating activities or operating cash flow)** The net amount of cash provided from operating activities.

**Cash flow statement (statement of cash flows)** A financial statement that reconciles beginning-of-period and end-of-period balance sheet values of cash; consists of three parts: cash flows from operating activities, cash flows from investing activities, and cash flows from financing activities.

**Cash offering** A merger or acquisition that is to be paid for with cash; the cash for the merger might come from the acquiring company's existing assets or from a debt issue.

**Cash price or spot price** The price for immediate purchase of the underlying asset.

**Cash ratio** A liquidity ratio calculated as (cash + short-term marketable investments) divided by current liabilities; measures a company's ability to meet its current obligations with just the cash and cash equivalents on hand.

**Cash settlement** A procedure used in certain derivative transactions that specifies that the long and short parties engage in the equivalent cash value of a delivery transaction.

**Cash-flow-statement-based accruals ratio** The difference between reported net income on an accrual basis and the cash flows from operating and investing activities compared to the average net operating assets over the period.

**Cash-flow-statement-based aggregate accruals** The difference between reported net income on an accrual basis and the cash flows from operating and investing activities.

**Central bank** A bank's bank and a public authority that regulates the nation's depository institutions and controls the quantity of money.

**Central limit theorem** A result in statistics that states that the sample mean computed from large samples of size $n$ from a population with finite variance will follow an approximate normal distribution with a mean equal to the population mean and a variance equal to the population variance divided by $n$.

**Centralized risk management or companywide risk management** When a company has a single risk management group that monitors and controls all of the risk-taking activities of the organization. Centralization permits economies of scale and allows a company to use some of its risks to offset other risks. See also *enterprise risk management.*

**Chain rule of forecasting** A forecasting process in which the next period's value as predicted by the forecasting equation is substituted into the right-hand side of the equation to give a predicted value two periods ahead.

**Characteristic line** Regression line that indicates the systematic risk (beta) of a risky asset.

**Chart of accounts** A list of accounts used in an entity's accounting system.

**Cheapest to deliver** A bond in which the amount received for delivering the bond is largest compared with the amount paid in the market for the bond.

**Cherry-picking** When a bankrupt company is allowed to enforce contracts that are favorable to it while walking away from contracts that are unfavorable to it.

**Classical** A macroeconomist who believes that the economy is self-regulating and that it is always at full employment.

**Classified balance sheet** A balance sheet organized so as to group together the various assets and liabilities into subcategories (e.g., current and noncurrent).

**Clean-surplus accounting** The bottom-line income reflects all changes in shareholders' equity arising from other than owner transactions. In the absence of owner transactions, the change in shareholders' equity should equal net income. No adjustments such as translation adjustments bypass the income statement and go directly to shareholders equity.

**Clearinghouse** An entity associated with a futures market that acts as middleman between the contracting parties and guarantees to each party the performance of the other.

**Clientele effect** The preference some investors have for shares that exhibit certain characteristics.

**Closeout netting** Netting the market values of *all* derivative contracts between two parties to determine one overall value owed by one party to another in the event of bankruptcy.

**Coefficient of variation (CV)** The ratio of a set of observations' standard deviation to the observations' mean value.

**Cointegrated** Describes two time series that have a long-term financial or economic relationship such that they do not diverge from each other without bound in the long run.

**Collar** An option strategy involving the purchase of a put and sale of a call in which the holder of an asset gains protection below a certain level, the exercise price of the put, and pays for it by giving up gains above a certain level, the exercise price of the call. Collars also can be used to provide protection against rising interest rates on a floating-rate loan by giving up gains from lower interest rates.

**Collusive agreement** An agreement between two (or more) producers to restrict output, raise the price, and increase profits.

**Combination** A listing in which the order of the listed items does not matter.

**Command system** A method of allocating resources by the order (command) of someone in authority. In a firm a managerial hierarchy organizes production.

**Commercial paper** Unsecured short-term corporate debt that is characterized by a single payment at maturity.

**Commission brokers** Employees of a member firm who buy or sell securities for the customers of the firm.

**Committed lines of credit** A bank commitment to extend credit up to a pre-specified amount; the commitment is considered a short-term liability and is usually in effect for 364 days (one day short of a full year).

**Commodity forward** A contract in which the underlying asset is oil, a precious metal, or some other commodity.

**Commodity futures** Futures contracts in which the underlying is a traditional agricultural, metal, or petroleum product.

**Commodity option** An option in which the asset underlying the futures is a commodity, such as oil, gold, wheat, or soybeans.

**Commodity swap** A swap in which the underlying is a commodity such as oil, gold, or an agricultural product.

**Common size statements** Financial statements in which all elements (accounts) are stated as a percentage of a key figure such as revenue for an income statement or total assets for a balance sheet.

**Common-size analysis** The restatement of financial statement items using a common denominator or reference item that allows one to identify trends and major differences; an example is an income statement in which all items are expressed as a percent of revenue.

**Company fundamental factors** Factors related to the company's internal performance, such as factors relating to earnings growth, earnings variability, earnings momentum, and financial leverage.

**Company share-related factors** Valuation measures and other factors related to share price or the trading characteristics of the shares, such as earnings yield, dividend yield, and book-to-market value.

**Comparable company**  A company that has similar business risk; usually in the same industry and preferably with a single line of business.

**Competitive bid**  An underwriting alternative wherein an issuing entity (governmental body or a corporation) specifies the type of security to be offered (bonds or stocks) and the general characteristics of the issue, and the issuer solicits bids from competing investment banking firms with the understanding that the issuer will accept the highest bid from the bankers.

**Complement**  In probability, with reference to an event $S$, the event that $S$ does not occur; in economics, a good that is used in conjunction with another good.

**Completed contract**  A method of revenue recognition in which the company does not recognize any revenue until the contract is completed; used particularly in long-term construction contracts.

**Completely diversified portfolio**  A portfolio in which all unsystematic risk has been eliminated by diversification.

**Component cost of capital**  The rate of return required by suppliers of capital for an individual source of a company's funding, such as debt or equity.

**Compounding**  The process of accumulating interest on interest.

**Comprehensive income**  The change in equity of a business enterprise during a period from nonowner sources; includes all changes in equity during a period except those resulting from investments by owners and distributions to owners; comprehensive income equals net income plus other comprehensive income.

**Conditional expected value**  The expected value of a stated event given that another event has occurred.

**Conditional heteroskedasticity**  Heteroskedasticity in the error variance that is correlated with the values of the independent variable(s) in the regression.

**Conditional probability**  The probability of an event given (conditioned on) another event.

**Conditional variances**  The variance of one variable, given the outcome of another.

**Confidence interval**  A range that has a given probability that it will contain the population parameter it is intended to estimate.

**Conglomerate merger**  A merger involving companies that are in unrelated businesses.

**Consistency**  A desirable property of estimators; a consistent estimator is one for which the probabil-

ity of estimates close to the value of the population parameter increases as sample size increases.

**Consistent**  With reference to estimators, describes an estimator for which the probability of estimates close to the value of the population parameter increases as sample size increases.

**Consolidation**  The combining of the results of operations of subsidiaries with the parent company to present financial statements as if they were a single economic unit. The asset, liabilities, revenues and expenses of the subsidiaries are combined with those of the parent company, eliminating intercompany transactions.

**Consolidation phase**  Phase in the investment life cycle during which individuals who are typically past the midpoint of their career have earnings that exceed expenses and invest them for future retirement or estate planning needs.

**Constant maturity swap or CMT swap**  A swap in which the floating rate is the rate on a security known as a constant maturity treasury or CMT security.

**Constant maturity treasury or CMT**  A hypothetical U.S. Treasury note with a constant maturity. A CMT exists for various years in the range of 2 to 10.

**Constant returns to scale**  Features of a firm's technology that lead to constant long-run average cost as output increases. When constant returns to scale are present, the *LRAC* curve is horizontal.

**Construct the portfolio**  Given the strategy and economic outlook, what specific stocks and/or bonds will be put into the portfolio at the present time that are consistent with the client's policy statement.

**Consumer Price Index (CPI)**  An index that measures the average of the prices paid by urban consumers for a fixed "basket" of the consumer goods and services.

**Consumer surplus**  The value (or marginal benefit) of a good minus the price paid for it, summed over the quantity bought.

**Contango**  A situation in a futures market where the current futures price is greater than the current spot price for the underlying asset.

**Contestable market**  A market in which firms can enter and leave so easily that firms in the market face competition from potential entrants.

**Contingent claims**  Derivatives in which the payoffs occur if a specific event occurs; generally referred to as options.

**Continual monitoring**  The constant evaluation of the economic environment, the policy statement, and the portfolio to ensure that it is consistent with the policy statement. Also involves evaluating performance to determine if changes are required in the portfolio, the strategy, or the policy statement.

**Continuous market** A market where stocks are priced and traded continuously by an auction process or by dealers when the market is open.

**Continuous random variable** A random variable for which the range of possible outcomes is the real line (all real numbers between $-\infty$ and $+\infty$ or some subset of the real line.

**Continuous time** Time thought of as advancing in extremely small increments.

**Continuously compounded return** The natural logarithm of 1 plus the holding period return, or equivalently, the natural logarithm of the ending price over the beginning price.

**Contra account** An account that offsets another account.

**Contribution margin** The amount available for fixed costs and profit after paying variable costs; revenue minus variable costs.

**Controlling interest** An investment where the investor exerts control over the investee, typically by having a greater than 50 percent ownership in the investee.

**Convenience yield** The nonmonetary return offered by an asset when the asset is in short supply, often associated with assets with seasonal production processes.

**Conventional cash flow** A conventional cash flow pattern is one with an initial outflow followed by a series of inflows.

**Conversion factor** An adjustment used to facilitate delivery on bond futures contracts in which any of a number of bonds with different characteristics are eligible for delivery.

**Convertible debt** Debt with the added feature that the bondholder has the option to exchange the debt for equity at prespecified terms.

**Cooperative equilibrium** The outcome of a game in which the players make and share the monopoly profit.

**Core inflation rate** A measure of inflation based on the core CPI—the CPI excluding food and fuel.

**Corporate governance** The system of principles, policies, procedures, and clearly defined responsibilities and accountabilities used by stakeholders to overcome the conflicts of interest inherent in the corporate form.

**Corporate raider** A person or organization seeking to profit by acquiring a company and reselling it, or seeking to profit from the takeover attempt itself (e.g. greenmail).

**Corporation** A legal entity with rights similar to those of a person. The chief officers, executives, or top managers act as agents for the firm and are legally entitled to authorize corporate activities and to enter into contracts on behalf of the business.

**Correlation** A number between $-1$ and $+1$ that measures the co-movement (linear association) between two random variables.

**Correlation analysis** The analysis of the strength of the linear relationship between two data series.

**Correlation coefficient** A standardized measure of the relationship between two variables that ranges from $-1.00$ to $+1.00$.

**Cost averaging** The periodic investment of a fixed amount of money.

**Cost of capital** The rate of return that suppliers of capital require as compensation for their contribution of capital.

**Cost of carry** The cost associated with holding some asset, including financing, storage, and insurance costs. Any yield received on the asset is treated as a negative carrying cost.

**Cost of carry model** A model for pricing futures contracts in which the futures price is determined by adding the cost of carry to the spot price.

**Cost of debt** The cost of debt financing to a company, such as when it issues a bond or takes out a bank loan.

**Cost of goods sold** For a given period, equal to beginning inventory minus ending inventory plus the cost of goods acquired or produced during the period.

**Cost of preferred stock** The cost to a company of issuing preferred stock; the dividend yield that a company must commit to pay preferred stockholders.

**Cost recovery method** A method of revenue recognition in which the seller does not report any profit until the cash amounts paid by the buyer—including principal and interest on any financing from the seller—are greater than all the seller's costs for the merchandise sold.

**Cost structure** The mix of a company's variable costs and fixed costs.

**Cost-push inflation** An inflation that results from an initial increase in costs.

**Council of Economic Advisers** The President's council whose main work is to monitor the economy and keep the President and the public well informed about the current state of the economy and the best available forecasts of where it is heading.

**Covariance**   A measure of the co-movement (linear association) between two random variables.

**Covariance matrix**   A matrix or square array whose entries are covariances; also known as a variance–covariance matrix.

**Covariance stationary**   Describes a time series when its expected value and variance are constant and finite in all periods and when its covariance with itself for a fixed number of periods in the past or future is constant and finite in all periods.

**Covered call**   An option strategy involving the holding of an asset and sale of a call on the asset.

**Covered interest arbitrage**   A transaction executed in the foreign exchange market in which a currency is purchased (sold) and a forward contract is sold (purchased) to lock in the exchange rate for future delivery of the currency. This transaction should earn the risk-free rate of the investor's home country.

**Credit**   With respect to double-entry accounting, a credit records increases in liability, owners' equity, and revenue accounts or decreases in asset accounts; with respect to borrowing, the willingness and ability of the borrower to make promised payments on the borrowing.

**Credit analysis**   The evaluation of credit risk; the evaluation of the creditworthiness of a borrower or counterparty.

**Credit derivatives**   A contract in which one party has the right to claim a payment from another party in the event that a specific credit event occurs over the life of the contract.

**Credit risk or default risk**   The risk of loss caused by a counterparty's or debtor's failure to make a promised payment.

**Credit scoring model**   A statistical model used to classify borrowers according to creditworthiness.

**Credit spread option**   An option on the yield spread on a bond.

**Credit swap**   A type of swap transaction used as a credit derivative in which one party makes periodic payments to the other and receives the promise of a payoff if a third party defaults.

**Credit VAR, Default VAR, or Credit at Risk**   A variation of VAR that reflects credit risk.

**Credit-linked notes**   Fixed-income securities in which the holder of the security has the right to withhold payment of the full amount due at maturity if a credit event occurs.

**Creditworthiness**   The perceived ability of the borrower to pay what is owed on the borrowing in a timely manner; it represents the ability of a company to withstand adverse impacts on its cash flows.

**Cross elasticity of demand**   The responsiveness of the demand for a good to a change in the price of a substitute or complement, other things remaining the same. It is calculated as the percentage change in the quantity demanded of the good divided by the percentage change in the price of the substitute or complement.

**Cross-product netting**   Netting the market values of all contracts, not just derivatives, between parties.

**Cross-sectional analysis**   Analysis that involves comparisons across individuals in a group over a given time period or at a given point in time.

**Cross-sectional data**   Observations over individual units at a point in time, as opposed to time-series data.

**Crowding-out effect**   The tendency for a government budget deficit to decrease investment.

**Cumulative distribution function**   A function giving the probability that a random variable is less than or equal to a specified value.

**Cumulative relative frequency**   For data grouped into intervals, the fraction of total observations that are less than the value of the upper limit of a stated interval.

**Currency**   The notes and coins held by individuals and businesses.

**Currency drain ratio**   The ratio of currency to deposits.

**Currency forward**   A forward contract in which the underlying is a foreign currency.

**Currency option**   An option that allows the holder to buy (if a call) or sell (if a put) an underlying currency at a fixed exercise rate, expressed as an exchange rate.

**Currency swap**   A swap in which each party makes interest payments to the other in different currencies.

**Current assets, or liquid assets**   Assets that are expected to be consumed or converted into cash in the near future, typically one year or less.

**Current cost**   With reference to assets, the amount of cash or cash equivalents that would have to be paid to buy the same or an equivalent asset today; with reference to liabilities, the undiscounted amount of cash or cash equivalents that would be required to settle the obligation today.

**Current credit risk**   The risk associated with the possibility that a payment currently due will not be made.

**Current exchange rate**   For accounting purposes, the spot exchange rate on the balance sheet date.

**Current income**   A return objective in which the investor seeks to generate income rather than capital gains; generally a goal of an investor who wants to supplement earnings with income to meet living expenses.

**Current liabilities** Short-term obligations, such as accounts payable, wages payable, or accrued liabilities, that are expected to be settled in the near future, typically one year or less.

**Current rate method** Approach to translating foreign currency financial statements for consolidation in which all assets and liabilities are translated at the current exchange rate. The current rate method is the prevalent method of translation.

**Current ratio** A liquidity ratio calculated as current assets divided by current liabilities.

**Current taxes payable** Tax expenses that have been recognized and recorded on a company's income statement but which have not yet been paid.

**Cyclical change** An economic trend arising from the ups and downs of the business cycle.

**Cyclical company** A firm whose earnings rise and fall with general economic activity.

**Cyclical stock** A stock with a high beta; its gains typically exceed those of a rising market and its losses typically exceed those of a falling market.

**Cyclical surplus or deficit** The actual surplus or deficit minus the structural surplus or deficit.

**Cyclical unemployment** The fluctuating unemployment over the business cycle.

**Daily settlement** See *marking to market*.

**Data mining** The practice of determining a model by extensive searching through a dataset for statistically significant patterns.

**Day trader** A trader holding a position open somewhat longer than a scalper but closing all positions at the end of the day.

**Days of inventory on hand (DOH)** An activity ratio equal to the number of days in the period divided by inventory turnover over the period.

**Days of sales outstanding (DSO)** An activity ratio equal to the number of days in the period divided by receivables turnover.

**Dead-hand provision** A poison pill provision that allows for the redemption or cancellation of a poison pill provision only by a vote of continuing directors (generally directors who were on the target company's board prior to the takeover attempt).

**Deadweight loss** A measure of inefficiency. It is equal to the decrease in total surplus that results from an inefficient level of production.

**Dealing securities** Securities held by banks or other financial intermediaries for trading purposes.

**Debit** With respect to double-entry accounting, a debit records increases of asset and expense accounts or decreases in liability and owners' equity accounts.

**Debt covenants** Agreements between the company as borrower and its creditors.

**Debt incurrence test** A financial covenant made in conjunction with existing debt that restricts a company's ability to incur additional debt at the same seniority based on one or more financial tests or conditions.

**Debt rating approach** A method for estimating a company's before-tax cost of debt based upon the yield on comparably rated bonds for maturities that closely match that of the company's existing debt.

**Debt ratings** An objective measure of the quality and safety of a company's debt based upon an analysis of the company's ability to pay the promised cash flows, as well as an analysis of any indentures.

**Debt with warrants** Debt issued with warrants that give the bondholder the right to purchase equity at prespecified terms.

**Debt-to-assets ratio** A solvency ratio calculated as total debt divided by total assets.

**Debt-to-capital ratio** A solvency ratio calculated as total debt divided by total debt plus total shareholders' equity.

**Debt-to-equity ratio** A solvency ratio calculated as total debt divided by total shareholders' equity.

**Decentralized risk management** A system that allows individual units within an organization to manage risk. Decentralization results in duplication of effort but has the advantage of having people closer to the risk be more directly involved in its management.

**Deciles** Quantiles that divide a distribution into 10 equal parts.

**Decision rule** With respect to hypothesis testing, the rule according to which the null hypothesis will be rejected or not rejected; involves the comparison of the test statistic to rejection point(s).

**Declaration date** The day that the corporation issues a statement declaring a specific dividend.

**Declining trend channel** The range defined by security prices as they move progressively lower.

**Deductible temporary differences** Temporary differences that result in a reduction of or deduction from taxable income in a future period when the balance sheet item is recovered or settled.

**Deep in the money** Options that are far in-the-money.

**Deep out of the money** Options that are far out-of-the-money.

**Default risk premium** An extra return that compensates investors for the possibility that the borrower will fail to make a promised payment at the contracted time and in the contracted amount.

**Defensive company**   Firms whose future earnings are likely to withstand an economic downturn.

**Defensive interval ratio**   A liquidity ratio that estimates the number of days that an entity could meet cash needs from liquid assets; calculated as (cash + short-term marketable investments + receivables) divided by daily cash expenditures.

**Defensive stock**   A stock whose return is not expected to decline as much as that of the overall market during a bear market (a beta less than one).

**Deferred tax assets**   A balance sheet asset that arises when an excess amount is paid for income taxes relative to accounting profit. The taxable income is higher than accounting profit and income tax payable exceeds tax expense. The company expects to recover the difference during the course of future operations when tax expense exceeds income tax payable.

**Deferred tax liabilities**   A balance sheet liability that arises when a deficit amount is paid for income taxes relative to accounting profit. The taxable income is less than the accounting profit and income tax payable is less than tax expense. The company expects to eliminate the liability over the course of future operations when income tax payable exceeds tax expense.

**Defined-benefit pension plans**   Plan in which the company promises to pay a certain annual amount (defined benefit) to the employee after retirement. The company bears the investment risk of the plan assets.

**Defined-contribution pension plans**   Individual accounts to which an employee and typically the employer makes contributions, generally on a tax-advantaged basis. The amounts of contributions are defined at the outset, but the future value of the benefit is unknown. The employee bears the investment risk of the plan assets.

**Definitive merger agreement**   A contract signed by both parties to a merger that clarifies the details of the transaction, including the terms, warranties, conditions, termination details, and the rights of all parties.

**Degree of confidence**   The probability that a confidence interval includes the unknown population parameter.

**Degree of financial leverage (DFL)**   The ratio of the percentage change in net income to the percentage change in operating income; the sensitivity of the cash flows available to owners when operating income changes.

**Degree of operating leverage (DOL)**   The ratio of the percentage change in operating income to the percentage change in units sold; the sensitivity of operating income to changes in units sold.

**Degree of total leverage**   The ratio of the percentage change in net income to the percentage change in units sold; the sensitivity of the cash flows to owners to changes in the number of units produced and sold.

**Degrees of freedom (df)**   The number of independent observations used.

**Delivery**   A process used in a deliverable forward contract in which the long pays the agreed-upon price to the short, which in turn delivers the underlying asset to the long.

**Delivery option**   The feature of a futures contract giving the short the right to make decisions about what, when, and where to deliver.

**Delta**   The relationship between the option price and the underlying price, which reflects the sensitivity of the price of the option to changes in the price of the underlying.

**Delta hedge**   An option strategy in which a position in an asset is converted to a risk-free position with a position in a specific number of options. The number of options per unit of the underlying changes through time, and the position must be revised to maintain the hedge.

**Delta-normal method**   A measure of VAR equivalent to the analytical method but that refers to the use of delta to estimate the option's price sensitivity.

**Demand for money**   The relationship between the quantity of money demanded and the interest rate when all other influences on the amount of money that people wish to hold remain the same.

**Demand-pull inflation**   An inflation that results from an initial increase in aggregate demand.

**Dependent**   With reference to events, the property that the probability of one event occurring depends on (is related to) the occurrence of another event.

**Dependent variable**   The variable whose variation about its mean is to be explained by the regression; the left-hand-side variable in a regression equation.

**Depository institution**   A firm that takes deposits from households and firms and makes loans to other households and firms.

**Depreciation**   The process of systematically allocating the cost of long-lived (tangible) assets to the periods during which the assets are expected to provide economic benefits.

**Derivative**   A financial instrument whose value depends on the value of some underlying asset or factor (e.g., a stock price, an interest rate, or exchange rate).

**Derivatives dealers** Commercial and investment banks that make markets in derivatives.

**Derived demand** Demand for a factor of production, which is derived from the demand for the goods and services produced by that factor.

**Descriptive statistics** The study of how data can be summarized effectively.

**Designated fair value instruments** Financial instruments that an entity chooses to measure at fair value per IAS 39 or SFAS 159. Generally, the election to use the fair value option is irrevocable.

**Desired reserve ratio** The ratio of reserves to deposits that banks want to hold.

**Diff swaps** A swap in which the payments are based on the difference between interest rates in two countries but payments are made in only a single currency.

**Diffuse prior** The assumption of equal prior probabilities.

**Diluted EPS** The EPS that would result if all dilutive securities were converted into common shares.

**Diluted shares** The number of shares that would be outstanding if all potentially dilutive claims on common shares (e.g., convertible debt, convertible preferred stock, and employee stock options) were exercised.

**Diminishing balance method** An accelerated depreciation method, i.e., one that allocates a relatively large proportion of the cost of an asset to the early years of the asset's useful life.

**Diminishing marginal returns** The tendency for the marginal product of an additional unit of a factor of production to be less than the marginal product of the previous unit of the factor.

**Direct debit program** An arrangement whereby a customer authorizes a debit to a demand account; typically used by companies to collect routine payments for services.

**Direct financing lease** A type of finance lease, from a lessor perspective, where the present value of the lease payments (lease receivable) equals the carrying value of the leased asset. The revenues earned by the lessor are financing in nature.

**Direct format (direct method)** With reference to the cash flow statement, a format for the presentation of the statement in which cash flow from operating activities is shown as operating cash receipts less operating cash disbursements.

**Direct write-off method** An approach to recognizing credit losses on customer receivables in which the company waits until such time as a customer has defaulted and only then recognizes the loss.

**Dirty-surplus accounting** Accounting in which some income items are reported as part of stockholders' equity rather than as gains and losses on the income statement; certain items of comprehensive income bypass the income statement and appear as direct adjustments to shareholders' equity.

**Dirty-surplus items** Direct adjustments to shareholders' equity that bypass the income statement.

**Disbursement float** The amount of time between check issuance and a check's clearing back against the company's account.

**Discount** To reduce the value of a future payment in allowance for how far away it is in time; to calculate the present value of some future amount. Also, the amount by which an instrument is priced below its face value.

**Discount interest** A procedure for determining the interest on a loan or bond in which the interest is deducted from the face value in advance.

**Discount rate** The interest rate at which the Fed stands ready to lend reserves to depository institutions.

**Discounted cash flow analysis** In the context of merger analysis, it is an estimate of a target company's value found by discounting the company's expected future free cash flows to the present.

**Discouraged workers** People who are available and willing to work but have not made specific effort to find a job in the previous four weeks.

**Discrete random variable** A random variable that can take on at most a countable number of possible values.

**Discrete time** Time thought of as advancing in distinct finite increments.

**Discretionary fiscal policy** A fiscal action that is initiated by an act of Congress.

**Discriminant analysis** A multivariate classification technique used to discriminate between groups, such as companies that either will or will not become bankrupt during some time frame.

**Diseconomies of scale** Features of a firm's technology that lead to rising long-run average cost as output increases.

**Dispersion** The variability around the central tendency.

**Disposable income** Aggregate income minus taxes plus transfer payments.

**Divestiture** The sale, liquidation, or spin-off of a division or subsidiary.

**Dividend discount model (DDM)** A technique for estimating the value of a stock issue as the present value of all future dividends.

**Dividend discount model based approach** An approach for estimating a country's equity risk premium. The market rate of return is estimated as the sum of the dividend yield and the growth rate in dividends for a market index. Subtracting the risk-free rate of return from the estimated market return produces an estimate for the equity risk premium.

**Dividend payout policy** The strategy a company follows with regard to the amount and timing of dividend payments.

**Dividend payout ratio** The ratio of cash dividends paid to earnings for a period.

**Dividends per share** The dollar amount of cash dividends paid during a period per share of common stock.

**Dominant strategy equilibrium** A Nash equilibrium in which the best strategy for each player is to cheat (deny) regardless of the strategy of the other player.

**Double declining balance depreciation** An accelerated depreciation method that involves depreciating the asset at double the straight-line rate. This rate is multiplied by the book value of the asset at the beginning of the period (a declining balance) to calculate depreciation expense.

**Double taxation** Corporate earnings are taxed twice when paid out as dividends. First, corporate earnings are taxed regardless of whether they will be distributed as dividends or retained at the corporate level, and second, dividends are taxed again at the individual shareholder level.

**Double-entry accounting** The accounting system of recording transactions in which every recorded transaction affects at least two accounts so as to keep the basic accounting equation (assets = liabilities + owners' equity) in balance.

**Down transition probability** The probability that an asset's value moves down in a model of asset price dynamics.

**Downstream** A transaction between two affiliates, an investor company and an associate company such that the investor company records a profit on its income statement. An example is a sale of inventory by the investor company to the associate.

**Drag on liquidity** When receipts lag, creating pressure from the decreased available funds.

**Dummy variable** A type of qualitative variable that takes on a value of 1 if a particular condition is true and 0 if that condition is false.

**Duopoly** A market structure in which two producers of a good or service compete.

**DuPont analysis** An approach to decomposing return on investment, e.g., return on equity, as the product of other financial ratios.

**Duration** A measure of an option-free bond's average maturity. Specifically, the weighted average maturity of all future cash flows paid by a security, in which the weights are the present value of these cash flows as a fraction of the bond's price. A measure of a bond's price sensitivity to interest rate movements.

**Dutch Book theorem** A result in probability theory stating that inconsistent probabilities create profit opportunities.

**Dynamic hedging** A strategy in which a position is hedged by making frequent adjustments to the quantity of the instrument used for hedging in relation to the instrument being hedged.

**Earnings at risk (EAR)** A variation of VAR that reflects the risk of a company's earnings instead of its market value.

**Earnings expectation management** Attempts by management to influence analysts' earnings forecasts.

**Earnings game** Management's focus on reporting earnings that meet consensus estimates.

**Earnings management activity** Deliberate activity aimed at influencing reporting earnings numbers, often with the goal of placing management in a favorable light; the opportunistic use of accruals to manage earnings.

**Earnings multiplier model** A technique for estimating the value of a stock issue as a multiple of its future earnings per share.

**Earnings per share** The amount of income earned during a period per share of common stock.

**Earnings surprise** A company announcement of earnings that differ from analysts' prevailing expectations.

**Economic depreciation** The change in the market value of capital over a given period.

**Economic efficiency** A situation that occurs when the firm produces a given output at the least cost.

**Economic exposure** The risk associated with changes in the relative attractiveness of products and services offered for sale, arising out of the competitive effects of changes in exchange rates.

**Economic order quantity–reorder point** An approach to managing inventory based on expected demand and the predictability of demand; the ordering point for new inventory is determined based on the costs of ordering and carrying inventory, such that the total cost associated with inventory is minimized.

**Economic profit**   A firm's total revenue minus its total cost.

**Economic rent**   Any surplus—consumer surplus, producer surplus or economic profit. The income received by the owner of a factor of production over and above the amount required to induce that owner to offer the factor for use.

**Economies of scale**   Features of a firm's technology that lead to a falling long-run average cost as output increases. In reference to mergers, it is the savings achieved through the consolidation of operations and elimination of duplicate resources.

**Economies of scope**   Decreases in average total cost that occur when a firm uses specialized resources to produce a range of goods and services.

**Effective annual rate**   The amount by which a unit of currency will grow in a year with interest on interest included.

**Effective annual yield (EAY)**   An annualized return that accounts for the effect of interest on interest; EAY is computed by compounding 1 plus the holding period yield forward to one year, then subtracting 1.

**Efficiency**   In statistics, a desirable property of estimators; an efficient estimator is the unbiased estimator with the smallest variance among unbiased estimators of the same parameter.

**Efficiency wage**   A real wage rate that is set above the equilibrium wage rate and that balances the costs and benefits of this higher wage rate to maximize the firm's profit.

**Efficient capital market**   A market in which security prices rapidly reflect all information about securities.

**Efficient frontier**   The portion of the minimum-variance frontier beginning with the global minimum-variance portfolio and continuing above it; the graph of the set of portfolios offering the maximum expected return for their level of variance of return.

**Efficient portfolio**   A portfolio offering the highest expected return for a given level of risk as measured by variance or standard deviation of return.

**Elastic demand**   Demand with a price elasticity greater than 1; other things remaining the same, the percentage change in the quantity demanded exceeds the percentage change in price.

**Elasticity**   A measure of sensitivity; the incremental change in one variable with respect to an incremental change in another variable.

**Elasticity of supply**   The responsiveness of the quantity supplied of a good to a change in its price, other things remaining the same.

**Electronic funds transfer**   The use of computer networks to conduct financial transactions electronically.

**Empirical probability**   The probability of an event estimated as a relative frequency of occurrence.

**Employment Act of 1946**   A landmark Congressional act that recognizes a role for government actions to keep unemployment low, the economy expanding, and inflation in check.

**Employment-to-population ratio**   The percentage of people of working age who have jobs.

**Enhanced derivatives products companies (EDPC)**   A type of subsidiary engaged in derivatives transactions that is separated from the parent company in order to have a higher credit rating than the parent company.

**Enterprise risk management**   A form of *centralized risk management* that typically encompasses the management of a broad variety of risks, including insurance risk.

**Equitizing cash**   A strategy used to replicate an index. It is also used to take a given amount of cash and turn it into an equity position while maintaining the liquidity provided by the cash.

**Equity**   Assets less liabilities; the residual interest in the assets after subtracting the liabilities.

**Equity carve-out**   A form of restructuring that involves the creation of a new legal entity and the sale of equity in it to outsiders.

**Equity forward**   A contract calling for the purchase of an individual stock, a stock portfolio, or a stock index at a later date at an agreed-upon price.

**Equity method**   A basis for reporting investment income in which the investing entity recognizes a share of income as earned rather than as dividends when received. These transactions are typically reflected in Investments in Associates or Equity Method Investments.

**Equity options**   Options on individual stocks; also known as stock options.

**Equity risk premium**   The expected return on equities minus the risk-free rate; the premium that investors demand for investing in equities.

**Equity swap**   A swap transaction in which at least one cash flow is tied to the return to an equity portfolio position, often an equity index.

**Error autocorrelation**   The autocorrelation of the error term.

**Error term**   The portion of the dependent variable that is not explained by the independent variable(s) in the regression.

**Estimate**   The particular value calculated from sample observations using an estimator.

**Estimated (or fitted) parameters** With reference to regression analysis, the estimated values of the population intercept and population slope coefficient(s) in a regression.

**Estimated rate of return** The rate of return an investor anticipates earning from a specific investment over a particular future holding period.

**Estimation** With reference to statistical inference, the subdivision dealing with estimating the value of a population parameter.

**Estimator** An estimation formula; the formula used to compute the sample mean and other sample statistics are examples of estimators.

**Eurodollar** A dollar deposited outside the United States.

**European-style option or European option** An option contract that can only be exercised on its expiration date.

**Event** Any outcome or specified set of outcomes of a random variable.

**Event study** Research that examines the reaction of a security's price to a specific company, world event, or news announcement.

**Excess kurtosis** Degree of peakedness (fatness of tails) in excess of the peakedness of the normal distribution.

**Excess reserves** A bank's actual reserves minus its desired reserves.

**Exchange for physicals (EFP)** A permissible delivery procedure used by futures market participants, in which the long and short arrange a delivery procedure other than the normal procedures stipulated by the futures exchange.

**Exchange ratio** The number of shares that target stockholders are to receive in exchange for each of their shares in the target company.

**Ex-dividend** Trading ex-dividend refers to shares that no longer carry the right to the next dividend payment.

**Ex-dividend date** The first date that a share trades without (i.e. "ex") the dividend.

**Exercise or exercising the option** The process of using an option to buy or sell the underlying.

**Exercise date** The day that employees actually exercise the options and convert them to stock.

**Exercise price (strike price, striking price, or strike)** The fixed price at which an option holder can buy or sell the underlying.

**Exercise rate or strike rate** The fixed rate at which the holder of an interest rate option can buy or sell the underlying.

**Exhaustive** Covering or containing all possible outcomes.

**Expected rate of return** The return that analysts' calculations suggest a security should provide, based on the market's rate of return during the period and the security's relationship to the market.

**Expected value** The probability-weighted average of the possible outcomes of a random variable.

**Expensed** Taken as a deduction in arriving at net income.

**Expenses** Outflows of economic resources or increases in liabilities that result in decreases in equity (other than decreases because of distributions to owners); reductions in net assets associated with the creation of revenues.

**Expiration date** The date on which a derivative contract expires.

**Exposure to foreign exchange risk** The risk of a change in value of an asset or liability denominated in a foreign currency due to a change in exchange rates.

**External diseconomies** Factors outside the control of a firm that raise the firm's costs as the industry produces a larger output.

**External economies** Factors beyond the control of a firm that lower the firm's costs as the industry produces a larger output.

**External efficiency** A market in which prices adjust quickly to new information regarding supply or demand. Also referred to as *informational efficiency*.

**External growth** Company growth in output or sales that is achieved by buying the necessary resources externally (i.e., achieved through mergers and acquisitions).

**Externality** The effect of an investment on other things besides the investment itself.

**Face value (also principal, par value, stated value, or maturity value)** The amount of cash payable by a company to the bondholders when the bonds mature; the promised payment at maturity separate from any coupon payment.

**Factor** A common or underlying element with which several variables are correlated.

**Factor risk premium (or factor price)** The expected return in excess of the risk-free rate for a portfolio with a sensitivity of 1 to one factor and a sensitivity of 0 to all other factors.

**Factor sensitivity (also factor betas or factor loadings)** A measure of the response of return to each unit of increase in a factor, holding all other factors constant.

**Fair market value** The market price of an asset or liability that trades regularly.

**Fair value** The amount at which an asset could be exchanged, or a liability settled, between knowledgeable, willing parties in an arm's-length transaction; the price that would be received to sell an asset or paid to transfer a liability in an orderly transaction between market participants.

**Federal budget** The annual statement of the outlays and tax revenues of the government of the United States, together with the laws and regulations that approve and support those outlays and taxes.

**Federal funds rate** The interest rate that the banks charge each other on overnight loans.

**Federal Open Market Committee** The main policy-making organ of the Federal Reserve System.

**Federal Reserve System (the Fed)** The central bank of the United States.

**Fiduciary call** A combination of a European call and a risk-free bond that matures on the option expiration day and has a face value equal to the exercise price of the call.

**FIFO method** The first in, first out, method of accounting for inventory, which matches sales against the costs of items of inventory in the order in which they were placed in inventory.

**Filter rule** A trading rule that recommends security transactions when price changes exceed a previously determined percentage.

**Finance lease (capital lease)** Essentially, the purchase of some asset by the buyer (lessee) that is directly financed by the seller (lessor).

**Financial analysis** The process of selecting, evaluating, and interpreting financial data in order to formulate an assessment of a company's present and future financial condition and performance.

**Financial distress** Heightened uncertainty regarding a company's ability to meet its various obligations because of lower or negative earnings.

**Financial flexibility** The ability to react and adapt to financial adversities and opportunities.

**Financial futures** Futures contracts in which the underlying is a stock, bond, or currency.

**Financial leverage** The extent to which a company can effect, through the use of debt, a proportional change in the return on common equity that is greater than a given proportional change in operating income; also, short for the financial leverage ratio.

**Financial leverage ratio** A measure of financial leverage calculated as average total assets divided by average total equity.

**Financial reporting quality** The accuracy with which a company's reported financials reflect its operating performance and their usefulness for forecasting future cash flows.

**Financial risk** The risk that environmental, social, or governance risk factors will result in significant costs or other losses to a company and its shareholders; the risk arising from a company's obligation to meet required payments under its financing agreements.

**Financing activities** Activities related to obtaining or repaying capital to be used in the business (e.g., equity and long-term debt).

**Firm** An economic unit that hires factors of production and organizes those factors to produce and sell goods and services.

**First-differencing** A transformation that subtracts the value of the time series in period $t-1$ from its value in period $t$.

**First-order serial correlation** Correlation between adjacent observations in a time series.

**Fiscal imbalance** The present value of the government's commitments to pay benefits minus the present value of its tax revenues.

**Fiscal policy** The government's attempt to achieve macroeconomic objectives such as full employment, sustained long-term economic growth, and price level stability by setting and changing tax rates, making transfer payments, and purchasing goods and services.

**Fixed asset turnover** An activity ratio calculated as total revenue divided by average net fixed assets.

**Fixed charge coverage** A solvency ratio measuring the number of times interest and lease payments are covered by operating income, calculated as (EBIT + lease payments) divided by (interest payments + lease payments).

**Fixed costs** Costs that remain at the same level regardless of a company's level of production and sales.

**Fixed rate perpetual preferred stock** Nonconvertible, noncallable preferred stock that has a fixed dividend rate and no maturity date.

**Fixed-income forward** A forward contract in which the underlying is a bond.

**Flat trend channel** The range defined by security prices as they maintain a relatively steady level.

**Flip-in pill** A poison pill takeover defense that dilutes an acquirer's ownership in a target by giving other existing target company shareholders the right to buy additional target company shares at a discount.

**Flip-over pill** A poison pill takeover defense that gives target company shareholders the right to purchase shares of the acquirer at a significant discount to the market price, which has the effect of causing dilution to all existing acquiring company shareholders.

**Float** In the context of customer receipts, the amount of money that is in transit between payments made by customers and the funds that are usable by the company.

**Float factor**   An estimate of the average number of days it takes deposited checks to clear; average daily float divided by average daily deposit.

**Floating-rate loan**   A loan in which the interest rate is reset at least once after the starting date.

**Floor**   A combination of interest rate put options designed to hedge a lender against lower rates on a floating-rate loan.

**Floor brokers**   Independent members of an exchange who act as brokers for other members.

**Floor traders or locals**   Market makers that buy and sell by quoting a bid and an ask price. They are the primary providers of liquidity to the market.

**Floored swap**   A swap in which the floating payments have a lower limit.

**Floorlet**   Each component put option in a floor.

**Flotation cost**   Fees charged to companies by investment bankers and other costs associated with raising new capital.

**Foreign currency transactions**   Transactions that are denominated in a currency other than a company's functional currency.

**Forward contract**   An agreement between two parties in which one party, the buyer, agrees to buy from the other party, the seller, an underlying asset at a later date for a price established at the start of the contract.

**Forward integration**   A merger involving the purchase of a target that is farther along the value or production chain; for example, to acquire a distributor.

**Forward price or forward rate**   The fixed price or rate at which the transaction scheduled to occur at the expiration of a forward contract will take place. This price is agreed on at the initiation date of the contract.

**Forward rate agreement (FRA)**   A forward contract calling for one party to make a fixed interest payment and the other to make an interest payment at a rate to be determined at the contract expiration.

**Forward swap**   A forward contract to enter into a swap.

**Four-firm concentration ratio**   A measure of market power that is calculated as the percentage of the value of sales accounted for by the four largest firms in an industry.

**Free cash flow**   The actual cash that would be available to the company's investors after making all investments necessary to maintain the company as an ongoing enterprise (also referred to as free cash flow to the firm); the internally generated funds that can be distributed to the company's investors (e.g., shareholders and bondholders) without impairing the value of the company.

**Free cash flow hypothesis**   The hypothesis that higher debt levels discipline managers by forcing them to make fixed debt service payments and by reducing the company's free cash flow.

**Free cash flow to equity**   The cash flow available to a company's common shareholders after all operating expenses, interest, and principal payments have been made, and necessary investments in working and fixed capital have been made.

**Free cash flow to the firm**   The cash flow available to the company's suppliers of capital after all operating expenses have been paid and necessary investments in working capital and fixed capital have been made.

**Frequency distribution**   A tabular display of data summarized into a relatively small number of intervals.

**Frequency polygon**   A graph of a frequency distribution obtained by drawing straight lines joining successive points representing the class frequencies.

**Frictional unemployment**   The unemployment that arises from normal labor turnover—from people entering and leaving the labor force and from the ongoing creation and destruction of jobs.

**Friendly transaction**   A potential business combination that is endorsed by the managers of both companies.

**Full employment**   A situation in which the quantity of labor demanded equals the quantity supplied. At full employment, there is no cyclical unemployment—all unemployment is frictional and structural.

**Full-employment equilibrium**   A macroeconomic equilibrium in which real GDP equals potential GDP.

**Full price**   The price of a security with accrued interest.

**Functional currency**   The currency of the primary economic environment in which an entity operates.

**Fundamental beta**   A beta that is based at least in part on fundamental data for a company.

**Fundamental factor models**   A multifactor model in which the factors are attributes of stocks or companies that are important in explaining cross-sectional differences in stock prices.

**Future value (FV)**   The amount to which a payment or series of payments will grow by a stated future date.

**Futures commission merchants (FCMs)** Individuals or companies that execute futures transactions for other parties off the exchange.

**Futures contract** A variation of a forward contract that has essentially the same basic definition but with some additional features, such as a clearing-house guarantee against credit losses, a daily settlement of gains and losses, and an organized electronic or floor trading facility.

**Futures exchange** A legal corporate entity whose shareholders are its members. The members of the exchange have the privilege of executing transactions directly on the exchange.

**Gains** Asset inflows not directly related to the ordinary activities of the business.

**Game theory** A tool that economists use to analyze strategic behavior—behavior that takes into account the expected behavior of others and the recognition of mutual interdependence.

**Gamma** A numerical measure of how sensitive an option's delta is to a change in the underlying.

**Generalized least squares** A regression estimation technique that addresses heteroskedasticity of the error term.

**Generational accounting** An accounting system that measures the lifetime tax burden and benefits of each generation.

**Generational imbalance** The division of the fiscal imbalance between the current and future generations, assuming that the current generation will enjoy the existing levels of taxes and benefits.

**Geometric mean** A measure of central tendency computed by taking the $n$th root of the product of $n$ non-negative values.

**Gifting phase** Phase in the investment life cycle during which individuals use excess assets to financially assist relatives or friends, establish charitable trusts, or construct trusts to minimize estate taxes.

**Giro system** An electronic payment system used widely in Europe and Japan.

**Goodwill** An intangible asset that represents the excess of the purchase price of an acquired company over the value of the net assets acquired.

**Government debt** The total amount that the government has borrowed. It equals the sum of past budget deficits minus the sum of past budget surpluses.

**Government expenditure multiplier** The magnification effect of a change in government expenditure on goods and services on equilibrium expenditure and real GDP.

**Grant date** The day that options are granted to employees; usually the date that compensation

expense is measured if both the number of shares and option price are known.

**Greenmail** The purchase of the accumulated shares of a hostile investor by a company that is targeted for takeover by that investor, usually at a substantial premium over market price.

**Gross profit (gross margin)** Sales minus the cost of sales (i.e., the cost of goods sold for a manufacturing company).

**Gross profit margin** The ratio of gross profit to revenues.

**Grouping by function** With reference to the presentation of expenses in an income statement, the grouping together of expenses serving the same function, e.g. all items that are costs of goods sold.

**Grouping by nature** With reference to the presentation of expenses in an income statement, the grouping together of expenses by similar nature, e.g., all depreciation expenses.

**Growth company** A company that consistently has the opportunities and ability to invest in projects that provide rates of return that exceed the firm's cost of capital. Because of these investment opportunities, it retains a high proportion of earnings, and its earnings grow faster than those of average firms.

**Growth investors** With reference to equity investors, investors who seek to invest in high-earnings-growth companies.

**Growth option or expansion option** The ability to make additional investments in a project at some future time if the financial results are strong.

**Growth stock** A stock issue that generates a higher rate of return than other stocks in the market with similar risk characteristics.

**Harmonic mean** A type of weighted mean computed by averaging the reciprocals of the observations, then taking the reciprocal of that average.

**Hedge ratio** The relationship of the quantity of an asset being hedged to the quantity of the derivative used for hedging.

**Hedging** A general strategy usually thought of as reducing, if not eliminating, risk.

**Held-for-trading securities (trading securities)** Debt or equity financial assets bought with the intention to sell them in the near term, usually less than three months; securities that a company intends to trade.

**Held-to-maturity investments** Debt (fixed-income) securities that a company intends to hold to maturity; these are presented at their original cost, updated for any amortization of discounts or premiums.

**Herfindahl–Hirschman Index**   A measure of market concentration that is calculated by summing the squared market shares for competing companies in an industry; high HHI readings or mergers that would result in large HHI increases are more likely to result in regulatory challenges.

**Heteroskedastic**   With reference to the error term of a regression, having a variance that differs across observations.

**Heteroskedasticity**   The property of having a non-constant variance; refers to an error term with the property that its variance differs across observations.

**Heteroskedasticity-consistent standard errors**   Standard errors of the estimated parameters of a regression that correct for the presence of heteroskedasticity in the regression's error term.

**Histogram**   A bar chart of data that have been grouped into a frequency distribution.

**Historical cost**   In reference to assets, the amount paid to purchase an asset, including any costs of acquisition and/or preparation; with reference to liabilities, the amount of proceeds received in exchange in issuing the liability.

**Historical equity risk premium approach**   An estimate of a country's equity risk premium that is based upon the historical averages of the risk-free rate and the rate of return on the market portfolio.

**Historical exchange rates**   For accounting purposes, the exchange rates that existed when the assets and liabilities were initially recorded.

**Historical method**   A method of estimating VAR that uses data from the returns of the portfolio over a recent past period and compiles this data in the form of a histogram.

**Historical simulation (or back simulation)**   Another term for the historical method of estimating VAR. This term is somewhat misleading in that the method involves not a *simulation* of the past but rather what *actually happened* in the past, sometimes adjusted to reflect the fact that a different portfolio may have existed in the past than is planned for the future.

**Holder-of-record date**   The date that a shareholder listed on the corporation's books will be deemed to have ownership of the shares for purposes of receiving an upcoming dividend; two business days after the ex-dividend date.

**Holding period return**   The return that an investor earns during a specified holding period; a synonym for total return.

**Holding period yield (HPY)**   The return that an investor earns during a specified holding period; holding period return with reference to a fixed-income instrument.

**Homogenization**   Creating a contract with standard and generally accepted terms, which makes it more acceptable to a broader group of participants.

**Homoskedasticity**   The property of having a constant variance; refers to an error term that is constant across observations.

**Horizontal analysis**   Common-size analysis that involves comparing a specific financial statement with that statement in prior or future time periods; also, cross-sectional analysis of one company with another.

**Horizontal common-size analysis**   A form of common-size analysis in which the accounts in a given period are used as the benchmark or base period, and every account is restated in subsequent periods as a percentage of the base period's same account.

**Horizontal merger**   A merger involving companies in the same line of business, usually as competitors.

**Hostile transaction**   An attempt to acquire a company against the wishes of the target's managers.

**Hurdle rate**   The rate of return that must be met for a project to be accepted.

**Hypothesis**   With reference to statistical inference, a statement about one or more populations.

**Hypothesis testing**   With reference to statistical inference, the subdivision dealing with the testing of hypotheses about one or more populations.

**Identifiable intangible**   An intangible that can be acquired singly and is typically linked to specific rights or privileges having finite benefit periods (e.g., a patent or trademark).

**If-converted method**   A method for accounting for the effect of convertible securities on earnings per share (EPS) that specifies what EPS would have been if the convertible securities had been converted at the beginning of the period, taking account of the effects of conversion on net income and the weighted average number of shares outstanding.

**Impairment**   Diminishment in value as a result of carrying (book) value exceeding fair value and/or recoverable value.

**Impairment of capital rule**   A legal restriction that dividends cannot exceed retained earnings.

**Implicit rental rate**   The firm's opportunity cost of using its own capital.

**Implied repo rate**   The rate of return from a cash-and-carry transaction implied by the futures price relative to the spot price.

**Implied volatility**   The volatility that option traders use to price an option, implied by the price of the option and a particular option-pricing model.

**Implied yield**   A measure of the yield on the underlying bond of a futures contract implied by pricing it as though the underlying will be delivered at the futures expiration.

**Imputation**   In reference to corporate taxes, a system that imputes, or attributes, taxes at only one level of taxation. For countries using an imputation tax system, taxes on dividends are effectively levied only at the shareholder rate. Taxes are paid at the corporate level but they are *attributed* to the shareholder. Shareholders deduct from their tax bill their portion of taxes paid by the company.

**Incentive system**   A method of organizing production that uses a market-like mechanism inside the firm.

**Income**   Increases in economic benefits in the form of inflows or enhancements of assets, or decreases of liabilities that result in an increase in equity (other than increases resulting from contributions by owners).

**Income elasticity of demand**   The responsiveness of demand to a change in income, other things remaining the same. It is calculated as the percentage change in the quantity demanded divided by the percentage change in income.

**Income statement (statement of operations or profit and loss statement)**   A financial statement that provides information about a company's profitability over a stated period of time.

**Income tax paid**   The actual amount paid for income taxes in the period; not a provision, but the actual cash outflow.

**Income tax payable**   The income tax owed by the company on the basis of taxable income.

**Income tax recoverable**   The income tax expected to be recovered, from the taxing authority, on the basis of taxable income. It is a recovery of previously remitted taxes or future taxes owed by the company.

**Incremental cash flow**   The cash flow that is realized because of a decision; the changes or increments to cash flows resulting from a decision or action.

**Independent**   With reference to events, the property that the occurrence of one event does not affect the probability of another event occurring.

**Independent and identically distributed (IID)**   With respect to random variables, the property of random variables that are independent of each other but follow the identical probability distribution.

**Independent projects**   Independent projects are projects whose cash flows are independent of each other.

**Independent variable**   A variable used to explain the dependent variable in a regression; a right-hand-side variable in a regression equation.

**Index amortizing swap**   An interest rate swap in which the notional principal is indexed to the level of interest rates and declines with the level of interest rates according to a predefined schedule. This type of swap is frequently used to hedge securities that are prepaid as interest rates decline, such as mortgage-backed securities.

**Index option**   An option in which the underlying is a stock index.

**Indexing**   An investment strategy in which an investor constructs a portfolio to mirror the performance of a specified index.

**Indirect format (indirect method)**   With reference to cash flow statements, a format for the presentation of the statement which, in the operating cash flow section, begins with net income then shows additions and subtractions to arrive at operating cash flow.

**Induced taxes**   Taxes that vary with real GDP.

**Inelastic demand**   A demand with a price elasticity between 0 and 1; the percentage change in the quantity demanded is less than the percentage change in price.

**Inflation premium**   An extra return that compensates investors for expected inflation.

**Inflation rate**   The annual percentage change in the price level.

**Inflation rate targeting**   A monetary policy strategy in which the central bank makes a public commitment to achieve an explicit inflation rate and to explain how its policy actions will achieve that target.

**Inflationary gap**   The amount by which real GDP exceeds potential GDP.

**Information**   An attribute of a good market that includes providing buyers and sellers with timely, accurate information on the volume and prices of past transactions and on all currently outstanding bids and offers.

**Information ratio (IR)**   Mean active return divided by active risk.

**Informationally efficient market**   A more technical term for an efficient capital market that emphasizes the role of information in setting the market price.

**Initial margin requirement**   The margin requirement on the first day of a transaction as well as on any day in which additional margin funds must be deposited.

**Initial public offering (IPO)** A new issue by a firm that has no existing public market.

**In-sample forecast errors** The residuals from a fitted time-series model within the sample period used to fit the model.

**Instability in the minimum-variance frontier** The characteristic of minimum-variance frontiers that they are sensitive to small changes in inputs.

**Installment** Said of a sale in which proceeds are to be paid in installments over an extended period of time.

**Installment method (installment-sales method)** With respect to revenue recognition, a method that specifies that the portion of the total profit of the sale that is recognized in each period is determined by the percentage of the total sales price for which the seller has received cash.

**Instrument rule** A decision rule for monetary policy that sets the policy instrument at a level that is based on the current state of the economy.

**Intangible assets** Assets lacking physical substance, such as patents and trademarks.

**Interest coverage** A solvency ratio calculated as EBIT divided by interest payments.

**Interest rate** A rate of return that reflects the relationship between differently dated cash flows; a discount rate.

**Interest rate call** An option in which the holder has the right to make a known interest payment and receive an unknown interest payment.

**Interest rate cap or cap** A series of call options on an interest rate, with each option expiring at the date on which the floating loan rate will be reset, and with each option having the same exercise rate. A cap in general can have an underlying other than an interest rate.

**Interest rate collar** A combination of a long cap and a short floor, or a short cap and a long floor. A collar in general can have an underlying other than an interest rate.

**Interest rate floor or floor** A series of put options on an interest rate, with each option expiring at the date on which the floating loan rate will be reset, and with each option having the same exercise rate. A floor in general can have an underlying other than the interest rate.

**Interest rate forward** (See *forward rate agreement*)

**Interest rate option** An option in which the underlying is an interest rate.

**Interest rate parity** A formula that expresses the equivalence or parity of spot and forward rates, after adjusting for differences in the interest rates.

**Interest rate put** An option in which the holder has the right to make an unknown interest payment and receive a known interest payment.

**Interest rate swap** A swap in which the underlying is an interest rate. Can be viewed as a currency swap in which both currencies are the same and can be created as a combination of currency swaps.

**Intergenerational data mining** A form of data mining that applies information developed by previous researchers using a dataset to guide current research using the same or a related dataset.

**Internal rate of return (IRR)** The discount rate that makes net present value equal 0; the discount rate that makes the present value of an investment's costs (outflows) equal to the present value of the investment's benefits (inflows).

**Interquartile range** The difference between the third and first quartiles of a dataset.

**Interval** With reference to grouped data, a set of values within which an observation falls.

**Interval scale** A measurement scale that not only ranks data but also gives assurance that the differences between scale values are equal.

**In-the-money** Options that, if exercised, would result in the value received being worth more than the payment required to exercise.

**Intrinsic value or exercise value** The value obtained if an option is exercised based on current conditions.

**Inventory** The unsold units of product on hand.

**Inventory blanket lien** The use of inventory as collateral for a loan. Though the lender has claim to some or all of the company's inventory, the company may still sell or use the inventory in the ordinary course of business.

**Inventory turnover** An activity ratio calculated as cost of goods sold divided by average inventory.

**Inverse floater** A floating-rate note or bond in which the coupon is adjusted to move opposite to a benchmark interest rate.

**Investing activities** Activities which are associated with the acquisition and disposal of property, plant, and equipment; intangible assets; other long-term assets; and both long-term and short-term investments in the equity and debt (bonds and loans) issued by other companies.

**Investment decision process** Estimation of intrinsic value for comparison with market price to determine whether or not to invest.

**Investment opportunity schedule** A graphical depiction of a company's investment opportunities ordered from highest to lowest expected return. A company's optimal capital budget is found where the investment opportunity schedule intersects with the company's marginal cost of capital.

**Investment strategy**  A decision by a portfolio manager regarding how he or she will manage the portfolio to meet the goals and objectives of the client. This will include either active or passive management and, if active, what style in terms of top-down or bottom-up or fundamental versus technical.

**IRR rule**  An investment decision rule that accepts projects or investments for which the IRR is greater than the opportunity cost of capital.

**Joint probability**  The probability of the joint occurrence of stated events.

**Joint probability function**  A function giving the probability of joint occurrences of values of stated random variables.

**Joint venture**  An entity (partnership, corporation, or other legal form) where control is shared by two or more entities called venturers.

**Just-in-time method**  Method of managing inventory that minimizes in-process inventory stocks.

**Keynesian**  A macroeconomist who believes that left alone, the economy would rarely operate at full employment and that to achieve full employment, active help from fiscal policy and monetary policy is required.

**Keynesian cycle theory**  A theory that fluctuations in investment driven by fluctuations in business confidence—summarized in the phrase "animal spirits"—are the main source of fluctuations in aggregate demand.

**k-percent rule**  A rule that makes the quantity of money grow at a rate of $k$ percent a year, where $k$ equals the growth rate of potential GDP.

**kth Order autocorrelation**  The correlation between observations in a time series separated by $k$ periods.

**Kurtosis**  The statistical measure that indicates the peakedness of a distribution.

**Labor force**  The sum of the people who are employed and who are unemployed.

**Labor force participation rate**  The percentage of the working-age population who are members of the labor force.

**Labor union**  An organized group of workers whose purpose is to increase wages and to influence other job conditions.

**Laddering strategy**  A form of active strategy which entails scheduling maturities on a systematic basis within the investment portfolio such that investments are spread out equally over the term of the ladder.

**Laffer curve**  The relationship between the tax rate and the amount of tax revenue collected.

**Law of diminishing returns**  As a firm uses more of a variable input, with a given quantity of other inputs (fixed inputs), the marginal product of the variable input eventually diminishes.

**Law of one price**  The condition in a financial market in which two equivalent financial instruments or combinations of financial instruments can sell for only one price. Equivalent to the principle that no arbitrage opportunities are possible.

**Legal monopoly**  A market structure in which there is one firm and entry is restricted by the granting of a public franchise, government license, patent, or copyright.

**Legal risk**  The risk that failures by company managers to effectively manage a company's environmental, social, and governance risk exposures will lead to lawsuits and other judicial remedies, resulting in potentially catastrophic losses for the company; the risk that the legal system will not enforce a contract in case of dispute or fraud.

**Legislative and regulatory risk**  The risk that governmental laws and regulations directly or indirectly affecting a company's operations will change with potentially severe adverse effects on the company's continued profitability and even its long-term sustainability.

**Leptokurtic**  Describes a distribution that is more peaked than a normal distribution.

**Lessee**  The party obtaining the use of an asset through a lease.

**Lessor**  The owner of an asset that grants the right to use the asset to another party.

**Level of significance**  The probability of a Type I error in testing a hypothesis.

**Leverage**  In the context of corporate finance, leverage refers to the use of fixed costs within a company's cost structure. Fixed costs that are operating costs (such as depreciation or rent) create operating leverage. Fixed costs that are financial costs (such as interest expense) create financial leverage.

**Leveraged buyout (LBO)**  A transaction whereby the target company management team converts the target to a privately held company by using heavy borrowing to finance the purchase of the target company's outstanding shares.

**Leveraged floating-rate note or leveraged floater**  A floating-rate note or bond in which the coupon is adjusted at a multiple of a benchmark interest rate.

**Leveraged recapitalization**  A post-offer takeover defense mechanism that involves the assumption of a large amount of debt that is then used to finance share repurchases; the effect is to dramatically change the company's capital structure while attempting to deliver a value to target shareholders in excess of a hostile bid.

**Liabilities** Present obligations of an enterprise arising from past events, the settlement of which is expected to result in an outflow of resources embodying economic benefits; creditors' claims on the resources of a company.

**LIFO layer liquidation (LIFO liquidation)** With respect to the application of the LIFO inventory method, the liquidation of old, relatively low-priced inventory; happens when the volume of sales rises above the volume of recent purchases so that some sales are made from relatively old, low-priced inventory.

**LIFO method** The last in, first out, method of accounting for inventory, which matches sales against the costs of items of inventory in the reverse order the items were placed in inventory (i.e., inventory produced or acquired last are assumed to be sold first).

**LIFO reserve** The difference between inventory reported at FIFO and inventory reported at LIFO (FIFO inventory value less LIFO inventory value).

**Likelihood** The probability of an observation, given a particular set of conditions.

**Limit down** A limit move in the futures market in which the price at which a transaction would be made is at or below the lower limit.

**Limit move** A condition in the futures markets in which the price at which a transaction would be made is at or beyond the price limits.

**Limit order** An order that lasts for a specified time to buy or sell a security when and if it trades at a specified price.

**Limit pricing** The practice of setting the price at the highest level that inflicts a loss on an entrant.

**Limit up** A limit move in the futures market in which the price at which a transaction would be made is at or above the upper limit.

**Linear association** A straight-line relationship, as opposed to a relationship that cannot be graphed as a straight line.

**Linear interpolation** The estimation of an unknown value on the basis of two known values that bracket it, using a straight line between the two known values.

**Linear regression** Regression that models the straight-line relationship between the dependent and independent variable(s).

**Linear trend** A trend in which the dependent variable changes at a constant rate with time.

**Liquid** Term used to describe an asset that can be quickly converted to cash at a price close to fair market value.

**Liquidation** To sell the assets of a company, division, or subsidiary piecemeal, typically because of bankruptcy; the form of bankruptcy that allows for the orderly satisfaction of creditors' claims after which the company ceases to exist.

**Liquidity** The ability to buy or sell an asset quickly and at a reasonable price based on information. A company's ability to satisfy its short-term obligations using assets that are most readily converted into cash; the ability to trade a futures contract, either selling a previously purchased contract or purchasing a previously sold contract.

**Liquidity premium** An extra return that compensates investors for the risk of loss relative to an investment's fair value if the investment needs to be converted to cash quickly.

**Liquidity ratios** Financial ratios measuring the company's ability to meet its short-term obligations.

**Liquidity risk** The risk that a financial instrument cannot be purchased or sold without a significant concession in price due to the size of the market.

**Living wage** An hourly wage rate that enables a person who works a 40-hour work week to rent adequate housing for not more than 30 percent of the amount earned.

**Local currency** The currency of the country where a company is located.

**Lockbox system** A payment system in which customer payments are mailed to a post office box and the banking institution retrieves and deposits these payments several times a day, enabling the company to have use of the fund sooner than in a centralized system in which customer payments are sent to the company.

**Locked limit** A condition in the futures markets in which a transaction cannot take place because the price would be beyond the limits.

**Logit model** A qualitative-dependent-variable multiple regression model based on the logistic probability distribution.

**Log-linear model** With reference to time-series models, a model in which the growth rate of the time series as a function of time is constant.

**Log-log regression model** A regression that expresses the dependent and independent variables as natural logarithms.

**London Interbank Offer Rate (LIBOR)** The Eurodollar rate at which London banks lend dollars to other London banks; considered to be the best representative rate on a dollar borrowed by a private, high-quality borrower.

**Long**   The buyer of a derivative contract. Also refers to the position of owning a derivative.

**Long run** A period of time in which the quantities of all resources can be varied.

**Longitudinal data**   Observations on characteristic(s) of the same observational unit through time.

**Long-lived assets (or long-term assets)**   Assets that are expected to provide economic benefits over a future period of time, typically greater than one year.

**Long-run aggregate supply**   The relationship between the quantity of real GDP supplied and the price level in the long run when real GDP equals potential GDP.

**Long-run average cost curve** The relationship between the lowest attainable average total cost and output when both plant size and labor are varied.

**Long-run industry supply curve**   A curve that shows how the quantity supplied by an industry varies as the market price varies after all the possible adjustments have been made, including changes in plant size and the number of firms in the industry.

**Long-run macroeconomic equilibrium**   A situation that occurs when real GDP equals potential GDP—the economy is on its long-run aggregate supply curve.

**Long-run Phillips curve**   A curve that shows the relationship between inflation and unemployment when the actual inflation rate equals the expected inflation rate.

**Long-term contract**   A contract that spans a number of accounting periods.

**Long-term debt-to-assets ratio**   The proportion of a company's assets that is financed with long-term debt.

**Long-term equity anticipatory securities (LEAPS)** Options originally created with expirations of several years.

**Long-term liability**   An obligation that is expected to be settled, with the outflow of resources embodying economic benefits, over a future period generally greater than one year.

**Long-term, high-priority goal**   A long-term financial investment goal of personal importance that typically includes achieving financial independence, such as being able to retire at a certain age.

**Look-ahead bias**   A bias caused by using information that was unavailable on the test date.

**Losses**   Asset outflows not directly related to the ordinary activities of the business.

**Lower bound**   The lowest possible value of an option.

**Lower-priority goal**   A financial investment goal of lesser personal importance, such as taking a luxurious vacation or buying a car every few years.

**M1**   A measure of money that consists of currency and traveler's checks plus checking deposits owned by individuals and businesses.

**M2**   A measure of money that consists of M1 plus time deposits, savings deposits, and money market mutual funds, and other deposits.

**Macaulay duration**   The duration without dividing by 1 plus the bond's yield to maturity. The term, named for one of the economists who first derived it, is used to distinguish the calculation from modified duration. See also *modified duration*.

**Macroeconomic factor**   A factor related to the economy, such as the inflation rate, industrial production, or economic sector membership.

**Macroeconomic factor model**   A multifactor model in which the factors are surprises in macroeconomic variables that significantly explain equity returns.

**Macroeconomic long run**   A time frame that is sufficiently long for the real wage rate to have adjusted to achieve full employment: real GDP equal to potential GDP, unemployment equal to the natural unemployment rate, the price level is proportional to the quantity of money, and the inflation rate equal to the money growth rate minus the real GDP growth rate.

**Macroeconomic short run**   A period during which some money prices are sticky and real GDP might be below, above, or at potential GDP and unemployment might be above, below, or at the natural rate of unemployment.

**Maintenance margin**   The required proportion that the investor's equity value must be to the total market value of the stock. If the proportion drops below this percent, the investor will receive a margin call.

**Maintenance margin requirement**   The margin requirement on any day other than the first day of a transaction.

**Managerialism theories**   Theories that posit that corporate executives are motivated to engage in mergers to maximize the size of their company rather than shareholder value.

**Manufacturing resource planning (MRP)**   The incorporation of production planning into inventory management. A MRP analysis provides both a materials acquisition schedule and a production schedule.

**Margin**   The percent of cost a buyer pays in cash for a security, borrowing the balance from the broker. This introduces leverage, which increases the risk of the transaction. Also the amount of money that a trader deposits in a margin account. In futures markets, there is no borrowing so the margin is more of a down payment or performance bond.

**Margin call** A request by an investor's broker for additional capital for a security bought on margin if the investor's equity value declines below the required maintenance margin.

**Marginal cost** The opportunity cost of producing one more unit of a good or service. It is the best alternative forgone. It is calculated as the increase in total cost divided by the increase in output.

**Marginal cost pricing rule** A rule that sets the price of a good or service equal to the marginal cost of producing it.

**Marginal product** The increase in total product that results from a one-unit increase in the variable input, with all other inputs remaining the same. It is calculated as the increase in total product divided by the increase in the variable input employed, when the quantities of all other inputs are constant.

**Marginal revenue** The change in total revenue that results from a one-unit increase in the quantity sold. It is calculated as the change in total revenue divided by the change in quantity sold.

**Marginal revenue product** The change in total revenue that results from employing one more unit of a factor of production (labor) while the quantity of all other factors remains the same. It is calculated as the increase in total revenue divided by the increase in the quantity of the factor (labor).

**Marginal tax rate** The part of each additional dollar in income that is paid as tax.

**Market** The means through which buyers and sellers are brought together to aid in the transfer of goods and/or services.

**Market order** An order to buy or sell a security immediately at the best price available.

**Market portfolio** The portfolio that includes all risky assets with relative weights equal to their proportional market values.

**Market power** The ability to influence the market, and in particular the market price, by influencing the total quantity offered for sale.

**Market price of risk** The slope of the capital market line, indicating the market risk premium for each unit of market risk.

**Market rate** The rate demanded by purchasers of bonds, given the risks associated with future cash payment obligations of the particular bond issue.

**Market risk** The risk associated with interest rates, exchange rates, and equity prices.

**Market risk premium** The expected excess return on the market over the risk-free rate.

**Market-oriented investors** With reference to equity investors, investors whose investment disciplines cannot be clearly categorized as value or growth.

**Marking to market** A procedure used primarily in futures markets in which the parties to a contract settle the amount owed daily. Also known as the *daily settlement.*

**Markowitz decision rule** A decision rule for choosing between two investments based on their means and variances.

**Mark-to-market** The revaluation of a financial asset or liability to its current market value or fair value.

**Matching principle** The accounting principle that expenses should be recognized when the associated revenue is recognized.

**Matching strategy** An active investment strategy that includes intentional matching of the timing of cash outflows with investment maturities.

**Materiality** The condition of being of sufficient importance so that omission or misstatement of the item in a financial report could make a difference to users' decisions.

**Matrix pricing** In the fixed income markets, to price a security on the basis of valuation-relevant characteristics (e.g. debt-rating approach).

**Maturity premium** An extra return that compensates investors for the increased sensitivity of the market value of debt to a change in market interest rates as maturity is extended.

**McCallum rule** A rule that makes the growth rate of the monetary base respond to the long-term average growth rate of real GDP and medium-term changes in the velocity of circulation of the monetary base.

**Mean** The sum of all values in a distribution or dataset, divided by the number of values summed; a synonym of arithmetic mean.

**Mean absolute deviation** With reference to a sample, the mean of the absolute values of deviations from the sample mean.

**Mean excess return** The average rate of return in excess of the risk-free rate.

**Mean rates of return** The average of an investment's returns over an extended period of time.

**Mean reversion** The tendency of a time series to fall when its level is above its mean and rise when its level is below its mean; a mean-reverting time series tends to return to its long-term mean.

**Mean–variance analysis** An approach to portfolio analysis using expected means, variances, and covariances of asset returns.

**Means of payment** A method of settling a debt.

**Measure of central tendency**  A quantitative measure that specifies where data are centered.

**Measure of location**  A quantitative measure that describes the location or distribution of data; includes not only measures of central tendency but also other measures such as percentiles.

**Measurement scales**  A scheme of measuring differences. The four types of measurement scales are nominal, ordinal, interval, and ratio.

**Median**  The value of the middle item of a set of items that has been sorted into ascending or descending order; the 50th percentile.

**Merger**  The absorption of one company by another; that is, two companies become one entity and one or both of the pre-merger companies ceases to exist as a separate entity.

**Mesokurtic**  Describes a distribution with kurtosis identical to that of the normal distribution.

**Minimum efficient scale**  The smallest quantity of output at which the long-run average cost curve reaches its lowest level.

**Minimum wage**  A regulation that makes the hiring of labor below a specified wage rate illegal. The lowest wage at which a firm may legally hire labor.

**Minimum-variance frontier**  The graph of the set of portfolios that have minimum variance for their level of expected return.

**Minimum-variance portfolio**  The portfolio with the minimum variance for each given level of expected return.

**Minority active investments**  Investments in which investors exert significant influence, but not control, over the investee. Typically, the investor has 20 to 50% ownership in the investee.

**Minority interest (noncontrolling interest)**  The proportion of the ownership of a subsidiary not held by the parent (controlling) company.

**Minority passive investments (passive investments)**  Investments in which the investor has no significant influence or control over the operations of the investee.

**Mismatching strategy**  An active investment strategy whereby the timing of cash outflows is not matched with investment maturities.

**Mixed factor models**  Factor models that combine features of more than one type of factor model.

**Mixed offering**  A merger or acquisition that is to be paid for with cash, securities, or some combination of the two.

**Modal interval**  With reference to grouped data, the most frequently occurring interval.

**Mode**  The most frequently occurring value in a set of observations.

**Model risk**  The use of an inaccurate pricing model for a particular investment, or the improper use of the right model.

**Model specification**  With reference to regression, the set of variables included in the regression and the regression equation's functional form.

**Modified duration**  A measure of a bond's price sensitivity to interest rate movements. Equal to the Macaulay duration of a bond divided by one plus its yield to maturity.

**Monetarist**  A macroeconomist who believes that the economy is self-regulating and that it will normally operate at full employment, provided that monetary policy is not erratic and that the pace of money growth is kept steady.

**Monetarist cycle theory**  A theory that fluctuations in both investment and consumption expenditure, driven by fluctuations in the growth rate of the quantity of money, are the main source of fluctuations in aggregate demand.

**Monetary assets and liabilities**  Assets and liabilities with value equal to the amount of currency contracted for, a fixed amount of currency. Examples are cash, accounts receivable, mortgages receivable, accounts payable, bonds payable, and mortgages payable. Inventory is not a monetary asset. Most liabilities are monetary.

**Monetary base**  The sum of Federal Reserve notes, coins and banks' deposits at the Fed.

**Monetary policy**  The Fed conducts the nation's monetary policy by changing interest rates and adjusting the quantity of money.

**Monetary policy instrument**  A variable that the Fed can control directly or closely target.

**Monetary/nonmonetary method**  Approach to translating foreign currency financial statements for consolidation in which monetary assets and liabilities are translated at the current exchange rate. Nonmonetary assets and liabilities are translated at historical exchange rates (the exchange rates that existed when the assets and liabilities were acquired).

**Money**  Any commodity or token that is generally acceptable as the means of payment.

**Money market**  The market for short-term debt instruments (one-year maturity or less).

**Money market yield (or CD equivalent yield)**  A yield on a basis comparable to the quoted yield on an interest-bearing money market instrument that pays interest on a 360-day basis; the annualized holding period yield, assuming a 360-day year.

**Money multiplier**  The ratio of the change in the quantity of money to the change in the monetary base.

**Moneyness**   The relationship between the price of the underlying and an option's exercise price.

**Money-weighted rate of return**   The internal rate of return on a portfolio, taking account of all cash flows.

**Monitoring costs**   Costs borne by owners to monitor the management of the company (e.g., board of director expenses).

**Monopolistic competition**   A market structure in which a large number of firms compete by making similar but slightly different products.

**Monopoly**   A market structure in which there is one firm, which produces a good or service that has no close substitutes and in which the firm is protected from competition by a barrier preventing the entry of new firms.

**Monopsony**   A market in which there is a single buyer.

**Monte Carlo simulation method**   An approach to estimating a probability distribution of outcomes to examine what might happen if particular risks are faced. This method is widely used in the sciences as well as in business to study a variety of problems.

**Moving average**   The continually recalculating average of security prices for a period, often 200 days, to serve as an indication of the general trend of prices and also as a benchmark price.

**Multicollinearity**   A regression assumption violation that occurs when two or more independent variables (or combinations of independent variables) are highly but not perfectly correlated with each other.

**Multiple linear regression model**   A linear regression model with two or more independent variables.

**Multiple R**   The correlation between the actual and forecasted values of the dependent variable in a regression.

**Multiplication rule for probabilities**   The rule that the joint probability of events A and B equals the probability of A given B times the probability of B.

**Multi-step format**   With respect to the format of the income statement, a format that presents a subtotal for gross profit (revenue minus cost of goods sold).

**Multivariate distribution**   A probability distribution that specifies the probabilities for a group of related random variables.

**Multivariate normal distribution**   A probability distribution for a group of random variables that is completely defined by the means and variances of the variables plus all the correlations between pairs of the variables.

**Mutually exclusive events**   Events such that only one can occur at a time.

**Mutually exclusive projects**   Mutually exclusive projects compete directly with each other. For example, if Projects A and B are mutually exclusive, you can choose A or B, but you cannot choose both.

**n Factorial**   For a positive integer $n$, the product of the first $n$ positive integers; 0 factorial equals 1 by definition. $n$ factorial is written as $n!$.

**Nash equilibrium**   The outcome of a game that occurs when player A takes the best possible action given the action of player B and player B takes the best possible action given the action of player A.

**Natural monopoly**   A monopoly that occurs when one firm can supply the entire market at a lower price than two or more firms can.

**Natural unemployment rate**   The unemployment rate when the economy is at full employment. There is no cyclical unemployment; all unemployment is frictional, structural, and seasonal.

**Near-term, high-priority goal**   A short-term financial investment goal of personal importance, such as accumulating funds for making a house down payment or buying a car.

**Needs-tested spending**   Government spending on programs that pay benefits to suitably qualified people and businesses.

**Negative serial correlation**   Serial correlation in which a positive error for one observation increases the chance of a negative error for another observation, and vice versa.

**Negotiated sales**   An underwriting arrangement wherein the sale of a security issue by an issuing entity (governmental body or a corporation) is done using an investment banking firm that maintains an ongoing relationship with the issuer. The characteristics of the security issue are determined by the issuer in consultation with the investment banker.

**Net asset balance sheet exposure**   When assets translated at the current exchange rate are greater in amount than liabilities translated at the current exchange rate. Assets exposed to translation gains or losses exceed the exposed liabilities.

**Net book value**   The remaining (undepreciated) balance of an asset's purchase cost. For liabilities, the face value of a bond minus any unamortized discount, or plus any unamortized premium.

**Net income (loss)**   The difference between revenue and expenses; what remains after subtracting all expenses (including depreciation, interest, and taxes) from revenue.

**Net liability balance sheet exposure** When liabilities translated at the current exchange rate are greater than assets translated at the current exchange rate. Liabilities exposed to translation gains or losses exceed the exposed assets.

**Net operating assets** The difference between operating assets (total assets less cash) and operating liabilities (total liabilities less total debt).

**Net operating cycle** An estimate of the average time that elapses between paying suppliers for materials and collecting cash from the subsequent sale of goods produced.

**Net operating profit less adjusted taxes, or NOPLAT** A company's operating profit with adjustments to normalize the effects of capital structure.

**Net present value (NPV)** The present value of an investment's cash inflows (benefits) minus the present value of its cash outflows (costs).

**Net profit margin (profit margin or return on sales)** An indicator of profitability, calculated as net income divided by revenue; indicates how much of each dollar of revenues is left after all costs and expenses.

**Net realizable value** Estimated selling price in the ordinary course of business less the estimated costs necessary to make the sale.

**Net revenue** Revenue after adjustments (e.g., for estimated returns or for amounts unlikely to be collected).

**Netting** When parties agree to exchange only the net amount owed from one party to the other.

**New classical** A macroeconomist who holds the view that business cycle fluctuations are the efficient responses of a well-functioning market economy bombarded by shocks that arise from the uneven pace of technological change.

**New classical cycle theory** A rational expectations theory of the business cycle that regards unexpected fluctuations in aggregate demand as the main source of fluctuations of real GDP around potential GDP.

**New issue** Common stocks or bonds offered by companies for public sale.

**New Keynesian** A macroeconomist who holds the view that not only is the money wage rate sticky but also that the prices of goods and services are sticky.

**New Keynesian cycle theory** A rational expectations theory of the business cycle that regards unexpected and currently expected fluctuations in aggregate demand as the main source of fluctuations of real GDP around potential GDP.

**Node** Each value on a binomial tree from which successive moves or outcomes branch.

**Nominal rate** A rate of interest based on the security's face value.

**Nominal risk-free interest rate** The sum of the real risk-free interest rate and the inflation premium.

**Nominal scale** A measurement scale that categorizes data but does not rank them.

**Nonconventional cash flow** In a nonconventional cash flow pattern, the initial outflow is not followed by inflows only, but the cash flows can flip from positive (inflows) to negative (outflows) again (or even change signs several times).

**Noncurrent** Not due to be consumed, converted into cash, or settled within one year after the balance sheet date.

**Noncurrent assets** Assets that are expected to benefit the company over an extended period of time (usually more than one year).

**Nondeliverable forwards (NDFs)** Cash-settled forward contracts, used predominately with respect to foreign exchange forwards.

**Nonlinear relation** An association or relationship between variables that cannot be graphed as a straight line.

**Nonmonetary assets and liabilities** Assets and liabilities that are not monetary assets and liabilities. Nonmonetary assets include inventory, fixed assets, and intangibles, and nonmonetary liabilities include deferred revenue.

**Nonparametric test** A test that is not concerned with a parameter, or that makes minimal assumptions about the population from which a sample comes.

**Nonrenewable natural resources** Natural resources that can be used only once and that cannot be replaced once they have been used.

**Nonstationarity** With reference to a random variable, the property of having characteristics such as mean and variance that are not constant through time.

**Normal backwardation** The condition in futures markets in which futures prices are lower than expected spot prices.

**Normal contango** The condition in futures markets in which futures prices are higher than expected spot prices.

**Normal distribution** A continuous, symmetric probability distribution that is completely described by its mean and its variance.

**Normal profit** The return that an entrepreneur can expect to receive on the average.

**Notes payable** Amounts owed by a business to creditors as a result of borrowings that are evidenced by (short-term) loan agreements.

*n*-Period moving average  The average of the current and immediately prior $n - 1$ values of a time series.

NPV rule  An investment decision rule that states that an investment should be undertaken if its NPV is positive but not undertaken if its NPV is negative.

Null hypothesis  The hypothesis to be tested.

Number of days of inventory  An activity ratio equal to the number of days in a period divided by the inventory ratio for the period; an indication of the number of days a company ties up funds in inventory.

Number of days of payables  An activity ratio equal to the number of days in a period divided by the payables turnover ratio for the period; an estimate of the average number of days it takes a company to pay its suppliers.

Number of days of receivables  Estimate of the average number of days it takes to collect on credit accounts.

Objective probabilities  Probabilities that generally do not vary from person to person; includes a priori and objective probabilities.

Objectives  The investor's goals expressed in terms of risk and return and included in the policy statement.

Off-balance sheet financing  Arrangements that do not result in additional liabilities on the balance sheet but nonetheless create economic obligations.

Off-market FRA  A contract in which the initial value is intentionally set at a value other than zero and therefore requires a cash payment at the start from one party to the other.

Offsetting  A transaction in exchange-listed derivative markets in which a party re-enters the market to close out a position.

Oligopoly  A market structure in which a small number of firms compete.

One-sided hypothesis test (or one-tailed hypothesis test)  A test in which the null hypothesis is rejected only if the evidence indicates that the population parameter is greater than (smaller than) $\theta_0$. The alternative hypothesis also has one side.

Open market operation  The purchase or sale of government securities—U.S. Treasury bills and bonds—by the Federal Reserve in the open market.

Operating activities  Activities that are part of the day-to-day business functioning of an entity, such as selling inventory and providing services.

Operating breakeven  The number of units produced and sold at which the company's operating profit is zero (revenues = operating costs).

Operating cycle  A measure of the time needed to convert raw materials into cash from a sale; it consists of the number of days of inventory and the number of days of receivables.

Operating lease  An agreement allowing the lessee to use some asset for a period of time; essentially a rental.

Operating leverage  The use of fixed costs in operations.

Operating profit (operating income)  A company's profits on its usual business activities before deducting taxes.

Operating profit margin (operating margin)  A profitability ratio calculated as operating income (i.e., income before interest and taxes) divided by revenue.

Operating return on assets (operating ROA)  A profitability ratio calculated as operating income divided by average total assets.

Operating risk  The risk attributed to the operating cost structure, in particular the use of fixed costs in operations; the risk arising from the mix of fixed and variable costs; the risk that a company's operations may be severely affected by environmental, social, and governance risk factors.

Operations risk or operational risk  The risk of loss from failures in a company's systems and procedures (for example, due to computer failures or human failures) or events completely outside of the control of organizations (which would include "acts of God" and terrorist actions).

Opportunity cost  The value that investors forgo by choosing a particular course of action; the value of something in its best alternative use.

Opportunity set  The set of assets available for investment.

Optimal capital structure  The capital structure at which the value of the company is maximized.

Optimal portfolio  The portfolio on the efficient frontier that has the highest utility for a given investor. It lies at the point of tangency between the efficient frontier and the curve with the investor's highest possible utility.

Optimizer  A specialized computer program or a spreadsheet that solves for the portfolio weights that will result in the lowest risk for a specified level of expected return.

Option  A financial instrument that gives one party the right, but not the obligation, to buy or sell an underlying asset from or to another party at a fixed price over a specific period of time. Also referred to as contingent claims.

**Option price, option premium, or premium** The amount of money a buyer pays and seller receives to engage in an option transaction.

**Ordinal scale** A measurement scale that sorts data into categories that are ordered (ranked) with respect to some characteristic.

**Ordinary annuity** An annuity with a first cash flow that is paid one period from the present.

**Ordinary least squares (OLS)** An estimation method based on the criterion of minimizing the sum of the squared residuals of a regression.

**Ordinary shares** (**common stock or common shares**) Equity shares that are subordinate to all other types of equity (e.g., preferred equity).

**Organic growth** Company growth in output or sales that is achieved by making investments internally (i.e., excludes growth achieved through mergers and acquisitions).

**Orthogonal** Uncorrelated; at a right angle.

**Other comprehensive income** Items of comprehensive income that are not reported on the income statement; comprehensive income minus net income.

**Other post-retirement benefits** Promises by the company to pay benefits in the future, other than pension benefits, such as life insurance premiums and all or part of health care insurance for its retirees.

**Other receivables** Amounts owed to the company from parties other than customers.

**Outcome** A possible value of a random variable.

**Outliers** Small numbers of observations at either extreme (small or large) of a sample.

**Out-of-sample forecast errors** The differences between actual and predicted value of time series outside the sample period used to fit the model.

**Out-of-sample test** A test of a strategy or model using a sample outside the time period on which the strategy or model was developed.

**Out-of-the-money** Options that, if exercised, would require the payment of more money than the value received and therefore would not be currently exercised.

**Output gap** Real GDP minus potential GDP.

**Overnight index swap (OIS)** A swap in which the floating rate is the cumulative value of a single unit of currency invested at an overnight rate during the settlement period.

**Overweighted** A condition in which a portfolio, for whatever reason, includes more of a class of securities than the relative market value alone would justify.

**Owners' equity** The excess of assets over liabilities; the residual interest of shareholders in the assets of an entity after deducting the entity's liabilities.

**Paired comparisons test** A statistical test for differences based on paired observations drawn from samples that are dependent on each other.

**Paired observations** Observations that are dependent on each other.

**Pairs arbitrage trade** A trade in two closely related stocks involving the short sale of one and the purchase of the other.

**Panel data** Observations through time on a single characteristic of multiple observational units.

**Parameter** A descriptive measure computed from or used to describe a population of data, conventionally represented by Greek letters.

**Parameter instability** The problem or issue of population regression parameters that have changed over time.

**Parametric test** Any test (or procedure) concerned with parameters or whose validity depends on assumptions concerning the population generating the sample.

**Partial regression coefficients or partial slope coefficients** The slope coefficients in a multiple regression.

**Partnership** A business owned and operated by more than one individual.

**Passive strategy** In reference to short-term cash management, it is an investment strategy characterized by simple decision rules for making daily investments.

**Payables turnover** An activity ratio calculated as purchases divided by average trade payables.

**Payer swaption** A swaption that allows the holder to enter into a swap as the fixed-rate payer and floating-rate receiver.

**Payment date** The day that the company actually mails out (or electronically transfers) a dividend payment.

**Payment netting** A means of settling payments in which the amount owed by the first party to the second is netted with the amount owed by the second party to the first; only the net difference is paid.

**Payoff** The value of an option at expiration.

**Payoff matrix** A table that shows the payoffs for every possible action by each player for every possible action by each other player.

**Payout ratio** The percentage of total earnings paid out in dividends in any given year (in per-share terms, DPS/EPS).

**Peak** The culmination of a bull market when prices stop rising and begin declining.

**Pecking order theory**   The theory that managers take into account how their actions might be interpreted by outsiders and thus order their preferences for various forms of corporate financing. Forms of financing that are least visible to outsiders (e.g., internally generated funds) are most preferable to managers and those that are most visible (e.g., equity) are least preferable.

**Per unit contribution margin**   The amount that each unit sold contributes to covering fixed costs—that is, the difference between the price per unit and the variable cost per unit.

**Percentage-of-completion**   A method of revenue recognition in which, in each accounting period, the company estimates what percentage of the contract is complete and then reports that percentage of the total contract revenue in its income statement.

**Percentiles**   Quantiles that divide a distribution into 100 equal parts.

**Perfect collinearity**   The existence of an exact linear relation between two or more independent variables or combinations of independent variables.

**Perfect competition**   A market in which there are many firms each selling an identical product; there are many buyers; there are no restrictions on entry into the industry; firms in the industry have no advantage over potential new entrants; and firms and buyers are well informed about the price of each firm's product.

**Perfect price discrimination**   Price discrimination that extracts the entire consumer surplus.

**Perfectly elastic demand**   Demand with an infinite price elasticity; the quantity demanded changes by an infinitely large percentage in response to a tiny price change.

**Perfectly inelastic demand**   Demand with a price elasticity of zero; the quantity demanded remains constant when the price changes.

**Performance appraisal**   The evaluation of risk-adjusted performance; the evaluation of investment skill.

**Performance guarantee**   A guarantee from the clearinghouse that if one party makes money on a transaction, the clearinghouse ensures it will be paid.

**Performance measurement**   The calculation of returns in a logical and consistent manner.

**Period costs**   Costs (e.g., executives' salaries) that cannot be directly matched with the timing of revenues and which are thus expensed immediately.

**Periodic rate**   The quoted interest rate per period; the stated annual interest rate divided by the number of compounding periods per year.

**Permanent differences**   Differences between tax and financial reporting of revenue (expenses) that will not be reversed at some future date. These result in a difference between the company's effective tax rate and statutory tax rate and do not result in a deferred tax item.

**Permutation**   An ordered listing.

**Perpetuity**   A perpetual annuity, or a set of never-ending level sequential cash flows, with the first cash flow occurring one period from now.

**Pet projects**   Projects in which influential managers want the corporation to invest. Often, unfortunately, pet projects are selected without undergoing normal capital budgeting analysis.

**Phillips curve**   A curve that shows a relationship between inflation and unemployment.

**Plain vanilla swap**   An interest rate swap in which one party pays a fixed rate and the other pays a floating rate, with both sets of payments in the same currency.

**Platykurtic**   Describes a distribution that is less peaked than the normal distribution.

**Point estimate**   A single numerical estimate of an unknown quantity, such as a population parameter.

**Point of sale**   Systems that capture transaction data at the physical location in which the sale is made.

**Poison pill**   A pre-offer takeover defense mechanism that makes it prohibitively costly for an acquirer to take control of a target without the prior approval of the target's board of directors.

**Poison puts**   A pre-offer takeover defense mechanism that gives target company bondholders the right to sell their bonds back to the target at a pre-specified redemption price, typically at or above par value; this defense increases the need for cash and raises the cost of the acquisition.

**Policy statement**   A statement in which the investor specifies investment goals, constraints, and risk preferences.

**Pooled estimate**   An estimate of a parameter that involves combining (pooling) observations from two or more samples.

**Pooling of interests accounting method**   A method of accounting in which combined companies were portrayed as if they had always operated as a single economic entity. Called pooling of interests under U.S. GAAP and uniting of interests under IFRS. (No longer allowed under U.S. GAAP or IFRS.)

**Population**   All members of a specified group.

**Population mean**   The arithmetic mean value of a population; the arithmetic mean of all the observations or values in the population.

**Population standard deviation**   A measure of dispersion relating to a population in the same unit of measurement as the observations, calculated as the positive square root of the population variance.

**Population variance**   A measure of dispersion relating to a population, calculated as the mean of the squared deviations around the population mean.

**Portfolio performance attribution**   The analysis of portfolio performance in terms of the contributions from various sources of risk.

**Portfolio possibilities curve**   A graphical representation of the expected return and risk of all portfolios that can be formed using two assets.

**Position trader**   A trader who typically holds positions open overnight.

**Positive serial correlation**   Serial correlation in which a positive error for one observation increases the chance of a positive error for another observation, and a negative error for one observation increases the chance of a negative error for another observation.

**Posterior probability**   An updated probability that reflects or comes after new information.

**Potential credit risk**   The risk associated with the possibility that a payment due at a later date will not be made.

**Potential GDP**   The value of production when all the economy's labor, capital, land, and entrepreneurial ability are fully employed; the quantity of real GDP at full employment.

**Power of a test**   The probability of correctly rejecting the null—that is, rejecting the null hypothesis when it is false.

**Precautionary stocks**   A level of inventory beyond anticipated needs that provides a cushion in the event that it takes longer to replenish inventory than expected or in the case of greater than expected demand.

**Pre-investing**   The strategy of using futures contracts to enter the market without an immediate outlay of cash.

**Prepaid expense**   A normal operating expense that has been paid in advance of when it is due.

**Present (price) value of a basis point (PVBP)**   The change in the bond price for a 1 basis point change in yield. Also called *basis point value* (BPV).

**Present value (PV)**   The present discounted value of future cash flows: For assets, the present discounted value of the future net cash inflows that the asset is expected to generate; for liabilities, the present discounted value of the future net cash outflows that are expected to be required to settle the liabilities.

**Presentation currency**   The currency in which financial statement amounts are presented.

**Pretax margin**   A profitability ratio calculated as earnings before taxes divided by revenue.

**Price ceiling**   A regulation that makes it illegal to charge a price higher than a specified level.

**Price continuity**   A feature of a liquid market in which there are small price changes from one transaction to the next due to the depth of the market.

**Price discovery**   A feature of futures markets in which futures prices provide valuable information about the price of the underlying asset.

**Price discrimination**   The practice of selling different units of a good or service for different prices or of charging one customer different prices for different quantities bought.

**Price elasticity of demand**   A units-free measure of the responsiveness of the quantity demanded of a good to a change in its price, when all other influences on buyers' plans remain the same.

**Price floor**   A regulation that makes it illegal to trade at a price lower than a specified level.

**Price limits**   Limits imposed by a futures exchange on the price change that can occur from one day to the next.

**Price relative**   A ratio of an ending price over a beginning price; it is equal to 1 plus the holding period return on the asset.

**Price taker**   A firm that cannot influence the price of the good or service it produces.

**Price to book value**   A valuation ratio calculated as price per share divided by book value per share.

**Price to cash flow**   A valuation ratio calculated as price per share divided by cash flow per share.

**Price to sales**   A valuation ratio calculated as price per share divided by sales per share.

**Price/earnings (P/E) ratio**   The number by which expected earnings per share is multiplied to estimate a stock's value; also called the *earnings multiplier.*

**Priced risk**   Risk for which investors demand compensation for bearing (e.g. equity risk, company-specific factors, macroeconomic factors).

**Price-setting option**   The operational flexibility to adjust prices when demand varies from forecast. For example, when demand exceeds capacity, the company could benefit from the excess demand by increasing prices.

**Price-weighted index**   An index calculated as an arithmetic mean of the current prices of the sampled securities.

**Primary market**   The market in which newly issued securities are sold by their issuers, who receive the proceeds.

**Principal**   The amount of funds originally invested in a project or instrument; the face value to be paid at maturity.

**Principal–agent problem**   The problem of devising compensation rules that induce an *agent* to act in the best interest of a *principal*.

**Prior probabilities**   Probabilities reflecting beliefs prior to the arrival of new information.

**Private placement**   A new issue sold directly to a small group of investors, usually institutions.

**Probability**   A number between 0 and 1 describing the chance that a stated event will occur.

**Probability density function**   A function with non-negative values such that probability can be described by areas under the curve graphing the function.

**Probability distribution**   A distribution that specifies the probabilities of a random variable's possible outcomes.

**Probability function**   A function that specifies the probability that the random variable takes on a specific value.

**Probit model**   A qualitative-dependent-variable multiple regression model based on the normal distribution.

**Producer surplus**   The price of a good minus its minimum supply-price, summed over the quantity sold.

**Product differentiation**   Making a product slightly different from the product of a competing firm.

**Production quota**   An upper limit to the quantity of a good that may be produced in a specified period.

**Production-flexibility**   The operational flexibility to alter production when demand varies from forecast. For example, if demand is strong, a company may profit from employees working overtime or from adding additional shifts.

**Profitability ratios**   Ratios that measure a company's ability to generate profitable sales from its resources (assets).

**Project sequencing**   To defer the decision to invest in a future project until the outcome of some or all of a current project is known. Projects are sequenced through time, so that investing in a project creates the option to invest in future projects.

**Projected benefit obligation**   Under U.S. GAAP, a measure used in estimating a defined-benefit pension plan's liabilities, defined as "the actuarial present value as of a date of all benefits attributed by the pension benefit formula to employee ser-

vice rendered prior to that date. The projected benefit obligation is measured using assumptions as to future compensation if the pension benefit formula is based on those future compensation levels."

**Proportionate consolidation**   A method of accounting for joint ventures where the venturer's share of the assets, liabilities, income and expenses of the joint venture are combined on a line-by-line basis with similar items on the venturer's financial statements.

**Protective put**   An option strategy in which a long position in an asset is combined with a long position in a put.

**Provision**   In accounting, a liability of uncertain timing or amount.

**Proxy fight**   An attempt to take control of a company through a shareholder vote.

**Proxy statement**   A public document that provides the material facts concerning matters on which shareholders will vote.

**Pseudo-random numbers**   Numbers produced by random number generators.

**Pull on liquidity**   When disbursements are paid too quickly or trade credit availability is limited, requiring companies to expend funds before they receive funds from sales that could cover the liability.

**Purchase method**   A method of accounting for a business combination where the acquiring company allocates the purchase price to each asset acquired and liability assumed at fair value. If the purchase price exceeds the allocation, the excess is recorded as goodwill.

**Purchased in-process research and development costs**   The costs of research and development in progress at an acquired company.

**Purchasing power gain**   A gain in value caused by changes in price levels. Monetary liabilities experience purchasing power gains during periods of inflation.

**Purchasing power loss**   A loss in value caused by changes in price levels. Monetary assets experience purchasing power losses during periods of inflation.

**Pure discount instruments**   Instruments that pay interest as the difference between the amount borrowed and the amount paid back.

**Pure factor portfolio**   A portfolio with sensitivity of 1 to the factor in question and a sensitivity of 0 to all other factors.

**Pure-play method**   A method for estimating the beta for a company or project; it requires using a comparable company's beta and adjusting it for financial leverage differences.

**Put** An option that gives the holder the right to sell an underlying asset to another party at a fixed price over a specific period of time.

**Put–call parity** An equation expressing the equivalence (parity) of a portfolio of a call and a bond with a portfolio of a put and the underlying, which leads to the relationship between put and call prices

**Put–call–forward parity** The relationship among puts, calls, and forward contracts.

***p*-Value** The smallest level of significance at which the null hypothesis can be rejected; also called the marginal significance level.

**Qualifying special purpose entities** Under U.S. GAAP, a special purpose entity structured to avoid consolidation that must meet qualification criteria.

**Qualitative dependent variables** Dummy variables used as dependent variables rather than as independent variables.

**Quantile (or fractile)** A value at or below which a stated fraction of the data lies.

**Quantity theory of money** The proposition that in the long run, an increase in the quantity of money brings an equal percentage increase in the price level.

**Quartiles** Quantiles that divide a distribution into four equal parts.

**Quick assets** Assets that can be most readily converted to cash (e.g., cash, short-term marketable investments, receivables).

**Quick ratio, or acid test ratio** A stringent measure of liquidity that indicates a company's ability to satisfy current liabilities with its most liquid assets, calculated as (cash + short-term marketable investments + receivables) divided by current liabilities.

**Quintiles** Quantiles that divide a distribution into five equal parts.

**Random number** An observation drawn from a uniform distribution.

**Random number generator** An algorithm that produces uniformly distributed random numbers between 0 and 1.

**Random variable** A quantity whose future outcomes are uncertain.

**Random walk** A time series in which the value of the series in one period is the value of the series in the previous period plus an unpredictable random error.

**Range** The difference between the maximum and minimum values in a dataset.

**Ratio scales** A measurement scale that has all the characteristics of interval measurement scales as well as a true zero point as the origin.

**Ratio spread** An option strategy in which a long position in a certain number of options is offset by a short position in a certain number of other options on the same underlying, resulting in a risk-free position.

**Rational expectation** The most accurate forecast possible, a forecast that uses all the available information, including knowledge of the relevant economic forces that influence the variable being forecasted.

**Real business cycle theory** A theory of the business cycle that regards random fluctuations in productivity as the main source of economic fluctuations.

**Real exchange rate** The relative price of foreign-made goods and services to U.S.-made goods and services.

**Real risk-free interest rate** The single-period interest rate for a completely risk-free security if no inflation were expected.

**Real wage rate** The quantity of goods and services that an hour's work can buy. It is equal to the money wage rate divided by the price level and multiplied by 100.

**Realizable value (settlement value)** With reference to assets, the amount of cash or cash equivalents that could currently be obtained by selling the asset in an orderly disposal; with reference to liabilities, the undiscounted amount of cash or cash equivalents expected to be paid to satisfy the liabilities in the normal course of business.

**Realized capital gains** Capital gains that result when an appreciated asset is sold; realized capital gains are taxable.

**Receivables turnover** An activity ratio equal to revenue divided by average receivables.

**Receiver swaption** A swaption that allows the holder to enter into a swap as the fixed-rate receiver and floating-rate payer.

**Recessionary gap** The amount by which potential GDP exceeds real GDP.

**Reference base period** The period in which the CPI is defined to be 100.

**Regime** With reference to a time series, the underlying model generating the times series.

**Registered competitive market makers (RCMMs)** Members of an exchange who are allowed to use their memberships to buy or sell for their own account within the specific trading obligations set down by the exchange.

**Registered traders** Members of the stock exchange who are allowed to use their memberships to buy and sell for their own account, which means they save commissions on their trading but they provide liquidity to the market, and they abide by exchange regulations on how they can trade.

**Regression coefficients**   The intercept and slope coefficient(s) of a regression.

**Regulatory risk**   The risk associated with the uncertainty of how derivative transactions will be regulated or with changes in regulations.

**Rejection point (or critical value)**   A value against which a computed test statistic is compared to decide whether to reject or not reject the null hypothesis.

**Relative dispersion**   The amount of dispersion relative to a reference value or benchmark.

**Relative frequency**   With reference to an interval of grouped data, the number of observations in the interval divided by the total number of observations in the sample.

**Relative-strength (RS) ratio**   The ratio of a stock price or an industry index value to a market indicator series, indicating the stock's or the industry's performance relative to the overall market.

**Renewable natural resources**   Natural resources that can be used repeatedly without depleting what is available for future use.

**Rent ceiling**   A regulation that makes it illegal to charge a rent higher than a specified level.

**Rent seeking**   The pursuit of wealth by capturing economic rent—consumer surplus, producer surplus, or economic profit.

**Reorganization**   Agreements made by a company in bankruptcy under which a company's capital structure is altered and/or alternative arrangements are made for debt repayment; U.S. Chapter 11 bankruptcy. The company emerges from bankruptcy as a going concern.

**Replacement value**   The market value of a swap.

**Report format**   With respect to the format of a balance sheet, a format in which assets, liabilities, and equity are listed in a single column.

**Reputational risk**   The risk that a company will suffer an extended diminution in market value relative to other companies in the same industry due to a demonstrated lack of concern for environmental, social, and governance risk factors.

**Required reserve ratio**   The minimum percentage of deposits that banks are required to hold as reserves.

**Reserve ratio**   The fraction of a bank's total deposits that are held in reserves.

**Reserves**   A bank's reserves consist of notes and coins in its vaults plus its deposit at the Federal Reserve.

**Residual autocorrelations**   The sample autocorrelations of the residuals.

**Residual claim**   The owners' remaining claim on the company's assets after the liabilities are deducted.

**Residual dividend approach**   A dividend payout policy under which earnings in excess of the funds necessary to finance the equity portion of company's capital budget are paid out in dividends.

**Residual loss**   Agency costs that are incurred despite adequate monitoring and bonding of management.

**Resistance level**   A price at which a technician would expect a substantial increase in the supply of a stock to reverse a rising trend.

**Retail method**   An inventory accounting method in which the sales value of an item is reduced by the gross margin to calculate the item's cost.

**Return on assets (ROA)**   A profitability ratio calculated as net income divided by average total assets; indicates a company's net profit generated per dollar invested in total assets.

**Return on common equity (ROCE)**   A profitability ratio calculated as (net income − preferred dividends) divided by average common equity; equal to the return on equity ratio when no preferred equity is outstanding.

**Return on equity (ROE)**   A profitability ratio calculated as net income divided by average shareholders' equity.

**Return on total capital**   A profitability ratio calculated as EBIT divided by the sum of short- and long-term debt and equity.

**Return prediction studies**   Studies wherein investigations attempt to predict the time series of future rates of return using public information. An example would be predicting above-average returns for the stock market based on the aggregate dividend yield—e.g., high dividend yield indicates above average future market returns.

**Revaluation**   The process of valuing long-lived assets at fair value, rather than at cost less accumulated depreciation. Any resulting profit or loss is either reported on the income statement and/or through equity under revaluation surplus.

**Revenue**   The amount charged for the delivery of goods or services in the ordinary activities of a business over a stated period; the inflows of economic resources to a company over a stated period.

**Reverse stock split**   A reduction in the number of shares outstanding with a corresponding increase in share price, but no change to the company's underlying fundamentals.

**Revolving credit agreements**   The strongest form of short-term bank borrowing facilities; they are in effect for multiple years (e.g., 3–5 years) and may have optional medium-term loan features.

**Rho**   The sensitivity of the option price to the risk-free rate.

**Ricardo-Barro equivalence**   The proposition that taxes and government borrowing are equivalent—a budget deficit has no effect on the real interest rate or investment.

**Rising trend channel**   The range defined by security prices as they move progressively higher.

**Risk averse**   The assumption about investors that they will choose the least risky alternative, all else being equal.

**Risk budgeting**   The establishment of objectives for individuals, groups, or divisions of an organization that takes into account the allocation of an acceptable level of risk.

**Risk governance**   The setting of overall policies and standards in risk management

**Risk management**   The process of identifying the level of risk an entity wants, measuring the level of risk the entity currently has, taking actions that bring the actual level of risk to the desired level of risk, and monitoring the new actual level of risk so that it continues to be aligned with the desired level of risk.

**Risk premium**   The expected return on an investment minus the risk-free rate.

**Risk-free asset**   An asset with returns that exhibit zero variance.

**Risk-neutral probabilities**   Weights that are used to compute a binomial option price. They are the probabilities that would apply if a risk-neutral investor valued an option.

**Risk-neutral valuation**   The process by which options and other derivatives are priced by treating investors as though they were risk neutral.

**Risky asset**   An asset with uncertain future returns.

**Robust**   The quality of being relatively unaffected by a violation of assumptions.

**Robust standard errors**   Standard errors of the estimated parameters of a regression that correct for the presence of heteroskedasticity in the regression's error term.

**Root mean squared error (RMSE)**   The square root of the average squared forecast error; used to compare the out-of-sample forecasting performance of forecasting models.

**Roy's safety first criterion**   A criterion asserting that the optimal portfolio is the one that minimizes the probability that portfolio return falls below a threshold level.

**Rule of 72**   The principle that the approximate number of years necessary for an investment to double is 72 divided by the stated interest rate.

**Runs test**   A test of the weak-form efficient market hypothesis that checks for trends that persist longer in terms of positive or negative price changes than one would expect for a random series.

**Safety stock**   A level of inventory beyond anticipated needs that provides a cushion in the event that it takes longer to replenish inventory than expected or in the case of greater than expected demand.

**Safety-first rules**   Rules for portfolio selection that focus on the risk that portfolio value will fall below some minimum acceptable level over some time horizon.

**Sales**   Generally, a synonym for revenue; "sales" is generally understood to refer to the sale of goods, whereas "revenue" is understood to include the sale of goods or services.

**Sales returns and allowances**   An offset to revenue reflecting any cash refunds, credits on account, and discounts from sales prices given to customers who purchased defective or unsatisfactory items.

**Sales risk**   Uncertainty with respect to the quantity of goods and services that a company is able to sell and the price it is able to achieve; the risk related to the uncertainty of revenues.

**Sales-type lease**   A type of finance lease, from a lessor perspective, where the present value of the lease payments (lease receivable) exceeds the carrying value of the leased asset. The revenues earned by the lessor are operating (the profit on the sale) and financing (interest) in nature.

**Salvage value**   The amount the company estimates that it can sell the asset for at the end of its useful life.

**Sample**   A subset of a population.

**Sample excess kurtosis**   A sample measure of the degree of a distribution's peakedness in excess of the normal distribution's peakedness.

**Sample kurtosis**   A sample measure of the degree of a distribution's peakedness.

**Sample mean**   The sum of the sample observations, divided by the sample size.

**Sample selection bias**   Bias introduced by systematically excluding some members of the population according to a particular attribute—for example, the bias introduced when data availability leads to certain observations being excluded from the analysis.

**Sample skewness**   A sample measure of degree of asymmetry of a distribution.

**Sample standard deviation**   The positive square root of the sample variance.

**Sample statistic or statistic**   A quantity computed from or used to describe a sample.

**Sample variance**   A sample measure of the degree of dispersion of a distribution, calculated by dividing the sum of the squared deviations from the sample mean by the sample size ($n$) minus 1.

**Sampling**   The process of obtaining a sample.

**Sampling distribution**   The distribution of all distinct possible values that a statistic can assume when computed from samples of the same size randomly drawn from the same population.

**Sampling error**   The difference between the observed value of a statistic and the quantity it is intended to estimate.

**Sampling plan**   The set of rules used to select a sample.

**Sandwich spread**   An option strategy that is equivalent to a short butterfly spread.

**Sarbanes–Oxley Act**   An act passed by the U.S. Congress in 2002 that created the Public Company Accounting Oversight Board (PCAOB) to oversee auditors.

**Scalper**   A trader who offers to buy or sell futures contracts, holding the position for only a brief period of time. Scalpers attempt to profit by buying at the bid price and selling at the higher ask price.

**Scatter plot**   A two-dimensional plot of pairs of observations on two data series.

**Scenario analysis**   Analysis that shows the changes in key financial quantities that result from given (economic) events, such as the loss of customers, the loss of a supply source, or a catastrophic event; a risk management technique involving examination of the performance of a portfolio under specified situations. Closely related to stress testing.

**Screening**   The application of a set of criteria to reduce a set of potential investments to a smaller set having certain desired characteristics.

**Search activity**   The time spent looking for someone with whom to do business.

**Seasoned equity issues**   New equity shares offered by firms that already have stock outstanding.

**Seats**   Memberships in a derivatives exchange.

**Secondary market**   The market in which outstanding securities are bought and sold by owners other than the issuers. Purpose is to provide liquidity for investors.

**Sector neutralizing**   Measure of financial reporting quality by subtracting the mean or median ratio for a given sector group from a given company's ratio.

**Securities Act of 1933**   An act passed by the U.S. Congress in 1933 that specifies the financial and other significant information that investors must receive when securities are sold, prohibits misrepresentations, and requires initial registration of all public issuances of securities.

**Securities Exchange Act of 1934**   An act passed by the U.S. Congress in 1934 that created the Securities and Exchange Commission (SEC), gave the SEC authority over all aspects of the securities industry, and empowered the SEC to require periodic reporting by companies with publicly traded securities.

**Securities offering**   A merger or acquisition in which target shareholders are to receive shares of the acquirer's common stock as compensation.

**Security market index**   An index created as a statistical measure of the performance of an entire market or segment of a market based on a sample of securities from the market or segment of a market.

**Security market line (SML)**   The graph of the capital asset pricing model.

**Segment debt ratio**   Segment liabilities divided by segment assets.

**Segment margin**   Segment profit (loss) divided by segment revenue.

**Segment ROA**   Segment profit (loss) divided by segment assets.

**Segment turnover**   Segment revenue divided by segment assets.

**Semideviation**   The positive square root of semivariance (sometimes called semistandard deviation).

**Semilogarithmic**   Describes a scale constructed so that equal intervals on the vertical scale represent equal rates of change, and equal intervals on the horizontal scale represent equal amounts of change.

**Semistrong-form efficient market hypothesis**   The belief that security prices fully reflect all publicly available information, including information from security transactions and company, economic, and political news.

**Semivariance**   The average squared deviation below the mean.

**Sensitivity analysis**   Analysis that shows the range of possible outcomes as specific assumptions are changed.

**Separation theorem**   The proposition that the investment decision, which involves investing in the market portfolio on the capital market line, is separate from the financing decision, which targets a specific point on the CML based on the investor's risk preference.

**Serially correlated**  With reference to regression errors, errors that are correlated across observations.

**Service period**  The period benefited by the employee's service, usually the period between the grant date and the vesting date.

**Settlement date or payment date**  The date on which the parties to a swap make payments.

**Settlement period**  The time between settlement dates.

**Settlement price**  The official price, designated by the clearinghouse, from which daily gains and losses will be determined and marked to market.

**Settlement risk**  When settling a contract, the risk that one party could be in the process of paying the counterparty while the counterparty is declaring bankruptcy.

**Share repurchase**  A transaction in which a company buys back its own shares. Unlike stock dividends and stock splits, share repurchases use corporate cash.

**Shark repellents**  A pre-offer takeover defense mechanism involving the corporate charter (e.g., staggered boards of directors and supermajority provisions).

**Sharpe ratio**  The average return in excess of the risk-free rate divided by the standard deviation of return; a measure of the average excess return earned per unit of standard deviation of return.

**Short**  The seller of a derivative contract. Also refers to the position of being short a derivative.

**Short run**  The period of time in which the quantity of at least one factor of production is fixed and the quantities of the other factors can be varied. The fixed factor is usually capital—that is, the firm has a given plant size.

**Shortfall risk**  The risk that portfolio value will fall below some minimum acceptable level over some time horizon.

**Short-run aggregate supply**  The relationship between the quantity of real GDP supplied and the price level when the money wage rate, the prices of other resources, and potential GDP remain constant.

**Short-run industry supply curve**  A curve that shows the quantity supplied by the industry at each price when the plant size of each firm and the number of firms in the industry remain the same.

**Short-run macroeconomic equilibrium**  A situation that occurs when the quantity of real GDP demanded equals the quantity of real GDP supplied—at the point of intersection of the *AD* curve and the *SAS* curve.

**Short-run Phillips curve**  A curve that shows the tradeoff between inflation and unemployment, when the expected inflation rate and the natural unemployment rate remain the same.

**Short sale**  The sale of borrowed securities with the intention of repurchasing them later at a lower price and earning the difference.

**Shutdown point**  The output and price at which the firm just covers its total variable cost. In the short run, the firm is indifferent between producing the profit-maximizing output and shutting down temporarily.

**Signal**  An action taken by an informed person (or firm) to send a message to uninformed people or an action taken outside a market that conveys information that can be used by the market.

**Simple interest**  The interest earned each period on the original investment; interest calculated on the principal only.

**Simple random sample**  A subset of a larger population created in such a way that each element of the population has an equal probability of being selected to the subset.

**Simple random sampling**  The procedure of drawing a sample to satisfy the definition of a simple random sample.

**Simulation**  Computer-generated sensitivity or scenario analysis that is based on probability models for the factors that drive outcomes.

**Simulation trial**  A complete pass through the steps of a simulation.

**Single-payment loan**  A loan in which the borrower receives a sum of money at the start and pays back the entire amount with interest in a single payment at maturity.

**Single-price monopoly**  A monopoly that must sell each unit of its output for the same price to all its customers.

**Single-step format**  With respect to the format of the income statement, a format that does not subtotal for gross profit (revenue minus cost of goods sold).

**Skewed**  Not symmetrical.

**Skewness**  A quantitative measure of skew (lack of symmetry); a synonym of skew.

**Sole proprietorship**  A business owned and operated by a single person.

**Solvency**  With respect to financial statement analysis, the ability of a company to fulfill its long-term obligations.

**Solvency ratios**  Ratios that measure a company's ability to meet its long-term obligations.

**Sovereign yield spread**  An estimate of the country spread (country equity premium) for a developing nation that is based on a comparison of bonds yields in country being analyzed and a developed country. The sovereign yield spread is the difference between a government bond yield in the country being analyzed, denominated in the currency of the developed country, and the Treasury bond yield on a similar maturity bond in the developed country.

**Spearman rank correlation coefficient**   A measure of correlation applied to ranked data.

**Special purpose entity (special purpose vehicle or variable interest entity)**   A non-operating entity created to carry out a specified purpose, such as leasing assets or securitizing receivables; can be a corporation, partnership, trust, limited liability, or partnership formed to facilitate a specific type of business activity.

**Specialist**   The major market maker on U.S. stock exchanges who acts as a broker or dealer to ensure the liquidity and smooth functions of the secondary stock market.

**Specific identification method**   An inventory accounting method that identifies which specific inventory items were sold and which remained in inventory to be carried over to later periods.

**Speculative company**   A firm with a great degree of business and/or financial risk, with commensurate high earnings potential.

**Speculative stock**   A stock that appears to be highly overpriced compared to its intrinsic valuation.

**Spending phase**   Phase in the investment life cycle during which individuals' earning years end as they retire. They pay for expenses with income from social security and returns from prior investments and invest to protect against inflation.

**Spin-off**   A form of restructuring in which shareholders of the parent company receive a proportional number of shares in a new, separate entity; shareholders end up owning stock in two different companies where there used to be one.

**Split-off**   A form of restructuring in which shareholders of the parent company are given shares in a newly created entity in exchange for their shares of the parent company.

**Split-rate**   In reference to corporate taxes, a split-rate system taxes earnings to be distributed as dividends at a different rate than earnings to be retained. Corporate profits distributed as dividends are taxed at a lower rate than those retained in the business.

**Spread**   An option strategy involving the purchase of one option and sale of another option that is identical to the first in all respects except either exercise price or expiration.

**Spurious correlation**   A correlation that misleadingly points towards associations between variables.

**Stagflation**   The combination of inflation and recession.

**Standard cost**   With respect to inventory accounting, the planned or target unit cost of inventory items or services.

**Standard deviation**   The positive square root of the variance; a measure of dispersion in the same units as the original data.

**Standard normal distribution (or unit normal distribution)**   The normal density with mean ($\mu$) equal to 0 and standard deviation ($\sigma$) equal to 1.

**Standardized beta**   With reference to fundamental factor models, the value of the attribute for an asset minus the average value of the attribute across all stocks, divided by the standard deviation of the attribute across all stocks.

**Standardizing**   A transformation that involves subtracting the mean and dividing the result by the standard deviation.

**Stated annual interest rate or quoted interest rate**   A quoted interest rate that does not account for compounding within the year.

**Stated rate (nominal rate or coupon rate)**   The rate at which periodic interest payments are calculated.

**Statement of cash flows (cash flow statement)**   A financial statement that reconciles beginning-of-period and end-of-period balance sheet values of cash; provides information about an entity's cash inflows and cash outflows as they pertain to operating, investing, and financing activities.

**Statement of changes in shareholders' equity (statement of owners' equity)**   A financial statement that reconciles the beginning-of-period and end-of-period balance sheet values of shareholders' equity; provides information about all factors affecting shareholders' equity.

**Statement of retained earnings**   A financial statement that reconciles beginning-of-period and end-of-period balance sheet values of retained income; shows the linkage between the balance sheet and income statement.

**Static trade-off theory of capital structure**   A theory pertaining to a company's optimal capital structure; the optimal level of debt is found at the point where additional debt would cause the costs of financial distress to increase by a greater amount than the benefit of the additional tax shield.

**Statistic**   A quantity computed from or used to describe a sample of data.

**Statistical factor models**   A multifactor model in which statistical methods are applied to a set of historical returns to determine portfolios that best explain either historical return covariances or variances.

**Statistical inference**　Making forecasts, estimates, or judgments about a larger group from a smaller group actually observed; using a sample statistic to infer the value of an unknown population parameter.

**Statistically significant**　A result indicating that the null hypothesis can be rejected; with reference to an estimated regression coefficient, frequently understood to mean a result indicating that the corresponding population regression coefficient is different from 0.

**Statistics**　The science of describing, analyzing, and drawing conclusions from data; also, a collection of numerical data.

**Statutory merger**　A merger in which one company ceases to exist as an identifiable entity and all its assets and liabilities become part of a purchasing company.

**Stock grants**　The granting of stock to employees as a form of compensation.

**Stock options (stock option grants)**　The granting of stock options to employees as a form of compensation.

**Stock purchase**　An acquisition in which the acquirer gives the target company's shareholders some combination of cash and securities in exchange for shares of the target company's stock.

**Stock-out losses**　Profits lost from not having sufficient inventory on hand to satisfy demand.

**Storage costs or carrying costs**　The costs of holding an asset, generally a function of the physical characteristics of the underlying asset.

**Straddle**　An option strategy involving the purchase of a put and a call with the same exercise price. A straddle is based on the expectation of high volatility of the underlying.

**Straight-line method**　A depreciation method that allocates evenly the cost of a long-lived asset less its estimated residual value over the estimated useful life of the asset.

**Strangle**　A variation of a straddle in which the put and call have different exercise prices.

**Strap**　An option strategy involving the purchase of two calls and one put.

**Strategies**　All the possible actions of each player in a game.

**Stratified random sampling**　A procedure by which a population is divided into subpopulations (strata) based on one or more classification criteria. Simple random samples are then drawn from each stratum in sizes proportional to the relative size of

each stratum in the population. These samples are then pooled.

**Stress testing**　A set of techniques for estimating losses in extremely unfavorable combinations of events or scenarios.

**Strip**　An option strategy involving the purchase of two puts and one call.

**Strong-form efficient market hypothesis**　The belief that security prices fully reflect all information from both public and private sources.

**Structural change**　Economic trend occurring when the economy is undergoing a major change in organization or in how it functions.

**Structural surplus or deficit**　The budget balance that would occur if the economy were at full employment and real GDP were equal to potential GDP.

**Structural unemployment**　The unemployment that arises when changes in technology or international competition change the skills needed to perform jobs or change the locations of jobs.

**Structured note**　A variation of a floating-rate note that has some type of unusual characteristic such as a leverage factor or in which the rate moves opposite to interest rates.

**Subjective probability**　A probability drawing on personal or subjective judgment.

**Subsidiary merger**　A merger in which the company being purchased becomes a subsidiary of the purchaser.

**Subsidy**　A payment made by the government to a producer.

**Sunk cost**　A cost that has already been incurred.

**Supply-side effects**　The effects of fiscal policy on employment, potential GDP, and aggregate supply.

**Support level**　A price at which a technician would expect a substantial increase in price and volume for a stock to reverse a declining trend that was due to profit taking.

**Surprise**　The actual value of a variable minus its predicted (or expected) value.

**Survey approach**　An estimate of the equity risk premium that is based upon estimates provided by a panel of finance experts.

**Survivorship bias**　The bias resulting from a test design that fails to account for companies that have gone bankrupt, merged, or are otherwise no longer reported in a database.

**Sustainable growth rate**　The rate of dividend (and earnings) growth that can be sustained over time for a given level of return on equity, keeping the capital structure constant and without issuing additional common stock.

**Swap** An agreement between two parties to exchange a series of future cash flows.

**Swap spread** The difference between the fixed rate on an interest rate swap and the rate on a Treasury note with equivalent maturity; it reflects the general level of credit risk in the market.

**Swaption** An option to enter into a swap.

**Symmetry principle** A requirement that people in similar situations be treated similarly.

**Synthetic call** The combination of puts, the underlying, and risk-free bonds that replicates a call option.

**Synthetic forward contract** The combination of the underlying, puts, calls, and risk-free bonds that replicates a forward contract.

**Synthetic index fund** An index fund position created by combining risk-free bonds and futures on the desired index.

**Synthetic put** The combination of calls, the underlying, and risk-free bonds that replicates a put option.

**Systematic factors** Factors that affect the average returns of a large number of different assets.

**Systematic risk** The variability of returns that is due to macroeconomic factors that affect all risky assets. Because it affects all risky assets, it cannot be eliminated by diversification.

**Systematic sampling** A procedure of selecting every $k$th member until reaching a sample of the desired size. The sample that results from this procedure should be approximately random.

**Takeover** A merger; the term may be applied to any transaction, but is often used in reference to hostile transactions.

**Takeover premium** The amount by which the takeover price for each share of stock must exceed the current stock price in order to entice shareholders to relinquish control of the company to an acquirer.

**Tangible assets** Long-term assets with physical substance that are used in company operations, such as land (property), plant, and equipment.

**Target balance** A minimum level of cash to be held available—estimated in advance and adjusted for known funds transfers, seasonality, or other factors.

**Target capital structure** A company's chosen proportions of debt and equity.

**Target company, or target** The company in a merger or acquisition that is being acquired.

**Target payout ratio** A strategic corporate goal representing the long-term proportion of earnings that the company intends to distribute to shareholders as dividends.

**Target semideviation** The positive square root of target semivariance.

**Target semivariance** The average squared deviation below a target value.

**Targeting rule** A decision rule for monetary policy that sets the policy instrument at a level that makes the forecast of the ultimate policy target equal to the target.

**Tax base (tax basis)** The amount at which an asset or liability is valued for tax purposes.

**Tax expense** An aggregate of an entity's income tax payable (or recoverable in the case of a tax benefit) and any changes in deferred tax assets and liabilities. It is essentially the income tax payable or recoverable if these had been determined based on accounting profit rather than taxable income.

**Tax incidence** The division of the burden of the tax between the buyer and the seller.

**Tax loss carry forward** A taxable loss in the current period that may be used to reduce future taxable income.

**Tax risk** The uncertainty associated with tax laws.

**Tax wedge** The gap between the before-tax and after-tax wage rates.

**Taxable income** The portion of an entity's income that is subject to income taxes under the tax laws of its jurisdiction.

**Taxable temporary differences** Temporary differences that result in a taxable amount in a future period when determining the taxable profit as the balance sheet item is recovered or settled.

**Taylor rule** A rule that sets the federal funds rate at the equilibrium real interest rate (which Taylor says is 2 percent a year) plus amounts based on the inflation rate and the output gap.

**$t$-Distribution** A symmetrical distribution defined by a single parameter, degrees of freedom, that is largely used to make inferences concerning the mean of a normal distribution whose variance is unknown.

**Technical analysis** Estimation of future security price movements based on past price and volume movements.

**Technological efficiency** A situation that occurs when the firm produces a given output by using the least amount of inputs.

**Technology** Any method of producing a good or service.

**Temporal method** A variation of the monetary/nonmonetary translation method that requires not only monetary assets and liabilities, but also nonmonetary assets and liabilities that are measured at their current value on the balance sheet date to be translated at the current exchange rate. Assets and liabilities are translated at rates consistent with the timing of their measurement value. This method is typically used when the functional currency is other than the local currency.

**Tender offer**   A public offer whereby the acquirer invites target shareholders to submit ("tender") their shares in return for the proposed payment.

**Tenor**   The original time to maturity on a swap.

**Termination date**   The date of the final payment on a swap; also, the swap's expiration date.

**Test statistic**   A quantity, calculated based on a sample, whose value is the basis for deciding whether or not to reject the null hypothesis.

**Theta**   The rate at which an option's time value decays.

**Third market**   Over-the-counter trading of securities listed on an exchange.

**Time series**   A set of observations on a variable's outcomes in different time periods.

**Time to expiration**   The time remaining in the life of a derivative, typically expressed in years.

**Time value or speculative value**   The difference between the market price of the option and its intrinsic value, determined by the uncertainty of the underlying over the remaining life of the option.

**Time value decay**   The loss in the value of an option resulting from movement of the option price toward its payoff value as the expiration day approaches.

**Time value of money**   The principles governing equivalence relationships between cash flows with different dates.

**Time-period bias**   The possibility that when we use a time-series sample, our statistical conclusion may be sensitive to the starting and ending dates of the sample.

**Time-series analysis**   An examination of a firm's performance data over a period of time.

**Time-series data**   Observations of a variable over time.

**Time-weighted rate of return**   The compound rate of growth of one unit of currency invested in a portfolio during a stated measurement period; a measure of investment performance that is not sensitive to the timing and amount of withdrawals or additions to the portfolio.

**Top-down analysis**   With reference to investment selection processes, an approach that starts with macro selection (i.e., identifying attractive geographic segments and/or industry segments) and then addresses selection of the most attractive investments within those segments.

**Total asset turnover**   An activity ratio calculated as revenue divided by average total assets.

**Total cost**   The cost of all the productive resources that a firm uses.

**Total fixed cost**   The cost of the firm's fixed inputs.

**Total invested capital**   The sum of market value of common equity, book value of preferred equity, and face value of debt.

**Total probability rule**   A rule explaining the unconditional probability of an event in terms of probabilities of the event conditional on mutually exclusive and exhaustive scenarios.

**Total probability rule for expected value**   A rule explaining the expected value of a random variable in terms of expected values of the random variable conditional on mutually exclusive and exhaustive scenarios.

**Total product**   The total output produced by a firm in a given period of time.

**Total return**   A return objective in which the investor wants to increase the portfolio value to meet a future need by both capital gains and current income reinvestment.

**Total return swap**   A swap in which one party agrees to pay the total return on a security. Often used as a credit derivative, in which the underlying is a bond.

**Total revenue**   The value of a firm's sales. It is calculated as the price of the good multiplied by the quantity sold.

**Total revenue test**   A method of estimating the price elasticity of demand by observing the change in total revenue that results from a change in the price, when all other influences on the quantity sold remain the same.

**Total variable cost**   The cost of all the firm's variable inputs.

**Tracking error**   The standard deviation of the difference in returns between an active investment portfolio and its benchmark portfolio; also called tracking error volatility, tracking risk, and active risk.

**Tracking portfolio**   A portfolio having factor sensitivities that are matched to those of a benchmark or other portfolio.

**Tracking risk**   The standard deviation of the differences between a portfolio's returns and its benchmark's returns; a synonym of active risk.

**Trade credit**   A spontaneous form of credit in which a purchaser of the goods or service is financing its purchase by delaying the date on which payment is made.

**Trade receivables (commercial receivables or accounts receivable)**   Amounts customers owe the company for products that have been sold as well as amounts that may be due from suppliers (such as for returns of merchandise).

**Trading securities (held-for-trading securities)** Securities held by a company with the intent to trade them.

**Transaction cost** The cost of executing a trade. Low costs characterize an operationally efficient market.

**Transaction exposure** The risk of a change in value between the transaction date and the settlement date of an asset or liability denominated in a foreign currency.

**Transactions motive** In the context of inventory management, the need for inventory as part of the routine production–sales cycle.

**Translation exposure** The risk associated with the conversion of foreign financial statements into domestic currency.

**Treasury bill** A negotiable U.S. government security with a maturity of less than one year that pays no periodic interest but yields the difference between its par value and its discounted purchase price.

**Treasury bond** A U.S. government security with a maturity of more than 10 years that pays interest periodically.

**Treasury note** A U.S. government security with maturities of 1 to 10 years that pays interest periodically.

**Treasury shares** Shares that were issued and subsequently repurchased by the company.

**Treasury stock method** A method for accounting for the effect of options (and warrants) on earnings per share (EPS) that specifies what EPS would have been if the options and warrants had been exercised and the company had used the proceeds to repurchase common stock.

**Tree diagram** A diagram with branches emanating from nodes representing either mutually exclusive chance events or mutually exclusive decisions.

**Trend** A long-term pattern of movement in a particular direction.

**Trimmed mean** A mean computed after excluding a stated small percentage of the lowest and highest observations.

**Trough** The culmination of a bear market at which prices stop declining and begin rising.

**Trust receipt arrangement** The use of inventory as collateral for a loan. The inventory is segregated and held in trust, and the proceeds of any sale must be remitted to the lender immediately.

**t-Test** A hypothesis test using a statistic (t-statistic) that follows a t-distribution.

**Two-sided hypothesis test (or two-tailed hypothesis test)** A test in which the null hypothesis is rejected in favor of the alternative hypothesis if the evidence indicates that the population parameter is either smaller or larger than a hypothesized value.

**Type I error** The error of rejecting a true null hypothesis.

**Type II error** The error of not rejecting a false null hypothesis.

**Unbiasedness** Lack of bias. A desirable property of estimators, an unbiased estimator is one whose expected value (the mean of its sampling distribution) equals the parameter it is intended to estimate.

**Unbilled revenue (accrued revenue)** Revenue that has been earned but not yet billed to customers as of the end of an accounting period.

**Unclassified balance sheet** A balance sheet that does not show subtotals for current assets and current liabilities.

**Unconditional heteroskedasticity** Heteroskedasticity of the error term that is not correlated with the values of the independent variable(s) in the regression.

**Unconditional probability (or marginal probability)** The probability of an event *not* conditioned on another event.

**Underlying** An asset that trades in a market in which buyers and sellers meet, decide on a price, and the seller then delivers the asset to the buyer and receives payment. The underlying is the asset or other derivative on which a particular derivative is based. The market for the underlying is also referred to as the spot market.

**Underweighted** A condition in which a portfolio, for whatever reason, includes less of a class of securities than the relative market value alone would justify.

**Unearned fees** Unearned fees are recognized when a company receives cash payment for fees prior to earning them.

**Unearned revenue (deferred revenue)** A liability account for money that has been collected for goods or services that have not yet been delivered; payment received in advance of providing a good or service.

**Unemployment rate** The number of unemployed people expressed as a percentage of all the people who have jobs or are looking for one. It is the percentage of the labor force who are unemployed.

**Unidentifiable intangible** An intangible that cannot be acquired singly and that typically possesses an indefinite benefit period; an example is accounting goodwill.

**Unit elastic demand**  Demand with a price elasticity of 1; the percentage change in the quantity demanded equals the percentage change in price.

**Unit root**  A time series that is not covariance stationary is said to have a unit root.

**Uniting of interests method**  A method of accounting in which combined companies were portrayed as if they had always operated as a single economic entity. Called pooling of interests under U.S. GAAP and uniting of interests under IFRS. (No longer allowed under U.S. GAAP or IFRS.)

**Units-of-production method**  A depreciation method that allocates the cost of a long-lived asset based on actual usage during the period.

**Univariate distribution**  A distribution that specifies the probabilities for a single random variable.

**Unlimited funds**  An unlimited funds environment assumes that the company can raise the funds it wants for all profitable projects simply by paying the required rate of return.

**Unrealized capital gains**  Capital gains that reflect the price appreciation of currently held unsold assets.

**Unsystematic risk**  Risk that is unique to an asset, derived from its particular characteristics. It can be eliminated in a diversified portfolio.

**Unweighted index**  An indicator series affected equally by the performance of each security in the sample regardless of price or market value. Also referred to as an *equal-weighted series*.

**Up transition probability**  The probability that an asset's value moves up.

**Upstream**  A transaction between two affiliates, an investor company and an associate company such that the associate company records a profit on its income statement. An example is a sale of inventory by the associate to the investor company.

**Utilitarianism**  A principle that states that we should strive to achieve "the greatest happiness for the greatest number of people."

**Valuation**  The process of determining the value of an asset or service.

**Valuation allowance**  A reserve created against deferred tax assets, based on the likelihood of realizing the deferred tax assets in future accounting periods.

**Valuation process**  Part of the investment decision process in which you estimate the value of a security.

**Valuation ratios**  Ratios that measure the quantity of an asset or flow (e.g., earnings) in relation to the price associated with a specified claim (e.g., a share or ownership of the enterprise).

**Value**  The amount for which one can sell something, or the amount one must pay to acquire something.

**Value at risk (VAR)**  A money measure of the minimum value of losses expected during a specified time period at a given level of probability.

**Value investors**  With reference to equity investors, investors who are focused on paying a relatively low share price in relation to earnings or assets per share.

**Value stocks**  Stocks that appear to be undervalued for reasons besides earnings growth potential. These stocks are usually identified based on high dividend yields, low *P/E* ratios, or low price-to-book ratios.

**Value-weighted index**  An index calculated as the total market value of the securities in the sample. Market value is equal to the number of shares or bonds outstanding times the market price of the security.

**Variable costs**  Costs that fluctuate with the level of production and sales.

**Variance**  The expected value (the probability-weighted average) of squared deviations from a random variable's expected value.

**Variation margin**  Additional margin that must be deposited in an amount sufficient to bring the balance up to the initial margin requirement.

**Vega**  The relationship between option price and volatility.

**Velocity of circulation**  The average number of times a dollar of money is used annually to buy the goods and services that make up GDP.

**Venturers**  The owners of a joint venture. Each is active in the management and shares control of the joint venture.

**Vertical analysis**  Common-size analysis using only one reporting period or one base financial statement; for example, an income statement in which all items are stated as percentages of sales.

**Vertical common-size analysis**  The most common type of common-size analysis, in which the accounts in a given period are compared to a benchmark item in that same year.

**Vertical merger**  A merger involving companies at different positions of the same production chain; for example, a supplier or a distributor.

**Vested benefit obligation**  Under U.S. GAAP, a measure used in estimating a defined-benefit pension plan's liabilities, defined as the "actuarial present value of vested benefits."

**Vested benefits**  Future benefits promised to the employee regardless of continuing service. Benefits typically vest after a specified period of service or a specified period of service combined with age.

**Vesting date**   The date that employees can first exercise stock options; vesting can be immediate or over a future period.

**Volatility**   As used in option pricing, the standard deviation of the continuously compounded returns on the underlying asset.

**Warehouse receipt arrangement**   The use of inventory as collateral for a loan; similar to a trust receipt arrangement except there is a third party (i.e., a warehouse company) that supervises the inventory.

**Weak-form efficient market hypothesis**   The belief that security prices fully reflect all security market information.

**Weighted average cost method**   An inventory accounting method that averages the total cost of available inventory items over the total units available for sale.

**Weighted mean**   An average in which each observation is weighted by an index of its relative importance.

**Weighted-average cost of capital**   A weighted average of the after-tax required rates of return on a company's common stock, preferred stock, and long-term debt, where the weights are the fraction of each source of financing in the company's target capital structure.

**White knight**   A third party that is sought out by the target company's board to purchase the target in lieu of a hostile bidder.

**White squire**   A third party that is sought out by the target company's board to purchase a substantial minority stake in the target—enough to block a hostile takeover without selling the entire company.

**White-corrected standard errors**   A synonym for robust standard errors.

**Winner's curse**   The tendency for the winner in certain competitive bidding situations to overpay, whether because of overestimation of intrinsic value, emotion, or information asymmetries.

**Winsorized mean**   A mean computed after assigning a stated percent of the lowest values equal to one specified low value, and a stated percent of the highest values equal to one specified high value.

**Working capital**   The difference between current assets and current liabilities.

**Working capital management**   The management of a company's short-term assets (such as inventory) and short-term liabilities (such as money owed to suppliers).

**Working capital turnover**   A comparison of revenues with working capital to produce a measure that shows how efficiently working capital is employed.

**Working-age population**   The total number of people aged 15 years and over.

**Yield**   The actual return on a debt security if it is held to maturity.

**Yield beta**   A measure of the sensitivity of a bond's yield to a general measure of bond yields in the market that is used to refine the hedge ratio.

**Yield spread**   The difference between the yield on a bond and the yield on a default-free security, usually a government note, of the same maturity. The yield spread is primarily determined by the market's perception of the credit risk on the bond.

**Yield to maturity**   The annual return that an investor earns on a bond if the investor purchases the bond today and holds it until maturity.

**Zero-cost collar**   A transaction in which a position in the underlying is protected by buying a put and selling a call with the premium from the sale of the call offsetting the premium from the purchase of the put. It can also be used to protect a floating-rate borrower against interest rate increases with the premium on a long cap offsetting the premium on a short floor.

real GDP and, V2: 302–303
by reason, V2: 297–298
sources of, V2: 297–298
structural unemployment, V2: 301
types of, V2: 300–301
vital signs, V2: 289–290
wages, V2: 290–296
aggregate hours, V2: 294
employment-to-population ratio,
V2: 293–294
labor force participation, V2: 292
labor market indicators,
V2: 291–294
*National Income and Product
Accounts*, V2: 296
population survey, V2: 290–291
real wage rate, V2: 294–296
U.S. Census Bureau, V2: 290
joint unlimited liability, V2: 106
joint ventures, V3: 411n4
JP Morgan Chase, General Electric,
swap, V6: 133–136
judgment in accounts, entries, security
analysis, financial statements,
V3: 68–69
just-in-time, method of, V4: 114

**K**
Kahn, Robert L., V1: 456
Kansai Commodities Exchange, V6: 14
Kansas City Board of Trade, V6: 14
Kaplan, Paul, V4: 55
Kaserer, Christoph, V4: 66
Keynes, John Maynard, V2: 254, 336
Keynesian theory, V2: 337, 398
aggregate supply response,
V2: 336–337
defined, V2: 398
policy response needed, V2: 337
kinked demand curve model, V2: 226
Kmart, return on assets, bankruptcy,
DuPont analysis, V4: 139–141
knowledge of law, professional
standard, V1: 12, 15–21
Koedijk, Kees, V4: 68–69
Kohl's, V4: 91
Korea Futures Exchange, V6: 14, 85
Korea Stock Exchange, V6: 14, 62, 85
Korean stock index, V6: 15
Kotlikoff, Laurence, V2: 428
Kraft
consolidated statements of earnings,
V3: 136
gross profit margin, V3: 179
Krueger, Alan, V2: 72
kurtosis, V1: 302–305, 392n17
defined, V1: 302
in return distributions, V1: 302–305
Kydland, Finn, V2: 398

**L**
labor
demand for, V2: 260
elasticity of supply, V2: 69
labor demand curve, V2: 256–257
labor intensity, V2: 261
labor market, V2: 68–73, 253–264,
283–285
changes in demand for labor,
V2: 258–260
capital, V2: 260
price of output, V2: 259
technology, V2: 260
changing face of, V2: 293
demand for labor, V2: 255
elasticity of demand for labor,
V2: 261–262
capital for labor, V2: 261–262
for good produced, V2: 261
labor intensity, V2: 261
equivalence of conditions, profit
maximization, V2: 257–258
federal minimum wage, effects,
V2: 72–73
labor demand curve, V2: 256–257
labor market equilibrium,
V2: 263–264
demand for labor, V2: 264
equilibrium, V2: 264
supply of labor, V2: 264
living wage, V2: 73
marginal revenue product,
V2: 255–256
diminishing marginal revenue
product, V2: 256
market demand, V2: 260
minimum wage, V2: 71–73
inefficiency of, V2: 71–72
participation, V2: 292
real business cycle, V2: 400
supply of labor, V2: 262–263
changes, V2: 263
income effect, V2: 262
labor curve, V2: 262–263
market supply, V2: 263
substitution effect, V2: 262
labor market equilibrium,
V2: 263–264
demand for labor, V2: 264
equilibrium, V2: 264
supply of labor, V2: 264
labor market flows, V2: 297
labor market indicators, V2: 291–294
labor market power, V2: 264–271
efficiency wages, V2: 271
labor unions, V2: 265–270
AFL-CIO, V2: 265
minimum wage, V2: 270
monopoly, V2: 269–270

union-nonunion wage gap,
V2: 267–268
monopsony, V2: 268–270
minimum wage, V2: 270
labor unions, V2: 265–270
AFL-CIO, V2: 265
minimum wage, V2: 270
monopoly, V2: 269–270
monopsony
labor market, V2: 268–269
minimum wage, V2: 270
union-nonunion wage gap,
V2: 267–268
Laffer, Arthur B., V2: 421
Laffer curve, V2: 422
defined, V2: 421
landfill site, depreciated, V3: 357n10
last-in, first-out inventory method. *See*
LIFO inventory method
later-stage financing, V6: 200
law of diminishing returns, V2: 132
law of one price, V6: 21, 21n19
Lazear, Edward P., V2: 412
leases, V3: 445–464, V4: 46
advantages of, V3: 445–446
capital leases *vs.* operating leases,
V3: 446–464
finance leases *vs.* operating leases,
V3: 446–464
lessee, accounting, reporting by,
V3: 447–457
lessor, accounting, reporting by,
V3: 458–464
long-term
direct financing finance lease *vs.*
operating lease for lessor,
V3: 458–461
finance *vs.* operating lease for
lessee, V3: 447–453
operating leases, treating as
finance leases for lessee,
V3: 454–457
leaving employer, V1: 70–71
legal monopoly, V2: 181
legalized gambling, derivatives and,
V6: 20–21
Lehman Brothers Treasury Bond
Index, V4: 228, 230
Leibowitz, Martin, V5: 140
leisure, opportunity cost of, V2: 262
lending facility covenant breached,
V1: 390–391
lending long, V2: 353
leptokurtic, V1: 303
leptokurtic distribution, V1: 302
lessee, V3: 607n16
levels of service, disclosure of, V1: 58
leverage, risk-return possibilities with,
V4: 254